Performance Appraisal

State of the Art in Practice

James W. Smither, *Editor*

Foreword by Manuel London

JOSSEY-BASS
A Wiley Company
San Francisco

Published by

JOSSEY-BASS
A Wiley Imprint
www.josseybass.com

Jossey-Bass books and products are available through most bookstores. To contact Jossey-Bass directly, call (888) 378-2537, fax to (800) 605-2665, or visit our website at www.josseybass.com.

Substantial discounts on bulk quantities of Jossey-Bass books are available to corporations, professional associations, and other organizations. For details and discount information, contact the special sales department at Jossey-Bass.

We at Jossey-Bass strive to use the most environmentally sensitive paper stocks available to us. Our publications are printed on acid-free recycled stock whenever possible, and our paper always meets or exceeds minimum GPO and EPA requirements.

Library of Congress Cataloging-in-Publication Data

Performance appraisal: state of the art in practice / James W. Smither, editor; foreword by Manuel London.—1st ed.
p.   cm.—(Jossey-Bass business & management series) (Jossey-Bass social and behavioral science series)
Includes bibliographical references and indexes.
ISBN 0-7879-0945-9
1. Employees—Rating of—United States. 2. Performance standards—United States. 3. Personnel management—United States.
I. Smither, James W. II. Series. III. Series: Jossey-Bass social and behavioral science series.
HF5549.5.R3P4734 1998
658.3'125—dc21   98-9568

FIRST EDITION
HB Printing   10 9 8 7 6 5

A joint publication in
The Jossey-Bass Business & Management Series
and
The Jossey-Bass Social & Behavioral Science Series

Society for Industrial and Organizational Psychology
Professional Practice Series

SERIES EDITOR

Manuel London
State University of New York, Stony Brook

EDITORIAL BOARD

Lawrence Fogli
Core Corporation

Nita R. French
French & Associates

A. Catherine Higgs
Allstate Insurance Company

Allen I. Kraut
Baruch College
City University of New York

Edward L. Levine
University of South Florida

Kenneth Pearlman
AT&T

Walter W. Tornow
Center for Creative Leadership

To Robin, Amy, and Sean

Contents

Part Three: Linking Appraisal to the Larger Human Performance System

Foreword

This volume is part of the Professional Practice Series sponsored by the Society for Industrial and Organizational Psychology. The books in the series address contemporary ideas and problems, focus on how to get things done, and provide state-of-the-art technology based on theory and research from industrial and organizational psychology. We try to cover the needs of practitioners and those being trained for practice.

Four earlier volumes in this series, under the senior editorship of Douglas W. Bray, were published by Guilford Press and are now distributed by Jossey-Bass. Bray edited *Working with Organizations and Their People* (1991). The book examines the role of industrial and organizational psychologists as practitioners involved in evaluation, training, and organization development.

Susan E. Jackson edited the second book, *Diversity in the Workplace* (1992), which offers cases and methods for creating and assessing a diverse workplace, managing workplace diversity through personal growth and team development, and strategic initiatives to manage workplace diversity.

Abraham K. Korman's *Human Dilemmas in Work Organizations: Strategies for Resolution* (1994) considers the expanding world of the human resource practitioner. Readings describe programs for employee assistance, stress management, marginal performers, reorganizations, employee ethics, and elder care.

Ann Howard's book, *Diagnosis for Organizational Change* (1994), focuses on organizational diagnosis for design and development. Authors examine the assessment of human talent for staffing and training. They also provide an overview of the high-involvement workplace with a consideration of organization cultures, reward systems, and work teams.

As the new senior editor of the Professional Practice Series under our new publisher, Jossey-Bass, I edited *Employees, Careers, and Job Creation* (1995). This book examines ways human resource development programs contribute to an organization's viability and growth in tough economic times. It describes programs that help employees maintain their value to their firm or find new employment after organizational downsizing. It shows how organizations, government, and universities can work together to help employees create new ventures and career opportunities.

Allen I. Kraut edited *Organizational Surveys: Tools for Assessment and Change*, which appeared in the series in 1996. This book demonstrates the value of surveys for diagnosis of individual and organizational strengths and weaknesses, communication of organizational culture and expectations, and evaluation of human resource policies and programs. Cases describe best practices and methods by which organizations share items and compare results. The book shows how to link survey results to measures of organization effectiveness such as customer satisfaction, financial performance, and employee turnover. Also, it addresses tough issues such as holding managers accountable for survey results and avoiding treating survey results as necessarily reliable and valid data about individual capabilities.

The current volume, edited by James W. Smither, provides state-of-the-art methods for performance management. The authors recognize the strategic, systemic role of a performance appraisal process that evaluates employees on behaviors that are important to organizational success and ties the appraisal results to rewards and development. The book addresses current legal and societal issues in appraisal, including equal employment opportunity and disability legislation and judicial rulings. The goal is to design a performance appraisal process that is fair and applies in different organizational situations (such as teams) and contexts (multinational corporations). New forms of appraisal are described, such as 360-degree (multisource) survey feedback and self-assessment. The book shows how to increase rater accuracy and how to use appraisal for employee development. Overall, the book is a valuable resource to practitioners who want to evaluate and revamp their appraisal systems to meet the changing needs of their organizations.

My editorial board contributed to this effort by setting the direction for the series and ensuring the high-quality results represented here. I would like to thank the board members: Lawrence Fogl, Nita French, Catherine Higgs, Allen Kraut, Edward Levine, Kenneth Pearlman, and Walter Tornow. Also, I am grateful to the Society for Industrial and Organizational Psychology for sponsoring the series and supporting this volume.

February 1998   Manuel London
         State University of New York
         Series Editor

Preface

This book was written for practitioners in human resources and industrial-organizational psychology. For years, many practitioners have been frustrated by the absence of useful information about designing and implementing performance appraisal processes and systems. On one hand, academic journals have offered a great deal of very esoteric (and entirely impractical) scholarly research dealing with how people attend to, encode, recall, and evaluate human behavior. On the other hand, practitioner magazines toss out a seemingly unending supply of ideas and personal testimonials of unknown quality.

This book has sought to fill a gap. Its purpose is to present the implications of theory and research for practice. Practitioners who read it will discover the practical implications of the most current research and innovations in this area.

Our goal was to distill lessons of research that could be of value to practitioners, and to avoid the too-often esoteric, arcane, and impractical musings of academics who have no sense of how the real world works. Practitioners can learn the extent to which their own practice in this area matches our best knowledge. In this manner, the book can serve as a guide for practitioners who are faced with important questions about the design of performance appraisal processes and systems. In each chapter, we wanted to give you an up-to-date view of what we know about performance appraisal issues, and offer ideas that can help guide your efforts to design performance appraisal and management systems. I think the authors have succeeded and I hope you will think so too.

Overview of Chapters

In Chapter One, John Bernardin, Christine Hagan, Jeffrey Kane, and Peter Villanova begin by describing the frustrations that many organizations and employees have with performance appraisals. They note the recent trend to use the term *performance management* rather than *performance appraisal*—but point out that too often there is little change in the actual practice of appraisal and related human resource systems. The authors argue that there are some approaches to performance management that are preferable regardless of a firm's strategy. Specifically, they argue persuasively that an effective performance management system must focus on performance (not traits) and performance dimensions and standards that are derived from the expectations of external and internal customers. They also emphasize the importance of explicitly assessing contextual performance (contributions beyond formal or technical role expectations) and factors that may constrain (or facilitate) performance. They describe how firms such as Office Depot, Tiffany's of New York, Ritz-Carlton, Interim Temporary Services, Harley Davidson, the Limited, the Gap, Andersen Consulting, and Weyerhaeuser are responding to these challenges.

There are few practitioners who haven't lost more than a little sleep while worrying about legal issues and appraisals. This is an enormously complicated area (and it seems to get more confusing every year). In Chapter Two, Stanley Malos, an attorney and industrial-organizational psychologist, addresses a very wide range of legal issues that should be of concern to every practitioner, including employment at will, negligence, defamation, misrepresentation, seniority, just cause, progressive discipline, flexible job designs, security and privacy, and workplace violence. He reviews important legal principles (for example, disparate treatment and disparate impact) and describes numerous court cases dealing with discrimination based on gender, race, national origin, age, or disability (under Title VII of the Civil Rights Act of 1964, state fair employment practices acts, the Equal Pay Act of 1963, the Civil Rights Act of 1991, the Age Discrimination in Employment Act, the Rehabilitation Act of 1973, and the Americans with Disabilities Act). Malos briefly describes key elements from over fifty cases (from district and appellate courts, and from arbitration) that illustrate many of the key issues and nuances of employment law. Throughout the chapter, he offers many useful recommendations concerning substantive and procedural aspects of appraisal.

In Chapter Three, Donald Davis describes how three international human resource strategies (exportive, adaptive, and integrative) affect appraisals in international settings, especially focusing on the need for control versus the need to adapt to local conditions. He illustrates the implications of social conditions (economic, demographic, legal) and cultural values for appraisal practices. He then shows how to develop performance criteria (including unit-level, task performance, and contextual performance such as cross-cultural adjustment and skills) that reflect the firm's international human resource strategy. He discusses several limiting conditions (such as the effect of accounting and financial practices on unit-level measures and the extent to which cultural differences between the local assignment and the home country make adjustment very difficult) that must be considered when conducting international appraisals. Davis also shows how cultural factors affect the choice of raters and the way that feedback is provided (for example, in high-context cultures the emphasis is on listening and communication is less direct and precise). He also addresses cultural issues associated with the way (or extent to which) rewards are linked to performance.

In Chapter Four, Robert Cardy first describes the key elements of quality environments (such as a customer orientation with a prevention approach to errors) and then tackles the common proposal among quality advocates that performance appraisal should be eliminated, primarily because (in their view) performance is due largely to system factors (such as machinery, materials, supervision, organizational climate) rather than person characteristics. In contrast, traditional human resource management views employee ability and motivation as important sources of performance differences. Cardy demonstrates that there are reliable individual differences that affect performance (for example, witness the predictive validity of many selection techniques) and proposes an expanded model of appraisal that incorporates elements of both traditional and quality viewpoints. Specifically, he proposes that system factors should be explicitly assessed (for example, by generating specific descriptions of system factors using a critical incident technique). This proposal is very similar to the recommendation from Bernardin and his colleagues that situational constraints should be evaluated and discussed during the appraisal process. Cardy also describes other changes in appraisal practices that need to change in quality environments, including performance standards (defined by customers), content (emphasizing interpersonal skills and initiative), and rating sources (peers, customers).

Everyone knows, at least at a gut level, that politics can play an important role in performance appraisals. In Chapter Five, Steve Kozlowski, Georgia Chao, and Robert Morrison view appraisal politics as a fact of life in nearly all organizations. They argue that when intentional rating distortions are the norm in an organization, a failure to engage in appraisal politics may be maladaptive for ratees and the organization. For example, raters who do not distort their ratings may inadvertently hurt their ratees' career prospects. The authors describe a case study that illustrates how raters learn to distort their ratings to satisfy (apparently) incompatible goals, distinguishing among ratees for purposes of promotion (or other rewards) while motivating those ratees who will not be promoted. In the study, appraisal politics seems to have developed to accomplish important organizational goals (to identify the best performers) in spite of an ineffective appraisal system. In such a situation, efforts to control or eliminate appraisal politics may themselves be maladaptive. Similarly, Kozlowski and his colleagues point out that not all ratee impression management is deceptive. They note that the dilemma is identifying when appraisal politics (or impression management) is adaptive, and when it is dysfunctional.

In Chapter Six, Stephen Gilliland and Jay Langdon describe three aspects of fairness: procedural fairness (the fairness of procedures used to arrive at outcomes), interpersonal fairness (the fairness of interpersonal treatment and communication), and outcome fairness (the fairness of the decision and of outcomes such as pay associated with the decision). They review research showing that employees' perceptions of appraisal fairness are related to acceptance of evaluations, satisfaction with the process, (modest) changes in performance, trust in the supervisor, organizational commitment, and intentions to stay with the organization. They provide specific recommendations and organizational examples that illustrate how to increase fairness in each of three aspects of the performance appraisal process: system development (creating appraisal instruments, communicating objectives), appraisal (observing and evaluating performance, making reward decisions), and providing feedback (communication of ratings and rewards).

In Chapter Seven, Richard Reilly and Jack McGourty note that traditional human resource functions such as appraisal and compensation were designed for individuals, and can create dysfunction when applied in team settings. If organizations want to send the message that team performance is key to organizational success, then it is necessary to appraise the performance of the team as a unit. They offer clear, step-by-step recommendations (and many vivid examples) for appraising three classes of behavior in team settings: individual competencies (such as knowledge and skills related to organizationally valued performance), individual team member performance (that is, how each individual contributes to team performance via communication, collaboration, and supporting the team's goal setting and decision making), and performance at the team level. They describe how to conduct a team job analysis and provide guidance about the kinds of team-level outcomes that are appropriate to measure.

In Chapter Eight, Anthony Dalessio provides a remarkably comprehensive guide to implementing multisource feedback (sometimes referred to as 360-degree feedback) programs. He discusses the kinds of validity and reliability information that practitioners should consider and reviews research indicating that raters should be anonymous, that rating quality will be higher when results are used for developmental rather than administrative purposes (such as pay), that self-other discrepancies are associated with poor performance, that participants should seek negative feedback from others, and that multisource feedback is associated with moderate performance improvements (especially for participants who were initially rated poorly or who overevaluated themselves). Dalessio then discusses and offers concrete recommendations concerning a host of important issues including linking the process to the firm's strategic objectives, gaining support from senior leaders, deciding whether to use the results for developmental or administrative purposes, communication about the program, working with external consultants, identifying competencies to be assessed, constructing questionnaires, choosing response scales, collecting verbatim comments, selecting and training raters, distributing and collecting questionnaires, structuring feedback reports, and facilitating feedback. The chapter also covers follow-up activities and program evaluation.

In Chapter Nine, Leanne Atwater describes eight ways that self-assessment can contribute to effective appraisals, while also noting the problems it can occasionally create. She describes how biographical characteristics (such as age, tenure, gender, minority status) and other individual characteristics (intelligence, self-esteem, narcissism) can affect self-assessments. She makes a compelling case for the problems that arise for employees whose self-view differs widely from the way others view them. Simply stated, employees who see themselves the way others see them are better able to regulate their behavior, more likely to be effective performers, and less likely to experience career derailment. Atwater reviews several approaches to self-assessment (for example, both-rate, joint appraisal, or self-only appraisal) and describes ways to increase the accuracy of self-ratings and maximize the value of formal or informal feedback.

In Chapter Ten, Mirian Graddick and Pamela Lane note that 40 percent of executives in a recent study had not received a formal appraisal in the preceding year, even though all their organizations required such appraisals and nearly all the executives had a strong desire to receive a constructive performance review. Those who had received appraisals were generally frustrated by the quality of the process. Graddick and Lane describe how firms such as Eastman Kodak, American Express, Honeywell, and AT&T are handling these challenges. They describe the variety of financial and nonfinancial measures that are being used to assess how effectively executives meet the interests of shareholders, customers, and employees. They describe several approaches for developing competency models for executives, emphasize the importance of linking executive performance to compensation (as well as the difficulties of doing so), offer recommendations for evaluating CEOs, and describe the increasing use of multisource feedback and executive coaches. Moreover, they offer many practical insights that reflect their hands-on experience (as well as research) in this area.

In Chapter Eleven, Neil Hauenstein provides many practical recommendations and specific examples of how rater training can be enhanced. He describes the most common approach to rater training (sometimes called *rater error training*) where raters are encouraged to avoid halo and leniency errors and are shown examples of desirable and undesirable rating distributions, and he argues persuasively that this approach to rater training should be abandoned. Instead, he describes essential features that should be included in most rater training efforts (including explanations of performance dimensions coupled with the opportunity to make practice ratings and receive feedback about those ratings). He also describes rater training approaches that, based on research, are likely to increase the accuracy of raters' observations and ratings (such as frame-of-reference training, rater variability training, and behavioral observation training). Examples of these approaches are presented and the situations (for example, rating purpose—administrative versus developmental, and rating format—subjective versus quantitative) for which each approach is best suited are discussed. He also addresses the issue of training raters to give effective feedback. Using feedback intervention theory and research, he emphasizes the value of descriptive, task-level feedback (which shows the worker how to do the task better) and points out the damage that often results from feedback that focuses on the employee's self-image ("you're not a team player").

In Chapter Twelve, Paul Squires and Seymour Adler note that even accurate appraisals often provide little diagnostic value. They argue that, to guide training, appraisals need to identify the reasons underlying current skill levels. Drawing on research from cognitive psychology, they illustrate how to develop appraisals that are based on mental process models. These mental process models describe the knowledge (and structure of knowledge), executive control (or metacognitive) processes, and social-cognitive and emotional processes (such as self-efficacy) that distinguish expert from novice performers. Training interventions then seek to help teach novices the knowledge structures and executive control processes used by experts. Squires and Adler also describe many innovative examples of firms that use third-party, external assessors to provide developmental appraisals.

In Chapter Thirteen, Robert Heneman and Maria Gresham address the critical issue of how to link appraisal and compensation. They describe performance-based pay plans that can be linked to individual, group, and organizational performance, and they summarize research showing that performance-based pay generally has an impact on productivity that is equal to or exceeds the impact of other human resource interventions. They also identify the pay plans that appear best suited for a variety of business objectives (customer service, quality, productivity, cost reduction, profit, employee development) and for traditional versus involvement cultures. Finally, they discuss a host of implementation issues such as pay secrecy, split reviews, fairness, and measurement.

In the closing chapter, I try to summarize the insights and prescriptions from all the authors who contributed to this volume. In doing so, I sketch a picture of the features likely to be found in a state-of-the-art performance appraisal and management system.

Acknowledgments

I have heard that editing a book like this can be a lot of work. But to me it was fun, not work. I was given the opportunity to outline a volume that would help bridge the gap between theory, research, and practice in performance appraisal. I was able to select the authors who were best suited to write about each issue. Then I had the treat of being the first to read what each author had to say. Think about it. Imagine being given the chance to pick people you admire to write about things that interest you. All in all, a delightful experience.

A book like this happens only through the good will, talent, and effort of many people. First, I thank Manuel London, editor of the Professional Practice Series, for giving me the opportunity to edit this volume and for all his encouragement in this and many other endeavors. Second, I am grateful to the Society for Industrial and Organizational Psychology for sponsoring this series and volume. Third, thanks are due to the Editorial Board of the Professional Practice Series, who offered constructive ideas that helped shape the content of this book: Lawrence Fogli, Nita French, Catherine Higgs, Allen Kraut, Edward Levine, Kenneth Pearlman, and Walter Tornow. Fourth, thanks to Mike Campion who helped identify some authors for this volume. Fifth, special thanks is due to the thirteen reviewers. Each brought a special perspective and talent to their reviews. Together, they played an invaluable role in shaping the content and style of these chapters.

Rich Buda	Dick Reilly
Mike Campion	Sara Rynes
Nita French	Ron Stoffey
Walt Jordan	Bernadette Taylor
Jerry Kehoe	Mary Tenopyr
Manny London	Mike Warech
Ken Pearlman	

Sixth, I am deeply indebted to all the authors. Each contributed an enormous amount of time, energy, and expertise. In a very real sense, this is their book, not mine. Finally, I thank my parents, family, and friends, especially Robin, Amy, and Sean, for their enduring patience and love. I dedicate this book to them.

February 1998   James W. Smither
Philadelphia, Pennsylvania

The Authors

JAMES W. SMITHER is professor in the Management Department and Lindback Chair in the School of Business Administration at La Salle University. He received his B.A. degree in psychology (1972) from La Salle University, an M.A. degree in education (1973) from Seton Hall University, another M.A. degree in industrial-organizational psychology (1981) from Montclair State University, and a Ph.D. degree in industrial-organizational psychology (1985) from Stevens Institute of Technology.

Smither has published many articles in journals such as *Personnel Psychology, Journal of Applied Psychology,* and *Organizational Behavior and Human Decision Processes.* He is currently associate editor of *Personnel Psychology* and has been a member of its editorial board since 1991. He has also served as a reviewer for many other journals. Most of his career has been spent outside an academic setting. Before coming to La Salle in 1992, he worked in corporate human resources for AT&T. He has also worked as a rehabilitation counselor and executive director in nonprofit organizations. He continues to consult in the areas of management development and human resources for firms such as AT&T, Lucent Technologies, Deloitte & Touche, and Crown Cork & Seal.

Seymour Adler is currently senior vice president at Assessment Solutions, Incorporated (ASI). Adler is a principal of ASI and heads the research and development organization at ASI. He has served as a professor of psychology in the School of Business at Stevens Institute of Technology for twelve years and is currently on the faculty of New York University. He received his Ph.D. degree in industrial-organizational psychology from New York University in 1975.

Leanne E. Atwater received a Ph.D. degree in organizational psychology from Claremont Graduate School. Her present position is associate professor of management at Arizona State University West, where she teaches organizational behavior and human resource management. She is also the cofounder of Atwater Management Consulting and a corresponding fellow in the Center for Leadership Studies. Before joining academia, Atwater worked as a personnel research psychologist for the Department of the Navy and taught leadership at the U.S. Naval Academy. She introduced upward feedback into the training of midshipmen at the academy in 1988. Atwater has published many refereed journal articles on the subjects of leadership, upward feedback, and self-awareness. She is the book review editor for *Leadership Quarterly,* serves on the editorial review board for *Group and Organization Management,* and is an ad hoc reviewer for a number of other scholarly journals. She has done consulting and supervisory training for numerous private and public sector companies, often including upward and 360-degree feedback interventions. Organizations in which she has consulted include Loral Defense Systems, Lockheed-Martin, US West, Motorola, Scottsdale Insurance, Universal Instruments, Cyrus Copper, Resource Recycling Technologies, the Social Security Administration, the IRS, the U.S. Department of Labor, the U.S. Navy, the City of Phoenix, Coleman Spas, and the Arizona Department of Public Safety.

H. John Bernardin is a university research professor at Florida Atlantic University. He received his Ph.D. degree from Bowling Green State University. His research interests include performance measurement and personnel selection. He is the former editor of *Human Resource Management Review* and has authored over fifty articles on the subject of performance measurement. His latest book is *Human Resource Management: An Experiential Approach* (1998).

Robert L. Cardy is professor of management in the College of Business at Arizona State University. He is cofounder and editor of the *Journal of Quality Management.* He received his B.S. (1976) and M.A. (1978) degrees in psychology from Central Michigan University and his Ph.D. degree (1982) in industrial-organizational psychology from Virginia Tech.

Georgia T. Chao is associate professor of organizational behavior and head of the Asian Pacific Economic Cooperation Study Center at the Eli Broad Graduate School of Management, Michigan State University. Her research interests include organizational socialization, international human resource management, and career de velopment. Her most recent work examines intercultural aspects of organizational behavior among multinational corporations operating in the Asia-Pacific Rim. She has trained executives on impression management tactics and performance appraisals. Chao serves on the editorial boards of the *Journal of Applied Psychology* and the *International Journal of Selection and Assessment*. Chao received her M.S. (1978) and Ph.D. (1982) degrees in industrial and organizational psychology from The Pennsylvania State University.

Anthony T. Dalessio is a staff director at Bell Atlantic, where he works as an internal consultant with numerous client organizations on the development and implementation of selection tests, assessments, interviews, certification programs, multisource feedback processes, and organizational surveys. Prior to working in the telecommunications industry, he was a director at the Life Insurance Marketing and Research Association (LIMRA), where he managed projects on insurance agent selection and turnover, as well as nationwide surveys on agents' attitudes, productivity, and markets. He has been a faculty member in the industrial-organizational psychology programs at Old Dominion University and the University of Missouri–St. Louis, and has worked as a consultant for the National Aeronautics and Space Administration (NASA) on survey and selection projects. He received his Ph.D. degree in industrial-organizational psychology from Bowling Green State University in 1983.

Donald D. Davis (Ph.D., Michigan State University) is professor of psychology and management at Old Dominion University, where he has worked since 1982. He served as director of the doctoral program in industrial and organizational psychology there from 1986 until 1993. During the 1995–96 academic year he was a Fulbright professor of business administration at Wuhan University, one of China's oldest and most prestigious universities. He has published *Managing Technological Innovation* and a number of journal articles and book chapters on technological innovation, organization change, and Chinese organization and management practices. He serves on the editorial board of the *Journal of High*

Technology Management Research. He has consulted with nearly one hundred organizations throughout the United States and abroad. He has been active in the Society for Industrial and Organizational Psychology (SIOP), serving on numerous committees and as chair of the External Affairs Committee. He cofounded (with Frank Landy) and served as chair of SIOP's International Affairs Committee. In his spare time he teaches and studies t'ai chi ch'uan.

Stephen W. Gilliland is associate professor of management and policy in the College of Business and Public Administration at the University of Arizona. He received his Ph.D. degree in 1992 from Michigan State University and previously taught at Louisiana State University. He is the 1997 recipient of the Ernest J. McCormick Award for Early Career Contributions from the Society for Industrial and Organizational Psychology. He currently serves on the editorial boards of the *Academy of Management Journal, Journal of Applied Psychology,* and *Personnel Psychology.* His research interests include organizational justice, individual decision making, and the application of these areas to human resource policies and procedures. He has published numerous articles on fairness and justice in human resource management.

Mirian M. Graddick is Vice President–Human Resources–Business Effectiveness at AT&T. Graddick joined the company in 1981 and has held a variety of assignments in human resources, including the design and validation of entry-level selection tests, management of an assessment center designed to evaluate middle management potential, management development, human resource planning, management of executive education programs, development of corporate high-potential programs, and succession planning. Graddick has conducted research and written several papers on topics such as the analysis of managerial jobs, the advancement of women into middle and upper management, the selection and development of U.S. expatriates, integrating business planning and human resource planning, and corporate philosophies of management development. Graddick received her B.A. degree in psychology from Hampton University (1975) and her M.S. and Ph.D. degrees from Penn State University in industrial-organizational psychology (1978, 1991). She is a member of the American Psychological Association and is actively involved in the Society for Industrial and Organizational Psychology. In 1990, Graddick was the recipient of AT&T's Catherine B. Cleary Management Award. She serves on the Board of the National Medical Fellowships.

Maria T. Gresham is a doctoral student at the Ohio State University in the Department of Management and Human Resources. She is specializing in organizational behavior and human resources. Her research interests include compensation systems in innovative firms, the management of temporary and core employee relationships, and the effectiveness of virtual organizations.

Christine M. Hagan is a doctoral candidate at Florida Atlantic University's College of Business. She has over twenty years' experience in human resource management in a variety of industries. She serves as a lecturer in the Business School at the University of Miami. Her research interests include customer appraisal, contingency workers, and human resource effectiveness.

Neil M. A. Hauenstein is associate professor of psychology at Virginia Polytechnic Institute and State University, where he also serves as director of the industrial and organizational psychology graduate program. He received his B.A. degree (1979) in psychology from Ohio Northern University and his M.A. (1983) and Ph.D. (1987) degrees from the University of Akron.

Robert L. Heneman is director of graduate programs in labor and human resources and is associate professor of management and human resources in the Max M. Fisher College of Business at the Ohio State University. He received his Ph.D. degree in labor and industrial relations from Michigan State University, an M.A. degree in labor and industrial relations from the University of Illinois at Urbana-Champaign, and a B.A. degree in economics and psychology from Lake Forest College. Prior to joining the Ohio State University, he worked as a human resource specialist for Pacific Gas & Electric Company. His primary areas of research, teaching, and consulting are in performance management, compensation, staffing, and work design. He is on the editorial boards of *Human Resource Management Review, Human Resource Management Journal, Human*

Resource Planning, and *Compensation and Benefits Review.* He has written two books, *Merit Pay: Linking Pay Increases to Performance Ratings* (1992) and *Staffing Organizations* (1997). He has consulted with over fifty public and private sector organizations including IBM, BancOne, Time Warner, Whirlpool, the Limited, Borden, and the states of Ohio, Michigan, and Georgia. Heneman is past division chair, program chair, and Executive Committee member for the Human Resources Division of the Academy of Management. He is also a member of the certification program faculty of the American Compensation Association (ACA) and has served on the research and education committees of the ACA.

Jeffrey S. Kane is associate professor of management at Texas A&M University. He received his Ph.D. degree in organizational psychology from the University of Michigan. His research interests include performance measurement and appraisal and computer adaptations of personnel activities. He is the founder and former editor of *Human Resource Management Review* and the author of numerous articles on performance management and appraisal.

Steve W. J. Kozlowski is professor of organizational psychology at Michigan State University. His major research interests focus on organizational innovation and change, and on the processes by which people adapt to the new and unfamiliar. These interests are represented by his work on organizational downsizing, technology implementation, continuous learning, training adaptive teams, leadership and team development, climate, socialization, and performance appraisal. In his applied work, Kozlowski consults in his specialty areas with private industry and federal agencies, including the Naval Air Warfare Center Training Systems Division, Navy Personnel Research and Development Center, and the Army Research Institute. He is a fellow of the American Psychological Association and the Society for Industrial and Organizational Psychology. He serves on the editorial boards of the *Journal of Applied Psychology* and the *Academy of Management Journal.* Kozlowski received his M.S. (1979) and Ph.D. (1982) degrees in industrial and organizational psychology from The Pennsylvania State University.

Pamela Lane is Human Resources Director–Executive Remuneration at AT&T. Lane joined the company in 1983 and has spent twelve years in the area of executive compensation and benefits. In the mid-nineties, she led an effort within AT&T to define and link measures of performance with shareholder, customer, and employee stakeholder groups. Lane received a B.A. degree in English from Cornell University.

Jay C. Langdon is a doctoral student in the Department of Management and Policy in the College of Business and Public Administration at the University of Arizona. He received his B.S. degree in human resource management in 1996. His research interests include organizational justice and service in human resource management, and space and planetary science. Langdon currently serves as deputy science team leader for the University of Arizona's Student Satellite Project (SSP) and is focused on the interdisciplinary nature of learning in the development of a highly complex functional system.

Stanley B. Malos earned his J.D. degree from the University of California, Los Angeles, School of Law and his Ph.D. degree from Purdue University. Malos currently is associate professor of management/human resource management at San Jose State University's College of Business, where he conducts research on topics including career mobility, affirmative action, and legal issues in human resource management. Malos has practiced trial law in Washington and Alaska, has published in the *Academy of Management Review* and the *Industrial-Organizational Psychologist,* and has presented numerous papers at professional conferences. He is also an accomplished jazz trumpet player and an avid scuba diver.

Jack McGourty received his Ph.D. degree from Stevens Institute of Technology. He is a principal of Assessment Alternatives, a management consulting firm focusing on both employee and organizational assessment and development. He is also a senior researcher for the Stevens Alliance for Technology Management and a research professor at New Jersey Institute of Technology. He is also assessment director for the National Science Foundation's Gateway Coalition (led by Drexel University), focusing on the institutionalization of team assessment processes in undergraduate educational curricula. He has an active program of research and consulting in the area of team development, innovation, and technology-oriented competencies.

Robert F. Morrison joined the Navy Personnel Research and Development Center (NPRDC) as head of the Career Development Systems Division in March 1976. He became a senior scientist in April 1990 and emeritus in 1996. His special area of interest is the career concerns, decisions, behavior, and development of officer, managerial, and professional personnel. Prior to joining NPRDC, he was an associate professor of organization behavior at the University of Toronto's Faculty of Management Studies and operated his own consulting firm. Previously, Morrison had served in personnel research, management development, and employee relations positions for The Sun Company, The Martin Company, The Mead Corporation, and Mobil Oil Company. He is a fellow of the Society for Industrial and Organizational Psychology and the American Psychological Society. He earned an M.S. degree from Iowa State University and a Ph.D. degree in industrial psychology from Purdue University.

Richard R. Reilly received his Ph.D. degree from the University of Tennessee in 1969 and has been a research psychologist at The Educational Testing Service and AT&T. He is a fellow of the American Psychological Association and the American Psychological Society. Since 1982 Reilly has been on the faculty of Stevens Institute of Technology in Hoboken, New Jersey, where he is currently a professor in the Wesley J. Howe School of Technology Management. He is also president of Assessment Alternatives, a management consulting firm located in Florham Park, New Jersey. He has published over fifty articles and several book chapters dealing with topics related to assessment and appraisal. His current research is focused on issues related to team effectiveness and the measurement of team performance.

Paul Squires is currently vice president of consulting services for the Training and Development Division of Assessment Solutions, Incorporated (ASI). Previously, Squires was employed at Lucent Technologies and AT&T for seventeen years, where he worked as an industrial psychologist in numerous roles including selection and testing, employment, human resource information systems, and training and development. Squires received his Ph.D. degree in educational psychology from Fordham University in 1982.

Peter Villanova is associate professor in the Department of Management at Appalachian State University. He received his Ph.D. degree in industrial psychology from Virginia Polytechnic Institute and State University. His research interests include criterion problems, personnel selection, and performance measurement. He serves on the editorial board of *Human Resource Management Review* and coauthored a 1992 *Journal of Applied Psychology* monograph titled "The Criterion Problem."

PART 1

The Performance Appraisal Environment

CHAPTER 1

Effective Performance Management

A Focus on Precision, Customers, and Situational Constraints

H. John Bernardin
Christine M. Hagan
Jeffrey S. Kane
Peter Villanova

The appraisal of performance appraisal is not good. The *Wall Street Journal* reported that "in almost every major survey, most employees who get . . . evaluations and most supervisors who give them rate the process a resounding failure" (Schellhardt, 1996, p. 41). The Society of Human Resource Management concluded that over 90 percent of appraisal systems are unsuccessful, and a 1993 survey by Development Dimensions Incorporated found that most employers expressed "overwhelming" dissatisfaction with their performance management (PM) systems (Smith, Hornsby, & Shirmeyer, 1996). Other surveys have reported similar negative results (Antonioni, 1994; Bernardin & Villanova, 1986; Bretz, Milkovich, & Read, 1992).

Lawler (1994) summarized the dissatisfaction this way: "the problem—and it is well documented—is that most performance appraisal systems do not motivate individuals nor guide their development effectively" (p. 16). In fact, our review of the appraisal and the performance management literature indicates that, regardless of a program's stated purpose (for example, employee feedback, development, compensation, and so on), few studies report positive effects.

Numerous organizations provide anecdotal evidence supporting these statistics. In each of three consecutive years, Pratt and Whitney, the jet engine division of United Technologies, made radical changes to their performance management system. The results of their third-year program led to a huge class action lawsuit and a large out-of-court settlement. Despite all claims regarding their state-of-the-art human resource management (HRM) practices, IBM found it necessary to create a new appraisal system in order to do its massive performance-based restructuring in the early 1990s. Merck, the giant and highly successful pharmaceutical company, made substantial changes in its expensive performance management system because of a lack of variability in the ratings.

Perhaps as a result of all this dissatisfaction, some practitioners argue that traditional top-down supervisory appraisal is not an effective tool for performance management purposes and, in particular, for performance improvement purposes. At least one survey reports an increase in the use of nontraditional appraisal approaches, such as appraisal-by-exception-only, or nonstandardized narrative reviews (Smith et al., 1996). In fact, there is so much displeasure with *performance appraisal* (PA) systems that the very term PA has been virtually censored from our vocabulary and has been replaced with the moniker *performance management* (PM) systems. A plethora of consulting firms now market services and software related to performance management systems. How often has anyone in recent years heard the term PA mentioned favorably? Yet, how often have we heard the term PM substituted for essentially the same practice?

Beer, Ruh, Dawson, McCaa, and Kavanagh (1978) may have been the first to use the term *performance management*. Describing the development, implementation, and evaluation of a PM system for managers at Corning Glass, the program involved a network of related, interactive components, aimed primarily at the individual or work group level, the ultimate purpose of which was to improve organizational effectiveness. Performance appraisal was at the center of the program. This new systems approach, however, meant that individual or group performance was assessed based on an "organizational purpose" perspective. In addition, assessment information was extended to multiple uses, including such areas as employee feedback, promotions, succession planning, terminations, and compensation.

Three Prescriptions for More Effective PM

Our review of research, practice, and litigation related to performance appraisal and management leads us to propose that there are some things that can be done to improve the effectiveness of these systems. We propose that the effects of PM systems will be more positive if and when certain prescriptions are followed that have generally not been heeded by practitioners. These prescriptions are:

- Precision in the definition and measurement of performance is a key element of effective PM.
- The content and measurement of performance should derive from internal and external customers.
- The PM system should incorporate a formal process for investigating and correcting for the effects of situational constraints on performance.

Exhibit 1.1 presents these prescriptions, plus some specific recommendations subsumed under each of them.

HR professionals should keep in mind that any time a PM system is constructed, many factors will come into play. However, in spite of the general pessimism about performance appraisal, it is our belief that when these prescriptions are adopted, PM has the potential to significantly improve organizational effectiveness.

Exhibit 1.2 presents a summary of survey results regarding performance management practices that support the emphasis we are placing on these three prescriptions in the chapter.

The survey results are derived from responses to a questionnaire completed by over 167 administrators, raters, and people who were evaluated using 84 different PM systems in 35 different organizations (Bernardin & Villanova, 1986). These results underscore the importance of the three PM prescriptions for effectiveness if the ultimate purpose of the PM system is to improve the performance of the human resources within the organization. We

Exhibit 1.1. Prescriptions for Effective Performance Management.

1. Strive for as much precision in defining and measuring performance dimensions as is feasible.

   Define performance with a focus on valued outcomes.

   Outcome measures can be defined in terms of relative frequencies of behavior.

   Prescription applies regardless of corporate strategy.

   Define performance dimensions by combining functions with aspects of value (that is, quantity, quality, timeliness, cost-effectiveness, need for supervision, or interpersonal impact).

   Incorporate the measurement of contextual performance into PM system.

2. Link performance dimensions to meeting internal and external customer requirements.

   Internal customer definitions of performance should be linked to external customer satisfaction.

3. Incorporate the measurement of situational constraints into the PM system.

   Focus attention on perceived constraints on performance through self- and supervisory rating process.

Exhibit 1.2. Key Points of Survey Results.

1. The majority of people who are rated less than the highest on a rating scale disagree with the rating more than they agree. More specific performance content as a basis for the appraisal reduces this effect but a majority nonetheless still disagree with the rating more than they agree.

2. The majority of the people who disagree with the rating are less motivated and less satisfied with their jobs after the appraisal.

3. The majority of these people report having "little or no idea" how to improve their performance.

4. The differences between self- and supervisory appraisals are largely a function of perceptions related to factors perceived to be beyond the control of the performers.

5. Performers make more external attributions while observers make more internal attributions.

will address each of these prescriptions in the sections to follow. While the three prescriptions have received relatively little research attention, the research that has been conducted generally supports our recommendations. This research is described within the chapter.

All the attention paid to performance appraisal in general is testimony to its potentially pivotal role in influencing organizational performance and effectiveness. Thus it is unfortunate that neither concern about nor passion for a subject matter can be directly translated into operational recommendations that are guaranteed to succeed (Borman, 1991). Central to our perspective is the view that the most effective PM systems recognize that appraisal is not an end in itself; rather, it is a critical component of a much broader set of human resource practices that should be clearly linked to business performance, personal and organizational development, and corporate strategy and culture (Ulrich, 1997).

While it is our view that no single PM system is ideal for all jobs and for all purposes in all organizations, we also believe that some alternatives stand out as preferable under all circumstances, regardless of the particular strategy or culture. We characterize these as noncontingent choices or best practice elements. We believe that the three prescriptions—precision in measurement, customer focus, and consideration of situational constraints—fall into this best practices category and that these best practice prescriptions apply regardless of the corporate strategy.

Precision in PM Content: Definition and Measurement

Precision in both defining and in measuring performance is critical to effective performance management. In fact, before designing any appraisal or PM program, it is necessary to develop a clear understanding of exactly what is meant by "work performance." We define *performance* as the record of outcomes produced on a specified job function, activity, or behavior during a specified time period (Bernardin & Beatty, 1984). Within this definition, performance on a job as a whole would be equal to the sum (or average) of performance on the critical job functions or behaviors. With this outcomes-based definition, performance is something that is separate and distinct from the person who produced it or

n's characteristics. Unfortunately, many PM programs
cus on the person rather than on the person's performance.
There still seems to be confusion about the distinction between
measures of performance and evaluations of the performer's personal traits or, more recently, competencies.

Measuring Competencies
Versus Measuring Performance

Increasingly, we note a trend in evaluating the extent to which
ratees possess certain "competencies." This trend concerns us
because these so-called competencies look a whole lot like the old
traits that have been condemned in a plethora of articles on
appraisal. As an illustration, the managerial competencies used by
the American Management Association include self-confidence,
positive regard, self-control, spontaneity, stamina, and adaptability
(Parry, 1996). Competencies such as these can be a useful component in a program of personal development or perhaps in defining
elements of a job function. But an assessment of my competencies
is not a measure of my performance. PM systems should focus on a
record of outcomes. An assessment of skills, traits, competencies,
knowledge, or abilities of the performers could of course be helpful for employee development—but if alleged competencies such
as self-control and stamina are to be assessed, perhaps performance
tests and clinical assessment are a better way to go.

PM can (and should) focus on *the record of outcomes* that the person (or persons) actually achieved on the job. There is nothing
wrong with assessing what the person possesses by way of any of
these areas; we're just not measuring performance when we do so.
We can assess the extent to which a person possesses certain technical skills through ratings by those familiar with a person's skills
(although it would probably be better to use some form of test). It
is the manifestation of those skills on the job in the form of outcomes that constitutes performance. We can assess L.A. Laker
Shaquille O'Neil's psychomotor skills, his height, and his weight,
all of which may be predictors or correlates of his performance.
But his foul-shooting in 1996 was 46 percent and that is one element of his performance.

Stark, Luther, and Valvano (1996) describe high levels of disagreement among managers at Jaguar Cars when the managers

received low ratings on a competency they label "integrity." While Jaguar had developed behavioral definitions of integrity, the overall rating on this factor was the major source of the disagreement. Perhaps an elimination of such competency labels would help focus the fifteen managers' attention on actual behavior and the outcomes that result from the behavior. Office Depot evaluates its store managers on their "personal maturity." Needless to say, store managers often disagree with ratings indicating they need work on their personal maturity. Managers had far less difficulty understanding a rating reflecting "loses temper in disagreements with associates."

Corporate Strategy and PM Characteristics

In a frequently cited *Harvard Business Review* article, Treacy and Wiersema (1993) present a model of three paths to competitive advantage. These three paths are operational excellence, product leadership strategy, and customer intimacy strategy. Beatty and Schneier (1997) present an excellent summary of this model and its implications for human resource practice. Numerous successful companies are cited as examples for each of these three corporate strategies. It is further suggested that PM systems should be structurally different as a function of the strategy (Gubman, 1995). However, in our interviews with corporate representatives from these companies who were familiar with their performance appraisal and management systems, we found no differences in PM system characteristics as a function of the strategy in which they were classified (Bernardin & Kane, 1997). For example, Gubman hypothesized a closer linkage between customer satisfaction data and PM criteria for the "customer intimacy" companies. We found no stronger connection between customer satisfaction data and employee PM measures for this strategy. However, we did find a relatively stronger connection between customer satisfaction data, formal PM systems, and important personal outcomes (for example, rewards and recognitions) for almost all the highly successful companies cited in these articles *regardless of their particular hypothesized strategy.*

Gubman (1995) also suggests that successful corporations following the operational excellence path are more likely to have more specific and clearly defined performance standards than successful firms representing the other two paths. Again, our interviews did not find more precision in the definitions of performance for "operational excellence" firms. Rather, our interviews found relatively greater precision in criterion measurement for those companies identified as effective regardless of their strategy when compared to a control group of companies not identified as effective representations of one of the three strategies.

Cardy (1997) also suggests that such precision "may not be possible in complex and dynamic environments. Process control may also philosophically and operationally work against empowerment and innovation attempts" (pp. 12–13). We believe empowerment as related to PM can be fostered by having those who are empowered define the record of performance outcomes with more clarity. Performers can be empowered to define their own outcomes as they relate to their customers. One thing is certain. The empowered will have to compile some record of outcomes or they will not be empowered for long. The same argument applies to those involved in creative or innovative enterprises. So-called creative workers who produce no outcomes will not be employed for long in even the most creative of enterprises.

The bottom line seems clear: Precision in the measurement of outcomes is key to the effective implementation and maintenance of a corporate strategy regardless of that strategy (Beatty & Schneier, 1997).

Should We Measure Behaviors or Outcomes in PM Systems?

Many performance appraisal experts would not agree with our definition of performance as a record of outcomes. Most scholars advocate that performance appraisal should focus on behaviors rather than on the results or outcomes that derive from those behaviors (for example, Murphy & Cleveland, 1991; Latham, 1986). Those who may disagree with us argue that there are too many problems and biases besetting the measurement of results-based criteria. Feldman (1992) states that "performance numbers" may be "seriously misleading or absent altogether," and he argues that "artistic or creative jobs" cannot be evaluated at all except in terms of purely subjective judgments. Murphy and Cleveland state that "performance must ultimately be defined in terms of behaviors . . . the domain of performance is best defined as a domain of behaviors rather than a set of outcomes" (p. 92).

Our view is that outcomes must be the critical component of a PM system, that the definitions of outcomes should be derived from critical internal and external *customers* (discussed later in this chapter), and that outcomes can be defined and measured for virtually any job. Behaviors can (and should) be a part of any definition of performance as long as a consequence or outcome can be theoretically linked to the behavior (Olian & Rynes, 1991). Bernardin (1992) borrowed a quote from a Digital Equipment Corporation manager: "If the behaviors don't produce a result that is useful to the boss, the behaviors don't count." While we disagree with the focus on "the boss" here instead of "the customer," we agree that the basic sentiment is a realistic and appropriate one. Becker, Huselid, Pickus, and Spratt (1997) put it succinctly: "HR matters when it can point to human capital problems that limit the ability of the firm to achieve important business priorities and can provide HR solutions to those problems. Adopting the latest appraisal methodology, for example, only creates value when it can be evaluated within this context" (p. 45).

The academic disagreement regarding the content of appraisal can be reconciled with our definition of outcomes. We include in our definition of a performance outcome the frequency that a performer exhibits a behavior related to some aspect of value such as quantity, quality, or cost. For example, the *record of outcomes* for the behavior "seeks input from knowledgeable parties before making a decision" is the frequency of this behavior relative to all possible occasions in which a manager had an opportunity to seek expertise before making a decision. Another example of an outcome for a manager's job is "identifies legitimate situational constraints on the performance of his or her associates." At the Federal Aviation Administration, air traffic controllers rated their supervisors on the extent to which this behavior was exhibited relative to all the occasions when situational constraints had an impact on associates' work. A related item requiring a rating of frequency was "took action to reduce or eliminate job factors that interfered with my ability to do my work."

As another example of our concept of performance outcomes, let us consider this chapter as one outcome from the record of outcomes produced by the four authors. We all work for universities that have mission statements involving advancing knowledge in certain academic disciplines. Under the job function "Research," the four authors obviously published one chapter in a professional series book. While researching the topic and the act of writing this chapter are obvious behaviors related to our performance, it was the publication of this *one* chapter that at least theoretically contributes to the mission statement of our universities. This single outcome is first a measure of the quantity of our research records. The quality aspect of this record is surely more important in terms of the mission statement and of course more difficult to measure, particularly if we rely on our respective managers to evaluate quality. This chapter then constitutes one outcome from our record of outcomes for a defined period of time. Your appraisal of this outcome and the other chapters in this book constitutes a theoretical external customer's assessment of the quality of this outcome.

Among the companies that embrace this conceptualization of performance outcomes in combination with so-called objective data are Ritz-Carlton Hotels, Pizza Hut, Digital Equipment, Burger King, Jaguar Cars, Office Depot, Monsanto, and Blockbuster Video. These organizations combine internal and external customer-based survey data with countable results in order to derive a composite performance score for managers, work units, stores, districts, and even regions (Kane & Russell, 1998). At Office Depot, for example, frequency assessments on these outcomes are combined with the so-called objective measures of performance such as profit and loss data, shrinkage, sales, employee turnover, mystery shopper ratings, and training completed to provide the full record of performance for store managers and district managers. These outcomes are then assessed for effectiveness based on unit or corporate objectives (Pace & Bounds, 1991).

Information systems now allow for more useful (and valid) interpretation of such data and adjustment of almost all countable results to facilitate a fairer and more relevant PM system (Ghorpade & Chen, 1995; Heilmann, 1994). For example, turnover rates for store associates at Office Depot are considered and corrected in the context of the unemployment rate for the store's geographical area. Sales results are considered and adjusted in the context of both competitor and Office Depot corporate behavior (for example, new stores).

Countable results and relative frequencies of outcomes from exhibited behaviors can all be appraised in terms of six aspects of value. Quantity is but one aspect of the value of our work. Quality is another and more important aspect. Next, we discuss the six aspects of value in which all performance outcomes can be classified.

Value in the Definition of Performance

Tiffany's of New York evaluates its managers on a job function called "Decision-Making in Non-Routine Situations." The effectiveness with which a manager carries out this function could be described in terms of six different possible outcomes or aspects of value: quantity, quality, timeliness, cost-effectiveness, need for supervision, and interpersonal impact. At Tiffany's, raters consider the *quantity* and the *quality* of such decisions in terms of their accuracy or effectiveness, and the *timeliness* of such decisions in the sense of whether they are made in time to allow for effective implementation. We might also consider the *cost-effectiveness* of these decisions in the sense of whether they adequately account for the cost implications among the available alternatives. Managers could also be evaluated on the *interpersonal impact* of such decision making in the sense of considering issues like the equity of the workload the decisions imposed on work associates. In addition, we might consider the extent to which a manager had a *need for supervision* to attain a given outcome level.

Given all these possible ways in which performance on the decision-making function can be valued, it becomes apparent that eliciting a single rating on the overall performance of such a function could be difficult. How can we be sure that a rater considers all the relevant aspects of value for a particular function? How can we be sure that any two raters are attaching the same relative weights to the outcomes in arriving at their overall judgment on the function? The answer is that when we elicit ratings on job functions as a whole, we can't be sure of any of these things—we effectively abdicate control of the appraisal to the whims of raters. One remedy for this situation is to define (and ultimately rate) each element of appraisal content in terms of a job function and only one of its relevant aspects of value. This approach also applies to PM systems calling for work standards, performance goals, or objectives. (Our review of both PM literature and real-world practices indicates that there is very little, if any, operational distinction among the terms *standards, goals,* or *objectives;* the terms appear to be used interchangeably.) Precise definition of these different aspects of performance outcomes is a critical component of our first prescription for more effective PM.

It is possible that other aspects of value may emerge as relevant bases on which to assess performance on job functions or behaviors, and that one or more of the aspects of value could be subsumed under another criterion. For example, an argument could be made that need for supervision could be subsumed under cost-effectiveness. We have found that these six have successfully encompassed the important dimensions along which the value of performance can vary.

We will refer to the combination of a job function with one aspect of value as a *performance dimension.* Exhibit 1.3 presents examples of performance dimensions that apply this model for performance measurement. The first example combines a monitoring function with the quality aspect of value and provides three anchors to define effectiveness. The second dimension combines the timeliness aspect with a controlling function. The effectiveness definitions, values, weights for the dimensions, and the ultimate ratings on the dimension should be determined by a sample of critical internal and external customers (discussed later in this chapter).

Factors to Consider in Dimension Selection

As we discuss later, the definition and selection of the performance dimensions to be used should derive from those internal and external customers of the workers' or work units' outcomes. However, while importance for critical internal and external customers is the essential criterion for defining and assessing dimensions, other issues should also be assessed in selecting the dimensions to be included and determining whether assessments should be made on individual workers or work units.

First, if raters cannot observe the population or a representative sample of each employee's performance, or if they cannot provide data for the record of frequency for the exhibited outcome, then the dimension should not be included in the PM system. Sec-

Exhibit 1.3. Examples of Performance Dimensions.

Quality in MONITORING. When this manager received a higher-level inquiry concerning subordinates' work outputs or progress toward objectives:

(HIGH): Furnished information in response to the inquiry that was COMPLETELY ACCURATE with respect to both the central questions posed by the inquiry and the supporting details.

(MED): Furnished information that was accurate with respect to ALL of the central questions posed by the inquiry but inaccurate with respect to MOST of the supporting details.

(LOW): Furnished information that was inaccurate with respect to one or more of the central questions posed by the inquiry.

Timeliness in CONTROLLING. When this manager became aware of a deviation from standards or schedules by a subordinate individual or work unit:

(HIGH): Intervened early enough so that subordinates didn't have to ignore other duties to correct the deviations before unacceptable costs or schedule overruns had occurred.

(MED): Intervened so late that subordinates had to ignore most other duties to correct the deviations before unacceptable costs or schedule overruns had occurred.

(LOW): Intervened too late for the subordinates to correct the deviations before unacceptable costs or schedule overruns had occurred.

---

ond, it is advisable to avoid including any dimension where employees might easily manipulate the rater's impression of how effectively they are performing. The inclusion of such a dimension will only undermine the entire PM system and contribute nothing positive. Third, employee performance on each dimension should not be dependent on the performance of other employees. If the dimension is important to critical customers but the outcomes can only be linked to the work group, the assessment should be made at the group or unit level.

The Need for Specificity in Goals, Objectives, and Standards

Once an organization identifies the important performance dimensions, specific definition of the dimensions and the levels of effectiveness of the dimensions is critical. Surveys indicate that the majority of companies use some form of standards-based or management-by-objectives PM systems (for example, Bretz, Milkovich, & Read, 1992). But Bernardin, Hagan, and Hennessey (1995) found that fewer than 25 percent of the standards or objectives written for or by managers had a moderate (or greater) level of specificity in the definition of the outcome or the performance level. While the words *quality* and *quantity* were often mentioned in the standard, for example, most standards provided no specificity on these aspects of value. It should come as no surprise that raters and ratees often disagreed over exactly what constituted a given level of performance or whether a standard had been met or exceeded (see Exhibit 1.2).

Performance standards have been defined as levels of performance that correspond to predesignated levels of effectiveness (Bernardin & Beatty, 1984). As such, they convey critical information that affects all appraisal participants. From a rater's point of view, standards form the frame of reference within which to judge a ratee's performance. Depending on the nature of the standards, this comparison can range from a matching process involving a binary determination (for example, yes/no) to a complex integration process in which a rater assigns values to each performance element, then combines them to arrive at an overall evaluation (Murphy & Cleveland, 1995). The values assigned can be (and should be) linked to the achievement of important business objectives.

From a ratee's point of view, performance standards are an important communication mechanism through which employees decipher what is expected of them (Bobko & Colella, 1994). From an organization's point of view, performance standards are a key factor in creating a job-content foundation for an appraisal process and serve as a mechanism for communicating what the organization means by "high performance." Standards can thus be a key linking pin that aligns employee efforts with organizational strategies, goals, and objectives.

It is no surprise that many discussions about appraisal include the assertion that clear, specific performance standards, rather than ambiguous standards or no standards, will improve the overall accuracy and effectiveness of an appraisal process (for example, Kane & Russell, 1998). However, little empirical research has been directed at performance standards: their attributes, how they develop, and the results that occur when they are poorly designed or absent (Murphy & Cleveland, 1995). This is particularly surprising when one considers the amount of research attention that has been directed at employment standards (Bobko & Colella, 1994). In fact, we found few real-world studies that investigated the effects of performance standard specificity, measurability, and objectivity on rating effectiveness. Both Bernardin, Hagan, and Hennessey (1995) and Schrader and Steiner (1996) found strong effects for the value of more specific and objective performance standards. Viswesvaran, Ones, and Schmidt (1996) also found higher interrater reliabilities for less ambiguous standards. Of course, aside from the direct potential performance enhancement effects that clear and specific standards provide, they also serve an important bias-suppression effect that may not only reduce instances of employee grievance but also promote perceptions of fairness with the PM system (Kane & Russell, 1998; Taylor, Tracy, Renard, Harrison, & Carroll, 1995).

Several management theories have been built on the core assumption that clear, unambiguous expectations or standards are an important element of effectiveness. Bobko and Colella (1994) provide an extensive review of such related literature. From goal-setting research, they cite evidence to support the following contentions: performance standards directly influence an individual's self-set goals; an individual's personal goals regulate actions; and those aspiring to achieve difficult, specific goals perform better than those who work toward easy, vague, or no goals (for example, Locke, Shaw, Saari, & Latham, 1981). Similarly, feedback theory research suggests that specific information concerning one's performance positively influences future effectiveness (Tubbs, 1986). Specific performance standards play an important role when used as the foundation for developing such performance feedback. Using the intersection of goal-setting and feedback theory, Bobko and Colella (1994) offer the following research hypothesis: "Performance standards that are defined in specific . . . terms will lead to greater motivation, and consequently greater performance, than those that are vaguely defined" (p. 14).

According to the path-goal theory of leadership, one of the key strategic functions of a leader is path clarification: that is, to clarify for subordinates the specific kinds of behaviors that will lead to effective goal accomplishment (Evans, 1970).

Over forty years ago, when the earliest foundations for management by objectives (MBO) were being formulated, the value of clear, precise goals or targets was a basic underlying assumption of the method (see Drucker, 1954, pp. 126–127).

In spite of this research and theory, some scholars have been skeptical. Milkovich and Wigdor (1991) asserted that "the search for a high degree of precision in measurement does not appear to be economically viable in most applied settings; many believe that there is little to be gained from such a level of precision" (p. 3). Although it is not clear from the text, justification for this position appears to be based on conclusions from research concerning rating formats and, more recently, from research concerning the cognitive aspects of performance appraisal (for example, Landy & Farr, 1980). We disagree with this conclusion. First, albeit limited, the empirical studies on the subject support the call for precision in performance definition and measurement (for example, Bernardin, 1992; Bernardin & Smith, 1981). Second, any assertions based on research from cognitive psychology *must* include the acknowledgment that virtually all of this research was conducted in laboratory settings that typically lacked the characteristics necessary for generalizing the findings directly to real-world settings (Bernardin & Villanova, 1986). For example, few laboratory studies involve working relationships between raters and ratees, and the ratings have no administrative significance. Finally, we believe that case studies, survey evidence, and substantial research from related fields (goal setting, feedback, leadership, MBO) supports our view as well (for example, Tubbs, 1986; Wright & Kacmar, 1994). Merck, for example, placed great emphasis on the precision of measurement in its PM system and held managers accountable for the quality of the performance objectives that were the basis of the Merck PM system. The objectives were reviewed not only for their measurability but also for their relationship to critical business objectives. In fact, these changes in the PM system correlated positively with return on assets (Murphy, 1993). One correlational study also supports the importance of precision in measurement. McDonald and Smith

(1995) found that companies with relatively higher profits, higher stock value, and significantly higher return on equity used more precise definitions of performance that were linked to specific corporate objectives.

To summarize, then, precision in the definition of performance and in setting performance standards is critical in creating and sustaining an effective PM system. The research relevant to this proposition from a variety of research trails is compelling. As a foundation for rater assessments, formal standards, goals, or objectives focus rater attention on established performance criteria and limit the opportunity for extraneous, irrelevant factors to contaminate rater judgment. As Drucker recommended decades ago, the consideration and limiting of these external constraints, when combined with greater precision in the definition of performance, should result in more effective PM.

How Much Specificity for PM Dimensions?

In general, we would say that striving to achieve precision in performance definition and measurement is a best practice and applies to all appraisal situations in which the purpose of the appraisal is to facilitate improvement in performance. The HR professional should be prepared to exercise a degree of judgment in identifying the optimal level of specificity. Positions contain a collection of activities that typically range from the general, such as human relations activities and administrative responsibilities, to the highly specific, such as listening to both parties in a conflict before deciding on a resolution, maintaining records of instances of corrective communications to employees, and of the way a leader communicates assignments to employees. We view the decision concerning degree of specificity as a trade-off between a focus on individual performance information versus the need to compare individual appraisal scores. On one hand, precision enhances appraisal's potential as an organization communications vehicle. Employees are better able to direct their own performance efforts when they know what is expected of them. Thus greater specificity should create more effective performance. And, of course, improved effectiveness is a primary goal of PM systems. On the other hand, the greater the level of specificity, the more different things there will be to assess for each ratee. Here, the multiple purposes of the PM system should provide guidance to the HR professional. Particularly when the ratings are to be used to compare performers for pay or promotional considerations, it is usually preferable to formulate the job functions that must be observed to be assessed at a broader level so that performer scores can be legitimately compared. However, there are also occasions when more detailed and specific definitions of outcomes, functions, tasks, behaviors, or activities should be the constructs to be assessed even when scores must be compared for an administrative purpose (for example, static job requirements with a finite number of important activities). Finally, performance appraisals that become the subject of litigation are more defensible when the basis of the appraisal is more specific (Bernardin, Hennessey, & Peyrefitte, 1995; see also Chapter Two in this volume).

Linking PM Dimensions to Customer Satisfaction Data

The survey data summarized in Exhibit 1.2 also show that employees have a clearer understanding of what constitutes effective performance when the definition of performance is related to outcomes based on customer requirements. While many PM experts would agree that outcome or results measures can be derived in businesses focused on the production of goods, most contend that such data are more difficult to develop when organizations are engaged in providing services (for example, Cardy & Dobbins, 1994). Several well-documented characteristics of services differentiate them from the output of traditional production organizations: *intangibility* (that is, they are performances rather than objects); *heterogeneity* (that is, their performance often varies from producer to producer, from customer to customer, from day to day); and *inseparability* (that is, many services are produced only at the time they are consumed) (Parasuraman, Zeithaml, & Berry, 1988). Yi (1990) and Lengnick-Hall (1996) note that marketing literature reflects two views of customer satisfaction: as an *outcome,* and as an *experiential process* that occurs throughout consumption (see also Oliver & De Sarbo, 1988; Westbrook & Reilly, 1983).

Rust and Oliver (1994) further define successful services design and delivery as consisting of three distinct components: product design, service environment design, and service delivery. Designing the product itself involves identifying the specific features that will be embodied in the service. The environment involves designing the setting and the props that will be used to administer the service. The service delivery involves the way the service is, in fact, provided in a particular transaction, on a particular occasion. The first two of the three components are typically designed and built into the service (Rust & Oliver, 1994). The third focuses entirely on the actual service provision event, the perceptions concerning behaviors that occur, and the key results of the deliverer-customer interaction (for example, Bitner, Booms, & Mohr, 1994).

The third component (service delivery) suggests a critical role for employees in service industries that has largely been absent in traditional manufacturing organizations. Discussions of strategic HR planning usually focus on meeting or exceeding customer requirements as the ultimate criterion for strategic planning, the key to "strategic unity" and making HRM activities more relevant (for example, Ulrich, 1997). Within this model, then, ensuring that employees are properly selected, trained, appraised, and rewarded to respond effectively to this customer challenge should be a key element of an organization's HR strategy. We believe that linking well-defined customer outcomes with the PM dimensions is an ideal way to begin to create a high-performance, customer-focused organization. Whether individual performers or units of performance are assessed on these outcomes largely depends on whether it is possible (and practical) to assess at the individual performer level.

With this model of service marketing as a guideline, customer satisfaction is a function of the representative customer requirements and expectations regarding the services. The frequency with which these requirements are met for repeated services becomes the outcome measure. For example, Federal Express determined that customers calling for service expect to speak with a FedEx representative within ten seconds of the call going through. The frequency with which this expectation is met represents one quantity aspect of the service. Villanova (1992) presents a model for customer-based criterion development that is summarized in Exhibit 1.4. The stages of the model go from identification of critical customers to the determination of relevance weights for the performance dimensions.

Exhibit 1.4. Steps in the Development of Customer-Based Outcome Measures.

1. In the context of business unit performance data, benchmark data, customer-based research, and unit-level objectives, identify the products or services necessary to achieve the goals related to the requirements of the external customers.
2. Collect data on internal customer requirements and determine relationships with external customer requirements from Step 1.
3. Develop a priority list and importance weights for internal demands based on importance for external requirements. Data collection will yield customer-based PM criteria.
4. Consult with work unit on the products required based on unit-level goals from Steps 1 and 2. The product specifications should be derived from customer-based research—that is, customers determine the job specifications in terms of aspects of value (for example, quantity, timeliness, and especially quality).

This marketing orientation does not rule out the role of the manager or supervisor in the derivation of performance dimensions or in the ultimate performance appraisals. There are clearly some aspects of value that should be defined and assessed by a manager or supervisor that are also surely relevant to overall performance (for example, cost-effectiveness). Profit and loss statements remain the sine qua non of most management positions and PM systems, like all HR systems, should be assessed in this context.

In developing an operational blueprint for "horizontal"—that is, customer-focused—PA, McKinsey and Company specifically recommended tying strategic performance goals directly to customer satisfaction and ensuring that every position in the organization had maximum contact with customers and suppliers (Stewart, 1992). Within the HR research community, however, the attention that has been directed at customer feedback has been primarily in the context of multirater appraisal (Johnson, Olson, & Courtney, 1996). However, despite the strong interest in multisource appraisal, there has been relatively little research on the role of customers as a source of feedback (Johnson et al., 1996). Edwards and Ewen (1996) indicate that customer feedback provides valuable information to an organization—as an input to the production process, as a presence in the quality control area, as an opportunity to increase understanding about what customers value, and as information on which to base future product development efforts. London and Beatty (1993) argue that internal and external customer feedback could provide a source of competitive advantage, provided that the feedback is translated into specific outcomes that focus directly on creating customer value.

PM and Total Quality Management

For many years, academic research concerning the quality movement lagged behind the practitioners' world (Rust & Oliver, 1994). Some recent work in performance appraisal is now theoretically tied into the TQM movement (for example, Masterson & Taylor, 1996). Various conceptualizations of customer satisfaction, customer perception of quality, and customer perception about pure value have been offered (Bitner & Hubbert, 1994). Survey instruments such as SERVQUAL (Parasuraman, Berry, & Zeithaml, 1993) represent considerable progress in identifying and operationalizing the consumer constructs that influence purchasing behavior (De Sarbo, Huff, Rolandelli, & Choi, 1994). Similarly, studies focusing on customer or employee reactions to the processes that surround an organization's provision of a product or service have deepened our understanding of consumer behavior relative to customer-employee interactions (for example, Bitner, Booms, & Tetrault, 1990).

In spite of this attention, there is little research linking responses on these instruments with performance appraisal constructs, performance management, or other HR practices. We have arrived at a point where human resource scholars and practitioners should turn attention to the subject of customer feedback, its structure, and its potential role in defining PM content and focus. In particular, when PM is viewed as the total system of gathering relevant information, providing specific feedback to individuals and work groups, and applying such information for the improvement of organizational effectiveness, then customer feedback clearly holds promise.

There are case studies indicating that some organizations are aggressively trying to link customer feedback with HR practices. The Ritz-Carlton has followed this model, not only linking specific items on its customer satisfaction instrument with the constructs defining its PM system, but also using a performance weighting system based on the predictive value of each item for overall customer satisfaction. The PM data are then linked to bonus points in the compensation system. Office Depot links responses from its annual Customer Satisfaction Measurement Program to specific performance standards for managers assigned to particular industrial segments. The managerial pay-for-performance system is then tied to an assessment of performance relative to these standards. Harley Davidson developed a customer satisfaction instrument for retailers selling its product and then linked the satisfaction data with managerial process improvement assessments. Some companies now tie PM criteria to the results of evaluations from so-called professional customers or mystery shoppers. We will examine this approach to linking PM constructs to customer satisfaction next.

The Use of Mystery Shoppers

The retail industry has made noteworthy efforts in soliciting customer feedback through its use of mystery shopping. Typically, this involves contracting with an organization to provide anonymous individuals who periodically shop in the store, evaluating and reporting about the experience from a customer's viewpoint. Mystery shoppers usually review a predetermined menu of variables for each store they visit, based on criteria established by the retail organization. At the Limited and the GAP, for example, mystery shoppers follow a script to test the extent to which store employees adhere to their training regarding customer interactions.

The use of mystery shopping has become so popular that in 1994, one contractor reported a professional shopping staff of 8,800 and a business that was growing at the rate of 50 percent per year (Helliker, 1994). Other organizations, including Burger King, Neiman Marcus, Hyatt Hotels, Hertz Auto Rentals, Barney's New York, and Revco Drug Stores have had extensive experience using mystery shoppers to obtain customer-based information.

One corporate example of linking PM criteria to mystery shopper data is Office Depot. There, mystery shopping data is converted into a Customer Satisfaction Index (CSI) that also includes customer complaints. The CSI is then compiled and reported to each store manager once a month. The data, aggregated across the year, becomes a key determinant of each manager's annual appraisal, bonus, base salary increase, and objectives for the next appraisal cycle.

Our literature search turned up no systematic study of the validity and reliability of mystery shopping, nor has the effect of mystery shopping on business performance been rigorously examined. It is our belief that the ability of mystery shopping to materially influence organizational effectiveness will be directly tied to the degree to which key customer requirements—which are predictive of actual purchase behavior—are identified. These customer requirements are then translated into mystery shopping criteria, and then gathered with a high level of precision.

Bolton and Drew (1994) express concern that criteria full of purely objective efficiency data are easiest to identify and contract out, so mystery shoppers are focusing most often on issues such as determining the length of time that it takes an associate to approach them, or how long they await final service delivery, or the number of times the telephone rings before it is answered, or the number of different individuals that become involved when a customer request strays from the norm. These measures are effective customer measures *only* when they capture information that real customers value highly. In other words, if an organization's source of competitive advantage is price or convenience or uniqueness of service features, or value in relation to competitors, then the efficiency measures mentioned here may create an inaccurate or a mixed signal to employees about the performance efforts that have real value.

The Selection of External Customers

A critical issue is the identification of external customers for the purpose of soliciting performance feedback. In niche businesses, this may be relatively simple. But often the decision is not so clearcut. For example, when the recipient of the service is different from the payer—as is the case in health care and in other types of insured services—who is the customer? In retail operations, particularly in high-volume, low-price businesses, finding the shoppers whose feedback is generally representative of the cross-section of customers presents a considerable dilemma. Typically, an organization must recognize that it has a variety of customers, that different customers have different needs, and that an organization cannot satisfy all customer needs equally (Shapiro, 1988).

All customers are important—but invariably some are more important than others. Collaboration among various functions is important when pinpointing the key target accounts and market segments (Shapiro, 1988, p. 121).

Thus choosing customers whose feedback is valued becomes a key strategic decision. Once these customers are identified, the question becomes how easily can an organization access them for a survey? A rental car company may survey all customers (or a random selection of all customers) eight weeks after their rental experience with the organization. Since rental car customers must show valid drivers' licenses with names and addresses, customers should be readily accessible by mail. Without such information and access, the validity and reliability of customer feedback could be a problem. Organizations that rely solely on customer complaints, or on customers who agree to complete voluntary surveys, must deal with the possibility that the feedback is not representative of the typical or key customers. Under such circumstances, it may be tempting for an organization to avoid such problems in favor of a mystery shopping approach to obtain feedback.

We see at least two general applications for customer feedback in an appraisal context. First, when an individual occupies a key boundary-spanning role linking the customer with the organization, the customer may be in the best position to judge individual performance.

Andersen Consulting, for example, places considerable weight on what the customers say about the performance of the Andersen associate assigned to a particular client and project. Andersen is among the large consulting firms that have taken advantage of the trend toward outsourcing HR functions and projects and assuming a key boundary-spanning role with the customer. Some Andersen employees work full time for particular clients in HR and other functional areas. Needless to say, the customer needs to be pleased with the work.

A second purpose is to gather more general, systematic information so as to determine whether the organization is ready to respond to what customers want, when they want it, and how they want it (Bolton & Drew, 1994). These data thus have the potential to integrate marketing strategies with HR activities and personnel policies. Attention should be directed at how customer feedback is specifically applied within organizations to shape performance management practice. A key question here would be, given particular marketing strategies, which HR interventions respond most effectively and efficiently to customer feedback?

The Role of Internal Customers to Derive PM Dimensions

Thus far, our discussion has focused on external customers (or their surrogates) as a source for performance dimension development. However, performance feedback emanating from internal customers holds considerable promise as well (Sulzer-Azaroff & Harshbarger, 1995). When one of us asked an organization's associates to define an internal customer, one answered that it was a "a guy who comes in to pay his bill." This is not what we had in mind. *Internal customers* are the organization's recipients of vital products or services provided by that same organization's internal suppliers. Such internal products and services must of course be linked to the real external customers who purchase the products or services being offered for sale (Villanova, 1992). Hauser, Simester, and Wernerfelt (1996) suggest that an internal customer focus is a logical next move to drive a marketing orientation deep within an organization once the organization implements an external customer feedback process, noting two advantages to such an approach. First, an internal customer focus may better align internal supplier objectives with firm objectives, since they sometimes conflict (Heilmann, 1994). Second, especially when technical skills are involved, the internal customer may be in the best position to accurately appraise the effectiveness of specific outcomes and also to report on what specific functions contribute to the fulfillment of external satisfaction criteria. This internal outcome assessment, if properly aligned with customer expectations, should be theoretically predictive of external customer satisfaction. A third advantage is that performance appraisal by internal customers may foster a consistent, market-oriented cultural norm throughout the entire organization. This is important particularly if the focus on customers becomes blurred the deeper into the organization one ventures. For example, the Metropolitan Life Insurance Company of

New York determined that only 25 percent of its employees were engaged in directly servicing external customers (Zeithaml, Parasuraman, & Berry, 1990). Presumably, the remaining 75 percent of the organization is involved in providing some form of support functions related to servicing customer needs. In this type of case, internal customer appraisal may drive a customer-focus culture deeper into the firm (Hauser et al., 1996) and buttress the view that an organization is a collection of upstream-downstream, value-adding, customer-focused activities. Weyerhaeuser uses "customer requirements analysis deployment" to coordinate staff support departments such as HR with line departments such as sales and marketing. The supplier departments receive a formal evaluation from their internal customers (McLaurin & Bell, 1993).

Our emphasis on developing a PM system that includes an internal customer focus is consistent with Deming's first prescription for successful performance appraisal: organizations must clearly and consistently communicate the firm's mission or constancy of purpose (Cardy & Dobbins, 1994; Deming, 1986). What better way to do this than through institutionalizing the customer perspective inside the organization?

Internal and external customers should play a critical role in determining the content that is the basis for the appraisals of the supplier (Antonioni, 1994). If their assessments are to be sought as inputs to the appraisal, then they should also be involved in defining the dimensions of performance.

The current interest and recent supportive evidence involving the "upward appraisal" of managers and supervisors by their subordinates assumes that managers and supervisors should be supplying something for their work unit as they strive to achieve results through their group (London & Smither, 1995; Smither et al., 1995). Multirater systems that incorporate an internal and external customer focus for the derivation of PM constructs and the identification of raters should ultimately facilitate an integration of the PM system.

The Role of Context in Measuring Performance

Internal customers are also invaluable for the appraisal of *contextual performance* (Borman & Motowidlo, 1993). Contextual performance includes work behaviors that have "added value to the firm" above and beyond the technical core of performance. These behaviors may include spontaneously offering suggestions for improving work processes, taking the initiative to repair broken machinery, maintaining good relationships, assisting coworkers, and providing mentoring for younger workers.

These types of behaviors are also referred to as *organizational citizenship* behaviors (for example, Podsakoff, Ahearne, & MacKenzie, 1997). Accordingly, a good organizational citizen is an employee who contributes beyond the formal role expectations of a job as might be detailed in a job description. Such employees are positively disposed to take on alternative job assignments, respond cheerfully to requests for assistance from others, are interpersonally tactful, arrive at work on time, and may often stay later than required to complete a task. These are contributions to organizational success that may not be formally recognized by the PM system (that is, do not serve as criteria for decision making) but that have been repeatedly shown to influence supervisors' ratings of subordinate performance just the same (for example, Van Scotter & Motowidlo, 1996).

The need to formally recognize contextual contributions to overall performance arises for three main reasons:

- Contextual performance operates to either support or inhibit technical production and can thus facilitate individual-, group-, and system-level outcomes.
- Omission of legitimate components of the contextual performance domain places raters in a compromised position where they might adjust ratings of technical performance to account for contextual performance.
- Significant contributions to individual, group, and system performance may go unrecognized and unrewarded, thus reducing their likelihood in the future.

Although contextual performance may contribute in its own right to individual effectiveness by enhancing an individual's leadership position or by developing additional skills that improve efficiency, the value of contextual performance is more often in the way of supporting the organizational, social, and psychological environment that surrounds the technical core of production behavior.

One important implication of contextual performance is that it serves a system maintenance function (Dobbins, Cardy, Facteau, & Miller, 1993; Murphy & Cleveland, 1995). Just as situational leadership theories posit that a leader's directive and task-centered behaviors function best when leader-member relations are positive and the position power of the leader is strong (Fiedler, 1967; Hersey & Blanchard, 1988), contextual performance facilitates the translation of productive effort into productive results. In this way, contextual performance can be construed as a resource variable much like those described by Peters and O'Connor (1980) in the framework of situational constraints. In the absence of a supportive work context, it may be that much more difficult to translate productive behavior into results or even to engage in productive behaviors (Peters, Chassie, Lindholm, O'Connor, & Kline, 1982).

The failure to recognize contextual performance will result not only in problems with the PM system but, more important, could ultimately be deleterious to unit performance (Villanova, 1996). There is no question that contextual issues can bias ratings.

Research has established that contextual performance accounts for as much, if not more, of the variance in supervisory ratings of performance as the actual production records (MacKenzie, Podsakoff, & Fetter, 1991) or the employee's technical performance (for example, Van Scotter & Motowidlo, 1996). Perhaps it isn't surprising that managers rate the performance of more compliant and helpful workers higher than what they would deserve if the appraisal were based solely on their actual production. For example, in a study that presaged the current emphasis placed on contextual performance, Grey and Kipnis (1976) demonstrated that supervisory ratings of performance for compliant workers were contingent on the proportion of noncompliant workers in the rater's work group; as the proportion of noncompliant workers in a group increased, so did the ratings given to compliant workers by their supervisors. Ivancevich (1983) also found that supervisory ratings of subordinates were contingent on the proportion of subordinates who were performing poorly in the supervisor's work group.

It is likely that the contextual contribution of these workers promotes managers' leadership positions in the group, allows them to delegate more group maintenance functions to others, and reduces the need for management or supervisory behaviors. Omit-ting contextual performance from the formal criterion domain of a PM system places the manager in a quandary. In the first place, performance ratings that are influenced by contextual considerations but aren't substantiated by the production data open the door to accusations of bias and favoritism. However, if managers rate their more compliant and dedicated subordinates solely on the basis of their technical performance, they may extinguish behaviors that promote the leaders' own position in the group and, more important, facilitate present and future technical performance among group members.

Villanova's (1992) customer-based model for developing performance criteria could be extended to include contextual performance factors as they relate to the six aspects of value we described earlier (that is, quantity, timeliness, quality, need for supervision, cost effectiveness, interpersonal impact). In fact, several of the behavioral and result measures described by Borman and Motowidlo (1993) could be subsumed within the "interpersonal impact" aspect of value for particular work functions. Contextual performance contributions such as mentoring, facilitating a pleasant work environment, and compliance with organizational and subunit policies and procedures may have implications for several value aspects.

If performance is defined at a more specific task, behavior or activity level, contextual performance could be (and should be) represented in appropriate performance dimensions. Such a representation should be accomplished as dimensions are derived with an internal customer focus and multirater systems are employed that include peer and subordinate assessments (Antonioni, 1994). Faison, the North Carolina–based commercial real estate company, places considerable weight on the contextual performance of its managers in conjunction with a highly quantitative MBO system. Over twenty items describe contextual performance as related to leadership and teamwork. Peers and subordinates rate most of these items. For example, managers are rated on the extent to which they "openly share information and ideas" and "encourage trust and open communication."

To summarize, then, we believe that the subject of customer-based appraisal—both internal and external—holds great promise for organizations and PM systems. The strong trend toward multirater systems is certainly compatible with the marketing conceptualization of defining performance from the perspective of internal (for example, peers, subordinates) and external customers (for example, mystery shoppers, real customers). Research should focus on conditions under which customer feedback provides particular advantage, the processes associated with collecting valid, reliable, useful information, and the effectiveness of various HR interventions designed to respond to such feedback or appraisal results (Johnson, Olson, & Courtney, 1996).

The Context of Performance: Measuring and Correcting for Constraints

Our third prescription for more effective PM concerns the role of situational constraints and causal attributions on the PM process. We recommend methods that could formally consider, account for, and (hopefully) reduce such constraints.

As the survey results summarized in Exhibit 1.2 indicate, raters and ratees often disagree on the extent to which situational constraints have affected performance. In general, raters do not regard constraints on performance as a very serious problem hindering the attainment of desired outcomes—while those performing the work believe constraints are a serious problem. This disagreement translates into dysfunctional reactions to the PM system and performance ratings. A major goal for a PM system should be to eliminate or reduce the effects of situational constraints on performance, whether those constraints are real or imagined, and to facilitate maximal performance and greater understanding regarding the causes of performance.

Situational Influences on Performance

Circumstances beyond a performer's control can have the effect of either facilitating or constraining the level of performance achieved (Kane, 1986). The survey results summarized in Exhibit 1.2 document the extent to which raters and ratees differ on the impact of extraneous situational factors such as coworker performance, equipment and supply problems, or poor training. While there are certainly situational facilitators that boost performance (for example, cooperative coworkers), constraints on performance are of greater

interest because they tend to account for a great deal of the disagreement between raters and ratees, disagreements that often translate into costly difficulties for the organization (Dobbins et al., 1993).

The proponents of the Total Quality Movement (TQM) emphasize the extent to which system factors can constrain performance (for example, Masterson & Taylor, 1996; Waldman, 1994).
Indeed, the father of TQM, W. Edwards Deming (1986), has
claimed that such situational factors account for 94 percent of the
variance in performance, 90 percent of which is the result of "common causes" that are beyond the control of the performer.

A majority of workers from one survey felt that factors beyond
their control had a "significant impact" on their own performance
(Bernardin & Villanova, 1986). A majority of respondents also
maintained that their supervisors did not adequately understand
the impact of such factors on their own performance (Bernardin,
1992). Perceptions of the impact of constraints may also explain
discrepancies between self- and supervisory performance evaluations (Bernardin, 1989).

All of us do self-appraisals. Whether there is a formal system of
self-appraisal or not, most of us compare our appraisals to those
made by our supervisors. The survey results summarized in Exhibit
1.2 also reported that 59 percent of workers across a variety of jobs
disagreed or strongly disagreed with the performance rating given
by their supervisors whenever the supervisor's appraisal was at less
than the highest level for that rating scale.

Not only do discrepancies in self- versus supervisory evaluations
have an effect on subsequent worker behavior, they are also related
to very costly grievance and appeal processes when evaluations are
tied to important personnel decisions—merit pay, selection, promotions, discharges, and so on. Thus, regardless of whether we are
talking about employee motivation, turnover, group cohesion, or
monetary costs, the effects of discrepancies in self- versus supervisory evaluations on the PM system are indeed great (Bernardin,
1989; Cardy & Dobbins, 1994).

The Fundamental Attribution Error

Research on attribution theory may provide an explanation for
these discrepancies. In their review of actor/observer biases in attributions of causality, Jones and Nisbett (1972) noted that there is a

tendency for actors (that is, performers) to attribute less than perfect performance to factors that were beyond their control while observers (for example, supervisors) tend to attribute the same outcomes to stable personal characteristics or dispositions such as ability or motivation. A great deal of research since 1972 documents the pervasive nature of this "fundamental attribution error" (Van Boven & Gilovich, 1997).

Workers doing poorly on the job often have a different perspective on a problem than the supervisor does, particularly when the supervisor has never performed the work. In attempting to explain inadequate performance, the worker may point to various external constraints on performance such as lack of supplies, unpredictable workload, troublesome coworkers, ambiguous job assignments, and so on. The supervisor very often disagrees with employees on the extent to which different factors constrained their performance (Pooyan et al., 1982; Zuckerman, 1979). The supervisor is often convinced that the worker lacks some enduring quality such as aptitude or motivation. The supervisor is also less likely to be cognizant of contextual performance factors that constrain individual performance.

A 1995 *Detroit News* report card on the Detroit Red Wings provides a nice illustration of the "fundamental attribution error." After the Red Wings were swept four straight games by the New Jersey Devils for hockey's Stanley Cup, a *News* reporter gave Red Wing forward Ray Sheppard an "F" for his performance. The reporter theorized that Sheppard lacked "motivation and desire" in the Cup final but did allow that "granted, he had a broken wrist." Just maybe Mr. Sheppard might have placed a little more attributional weight on the broken wrist and less on his alleged motivational problems.

This type of disagreement over attributions may not only be at the root of the discrepancies between self- and supervisory appraisals, it may also be a key element in the employee's motivation regarding future performance. Abundant empirical evidence supports the contention that perceived work constraints reduce aspiration levels (for example, Phillips & Freedman, 1984; Villanova, 1996). Disagreement on why goals were not achieved may result in lower commitment to future goals or outright abandonment of goals assigned by supervisors. This is particularly likely in instances where a worker had previously enjoyed considerable latitude over the setting of goals and now faces closer scrutiny of and less control over the goals that are established (Austin, 1989).

PM procedures that focus on perceived situational constraints should reduce differential attributions of performance and ultimately reduce differences in self- versus supervisory performance evaluations. An ancillary benefit could be increased commitment to negotiated or assigned goals. In addition, such procedures will focus attention on external factors that, whether real or illusory, should be a major concern for management. This focus on situational constraints should also give managers and supervisors charged with achieving results an appropriate perspective on their jobs. Attending to real constraints on unit performance should be a major focus of any manager's job.

Accounting for the Influence of Situational Factors

The existence of situational facilitators and constraints raises the question of how to account for their influence in PM systems (Austin, 1989). Clearly, it is unfair from the organization's perspective to reward someone for a given level of effectiveness achieved under conditions when situational facilitators made the achieved level easier to achieve relative to others competing for the same rewards. Similarly, it is unfair to employees to blame them for failing to achieve levels that were made impossible to achieve by situational constraints (Dobbins et al., 1993).

Most organizations use PM systems that tacitly allow raters to add or subtract fudge factors to adjust for situational influences. This informal correction fails to control for potentially wide differences between raters in their recognition of—and willingness to adjust for—such influences.

Bernardin (1989) argues for explicit ratings by supervisors of factors that may facilitate or impede performance so that adjustments to ratings, if made, are documented in an employee's work record. Recognizing that performance management is a two-way street, Dobbins et al. (1993) also champion this approach for the purpose of not only providing a more accurate record of employee performance but also as a record of management's response to correct constraints that could be addressed through managerial intervention. Thus the accountability feature of including a descriptive record of constraints works both ways.

Performance Distribution Assessment (PDA), proposed by Kane (1986), employs explicit provisions to account for situational influences. Specifically, PDA elicits from the rater (preferably in consensus with the ratee) an estimate of the best performance distribution possible to achieve during the appraisal period. The actual distribution achieved is also reported, and the scoring system expresses the proximity of the actual distribution to the best possible one. Thus any given level of accomplishment is valued less to the extent that situational facilitators made it easier to attain all levels of achievement (or simply raised the ceiling of feasibility to higher levels) than would be the case under normal circumstances. The method also accounts for (and corrects for) the influence of situational constraints by reflecting their effect of lowering the ceiling of feasibility and thereby elevating the degree of effectiveness attributed to any given level of accomplishment.

While some research has confirmed its effectiveness (for example, Kane, 1998), considerably more needs to be done, especially in applied settings, to establish the effectiveness and practical feasibility of the approach. However, in organizations where situational influences are of particular concern as sources of unfairness in appraisals, the PDA method exists as a potential solution to consider. In addition, the data that are gathered from the PDA method allow for other HR interventions directed at the most serious and valid constraints on a unit's performance (Kane, 1998).

A PM Intervention to Identify and Reduce External Constraints

Bernardin (1989) introduced attributional training to focus the attention of the supervisor and the subordinate on the perceived effects of constraints on specific dimensions or elements of performance. One assumption of attributional training is that some type of behavior-based or results-based PM system is in place. The approach is also appropriate for appraisal systems that call for individualized or group performance standards, goals, or objectives.

A spreadsheet matrix is prepared with the columns made up of the performance dimensions and the rows listing all potential constraints on performance (Bernardin & Beatty, 1984, p. 149). One method has the supervisor and the subordinate independently considering and rating the subordinate's *maximum potential* for performance on each dimension since the last appraisal period. In addition, the performer and the observer also indicate the extent to which each of the constraints deterred this potential for the present appraisal period. Each rater is also asked to record specific examples for each relevant combination of dimension and constraint. Exhibit 1.5 presents an example of such a matrix for the director of a research and development center.

Most cells of the matrix should be empty because most constraints did not have a significant impact on performance for that specific period of time. Participants are encouraged to write very specific examples of how a given constraint affected a given performance dimension. For example, the director of the research center indicates that a change in his work assignment was a constraint on his performance related to "assisting center researchers."

The supervisor and the subordinate then exchange their completed matrices and are given an opportunity to study them (the supervisor may also want to verify some of the subordinate's information). A more efficient approach calls for the performer to submit the completed matrix to the supervisor, who considers the self-appraisals and perceived constraints when appraising the subordinate's performance. The performance appraisal meeting should focus on the constraining cells, particularly where there are discrepancies in the ratings in the constraint cells for a given dimension. The supervisors should allow the subordinates an opportunity to fully explain any of the cells the subordinates have selected that the supervisors did not regard as important constraints. The discussion should concentrate on specifically how and how often a constraint affected performance on a given performance dimension.

This phase in the PM system could end with an agreement that certain cells in the matrix are genuine and significant problems to which supervisory time and effort should be committed. The most important phase of the discussion is future oriented. The supervisor and subordinate should now concentrate on what each can do to limit or eliminate the relevant constraints. Where feasible, supervisors should commit to attending to those constraints for which

Exhibit 1.5. A Performance/Constraint Matrix (R&D Director).

Constraints	Performance Dimensions			
	Assisting Center Researchers	Generating Research Grants	Organizing and Conducting Seminars	Conducting Research
Absenteeism/turnover		a		
Slow procedures				
Clerical support		b		b
Supply shortage				
Excessive restrictions	c	d		
Working conditions				
Poor coworker performance				
Poor subordinate performance			e	f
Poor manager performance				
Inefficient structure				
Excessive reporting requirements				
Workloads				
Change in administrative policy				
Coworker pressure				
Change in work assignment	k,h	k,h	k,h	k,h
Lack of equipment				
Inadequate communication				i
Raw material problem				
Economic conditions				j
Lack of (or poor) training				

Exhibit 1.5. A Performance/Constraint Matrix
(R&D Director), cont'd.

Constraints	*Goals*
a. Loss of departmental secretary precluded proposal writing for two months	a. Proposed backup clerical support for excessive work loads; have plan by 3/1
b. Secretary worked on unrelated project for two months	b. Develop more detailed job description and chain of command for secretaries, that is, only one boss; submit plan by 3/1
c. Grant support lifted from four recipients due to lack of funds	c. Review committee will be made aware of total funds awailable
d. No money allotted for hiring grantsperson as promised	d. Conduct search to determine if part-time person can be identified; write announcement by 2/15
e. Staff rarely attended seminars although they were scheduled on payday	
f. Staff member failed to do literature review in a collaborative research project	
h. Given new responsibility for compensation policy and computer records (not on original job description)	h. Provide written charge in the future
i. Failure of management to provide written charge for compensation project resulted in time being wasted in clarification with divisions	i. Get commitment from management to attend all executive-level meetings
j. Severe reduction in research budget has precluded three pilot projects that had great potential for external funding	j. More active search for external dollars. Will review foundation interests; submit report by 4/1
k. Asked to conduct seminar at last moment due to funding problem; took 15 percent of my time away from all assignments	k. Will do survey to determine what time would be most favorable; report attendance to director (will submit report in two months)

they are responsible or which they can at least investigate. For example, as depicted in Exhibit 1.5, completion of the unexpected project assigned to the director regarding the new compensation system for center researchers could be facilitated if the supervisor could successfully negotiate certain data access with other supervisors. Subordinates might attribute problems for certain dimensions to shortages of supplies. The supervisor could investigate this supply problem and, if it turned out to be significant, take action to alleviate it.

The final phase of attributional training should be based on investigating specific constraints on performance. The supervisor and subordinate agree to meet on a future date to assess the status of the important constraints. This approach will focus the meeting on the relevant constraints and the extent to which their impact has been reduced by the supervisor's or the subordinate's actions.

The attributional approach meets the requirements for timely and specific feedback and should be less traumatic than an annual or semiannual meeting that covers a plethora of topics. Once the performance/constraint matrix is completed the first time, the entire process should be relatively painless for the supervisors and subordinates. The matrix can then be incorporated into normal work and planning and review or MBO procedures.

Research on the effects of attributional training found reduced discrepancies between self- and supervisory appraisals and increased overall performance for the work unit. In addition, one year after the training, ratees who had participated indicated that fewer constraints had hindered their performance and that they had greater control of their work outcomes (Bernardin & Beatty, 1984, p. 149). This formal consideration of situational constraints also enhanced perceptions of fairness and due process for the PM system, an important ancillary benefit (Folger, Konovsky, & Cropanzano, 1992; Taylor et al., 1995).

Conclusion

This chapter offers three prescriptions for developing and sustaining effective performance management systems that link PM content and its assessment to customer-defined criteria for effective performance. *Customers* is used here to refer to both the internal and external consumers of an employee's work outcomes. The inclusion of this constituency in the design of PM systems and the assessment and management of performance is intended to complement, not replace, traditional constituencies used to perform these functions, such as managers, supervisors, peers, and subordinates. What we thus advocate are multiperspective PM systems that include as one of the key sources of input the perspectives of the internal and external consumers of employee and group work products.

Although we have firm conceptual and empirical grounds for our recommendations, much research remains to be done to compare the effectiveness of alternative approaches to these activities. We believe that measurement precision is a worthwhile goal to strive for. The fact that this goal has proven elusive in the past does not, in our view, invalidate it. Recent developments in assessment methods raise new hope that previously unachievable accuracy levels are within our reach (Kane, 1998). We believe that efforts to upgrade the accuracy with which performance assessments are elicited should be suspended only when the cost of additional increments of accuracy outweigh their benefits.

We further believe that the attributional problems that we discussed can be reduced with improved precision in measurement. You will also note from Exhibit 1.2 that ratees and raters were more likely to agree on the level of performance as a function of the precision in the measurement tools. Greater appraisal agreement also implies greater attributional agreement.

Precision in measurement should also facilitate the identification of legitimate constraints on performance that should require the attention of management. Such an orientation in PM systems is compatible with TQM processes seeking to reduce system variance.

We also recognize that performance appraisals are widely used to achieve political purposes rather than to accurately report a record of performance outcomes (Ferris, Judge, Rowland, & Fitzgibbons, 1994). This is largely due to the fact that existing PM systems, including the plethora of competency-based systems being marketed today, are so readily amenable to such distortion, as well as to the prevalence of organizational cultures that tacitly approve of it. We believe that such manipulation of appraisals leads not to enhanced organizational effectiveness but rather to the opposite effect. We are convinced that organizations should strive to make accurate performance assessments the basis for all selection and reward decisions. Only in this way can aggregated gains in individual effectiveness lead to overall gains in organizational effectiveness.

References

Antonioni, D. (1994). Improve the performance management process before discontinuing performance appraisals. *Compensation and Benefits Review, 26*(3), 29–37.

Austin, J. T. (1989). Effects of shifts in goal origin on goal acceptance and attainment. *Organizational Behavior and Human Decision Processes, 46,* 315–335.

Beatty, R. W., & Schneier, C. E. (1997). New HR roles to impact organizational performance: From "partners" to "players." *Human Resource Management, 36,* 29–38.

Becker, B. E., Huselid, M. A., Pickus, P. S., & Spratt, M. F. (1997). HR as a source of shareholder value: Research and recommendations. *Human Resource Management, 36,* 39–48.

Beer, M., Ruh, R., Dawson, J. A., McCaa, B. B., & Kavanagh, M. J. (1978). A performance management system: Research, design, introduction, and evaluation. *Personnel Psychology, 31,* 505–535.

Bernardin, H. J. (1989). Increasing the accuracy of performance measurement: A proposed solution to erroneous attributions. *Human Resource Planning, 12,* 239–250.

Bernardin, H. J. (1992). The "analytic" framework for customer-based performance content development and appraisal. *Human Resource Management Review, 2,* 81–102.

Bernardin, H. J., & Beatty, R. W. (1984). *Performance appraisal: Assessing human behavior at work.* Boston: Kent.

Bernardin, H. J., Hagan, C. M., & Hennessey, H. (1995). *The effects of criterion specificity and managerial accountability on appraisal effectiveness.* Paper presented at the annual meeting of the Academy of Management, Vancouver, Canada.

Bernardin, H. J., Hennessey, H. W., & Peyrefitte, J. (1995). Age, racial, and gender bias as a function of criterion specificity: A test of expert testimony. *Human Resource Management Review, 5,* 63–77.

Bernardin, H. J., & Kane, J. S. (1997). *The relationship between corporate strategy and characteristics of performance management systems.* Unpublished manuscript. Administrative Systems Center, Boca Raton, FL.

Bernardin, H. J., & Smith, P. C. (1981). A clarification of some issues regarding the development and use of behaviorally anchored rating scales. *Journal of Applied Psychology, 66,* 458–463.

Bernardin, H. J., & Villanova, P. J. (1986). Performance appraisal. In E. A. Locke (Ed.), *Generalizing from laboratory to field settings* (pp. 43–62). San Francisco. New Lexington Press.

Bitner, M. J., Booms B. H., & Mohr, L. A. (1990). Critical service encounters: The employee's viewpoint. *Journal of Marketing, 58*(5), 95–106

Bitner, M. J., Booms, B. H., & Tetrault, M. S. (1990). The service encounter: Diagnosing favorable and unfavorable incidents. *Journal of Marketing, 54*(1), 71–84.

Bitner, M. J., & Hubbert, A. R. (1994). Encounter satisfaction versus overall satisfaction versus quality. In R. T. Rust & R. L. Oliver (Eds.), *Service quality: New directions in theory and practice* (pp. 72–94). Thousand Oaks, CA: Sage.

Bobko, P., & Colella, A. (1994). Employee reactions to performance standards: A review and research propositions. *Personnel Psychology, 47,* 1–36.

Bolton, R. N., & Drew, J. H. (1994). Linking customer satisfaction to service operations and outcomes. In R. T. Rust & R. L. Oliver (Eds.), *Service quality: New directions in theory and practice* (pp. 173–200). Thousand Oaks, CA: Sage.

Borman, W. C. (1991). Job behavior, performance, and effectiveness. In M. D. Dunnette & L. M. Hough (Eds.), *Handbook of industrial and organizational psychology: Vol. 2* (2nd ed., pp. 271–326). Palo Alto, CA: Consulting Psychologists Press.

Borman, W. C., & Motowidlo, S. J. (1993). Expanding the criterion domain to include elements of contextual performance. In N. Schmitt & W. C. Borman (Eds.), *Personnel selection in organizations* (pp. 71–98). San Francisco: Jossey-Bass.

Bretz, R. D., Jr., Milkovich, G. T., & Read, W. (1992). The current state of performance appraisal research and practice: Concerns, directions, and implications. *Journal of Management, 18,* 321–352.

Cardy, R. L. (1997). Process and outcomes: A performance management paradox? *News: Human Resources Division, 21*(1), 12–14.

Cardy, R. L., & Dobbins, G. H. (1994). *Performance appraisal: Alternative perspectives.* Cincinnati, OH: South-Western.

Deming, W. E. (1986). *Out of the crisis.* Cambridge, MA: MIT Center for Advanced Engineering Study.

De Sarbo, W. S., Huff, L., Rolandelli, M. M., & Choi, J. (1994). On the measurement of perceived service quality: A conjoint analysis approach. In R. T. Rust & R. L. Oliver (Eds.), *Service quality: New directions in theory and practice* (pp. 201–222). Thousand Oaks, CA: Sage.

Dobbins, G. H., Cardy, R. L., Facteau, J. D., & Miller, J. S. (1993). Implications of situational constraints on performance evaluation and performance management. *Human Resource Management Review, 3,* 105–128.

Drucker, P. F. (1954). *The practice of management.* New York: HarperCollins.

Edwards, M. R., & Ewen, A. J. (1996). *360-degree feedback: The powerful new model for employee assessment and performance improvement.* NY: AMACOM.

Evans, M. G. (1970). The effects of supervisory behavior on the path-goal relationship. *Organizational Behavior and Human Performance, 55,* 277–298.

Feldman, D. (1992). The case for non-analytic performance appraisal. *Human Resource Management Review, 2,* 9–35.

Ferris, G. R., Judge, T. A., Rowland, K. M., & Fitzgibbons, D. E. (1994). Subordinate influence and the performance evaluation process: Test of a model. *Organizational Behavior and Human Decision Processes, 58,* 101–135.

Fiedler, F. (1967). *A theory of leadership effectiveness.* New York: McGraw-Hill.

Folger, R., Konovsky, M. A., & Cropanzano, R. (1992). A due process metaphor for performance appraisal. In B. M. Staw & L. L. Cummings (Eds.), *Research in organizational behavior* (pp. 129–177). Greenwich, CT: JAI Press.

Ghorpade, J., & Chen, M. M. (1995). Creating quality-driven performance appraisal systems. *Academy of Management Executive 9,* 32–39.

Grey, R. J., & Kipnis, D. (1976). Untangling the performance appraisal dilemma: The influence of perceived organizational context on evaluative processes. *Journal of Applied Psychology 61,* 329–335.

Gubman, E. L. (1995). Aligning people strategies with customer value. *Compensation and Benefits Review, 27*(1), 15–22.

Hauser, J. R., Simester, D. I., & Wernerfelt, B. (1996, August). Internal customers and internal suppliers. *Journal of Marketing Research,* pp. 276–280.

Heilmann, R. L. (1994). The alignment matrix. *Quality Progress, 27,* 75–78.

Helliker, K. (1994, November 30). Smile: That cranky shopper may be a store spy. *Wall Street Journal,* p. B1.

Hersey, P., & Blanchard, K. H. (1988). *Management of organizational behavior: Utilizing human resources* (5th ed.). Upper Saddle River, NJ: Prentice Hall.

Ivancevich, J. M. (1983). Contrast effects in performance evaluation and reward practices. *Academy of Management Journal, 26,* 465–476.

Johnson, J. W., Olson, A. M., & Courtney, C. L. (1996). Implementing multiple perspective feedback: An integrated framework. *Human Resource Management Review, 6,* 253–277.

Jones, E., & Nisbett, R. (1972). The actor and the observer: Divergent perceptions of the causes of behavior. In E. F. Jones, D. Kanouse, H. H. Kelley, R. E. Nisbett, S. Valins, & B. Weiner (Eds.), *Attribution: Perceiving the causes of behavior* (pp. 79–94). Morristown, NJ: General Learning Press.

Kane, J. S. (1986). Performance distribution assessment. In R. A. Berk (Ed.), *Performance assessment: Methods and applications* (pp. 237–274). Baltimore: Johns Hopkins University Press.

Kane, J. S., & Russell, J. E. A. (1998). Performance appraisal and management. In H. J. Bernardin & J. E. A.. Russell (Eds.), *Human resource management: An experiential approach* (pp. 237–272). Burr Ridge, IL: Irwin/McGraw-Hill.

Landy, F. J., & Farr, J. L. (1980). Performance rating. *Psychological Bulletin, 87,* 72–107.

Latham, G. P. (1986). Job performance and appraisal. In C. L. Cooper & I. Robertson (Eds.), *International review of industrial and organizational psychology* (pp. 117–155). New York: Wiley.

Lawler, E. E., III. (1994). Performance management: The next generation. *Compensation and Benefits Review, 26*(3), 16–19.

Lengnick-Hall, C. A. (1996). Customer contributions to quality: A different view of the customer-oriented firm. *Academy of Management Review, 21,* 791–824.

Locke, E. A., Shaw, K. N., Saari, L. M., & Latham, G. P. (1981). Goal setting and task performance, 1969–1980. *Psychological Bulletin, 90,* 125–152.

London, M., & Beatty, R. W. (1993). 360-degree feedback as a competitive advantage. *Human Resource Management, 32,* 353–372.

London, M., & Smither, J. W. (1995). Can multisource feedback change perceptions of goal accomplishment, self-evaluations, and performance-related outcomes? Theory-based applications and directions for research. *Personnel Psychology, 48,* 803–839.

MacKenzie, S. B., Podsakoff, P. M., & Fetter, R. (1991). Organizational citizenship behavior and objective productivity as determinants of managerial evaluations of salespersons' performance. *Organizational Behavior and Human Decision Processes, 50,* 123–150.

Masterson, S. S., & Taylor, M. S. (1996). Total quality management and performance appraisal. *Journal of Quality Management, 1,* 67–89.

McDonald, D., & Smith, A. (1995). A proven connection: Performance management and business results. *Compensation and Benefits Review, 27*(1), 59–64.

McLaurin, D. L., & Bell, S. (1993). Making customer service more than just a slogan. *Quality Progress, 26,* 35–39.

Milkovich, G. T., & Wigdor, A. K. (Eds.). (1991). *Pay for performance: Evaluating performance appraisal and merit pay*. Washington, DC: Committee on Performance Appraisal for Merit Pay, Commission on Behavioral and Social Sciences and Education, National Research Council.

Murphy, K. J. (1993, Spring). Performance measurement and appraisal: Merck tries to motivate managers to do it right. *Employee Relations Today*, pp. 47–62.

Murphy, K. R., & Cleveland, J. N. (1991). *Performance appraisal: An organizational perspective*. Needham Heights, MA: Allyn & Bacon.

Murphy, K. R., & Cleveland, J. N. (1995). *Understanding performance appraisal: Social, organizational, and goal-based perspectives*. Thousand Oaks, CA: Sage.

Olian, J. D., & Rynes, S. L. (1991). Making total quality work: Aligning organizational processes, performance measures, and stakeholders. *Human Resource Management, 30,* 303–330.

Oliver, R. L., & De Sarbo, W. S. (1988). Response determinants in satisfaction judgments. *Journal of Consumer Research, 14,* 495–507.

Pace, L. A., & Bounds, G. M. (1991). The role of the employee in improving competitiveness. In M. J. Stahl & G. M. Bounds (Eds.), *Competing globally through customer value: The management of strategic suprasystems* (pp. 189–206). New York: Quorum Books.

Parasuraman, A., Berry, L. L., & Zeithaml, V. A. (1993). More on improving service quality measurement. *Journal of Retailing, 69,* 140–147.

Parasuraman, A., Zeithaml, V., & Berry, L. (1988). SERVQUAL: A multiple-item scale for measuring consumer perceptions of service quality. *Journal of Retailing, 64,* 12–40.

Parry, S. B. (1996, July). The quest for competencies. *Training*, pp. 48–53.

Peters, L. H., Chassie, M. B., Lindholm, H. R., O'Connor, E. J., & Kline, C. R. (1982). The joint influence of situational constraints and goal setting on performance and affective outcomes. *Journal of Management, 8,* 7–20.

Peters, L. H., & O'Connor, E. J. (1980). Situational constraints and work outcomes: The influence of a frequently overlooked construct. *Academy of Management Review, 5,* 391–397.

Phillips, J. S., & Freedman, S. M. (1984). Situational performance constraints and task characteristics: Their relationship to motivation and satisfaction. *Journal of Management, 10,* 321–331.

Podsakoff, P. M., Ahearne, M., & MacKenzie, S. B. (1997). Organizational citizenship behavior and the quantity and quality of work group performance. *Journal of Applied Psychology, 82,* 262–270.

Pooyan, A., O'Connor, E. J., Peters, L. H., Quick, J. C., Jones, N. D., & Kulisch, A. (1982, April). *Supervisory/subordinate differences in perceptions of situational constraints: Barriers are in the eye of the beholder.* Paper presented at the Southwest Academy of Management Meeting, Phoenix, AZ.

Rust, R. T., & Oliver, R. L. (1994). Service quality: Insights and managerial implications from the frontier. In R. T. Rust & R. L. Oliver (Eds.), *Service quality: New directions in theory and practice* (pp. 1–20). Thousand Oaks, CA: Sage.

Schellhardt, T. (1996, November 19). Annual agony: It's time to evaluate your work and all involved are groaning. *Wall Street Journal,* p. A1.

Schrader, B. W., & Steiner, D. D. (1996). Common comparison standards: An approach to improving agreement between self and supervisory performance ratings. *Journal of Applied Psychology, 81,* 813–820.

Shapiro, B. P. (1988). What the hell is "market orientated"? *Harvard Business Review, 66,* 119–125.

Smith, B., Hornsby, J. S., & Shirmeyer, R. (1996, Summer). Current trends in performance appraisal: An examination of managerial practice. *SAM Advanced Management Journal,* pp. 10–15.

Smither, J. W., London, M., Vasilopoulos, N. L., Reilly, R. R., Millsap, R. E., & Salvemini, N. (1995). An examination of the effects of an upward feedback program over time. *Personnel Psychology, 48,* 1–34.

Stark, M. J., Luther, W., & Valvano, S. (1996). Jaguar Cars drives toward competency-based pay. *Compensation and Benefits Review, 28*(6), 34–39.

Stewart, T. A. (1992, May 18). The search for the organization of tomorrow. *Fortune,* pp. 92–98.

Sulzer-Azaroff, B., & Harshbarger, D. (1995). Putting fear to flight. *Quality Progress, 28,* 61–65.

Taylor, M. S., Tracy, K. B., Renard, M. K., Harrison, J. K., & Carroll, S. J. (1997). Due process in performance appraisal: A quasi-experiment in procedural justice. *Administrative Science Quarterly, 40,* 495–523.

Treacy, M., & Wiersema, F. (1993). Customer intimacy and other value disciplines. *Harvard Business Review, 21*(1), 15–22.

Tubbs, M. (1986). Goal setting: A meta-analytic examination of the empirical evidence. *Journal of Applied Psychology, 71,* 474–483.

Ulrich, D. (1997). Judge me more by my future than by my past. *Human Resource Management, 36,* 5–8.

Van Boven, L. D., & Gilovich, T. (1997, May). *Intuitive awareness of the fundamental attribution error: Do actors know how they are seen by observers?* Paper presented at the annual meeting of the American Psychological Society, Washington, DC.

Van Scotter, J. R., & Motowidlo, S. J. (1996). Interpersonal facilitation and job dedication as separate facets of contextual performance. *Journal of Applied Psychology, 81,* 525–531.

Villanova, P. (1992). A customer-based model for developing job performance criteria. *Human Resource Management Review, 2,* 103–114.

Villanova, P. (1996). Predictive validity of situational constraints in general versus specific performance domains. *Journal of Applied Psychology, 81,* 532–547.

Viswesvaran, C., Ones, D. S., & Schmidt, F. L. (1996). Comparative analysis of the reliability of job performance ratings. *Journal of Applied Psychology, 81,* 557–574.

Waldman, D. A. (1994). The contributions of total quality management to a theory of work performance. *Academy of Management Review, 19,* 510–536.

Westbrook, R. A., & Reilly, M. D. (1983). Value-percept disparity: An alternative to the disconfirmation of expectations theory of consumer satisfaction. In R. P. Bagozzi & A. M. Tybout (Eds.), *Advances in consumer research* (pp. 256–261). Ann Arbor, MI: Association for Consumer Research.

Wright, P. M., & Kacmar, K. M. (1994). Goal specificity as a determinant of goal commitment and goal change. *Organizational Behavior and Human Decision Processes, 59,* 242–260.

Yi, Y. (1990). A critical review of consumer satisfaction. In V. A. Zeithamal (Ed.), *Review of marketing* (pp. 68–123). Chicago: American Marketing Association.

Zeithaml, V. A., Parasuraman, A., & Berry, L. L. (1990). *Delivering quality service: Balancing customer perceptions and expectations.* New York: Free Press.

Zuckerman, M. (1979). Attribution of success and failure revisited: The motivational bias is alive and well in attribution theory. *Journal of Personality, 47,* 245–287.

CHAPTER 2

Current Legal Issues in Performance Appraisal

Stanley B. Malos

To say that the importance of legal issues in performance appraisal has skyrocketed in recent years would be something of an understatement. When I began my research for this chapter by searching various computer databases, I found almost five hundred published judicial and arbitration decisions from just the last several years that involve performance appraisals in one form or another! Many of these decisions turned out merely to contain evidence of favorable performance, offered to show that an individual was qualified for a particular job, and to raise an inference that the reason for refusing to hire, promote, or retain that person must have been discriminatory (see *McDonnell Douglas Corp.* v. *Green,* 411 U.S. 792 [1973]). However, the sheer number of cases underscores a critical reality for today's industrial-organizational psychologist or human resource practitioner: it is almost inevitable that one or more elements of your organization's performance appraisal system will attract legal scrutiny at some point in time. This likely scrutiny is particularly worrisome when considering the potential for jury trials, compensatory and punitive damages, and other burdens imposed in discrimination cases under the Civil Rights Act of 1991.

In this chapter, I offer a foundation for recognizing aspects of performance appraisals that are likely to wind up in litigation, and for modifying those that have caused problems for employers in a variety of legal disputes. I begin with an overview of performance appraisals as they relate to the nature of the employment relationship. I then examine specific appraisal processes and potential liability under Title VII of the Civil Rights Act of 1964 (Title VII), the Civil Rights Act of 1991 (CRA 1991), the Age Discrimination in Employment Act (ADEA), the Americans with Disabilities Act (ADA), the Equal Pay Act, and tort theories such as *negligence* (breach of duty to conduct appraisals with due care), *defamation* (disclosure of untrue unfavorable performance information that damages the reputation of the employee), and *misrepresentation* (disclosure of untrue favorable performance information that presents a risk of harm to prospective employers or third parties). Next, I take a closer look at substantive and procedural aspects of performance appraisals and the legal defensibility of employment decisions. I also examine discipline and related performance issues that arise under union and other employment contracts. I conclude with a discussion of emerging legal issues in performance appraisal such as those related to flexible job designs, security and privacy, and workplace violence. Although I do not offer legal advice (knowledgeable local counsel should be consulted when specific questions arise), I do provide practical suggestions for the design and implementation of legally sound performance appraisal systems throughout the chapter.

Performance Appraisals and the Employment Relationship

Initial selection tests typically become involved in legal disputes because a desired employment relationship does *not* emerge as a result of a given test. Performance appraisals, on the other hand, become central to disputes that arise after an employment relationship has been established. Performance and other ratings are used to select present employees for merit pay, promotion, training, retention, transfer, discipline, demotion, or termination. The nature of the employment relationship, as well as the nature of the employment decision, must be considered to determine the potential for performance evaluations to fuel discrimination and other types of lawsuits such as those under the Fair Labor Standards Act (FLSA) and the Family and Medical Leave Act (FMLA).

Performance Appraisals and Employment at Will

Where there are no express contract terms that govern performance appraisals, courts have allowed employers a good deal of latitude to determine how to evaluate their employees (Gomez-Mejia,
Balkin, & Cardy, 1995). However, even in an *employment at will* relationship, under which either the employer or the employee may
terminate the employment relationship at any time, an employer's
discretion is not entirely without limits. As Koys, Briggs, and Grenig
(1987) have pointed out, courts vary by jurisdiction in their recognition of the *at will* doctrine as a matter of state contract and labor
law. Moreover, courts have found employers liable under numerous exceptions to the doctrine. These exceptions include implied
contract (as where an obligation to terminate only for just cause
arises based on verbal promises or statements in an employee handbook) and violation of public policy (as where an employee is terminated after complaining of harassment or accusing the employer
of other misconduct). Potential liability for defamation or negligence also may restrict, in practical terms, the manner in which
employers can manage and appraise performance. As the following examples illustrate, performance appraisals also may figure in
determining the very nature of the employment relationship. This
can in turn determine the effect of laws such as the FLSA, the
ADEA, Title VII, and the FLMA.

Table 2.1 presents a summary of selected legal principles and laws
that relate to performance appraisals and the nature of the employment relationship. Further details and examples from the cases are
provided in the following section.

Implied Contracts and Public Policy

Mathewson v. *Aloha Airlines,* 152 LRRM 2986 (Haw. 1996) provides
an interesting example of both the implied contract and public
policy exceptions to the *at will* doctrine. In that case, Mathewson,
an Aloha Airlines pilot, disputed his termination, which occurred
just two weeks before a one-year *at will* probationary period would
have expired. The termination was supposedly based on poor performance ratings, particularly those in peer evaluations by fellow
pilots. However, it turns out that Mathewson had been blacklisted
by the pilots' union for having worked as a scab for another airline

Table 2.1. Summary of Selected Legal Principles and Laws Relating to Performance Appraisals and the Employment Relationship.

Legal Principle or Law	Summary	Relationship to Performance Appraisals and the Employment Relationship
Employment at will	Status under which the employer or employee may end an employment relationship at any time	Allows the employer considerable latitude in determining whether, when, and how to appraise performance
Implied contract	Nonexplicit agreement that affects some aspect of the employment relationship	May restrict manner in which employer can use appraisal results (for example, may prevent termination unless for cause)
Violation of public policy	Determination that given action is adverse to the public welfare and is therefore prohibited	May restrict manner in which employer can use appraisal results (for example, may prevent retaliation for reporting illegal conduct by employer)
Negligence	Breach of duty to conduct performance appraisals with due care	Potential liability may require employer to inform employee of poor performance and provide opportunity to improve
Defamation	Disclosure of untrue unfavorable performance information that damages an employee's reputation	Potential liability may restrict manner in which negative performance information can be communicated to others
Misrepresentation	Disclosure of untrue favorable performance information that causes risk of harm to others	Potential liability may restrict willingness of employer to provide references altogether, even for good former employees
Fair Labor Standards Act (FLSA)	Imposes (among other things) obligation to pay overtime to nonexempt (nonmanagerial) employees	Fact that employee conducts appraisals may influence determination that employee functions as supervisor or manager and is therefore exempt
Family and Medical Leave Act (FMLA)	Imposes (among other things) obligation to reinstate employee returning from leave to similar position	Subjecting employee to new or tougher appraisal procedures upon return may suggest that employee has not been given similar position of employment

during a union strike. The Hawaii Supreme Court held that the employer had violated both an implied contract to provide fair, unbiased evaluations (based on parts of the company's Flight Operations Manual), and public policy against discrimination based on nonmembership in a labor organization (a right protected under state and federal labor law).

In another case that illustrates the importance of state law in this area, a California appellate court found it necessary to overturn a lower court ruling on the *at will* issue in *Haycock* v. *Hughes Aircraft,* 10 IER Cases 1612 (Cal. App. 1994). Even though California labor law creates a presumption of *at will* employment, that presumption can be overcome by an implied agreement not to terminate except for just cause. Evidence suggested that, because of such an agreement, Hughes had fraudulently altered favorable evaluations of a twenty-five-year employee, without his knowledge, to justify a "for cause" termination rather than a layoff under which he would have been protected by the company's appraisal review mechanisms and seniority preferences. For an analogous case in the whistleblowing context, see *Robertson* v. *Alabama Department of Economic and Community Affairs,* 4 AD Cases 1749 (D. Ala. 1995), which upheld, on public policy grounds, Robertson's claim that the employer had lowered her appraisal results in retaliation for supporting a coworker's sex discrimination complaint, and for accusing the employer of misapplying federal funds.

Performance Appraisals and the Existence of an Employment Relationship

The very fact that performance is evaluated can influence the determination that an employment relationship exists, as well as the nature of that relationship. In *EEOC* v. *Johnson & Higgins,* 71 FEP Cases 818 (2d Cir. 1996), Johnson & Higgins (J&H) appealed from a lower court ruling that its mandatory retirement policy for directors reaching age sixty-two violated the ADEA. J&H argued that the ADEA did not apply because their directors were not "employees" within the meaning of the Act, but instead maintained a "fundamentally entrepreneurial relationship" similar to a partnership. The Court of Appeals held in favor of the Equal Employment Opportunity Commission (EEOC), however, finding an employment relationship (and thus an ADEA violation) based on the fact that J&H's senior board members reviewed directors' performance annually, and the results determined directors' compensation to a great extent.

In a somewhat different context, the fact that appraisals were conducted led the court in *Sturm* v. *TOC Retail Inc.*, 2 WH Cases 2d 628 (D.C. Ga. 1994), to dismiss Sturm's claim for overtime pay under the FLSA. Because Sturm, a convenience store employee, was responsible for evaluating the performance of two or more employees to determine their raises and continued employment, the Court found that Sturm's duties were primarily managerial, and that he therefore was exempt from the overtime provisions of the Act.

Fair performance evaluations have been held to be tangible job benefits, and interference with those benefits may give rise to liability for harassment under Title VII (see, for example, *Ton* v. *Information Resources Inc.*, 70 FEP Cases 355 [N.D. Ill. 1996], in which Ton was issued an "indefensibly harsh" performance evaluation in retaliation for rejecting his manager's sexual advances). However, an unfavorable review, without some sort of harm to the employee, is not actionable. In *Smart* v. *Ball State University*, 71 FEP Cases 495, 498 (7th Cir. 1996), Smart, a tree surgeon trainee, filed an EEOC complaint against the university claiming gender discrimination under Title VII. She later claimed that the university had retaliated against her for that complaint by applying more formal and stringent evaluation procedures, which resulted in less favorable reviews. Nevertheless, Smart successfully completed her training and got a job with the university as a full-fledged tree surgeon. In upholding dismissal of Smart's lawsuit, the Court of Appeals noted that Smart had failed to establish a causal connection between her negative evaluations and any sort of adverse employment action. The Court acknowledged that "adverse employment action" has been defined broadly, and is not limited to tangible losses such as discharge or reduction in pay. However, the Court explained further that "not everything that makes an employee unhappy is an actionable adverse action. Otherwise, minor and even trivial employment actions . . . could form the basis of a discrimination suit." This language illustrates that most courts are reluctant to pass judgment on the general fairness of an organization's employment practices unless discrimination or some other improper outcome can be shown (see generally Barrett & Kernan, 1987).

Issues involving performance appraisals and the employment relationship also have arisen under the FMLA. In *Patterson* v. *Alltel Information Services,* 3 WH Cases 2d. 406 (D. Maine 1996), Patterson claimed that Alltel violated the FMLA when, on his return from medical leave for work-related stress, he was relegated to "special projects" and received unfavorable evaluations that eventually led to his layoff as part of a companywide reduction in force (RIF). The Court, however, dismissed Patterson's claim that he had suffered a postleave change in his "position of employment" (an FMLA violation) that led to poor performance and his eventual layoff. Alltel was able to establish that Patterson's performance had been rated poorly prior to any change in position, and that he would have been laid off even had he not gone on leave.

Practical Suggestions

As discussed in greater detail later in this chapter, timely and consistent documentation of performance information in accordance with established practices can be critical to the successful defense of a variety of legal disputes. However, as the cases digested in previous paragraphs demonstrate, performance appraisals may be construed by courts to affect the nature and existence of employment relationships in ways that were neither contemplated nor desired by the employer. To limit the extent to which this can occur, employers should consider drafting job offers, employee handbooks, and other employment documents to include express *at will* language that refers explicitly to performance appraisals (see Exhibit 2.1).

This language might state, for example, that employment is understood to be *at will,* that the employer expressly reserves the right to discharge the employee at any time for any reason with or without cause and with or without notice, and that nothing in the employer's policies, practices, or procedures, including performance appraisals, should be construed as conferring any right upon the employee to continued employment. Management also could expressly reserve the right to unilaterally alter the terms and conditions of employment, including the manner in which performance may or may not be appraised.

Further, unless limited by explicit contract language to the contrary, employment documents should make it clear that the employer

Exhibit 2.1. Practical Suggestions for Limiting Performance Appraisals' Unwanted Effects on the Employment Relationship.

Consider drafting job offers, employee handbooks, and other employment documents, for signature by the employee, to include express *at will* language that refers explicitly to performance appraisals. Such language might state

- That employment is understood to be *at will*
- That the employer expressly reserves the right to discharge the employee at any time for any reason with or without cause and with or without notice
- That nothing in the employer's policies, practices, or procedures, including performance appraisals, should be construed as conferring any right upon the employee to continued employment
- That the employer expressly reserves the right to unilaterally alter the terms and conditions of employment, including the manner in which performance is or is not appraised
- That the employer is under no obligation to appraise performance
- That neither the fact that appraisals are or are not conducted, nor the manner in which they may be conducted, should be construed as giving rise to a "just cause" requirement for terminating the employment relationship
- That performance appraisals and other evaluation procedures should in no way be considered in any other manner in determining the existence or nature of any employment relationship that may be found to exist between the parties

is under no obligation to appraise performance, and that neither the fact that appraisals are or are not conducted, nor the manner in which they may be conducted, should be construed as giving rise to a "just cause" requirement for terminating the employment relationship. In summary, employment documentation, signed by the employee, should set forth clearly the express intention and understanding of both the employer and the employee that performance appraisals and other evaluation procedures should in no way be considered in determining the existence or nature of any employment relationship that may be found to exist between the parties.

Such language should, at a minimum, make it more difficult for disgruntled current and former employees to rely on performance appraisals and related procedures to the detriment of the employer.

Employment Discrimination Theories and the Type of Employment Decision

Both the theory used to prove discrimination (disparate treatment or disparate impact), and the type of employment decision (for example, compensation, promotion, layoff, or discharge), are likely to determine when and how performance appraisals will figure in discrimination cases. Previous reviews (Burchett & De Meuse, 1985; Martin & Bartol, 1991; Martin, Bartol, & Levine, 1986; Veglahn, 1993) digest a good deal of earlier case law and arbitration decisions that address these issues. I therefore focus on recent developments.

Table 2.2 presents a summary of selected legal principles and laws that can relate to performance appraisals and potential liability for employment discrimination. For those who may not be familiar with this area of the law, I provide a more detailed summary of discrimination analysis under disparate treatment and disparate impact theories, which may be applied to any of the substantive laws—for example, Title VII, ADEA, ADA—under which employers are often accused of discrimination. I also discuss briefly how the employer's defense strategy will differ with the nature of the employment decision in question. Examples from the cases follow the table.

Disparate Treatment

Most discrimination cases that involve performance appraisal allege disparate treatment. In these cases, employees claim that they were intentionally treated differently because of their gender, race, ethnic background, national origin, age, disability, or other status protected under state or federal law. An employee can establish a *prima facie* case (raise an inference) of discrimination either by presenting direct evidence of discrimination (for example, racist or sexist remarks that appear to have influenced the employment decision), or by showing that he or she was qualified and available for a position but was rejected under circumstances that suggest unlawful discrimination (*Texas Department of Community Affairs* v. *Burdine*,

**Table 2.2. Summary of Selected Legal Principles
and Laws Relating to Performance Appraisals
and Employment Discrimination.**

Legal Principle or Law	Summary	Relationship to Performance Appraisals and Employment Discrimination
Disparate treatment	Intentional discrimination; improper distinctions among individuals based on protected status (age, race, sex)	Results of invalid, biased, or subjective performance appraisals may be involved in trying to justify employment decisions that are based on discriminatory motives
Disparate (adverse) impact	Unintentional discrimination; arises from employment practices that appear neutral but adversely affect those with protected status	Invalid appraisal practices or absence of safeguards can operate to exclude qualified protected class members from employment opportunities more often than nonmembers
Title VII of the Civil Rights Act of 1964 (Title VII)	Outlaws discrimination based on race, color, sex, religion, or national origin	Provides protection against use of appraisal procedures and results to perpetrate discrimination
State fair employment practices acts	Provide protection similar to Title VII; laws vary by state	Similar to above
Equal Pay Act of 1963	Prohibits gender-based differences in pay for equal work, subject to limited exceptions	Appraisal results can be used to invoke and justify exceptions (for example, merit-based pay distinctions)
Civil Rights Act of 1991 (CRA 1991)	Allows jury trials and compensatory and punitive damages in discrimination cases; alters burden of proof and other technical aspects of some cases	Reduces plaintiffs' burden of identifying particular employment practices (for example, performance appraisals) that caused discrimination if effects cannot be separated from those of other practices
Age Discrimination in Employment Act (ADEA)	Prohibits employment discrimination based on age of forty or over	Provides protection against use of appraisal procedures and results to perpetrate age-based discrimination

**Table 2.2. Summary of Selected Legal Principles
and Laws Relating to Performance Appraisals
and Employment Discrimination, cont'd.**

Legal Principle or Law	Summary	Relationship to Performance Appraisals and Employment Discrimination
Americans with Disabilities Act of 1990	Prohibits employment discrimination based on disability, record of disability, or perception of disability	Limits appraisal criteria to essential job functions and may require reasonable accommodation as to how performance is appraised
Rehabilitation Act of 1973	Similar to ADA; applies to federal contractors	Similar to above

450 U.S. 248 [1981]). This most commonly is done according to *McDonnell Douglas Corp.* v. *Green,* 411 U.S. 792 (1973), by showing that the employee (1) belongs to a protected class; (2) applied for and was qualified for a job opening; (3) was rejected; and (4) the job remained open while the employer continued to seek similarly qualified applicants or hired an individual not a member of the same protected class. Under the now well-accepted burden-shifting process of *McDonnell Douglas,* the employer then must articulate a legitimate, nondiscriminatory reason (typically a performance-related one) for its action. If the employer can do so, the employee then must show that the employer's stated reason was a pretext for a discriminatory decision. In so-called *mixed motive* cases (those where decisions are based partly on discriminatory motives but also on performance), an employer still can avoid liability for compensatory and punitive damages, reinstatement, back pay, and similar relief otherwise available under substantive law, if it can convince the fact-finder that it would have made the same decision even had it not taken improper factors (for example, gender) into account (*Price Waterhouse* v. *Hopkins,* 109 S.Ct. 1775 [1989]; CRA 1991, section 107[a]). This defense is not available, however, in cases where protected class status (for example, age) is clearly used as a limiting

criterion in the employment decision (see, for example, *EEOC* v. *Johnson & Higgins,* where J&H unsuccessfully tried to defend its age-based mandatory retirement policy by claiming that it enabled the company to plan its succession in an orderly fashion).

Disparate (Adverse) Impact

Performance appraisals figure less prominently in disparate impact cases, in which a seemingly neutral employment practice may have an unintentional but nonetheless discriminatory effect. In such cases, employees must demonstrate a causal connection between a specific employment practice (for example, performance appraisals) and a discriminatory result, unless the elements of the employer's decision-making process are not capable of separation for purposes of analysis (Civil Rights Act of 1991; *Wards Cove Packing Co.* v. *Atonio,* 490 U.S. 642 [1989]). Appraisal results then can be used to rebut plaintiffs' (usually statistical) evidence of an improper disparity in promotion, layoff, or other employment decisions (*EEOC* v. *Texas Instruments, Inc.,* 72 FEP Cases 980 [5th Cir. 1996]; *Griggs* v. *Duke Power Co.,* 401 U.S. 424 [1971]; *Watson* v. *Fort Worth Bank & Trust Co.,* 108 S.Ct. 2777 [1988]). Here, the burden-shifting process parallels that of disparate treatment cases; the employer must show that the challenged practice bears a "manifest relationship" to job performance consistent with "business necessity." A common articulation of this burden is to show that the challenged practice "is significantly related to the legitimate goals of the employer," *Wards Cove,* 490 U.S. at 659. (The *Wards Cove* case, while subject to attack during the legislative process, was not expressly overturned by CRA 1991, and is still considered by leading commentators to provide viable guidance in this context; see Cathcart & Snyderman, 1997.) The employee then may establish pretext if he or she can show that other appraisal practices would have served the employer's interests without such a discriminatory effect (*Albemarle Paper Co.* v. *Moody,* 422 U.S. 405 [1975]).

Nature of the Employment Decision

The employer's defense strategy typically will differ depending on the nature of the employment decision (Martin & Bartol, 1991). In failure-to-promote cases, employers use appraisals to show that the person selected for the promotion is likely to perform in the higher position better than the plaintiff. In layoff or discharge cases, employers use appraisals to show that the plaintiff was already performing poorly in comparison either to peers (layoff cases) or to some minimum standard of acceptable performance (discharge cases). In merit pay cases, employers compare the plaintiff's performance with specific compensation criteria.

I now present examples of recent cases that involve Title VII, the Equal Pay Act, the ADEA, the ADA, and other theories of recovery. Because of the rapidly growing number of cases that involve performance appraisals, I only had room to include a limited number of cases. I therefore decided to offer a mix of appellate, trial court, and arbitration decisions to provide the reader with a feel for both the legal and factual issues that tend to be in dispute. I omitted cases in which favorable appraisal results were used solely to establish a *prima facie* case, because these usually were not very instructive for practitioners. Instead, I focused on cases where the employer's defense relied on poor performance appraisals to demonstrate a legitimate, nondiscriminatory reason for its actions, or that it would have taken the same action irrespective of possible discrimination in a mixed motive case. I also included cases where favorable appraisals were used to show pretext, which is often the determinative issue in contemporary discrimination litigation.

Discrimination Cases Under Title VII, State Fair Employment Practices Laws, and the Equal Pay Act

Title VII of the Civil Rights Act of 1964 makes it unlawful to discriminate against any individual with respect to compensation, terms, conditions, or privileges of employment, because of race, color, religion, sex, or national origin. State fair employment practices acts, which vary by jurisdiction, contain similar prohibitions that provide at least as much protection as federal law, and sometimes carry procedural or strategic advantages for plaintiffs. The Equal Pay Act provides protection against wage discrimination on the basis of gender "for equal work on jobs the performance of which requires equal skill, effort, and responsibility, and which are performed under similar working conditions," 29 U.S.C. Section 206 (d)(1). Violations of the Act are inferred if the employer pays different wages to an employee of the opposite sex for substantially equal work. The employer then may defend by showing that any wage discrepancy resulted from a bona fide seniority system, performance or merit-based distinctions, piece-rate or other production-based systems, or some legitimate factor other than gender (*Corning Glass Works* v. *Brennan,* 417 U.S. 188 [1974]).

Several recent cases in this area involve professionals such as college professors, attorneys, and engineers. In *Fisher* v. *Vassar College,* 70 FEP Cases 1155 (2d Cir. 1995), Fisher, a biology professor, was denied tenure at Vassar and claimed discrimination based on sex, marital status, age discrimination, and violation of the Equal Pay Act. Vassar based its decision on the biology department's recommendation, outside evaluations, and student comments, all of which were reviewed by the college dean and a collegewide faculty committee. The department's evaluation focused on scholarship, service, teaching ability, and leadership (all of which were found wanting), but also noted Fisher's eight-to-nine-year hiatus to raise a family before returning to work and coming up for tenure review. After trial in a factually complex case, the District Court concluded that Fisher had met the recognized qualifications for tenure, that the department's evaluations were biased and pretextual, and awarded her more than $600,000 in damages.

On appeal, a panel of the Second Circuit reversed. The Court agreed that Fisher had established a *prima facie* case of discrimination, and that Vassar had articulated a legitimate, nondiscriminatory reason for denying her tenure (the department's negative evaluation of Fisher's performance). It also seemed inclined to agree that Vassar's tenure review was pretextual, in that its tenure standards were unclear and unspecified, and the tenure committee had selectively excluded favorable information about Fisher's performance. However, citing *St. Mary's Honor Ctr.* v. *Hicks,* 113 S.Ct. 2742, 2752 (1993), the Court pointed out that it is not enough merely to show pretext; the plaintiff must prove that the employer's articulated reason is a pretext *for discrimination.* The Court found the evidence insufficient to establish that Vassar's denial of tenure was discriminatory. It also rejected Fisher's Equal Pay Act claim because the higher-paid male to whom Fisher compared herself had been on the tenure track several years longer than Fisher, which established a legitimate differential based on factors other than gender.

Jiminez v. *Mary Washington College,* 67 FEP Cases 1867 (4th Cir. 1995), is another case that illustrates judicial reluctance to second-guess the merits of promotion decisions, particularly when the performance being evaluated lies within the decision makers' substantive expertise. In *Jiminez,* the District Court found that the college had discriminated in denying Jiminez tenure based on race (black) and national origin (Trinidad). As in *Fisher,* tenure decisions were based on evaluations of service, scholarship, and teaching effectiveness. Although Jiminez's service was appraised highly, he had failed to publish adequately or complete his doctoral dissertation in six years with the college. He also had received consistently low ratings from students. However, Jiminez argued that these ratings were due to a concerted effort by a group of white students to have him removed. The Court found that Jiminez had established a *prima facie* case of discrimination, and that the college had rebutted it (based on poor performance), but that Jiminez had shown pretext (the college's failure to disregard "racially tainted" teaching evaluations).

The Court of Appeals reversed. Noting that courts typically "review professional employment decisions with great trepidation," the Court found (as in *Fisher*) that, even had the college's determination of poor performance (due to other, "untainted" bad evaluations and failure to defend his dissertation) been pretextual, Jiminez still had failed to establish discrimination.

Byrd v. *Ronayne,* 68 FEP Cases 769 (1st Cir. 1995) illustrates a similar analysis in the law firm context. Byrd, a law firm associate, was terminated after client complaints about the quality of her work. She sued, accusing the firm of Title VII sex discrimination, an Equal Pay Act violation, and retaliatory discharge based on her previous filing of an EEOC complaint. Byrd had received bonuses and favorable reviews notwithstanding some acknowledged performance difficulties, but the District Court found that she had failed to establish a *prima facie* case under *McDonnell Douglas,* because her documented poor performance indicated she was not qualified for her job.

The Court of Appeals agreed, but went further. It ruled that, even had Byrd been able to make out a *prima facie* case, she had failed to raise sufficient evidence of pretext (via the bonuses and favorable reviews) because her performance clearly was poor at the time of her discharge. The Court also upheld dismissal of Byrd's Equal Pay Act claim, because she failed to show that her duties were similar to a more highly paid male associate, or that this associate (who also generated more billings) had a similar record of client complaints and performance problems.

For an analogous case in which the employer also prevailed, see *EEOC* v. *Lousiana Network*, 1 WH Cases 2d 435 (D. La. 1992). In that case, the court found that a radio station did not violate Title VII or the Equal Pay Act when it paid a female news anchor less than a male anchor who had superior experience and on-air presentation skills, as documented in written performance appraisals. A note of caution is in order here, however. Although the employers prevailed in these cases, the facts underlying the pretext claim in *Byrd* illustrate the danger of trying to be kind to a poor performer by continuing to give good evaluations in the face of known performance problems. This issue is discussed in greater detail in later portions of this chapter.

Amirmokri v. *Baltimore Gas & Electric Co.,* 68 FEP Cases 809 (4th Cir. 1995), presents another situation where the employer successfully defended a Title VII claim, here for failure to promote based on national origin. In this case, the employer relied on evidence that the promoted employee had performance evaluations superior to Amirmokri's. Although Amirmokri, an engineer of Iranian descent, made out a *prima facie* case under *McDonnell Douglas,* the employer was able to show that the person promoted was more qualified, based on objective performance evaluations and subjective factors such as interpersonal skills and ability to lead a team. The District Court also rejected Amirmokri's pretext claim, and dismissed his discrimination case altogether. However, based on evidence that Amirmokri was called names including "the ayatollah," "the local terrorist," and "camel jockey," the Court of Appeals allowed the case to go to trial on the issue of hostile environment harassment (EEOC and Supreme Court rulings have interpreted Title VII to prohibit harassment based on national origin as well as gender and other protected status). The Court also ordered a trial on Amirmokri's claim for constructive discharge, which alleged that the hostility of the working environment was so intolerable that a reasonable person would have felt compelled to leave the job. The Court focused on evidence that Amirmokri's supervisor had intentionally embarrassed him by assigning him impossible tasks and telling coworkers that he was incompetent, which may have negatively affected both his performance and its evaluation. The case illustrates that defensible performance appraisals alone may not ensure success in court, because conduct related to the evaluation process can give rise to liability under more than one legal theory.

Kerr-Selgas v. *American Airlines,* 69 FEP Cases 944 (1st Cir. 1995) is another Title VII harassment case. In this one, a male supervisor gave his female employee a negative performance evaluation shortly after she rejected his sexual advances. Although the case deals primarily with procedural issues unrelated to performance appraisals, the employer's failure to take proper and timely action against the supervisor led a jury to award $1.2 million for discrimination, retaliation, and invasion of privacy (see also *Ton* v. *Information Resources,* a same-sex harassment case in which the plaintiff's performance was rated poorly after he refused his manager's sexual advances).

Finally, affirmative action policies were at the heart of a white male's complaint of reverse discrimination in *Whalen* v. *Rubin,* 71 FEP Cases 1170, 1174 (7th Cir. 1996). Whalen, an IRS appeals officer who was both a lawyer and a CPA, was passed over for a promotion, which went to a woman named Price. Price was ranked as the most qualified among seven candidates, while Whalen tied for last on the list. An IRS panel of interviewers unanimously chose Price as the best person for the job, based on her substantial experience as an acting supervisor and her completion of a pre-management training course. Whalen countered that Price's selection was tainted, because the IRS maintained an affirmative action plan and provided bonuses to employees based on their "success" with equal employment opportunity. The Court of Appeals rejected this argument, and held that Whalen had failed to establish a direct causal link between the IRS's affirmative action policy and his inferior performance ratings: "the mere existence of an affirmative action policy is . . . insufficient to prove that the IRS actually intentionally discriminated against Whalen." For an analogous holding under New Jersey state law, see *Wachstein* v. *Slocum,* 67 FEP Cases 587 (N.J. App. 1993).

Age Discrimination Cases Under the ADEA

As the average age of the American worker continues to increase, so does the number of age discrimination lawsuits, including those claiming age-related biases in performance appraisals (see Miller, Kaspin, & Schuster, 1990; Perry, Kulik, & Bourhis, 1996). The ADEA as originally passed protected employees between the ages of forty and sixty-five against discrimination "with respect to compensation, terms, conditions, or privileges of employment," or classification that would "tend to deprive any individual of employment opportunities or otherwise adversely affect [that individual's] status as an employee," 29 U.S.C. sections 623(a)(1)-(2). The Act was later amended to raise the upper limit to seventy, and amended again (in 1986) to remove the upper limit entirely. Although employers have been able to defend quite a few of these cases successfully, employees continue to succeed where they can show that performance evaluations were manipulated to justify age-based discrimination.

For example, in *Starceski* v. *Westinghouse Electric Corp.*, 67 FEP Cases 1184 (3rd Cir. 1995), the Court of Appeals affirmed a jury verdict for Starceski, a sixty-three-year-old senior engineer and thirty-six-year Westinghouse employee, based on evidence that a supervisor had directed another employee to doctor Starceski's evaluations to reflect poor performance. Starceski was able to show that managers were told to transfer jobs away from older workers in anticipation of an RIF, that five of six workers laid off were over forty, that the average age of the work group after these layoffs was under forty, and that several of those who were not laid off had lower performance evaluations than he did. Under these circumstances, the Court rejected Westinghouse's claim that it would have laid Starceski off even had it not considered his age.

A similar result often occurs where a long history of good performance is suddenly followed by the bad evaluation of an age-protected worker just before a layoff. In *Woodman* v. *Haemonetics Corp.*, 67 FEP Cases 838, 840 (1st Cir. 1995) the Appellate Court reversed dismissal of Woodman's ADEA claim, in part because of a supervisor's statement that "these damn people [management]—they want younger people here." The Court found that this statement and other evidence warranted a trial on the issue of pretext and discriminatory intent. See also *Brewer* v. *Quaker State Refining*

Corp., 69 FEP Cases 753, 759 (3rd Cir. 1995), in which Brewer's receipt of a bonus shortly before his discharge, and a performance memorandum stating that plaintiff "is fifty-three years old, which presents another problem," amounted to circumstantial evidence of age discrimination that required a trial on the issue of the "corporate culture in which the employment decision to discharge Brewer was made."

The employer fared better in *Thomas* v. *IBM,* 67 FEP Cases 270 (10th Cir. 1995). In that case, Thomas's ADEA and fraudulent evaluation claims were dismissed by the District Court, a decision upheld on appeal. Thomas claimed but could not demonstrate that IBM gave her undeservedly low performance evaluations because of her age to induce her to accept early retirement or an extended leave of absence. The case contains an interesting discussion of IBM's performance ranking system, through which employees ranked low in terms of their "relative contribution to IBM's business" find their positions at risk. In upholding dismissal of Thomas's claims, the Court noted that IBM's appraisal system appeared to contain safeguards designed to minimize possible bias (these aspects of appraisals are discussed later on).

EEOC v. *Texas Instruments, Inc.,* 72 FEP Cases 980 (5th Cir. 1996) presents a case in which the employer found itself in the unusual position of having to argue that its appraisal system was essentially worthless for evaluating performance in determining whom to lay off during an RIF. The Court ruled in favor of Texas Instruments (TI), notwithstanding evidence of age-related comments and disregard of its own seniority system and appraisal results. Unlike *Woodman* v. *Haemonetics Corp.,* the Court in this case found remarks to the effect that "his age got him" and that TI "had to make room for some of the younger supervisors" to be "stray remarks" that were insufficient to rebut TI's stated reasons for discharging six supervisors who were in their fifties. In an age of rapidly changing technology, the Court accepted as nonpretextual TI's claim that it disregarded both seniority preferences and favorable appraisals because to adhere to their use would have caused TI to retain highly paid supervisors whose willingness or ability to learn new technology was questionable. TI's evaluations and "Key Personnel Assessment" rankings apparently were not designed to make fine distinctions among employees; the former clustered ratings tightly around group medians, whereas the latter merely reflected departmental pay differentials among employees.

The Court also accepted TI's argument that favorable performance ratings on present jobs were not necessarily relevant to determining ability to perform post-RIF duties that required mastery of sophisticated computer software and other new resources in a rapidly changing technological environment. However, it is not clear that these arguments would prevail in all jurisdictions. Practitioners would be well advised to keep job descriptions, performance criteria, and appraisal processes updated to the greatest extent practicably possible.

Finally, *Fisher* v. *Vassar College,* discussed earlier in the context of Title VII, also contained an ADEA claim that was dismissed without trial. Despite evidence that eight other tenured faculty at Vassar were at least nine years younger than Fisher when they were tenured—and a colleague's statement that Fisher "was too old to ever become tenured"—the Court of Appeals upheld dismissal of her case because the sample of younger tenured faculty was too small to permit meaningful inferences about discrimination, and because Fisher's extended hiatus from academia prior to entering the tenure track explained any age discrepancy without the need to infer discrimination.

Disability Discrimination Cases Under the ADA and Rehabilitation Act of 1973

The ADA prohibits an employer from discriminating in employment, based on a known physical or mental impairment, against a qualified individual with a disability. A "qualified individual with a disability" is defined as an individual substantially limited in one or more major life activities who, with or without a reasonable accommodation, can perform the essential functions of the position that the individual desires or holds; 42 U.S.C. Section 12111; 29 C.F.R. Section 1630.2(m). The ADA also prohibits discrimination based on a record of impairment or perception of impairment ("regarded as" cases). The Rehabilitation Act contains similar proscriptions for employers with federal funding or federal contracts, and tends to be used primarily in cases where the alleged discrimination took place before the effective date of the ADA (July 1992).

Growing recognition that a wide variety of conditions may be construed as disabilities (particularly in the area of stress-related and other mental impairments) has led to a rapid increase in the number of claims filed under these statutes, and perhaps to a judicial reluctance to expand the scope of liability in the courts. In the context of performance appraisals, these cases usually turn on whether the employer knew or had reason to know of the employee's disability, whether the employee was qualified, or whether the employee was evaluated on something other than the job's essential functions.

For example, in *Hedberg* v. *Indiana Bell Telephone Co.*, 4 AD Cases 65, 69 (7th Cir. 1995), the employer was undergoing an RIF based on relative performance rankings. It terminated Hedberg in part based on low rating scores on a written evaluation form and in part based on appraisal comments about problems with interpersonal skills, not coming to work on time, and his "work ethic." Unknown to the company, Hedberg suffered from a condition called primary amyloidosis, a disease that can cause chronic fatigue symptoms. The District Court dismissed Hedberg's ADA claim because it concluded that the disease was not a "known disability" within the meaning of the Act. The Court of Appeals affirmed, noting that, unlike most discrimination claims in which the protected characteristic of the plaintiff (for example, race or gender) is obvious to the employer, there are situations in which an employer clearly does not know about an employee's disability. The Court reasoned that an employer cannot fire an employee "because of" a disability of which it has no knowledge. Here, the employer maintained that it fired Hedberg primarily based on low written evaluations, but the Court offered that, even had they fired him for perceived lack of "work ethic," they would not have violated the ADA:

> Employers fire people every day. Perhaps the most common criterion for choosing whom to fire is which employees perform a job better or worse than others. Allowing liability when an employer indisputably had no knowledge of the disability but knew of the disability's effects . . . would create an enormous sphere of potential liability. Tardiness and laziness have many causes, few of them based in illness. The ADA hardly requires that merely because

some perceived tardiness and laziness is rooted in disability, an employer who has not been informed of the disability is bound to retain all apparently tardy and lazy employees on the chance that they may have a disability that causes their behavior. The ADA does not require clairvoyance. [Moreover] even when the employer does know of an employee's disability . . . the employer may [still] fire the employee because he cannot perform his job adequately [with or without a reasonable accommodation], i.e., [if] he is not a "qualified individual" within the meaning of the ADA.

For a case in which the employer did use negative appraisals to show that the employee was not qualified for her job, see *Demming* v. *Housing Authority,* 4 AD Cases 1593 (8th Cir. 1995), in which Demming claimed that her discharge occurred because she had been hospitalized for thyroid cancer, but could not establish that performance factors unrelated to her disability were not the real reason for her discharge.

Qualification for a job, essential functions of the job, and employer knowledge of the employee's disability all were involved in *Lewis* v. *Zilog, Inc.,* 4 AD Cases 1787 (N.D. Ga. 1995). In that case, Lewis was diagnosed with bipolar mood disorder, a condition she claimed resulted in part from a stressful meeting about a written performance evaluation that cited her need to improve relationships with others. Lewis had a history of yelling at coworkers and exhibiting attitude and mood swings. During the meeting, she jumped up and ran around the office, blamed others for various problems, and sliced a photo of her supervisor into small pieces. Lewis later claimed to be totally disabled, took the second of two medical leaves, filed for long-term disability benefits, and was terminated for exceeding the allowable maximum leave under company policy. She sued Zilog under Title VII and the ADA.

Zilog moved to dismiss Lewis's ADA claims, conceding that Lewis had a disability within the meaning of the Act, but denying that it had been aware of any disability during Lewis's employment, and denying that she was a "qualified individual with a disability" for ADA purposes. The Court granted Zilog's motion, ruling that Lewis's benefit-related assertions that she was unable to work proved that she could not perform the essential functions of her job (her psychiatrist was unable to suggest a reasonable accommodation that would have allowed her to return to work). The

Court also found that Zilog's termination of Lewis in accordance with its own medical leave policy was a legitimate nondiscriminatory reason, and rejected any claim of pretext. Zilog had terminated other individuals in accordance with its policy, and the Court found no evidence that Zilog knew Lewis had bipolar mood disorder even though coworkers were aware that she suffered from stress and took the drug Prozac.

Olson v. *General Electric Astrospace,* 6 AD Cases 270, 275 (3rd Cir. 1996) further illustrates how evidence offered to prove one element of an ADA claim (for example, "qualified individual") can be used to negate a different element (for example, "individual with a disability"). Olson had been laid off during an RIF after a history of hospitalization for depression and a possible sleep disorder. Olson's supervisor, in a written performance evaluation prior to Olson's layoff, questioned his work habits and commitment to his department because of "an unusual amount of time off for personal illness reasons." Olson later was interviewed for rehire by the same supervisor, who recommended a different candidate to a superior who was responsible for making the actual hire decision. This superior accepted the recommendation to hire the other candidate, and Olson sued, claiming an ADA violation.

Olson's ADA claim was dismissed by the District Court, because evidence that he was able to perform his duties despite any psychological problems (that is, that he was qualified for the job) "ironically establish[ed] that he was not substantially limited in a major life activity." The Court of Appeals agreed with this analysis as far as it went, but ordered a trial on the issue of whether Olson had been "regarded as" having a disability. Even though the hiring decision was made by a person who claimed to have no knowledge of Olson's medical history, the fact that this person's decision was influenced by the recommendation of a supervisor who did have such knowledge raised a factual issue that needed a trial to resolve. This case suggests that supervisors should be better trained to recognize potential "regarded as" liability, and that review mechanisms and other safeguards should be installed to ensure that potentially tainted recommendations are not involved in hiring, promotion, and related employment decisions.

Two recent cases involving human immunodeficiency virus (HIV) further illustrate the nuances of ADA actions where the disability is not obvious or clearly known to the employer. In *R.G.H.* v. *Abbott Laboratories,* 4 AD Cases 289 (N.D. Ill. 1995), R.G.H., a research biochemist, tested positive for HIV after accidental exposure to the virus in one of Abbott's labs. After a number of favorable appraisals and raises, he was turned down for two promotions, the first because a better-qualified applicant was selected, and the second because of deficient performance evaluations. R.G.H. alleged an ADA violation, but the Abbott employees who made these decisions established that they were ignorant of his HIV status, and he was unable to present evidence as to the role played by any perceived or actual disability in either outcome.

The HIV-infected plaintiff in *Runnenbaum* v. *NationsBank of Maryland,* 5 AD Cases 1602 (4th Cir. 1996), faced a similar problem (dismissal) at the District Court level, and appealed. A panel of the 4th Circuit, in a split decision, reversed and remanded for trial. The majority found accusations that Runnenbaum failed to complete certain "training tasks" or present a "professional image" to be potentially pretextual, because the bulk of his performance appraisals were positive or outstanding. The dissent seemed unwilling to interfere with the professional judgment of the employer.

Finally, *Borkowski* v. *Valley Central School District,* 4 AD Cases 1264 (2d Cir. 1995), involved a number of performance-related ADA issues, including reasonable accommodation and essential functions, in the context of a teacher tenure denial. Borkowski, an elementary school teacher, had sustained serious head injuries in a motor vehicle accident. Although she recovered substantially, she continued to experience difficulties with memory, concentration, and dealing with multiple stimuli simultaneously. These problems led to difficulties controlling students in her classes, as noted by an observer during an unannounced classroom visit. Overall, Borkowski received mixed performance reviews, and was denied tenure. She unsuccessfully sought reconsideration due to her disability, and sued under the Rehabilitation Act.

On appeal, while acknowledging the school district's discretionary authority to make tenure decisions, the Court ruled that the district had acted improperly in refusing to consider whether Borkowski could have performed the essential functions of her position with a reasonable accommodation, such as providing a teaching assistant to help her control her classes (the Court also questioned whether classroom control really was an essential function of the job). The Court further noted that Section 504 of the ADA requires an employer to ensure that its evaluative techniques measure the job-related skills of an individual with a disability, not the disability itself. This raises a further issue as to whether the practice of using unannounced classroom visits to evaluate Borkowski's performance might have been an ADA violation in and of itself.

The Court's language in *Borkowski* makes clear that employers may need to make reasonable accommodations not only with respect to how jobs are to be performed, but also with respect to the manner in which performance is to be evaluated. Employers must take care to ensure that only the essential functions of the job are evaluated, and that only performance is used to make employment-related decisions. In addition, although the ADA prohibits discrimination on the basis of "known" disabilities, and it is generally the responsibility of the employee to request a reasonable accommodation, there is a trend toward requiring the employer to engage in an interactive process with the employee to provide an accommodation even without an explicit request (Fram, 1997). It thus would seem beneficial to establish mechanisms through which individuals can help employers become aware of potential disabilities on a confidential basis. Such mechanisms might help avoid potential invasions of privacy or liability for discrimination based on the perception of a disability that could arise if an employer's direct inquiry about the possible need for an accommodation were to offend or stigmatize a particular employee. Taking such steps might increase both the chances of identifying problematic situations proactively, and of defending discrimination claims in court with a showing of good faith efforts to comply with the requirements of the ADA.

For example, the employer might post a notice setting forth its intention, in accordance with federal law, to make necessary modifications to break down workplace barriers to effective job performance, and that employees knowing of any such barriers should identify them in confidence to a designated individual. Using this sort of language could help avoid drawing undue attention to disabled employees' impairments and the disability-based nature of the notice. Supervisors also should be trained to identify, during appraisal processes and otherwise, employees whose performance suggests that reasonable accommodation of a physical or mental impairment might be in order. Supervisors then should explore with the employee, discretely and on an interactive basis, the need for and nature of any such accommodation.

Tort Liability Arising out of Performance Appraisals

Performance evaluation processes can also cause problems for employers under state tort law theories such as infliction of emotional distress, negligence, defamation, or misrepresentation. Emotional distress cases usually involve fact-specific disputes over the outrageousness of conduct such as harassment, and are not discussed further here. Negligence cases have declined in frequency, so I address them only briefly. Defamation actions have become more common, and misrepresentation is a relatively new player in the appraisal context. Taken together, these types of cases underscore the need to perform appraisals and communicate their results with a great deal of care.

Negligence

Negligence claims require a showing that the employer owed a duty to conduct performance appraisals with due care, and that this duty was violated. Because of the *employment at will* doctrine, such a duty, where it exists, is usually found in some form of employment contract (see, for example, *Mathewson* v. *Aloha Airlines*). Interestingly, cases in this area may involve complaints about *favorable* evaluations, as where an employer fails to notify an employee through the appraisal process that performance is inadequate, and terminates the employee without providing an opportunity to improve (for example, *Mann* v. *J. E. Baker Co.*, 52 FEP Cases 1111 [D. Pa. 1990]). Liability may also arise where the employer communicates favorable but untrue information about a former employee's performance and causes a substantial risk of harm to others by doing so (see *Randi W., a Minor,* v. *Muroc Joint Unified School District et al.*, 97 Cal. Daily Op. Serv. 614 [1997], discussed more fully later in this chapter).

Some courts formerly allowed cases to proceed on both negligence and breach of contract theories simultaneously (for example, *Schipani* v. *Ford Motor Co.*, 30 FEP Cases 361 [Mich. App.

1981]). However, courts in most jurisdictions have refused to recognize a tort claim for negligent evaluation (which might draw a larger damage award) unless the appraisal-related conduct can be distinguished from breach of a duty imposed by contract (for example, *Mooneyham v. Smith Kline & French Labs*, 55 FEP Cases 1777 [W.D. Mich. 1990]; *Haas v. Montgomery Ward & Co.*, 43 FEP Cases 188 [6th Cir. 1987]). For practical reasons, most of these cases now tend to involve the employer's alleged failure to follow its own performance management or progressive discipline procedures, as specified in a collective bargaining or other employment contract. These types of cases are addressed later in this chapter in connection with the legal defensibility of appraisal procedures. As discussed more fully later on, it is a good idea to ensure that poorly performing employees are notified of work-related problems, so they cannot later claim that they would have improved but for the employer's failure to properly manage their performance.

Defamation

To establish defamation arising out of a negative performance appraisal, an employee must prove (1) that the appraisal contained a false assertion of fact (rather than a subjective opinion incapable of objective verification; for example, "Smith missed important deadlines on two occasions," rather than "Smith is difficult to deal with"); (2) that the assertion was "published" (that is, communicated to some third party); and (3) that the published falsehood injured the employee's reputation (*Isaacson v. Keck, Mahin & Cate*, 61 FEP Cases 1145 [N.D. Ill. 1993]). Because statements that disparage a person's profession or occupation have been held to be *defamatory per se* (that is, not requiring proof of actual injury), the employer's defense usually relies on lack of publication or a claim of privilege. In general, there is a qualified privilege to communicate, in good faith (without malice), accurate appraisal results, if the employer is under a duty to do so or shares a common interest with the recipient in the subject matter.

For example, in *Thompto v. Coburn's Inc.*, 10 IER Cases 263 (N.D. Iowa 1994), Thompto, a deli manager, was fired because she failed to meet performance goals for profits, labor costs, and customer complaints. She sued for wrongful discharge and defamation after

Coburn's gave information about her dismissal to Job Service, civil rights investigators, and department managers. The Court rejected Thompto's claims, however, ruling that Coburn's had a qualified privilege because it was required to cooperate with state agencies to establish the basis for Thompto's termination, and because the other recipients of the information held a shared interest in its subject.

Misrepresentation: Walking the Tightrope Between Negligence and Defamation

A recent case illustrates the difficult balancing act employers must perform with regard to job performance information. In *Randi W., a Minor,* v. *Muroc Joint Unified School District et al.,* the California Supreme Court held that although an employer is not often accountable for failing to disclose negative information about a former employee, it may be held liable if a recommendation *affirmatively misrepresents that a former employee's performance was favorable* when such a misrepresentation might present a *substantial and foreseeable risk of harm* to a prospective employer or third party.

Randi W., a thirteen-year-old female middle school student, accused her vice principal, Gadams, of sexual molestation. Gadams had obtained his position through a college placement office, which had received letters from Gadams's previous employers that described him as "an upbeat, enthusiastic administrator who relates well to the students" and contained glowing praise for Gadams's "genuine concern" for students, "outstanding rapport" with everyone, and contribution to achieving "a safe, orderly, and clean environment for students and staff." One of the former employers recommended him "without reservation"; the other energetically concluded that it "wouldn't hesitate to recommend Mr. Gadams for any position!" However, evidence indicated that both employers knew that Gadams had had previous performance problems that included hugging female junior high school students, giving them massages, and making sexual overtures. One of the former employers even had disciplined Gadams in connection with sexual harassment charges that included "sexual touching" of female students, and had pressured Gadams to resign.

Lawyers for Randi W. sued based on negligent misrepresentation and related theories. In the trial court, defendants successfully moved to dismiss on the grounds that they owed no legal duty to

Randi W. The Court of Appeals reinstated the case, however, and the Supreme Court agreed. The Court reasoned that, although employers have no duty to say anything about former employees' performance, when they choose to communicate such information, there is a duty to use reasonable care in doing so. The Court held that defendants should have foreseen that future prospective employers would rely on these favorable letters and decide to hire Gadams, placing students such as Randi W. at risk.

The Court was not persuaded by the employers' arguments that the threat of tort liability would unduly restrict the flow of information and impede job applicants from finding new employment, and that no reasonable person would assume that a letter of recommendation contains the whole truth about a candidate's performance background and character. However, perhaps concerned about the growing number of employers who have reluctantly adopted uniform "no comment" policies (many now refuse to provide any references whatsoever even for stellar former employees), the Court carefully limited its ruling to situations that present "a substantial foreseeable risk of physical injury to the prospective employer or third persons," and which in fact result in such harm. The potential applicability of this holding to a broader range of workplace violence cases is discussed later in this chapter.

What to Do

A review of the cases digested in this section discloses a number of ways in which performance appraisals can give rise to unexpected employer liability for discrimination, harassment, constructive discharge, and related theories of liability. Some suggestions for limiting such liability are summarized in Table 2.3.

Performance Appraisals and the Legal Defensibility of Employment Decisions

Performance appraisals sometimes have been treated as tests in employment litigation, and are theoretically subject to the Uniform Guidelines on Employee Selection (41 C.F.R. 60, et seq.; see *Brito v. Zia Co.*, 478 F.2d 1200 [10th Cir. 1973]; *Albemarle Paper Co. v. Moody*, 422 U.S. 405 [1975]). However, Barrett and Kernan (1987) have argued that performance appraisals are better understood as criteria

**Table 2.3. Practical Suggestions for
Limiting Discrimination and Related Legal Liability
in the Context of Performance Appraisals.**

Legal Theory	Suggestion for Limiting Potential Liability
Harassment or constructive discharge	Require employees to notify employer of any conditions related to job, job performance, or appraisals (for example, supervisor bias or improper conduct) that allegedly are so severe as to require quitting; establish and consistently follow procedures to promptly investigate and eliminate any such offending conditions or conduct by supervisors or other employees to avoid claim that employer tacitly accepted or approved of harassment
Age discrimination	Train supervisors to avoid age-loaded comments in verbal or written appraisals; update performance criteria as technology changes to avoid pretext claims when older workers are laid off for lack of newer skills
Disability discrimination	Review recommendations and appraisal results for evidence of perceived ("regarded as") discrimination; ensure that only essential functions are evaluated; train supervisors to identify reasonable accommodations in performance criteria and appraisal procedures on an interactive basis in a discrete and confidential manner
Defamation or misrepresentation	Establish procedures to control or avoid providing false performance information (favorable or unfavorable)
Negligence	Keep employees advised if performance is poor so they cannot contest discharge by claiming performance would have improved but for faulty evaluation process

correlated with tests, given that there are usually no other performance standards whose correspondence with appraisal results can be independently assessed. In practice, courts have appeared not to pay much attention to formal notions of reliability or validity (Beck-Dudley & McEvoy, 1991), and these issues have rarely been discussed explicitly in reported cases. However, they do appear implicitly in many instances. For example, in a sample of 295 federal appellate discrimination opinions through 1995, Werner and Bolino (1997) found support for the importance of job analysis, written instructions, employee review of results, and triangulation among raters in predicting case outcomes. These and other notions of fairness, accuracy, validity, and due process continue to appear in many legal opinions.

A number of review articles have examined performance evaluations in the case law, and have offered recommendations that appear to relate favorably to the legal defensibility of employment decisions (for example, Ashe & McRae, 1985; Barrett & Kernan, 1987; Beck-Dudley & McEvoy, 1991; Bernardin, Kane, Ross, Spina, & Johnson, 1995; Burchett & De Meuse, 1985; Cascio & Bernardin, 1981; Lubben, Thompson, & Klasson, 1980; Martin & Bartol, 1991; Martin, Bartol, & Levine, 1986; Veglahn, 1993). These reviews represent a consensus regarding substantive and procedural recommendations for legally sound evaluation practices that remain valuable today.

Cases Involving Substantive Aspects of Performance Appraisal

Recent cases concerning the content of performance appraisals have addressed subjectivity, job-relatedness, specificity, and consistency. These cases illustrate both good and not-so-good examples for practice. Exhibit 2.2 summarizes substantive recommendations in this area.

Subjectivity and Job-Relatedness of the Criteria

In *Eldred* v. *Consolidated Freightways*, 71 FEP Cases 33 (D. Mass. 1995), Eldred, a female dispatcher, was denied a promotion based on her male supervisor's "gut feeling" that she lacked "aggressiveness" and

**Exhibit 2.2. Substantive Recommendations for
Legally Sound Performance Appraisals.**

Appraisal *criteria*

- Should be objective rather than subjective
- Should be job-related or based on job analysis
- Should be based on behaviors rather than traits
- Should be within the control of the ratee
- Should relate to specific functions, not global assessments
- Should be communicated to the employee

Note: Recommendations summarized here are drawn in part from Ashe & McRae, 1985; Barrett & Kernan, 1987; Beck-Dudley & McEvoy, 1991; Bernardin, Kane, Ross, Spina, & Johnson, 1995; Burchett & De Meuse, 1985; Cascio & Bernardin, 1981; Lubben, Thompson, & Klasson, 1980; Martin & Bartol, 1991; Martin, Bartol, & Levine, 1986; Veglahn, 1993; and recent cases. Recommendations were extracted, consolidated across articles, and supplemented by the author.

was too "soft" with Consolidated's drivers. In ruling for Eldred on her sex discrimination claim, the Court noted that this "gut feeling" was neither reliable nor accurate (the person selected for the promotion turned out to perform poorly), and that the employer's stated reliance on subjective criteria that were not shown to be related to job performance supported a finding of gender bias.

Similarly, in *City of Indian Harbor Beach,* 103 LA 634, 637 (Arb. 1994), the city denied one of its police officers a merit pay increase despite overall performance ratings that were high enough to warrant a raise. The city argued that it never intended for merit increases to be based solely on performance ratings, because evaluations are performed by the immediate supervisor, who typically belongs to the same union as the employee. The arbitrator, however, emphatically rejected any suggestion that management should be allowed to consider other, more subjective factors in its merit pay determinations. In sustaining the officer's grievance, the arbitrator found that the city had not shown its merit pay determinations to be "based upon evidence and standards that are reasonable, demonstrable, and objective."

On the other hand, in *Thomas* v. *IBM,* 67 FEP Cases at 276, IBM was able to successfully defend accusations of age discrimination, in part because its appraisal system "contained safeguards to minimize the possibility for unlawful bias or discrimination, such as a written performance plan, *objective criteria,* a requirement that the supervisor specify in writing the reasons for each rating, and an independent review of the supervisor's evaluation by the second-level manager" (emphasis added).

Interestingly, in *Amirmokri,* the court found it permissible to use subjective criteria such as interpersonal skills and team leadership to justify promoting another employee over Amirmokri, and stated that it would have reached the same conclusion even if Amirmokri's education and experience had been objectively superior to the employee selected. Thus, it appears possible that courts may be more willing to accept the favorable use of subjective criteria to justify a positive employment decision than they are to accept the unfavorable use of such criteria to justify a negative one. Employers should take care to document both types of decisions in any event.

Specificity and Consistency of Performance Criteria and Their Application

In addition to *Thomas* v. *IBM,* which lauded the use of specific reasons for individual facet ratings, several other cases have dealt with the specificity of criteria and the consistency of their application across individuals or over time. For example, in *Fisher* v. *Vassar College,* the District Court had examined Vassar's "unclear and unspecified" tenure criteria (teaching, scholarship, service, and leadership), and found them to be "disingenuous" and pretextual as applied. However, the Court of Appeals's reversal in favor of Vassar suggests that in promotion cases involving academics and other professionals, such criteria may be deferred to because these decisions are inherently subjective. Fisher had been able to point out inconsistencies in the way performance criteria were applied to other professors ahead of her on the tenure track, but to no avail. The Court even commented that "it is difficult to conceive of tenure standards that would be objective and quantifiable" (70 FEP Cases at 1165).

Woodman v. *Haemonetics Corp.* also involved the use of general, global criteria that were inconsistently applied. In that case, performance criteria were changed, in response to a directive from a recently promoted executive, to emphasize "flexibility" (for example, susceptibility to cross-training and multiple responsibilities) and "participation" (for example, capacity to provide suggestions for efficiency improvements). After ten years of good reviews, Woodman's performance was rated unsatisfactory, and he was terminated in an RIF. The court focused closely on changes in Woodman's performance ratings after the switch to these new criteria to find that Woodman had made a showing of pretext that was sufficient to go to trial on his ADEA claim.

Cases Involving Procedural Aspects of Performance Appraisal

Recent cases concerning performance appraisal have addressed the presence or absence of many of the procedural safeguards recommended by previous authors, as summarized in Exhibit 2.3. The absence of such safeguards generally has not been fatal to the employer unless some other impropriety (for example, discrimination) or harm to the employee could be shown. On the other hand, where such safeguards do exist, both the employer and employee have been expected to observe and abide by them. Frankly, it is difficult to discern a noticeable pattern in this area, and it appears that the legal viability of appraisal procedures will depend on the facts and circumstances of each case.

Standardized Procedures and Rater Training

In *Kelly* v. *Drexel University,* 5 AD Cases 1101 (E.D. Pa. 1995), the Court rejected Kelly's argument that his position was eliminated because of age or disability discrimination. Despite the employer's failure to systematically evaluate employees' performance, or to provide equal employment opportunity training for raters, the Court could find no evidence that the employer's stated reasons— lack of computer proficiency and inability to adapt to a heavier workload—were not the real reasons for Kelly's dismissal.

Procedures and Performance Deficiencies Communicated to the Ratee

In *Salt Lake City VA Medical Center,* 103 LA 285 (Arb. 1994), the arbitrator rejected a housekeeper's grievance based on the employer's failure to inform him of the requirements for a higher performance rating. The grievant's overall rating was "fully successful,"

Exhibit 2.3. Procedural Recommendations for Legally Sound Performance Appraisals.

Appraisal *procedures*

- Should be standardized and uniform for all employees within a job group
- Should be formally communicated to employees
- Should provide notice of performance deficiencies and of opportunities to correct them
- Should provide access for employees to review appraisal results
- Should provide formal appeal mechanisms that allow for employee input
- Should use multiple, diverse, and unbiased raters
- Should provide written instructions and training for raters
- Should require thorough and consistent documentation across raters that includes specific examples of performance based on personal knowledge
- Should establish a system to detect potentially discriminatory effects or abuses of the system overall

Note: Recommendations summarized here are drawn in part from Ashe & McRae, 1985; Barrett & Kernan, 1987; Beck-Dudley & McEvoy, 1991; Bernardin, Kane, Ross, Spina, & Johnson, 1995; Burchett & De Meuse, 1985; Cascio & and Bernardin, 1981; Lubben, Thompson, & Klasson, 1980; Martin & Bartol, 1991; Martin, Bartol, & Levine, 1986; Veglahn, 1993; and recent cases. Recommendations were extracted, consolidated across articles, and supplemented by the author.

and he had been provided with the standards for that rating under the applicable collective bargaining agreement. On the other hand, in *Peoples Natural Gas,* 105 LA 37 (Arb. 1995), an employee terminated for unsatisfactory performance in a new job was reinstated, based on the employer's failure to follow through on its agreed plan of action to provide adequate training and monitor the employee's level of improvement.

Ratee Access and Input

In *Demming* v. *Housing Authority,* Demming's failure to take advantage of notice and opportunity to respond to an explicit forty-nine-point performance evaluation was used to support her termination and reject her ADA claim. Similarly, in *Town of Bedford*, 106 LA 967 (Arb. 1996), a police sergeant's refusal to cooperate in his own performance evaluation by submitting information that he wanted the employer to consider proved fatal to his grievance to upwardly amend his appraisal results. On the other hand, in *Haycock* v. *Hughes Aircraft*, the employer's failure to submit a fraudulently altered performance appraisal to Haycock for his signature pursuant to company policy supported his claim of pretext, and helped sustain his implied contract and defamation claims.

Multiple Raters (Self, Peers, Clients, Others)

In *Whalen* v. *Rubin*, the employer's use of multiple raters who independently decided that an employee other than Whalen was most qualified for a promotion helped negate Whalen's reverse discrimination claim. In *Byrd* v. *Ronayne*, client comments and an associate attorney's candid self-evaluation that acknowledged performance deficiencies helped sustain the firm's decision to terminate her. In *McLee* v. *Chrysler Corp.*, 73 FEP Cases 751 (2nd Cir. 1997), a warehouse supervisor's own admissions conceding the truth of negative performance ratings also helped undermine any claim that his termination was racially motivated or pretextual. And in *Golder* v. *Lockheed Sanders*, Inc., 71 FEP Cases 1425 (D.N.H. 1996), peer evaluations helped support Golder's performance-based dismissal during an RIF over his unsubstantiated objections that they were unreliable, overly subjective, generally unfair, and a pretext for age discrimination.

On the other hand, in *Mathewson* v. *Aloha Airlines*, peer evaluations were found to be pretextual and retaliatory against a pilot who had crossed picket lines during the pilot union's strike against a different airline. And in *Jiminez* v. *Mary Washington College*, potentially collusive and racially motivated student ratings led the District Court to sustain Jiminez's claim of discriminatory tenure denial (although this decision was reversed on appeal because the College's performance-based reasons could not be shown to be pretextual). Conversely, in *Hampton* v. *Tinton Falls Police Dept.*, 72 FEP Cases 101 (3rd Cir. 1996), a police department's *disregard* of a black lieutenant's recommendation to promote a black sergeant raised a factual issue as to whether favorable performance information was improperly ignored because the rater and ratee were the same race.

In sum, these latter cases suggest that where peers and other untrained or potentially biased evaluators are used, the results should be weighed with caution against more systematic criteria, so that trait-based ratings are avoided and objectivity, job-relatedness, and other substantive safeguards are preserved. For example, procedures could be developed to ensure that appraisal results leading to negative employment decisions are reviewed systematically (or at least spot-checked) by industrial-organizational psychologists or HR professionals for evidence that age, gender, ethnicity, national origin, union status, or other improper factors may have influenced the outcome. Of course, where such review procedures do exist, they should be followed; see *Woodson* v. *Scott Paper Co.,* 73 FEP Cases 1237 (3rd Cir. 1997), in which the employer's failure to have its corporate review committee examine discrepancies between a black manager's low RIF ranking and his favorable past evaluations supported a jury's determination that Woodson was terminated in retaliation for filing a discrimination complaint with the state Human Rights Commission.

Documentation, Consistency, and Rater Knowledge of the Ratee's Performance

A supervisor's failure to document in writing purported performance deficiencies to support his "gut feeling" that another employee was better qualified for a promotion led the court in *Eldred* v. *Consolidated Freightways* to conclude that stated deficiencies were a pretext for gender discrimination. In *Woodman* v. *Haemonetics,* inconsistencies over time in Woodman's evaluations led the court to conclude that a sudden reduction in his ratings five days before his termination during an RIF was pretextual.

Conversely, consistency over time and across raters led to conclusions that low performance ratings for Dennis, a black transportation planner, and Plummer, a black hotel security director, were not racially motivated; *Dennis* v. *County of Fairfax,* 67 FEP Cases 1681 (4th Cir. 1995); *Plummer* v. *Marriott Corp.,* 71 FEP Cases 945 (La. App. 1995). And although the arbitrator in *Town of Bedford* found no problem with having a police sergeant evaluated by a lieutenant who worked a different shift and had only recently become his supervisor, the courts in *Cook* v. *Arrowsmith Shelburne, Inc.,* 69 FEP Cases 392 (2nd Cir. 1995), *Henderson & Bryan* v. *A.T.&T. Corp.,* and *Woodson* v. *Scott Paper Co.* relied partly on raters' lack of personal knowledge to sustain employees' claims that negative performance ratings came as a result of age, race, or gender discrimination.

Seniority, Just Cause, Discipline, and Related Performance Issues Under Union and Other Employment Contracts

If it is important to observe substantive and procedural safeguards in appraising performance generally, then it is critical to do so when those safeguards are mandated by the terms of an express or implied contract. Alleged violations of contractual appraisal provisions necessarily involve the analysis of case-specific language, so I do not deal with them at length in this chapter. However, some issues in this context are relevant to the overall viability of any organization's practices. Among these are seniority, the *just cause* standard, and progressive or positive discipline.

Seniority

The seniority issue frequently arises during an RIF that attempts to accommodate both longevity preferences and performance criteria. For example, in *Houston Lighting & Power Company,* 103 LA 179 (Arb. 1993), a union contract provided that "in the event of a permanent reduction in force, where ability, skill, and qualifications are equal, seniority shall govern." A number of laid-off employees filed grievances over individual decisions, but an arbitrator upheld the employer's overall system, by which supervisors used a special performance profile to classify individuals within a particular job category as marginal, average, or above average, and applied seniority criteria within these classifications. This system also was upheld by the Court of Appeals in a related case, in which the Court found the system "reasonably calculated to fairly accomplish the determination of utility, skill, and qualifications" using criteria that were "within the scope of contractually allowed factors," 151 LRRM at 2023 (5th Cir. 1995).

Failure to adhere to an *informal* seniority system during an RIF is not necessarily fatal to the employer if legitimate reasons for departing from prior practice are credibly put forth. In *EEOC* v.

Texas Instruments, Inc., the Court found that the need to retain employees who could "satisfy and adapt to a rapidly changing technological environment" justified laying off older supervisors over younger ones who possessed college degrees, superior computer skills, and other technological expertise (72 FEP Cases at 982). As mentioned earlier, however, it would be best to keep job descriptions and performance criteria updated to the greatest extent practicably possible.

The Just Cause Standard

Express or implied agreements not to terminate an employee except for just cause are among the most commonly litigated exceptions to the doctrine of *employment at will.* For example, the court's decision to uphold the employee's reinstatement in *Mathewson* v. *Aloha Airlines* was based in large part on an implied agreement that Mathewson would be evaluated only on his merits and qualifications, rather than on biased peer appraisals influenced by his perceived scab status. And in *Postville School District* v. *Billmeyer,* 152 LRRM 2401 (Iowa 1996), the Iowa Supreme Court refused to overturn an arbitrator's decision that failed to find evidence of the just cause that would have been required to support the school district's termination of an employee for alleged sexual misconduct outside the workplace. On the other hand, the arbitrator in *Linconview Local Board of Education,* 103 LA 854 (Arb. 1994), found no basis to apply a just cause standard in the Board of Education's decision to nonrenew the limited one-year contract of a teacher, so long as it abided by its procedural obligations with respect to its performance appraisal processes. These obligations, with which the board had complied, included evaluating the teacher twice a year based on actual classroom observation, conferring with the teacher and preparing written reports of evaluations, and providing copies of evaluations to the teacher.

Progressive or Positive Discipline

Both progressive and positive discipline procedures involve a series of steps that allow a problematic employee to improve performance before being discharged. Progressive discipline involves warnings and punishments of increasing severity, while positive discipline involves counseling and interventions of increasing intensity (Gomez-Mejia et al., 1995). In general, where either system is present, adhering to stated procedures will support the employer's discharge of the employee, whereas failure to do so will support the employee's allegation of improper motivation on the part of the employer.

For example, in *Hanchard* v. *Facilities Development Corp.*, 10 IER Cases 1004 (N.Y. App. 1995), the Facilities Development Corp. (FDC) employee handbook set forth a disciplinary plan with both positive and progressive features by which an employee of five or more years was to be provided performance counseling and a work plan to measure and guide improvement. The handbook also provided for the right to submit documentation and request a hearing prior to termination, and the right to be discharged only for "materially deficient work performance." Hanchard, an architect, had declining performance evaluations, became disruptive and insubordinate, was behind on most of his projects, and alienated both clients and coworkers. In a split decision, the Court rejected Hanchard's claim that his discharge was arbitrary and capricious, finding that the employer had "substantially complied" with its disciplinary procedures (the Court also found that Hanchard had failed to take advantage of the protections afforded to him). The dissent felt that FDC's compliance with its procedures had not been "substantial" enough.

For other cases in which the employer's adherence to its stated procedures led to a successful defense of its position, see *Gipson* v. *KAS Snacktime Co.*, 71 FEP Cases 1677 (E.D. Mo. 1994) (employee's failure to cooperate in personal development program offered by the employer negated claim of pretext in race discrimination case); *R.G.H.* v. *Abbott Laboratories* (employee's failure to respond to performance improvement plan over a six-month period negated claim of pretext in disability discrimination case); and *Samaritan Health System*, 106 LA 927 (Arb. 1996) (employer's substantial compliance with progressive discipline and performance evaluation procedures, coupled with employee's failure to challenge negative performance appraisal, supported employee's discharge for poor performance).

However, also see *Chertkova* v. *Connecticut General Life Insurance,* 71 FEP Cases 1006 (2nd Cir. 1996). In that case, a supervisor's abuse of the "performance improvement plan" process, in which so-called coaching sessions allegedly involved berating Chertkova behind closed doors and yelling comments such as "there is no chance! You are not going to be here!" was found to warrant reinstatement of her previously dismissed claims for constructive discharge and pretext in the context of sex discrimination. This case further underscores that disregard of proper appraisal procedures, whether by the employer or the employee, can cause problems in litigating discrimination and other kinds of legal disputes.

Emerging Legal Issues in Performance Appraisal

It has been estimated that almost 70 percent of the American populace now can claim membership in one or more protected classes under various antidiscrimination laws. This number can be expected to grow as increased immigration, greater longevity due to medical advances, and the widening scope of allowable mental health disabilities modify current demographics. As global competition and technology continue to drive RIFs and other restructuring, protected class status will continue to figure prominently in challenges to layoffs and discharges that employers claim were based on performance but employees claim were based on discrimination. The move toward "leaner, meaner" organizations, in which employees are expected to work harder and take on a wider range of responsibilities, will also increase the potential for performance appraisals to generate legal issues in emerging areas. Among these areas are flexible job designs, security and privacy, and workplace violence.

Flexible Job Designs

In the context of innovations such as team-based designs, Mirvis and Hall (1996) have noted the growing incidence of flexible firms, flexible jobs, and skill-based individual careers. Continuous learning, self-management, self-designed jobs, and flexible work roles are replacing rigid job descriptions and classification schemes. These changes carry implications for appraising performance, particularly with respect to demonstrating the job-relatedness or essential nature of performance criteria such as "interpersonal skills," "ability to lead a team," "flexibility," and "participation" (*Amirmokri* v. *Baltimore Gas & Electric; Woodman* v. *Haemonetics Corp.*). Although such criteria sometimes pass muster (as in *Amirmokri*), they also may form the basis for a claim of pretext (as in *Woodman*). This points out the need for employers to further define, refine, and validate flexible performance criteria, so as to be able to argue successfully in defense of discrimination claims that the use of such criteria serves a legitimate business function.

Security and Privacy

In re National Archives and Records Administration, 107 LA 123 (Arb. 1996) presents a case in which the high stakes often linked with favorable performance ratings (here, qualification for a promotion) led a National Archives employee to falsify his ratings by fraudulently altering one of his written appraisals. The employee, who had a top security clearance, was discharged for cause, in part because he had betrayed his position of trust with the agency. This points out the need for employers to develop appropriate security procedures to prevent similar occurrences, and to avoid compromising the privacy of other employees whose performance results may also be on file.

In *Sturm* v. *TOC,* security and surveillance actually were principal parts of a convenience store manager's performance appraisal duties, which perhaps takes the recommendation that evaluations should be based on personal knowledge to the extreme. Sturm's appraisal duties involved different forms of ongoing honesty testing, including baiting the cash register with extra cash, looking over employees' shoulders, and viewing video surveillance tapes. Given the severe problem with employee theft faced by many companies, and the increasing deference afforded to private employers in areas such as drug testing, it is probable that alleged invasions of privacy based on conduct such as that in *Sturm* will arise with increasing frequency in challenges to such practices. *Plummer* v. *Marriott Corp.,* a constructive discharge case, provides an example of such a challenge in connection with a polygraph test during an internal investigation of employee theft.

Workplace Violence

As noted earlier in connection with the *Randi W.* case, employers face increasing potential liability for nondisclosure of problematic employee performance, as when their affirmative misrepresentation that a former employee's performance was favorable presents a foreseeable risk of harm to others. With appraisal results continuing to figure prominently in layoffs and discharges, employee reactions to appraisers and appraisal processes seem increasingly likely to lead to injury, violence, or death in and outside the workplace. News media have reported such instances, as where an employee committed suicide by sticking his head into a giant circular saw when told by his supervisor that his already heavy workload standards would be increased yet again ("Firm Blamed," 1995). When an employee exhibits signals during an evaluation that suggest the possibility that such problems might exist (for example, symbolically decapitating one's supervisor during a meeting to discuss threatening behavior toward coworkers; *Lewis* v. *Zilog, Inc.*), it would not be surprising to see an employer held liable for related violence on the grounds that it knew or should have known that serious harm to the employee or others might result.

Although it remains difficult at best to predict who among the many employees exhibiting stress-related symptoms will actually resort to violence, the ADA imposes a duty on employers to provide reasonable accommodations to employees who suffer from mental disabilities, including those that might lead to such conduct. Opportunities for reduced stress, flexible workloads, and professional counseling might be appropriate first steps toward such an accommodation. Of course, in extreme cases, as where an employee poses "a direct threat to the health or safety of other individuals in the workplace," 42 U.S.C. Section 12113(b), there may be no choice but to remove the employee from the workplace. Employers can defend resulting discrimination claims on the grounds that the employee was not qualified under the ADA because he or she could not perform the essential functions of the job. Employers have successfully argued in such situations that the essential functions of any job include the ability to deal with criticism from supervisors and coworkers in a civil manner, and to refrain from violent behavior (see Fram, 1997; Willis, 1997).

Conclusions and Further Recommendations for Practice

As our economy continues increasingly to move toward a service and information emphasis, it seems inevitable that flexible, subjective performance criteria will remain in use, particularly at the professional and managerial level. As global competition continues increasingly to demand a customer focus and total quality orientation, it also seems inevitable that multiple sources of feedback (clients, subordinates, peers) will remain in use, perhaps at all levels of employment. As we have seen, both subjective criteria and biased or untrained raters can spawn discrimination claims that are difficult to defend. Where such criteria or raters are used, they would be best used in conjunction with objective criteria and trained, unbiased raters whose input is given greater (perhaps determinative) weight. This practice would preserve the benefits of multiple criteria and information sources, while also providing defenses to discrimination claims in the form of legitimate, nondiscriminatory reasons for adverse employment decisions or the absence of pretext. This practice also would support the mitigating defense, in a mixed motive case, that the employer would have made the same decision notwithstanding the use of arguably discriminatory factors.

I close by summarizing some additional recommendations from a noted practitioner in the employment law arena that become particularly relevant in termination cases (Cathcart, 1996). Employers should review appraisal procedures to ensure that employees are provided with an oral interview and a written statement of their appraisal, as well as the opportunity to acknowledge, in writing, receipt or review of the appraisal; that managers are encouraged to support candor in appraisals, to avoid central tendency or "friendliness" errors that can make subsequent demotions or discharges difficult to defend; and that appraisers are trained—and spot-checked from time to time—to identify and correct practices that might generate legal liability. Employers should also conduct a thorough pre-termination review of all information on potential candidates for discharge, and determine how other employees were treated who were subject to discretionary judgments of the same supervisor. Employers should consider the employee's seniority, the importance and specificity of alleged performance deficiencies, past practices in similar circumstances, the impartiality of evaluators, any extenuating circumstances, and compliance with company discipline and discharge procedures. Finally, the employer should consider any potential for defamation or invasion of employee privacy, as well as the manner in which the employee (and anyone else) will be told about the adverse decision.

I hope that these recommendations will increase the chances that your appraisal practices manage to avoid legal scrutiny. If, as has frequently become the case, however, your appraisal practices do wind up in litigation, I offer words that Obi-Wan Kenobi might have said: "May the Courts be with you."

References

Ashe, R. L., & McRae, G. S. (1985). Performance evaluations go to court in the 1980s. *Mercer Law Review, 36*, 887–905.

Barrett, G. V., & Kernan, M. C. (1987). Performance appraisal and terminations: A review of court decisions since *Brito* v. *Zia* with implications for personnel practices. *Personnel Psychology, 40*, 489–503.

Beck-Dudley, C. L., & McEvoy, G. M. (1991). Performance appraisals and discrimination suits: Do courts pay attention to validity? *Employee Responsibilities and Rights Journal, 4*, 149–163.

Bernardin, H. J., Kane, J. S., Ross, S., Spina, D. S., & Johnson, D. L. (1995). Performance appraisal design, development, and implementation. In G. R. Ferris, S. D. Rosen, & D. T. Barnum (Eds.), *Handbook of human resource management* (pp. 462–493). Cambridge, MA: Blackwell.

Burchett, S. R., & De Meuse, K. P. (1985). Performance appraisal and the law. *Personnel, 62*, 29–37.

Cascio, W. F., & Bernardin, H. J. (1981). Implications of performance appraisal litigation for personnel decisions. *Personnel Psychology, 34*, 211–226.

Cathcart, D. A. (1996). Employment termination litigation: Collateral tort theories and the multimillion dollar verdict: A 1994 update. In *Employment Discrimination and Civil Rights Actions in Federal and State Courts* (pp. 675–779). Philadelphia: American Law Institute.

Cathcart, D. A., & Snyderman, M. (1997). The Civil Rights Act of 1991. In P. M. Panken (Ed.), *Employment and labor law* (pp. 277–361). Philadelphia: American Law Institute.

Firm blamed for suicide. (1995, November 3). *San Jose Mercury News*, p. D1.

Fram, D. K. (1997). Expanded checklists for determining "disability," "qualified," and "reasonable accommodation" under the ADA. In *National Employment Law Institute Human Resources Workbook* (sec. 4, pp. 1–31). Larkspur, CA: NELI.

Gomez-Mejia, L. R., Balkin, D. B., & Cardy, R. L. (1995). *Managing human resources.* Upper Saddle River, NJ: Prentice Hall.

Koys, D. J., Briggs, S., & Grenig, J. (1987). State court disparity on employment-at-will. *Personnel Psychology, 40,* 565–577.

Lubben, G. L., Thompson, D. E., & Klasson, C. R. (1980, May-June). Performance appraisal: The legal implications of Title VII. *Personnel,* pp. 11–21.

Martin, D.C., & Bartol, K. M. (1991). The legal ramifications of performance appraisal: An update. *Employee Relations Law Journal, 17,* 257–286.

Martin, D.C., Bartol, K. M., & Levine, M. J. (1986). The legal ramifications of performance appraisal. *Employee Relations Law Journal, 12,* 370–395.

Miller, C. S., Kaspin, J. A., & Schuster, M. H. (1990). The impact of performance appraisal methods on Age Discrimination in Employment Act cases. *Personnel Psychology, 43,* 555–578.

Mirvis, P. H., & Hall, D. T. (1996). New organizational forms and the new career. In D. T. Hall (Ed.), *The career is dead—long live the career: A relational approach to careers* (pp. 72–101). San Francisco: Jossey-Bass.

Perry, E. L., Kulik, C. T., & Bourhis, A. C. (1996). Moderating effects of personal and contextual factors in age discrimination. *Journal of Applied Psychology, 81,* 628–647.

Veglahn, P. A. (1993, October). Key issues in performance appraisal challenges: Evidence from court and arbitration decisions. *Labor Law Journal,* pp. 595–606.

Werner, J. M., & Bolino, M. C. (1997). Explaining U.S. courts of appeals decisions involving performance appraisal: Accuracy, fairness, and validation. *Personnel Psychology, 50,* 1–24.

Willis, S. G. (1997). Stress-related disability claims under the ADA. *Practical Lawyer, 43,* 73–86.

CHAPTER 3

International Performance Measurement and Management

Donald D. Davis

The Thai office of Singapore Airlines reported difficulty with implementing its performance appraisal process. It seems that managers resisted providing negative comments because of their fear that such negative deeds would cause them to have bad karma and, as a consequence, they would be reincarnated at a lower level in their next life. Singapore Airlines allowed them to make local adaptations [Chee, 1994].

A Taiwanese manager at a Nike plant in Vietnam used a unique method of performance management for his subordinates, forcing them to run in circles around the plant until twelve workers fainted. The factory later had to apologize and pay 100,000 dong (about $10) to the workers and their families ["Nike Tries," 1997].

These examples illustrate the difficulty that firms have when they attempt to measure and manage the performance of employees from different nations and cultures. This chapter discusses important considerations for firms that need to measure and manage performance internationally.

Note: The author wishes to thank Wally Borman for his comments on an early draft of this chapter and also to thank Jim Smither and two anonymous reviewers for helping to keep his writing more firmly planted in the ground of practice. The chapter has greatly benefited from their suggestions.

Firms are struggling today to succeed in an environment filled with global complexity and heightened competition. Human resource practices play an important role in helping firms to succeed in this environment because they make firms stronger than their competitors and, as a result, yield competitive advantage (Porter, 1985, 1986). The most successful international companies today focus on developing the abilities, behaviors, and performance of individual managers (Bartlett & Ghoshal, 1990). Performance measurement and management (PMM) practices can contribute to achieving and sustaining global competitive advantage by enhancing the performance of managers and organizations. Stronger managers create stronger organizations. Stronger organizations grow and prosper.

This chapter discusses what must be considered when conducting PMM in the international context. The chapter is divided into four sections. The first section briefly discusses international human resource management strategy, which is shown to determine international PMM practices. The second section discusses social conditions and cultural values that influence the effectiveness of PMM practices. This section is important because social conditions and cultural differences limit the effectiveness of PMM practices and their success in helping to implement the firm's global strategy. The third section discusses international aspects of the following PMM practices: criterion development, methods of assessment, choice of raters, rater training, and performance management practices. The fourth and final section discusses a checklist that may be used to guide international PMM practice.

Throughout the chapter, where possible, I describe practices that rest on a foundation of empirical support. Prudent speculation is provided where empirical support is scarce. Best practices are provided to illustrate points in the discussion. Space allows only a broad discussion of the issues relevant to PMM practice in the international context rather than a deep analysis of any particular technique or practice.

International Human Resource Management

Human resource practices such as performance measurement are experiencing a shift in emphasis. Research and practice concerning PMM traditionally emphasized technique and methodology, for example, proper definition of criteria, accurate methods of appraisal, cognitive processes associated with making performance ratings, and appropriate methods for training raters (Landy & Farr, 1983). Recently, scientists and practitioners have begun to emphasize the importance of strategy when developing human resource management practices. This strategic perspective has been shown to be important in domestic organizations (Butler, Ferris, & Napier, 1991) as well as international and multinational organizations (Schuler, Dowling, & De Cieri, 1993). This emphasis on strategy is a logical extension of models of the performance appraisal process that view it as part of the surrounding organizational system (Mohrman, Resnick-West, & Lawler, 1989). This view of PMM is also popular in Europe (Drenth, in press; Sparrow & Hiltrop, 1997).

Like knowledge concerning how to coordinate and integrate diverse production technologies, human resource practices provide one of the core competencies of the firm (Prahalad & Hamel, 1990). This competency consists of tangible resources (for example, use of specific performance measurement forms and rater training programs) and intangible resources (for example, reputation, ability to negotiate successfully with national governments; Taylor, Beechler, & Napier, 1996). PMM practices form a fundamental human resource competency because they shape the behaviors that contribute to organizational effectiveness. Because both the outputs of the system, that is, employee behaviors, and the system itself combine to make the organization successful, PMM practices can provide unique advantages to the firm that are difficult for competitors to copy.

To provide competitive advantage, international human resource management (IHRM) practices must go beyond emphasis on mere technical practices, for example, tinkering with rating scale formats, to include an emphasis on the firm's strategic goals (Huselid, Jackson, & Schuler, 1997). PMM practices must address behaviors that help the firm achieve its strategic goals and objectives (Latham, 1984). When used in this manner, practices such as performance appraisal become a tool for ensuring successful execution of the firm's strategy, more than a method for guiding personnel administration decisions (Schneier, Shaw, & Beatty, 1991). While such a link is common today in theory, it is not always realized in practice.

Unfortunately, human resource professionals are not always involved in developing and executing global strategy. One senior manager sums up the situation as follows: "Human resource issues are considered when they are pertinent to the topic at hand, but we would never think of asking the HR people to participate in those strategic decisions. Although those guys are nice people, they are soft and they have little to contribute to the broader strategic issues of the firm" (Miller, Beechler, Bhatt, & Nath, 1986, p. 15).

Though a bit dated, this appraisal of human resource professionals is still accurate. Too many practitioners focus on technical concerns such as scale development and test validation and neglect a strategic perspective in their work.

Three International Human Resource Strategies

Firms going abroad must balance between the need to adapt to local conditions and the need to maintain homogeneity in practices throughout the firm's scattered locations (Rosenzweig & Singh, 1991). Firms must deal with people consistently on a worldwide basis. But to be effective locally, firms must adapt practices to local social and cultural conditions (Laurent, 1986). In this manner, the firm seeks "controlled variety" (Doz & Prahalad, 1986). This situation requires managers responsible for IHRM to maintain a balance between centralization and control on one hand, and decentralization and flexibility on the other. This balance is reflected in three general IHRM strategies (Taylor et al., 1996). Each of these strategies reflects different choices regarding the balance between global integration and national responsiveness (Harzing, 1995). Table 3.1 summarizes the three strategies.

Exportive Strategy

With this strategy, the multinational corporation (MNC) transfers HRM practices from its home country to each of its foreign units, which may be wholly owned subsidiaries or joint ventures. Each foreign unit uses the same PMM system regardless of national or cultural differences, thus enhancing homogeneity and control. This strategy is common during early stages of internationalization or when trained managers in the foreign location are scarce. This strategy yields the greatest control and uniformity in PMM practices, but it is the least flexible. This limited flexibility increases the

Table 3.1. International Human Resource Management Strategy and Performance Measurement and Management.

IHRM Strategy	Staffing Policy	Manager Type	PMM Practices	Advantages	Disadvantages
Exportive	Ethnocentric	PCNs	• Develop PMM system and practices in home country • Transfer PMM system and practices to foreign units	• Greatest control • Maintains homogeneity	• Least flexibility • Limited learning
Adaptive	Polycentric	HCNs	• Develop unique PMM system and practices in each foreign unit	• Greatest flexibility • Requires simple management skills	• Least control • Least learning
Integrative	Regiocentric Geocentric	PCNs, HCNs, TCNs, and Global	• Combine local PMM practices with PMM practices within region or from around the globe • Circulate best PMM practices within region or around the globe	• Flexible • Greatest learning • Moderate control	• Costly • Requires more complex management skills

likelihood that PMM practices will not be accepted or used as intended by local managers. Learning is limited because unique characteristics of the local situation are ignored.

Adaptive Strategy

With this strategy, MNCs adapt all IHRM practices to fit local social and cultural needs. Each of the MNC's foreign units may have unique PMM practices that may, in turn, be different from the MNC's domestic PMM practices. This strategy offers the greatest flexibility. It requires simple international management skills on the part of the central HR staff because of the great degree of decentralization. This strategy provides the least amount of control. Because little information gleaned from successful PMM practices is shared with headquarters or units in other nations, this strategy provides little opportunity for learning.

Integrative Strategy

With this strategy, MNCs attempt to take the best HRM practices from throughout the organization, regardless of national or cultural origin, in an attempt to create a global system. National and cultural conditions may be reflected in variation in PMM practices, and national and cultural variation that contributes to competitive advantage may be integrated into the MNC's PMM system. Control is balanced by the need for learning and flexibility. The integrative strategy reflects the need of MNCs to learn from IHRM practices and to view competition in a global manner. This global learning is important because it contributes to the ability of the organization to adapt to rapid change (Davis, 1995). Information is circulated chiefly through frequent communication. As a result, this strategy is expensive and difficult to manage. Despite these disadvantages, this strategy offers the greatest potential for helping the MNC meet the uncertain demands for change in the global environment.

International Staffing Issues

When creating international PMM practices, practitioners must consider the type of employees the firm uses overseas. The chief concern for each of these types is the fact that international employees straddle two or more cultures and must, therefore, satisfy performance expectations—which are often in conflict—in each of these cultures (Black & Gregerson, 1992). The following discussion of staffing issues is based on the work of Perlmutter (1969), Heenan and Perlmutter (1979), and Dowling, Schuler, and Welch (1994). These distinctions are used widely in the IHRM literature and are used here to highlight differences in PMM practices.

- *Ethnocentric staffing with parent country nationals.* The ethnocentric approach to staffing leads to the most important positions in foreign units being filled by managers from the country in which the headquarters firm is located. Such parent country nationals (PCNs), or expatriate managers, may be assigned abroad for short- or long-term stints, after which they return to the parent country to resume their careers. PCNs are most commonly used during early stages of internationalization or when there is a scarcity of trained managers in the foreign location. Their use most often accompanies the exportive IHRM strategy. PCNs wrestle with the conflict between the performance demands in their home country and the need to understand and adapt to the performance demands of the culture in which they are working.

- *Polycentric staffing with host country nationals.* With polycentric staffing, host country nationals (HCNs) are recruited to manage units located in their country. HCNs typically spend their entire careers in the host country. Each unit is treated independently by the parent firm. Such an emphasis reflects a preference for decentralization in human resource practices and often accompanies an adaptive IHRM strategy. Firms using an adaptive IHRM strategy may delegate responsibility for PMM practices to HCNs who manage the foreign unit. HCNs must grapple with the difference between the performance demands of their own culture and those of the culture in which the parent firm is located.

- *Regiocentric and geocentric staffing with third country nationals and global managers.* The regiocentric approach to staffing groups countries that lie in the same geographic region, for example, Western Europe, Southeast Asia, Latin America, and so forth. Staff are recruited and transferred throughout the region. This approach relies on use of third country nationals (TCNs)—that is, natives of countries other than that of the parent company who are hired to work in a host country foreign to them. TCNs must straddle the performance demands of three cultures—their native country, the country of the parent firm, and the country where the unit in which they are working is located.

The geocentric approach to staffing uses the best people for key positions throughout the organization regardless of nationality. Unlike ordinary international managers, who may focus on a foreign country or two, such global managers are virtually stateless. Global managers spend their career moving from nation to nation to develop their worldwide perspective and cross-cultural skills and to enhance individual and organizational learning in all parts of the organization (Adler & Bartholomew, 1992, p. 60). They may work within the same firm for their entire career or may operate as "free agents," moving from firm to firm. Asea Brown Boveri (ABB), one of the world's largest and most globally integrated builders of power plants and industrial factories, relies on developing global managers. ABB managers move their allegiance to the local affiliate to which they are assigned. When working in Mexico, an ABB manager who is blond, blue-eyed, and of German decent is more likely to report that he is Mexican than German; in previous assignments he may have described himself as Venezuelan at one time and as Spanish at another (Guyon, 1996).

The geocentric approach offers the greatest flexibility but is the most complex to manage. The following staffing assignments at Pepsi-Cola International, the international beverage division of PepsiCo, Inc., illustrate this flexibility and complexity (Fulkerson, 1997):

- An Indonesian moved to Baltimore
- An Indian sent to Singapore
- An African American U.S. Vietnam veteran posted to Vietnam
- A Pakistani Canadian sent to Kenya
- A Mexican sent to Indonesia
- A Russian sent to Boston
- A German sent to the Ukraine
- A Spaniard sent to London

Social and Cultural Differences and Performance Measurement and Management

Social conditions and cultural values moderate the relationship between IHRM strategy and PMM practices, as outlined in Figure 3.1. Despite the strength of the IHRM strategy, PMM practices fail to the degree that they do not fit the social conditions and cultural values

Figure 3.1. A Model of International Performance Measurement and Management Practices.

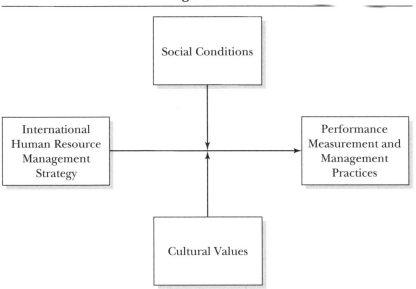

of the nation in which they take place. This failure of PMM practices makes it impossible to implement IHRM strategy successfully.

The influence of social and cultural differences on PMM practices can be seen in a joint venture involving Siemens, Toshiba, and IBM that is dedicated to creating a new type of memory chip at an IBM laboratory in New York (Browning, 1994). Siemens, in its briefing of expatriate engineers scheduled to depart for the United States, refers to America's "hamburger style" of management. American managers, Siemens states, prefer to criticize their subordinates gently. They start a performance feedback session with small talk, for example, "How's the family?" (the top hamburger bun). They then provide critical feedback (the hamburger). They close the session with more encouraging words (the bottom hamburger bun). German managers, on the other hand, provide only hamburger. And with Japanese managers, you get only the faintest smell of hamburger!

Examples of important social conditions include the economic, demographic, legal, professional, and historical features shown in Table 3.2. Countries with a large degree of state control intervention

Table 3.2. Influence of Social Conditions and Cultural Values on Performance Measurement and Management.

	Implications for Performance Measurement and Management Practices
Social Conditions	
Economy	
• Degree of state control	In nations with a large degree of state control of the economy, there is more emphasis on politics than performance when allocating rewards.
• Extent to which organizations are responsible for social development	Emphasis is on (over)staffing in nations where organizations are responsible for social development, with a weak link between performance and personnel decisions, such as firing or reward allocation.
• Infrastructure	Weak infrastructure—telecommunications, transportation, and so on—hampers performance and makes it more difficult to achieve strategic goals.
Social and demographic	
• Education and training	There may be greater receptiveness to performance measurement and performance-contingent rewards among the more educated and the highly trained.
• Race and ethnic relations, religion, gender roles, caste, and social class	Demographic characteristics influence all aspects of the relationship between rater and ratee.
• Common business practices	Some common business practices, such as bribery and nepotism, may influence performance ratings and reward allocation.
Legal	
• Industrial relations	National laws and regulations constrain all PMM practices.
• EEO laws and regulations	

History of foreign relations • History of colonization • Previous foreign interaction and incursion	Managers in nations with a history of foreign domination may be less receptive to foreign management practices. Managers in former colonies may be more receptive to management practices of nations that were once their colonial master, as in Francophone Africa.
Cultural Values	
Individualism versus collectivism	Represents extent of emphasis on needs of the individual versus needs of the group. Influences emphasis on individual or collective performance and rewards; different methods used to control behavior.
Power distance	Represents tolerance of social inequality and hierarchy in social relationships. Constrains choice of raters, for example, limited upward appraisal, 360-degree feedback, and employee involvement in the appraisal process.
Uncertainty avoidance	Represents tolerance for ambiguity and comfort with uncertainty. Influences directness and bluntness of feedback.
Masculinity versus femininity	Represents emphasis on clear, distinct social roles (masculine) or overlapping social roles (feminine). Greater emphasis on achievement with masculine values; greater emphasis on relationships with feminine values.
Short-term versus long-term orientation (Confucian dynamism)	High short-term orientation leads to less initiative and innovativeness and emphasis on social relations rather than performance. High long-term orientation results in greater commitment to making behavioral change after receiving performance feedback.

Table 3.2. Influence of Social Conditions and Cultural Values on Performance Measurement and Management, cont'd.

	Implications for Performance Measurement and Management Practices
Universalism versus particularism	Universalism emphasizes rule-based systems for controlling behavior. Particularism emphasizes individual differences and circumstances that are unique and that deserve exception. PMM practices are easier to implement in universalist cultures.
Neutral versus affective relationships	Represents extent to which reason (neutral) or emotion (affective) shapes behavior and are expressed openly. High affective likely to show immediate verbal and nonverbal emotional reaction to performance feedback, especially negative feedback.
Specific versus diffuse relationships	Represents extent to which we engage others in specific areas of life and single roles or aspects of personality or diffusely, in multiple roles and areas of life. Diffuseness leads to indirection and evasion in discussion of performance issues.
Achievement versus ascription	Represents extent to which status is accorded for achievement or for personal characteristics such as age, gender, social connections, education, caste. It is difficult to tie rewards to performance in ascriptive cultures.
Conceptions of time	Represents whether time is viewed as a linear series of events (sequential) or with past, present, and future all interrelated (synchronic) so that ideas about the future and memories from the past equally shape present behavior. Those who view time sequentially will see it as a resource to be conserved and will take a linear approach to PMM practice. Performance reviews will be tightly focused on discussion of past performance and future expectations.

Relationship to nature	Represents extent to which emphasis is placed on controlling nature or going along with its flow (harmony). Those who emphasize harmony with nature will be more forgiving of delays in meeting performance goals.
Harmony	Represents emphasis on getting along without conflict. Influences directness and bluntness of feedback, for example, low-harmony cultures may be more blunt. In high-harmony cultures, link between individual performance and rewards may be weak because of reluctance to stand out by receiving special treatment.
Allocation rules	Represents the norms used to guide distribution of rewards. Influences link between performance and rewards; rewards based on equity, equality, or need.

Source: Based on information provided in Erez (1994), Hoecklin (1995), Hofstede (1980, 1997), Schwartz (1992), and Trompenaars (1993).

in the economy, such as France, are likely to have reduced emphasis on work performance, a weak link between performance and rewards, and limited acceptance of PMM practices due to government restraint on management practices and a weakened competitive environment. Demographic factors influence receptiveness to formal PMM practices, choice of raters, and relationships between raters and ratees. As shown in the example at the beginning of this chapter, religious beliefs may influence the willingness to provide negative feedback. National laws constrain all business and IHRM choices including PMM practices. A country's colonial history may reduce receptiveness to foreign management practices and ideas in favor of indigenous practices. This is true to some degree in China (Davis, 1997).

Cultural values represent beliefs and preferences concerning action that are shared by most or all members of a society. These values are passed from one generation to the next through language and learning. Cultural values distinguish one human group from another and influence the manner in which people perceive and respond to the world around them, including the organizations in which they work. Common cultural values, the labels used most commonly to identify them, and their relationship with PMM practices are listed in Table 3.2. These values influence receptiveness to formal PMM practices, form and methods for providing feedback, links between performance and rewards, and interaction between rater and ratee.

A thorough study of social conditions and cultural values likely to influence PMM practices should begin once the site for the foreign unit has been identified. A number of electronic databases, such as ABI/Inform, PsycLit, Anthropological Index Online, Expanded Academic Index (Infotrac), Social Sciences Abstracts, Sociological Abstracts, and Sociofile, provide an easy starting point. Keywords to be used in the search can include the value labels listed in Table 3.2, PMM terms such as *performance, rewards,* or *compensation,* names of specific countries, and so forth. Other useful sources for cultural information related to IHRM include Harris and Moran (1996), Hoecklin (1995), Hofstede (1980, 1997), and Trompenaars (1993). Intercultural Press (P.O. Box 700, Yarmouth, ME 04096; http://www.bookmasters.com/interclt.htm) publishes profiles of numerous countries and cultures. Its Web page provides links to other sites related to culture, intercultural training, and global business.

Performance Measurement and Management Practices

When working abroad, managers must stretch beyond mere task performance to focus on culturally important features such as relationships with local government officials, outreach to employee family members, and so forth (Pucik, 1985). This view is consistent with recent attempts to expand conceptions of performance to include aspects of the context in which work behavior occurs, that is, contextual performance (Borman & Motowidlo, 1993). In the international context, contextual performance includes things such as cross-cultural adjustment, cross-cultural skill development, and learning. Table 3.3 provides a matrix of these factors at the unit and individual levels of performance. Task performance and contextual performance are discussed in more detail later in this chapter.

Developing Performance Criteria

Performance criteria must reflect the IHRM strategy. Firms may prefer to export criteria from the home country, allow the foreign unit to develop local criteria, or develop an integrative approach that combines use of global criteria with local criteria. Choice of IHRM strategy determines the relative emphasis on global and local criteria.

With an integrative strategy, global criteria reflect the home firm's central values and organization culture and are employed in all units of the MNC. At Pepsi-Cola International, values that underlie performance criteria emphasize leadership, high standards of personal performance, career and skill development, and balancing individual effort and teamwork (Fulkerson & Schuler, 1992). These values are represented in performance assessment throughout the world. Global criteria may be used in all units of the MNC to maintain homogeneity. Global criteria contribute to centralization and control and act to coordinate performance throughout the MNC.

Table 3.3. Performance Criteria in the International Context.

Performance Criteria	Potential Indicators
Unit Level	
• Financial	Profits, earnings growth, margins
• Market share	Expansion of number of and size of market niches based on customer-driven values and needs
• Productivity	Quantity of product or service output
• Management of social conditions	Reduction in strikes and labor unrest, receipt of critical government approvals and cooperation, uninterrupted supply of raw materials
• Quality	Reduction in scrap rate, errors, customer complaints
• Speed	Increase in customer response time, product cycle development
Individual Level	
Task behavior	
Goal achievement	
• Achievement of task goals	Achieve goals specified in performance plan, for example, increase sales by 15 percent, decrease turnover by 10 percent, speed up product delivery time by 10 percent
Managerial and supervisory behaviors	
• Decision making	Develop culturally sensitive decision-making style and procedures
• Leadership	Direct work of others successfully; communicate a vision of the unit's future and incorporate local priorities into this vision
• Technical knowledge	Fit technical knowledge to local needs

- Impact and influence
- Team building
- Career planning and development
- Feedback and coaching

- Fostering commitment

Contextual behavior

Organizational citizenship

- Helping and cooperating with others
- Working with enthusiasm

- Volunteering for activities

- Flexibility and openness to change
- Moral and ethical character

Cross-cultural adjustment

- Self and family
- Mental health
- Stress management

Get things done despite obstacles
Achieve successful team process consistent with cultural needs
Establish career plan within and across cultural boundaries for managers from different cultures
Provide performance feedback and coaching consistent with cultural values and employee needs
Strengthen employee attachment to unit and parent firm and foster motivation

Help others without being asked to do so

Speak positively and eagerly about work assignments; express passion and zeal about the future of the unit and its performance
Support or encourage others who have problems; this would include family members of employees in some cultures
Change opinions, beliefs, and attitudes when appropriate

Make decisions and take actions that meet ethical standards

Successful mental and physical adjustment
Absence of mental health symptoms such as depression
Use successful coping techniques such as exercise, meditation, development of social support networks

Table 3.3. Performance Criteria in the International Context, cont'd.

Performance Criteria	Potential Indicators
Cross-cultural skill development	
• Language	Improve competency in host country language
• Host culture	Learn host culture rites, rituals, practices, beliefs
• Intercultural competence	Aware of and sensitive to similarities and differences between parent culture and host culture; able to correctly interpret and evaluate behavior of host country natives
• Communication	Aware of and sensitive to similarities and differences in perception, cognition, and communication styles
• Managing face	Manage impact of self upon others; give and protect face of others
Learning	
• Networking	Develop alliances with customers, suppliers, vendors, potential collaborators in host country as well as with other MNC subsidiaries to form supportive network of long-term personal relationships with important others
• Dissemination of learning	Disseminate knowledge gleaned from host country to parent company and other units
• Continuous improvement	Improve quality of service and product, relationships with customers, suppliers, vendors, government officials
Limiting Conditions	
• Difficulty of assignment	Assess difference between parent and host cultures, harshness of living conditions
• Current versus potential	Distinguish between current performance and potential performance

Local criteria, on the other hand, may vary to reflect local conditions and will be different in each of the MNC's units, thus allowing the MNC to maintain needed flexibility. Using both global criteria and local criteria in PMM allows the MNC to maintain the desired balance between the need for control and flexibility.

Global and local criteria can serve several purposes. They may be used to validate selection batteries for expatriate and foreign managers, evaluate the effectiveness of predeparture training programs for expatriate managers, develop performance evaluation forms to assist with personnel decisions, and provide a control mechanism to connect the foreign unit to the MNC. The purpose for using criteria determines the choice of criteria that are used.

Job analysis should be used to develop criteria, but it must focus more broadly than the traditional emphasis on tasks performed in one job. Job analysis should also examine the manner in which tasks help implement strategy. Job analysis should consider multiple levels of analysis, that is, unit and team as well as individual, and the manner in which tasks are interrelated across these levels of analysis. Job analysis should consider elements of contextual performance as well as task performance.

Unit-Level Performance Criteria

Unit-level performance criteria represent outcomes at the strategic business unit (SBU) level of analysis and are usually linked to strategic goals. Unit-level measures include production levels, financial performance, increase in market share, quality, and successful management of external social conditions. Unit-level performance measures are most often used as a control mechanism, but they are sometimes used to assess the performance of expatriate managers who occupy key positions in the foreign unit (Pucik & Katz, 1986). Although unit-level measures allow close monitoring of the foreign unit's performance, they usually are influenced by factors that are not under the control of managers. For example, financial performance measures are misleading because accounting and financial procedures designed to minimize payment of foreign taxes tend to reduce apparent results, as do losses due to changes in foreign exchange rates. Although these financial practices obscure true performance of the unit, cash flow seems to offer an accurate estimate of unit performance (Dowling et al., 1994). Moreover, units in emerging markets such as India and Thailand may keep prices low to increase market share and thwart competition, a strategy used with great success by Japanese MNCs. Without adjustments for these other influences, the real contribution of managers to achievement of the organization's goals remains unknown. Moreover, exclusive emphasis on financial returns to judge performance may reduce managers' will to compete—being held accountable for outcomes out of their control can undercut their overall motivation on the job (Pucik, 1992, p. 72).

Performance criteria must include individual-level behaviors in addition to unit-level outcomes if they are to influence strategy implementation and increase competitive advantage (Ulrich, 1991). Unit-level measures of performance must be supplemented with behavioral measures that more accurately indicate the performance of individual managers who are being evaluated. Individual managerial behaviors must represent both task performance and contextual performance (Motowidlo, Borman, & Schmit, 1997).

Individual-Level Criteria: Task Performance

Motowidlo et al. (1997, p. 75) define two types of task performance. The first type includes activities that transform raw materials into goods and services, for example, selling products, operating production machinery, and so forth. The second type includes activities that serve those who produce goods and services, for example, purchasing, distributing, and managing and supervising. Both types of task performance occur in international organizations.

Goal achievement reflects the frequent use by U.S. MNCs of goal-setting as a managerial tool and ties task behavior to the strategy of the firm. These behaviors represent the first type of task performance related to production of goods and services. Managerial and supervisory behaviors reflect efforts to encourage others to work successfully. These behaviors represent the second type of task performance. Managerial and supervisory behaviors such as these are commonly included in PMM systems. In the international context, these behaviors must fit local cultural values. For example, autocratic decision making may be successful where power distance is high, as in Latin America, but may not be successful in countries such as Sweden where power distance is low.

Individual-Level Criteria: Contextual Performance

Motowidlo et al. (1997) define contextual performance as behaviors that help maintain the organizational, social, and psychological environment in which task performance occurs. This includes activities such as helping and cooperating with others, working with enthusiasm, volunteering for extra activities, and so on. These behaviors enable task behaviors and make them more efficient.

Several forms of contextual performance are important in the international context. These behaviors emphasize cross-cultural performance. Examples include cross-cultural adjustment, cross-cultural skill development, and learning. Each of these behaviors contributes to enhancing the organizational, social, and cultural environment in which task performance occurs.

Cross-cultural adjustment is key to the performance of managers working abroad. Cross-cultural adjustment is required for expatriate managers who go abroad, HCN managers assigned to the country of the parent firm, and TCN and global managers who must repeatedly adapt to different cultures. Unsuccessful cross-cultural adjustment is largely responsible for premature return rates of American expatriate managers (Kobrin, 1988). Without successful cross-cultural adjustment, it is impossible for the manager to establish needed relationships and pursue the business of the firm. Cross-cultural adjustment may be fostered by immersing oneself in the local culture rather than by remaining aloof and marginal (Berry, 1994).

Managers who travel with families must be concerned with cross-cultural adjustment of family members. Failure of family members to adapt to the host culture is a common cause of early return from foreign assignments. This maladjustment often results from lack of predeparture training, less enthusiasm about the assignment, and absence of organizational and other support systems (Black & Gregerson, 1991). Shell Internationale Petroleum, B.V., the giant English-Dutch oil and petroleum firm headquartered in London and the Hague, addresses family member needs through extensive predeparture training, use of spouse counselors, and development of social support networks consisting of repatriated family members (Solomon, 1996).

Merely having a family assistance program is not enough. Some firms, such as Motorola, have discovered that family assistance programs may go unused even when available (Pellico & Stroh, in press). Efforts must be made to ensure their use.

Family issues and their relationship to work performance are receiving greater attention (Zedeck, 1992), but assessment of family members' adjustment raises delicate questions concerning the authority of an employer to assess something so personal. Despite the need to monitor adjustment of family members, practitioners shall have to tread carefully here. This is best done informally.

Success in foreign assignments requires cross-cultural skills and abilities. Examples include knowledge of the host country language and culture, sensitivity to cross-cultural differences in expression and self-presentation, and so forth. Assessment of these skills should be part of any selection and predeparture training program for international managers (Black, Gregerson, & Mendenhall, 1992). Development of cross-cultural skills also should be monitored after foreign assignment. This attention sends a strong message about the importance of these skills.

Organizations that are capable of learning have a competitive advantage in the global environment (Bartlett & Ghoshal, 1989). Learning organizations have special characteristics that allow them to adapt and change more quickly (Senge, 1990). Many Japanese MNCs (Morishima, 1995) and some American MNCs such as Xerox (McGarry, 1994) use human resource practices quite effectively to create organizations that learn from their global practices. PMM practices can help these learning efforts.

Limiting Conditions

Limiting conditions may moderate performance. Differences between the home culture of the manager and the foreign culture in which he or she is working can make an assignment more difficult for one individual than for another. Some cultural transitions are more difficult to adapt to than others. Western managers have more difficulty adapting in India and Pakistan, East and Southeast Asia, the Middle East, and much of Africa than in other Western cultures (Torbiorn, 1982). Success in such transitions may require "cultural toughness"—that is, resilience and ability to deal with difficult situations (Mendenhall & Oddou, 1985). The difficulty of adjustment should be reflected in performance expectations and evaluations.

Another limiting condition is the relative emphasis on current versus potential performance and the evidence of "good faith" effort. These distinctions are common in Japanese performance evaluations (Pucik & Hatvany, 1983). Attention to these factors reflects concern for the means of achieving performance as well as its outcomes. Moreover, short-term lapses in performance may be forgiven when long-term improvement is expected. Such patience is necessary when units are located in developing nations where public infrastructure such as telecommunications and transportation delay swift progress or when the MNC is employing a strategy of low cost to increase market share.

Performance Measurement

Many techniques exist to measure performance. The advantages and disadvantages of each technique are widely known (Murphy & Cleveland, 1995). Fortunately, many of these techniques generalize to the international context. What changes across national boundaries is the manner in which these techniques are practiced, for example, the behaviors that are rated, who is asked to perform the rating, the manner in which feedback is provided, and so on. The following example illustrates this point.

National Rental Car employs a strategic, behaviorally based rating scale for the position of customer service representative (Beatty, 1989). Behaviors such as smiling, making eye contact, greeting customers, and solving customer problems are tied to the strategic goal of improving customer service. When used internationally, behaviors typical of the local culture would be measured. For example, in Japan, the angle of bowing for department store greeters as well as the proper back alignment and eye contact would be judged according to culturally defined standards. In nations having particularist rather than universalist values, such as Ghana and most other African nations, behaviors would be used that reflect loyalty and repaying of obligations in addition to following procedures and regulations (Blunt & Popoola, 1985, p. 109). In nations where nonquantitative techniques for assessment are preferred, strategic job behaviors may be observed so as to provide points for feedback and discussion rather than being measured formally and assigned quantitative ratings.

Some aspects of performance measurement are highly susceptible to cultural influence. Cultural differences exist in cognitive processes such as perception, information processing, causal attribution, and willingness to use extreme judgments on rating scales (Berry, Poortinga, Segall, & Dasen, 1992). These cultural differences are important in performance appraisal because of the extent to which cognitive processes influence performance ratings (De Nisi & Williams, 1988), and because social judgments such as those necessary to conduct performance ratings are especially susceptible to cultural influence (Smith & Peterson, 1988). For example, Indian managers are likely to rate more positively those who are loyal and have close personal relationships with them, while others will be rated negatively, regardless of actual performance (Sinha, 1994).

Members of different cultures may perceive different work-related behavior, use different mental categories to detect and represent ideal performance, categorize performance information differently, and associate different degrees of emotionality with the respective categories of work-related behaviors (see Segall, Dasen, Berry, & Poortinga, 1990, p. 162). These differences will influence choice of behaviors that are observed, remembered, and recorded when it is time to complete rating forms. These differences will also influence interaction in review sessions devoted to discussion of performance feedback and employee development.

Unfortunately, unlike research devoted to discovering similarity in work values such as that done by Hofstede (1980) and Trompenaars (1993), there is no empirical clustering of national cultures in terms of cognitive processes. Some studies have been conducted to determine national differences in use of rating scales, for example, demonstrating a modesty bias among Chinese raters (Farh, Dobbins, & Cheng, 1991), but empirical evidence of the influence of culture on the cognitive processes associated with performance rating is scant. Practitioners should encourage local development of rating procedures and training that reflect native cognitive processing.

Cultural differences exist in the communication process in which PMM practices are embedded. Hall (1976) distinguishes between high-context and low-context cultures. In high-context cultures, including most Eastern cultures such as Japan, much of the information to be conveyed during the communication process is located in the surrounding context shared by the sender and receiver. As a result, communication is less direct and precise. In low-context cultures, including most Western cultures such as the United States, most of the information is in the transmitted message itself. As a result, communication is more direct and precise.

In high-context cultures, the emphasis is on listening; in low-context cultures, the emphasis is on speaking (Gao, Ting-Toomey, & Gudykunst, 1996). This results in a deemphasis on the value of talk. For example, managers in China, a high-context culture, rank oral communication skills as least important for managerial success (Hildebrandt, 1988). In fact, glib Chinese managers are often objects of suspicion.

Differences in level of context influence several aspects of PMM (Harris & Moran, 1996, p. 26). In low-context cultures, there is an emphasis on fairness in the performance appraisal, the appraiser is assumed to be objective, feedback and criticism are direct, and appraisees may rebut their appraisal. In high-context cultures, there is an emphasis on employee development in the performance appraisal, the appraiser is assumed to be subjective, feedback and criticism are indirect and subtle, and appraisees may not rebut their appraisal.

Culture also influences choice of raters and methods of providing performance feedback. In cultures high in power distance, for example, those higher in status will resist receiving performance feedback from those lower in status. Cultures high in particularism will resist use of performance ratings to award pay bonuses, promotions, or developmental opportunities because of a preference for emphasizing special concerns such as friendship or need rather than performance. Those who value harmony, collectivism, and avoidance of uncertainty will have difficulty dealing with negative ratings and direct feedback. It will also be more difficult to employ 360-degree rating and feedback in such cultures.

In sum, people throughout the world process social information differently as a result of their culture. These cultural differences influence performance ratings. Local managers should be involved in development of performance measurement practices to ensure their fit with social conditions and cultural values.

Training Issues

Training should emphasize strategic goals and how individual performance contributes to unit effectiveness. Training should also explain how PMM practices increase individual and unit success. These points are important to emphasize because they represent assumptions that are not shared by managers throughout the world.

Frame-of-reference training should be used to improve rating accuracy and fairness. Frame-of-reference training provides a common set of standards regarding the behaviors used to define performance and indicators of success for each of these behaviors (Borman, 1979). Raters and ratees from different cultures should be trained to synchronize their perception and processing of performance information. Landis and Bhagat (1996) describe intercultural training methods that may be adapted for PMM training. Training methods that emphasize practice and skill development will be most effective (Black & Mendenhall, 1990).

Performance Management Practices

Performance management refers to practices used to help people manage their behavior to help the organization achieve its goals. In addition to use of performance measurement, described earlier, five practices are commonly used to manage international performance. These include rules and procedures, socialization, performance planning, feedback and coaching, and pay and compensation. Each of these practices is discussed in this section. Additionally, the need to align these practices with each other to form an integrated IHRM system is discussed.

- *Rules and procedures.* Rules and procedures are often used with an exportive IHRM strategy that emphasizes use of an ethnocentric staffing policy and PCNs. They are most useful for controlling behavior that may be unethical or illegal in the MNC's home country. For example, the Foreign Corrupt Practices Act in the United States forbids bribery of foreign officials despite the fact that such payments may be legal and expected in the country in which they are practiced. MNCs must discourage use of bribery abroad to avoid prosecution at home. Although rules and procedures are necessary to ensure some management behaviors, they have limited use as a general performance management tool due to their narrow focus and inflexibility.

- *Socialization.* Socialization in the international environment strives to ensure that employees throughout the world share similar organizational values. This practice works well with an integrative IHRM strategy that relies on a regiocentric or global staffing pattern and use of HCNs, TCNs, and global managers. Socialization is a more subtle and flexible control mechanism than reliance on rules and procedures. Socialization and emphasis on core values, such as the importance of personal accountability and valuing diversity, are essential for uniting managers into a cohesive global organization.

- *Performance planning.* Organizations are effective when they set proper goals and objectives and hold people accountable for meeting them. Performance plans signal the important values of the organization and help people to be accountable for achieving organizational goals. Performance plans should be flexible and dynamic. When working in fast-changing emerging markets, such as in Southeast Asia, plans should be updated more frequently than annually, the typical period for performance review. It will be easier to involve employees in performance planning in nations with values that accept participation in decision making.

- *Feedback and coaching.* Two types of feedback are useful: immediate feedback and developmental feedback. Immediate feedback is provided spontaneously in recognition of some type of exemplary work performance. This might include a particularly good report, a sale to a challenging customer, and so on. Developmental feedback identifies behavior to be targeted for more systematic change. It has more of a long-term focus than immediate feedback.

The method of providing feedback must be varied to fit local customs. Compliments and positive feedback are rewarding to people everywhere. Criticism and negative feedback elicit defensiveness. Indigenous methods for providing feedback should be used.

Coaching refers to efforts to change a group of behaviors. These behaviors should represent task and contextual performance. Feedback and coaching ensure that people are motivated to achieve the goals of the organization over time. Some organizations use specialized training for this. For example, General Motors sends promising engineers from its plants in Mexico to attend special management training and development programs at U.S. universities such as Stanford (Gowan & Lackey, 1996).

- *Compensation and rewards.* Cultures vary in the rules they use to allocate rewards. It is common in U.S. organizations to tie compensation and other rewards to individual or, more recently, to team performance. This practice derives from a value for equity in reward allocation. This is a strong American value that is not universal. Other countries may emphasize seniority, equality, or need in reward allocation. Compensation and reward practices should be adapted to fit local conditions. A blend of individual-based and team-based pay-for-performance will be successful in units using team-based forms of organization and units located in cultures sharing collectivist values.

As nations become more integrated into the global economy and have greater exposure to MNC management practices, pay-for-performance will become more widely accepted. The popularity of pay-for-performance is increasing in countries such as Malaysia and Singapore, where managers complain about the weak link between performance and rewards (Mills, 1994, 1995).

- *Need for alignment.* PMM practices must be aligned with individual, team, unit, and organizational goals. PMM data and practices should be used to support business planning and strategy development, selection and training of expatriate managers, career development, and promotion and succession planning.

Summary

The international context places special demands on human resource practices such as performance evaluation and performance management. Factors such as social conditions and cultural values not typically considered by domestic organizations become prominent when managing abroad. Table 3.4 summarizes important choices concerning PMM practices.

Practitioners must start by developing a strategic orientation. This strategic orientation consists of an international human resource strategy that is tied to the firm's global strategy. Integration should be emphasized as much as possible to enhance the opportunities to learn from cross-cultural experience around the globe.

Table 3.4. Doing International
Performance Measurement and Management.

PMM Practice	PMM Actions
Strategy formulation	• Develop international human resource management strategy that is linked with the firm's strategy for conducting international business.
	• Choose proper balance between centralized control and decentralized adaptation.
	• Include emphasis on learning to gain competitive advantage from overseas experience and to develop ability to adapt to change.
	• Choose ethnocentric, polycentric, regiocentric, or geocentric approach to staffing.
	• Involve HR managers from foreign units in creation of IHRM strategy.
	• Fit PMM practices to IHRM strategic goals.
Social and cultural analysis	• Analyze social conditions and cultural variables for each nation where foreign units will be located. Consider interactions among social conditions and cultural values.
	• Search electronic databases and other sources for information related to each factor and its potential impact on PMM and other related IHRM practices.
	• Involve subject matter experts and local managers in analysis.
Criterion development	• Conduct multilevel strategic job analysis.
	• Select criteria to represent both unit-level and individual-level performance.
	• Tie criteria to strategic goals and objectives of the unit.
	• Use unit-level criteria only for managers in key positions with ability to influence performance on these measures.
	• Emphasize both task performance and contextual performance in individual-level criteria.
	• Include measures of behaviors used to improve cross-cultural adjustment and performance to assess contextual performance.
	• Consider the limiting conditions when determining criteria and setting goals for performance.

Table 3.4. Doing International
Performance Measurement and Management, cont'd.

PMM Practice	PMM Actions
Implement performance measurement	• Emphasize culture-friendly behaviors that represent achievement of strategic goals.
	• Identify potential differences in cognitive processing of performance-related information; include this information in frame-of-reference training.
	• Recognize that quantitative ratings are not universally respected or accepted.
	• Use strategic goals to identify behaviors to observe and discuss in feedback sessions where quantitative ratings are not possible.
	• Identify relevant communication factors such as high and low context that influence the manner in which people will discuss and relate to performance issues.
	• Choose raters in a manner consistent with cultural values, for example, power distance and collectivism.
Provide training	• Train raters and ratees alike.
	• Explain how individual performance is related to strategic goals and effectiveness of foreign unit; emphasize shared responsibility.
	• Use frame-of-reference training to synchronize definition and perceptions of performance; clearly establish roles in the PMM process.
	• Identify and explain key behaviors and how to track them.
	• Explain role of cultural differences and how they may be expected to influence the PMM process.
	• Train raters in interpersonal and cross-cultural skills related to process.
	• Build skills in performance management rather than merely defending its importance.

Table 3.4. Doing International
Performance Measurement and Management, cont'd.

PMM Practice	PMM Actions
Implement performance management practices	• Employ full range of performance management practices; emphasize socialization to maintain flexibility.
	• Use performance measurement to provide foundation for performance management.
	• Align PMM practices with other human resource and organizational practices to ensure consistency and to gain leverage for organization change.
	• Do periodic follow-up of quality and timeliness of performance reviews.
	• Use performance management system to hold managers accountable for implementing and supporting the PMM process itself. For example, include efforts to socialize and develop subordinates in managers' performance review.
	• Use methods such as periodic surveys and focus groups to monitor and refine the PMM system.
	• Evaluate impact of PMM practices on unit performance to document utility of PMM system.

In each nation in which units are located, social conditions and cultural values should be evaluated to identify the extent to which they will influence HRM choices. HRM practices should fit as much as possible these social conditions and cultural values.

PMM practices should be used to bind together other IHRM practices such as socialization, training, selection, management development, and so forth to tie them to the firm's strategy and its culture. This connection allows the firm to achieve needed homogeneity. At the same time, IHRM choices must reflect local conditions to maintain needed flexibility. Joint optimization of homogeneity and local adaptation should be the goal. This may be achieved through use of global criteria to encourage homogeneity and local criteria to reflect unique local conditions.

Cultural differences in cognition and information processing, assumptions and beliefs about performance, and the communication process should be examined and reflected in training programs oriented to both raters and ratees. Training should focus on narrowing differences as much as possible to synchronize perceptions and judgments, use of the rating system, and reactions to it.

Finally, PMM must be managed as a subsystem of the organization. This means that PMM must be aligned with the organization's strategy, culture, structure, rewards, and processes devoted to leadership, motivation, communication, and decision making. Of course, PMM must also be aligned with other IHRM practices such as selection, training, and employee development.

Firms are struggling to compete successfully in a world filled with change and intense competition. Performance measurement and performance management can help firms meet this challenge.

References

Adler, N. J., & Bartholomew, S. (1992). Managing globally competent people. *Academy of Management Executive, 6*(3), 52–65.

Bartlett, C., & Ghoshal, S. (1989). *Managing across borders: The transnational solution.* Boston: Harvard Business School Press.

Bartlett, C., & Ghoshal, S. (1990, July-August). Matrix management: Not a structure, a frame of mind. *Harvard Business Review,* pp. 138–145.

Beatty, R. W. (1989). Competitive human resource advantage through the strategic management of performance. *Human Resource Planning, 12*(3), 179–194.

Berry, J. W. (1994). Acculturative stress. In W. J. Lonner & R. S. Malpass (Eds.), *Psychology and culture* (pp. 211–215). Needham Heights, MA.: Allyn & Bacon.

Berry, J. W., Poortinga, Y. H., Segall, M. H., & Dasen, P. R. (1992). *Cross-cultural psychology: Research and applications.* Cambridge, England: Cambridge University Press.

Black, J. S., & Gregerson, H. B. (1991). The other half of the picture: Antecedents of spouse cross-cultural adjustment. *Journal of International Business Studies, 22,* 461–467.

Black, J. S., & Gregerson, H. B. (1992, Summer). Serving two masters: Managing the dual allegiance of expatriate employees. *Sloan Management Review,* pp. 61–71.

Black, J. S., Gregerson, H. B., & Mendenhall, M. E. (1992). *Global assignments: Successfully expatriating and repatriating international managers.* San Francisco: Jossey-Bass.

Black, J. S., & Mendenhall, M. E. (1990). Cross-cultural training effectiveness: A review and theoretical framework for future research. *Academy of Management Review, 15,* 113–136.

Blunt, P., & Popoola, O. E. (1985). *Personnel management in Africa*. Reading, MA: Addison Wesley Longman.

Borman, W. C. (1979). Format and training effects on rating accuracy and rater errors. *Journal of Applied Psychology, 64,* 410–421.

Borman, W. C., & Motowidlo, S. J. (1993). Expanding the criterion domain to include elements of contextual performance. In N. Schmitt & W. C. Borman (Eds.), *Personnel selection in organizations* (pp. 71–98). San Francisco: Jossey-Bass.

Browning, E. S. (1994, May 3). Computer chip project brings rivals together, but the cultures clash. *Wall Street Journal,* pp. A1, A8.

Butler, J. E., Ferris, G. R., & Napier, N. K. (1991). *Strategy and human resources management*. Cincinnati: South-Western.

Chee, L. S. (1994). Singapore Airlines: Strategic human resource initiatives. In D. Torrington (Ed.), *International human resource management: Think globally, act locally* (pp. 143–159). Upper Saddle River, NJ: Prentice Hall.

Davis, D. D. (1995). Form, function, and strategy in the boundaryless organization. In A. Howard (Ed.), *The changing nature of work* (pp. 112–138). San Francisco: Jossey-Bass.

Davis, D. D. (1997). Change management and consulting in Chinese organizations. *Consulting Psychology Journal, 49,* 108–121.

De Nisi, A. S., & Williams, K. J. (1988). Cognitive approaches to performance appraisal. In G. Ferris & K. Rowland (Eds.), *Research in personnel and human resource management: Vol. 6* (pp. 108–155). Greenwich, CT: JAI Press.

Dowling, P. J., Schuler, R. S., & Welch, D. E. (1994). *International dimensions of human resource management* (2nd ed.). Belmont, CA: Wadsworth.

Doz, Y., & Prahalad, C. K. (1986). Controlled variety: A challenge for human resource management in the MNC. *Human Resource Management, 25*(1), 55–72.

Drenth, P. J. D. (in press). Personnel appraisal. In P. J. D. Drenth, H. Thierry, & C. J. de Wolff (Eds.), *Handbook of work and organizational psychology* (2nd ed.). Hillsdale, NJ: Erlbaum.

Erez, M. (1994). Toward a model of cross-cultural industrial and organizational psychology. In H. Triandis, M. Dunnette, & L. Hough (Eds.), *Handbook of industrial and organizational psychology* (2nd ed., pp. 559–607). Palo Alto, CA: Consulting Psychologists Press.

Farh, J. L., Dobbins, G. H., & Cheng, B. S. (1991). Cultural relativity in action: A comparison of self-ratings made by Chinese and U.S. workers. *Personnel Psychology, 44,* 129–147.

Fulkerson, J. R. (1997, April). Expats: The past, present, and future of global executives. In P. Caligiuri & L. K. Stroh (Chairs), *Current issues for managing global assignments in multinational organizations.*

Symposium conducted at the meeting of the Society for Industrial and Organizational Psychology, St. Louis, MO.

Fulkerson, J. R., & Schuler, R. S. (1992). Managing worldwide diversity at Pepsi-Cola International. In S. E. Jackson (Ed.), *Diversity in the workplace: Human resources initiatives* (pp. 248–276). New York: Guilford Press.

Gao, G., Ting-Toomey, S., & Gudykunst, W. B. (1996). Chinese communication processes. In M. H. Bond (Ed.), *The handbook of Chinese psychology* (pp. 280–293). Oxford, England: Oxford University Press.

Gowan, M., & Lackey, C. (1996). Doing the right things in Mexico. *Academy of Management Executive, 10*(1), 74–81.

Guyon, J. (1996, October 2). ABB fuses units with one set of values. *Wall Street Journal*, p. A15.

Hall, E. T. (1976). *Beyond culture.* New York: Anchor Books.

Harris, P. R., & Moran, R. T. (1996). *Managing cultural differences* (4th ed.). Houston: Gulf.

Harzing, A. W. (1995). Strategic planning in multinational corporations. In A. W. Harzing & J. Van Ruyssveldt (Eds.), *International human resource management: An integrated approach* (pp. 25–50). London: Sage.

Heenan, D., & Perlmutter, H. (1979). *Multinational organizational development: A social architecture perspective.* Reading, MA: Addison Wesley Longman.

Hildebrandt, H. W. (1988). A Chinese managerial view of business communication. *Management Communication Quarterly, 2*, 217–234.

Hoecklin, L. (1995). *Managing cultural differences: Strategies for competitive advantage.* Reading, MA: Addison Wesley Longman.

Hofstede, G. (1980). *Culture's consequences: International differences in work related values.* Thousand Oaks, CA: Sage.

Hofstede, G. (1997). *Culture and organizations: Software of the mind.* New York: McGraw-Hill.

Huselid, M. A., Jackson, S. E., & Schuler, R. S. (1997). Technical and strategic human resource management effectiveness as determinants of firm performance. *Academy of Management Journal, 40*, 171–188.

Kobrin, S. J. (1988). Expatriate reduction and strategic control in American multinational corporations. *Human Resource Management, 27*, 63–75.

Landis, D., & Bhagat, R. S. (Eds.). (1996). *Handbook of intercultural training* (2nd ed.). Thousand Oaks, CA: Sage.

Landy, F. J., & Farr, J. L. (1983). *The measurement of work performance: Methods, theory, and applications.* Orlando, FL: Academic Press.

Latham, G. P. (1984). The appraisal system as a strategic control. In C. J. Fombrun, N. M. Tichy, & M. A. Devanna (Eds.), *Strategic human resource management* (pp. 87–100). New York: Wiley.

Laurent, A. (1986). The cross-cultural puzzle of international human resource management. *Human Resource Management, 25,* 91 102.

McGarry, D. (1994). Playing the home and away teams. *Business Quarterly,
59*(2), 81–88.

Mendenhall, M. E., & Oddou, G. (1985). The dimensions of expatriate
acculturation: A review. *Academy of Management Review, 10,* 39–47.

Miller, E. L., Beechler, S., Bhatt, B., & Nath, R. (1986). The relationship
between the global strategic planning process and the human resource management function. *Human Resource Planning, 9*(1), 9–23.

Mills, C. (1994). *Performance management: What's hot—what's not: A study
of current and future practices in Malaysia.* Kuala Lumpur: Development Dimensions International and Malaysian Institute of Personnel Management.

Mills, C. (1995). *Performance management: Fact or fantasy: A study of current
and future practices in Singapore.* Singapore: Singapore Institute of
Management and Development Dimensions International.

Mohrman, A. J., Jr., Resnick-West, S. M., & Lawler, E. E., III. (1989). *Designing performance appraisal systems: Aligning appraisals and organizational realities.* San Francisco: Jossey-Bass.

Morishima, M. (1995). The Japanese human resource management system: A learning system. In L. F. Moore & P. D. Jennings (Eds.),
*Human resource management on the Pacific Rim: Institutions, practices,
and attitudes* (pp. 119–150). Hawthorne, NY: Walter de Gruyter.

Motowidlo, S. J., Borman, W. C., & Schmit, M. J. (1997). A theory of individual differences in task and contextual performance. *Human
Performance, 10,* 71–83.

Murphy, K. R., & Cleveland, J. N. (1995). *Understanding performance appraisal: Social, organizational, and goal-based perspectives.* Thousand
Oaks, CA: Sage.

Nike tries to quell exploitation charges. (1997, June 25). *Wall Street Journal,* p. A16.

Pellico, M. T., & Stroh, L. K. (in press). Spousal assistance programs: An
integral component of the international assignment. In Z. Aycan
(Ed.), *Expatriate management: Theory and research.* Greenwich, CT: JAI
Press.

Perlmutter, H. (1969, January-February). The tortuous evolution of the
multinational corporation. *Columbia Journal of World Business,* pp. 9–18.

Porter, M. E. (1985). *Competitive advantage: Creating and sustaining superior
performance.* New York: Free Press.

Porter, M. E. (Ed.). (1986). *Competition in global industries.* Cambridge, MA:
Harvard University Press.

Prahalad, C. K., & Hamel, G. (1990). The core competence of the corporation. *Harvard Business Review, 68*(3), 79–91.

Pucik, V. (1985). Strategic human resource management in a multinational firm. In H. V. Wortzel & L. H. Wortzel (Eds.), *Strategic management of multinational corporations: The essentials* (pp. 424–435). New York: Wiley.

Pucik, V. (1992). Globalization and human resource management. In V. Pucik, N. M. Tichy, & C. K. Barnett (Eds.), *Globalizing management: Creating and leading the competitive organization* (pp. 61–81). New York: Wiley.

Pucik, V., & Hatvany, N. (1983). Management practices in Japan and their impact on business strategy. In R. Lamb (Ed.), *Advances in strategic management: Vol. 1* (pp. 103–131). Greenwich, CT: JAI Press.

Pucik, V., & Katz, J. H. (1986). Information, control and human resource management in multinational firms. *Human Resource Management, 25,* 121–132.

Rosenzweig, P. M., & Singh, J. V. (1991). Organizational environments and the multinational enterprise. *Academy of Management Review, 16,* 340–361.

Schneier, C. E., Shaw, D. G., & Beatty, R. W. (1991). Performance measurement and management: A tool for strategy execution. *Human Resource Management, 30,* 279–301.

Schuler, R. S., Dowling, P., & De Cieri, H. (1993). An integrative framework of strategic international human resource management. *International Journal of Human Resource Management, 1,* 717–764.

Schwartz, S. (1992). Universals in the content and structure of values: Theoretical advances and empirical tests in 20 countries. In M. Zanna (Ed.), *Advances in experimental social psychology: Vol. 25* (pp. 1–65). Orlando, FL: Academic Press.

Segall, M. H., Dasen, P. R., Berry, J. W., & Poortinga, Y. H. (1990). *Human behavior in global perspective: An introduction to cross-cultural psychology.* Needham Heights, MA: Allyn & Bacon.

Senge, P. M. (1990). *The fifth discipline: The art and practice of the learning organization.* New York: Doubleday.

Sinha, J. B. P. (1994). Cultural embeddedness and the developmental role of industrial organizations in India. In H. C. Triandis, M. D. Dunnette, & L. M. Hough (Eds.), *Handbook of industrial and organizational psychology* (2nd ed., pp. 727–764). Palo Alto: Consulting Psychologists Press.

Smith, P. B., & Peterson, M. F. (1988). *Leadership, organizations and culture: An event management model.* London: Sage.

Solomon, C. M. (1996). Expats say: Help make us mobile. *Personnel Journal, 75*(7), 47–52.

Sparrow, P. R., & Hiltrop, J. M. (1997). Redefining the field of European human resource management: A battle between national mindsets and forces of business transition. *Human Resource Management, 36,* 201–219.

Taylor, S., Beechler, S., & Napier, N. (1996). Toward an integrative model of strategic international human resource management. *Academy of Management Review, 21,* 959–985.

Torbiorn, I. (1982). *Living abroad: Personal adjustment and personnel policy in the overseas setting.* New York: Wiley.

Trompenaars, F. (1993). *Riding the waves of culture.* London: Economist Books.

Ulrich, D. (1991). Using human resources for competitive advantage. In R. H. Kilmann & I. Kilmann (Eds.), *Making organizations competitive: Enhancing networks and relationships across boundaries* (pp. 129–155). San Francisco: Jossey-Bass.

Zedeck, S. (Ed.). (1992). *Work, families, and organizations.* San Francisco: Jossey-Bass.

CHAPTER 4

Performance Appraisal in a Quality Context:
A New Look at an Old Problem
Robert L. Cardy

Performance appraisal has been lamented by many managers as an unwelcome and difficult task. Not many people enjoy giving appraisals and probably not many enjoy receiving them. Researchers have also criticized appraisal for the amount of error and bias that can occur (Cardy & Dobbins, 1994). Further, dissatisfaction with appraisal is a common survey finding. Yet the appraisal and management of performance remains an important issue in organizations. Even though the role of evaluation may be uncomfortable for many, judgments of performance are needed if performance-contingent decisions, ranging from termination to pay increase and promotion, are to have any sort of rational basis. As employees, most of us want and need feedback—and performance appraisal is a systematic means for getting the feedback we need to improve. There is no doubt that the appraisal and management of human performance can be a difficult and error-ridden task. However, it is important to both the organizational and individual perspectives that the task still be done as effectively as possible.

The purpose of this chapter is to explore the topic of performance appraisal—through the frame of the quality perspective. My hope is that the chapter will give you a new perspective on the process of appraising and managing human performance and that you take away concrete steps that you might take to improve the appraisal process in your own organization. I would hasten to add that you should not expect to find here the recipe for the perfect appraisal system. I don't think such a recipe exists and those who might try to convince you that they can sell you such a recipe are simply after your wallet. The important thing is to listen to the customers of the process and to work toward improvement.

This exploration of performance appraisal begins with a brief overview of the quality orientation and its implications for performance appraisal. Next the general quality and traditional human resource management approaches are contrasted, followed by an examination of the traditional and quality approaches to performance appraisal. A potential resolution of the apparent conflict between the two approaches is then offered. The remainder of the chapter examines characteristics of performance appraisal that should maximize the effectiveness of appraisal in a quality organizational environment.

The Quality Orientation

A historical examination of the philosophy and practice of quality is beyond the scope of this chapter. The reader can consult other sources for a more thorough examination of the roots of the quality movement and nuances among the key representatives of the movement (for example, Deming, 1986; Ishikawa, 1985; Juran, 1989; Walton, 1986). The focus here will be on major characteristics of the quality approach and on similarities in philosophy and practices.

The quality orientation has been summarized and characterized by a number of researchers (see, for example, Waldman & Gopalakrishnan, 1996). Probably the two most fundamental characteristics of the quality approach are a customer orientation and a prevention approach to errors (Cardy & Dobbins, 1996). Customer satisfaction is the raison d'être for the quality approach. Improving customer satisfaction provides the motive force for quality practices and is the central reason for the practices associated with the quality approach. Customers of a product or service can be either internal or external to the organization. The customers are the focus of the quality process and determine the standards and directions for improving performance.

The customer focus produces a more fluid, open, and lateral organizational structure relative to the traditional structure of Western management (Cardy, Dobbins, & Carson, 1995). Rather than a top-down hierarchical framework that emphasizes vertical reporting relationships and that can create functional silos, the quality focus on the customer flattens out and integrates the processes and functions within an organization. Rather than satisfying the supervisor, the emphasis in a quality environment is on satisfying the customer. Effectively addressing the customer's needs and expectations means that functional blinders and internal power relationships need to be set aside so that the parts of the organization can work in concert. Another important aspect of the quality approach is an emphasis on prevention rather than detection of errors. The traditional Western approach to quality emphasizes the post hoc inspection process as a mechanism for ensuring adequate quality. The emphasis in the quality approach is on making inspection an integral part of the work process, rather than a separate function that occurs later. Deming, one of the most notable quality advocates, explicitly identified disadvantages to the traditional error detection system (for example, see Deming, 1986). One disadvantage is that not all defective products or inadequate service interactions can be identified by a separate review function. This fact will result in disgruntled customers and decreased demand for the organization's product or service. There are also direct costs in the production of errors due to the time and cost of materials associated with the creation of the defective product or inadequate service interaction. However, Deming argued that the most important costs of the detection system are the indirect costs. The indirect costs asserted by Deming to be associated with the detection approach include fear and loss of pride in workmanship. The post hoc evaluation by independent inspectors means that errors unrecognized and possibly not produced by the worker can be found and the worker may be held responsible for those outcomes. It is little wonder that Deming found the detection system to be a negative factor in the workplace.

The quality approach emphasizes the importance of striving to avoid committing errors in the first place. Workers are given the tools and responsibility for assessing the quality of their own work. Facility with statistical process control (SPC) techniques is important for measuring quality and determining sources of error. The quality approach decentralizes the traditional inspection function and integrates it into the work process itself (Cardy, Dobbins, & Carson, 1995).

The assumption that errors are largely due to system factors rather than worker characteristics is another important characteristic of the quality approach. This assumption can be thought of as underlying the prevention emphasis. Specifically, if errors are to be avoided, the most important means for doing this is a focus on the system, not on individual workers. Performance is mainly a function of system factors and improvement in this performance thus requires improvement in the system.

The quality approach has important implications for performance appraisal in particular and for human resource management (HRM) in general. A number of quality advocates have staunchly taken the position that the practice of appraisal should be abolished (for example, Deming, 1986; Halachmi, 1993; Scholtes, 1993). Among other issues, the fundamental problem with appraisal from the perspective of many quality advocates is that it holds workers responsible for outcomes that are beyond their control. If performance is largely due to system factors, then it makes little sense to assess the workers, since they contribute such a small amount to the performance outcomes.

Quality and HRM

A fundamental assumption of the quality approach is that system factors matter the most when it comes to performance. System factors refer to anything outside of individual workers. For example, machinery, materials, supervision, and even organizational climate may all be factors of the system that determine performance. Exhibit 4.1 presents a list of general categories of system factors that could influence performance. Deming (1986) has argued that system factors account for up to 95 percent of the variance in performance. However, this figure was simply an assertion based on no empirical evidence. Nonetheless, it is a figure routinely cited in the quality literature.

Given for now the assumption that system factors are the major determinant of performance, managers can improve worker performance by removing system barriers to maximal performance. The major thrust of the quality approach is continuous improvement in

Exhibit 4.1. General Categories of System Factors.

- Poor coordination of work activities with others
- Inadequate information, instructions, specifications, and so on
- Lack of needed equipment
- Inability to obtain raw materials, parts, supplies, and so on
- Inadequate financial resources
- Uncooperative coworkers or poor interpersonal relations
- Inadequate training
- Insufficient time to produce the quantity or quality of work required of the job
- Poor environmental conditions (for example, too cold, hot, noisy, or full of interruptions)
- Unexpected equipment breakdown

performance through improvements in the system. These system improvements begin with the identification and elimination of sporadic system influences that cause substantial variance in performance levels. Such influences are referred to as *special causes* and might include factors such as a bad shipment of materials, a machine not set up properly, and so on. Once these special causes are identified and eliminated, performance should be less erratic since the influences should all be stable system, or common, causes of performance. Once special causes are eliminated, the improvement effort then progresses to improving the system itself so that the level of performance increases and variance decreases.

Underlying the focus on system improvement is the quality assumption that people are intrinsically motivated to perform well. The emphasis from the quality perspective is on removing system barriers to performance. Removal of barriers is assumed to provide an opportunity for the natural motivation of workers to be released. The quality approach assumes that the motive force in workers is already there: it is simply a matter of removing the factors that block workers from performing at their maximum. As we will see, this is in sharp contrast to the approach taken by traditional HRM.

The field of HRM has focused on people rather than the system. A major assumption underlying HRM is, simply stated, people matter (Dobbins, Cardy, & Carson, 1991). Much of HRM is focused on measuring individual differences in workers in performance or characteristics believed to be related to performance. Systematic examination of job requirements is important in HRM so that individual differences important to the job can be identified, measured, and trained. Knowledge, skills, and abilities of workers are believed to be important and direct determinants of performance.

The HRM field has assumed that worker motivation is largely determined by extrinsic factors. While intrinsic motivation has sporadically been recognized as potentially important (for example, Deci, 1972), the thrust has been on setting extrinsic contingencies to maximize performance. Clear and difficult performance goals (Locke, Shaw, Saari, & Latham, 1981) and performance-contingent pay (for example, Gomez-Mejia & Balkin, 1989) are examples of the extrinsic motivation approach taken by HRM.

There is clearly a fundamental conflict between the quality and traditional HRM approaches. The two approaches differ sharply over what is considered to be the major determinant of performance and in the source of worker motivation to perform. The answer to the conflict lies not in which approach is right and which is wrong, but in recognizing that both approaches may be correct. The conflict between quality and HRM is analogous to the longstanding nature-nurture controversy in psychology. The nature proponents argued that characteristics of people were shaped by genetics while the nurture proponents argued that characteristics were shaped by environmental conditions. The two approaches have been merged into an interactionist approach (Kenrick & Funder, 1988) that recognizes both influences. A similar melding may be the most realistic and beneficial approach to identify how HRM can be shifted so that it plays an important role in a quality organizational environment.

Table 4.1 presents a listing of philosophical contrasts between traditional HRM and quality-oriented HRM. The contrasts are divided into process and content categories. *Process characteristics* refer to how the HRM function gets accomplished while *content characteristics* refer to what is focused on. The characteristics may be best thought of as extremes on continua. The contrasts make the philosophical distinctions clear but the sets of characteristics are not meant to accurately capture the HRM function in an organization. The process and content characteristics will be briefly

Table 4.1. Contrasts in Content and Process Characteristics.

	Traditional HRM	Quality-Oriented HRM
Process characteristics	Unilateral role	Consulting role
	Centralization	Decentralization
	Pull	Release
	Administrative	Developmental
Content characteristics	Singular	Pluralistic
	Compartmentalized	Holistic
	Worker-oriented	System-oriented
	Performance measures	Satisfaction measures
	Job-based	Person-based

described here, but further details can be found in Cardy and Dobbins (1996).

The process of traditional HRM is essentially described in the table as a top-down and centralized approach. The focus is on pulling people to do a better job and serving the administrative hierarchy in the organization. The process of traditional HRM is internally driven and fits with a traditional hierarchical organizational structure. In contrast, the process of a quality-oriented HRM function is more open and customer oriented, including constituent groups in the design and conduct of HRM functions. The focus of the quality HRM approach is on removing system barriers and on broadening and developing workplace skills so that workers can most effectively meet customer needs. The dynamic and continuous improvement nature of a quality environment means that broad skills, flexibility, and adaptability must be developed for performance to be at an effective level.

The content of traditional HRM is based on the relatively static and hierarchical structure of the traditional organization. Traditional HRM tends to be based on the notion that there is one best way of doing things. This monolithic approach probably comes from the centralized and hierarchical nature of a traditional organizational structure. Likewise, traditional HRM can be quite compartmentalized and specialized in its functions. Since worker characteristics are assumed to be important determinants of performance, the identification and measurement of worker characteristics is a focus of traditional HRM. Performance, as defined and measured within the organization, is a focus of traditional HRM. Finally, traditional HRM is based on the job as the primary level of analysis. Job analyses are done to identify duties and tasks and the characteristics needed to perform in each job.

The content of the quality HRM approach is much more variable, due to the various constituencies the HRM function must be responsive to. Rather than a reductionist approach and numerous job descriptions, a quality approach to HRM takes a more holistic view of the work environment. There are relatively few job descriptions and the team may be the broader unit of analysis. System factors are a focus in the quality HRM approach. The concept of *fit* is important, and the relationship between individual characteristics and the system of the organization is a concern. Customer satisfaction is a primary focus and may be used as the critical measure of performance. Finally, since static jobs may not exist, the quality approach to HRM focuses on the general person characteristics as the primary level of analysis. The dynamic environment means that the breadth of skills of employees and their abilities to adapt may be more important than their ability to perform a particular task at a particular time.

In sum, the quality and traditional HRM approaches sharply and fundamentally conflict. However, the conflict can be resolved by adapting HRM to fit within a quality organizational environment. The quality approach to HRM differs in a number of process and content respects from a traditional HRM approach. The quality HRM approach molds the pure person and system approaches embodied in the traditional HRM and quality approaches, respectively, and recognizes the importance of both factors.

Performance Appraisal

Performance appraisal has been the subject of countless theoretical and empirical research studies, yet remains one of the most disliked tasks in the workplace. This section will begin with a consideration of what performance appraisal is and then examine the quality advocates' admonition to eliminate appraisal. The rational and empirical bases for this advice will then be carefully considered. A model of quality-based appraisal will then be presented.

Definition or Start

Performance appraisal has been described as a process of identifying, observing, measuring, and developing human performance in organizations (Carroll & Schneier, 1982). This definition of appraisal is simple but consideration of its components is instructive. The *identification* component refers to the process of determining what aspects to focus on in the appraisal process. Obviously, these aspects should be performance-related criteria, but many ratees contend that evaluation is often significantly influenced by criteria that are irrelevant to performance. *Observation* means that all performance aspects must be directly and sufficiently observed so that fair and accurate judgments can be made. The *measurement* component of the definition might be considered the heart of appraisal. Somehow what is identified and observed must be evaluated. Unfortunately, raters may not share common standards to determine how good performance is. Idiosyncratic standards cause error and bias in ratings and can be a source of dissatisfaction for ratees. Finally, the *development* component refers to the future-oriented and improvement focus of appraisal. In practice, appraisal often focuses on the past as a way to justify the level of reward or punishment handed out to the ratee. This final component of the definition serves to remind us that the real value of appraisal is in improvement of performance.

The definition given here is much more a prescriptive than a descriptive definition of appraisal. Unfortunately, many of the components are neglected or done poorly in practice. Identification is often done in a unilateral fashion by the HRM department and a rating form is sent out from the "black box" of the department. Raters are often not trained in what should be observed or in evaluation standards. Development is often neglected and left up to the motivation and skills of individual raters. Administrative purposes are often the primary reasons for conducting appraisal. The raters, usually supervisors, need to justify their evaluations to the ratees and deal with frustration, disagreement, and possibly anger. Given this description of a typical appraisal situation, it is little wonder that dissatisfaction with appraisal is common in organizations (Cardy & Dobbins, 1994). Further, it is no surprise that raters dislike the task and often view it as a paper-shuffling bureaucratic exercise rather than a meaningful opportunity for exchange and improvement.

A number of quality advocates have even gone so far as to rec-ommend eliminating the practice of appraisal entirely. Given the state of the appraisal process in many organizations, many peo-ple—raters and ratees alike—would probably welcome the elimi-nation. Deming (1986) and some of his followers (for example, Scholtes, 1995) have been most vocal and explicit about the need to eliminate appraisal. Attacks on the practice of appraisal also come up on Internet list server (for example, HRNet) discussions and continue to be seen in the practitioner literature (for exam-ple, Halachmi, 1993), and, I'm sure, in hallways and lunchrooms of businesses across the globe. There are a number of reasons for dissatisfaction with appraisal that have been offered as part of the logical basis for eliminating appraisal.

Some of the major reasons offered for the elimination of ap-praisal include the assertion that most variance in performance is due to system factors rather than person factors, the observation that appraisal can undermine teamwork and encourage unhealthy interemployee competitiveness, and the belief that appraisal is an unreliable measurement process that leads to the creation of losers, cynics, and wasted human resources. These logical argu-ments have been reviewed by Cardy and Carson (1996), who have also offered a set of counterbalancing reasons from the employer and employee perspective for continuation of the practice of ap-praisal. Exhibit 4.2 summarizes the case for appraisal.

Discussion of each of these points can be found in the article by Cardy and Carson, but the points should largely be self-explanatory. These logical assertions that support the use of appraisal can be end-lessly countered with reasons for the elimination of appraisal. For example, someone who believes that appraisal is hopelessly error-filled and biased is unlikely to be convinced that appraisal should be done because people need feedback in order to improve. Even if the relation between feedback and performance improvement is ac-cepted as valid, appraisal can be rejected as a means for providing this feedback. What is needed to help resolve this issue is an exami-nation of the statistical basis for quality advocates' conclusion that appraisal should be eliminated. That is, why do quality advocates be-lieve that performance ratings are not meaningful?

The fundamental and statistical basis for the rejection of ap-praisal by many quality advocates is embodied in Deming's parable

Exhibit 4.2. Employee and Employer
Reasons for Conducting Appraisal.

Employer Perspective

1. Despite imperfect measurement, individual differences in performance can make a difference.

2. Documentation of performance appraisal and feedback may be needed for legal defense.

3. Appraisal provides a rational basis for constructing a bonus or merit system.

4. Appraisal dimensions and standards can operationalize strategic goals and clarify performance expectations.

5. Providing individual feedback is part of a performance management process.

6. Despite the traditional individual focus, appraisal criteria can include teamwork and teams can be the focus of appraisal.

Employee Perspective

1. Performance feedback is needed and desired.

2. Improvement in performance requires assessment.

3. Fairness requires that differences in performance levels across workers be measured and have an impact on outcomes.

4. Assessment and recognition of performance levels can motivate improved performance.

---

of the red beads (Walton, 1986). Deming devised a demonstration based on pulling beads out of a container and this demonstration was conducted at countless workshops he held.

Participants volunteered to act as workers and scoop out red and white beads from a container. The white beads represented acceptable products or service encounters while red beads represented defects. The volunteers were given goals, told to try harder, offered contingent pay, and generally subjected to traditional Western management practices. Of course, none of these efforts ever had any systematic impact on the numbers of red beads the workers draw from the container. The number of defects produced by the volunteers was determined by the proportion of red beads in the container, not by the effort or skill levels of the volunteer workers.

A major point of the red bead demonstration is that the system is a much more important determinant of performance than are individual workers. Deming contends that workers don't really make defects but are simply handed defects by the system. The ability and effort levels of workers are irrelevant when performance is determined by the system. Deming used the red bead demonstration as an analogy for the workplace and as a basis for creating a control chart. A *control chart* is an SPC tool used to determine if performance is due to stable system factors or to erratic special causes. Figure 4.1 presents a plot of fictitious data that might be generated by six volunteers across four trials of the red bead demonstration.

In Figure 4.1, upper and lower control limits have been calculated and placed on the control chart. The control limits are based on the variance in the observed performance levels, with wider control limits resulting from greater variability. The control limits are set at approximately 3.0 standard deviations above and below mean performance. If all the observed performance levels fall within the boundaries set by the control limits, the situation is said to be *in control*—that is, to be operating normally as a system without interference from its special causes. However, if observations are so erratic that some fall outside the control limit boundaries, the situation is out of control and special causes are in operation. It is only in this situation that individuals might be considered as a special cause. Of course, assuming a fairly stable situation that results in a normal distribution of performance, it is unlikely that performance levels beyond 3.0 standard deviations will be observed.

The red bead demonstration and the application of the control chart led Deming to two major conclusions: most variance in performance is due to system factors, and no meaningful performance differences exist when a performance situation is in control. That is, differences in performance that fall within control chart limits are not reliable and are due to random fluctuations. Thus performance differences within control chart limits cannot indicate systematic individual differences. System factors are obviously important determinants of performance and many organizations have realized tremendous improvements in their bottom lines by improving their systems. However, interpretation and application of the red bead demonstration appears to result in overloading important and systematic variance in performance.

Figure 4.1. The Red Bead Demonstration.

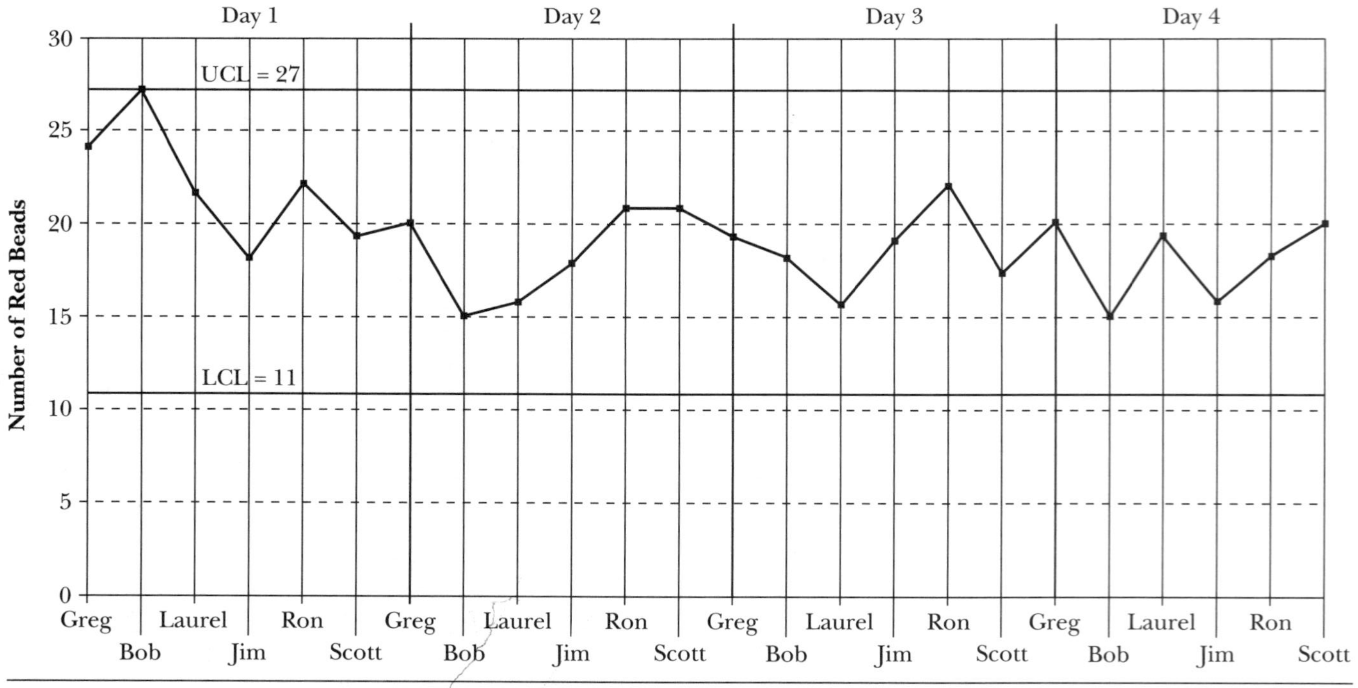

Given the assumptions underlying the red bead scenario, the conclusions that are drawn from it are inescapable and correct. If workers draw beads randomly, they are not responsible for the production of defects and the situation is in control. Any performance variance is due to random fluctuation. However, the red bead scenario may not be an accurate analogy for most workplaces.

There are probably very few workplaces in which individual differences in ability and motivation don't make noticeable impacts on performance. The skills and effort levels people bring to the workplace influence processes and outcomes. People are not interchangeable parts of a process. This truism can probably be most easily seen in the sports domain, where an injury to one player can seriously influence the effectiveness of a team and the outcome of a game. Individual differences in the workplace can also have an important influence on performance in an organization. For example, regardless of their using the same equipment, don't you sometimes notice that some grocery clerks are more efficient than others? Don't we all notice that some salespeople simply seem to care less than others? Of course, the critical issue here is whether these individual differences are really meaningful. Perhaps they exist but, as the control chart logic would indicate, the individual differences are not important unless they fall outside the upper or lower limits. This conclusion is not correct.

Consider another example of a work situation that, while in statistical control, is probably more representative of performance distributions in workplaces than is the red bead scenario. In most workplace situations, some portion of the performance differences among workers is systematic, rather than being entirely willy-nilly. The basis for this characteristic of the performance distribution rests on much more solid ground than subjective perception regarding sports and customer service. Specifically, the huge number of studies that find that scores on selection tests are correlated with job performance are a testament to the fact that there are systematic individual differences in performance. These correlations are usually in the range of .20 to .40, but these relatively small differences can make a tremendous difference over time (for example, Abelson, 1985; Hunter & Hunter, 1984).

Cardy and Carson (1996) directly investigated the potential impact of individual differences in performance using Monte Carlo (that is, computer simulation) methodology. The performance level of a fictitious target employee was set at either .2, .5, or .8 standard deviations above the mean of the work group. These are the values that Cohen (1992) has identified as representing small, medium, and large effect sizes, respectively. Cohen has described a medium effect size as a difference a careful observer could probably detect with the naked eye. A small effect size is difficult to detect, but not trivial, and the large effect is equidistant from the medium effect, but in the opposite direction.

The Monte Carlo study involved the generation of one thousand random observations with restrictions regarding the mean level of performance (either .2, .5, or .8 standard deviations above the average of the work group) and the consistency (standard deviation of performance) of the target employee. If each of the observations of the target employee are taken as representing a week's performance, the thousand observations would represent nearly twenty years of data. The process of generating the thousand observations was repeated 250 times.

An important finding of the study was that for even the highest-performing and most variable target employee only 1.3 percent of the resulting performance levels would exceed the 3.0 upper control limit. With less extreme average performance and lower variance, the likelihood that an above-average target employee's contributions would be noted with a control charting approach goes down substantially. The conclusion here is that higher and consistent performance of a worker would typically be lost in the noise of the variability of the work group's performance.

A critical question is whether the higher performance of employees, such as that depicted by the target employees, is practically significant. That is, even though the performance may rarely, if ever, exceed the control limit boundary, might the above-average performance constitute a contribution of practically meaningful size? Perhaps the most business-relevant and practically meaningful approach to this issue involves estimating the performance contribution of the target employee in dollar terms. A rule of thumb offered by researchers in the area of utility is that an employee who performs a standard deviation above average is worth about 40 percent of his or her salary more to the organization than an average employee (Schmidt, Hunter, Outerbridge, & Trattner, 1986). Let's take as an example an employee who earns $40,000 per year. Given the rule of thumb, a worker at one full standard deviation above average would be worth an additional $16,000 to the employer. For the target employees in the Monte Carlo study, the workers at .2, .5, and .8 standard deviations would be worth an additional $3,200, $8,000, and $12,800, respectively, relative to the average worker. These annual utility estimates can add up to sizable amounts when the effects are accrued across time or workers. Consider, for example, that a group of twenty employees performing .5 standard deviations above average would yield a benefit to the organization of $160,000. Over ten years, the benefit would total over $1.5 million. Of course, these dollar estimates would rise or fall depending upon salary levels, number of employees, and time period.

The computer simulation study makes clear that individual differences of practically important magnitudes can exist within a system that is statistically in control. The existence of reliable individual differences is attested to by the validity of selection techniques. The presence of these individual performance differences in the workplace leads to the conclusion that the quality contention that appraisal should be eliminated is in error. Individual differences may fall well within the boundaries set by control limits, yet be of practical importance. To ignore these performance differences is a disservice to the individual performers and to the organization. Further, not recognizing performance and not providing feedback and other outcomes based on performance levels will lead to less than maximal customer satisfaction, the principal motive force underlying quality efforts.

Expanded Model of Appraisal

As indicated earlier, there is a definite and fundamental conflict (Dobbins, Cardy, & Carson, 1991) between traditional HRM and quality. The HRM discipline has emphasized a main effect for person factors while the quality approach emphasizes a main effect for system factors. It is not that one approach is right and the other wrong. Rather, either approach alone is deficient. For example, we have seen that ignoring individual performance differences, even when all observations are within control chart limits, can overlook systematic and important variance in performance. The red bead demonstration as a basis for not conducting performance appraisal results in deficient measurement. Performance appraisal needs to be moved from person appraisal to an inclusive assessment of all the factors that influence performance. Only in this way can the performance measurement not be deficient.

Content

Upon initial examination, adapting appraisal to a quality environment seems quite straightforward. Essentially, what needs to be done is include in appraisal the initiatives and outcomes that make up the quality program. For example, one quality-oriented organization added quality aspects such as customer satisfaction ratings and adherence to quality principles to its appraisal system. While this approach may signal to workers the importance that the organization is placing on quality, it really doesn't address deficiencies with traditional appraisal and integrate appraisal with the quality context. As we will see, deeper changes to the appraisal system are needed to accomplish the goal of integrating appraisal with a quality environment.

A simple but fundamental change in performance appraisal is to include an assessment of system factors along with the typical assessment of the person who works within that system. The notion here is very simple: both person and system sets of factors need to be considered if a complete assessment leading to a rational approach to performance improvement is to be made. A generic set of system factors has been identified in the limited research on the issue (for example, Peters, O'Connor, & Eulberg, 1985), and the examples that were presented in Exhibit 4.1 are representative of these factors. These factors may all act to facilitate or inhibit performance, although the research focus has tended to be on the inhibition role. Exhibit 4.3 is an example of how these system factors might be presented as part of a rating form. The system factors would be evaluated in addition to whatever person factors are typically examined in the organization. As can be seen in the example rating form, the system factors have been categorized into various dimensions. The reader should be cautioned that this categorization was based simply on a logical consideration, not on an empirical factor analysis.

Exhibit 4.3. Situational Performance Factors.

Indicate for each item the appropriate score from the scale provided.

Very Adequate	More Than Adequate	About Right	Less Than Adequate	Considerably Lacking
1	2	3	4	5

Communication and coordination of work activities

1. Amount and relevance of training received ____

2. Information, instructions, and specifications needed ____
   to do the job

3. Coordination of work activities ____

4. Cooperation, communication, and relations between ____
   coworkers or others

Necessary Equipment

5. Equipment and tools necessary to do the job ____

6. Process for obtaining and retaining raw materials, ____
   parts, supplies, and so on

7. Dependability of equipment ____

Environmental Conditions

8. Conditions in which job is performed ____

Support

9. Availability of financial resources ____

10. Time allowed to produce quantity and quality of ____
    work required

There appears to have been only one attempt in the literature to develop a performance appraisal system that includes system factors (Kane, 1986). Kane's approach, called *performance distributional assessment,* involves numerous judgments concerning the frequency of various aspects of performance and the maximal performance that could have occurred given the operation of situational constraints. The complexity of the system and the number of judgments involved have probably been key factors in preventing the system from becoming widely recognized and applied.

There are some important considerations in regard to the assessment of system factors. First, the list of system factors presented here may be too generic and ambiguous. It would probably be a worthwhile activity to generate specific examples of the system factors that occur in an organization. The generic factors may all be represented with the approach, but in a way that is clear and appropriate to the organization. A process that might be followed for generating organizationally relevant and specific descriptions of system factors is the *critical incident technique* (Flanagan, 1954).This technique is used to generate behaviorally anchored rating scales (BARS) (Bernardin & Beatty, 1984), and it could be used to generate similar incident-anchored system scales. Just as with the development procedure for BARS, the process of generating system incidents may have spin-off benefits (Blood, 1974) such as making system problems clear to management that they may not have been aware of before.

Another important consideration in regard to system factors is that they may not all apply as system issues. In the empowered culture that usually is a key to implementing the quality approach (Cardy & Dobbins, 1996), some of the system factors may meld more into the domain of person factors. For example, in a traditional hierarchical system, the sufficiency of resources and the quality of supplies would likely be concerns that are external to the worker. However, in an empowered environment these same factors may be largely the responsibility of the workers. In this case, it may not be so apparent as to what should be considered person and system factors. The distinctions may require the input of both managers and subordinates (as in the critical incident technique). At a more individual level, it is possible that some of these system factors could be influenced by person characteristics. For example, a ratee who is uncooperative and difficult may complain that others don't cooperate when the problem actually lies within the ratee. While these examples highlight the difficulty that can be encountered in separating person from system factors, the contention in this chapter is that much can be gained by making the attempt to separate the two sources of influence on performance.

In addition to system factors, another important content issue in regard to appraisal is the measurement of person factors. The content of appraisal can be divided into one of three categories:

traits, behaviors, and results (Cardy & Dobbins, 1994). Traits have largely fallen into disfavor since their ambiguous nature may make them difficult to defend if legally challenged (Bernardin & Beatty, 1984). Ratee behaviors are more concrete and specific and are less subject to interpretation than are traits. Thus, behaviorally based appraisal systems are often recommended by appraisal researchers.

Results-based appraisal systems focus on the actual outcomes achieved by rates, with management-by-objectives being an example of this approach. A focus on results seems to be a fair, unbiased, and business-relevant basis for appraisal. However, a number of shortcomings of results-based appraisal have been pointed out (for example, see Cardy & Dobbins, 1994). For example, workers may develop a results-at-any-cost mentality and strive to obtain outcomes in ways that are dysfunctional for the organization. Perhaps the most important drawback to a focus on results is the fact that results are often beyond the control of the worker. Put another way, while objective outcomes may seem to be an appealing way to measure performance, they can be substantially affected by system factors. A simple example is the way the amount of sales by a salesperson may be dramatically affected by economic conditions. Should a responsive and reliable salesperson be reprimanded for a sales downturn that was caused by economic difficulties? This is exactly the type of problem that led Deming to condemn the practice of appraisal. Nonetheless, an organization that received a national award for quality rolled out a results-based appraisal system shortly after receiving the award. Certainly this approach to appraisal seems incompatible with a quality organization. However, a representative of the organization's HRM department defended the new system by arguing that not all parts of a large organization can be integrated. Perhaps integration can be difficult, but ignoring the issue in regard to appraisal and quality can undermine both systems.

Given the basic issue of the potential for both person and system factors to influence performance, it would seem best when attempting to assess the person to employ measures that are most cleanly and directly influenced by person factors and least influenced by system factors. A clean measure of performance due to person factors requires a measure that is least obscured by system factors.

While not a popular option, conceptual analysis of the appraisal content choices reveals that trait measures should most closely reflect person factors and be least influenced by system factors (Cardy, Caranikas-Walker, Sutton, & Wade, 1991). However, as stated previously, trait scales do suffer from ambiguity and questionable legal defensibility. Further, for purpose of performance improvement, appraisal of traits probably has little value as feedback. After all, traits are supposed to be rather stable characteristics of individuals. Negative evaluation on traits may seem an attack on the employee's self and likely evoke defensiveness. Further, it would probably be very difficult to determine how to improve in the trait domain.

A compromise solution is the use of behaviorally based appraisal. Trait inferences are actually summary labels that we give to patterns of behavior. The closeness between trait and behavioral scales can also be seen in the fact that most dimensions are actually traits that happen to be defined with behavioral examples that anchor each point on the scales. Thus traits can easily be rated using behavioral scales. This behavioral approach to assessing person factors should satisfy legal concerns while also limiting the influence of system factors.

The measurement of person factors in quality environments may require change in the dimensions assessed in appraisal. Specifically, the team and empowered nature of quality organizational environments may make interpersonal skills and initiative important aspects of performance. While these aspects of performance may not have been included in traditional appraisal systems, they may be central performance factors in quality environments. For example, oral communication skills, listening skills, and volunteering for projects are just some of the dimensions that may be critical to performance and therefore to appraisal in quality organizational environments.

In sum, the content of appraisal, if it is to provide for complete measurement, should include both person and system assessment. Conducting only a person assessment is deficient for the purpose of understanding all the influences on performance. In addition, the dimensions of the person assessment may be substantially changed in a quality environment. An important remaining issue is the process of appraisal. That is, a quality approach may lead to an expanded model of the content of appraisal—but what are the implications for how appraisal should be done? The following section addresses some of the salient process implications.

Process

Traditionally, appraisal involves once-a-year supervisory subjective judgment (Landy & Farr, 1980). As discussed earlier, an implicit characteristic of appraisal has been its focus on the person and disregard of the situation. The broadened content of appraisal brings with it some substantial and potentially positive changes to the process of appraisal.

Focus on Improvement

Appraisal is often disliked by both raters and ratees (Cardy & Dobbins, 1994). Probably a major reason for this is that appraisal has largely been a process of placing blame. Since appraisal has been focused on the person, the ratee has been presumed guilty of any performance deficiencies. With the more inclusive approach of including both person and system factors, there is the potential for shifting appraisal to a partnership between rater and ratee in an effort to improve performance rather than place blame. Rather than automatically focusing on the worker as the sole source of performance, the stage is set for examining the multiple causes of performance and what can be done about them.

To maximize the development of such a partnership, it is recommended that ratees conduct a self-appraisal using the same person and system dimensions as the rater. The disparity between rater and ratee assessments of system factors, instead of being simply a source of disagreement over evaluation standards, could illuminate areas of difficulty in the work situation that the rater may not have been aware of. The appraisal process can shift to a joint effort in identifying problems in both the person and system categories and in determining action plans. This is an opportunity for a fundamental change in the typical appraisal process that would be a positive and energizing change in an organization. There is potential for real collaboration and meaningful improvement in performance.

A negative potential for the expanded approach to appraisal should also be noted. Specifically, ratees may view a set of system factors on an appraisal form as an opportunity to make excuses for poor performance. A cynical view of the inclusion of system factors in appraisal is that the expanded model legitimizes excuse making. Ratees could take an approach that the best person rating can be obtained by convincing the rater that system factors posed serious constraints on performance. Thus impression management and negotiation skills may become an emphasis in the system. While this is a possible negative outcome, it would seem most likely to occur in an organizational culture marked by politics and low trust. A quality organizational environment emphasizes empowerment and trust of the workers. The expanded model of appraisal should work as a positive tool in such a culture. If low trust is a problem, then any improvement attempts, whether they consist of expanding appraisal or changes in some other domain, can be undermined.

Fit

The fit of employees with organizations has become increasingly recognized as an important consideration in the area of selection (Rynes & Gerhart, 1990). Interestingly, the potential importance of the construct does not seem to have been recognized on the criterion side. Expanding the model of appraisal to include person and system factors brings up the possibility of exploring the issue of how well the worker fits with the work situation. For example, some people may excel in an unstructured and chaotic work situation, while others may require a more structured and orderly environment to perform well. Assessing both person and system factors opens the opportunity to consider the role of person fit with the work situation in determining performance. I am not recommending that fit be included as part of the appraisal of a person's performance. However, the issue of fit should be addressed in a developmental fashion. Specifically, performance difficulties could arise from a mismatch between person and system characteristics. The possibilities for addressing such a mismatch involve changing either the person factors or the system characteristics of the work situation. The exploration and discussion of fit in appraisal review sessions could lead to changes in work situations that help maximize performance by better matching the workers.

Other outcomes might include training so that worker skills better match the work situation, or transferring workers so that better fits are achieved.

Diagnosing Cause

An important and focal change in the appraisal process is the emphasis that would be placed on accurately assessing the causes of performance. An outcome of expanding appraisal to include system factors will be concern with determining the causes of performance. Clearly, a basic distinction that must be made is determining whether an aspect of performance was caused by person or system factors. This distinction sounds simplistic and elementary, yet empirical research indicates that it may be a difficult and error-filled judgment (Cardy, Sutton, Carson, & Dobbins, 1990). Further, attribution theory (for example, Kelley, 1973; Weiner et al., 1972) and the body of empirical work it has produced indicates that differences in causal attributions between ratees and raters are likely common. This actor-observer bias (Jones & Nisbett, 1972) indicates that raters tend to view the worker as the cause of a poor performance episode, whereas the ratee tends to blame situational characteristics. This difference in causal attribution is not directly dealt with in the typical approach to appraisal. However, such differences in causal attributions will be made explicit by rater and ratee assessment of system factors in the expanded approach to appraisal.

Dealing explicitly with causal attributions is important for at least three reasons. First, causal attributions are often the unstated and implicit source of conflict between managers and subordinates. As discussed previously, the actor-observer bias can lead raters and ratees to different conclusions about the causes of performance. These causal attribution differences are probably seldom discussed but are implicitly revealed in the judgments, discussions, and recommendations. A worker may become negative and embittered over supervisory blame for what the worker perceives as difficult work situations. The manager may become frustrated with a difficult worker who doesn't seem to make the commitment needed to do the job. Unfortunately, the manager and subordinate may talk past each other but never directly confront the underlying issue of causal attributions. Causal attributions are often automatic and unconscious (Kelley, 1973) and usually seem to remain an implicit factor. It seems preferable to directly confront the issue of causal attributions, rather than let differences in these attributions simmer as a source of conflict.

A second reason for the importance of addressing causal attributions is that they influence evaluations. For example, poor performance attributed to the worker will likely result in a harsher evaluation of the person while attribution to the situation will likely result in more lenient evaluation of the person. Attribution as to the cause of performance may be a determinant of performance ratings as important as performance itself. It is important that causal attributions be as accurate as possible if performance evaluation and feedback are to be accurate and useful.

Finally, a third reason for the importance of causal attributions is that they drive the choices of remedies for performance problems. Poor performance attributed to the worker would call for actions such as training to correct the ability deficit that is assumed to exist within the person. Similarly, an attribution to the worker may lead to changes in the incentive system so that the worker will be sufficiently motivated to perform. In contrast, an external attribution for performance problems would lead to very different actions. For example, there may be a need to reduce conflicting assignments or to improve tools or materials. The actions may require management intervention. However, in an empowered situation, causal attributions to system factors may lead to a discussion of how the ratee could solve the system difficulty. Whether actions are taken by management, the ratee, or both, the actions would involve the quality-emphasized approach of removing system barriers to performance. Obviously, the attribution of cause for performance determines the action taken to improve performance. Once again, it is important that causal attributions be as accurate as possible so that investments in ineffective remedies can be avoided.

In addition to process, the topic of the source of appraisal should be considered. Judgments can be more or less meaningful and important due to the vantage point of the evaluator. As the old adage goes, "consider the source" before taking the judgment too seriously. In the following section, the topic of the source of appraisal will be briefly considered.

Source

The source of appraisal has traditionally been the worker's immediate supervisor. However, 360-degree appraisal has become increasingly popular in organizations so that self, peer, supervisory, subordinate, and customer sources of appraisal are more common. A limited amount of research has considered the lack of convergence that seems to typify the relationships among these sources (for example, Harris & Schaubroeck, 1988). A consideration of these findings is beyond the scope of this chapter. In regard to source, an important issue for the quality-based approach is to include sources who are most knowledgeable about the person and system factors that influence a worker's performance. Peers may have more observational opportunities and better insight into the operation of system factors than a worker's managers do. Whoever acts as evaluator should have an informed basis for doing so. The cost of adding additional sources of appraisal may not be worth it, particularly if the additional sources have limited observation of the worker.

The customer is a critical source of appraisal from a quality perspective. Customers of the worker, whether internal or external, need to be included in the appraisal process. The standards, or anchors, for assessing performance need to be set with the involvement of customers. Failure to include customers in the vital process of criterion development may mean that workers may be applauded for performance that seems important to their functional area but is irrelevant to the customers of the product or service. Including customers in determining what is important and how it should be valued is an important means for the organization to maximize customer satisfaction.

The involvement of customers with a major metropolitan police force provides an example of how the customer perspective can alter the meaning of performance (D. Brewster, personal communication, January 28, 1997). The police department established a community group to help examine its policies and procedures. This task force of citizens indicated that a ten-minute response time for some calls, such as burglary, was fine. The police force had been trying to achieve a response time of less than five minutes for such calls. The citizen group succeeded in convincing police officials that a case of a missing child calls for immediate and emergency reaction. Up to that point the police department had considered missing children a nonemergency situation until twenty-four hours had passed. The involvement of customers had important influences on the objectives and standards used in the police organization. In addition, the police department was able to perform better and develop a better understanding of the community's performance expectations. The involvement of customers, particularly in the development of criteria, is critical.

In sum, a quality organizational environment calls for changes in the content, process, and sources of appraisal. Exhibit 4.4 presents a summary of the suggestions that have been offered in this chapter. Quality programs are not a one-size-fits-all approach. Thus the appraisal recommendations are fairly generic and may need to be customized and embellished in order to best work in each particular quality environment. The intent of the suggestions is to provide some general direction for maximizing the effectiveness of performance appraisal in quality environments.

Summary and Conclusion

This chapter has contrasted the quality and HRM approaches to appraisal in the workplace. The quality contention that appraisal should be eliminated was examined in detail at the levels of logical rationale and statistical basis. It was concluded that individual differences are important and that performance appraisal is a necessary and important tool. It was recommended that the content of appraisal be expanded to include both person and system factors. It was argued that the inclusion of system factors would make appraisal less deficient. It was further recommended that the process of appraisal emphasize a partnership in performance improvement, a consideration of fit, and clear identification of causal factors. The importance of the customer in the appraisal process was emphasized.

The quality approach is not a fad. Certain labels, such as TQM and process reengineering, may come and go, but the quality emphasis will remain. Organizations will continue to be concerned

Exhibit 4.4. Content, Process, and Source Suggestions.

Content

- Include assessment of both person and system factors.
- Generate specific descriptions of system factors.
- Take a participative approach to distinguishing between person and system factors.
- Take a behavioral approach to measuring person factors.
- At the individual level, recognize that system factors may be influenced by person characteristics.

Process

- Shift appraisal to a partnership focused on improving performance rather than placing blame.
- Explore the possibility that differences between rater and ratee assessments of system factors indicate areas of difficulty in the work situation that the rater may not be aware of.
- Watch out for the tendency of ratees to use system factors as excuses, particularly in a climate with low trust.
- Use both person and system factors to allow for the determination and improvement of person fit with the work situation.
- Deal explicitly with causal attribution so that accurate diagnosis of performance can be made and effective remedies be introduced.

Source

- Include sources who are most knowledgeable about the person and system factors that influence the worker's performance.
- Involve both internal and external customers in setting standards and in assessing performance.

with customer satisfaction and quality processes and will probably continue to use techniques such as empowerment and SPC in their efforts. Performance appraisal is still a vital necessity in the new environment, but it needs to be adapted in important ways so that the practice maximally contributes to the quality effort. It is hoped that this chapter will help in making this transition.

References

Abelson, R. P. (1985). A variance explanation paradox: When a little is a lot. *Psychological Bulletin, 97,* 129–133.

Bernardin, H. J., & Beatty, R. W. (1984). *Performance appraisal: Assessing human behavior at work.* Boston: Kent.

Blood, M. R. (1974). Spin-offs from behavioral expectation scale procedures. *Journal of Applied Psychology, 59,* 513–515.

Cardy, R. L., Caranikas-Walker, F. C., Sutton, C. L., & Wade, K. (1991). Person and system sources of performance variance: Empirical findings. In G. H. Dobbins (Chair), *System approaches to performance appraisal: An alternative paradigm.* Symposium presented at the Annual Conference of the Society for Industrial and Organizational Psychology, Inc., St. Louis.

Cardy, R. L., & Carson, K. P. (1996). Total quality and the abandonment of performance appraisal: Taking a good thing too far? *Journal of Quality Management, 1,* 193–206.

Cardy, R. L., & Dobbins, G. H. (1994). *Performance appraisal: A consideration of alternative perspectives.* Cincinnati: South-Western.

Cardy, R. L., & Dobbins, G. H. (1996). Human resource management in a total quality organizational environment: Shifting from a traditional to a TQHRM approach. *Journal of Quality Management, 1,* 5–20.

Cardy, R. L., Dobbins, G. H., & Carson, K. P. (1995). TQM and HRM: Improving performance appraisal research, theory, and practice. *Canadian Journal of Administrative Sciences, 12,* 106–115.

Cardy, R. L., Sutton, C. L., Carson, K. P., & Dobbins, G. H. (1990). *Degree of responsibility: An empirical examination of person and system effects on performance ratings.* Paper presented at the Annual Academy of Management Meeting, San Francisco.

Carroll, S. J., & Schneier, C. E. (1982). *Performance appraisal and review systems: The identification of measurement, and development of performance in organizations.* Glenview, IL: Scott, Foresman.

Cohen, J. (1988). *Statistical power analysis for the behavioral sciences* (2nd ed.). Hillsdale, NJ: Erlbaum.

Cohen, J. (1992). A power primer. *Psychological Bulletin, 112,* 155–159.

Deci, R. L. (1972). The effects of contingent and non-contingent rewards and controls on intrinsic motivation. *Organizational Behavior and Human Performance, 8,* 217–229.

Deming, W. E. (1986). *Out of the crisis.* Cambridge, MA: MIT Center for Advanced Engineering Study.

Dobbins, G. H., Cardy, R. L., & Carson, K. P. (1991). Examining fundamental assumptions: A contrast of person and system approaches to human resource management. In K. N. Rowland & G. R. Ferris (Eds.), *Research in personnel and human resources management: Vol. 9* (pp. 1–38). Greenwich, CT: JAI Press.

Flanagan, J. C. (1954). The critical incident technique. *Psychological Bulletin, 51,* 327–358.

Gomez-Mejia, L. R., & Balkin, D. B. (1989). Effectiveness of individual and aggregate compensation strategies. *Industrial Relations, 28,* 431–445.

Halachmi, A. (1993). From performance appraisal to performance targeting. *Public Personnel Management, 22,* 323–344.

Harris, M. M., & Schaubroeck, J. (1988). A meta-analysis of self-supervisor, self-peer, and peer-supervisor ratings. *Personnel Psychology, 41,* 43–62.

Hunter, J. E., & Hunter, R. F. (1984). Validity and utility of alternative predictors of job performance. *Psychological Bulletin, 96,* 72–98.

Ishikawa, K. (1985). *What is total quality control? The Japanese way.* Upper Saddle River, NJ: Prentice Hall.

Jones, E. F., & Nisbett, R. E. (1972). The actor and the observer: Divergent perceptions of the causes of behavior. In E. F. Jones, D. Kanouse, H. H. Kelley, R. E. Nisbett, S. Valins, & B. Weiner (Eds.), *Attribution: Perceiving the causes of behavior* (pp. 79–94). Morristown, NJ: General Learning Press.

Juran, J. M. (1989). *Juran on leadership for quality: An executive handbook.* New York: Free Press.

Kane, J. S. (1986). Performance distribution assessment. In R. A. Berk (Ed.), *Performance assessment: Methods and applications* (pp. 237–274). Baltimore: Johns Hopkins University Press.

Kelley, H. H. (1973). The processes of causal attribution. *American Psychologist, 28,* 107–128.

Kenrick, D. T., & Funder, D. C. (1988). Profiting from controversy: Lessons from the person-situation debate. *American Psychologist, 43,* 23–34.

Landy, F. J., & Farr, J. L. (1980). Performance rating. *Psychological Bulletin, 87,* 72–107.

Locke, E. A., Shaw, K. N., Saari, L. M., & Latham, G. P. (1981). Goal setting and task performance: 1969–1980. *Psychological Bulletin, 90,* 125–152.

Peters, L. H., O'Connor, E. J., & Eulberg, J. R. (1985). Situational constraints: Sources, consequences, and future considerations. In K. N. Rowland & G. R. Ferris (Eds.), *Research in personnel and human resources management: Vol. 3* (pp. 79–114). Greenwich, CT: JAI Press.

Rynes, S., & Gerhart, B. (1990). Interviewer assessments of applicant "fit": An exploratory investigation. *Personnel Psychology, 43,* 13–34.

Schmidt, F. L., Hunter, J. E., Outerbridge, A. N., & Trattner, M. H. (1986). The economic impact of job selection methods on size, productivity, and payroll costs of the federal workforce: An empirically based demonstration. *Personnel Psychology, 39,* 1–29.

Scholtes, P. R. (1993, Summer). Total quality or performance appraisal: Choose one. *National Productivity Review,* pp. 349–363.

Scholtes, P. R. (1995, October). Performance appraisal: Obsolete and harmful. *Quality Magazine,* pp. 66–70.

Waldman, D. A., & Gopalakrishnan, M. (1996). Operational, organizational, and human resource factors predictive of customer perceptions of service quality. *Journal of Quality Management, 1,* 91–107.

Walton, M. (1986). *The Deming management method.* New York: Putnam.

Weiner, B., Frieze, I., Kukla, A., Reed, L., Rest, S., & Rosenbaum, R. (1972). Perceiving the causes of success and failure. In E. F. Jones, D. Kanouse, H. H. Kelley, R. E. Nisbett, S. Valins, & B. Weiner (Eds.), *Attribution: Perceiving the causes of behavior* (pp. 95–120). Morristown, NJ: General Learning Press.

CHAPTER 5

Games Raters Play
Politics, Strategies, and Impression Management in Performance Appraisal

Steve W. J. Kozlowski
Georgia T. Chao
Robert F. Morrison

Research designed to improve performance appraisal methods, rating formats, and rater training has been conducted for more than half a century. Organizations use performance appraisal to assess employee strengths and weaknesses, using the information to make decisions about rewards, promotion, and development. The practical importance of these decisions places a premium on the quality of appraisal information. Most of the research has focused on techniques designed to improve the psychometric quality and accuracy of ratings. In the 1980s, research shifted away from techniques to focus on rater cognition, still with the intention of improving judgmental accuracy. For the most part, this work has attempted to improve the quality of ratings by minimizing unintentional rating distortions.

Note: The case study research was supported under a Scientific Services Agreement (Contract No. DAALO3–86-D-0001) issued by Battelle Laboratories for the U.S. Army Research Office to Steve W. J. Kozlowski. The views, opinions, and findings contained in this chapter are those of the authors and should not be construed as an official position of their current or former organizations.

Several observers have noted that the focus on techniques and judgment processes has not yielded results that can be translated into improved performance appraisal systems. Although this concern is not new (for example, McGregor, 1957), a beneficial aspect of the recent debate is that it has focused attention on the organizational context as a critical neglected issue in performance appraisal. Most rating research has been inherently limited in its ability to model contextual factors in organizations that determine whether performance appraisal systems are effective or not (Banks & Murphy, 1985). These contextual factors have less to do with raters' *ability* to make accurate judgments and more to do with their *willingness* to accurately report the judgments they have made. Rather than the traditional focus on measurement reliability and validity (Landy & Farr, 1980), performance appraisal ratings may be regarded as outcomes of a goal-directed motivational process that occurs in a multifaceted organizational context (Cleveland & Murphy, 1992; Murphy & Cleveland, 1991). From this perspective, the organizational context provides a motivational impetus for raters to play political games, distorting their ratings to achieve organizational or personal goals. Moreover, unlike the traditional perspective, there is no assumption that intentional distortions are necessarily negative. Although they may be in some instances, they may also be well-intentioned adaptive responses to contextual demands.

Most theoretical models of the rating process incorporate contextual factors and acknowledge that rater errors may assume intentional as well as unintentional forms. Indeed, it is acknowledged that deliberate rating distortion is more prevalent than unintentional rater error (Bernardin & Villanova, 1986). In contrast to the focus on judgment and measurement accuracy, performance appraisal may be viewed as a discretionary, motivational, and political process that managers use to reward and punish subordinates (Longenecker, Sims, & Gioia, 1987; Longenecker, 1989) and influence organizational decision making (Kozlowski & Morrison, 1990). To the extent that rating politics are prevalent in organizations, a narrow focus on rating accuracy is probably misguided.

There has been relatively little research to explore contextual influences and the variety of creative, intentional reactions that they provoke (Harris, 1994). One of the challenges of researching appraisal politics is that it is difficult to model contextual factors in the laboratory, and difficult to observe politics directly in real appraisal contexts. As a consequence, research has tended to examine narrow conceptualizations of the context, such as appraisal purpose and rater accountability, and limited rater responses, such as rating leniency and accuracy. There has been less research attention to the richer and more complex contextual and political factors operative in organizations that are likely to engender more creative and strategic rating distortions.

How are we to deal with the intuitive certainty that politics are central to performance appraisal and the empirical ambiguity that stems from lack of attention to the phenomenon? We are not as pessimistic about understanding this problem as the limited research noted above might suggest. We believe that there is a solid foundation, from both the rater and ratee perspectives, for extrapolating "lessons learned" to help us understand the politics of performance appraisal.

For the rater perspective, there is reasonable convergence among theories regarding important organizational context and appraisal system factors that promote rater political behavior and rating distortions. Second, there is self-report research on appraisal politics that examines rater perceptions of the process (Longenecker et al., 1987; Longenecker, 1989) and the impetus for politics. And third, there are case studies that incorporate good qualitative descriptions of rater politics and motivating contextual factors (Bjerke, Cleveland, Morrison, & Wilson, 1987), coupled with empirical verification of the rating distortions (Kozlowski & Morrison, 1990). Moreover, critical incidents of appraisal politics that we have drawn from practicing managers corroborate theory, research, and case analyses.

For the ratee perspective, there is research that examines ratee perceptions of appraisal politics (Ashforth & Lee, 1990; Ferris, Frink, Bhawuk, Zhou, & Gilmore, 1996; Ferris et al., 1996; Ferris & King, 1991; Kumar & Ghadially, 1989; Voyer, 1994). Further research addresses ratee efforts to influence the appraisal process and its outcomes (Ashford & Northcraft, 1992; Chatman, Bell, & Staw, 1986; Giacalone, 1985; Kipnis & Schmidt, 1988; Tedeschi & Melburg, 1984; Thacker & Wayne, 1995; Wayne, 1995; Wayne & Kacmar, 1991).

In this chapter, we use this foundation to examine the interaction of the rater, ratee, and organizational system to understand factors that motivate political games with the performance appraisal process. We begin with an overview of appraisal theories, and identify factors that drive political processes. We review the empirical research on intentional rating errors, highlighting its limitations for an examination of rating politics. We next consider qualitative research, using a case analysis to describe and capture rater distortion strategies so as to demonstrate the operation of these political processes in context. Critical incident examples, based on our interactions with managers in the private sector, are used to illustrate concepts and the potential generalizability of these political processes. We then shift perspective to consider ratee efforts to influence the rating process through impression management, and the contribution of this practice to appraisal politics. Finally, we close with observations, implications, and recommendations.

Appraisal Process Theory and Research Theory

Researchers addressing subjective methods of performance appraisal have long recognized that ratings may contain error because of intentional as well as unintentional modifications by the rater (Landy & Farr, 1980; McGregor, 1957). Unintentional biases are generally regarded as a function of the rater's ability to make accurate judgments. They affect the rater's privately held evaluation and have been the province of research focused on the cognitive processes that distort human perception and judgment. In contrast, intentional bias is considered to be a result of the appraisal context operating through motivational factors that influence the rater's willingness to publicly share his or her private evaluation (Mohrman & Lawler, 1983). Although it is unlikely that the processes underlying intentional and unintentional biases are completely distinct (compare Hauenstein, 1992), it is a useful way for framing this basic research problem.

Appraisal Process Theory

Several models of the rating process have identified one or more contextual factors that may promote conscious manipulation of appraisals by raters (for example, De Cotiis & Petit, 1978; Ilgen &

Feldman, 1983; Kane & Lawler, 1979; Landy & Farr, 1980, 1983; Lawler, 1971; Mohrman & Lawler, 1983; Wherry, 1952). In general, these models have tended to focus on features of the *appraisal system* including its administrative policies, purposes, and degree of accountability (Kane & Lawler, 1979; Landy & Farr, 1983). Although given less theoretical and research attention, characteristics of the *organizational system* such as its culture, climate, socialization processes, and reward structure are also likely to play an important role in facilitating intentional distortions (Kozlowski & Morrison, 1990; Murphy & Cleveland, 1991).

Two key characteristics of the appraisal system include its purpose—that is, the consequences of appraisal—and the extent to which the rater is accountable for the ratings. Theory suggests that performance appraisal systems linked to desired outcomes (for example, pay, promotion, or job assignments) are likely to create conditions that motivate a rater to modify ratings (De Cotiis & Petit, 1978; Kane & Lawler, 1979; Landy & Farr, 1983; Lawler, 1971; Mohrman & Lawler, 1983; Wherry, 1952). Comments from managers on both ends of the performance rating process reflect this motivation to modify ratings:

- Earlier in the year, I had approached my manager requesting permission to transfer this particular engineer to another department for career development purposes. The request was refused and the engineer was very unhappy about it. I now rated the engineer a 5 [the top rating] to recognize his contributions, give him a maximum merit increase as partial compensation for stalling his career, and give him visibility for future promotional opportunities. *(Automobile Manufacturer)*

- During lean years, salaries were frozen for the general population of employees. This was not true for a select group, myself included, who were given minor increases. To my dismay, my [current performance] rating fell to the lowest rating I had ever received. The upshot of my complaint [to my manager] and his baseline premise was that while I had in fact performed well and his notes tried to convey this, his hands were to a great degree tied. There were many other employees within his group that had gone without salary increases for quite some time. Thus, in order to ensure harmony and maximize their gain this year, he was rating them higher to make up for their lost compensation over the prior four years. These comments reflect my dismay and the general feelings of frustration I have with the process at hand. *(Automobile Supplier)*

The motivation to modify formal rating procedures is particularly aroused when ratings activate conflicting goals (Kane & Lawler, 1979). For example, an organizational goal of providing accurate ratings so as to identify and promote the best performers will conflict with rater goals to maintain the climate for trust and interpersonal relationships within the workgroup. Accurately reported ratings that indicate imperfect performance can generate ratee defensiveness, especially when rewards are contingent on high ratings. As a result, raters may be reluctant to make distinctions among ratees when they are accountable and must confront the ratee with the evaluation (Kane & Lawler, 1979). Personal confrontation reduces the rater's propensity to make distinctions and increases rating leniency (Creswell, 1963). Mohrman and Lawler (1983) have suggested that raters strive for the best of all possible worlds in such conflicting situations. They attempt to create evaluations that appear favorable to the ratee—and still convey relevant information to the organization's decision makers.

Although previous paragraphs focus on appraisal system features and take an individual-level, motivational perspective, anecdotal reports suggest that intentional appraisal distortions may be commonplace in organizations (McGregor, 1957). Even recent advances in performance appraisal, such as 360-degree feedback, are not immune. As one manager described it:

- Because of the way that people are identified to provide 360-degree input, it is often the case that employees will provide input for some of the same people that will be providing input for them. Knowing this, there is a tendency to stress the positive and to downplay any problems, since the other person could read your comments about him before he writes his about you. *(Consulting Firm)*

If intentional distortions are commonplace, the contextual factors influencing appraisal politics are likely to go beyond features of the appraisal system, implicating organizational culture and climate, norms and values, and socialization processes. That is, there must be organizational mechanisms to rationalize, guide, and communicate intentional strategies. Under such circumstances, intentional distortions of the formal appraisal system may constitute an adaptive response. This broader perspective is rarely considered in performance appraisal research (Kozlowski & Morrison, 1990; Murphy & Cleveland, 1991).

Research Theory

Research addressing the appraisal context and rating distortions has tended to conceptualize both contextual factors and rater responses in relatively limited terms, focusing on appraisal purpose or accountability and rating leniency. For example, the use of appraisal ratings to make personnel decisions has been presumed to be the primary cause of high leniency that is often observed in actual performance appraisals. Indeed, the phenomenon of leniency is well documented in military officer appraisals (Curran, 1983; Pritchard, Peters, & Harris, 1973; Staff, Personnel Research Section, 1946; Sisson, 1948)—so much so that it spurred well-publicized efforts to reduce bias and control rating reports. This was the basis for research on the forced-choice rating format in the 1940s and 1950s by the Air Force (Highland & Berkshire, 1951), Army (Sisson, 1948), and Navy (Morrison & Maher, 1958; Waters & Wherry, 1962) in an effort to reduce leniency. Yet in spite of several format and training interventions, the problem continues to affect officer appraisals. Performance appraisals in business and industry are not immune; they also face significant leniency problems (Murphy & Cleveland, 1991). Similarly, adoption by industry of the format and training interventions developed by the military has also had little effect on reducing leniency (McGregor, 1957).

Research addressing this problem has tended to mirror the observations drawn from the previously described applied research. It has tended to contrast ratings obtained for research or developmental purposes with those obtained for administrative decisions (for example, promotion, salary, and termination), or situations in which the rater is not accountable with situations in which the rater must disclose the ratings to the ratee. Research or developmental ratings and ratings without accountability have typically been found to be less lenient and more accurate (Bernardin, Orban, & Carlyle, 1981; Heron, 1956; McIntyre, Smith, & Hassett, 1984; Meyer, Kay, & French, 1965; Murphy, Balzer, Kellam, & Armstrong, 1984; Sharon, 1970; Sharon & Bartlett, 1969; Taylor & Wherry, 1951; Williams, De Nisi, Blencoe, & Cafferty, 1985; Zedeck & Cascio,

1982). These findings suggest that administrative uses of the information activate a rater's motivation to report more positive information than the rater privately perceives to be appropriate.

A Broader Perspective on Appraisal Politics

Limitations in Appraisal Process Research

Although it is fair to conclude that appraisal purpose affects leniency and rating accuracy (Ilgen, Barnes-Farrell, & McKellin, 1993), it is also worth noting the limitations of this research. First, leniency is a limited conceptualization and operationalization of conscious rater distortions. It examines a simple response aggregated across ratees, and often raters as well. Theory and qualitative reports, however, suggest complex, differential rater responses. Indeed, where leniency is typical, it may prompt raters to use more subtle and creative distortions in an effort to distinguish among ratees who are all highly rated. To be consistent with theory, this argues for research that takes a broader view of appraisal distortions and studies the process at the appropriate level of analysis (for example, see Kozlowski, Kirsch, & Chao, 1986; Kozlowski & Kirsch, 1987). Research should allow different types of rater responses to be distinguished and complex reactions to be examined at the level of the rater.

Second, appraisal system features (purpose and accountability) are a narrow conceptualization of the rating context. With rare exceptions, most applied settings use performance appraisals to make decisions, and ratees often receive feedback or otherwise review their evaluations. We can assume that conflict between organizational and personal goals, and the resulting motivation to distort ratings, is a common occurrence. In effect, the factors most frequently researched lack variability across organizational settings, making other contextual influences more important to examine if we wish to understand factors that are relevant outside the laboratory. Thus, in addition to the appraisal system influences of purpose and accountability, organizational context factors also facilitate rating politics. Factors such as the perceived competitiveness for promotions and job assignments, the way performance appraisal is embedded in the organizational culture, and the presence of socialization mechanisms to acculturate raters to performance appraisal politics arc all potentially important contextual factors that may facilitate rating distortions (Kozlowski & Morrison, 1990; Murphy & Cleveland, 1991).

New Directions

This broader perspective of the appraisal context is not well represented in empirical research, but it is well supported by qualitative research. Qualitative studies have provided rich descriptions of appraisal politics from the perspective of the rater (Bjerke et al., 1987; Longenecker, 1989). Longenecker et al. (1987) reported findings compiled from interviews with sixty executives regarding the politics affecting performance ratings. They defined politics as deliberate rater efforts to balance goals under conflicting constraints. In the words of one of their informants, "There is really no getting around the fact that whenever I evaluate one of my people, I stop and think about the impact—the ramifications of my decisions on my relationship with the guy and his future here. . . . There are a lot of games played in the rating process and whether we admit it or not we are all guilty of playing them at our discretion" (p. 183). The interviews indicated that politics were invariably a part of the appraisal process because ratings affect subsequent interpersonal relations and trust, yield a written record subject to review by the ratee and others, and have a significant impact on ratees' pay and career advancement.

Politics mean modifying ratings to attain desired outcomes, such as helping someone attain a pay increase or promotion, kicking someone else in the pants, or making it clear to others that they have no future in the organization. Although the interviewees indicated that rating inflation was by far the most common distortion, deflation was also used to shock someone back to higher performance, punish a difficult employee, or create documentation of poor performance. A quote from one of Longenecker et al.'s interviewees reflects this perspective, "Accurately describing an employee's performance is really not as important as generating ratings that keep things cooking" (p. 185).

The study also indicated that culture tended to facilitate or inhibit rating distortions. For example, organizations where top executives engaged in and tolerated appraisal games were more likely to create a culture of appraisal politics that promoted rating distortions at lower levels. In contrast, organizations where executive management viewed appraisal as a sincere and serious process, invested effort to train and coach raters, and openly discussed the process were more likely to enact cultures that inhibited game playing in the rating process.

Appraisal Politics: A Case Study

The primary challenge of studying appraisal politics is the difficulty of capturing them in their natural context. Certainly, experience suggests that they occur, and retrospective interviews and survey reports say they occur, but hard evidence has tended to be lacking. Earlier we noted that empirical research on leniency as a rating distortion and techniques to control it were pioneered in the military. Because the military maintains archival ratings and has a highly structured performance appraisal process, it provides a setting in which a naturalistic study of appraisal politics is possible.

We conducted such a study, which to our knowledge is a unique example of objective data on the prevalence and nature of rating distortions in an actual organizational setting (Kozlowski & Morrison, 1990, 1991). The study combined qualitative description of the characteristics of the appraisal context and empirical analyses of appraisal ratings to capture different types of rater distortion strategies. Research identified organizational context factors that were reported to influence rater distortions (Morrison, Martinez, & Townsend, 1984). In addition, interviews (Bjerke et al., 1987) suggested several rating strategies used to balance competing rater goals.

We examined archival data for a sample of raters and ratees drawn from this organization and subject to these contextual influences. The formal organizational policy for performance appraisals provided a structure for establishing objective standards that could be compared with actual rater reporting behavior. Differences between appraisal data and what should have been reported based on organizational policy provided the means to capture intentional appraisal distortions. This approach made it possible to determine whether the contextual influences and rating strategies described in the qualitative research were actually represented in rater behavior. What follows is a description of the contextual factors in the organization and the distortion strategies that raters were expected to use.

The Context Surrounding the Rating Process

Motivating Influences

Curran (1983) has noted that appraisal for military officers is very similar to the process in industry. Raters and ratees tend to be in administrative, managerial, or technical-professional roles. The nature of the work necessitates ratings by a superior as the appraisal method. Moreover, there are a number of contextual influences that motivate raters to play games with the appraisals.

Promotions and future assignments are the most salient organizational rewards in the military (Curran, 1983). The timing of promotion decisions is relatively fixed compared to industry, although industry is also known to use fixed promotion schedules (Van Maanen & Schein, 1979). Officer *cohorts* (that is, officers of the same hierarchical rank and approximate tenure) compete for a limited number of promotion slots at certain windows of their tenure. Individuals who are not promoted on time with their cohort are considered in succeeding years, but the likelihood of promotion is markedly decreased. Those who are not eventually promoted are required to leave the organization. This up-or-out system creates the perception that promotion decisions are highly competitive.

Promotion decisions are made by central review boards using annual performance appraisals (Curran, 1983). Thus performance appraisals are highly salient to officer ratees and members of the boards. Ratings are reviewed by the ratees. Any rating that suggests negative information is considered career threatening (Sisson, 1948). This situation puts inflationary pressures on the ratings (Larson & Rimland, 1984) and produces conflicting goals for the rater.

Competing Rater Goals

Bjerke et al. (1987) have indicated that the rater's primary consideration in this organization is whether the ratee should be promoted to the next career-enhancing position. Therefore, ratings are completed so that ratees who deserve to move upward receive enhanced appraisals. However, raters also have to provide ratings for a significant proportion of ratees who, while not destined for highly desirable assignments, are nevertheless expected to be competent members of the organization. There are also a few low-potential ratees, but this latter group does not represent a problem for the rater or the rating system (Sisson, 1948). Distinguishing the pool of high-potential ratees from the second group without demotivating the latter, however, creates difficulties. The problem for the rater is to satisfy competing goals (Kane & Lawler, 1979)— ratings must distinguish among ratees for distant central review boards, but must also appear to be positive when reviewed by individual ratees.

The Organizational System and Rater Strategies

Bjerke et al. (1987) have described an appraisal culture where distortion strategies are used routinely to enhance or degrade ratings to satisfy competing rater goals. Moreover, they note several informal mechanisms within the organization that facilitate the diffusion of this cultural knowledge, in effect socializing raters by providing the information needed to engage in political strategies. Organizational representatives have reportedly described promotion board decision rules in presentations to organizational units (Holzbach, 1979; Morrison et al., 1984). Other mechanisms include mentoring of junior raters by more senior officers, informal discussion among peers, and materials distributed by assignment officers during training sessions (Bjerke et al., 1987).

Leniency is a persistent problem in most rating systems. When leniency is the norm, as it is in this organization, raters must resort to more complex distortions. The nature of this creative distortion is necessarily dependent on constraints set by the organization, its appraisal system, and the rating instrument. In the present case, the distortion strategies developed around two aspects of the appraisal form known to account for over two-thirds of the variance in promotion decisions (Holzbach, 1979; Morrison et al., 1984): the evaluation-comparison and the early promotion recommendation and ranking.

The evaluation-comparison is designed to provide a standard to help decision makers refine their interpretation of the ratee's overall performance rating. In the comparison procedure, the rater is to indicate the number of peers who receive overall evaluations above, below, or at the same level as the ratee. The peer group is defined by ratees in the same cohort within the rater's unit. This procedure is intended to provide a basis for determining the ratee's relative standing among peers. It also provides an opportunity for raters to modify the comparison aspect to better satisfy their competing goals.

The press for positive ratings makes leniency prevalent. Indeed, nearly all ratees receive the highest possible overall rating. In theory a ratee may have peers rated higher, lower, or at the same level, but in actuality, only the lower or same-level comparisons are relevant because there is nothing higher than the top rating. Moreover, because ratees expect to be rated higher than others in their peer group—the highest rating is "top 1 percent"—in practice only the lower comparison is employed by raters. Thus, the size of the comparison group reportedly rated below the ratee is the primary means of distorting the apparent value of the high overall rating. One strategy is to inflate the number of comparison officers rated below the ratee to enhance the ratee's evaluation. Receiving a high rating relative to a large comparison group is better than a high rating in a small group of reportedly lower-rated peers (Bjerke et al., 1987). The contrasting strategy is to deflate the size of the comparison group to degrade the value of the evaluation, without actually lowering the overall evaluation rating itself.

The early promotion recommendation is subject to parallel forms of distortion. Ratees recommended for early promotion— as most are in this sample—are ranked against their peers at the same hierarchical level who have also been recommended for early promotion. The total number recommended early is also reported to provide a comparison; being ranked near the top among many is better than being ranked high among a few. In addition, multiple ratees may be assigned the same rank order. In combination with the size of the peer-group comparison, subtle distinctions among ratees may be made. For example, all ratees may be ranked very high, but the comparison group for some ratees may be large (enhancing the high rank order), whereas the comparison group for other ratees may be small (degrading the high ranking).

Although some raters may use a single strategy uniformly, especially adept raters apply the various strategies differently across ratees, in an effort to distinguish more clearly among them, help them get promoted, and minimize interpersonal conflict. Thus, a rater may enhance, degrade, and report accurately across different ratees. Because appraisals are reviewed individually, out of context of the rater's set of cohort appraisals, application of these strategies is not obvious.

A hypothetical example may help to clarify the application of these strategies. Assume there are three ratees at the same hierarchical level and tenure in a rater's unit. The rater believes that all three are valuable to the organization, but wishes to make distinctions and maintain good interpersonal relations. In particular, the rater wants to significantly influence the career of ratee 1; aid the career of ratee 2, but not so much; and keep ratee 3 in line for future opportunities. All get the highest overall rating—top 1 percent—and are recommended for early promotion. They all look identical until the rater adjusts the size of the comparison groups. The evaluation-comparison group is reported to be fifteen for ratee 1, seven for ratee 2, and three for ratee 3. The early promotion recommendation and ranking follows a similar logic. Ratee 1 is ranked first of twelve reportedly recommended for early promotion. Ratee 2 is also ranked first, but of only five, while ratee 3 is ranked second of three. In reality, no such lower-rated or ranked peers exist—the rater simply invents phantoms to affect the weight of the comparison and the value of the rating to decision makers. The intent of this complex pattern of distortions would be to single out ratee 1 for a career-enhancing assignment, get ratee 2 promoted without enhancing the career to the same extent, and keep ratee 3 in line for promotion at a later time.

It should be noted that raters are not necessarily comfortable about distorting their ratings (Bjerke et al., 1987). Many raters feel a responsibility to provide appraisals that are as accurate as possible. However, for many others there is a sense that because most other raters use strategies, a good rater has to play politics to protect and enhance the careers of their best subordinates (Longenecker et al., 1987). To the extent that a strategy actually enhances the prospects of the best ratees, it may be interpreted as being in the best interests of the organization. *Indeed, if rating distortions are the norm, a failure to engage in appraisal politics may be maladaptive.*

Research Expectations

Given these motivating influences, rater goals, organizational context, and rater strategies, we anticipated several outcomes in actual rater behavior. First, high leniency as ratees approached their promotion window would create a condition in which more creative distortions were necessary to distinguish among ratees. Second, the factors inherent in the appraisal system context, the numerous and varied sources of knowledge for transmitting distortion strategies, and the competing rater goals suggested that rating modification strategies would be highly prevalent in this organization. And third, the strategies described in the qualitative research should be captured in the actual ratings, empirically substantiating the appraisal culture reported by this population of raters. Moreover, if the proposition that raters are attempting to satisfy competing goals has merit (providing apparently high ratings yet distinguishing among ratees), a substantial proportion of raters should engage in the complex distortion strategy, as it is most clearly relevant to making distinctions among ratees within units.

Research Approach

Rating Data

All performance appraisals reported throughout an officer's career are contained in an archive. Our investigation drew a sample that contained 167 raters, with 138 having two or more ratees and 29 having a single ratee. The 167 raters comprised 84 percent of 198 organizational units that formed the target population. Complete appraisals were available for all 602 ratees in the sample. Ratees had over a decade of service and were generally heads of units that were central to the primary mission of the organization. They were entering a major career transition that included promotion to upper management (Bjerke et al., 1987; Curran, 1983), and the opportunity to be selected for the focal position of their careers.

Appraisal Ratings

Because it is intended to be used for multiple purposes, the appraisal instrument used for officers is unusually comprehensive.

The administration of the system is specified in a detailed manual (NAVMILPERSCOMINST 1611.1, 1982). There is well-defined policy indicating under what circumstances an appraisal is to be completed, who is to render the ratings, and what qualities the performance dimensions are intended to assess. The appraisal instrument incorporates several rating and assessment sections. An evaluation on most of the performance dimensions is reported using one of nine categories: top 1 percent, top 5 percent, top 10 percent, top 30 percent, top 50 percent, bottom 50 percent, bottom 30 percent, marginal, and unsatisfactory. The evaluation for each performance dimension is actually based on ratings of several more specific behavioral indicators made on a separate appraisal worksheet. These specific ratings then guide the evaluation that is reported on the appraisal instrument. In addition to the conventional ratings, the appraisal instrument incorporates the comparative evaluations that were the focus of our effort to capture rater strategies. As we noted previously, our analyses were centered on these components because of their relevance to organizational decisions (Morrison et al., 1984). These rating and comparison evaluations included the overall evaluation-comparison and the early promotion recommendation and ranking. Although the instrument also has provision for a narrative report, we ignored this section to protect confidentiality and because prior research indicated that it was not particularly relevant to the phenomena of interest (Bjerke et al., 1987; Morrison et al., 1984).

Analyses and Findings

Conditions Facilitating Rating Games

Because ratees were approaching a critical promotion and assignment point in their careers, we anticipated that the ratings would be increasingly characterized by leniency. Table 5.1 shows response frequencies, means, and standard deviations for the most recent annual ratings on the twenty specific performance dimensions and overall evaluation for all ratees in the sample. Inspection of Table 5.1 reveals that extreme leniency and variance restriction permeated the ratings. Indeed, four of the ratings showed no variance at all; all officers were rated at the top. Even where some variability appeared, no more than 2.5 percent of the officers received evaluations lower than "top 1 percent."

Table 5.1. Descriptive Statistics for
Most Recent Annual Appraisal.

Performance Dimension	Rating	freq	M	SD
Specific aspects of performance				
Goal setting & achievement	0	591	.120	.151
	1	10		
	2	1		
Subordinate management & development	0	597	.008	.091
	1	2		
Working relations	0	598	.007	.081
	1	4		
Equipment & material management	0	600	.003	.058
	1	2		
Organization support	0	601	.003	.082
	2	1		
Response in stressful situation	0	597	.010	.115
	1	4		
Equal opportunity	0	602	.000	.000
Speaking ability	0	601	.002	.041
	1	1		
Writing ability	0	596	.010	.009
	1	6		
Speciality skills				
Seamanship	0	602	.000	.000
Airmanship	1	4		
	3	1		
Watch standing	0	602	.000	.000
Tactics	0	597	.008	.091
	1	5		
Leadership	0	593	.015	.121
	1	9		
Mission contribution				
Overall evaluation	0	593	.017	.140
	1	8		
	2	1		

Table 5.1. Descriptive Statistics for
Most Recent Annual Appraisal, cont'd.

Performance Dimension	Rating	freq	M	SD
Personal traits				
Judgment	0	593	.020	.181
	1	7		
	2	1		
	3	1		
Imagination	0	596	.010	.099
	1	6		
Analytic ability	0	598	.008	.108
	1	3		
	2	1		
Personal behavior	0	602	.000	.000
	—			
Forcefulness	0	590	.020	.140
	1	12		
Military bearing	0	600	.003	.058
	1	2		

Note: Lower ratings indicate superior performance: 0 = top 1 percent; 1 = top 5 percent; 2 = top 10 percent; 3 = top 20 percent. *Freq* indicates the frequency of endorsement of that rating for the sample of 602 ratees. Thus in excess of 98 percent of the ratees were rated in the top 1 percent. Rater $N = 167$.

We expected that this high degree of leniency would increase as ratees approached the critical promotion point. Figure 5.1 plots the overall evaluation mean and standard deviation over the ratees' tenure to illustrate this phenomenon. In Figure 5.1, the most recent appraisal fell within the promotion time window. Leniency and restriction became more severe as the officers became more senior and their key career window approached. With the exception of allowing the poorest performers to be identified (that is, by assigning any rating less than the maximum), the leniency and range restriction illustrated here rendered most of the conventional appraisal ratings useless (for example, Pritchard et al., 1973; Sisson, 1948).

Figure 5.1. Increases in Rating Leniency and Range Restriction as Ratees Approach Promotion Window.

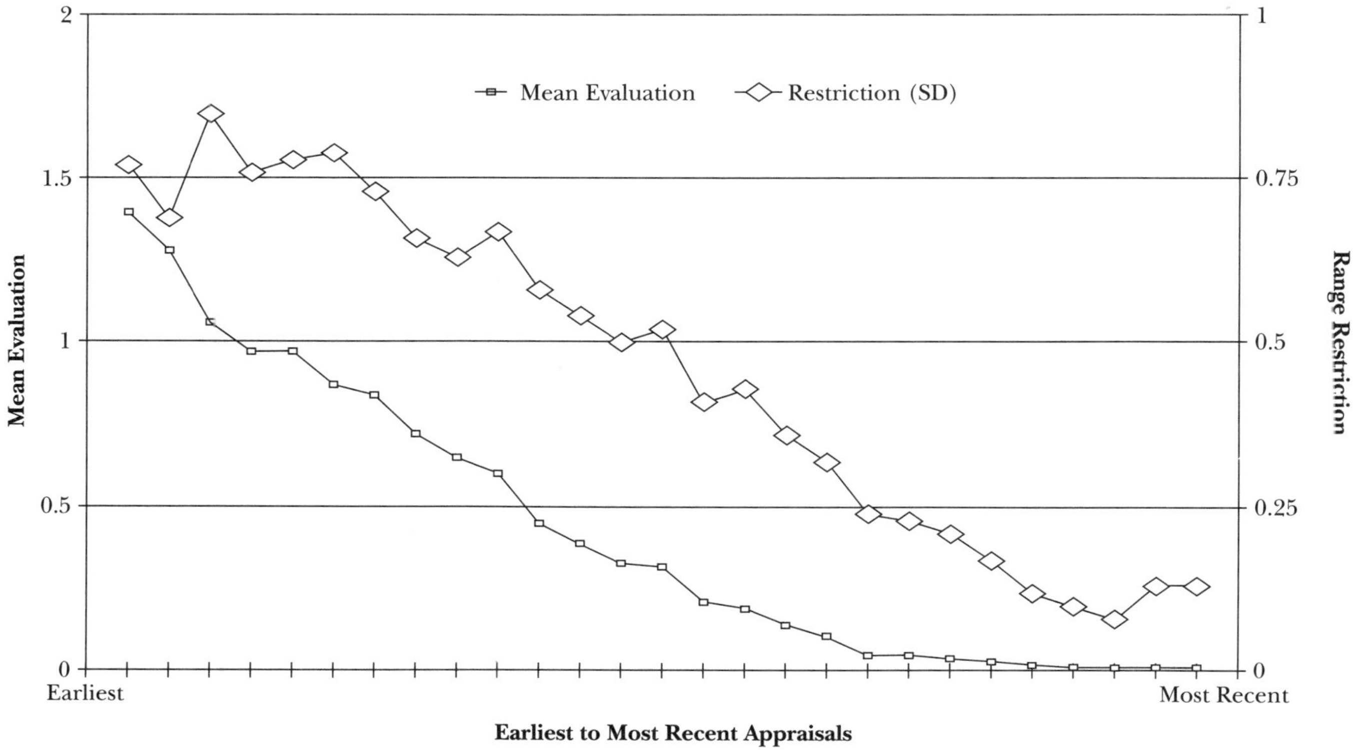

Note: Smaller values indicate greater leniency and restriction.

This excessive leniency created the necessity for raters to employ more complex strategies to distinguish among ratees and to help decision makers identify the most qualified subordinates. Two types of rater strategies, adjusting the comparison group size and altering rank orders, were used to make these distinctions. These strategies were applied to the overall evaluation-comparison and the early promotion ranking-comparison.

Adjusting Comparison Group Size

One set of rater strategies adjusted the size of the comparison groups that were reported in the ratee's evaluation-comparison and promotion-comparison portions of the appraisal. Although in theory, the comparison group could be higher than, equal to, or lower than the ratee, in practice, pressures for high evaluations ensured that the comparison group was limited to individuals reportedly rated below the ratee in question. Four strategies were possible. The first three represent uniform strategies applied by a rater to all ratees; the fourth strategy is any combination of the first three strategies, differentially applied across ratees.

- *Compliance:* A rater could adhere to formal policy. This is the assumed default of appraisal system designers and indicates no political game playing.
- *Inflation:* A rater could inflate the reported size of the comparison group with phantom peers to enhance a ratee's evaluation. Being rated or ranked higher than many of one's peers would raise the apparent evaluation of the target ratee.
- *Deflation:* In contrast, the rater could underreport the number of peers below the ratee. Deflation of the comparison group would degrade a high overall evaluation or ranking.
- *Complex:* Politically savvy raters could employ all the strategies across ratees.

For example, using the complex strategy, a rater might give the same high overall evaluation to two ratees, but overreport the number of peers in the comparison group (that is, those rated below) for the first ratee and underreport the number of ratees in the comparison group for the second ratee. This would have the effect of making the first ratee appear to be the stronger, even though both ratees have the same high rating. The use of complex strategies would imply that raters were attempting to distinguish among the ratees within their units.

Our analytic approach for capturing rater strategies was analogous to policy-capturing, except we classified raters by their distortion strategy as opposed to identifying what information was used to make a judgment. The procedure determined the actual statistics for a unit's ratees from the database and compared the actual statistics to the values reported by raters for each of their ratees. Primary analyses were conducted with the rater as the unit of analysis.

Evaluation-Comparison Distortions

One of the four strategies could be applied to the size of the evaluation-comparison group reported for each ratee. For this rating, the comparison group is supposed to be composed of all ratees at the same hierarchical level in the rater's unit. Percentages for raters using each strategy were computed for the entire sample, as well as for raters with multiple ratees and those with single ratees. Raters with single and multiple ratees were distinguished, because those with just one ratee could not deflate or use complex strategies. This is a consequence of capturing strategies by reference to actual data. If there is truly only one ratee with no cohort, under-reporting nonexistent peers is not logically possible—the rater cannot report less than zero, though it is still possible for the rater to distort by reporting any number greater than zero. The only strategies available for raters with one ratee were inflation through the reporting of phantom peers or compliance through accurate reports. Thus comparisons among the percentages reported for all raters are not meaningful in that raters did not all have equivalent opportunities to select among the strategies.

The multiple-ratee situation allowed raters much more latitude to use the full range of strategies; 18 percent complied, 49 percent inflated, 3 percent deflated, and 30 percent used the complex alternative. In contrast, raters with a single ratee were more likely to inflate (65 percent versus 49 percent) and comply (35 percent versus 18 percent). Overall, 79 percent of the raters distorted in some fashion. Table 5.2 gives the percentages in each category.

**Table 5.2. Distortion Strategies:
Adjusting the Size of the Comparison Group.**

Overall Evaluation Rating—Comparison

| | *Rater Distortion Strategy* | | | |
Rater Sample	*Comply*	*Inflate*	*Deflate*	*Complex*
All raters	21	52	2	25
Raters with one ratee	35	65	NA	NA
Raters with multiple ratees	18	49	3	30

Early Promotion Recommendation and Ranking—Comparison

| | *Rater Distortion Strategy* | | | |
Rater Sample	*Comply*	*Inflate*	*Deflate*	*Complex*
All raters	29	46	3	22
Raters with one ratee	41	59	NA	NA
Raters with multiple ratees	26	43	4	27

Note: Entries represent percentages of the specified rater sample. Rater $N = 167$; n for raters with one ratee was 29; n for raters with multiple ratees was 138. NA = not applicable.

Promotion-Comparison Distortions

When an officer is recommended for early promotion, and most are (89 percent in this sample), the rater is to indicate the number of peers that have also been recommended early along with the rank order of the target ratee. Thus the comparison group here is supposed to be limited to ratees at the same hierarchical level in the rater's unit who have also been recommended for early promotion. The same strategies are applicable to the reported size of the promotion-comparison group, because the number of comparison peers provides a standard against which the target ratee's rank order can be weighted. By manipulating the size of the comparison group, it is possible for a rater to give a high ranking and yet disguise from the ratee the actual value of that ranking to decision makers.

Percentages for the strategies used by the raters are also displayed in Table 5.2. The percentages across the entire sample are not directly comparable, because raters with only one ratee had only two logical alternatives (compliance or inflation). As shown in Table 5.2, raters with single ratees were more likely to comply than were raters with multiple ratees (41 percent versus 26 percent). In addition, raters with single ratees distorted by using inflation at a higher rate than raters with multiple ratees (59 percent versus 43 percent). Complex and deflation alternatives were used by 27 percent and 4 percent, respectively, of the raters with multiple ratees.

Overall, 71 percent of the raters distorted the size of the peer group used in the comparison. The proportion was higher for raters with multiple ratees (74 percent) than for raters with only one ratee (59 percent). This difference undoubtedly reflected the greater opportunity that raters with multiple ratees had to engage in strategic rating behavior. The proportion of raters modifying the size of the peer group used in the ranking comparisons was somewhat lower than the proportion applying the strategy to the evaluation-comparison ratings (71 percent versus 79 percent).

The Complex Strategy

Findings reported to this point have focused on the rater as the unit of analysis. Given that a substantial proportion of the raters used different strategies across ratees within their unit, an examination of ratee-level statistics for this subsample can reveal the probable intent behind the use of complex combinations of strategies. The subsample for this analysis contained only ratees ($n = 176$) whose raters employed complex strategies. For the evaluation-comparison, 42 percent of the ratees had cohort groups that were inflated in size, 35 percent had groups that were deflated, and 23 percent had groups that were in compliance. A similar pattern was revealed for the early promotion comparison group. The complex strategy resulted in inflation for 47 percent, deflation for 31 percent, and compliance for 23 percent of the ratees.

What is most interesting about these results is the much greater use of deflation as an aspect of the complex strategy relative to deflation as a uniformly applied strategy. Deflation as a consistent approach was the least used strategy (as shown in Table 5.2). However, as an aspect of the complex strategy, about one-third of the ratees were deflated. This suggests an attempt by the raters to better distinguish among ratees within the unit, without giving ratings that appeared low when considered in isolation.

Altering the Rank Order

A ranking procedure is predicated on an ordinal scale that sets some specific constraints on the process. If at least one ratee is recommended for early promotion, there should be one ratee with a rank of 1. Similarly, organizational policy dictates that rank-ordering should be contiguous and should correspond to the number of ratees recommended within the unit; there should be no gaps or multiple occurrences of the same ranks. However, in addition to the strategies for manipulating the size of the promotion-comparison group, the rank order of the ratees is subject to other modification strategies. Distinctions among ratees recommended for early promotion are made when multiple ratees are assigned the same rank order or some rank orders are omitted.

The constraints of the organizational policy create a problem when a rater believes that some ratees are good, but not among the very best. From the rater's perspective, no ratee may deserve to be given a rank of 1. Or a rater may have two or more ratees who are equivalent, and one ratee who deserves a somewhat lower appraisal. The rater could give all three ratees a rank of 2. Of the three ratees, two could have their ranks compared with an apparently large cohort, enhancing their ranking. The other ratee could be ranked within a small cohort, degrading somewhat the high rank. Although rating policy and the logic of the ranking procedure does not allow multiple ratees at the same rank order (multi-ranking), a rater may consider this a viable evaluation alternative.

Overall, 29 percent of the raters who recommended at least one person for early promotion ($n = 161$) did not provide any ratee with a rank of 1. Of those raters ($n = 130$) recommending two or more for early promotion, 32 percent gave the same rank order to two or more ratees at least once. The difference between the percentage of multiple rankings found in the data (43 percent) and the percentage of raters using multi-ranking (32 percent) indicates that some raters multi-ranked more than once. The extent to which multiple rankings occurred within different rank orders is as follows: rank 1 (17 percent), rank 2 (10 percent), rank 3 (6 percent), rank 4 (7 percent), rank 5 (1 percent), rank 6 (1 percent), and rank 7

(1 percent). These percentages clearly show that most of the multiple rankings occurred for the highest ranks, although the behavior also extended to the lower rank orders.

Lessons and Implications

One of the most striking findings of this descriptive research is that intentional distortions were highly prevalent in this sample. This finding strongly suggests that such intentional behavior was facilitated by organizational system and appraisal system features. We can speculate about contributing factors. The appraisal system had multiple uses, including development, but was the primary means for allocating highly valued rewards. It had been in place and unchanged for quite some time, allowing creative distortions to develop and become institutionalized. The distortion strategies were widely known and tolerated at the highest levels of the organization. A well-defined culture among raters and socialization mechanisms provided guidance about strategies that could be used to modify rating reports; this provided the means. Moreover, the ratees were approaching a career transition for which the appraisal ratings were critical, and the raters were required to review the evaluations with their subordinate ratees; this provided the motivation. A summary of these factors is shown in Exhibit 5.1.

We believe that the factors outlined in Exhibit 5.1 promote purposeful adaptations of the formal rating process. The impact of these contextual factors was reflected in the increasing leniency and restriction in the ratings as ratees approached the promotion transition; the ratings were uniformly high and were designed to be perceived positively by the ratees. Distinguishing among the highest potential ratees and those who were merely competent required more complex strategies. Thus the distortion strategies captured in this research were probably predicated on distinguishing performance and future potential levels among ratees for decision makers (Morrison et al., 1984). This type of adaptive behavior is consistent with the contention that raters in situations with conflicting goals will attempt to satisfy all contingencies.

Although most of the raters consistently inflated the comparison group, the most interesting raters were those who employed the complex strategy. The analyses indicated that complex-strategy

**Exhibit 5.1. Factors That Promote Appraisal Politics
and Rating Distortion Strategies.**

Appraisal System Factors

- Multiple uses for performance appraisal information
- Direct linkage between performance appraisal and highly desired, competitive organizational rewards
- Rater accountability for the rating to the ratee
- Competing rater goals
- Longevity of the performance appraisal instrument and system
- Systematic high leniency in the ratings
- Lack of surveillance

Organizational System Factors

- Tolerance, acceptance, even complicity in appraisal politics by executive management
- A culture and climate that rationalizes and supports appraisal politics
- Incorporation of distortion strategies into formal decision-making processes
- Multiple organizational (quasi-formal) mechanisms that disseminate distortion strategies to new generations of raters
- Informal socialization processes that transmit cultural folklore to new raters

raters deflated ratees to a much greater degree than raters in general, suggesting that they were attempting to better differentiate among their ratees. They more clearly distinguished some ratees, whose ratings were enhanced, from others, whose ratings were degraded. At the same time, the raters apparently endeavored to keep all the individual ratings positive. This suggests that complex-strategy raters are likely to be well aware of the politics of the appraisal process. They possess well-formed models of how the information is to be used for decision making and what their ratees expect, and make their ratings accordingly.

Given that rating distortions were quite prevalent in this sample, those raters who consistently complied with policy may have inadvertently lowered their ratees' career prospects. If this is the case, raters who failed to use adaptive strategies may have placed their ratees at a significant disadvantage relative to their peers in the tournament for promotion and career-enhancing assignments. When political strategies become part of the cultural norm, compliance with formal appraisal policy may be maladaptive for ratees *and* the organization.

These results suggest that politics typify the appraisal process in this organization. Certainly there are justifiable concerns about the generalizability of results given the nature of the sample. We acknowledge that military organizations have some unique contextual characteristics and appraisal processes that distinguish them from industrial settings. However, we do not believe that this presents a serious problem for the implications we will draw. First, the appraisal context, system characteristics, and problems examined in this study are well documented in each of the military services (for example, Curran, 1983; Egli, 1987; Ginovsky, 1988a, 1988b; Larson & Rimland, 1984; Mize, 1987; Pritchard et al., 1973; Sisson, 1948; Swenson, 1987). Thus, at minimum, the findings ought to generalize to other military contexts, which represent a significant population of organization members. Second, military organizations have been central in applied research on rater distortions providing documentation, format interventions, and training (Sisson, 1948; Bjerke et al., 1987). Many of the findings yielded by this research effort have been replicated in industrial settings (for example, Bernardin et al., 1981; Heron, 1956). Finally, the central implications we draw from these results are not founded on the specific contextual characteristics and rater responses examined in this study.

This last point is critical. The *specific* strategic behaviors captured in this research cannot be reproduced outside of the organization and appraisal context we investigated. From our perspective, however, that is not the issue. Rather, the issue is whether the phenomenon of strategic rating behavior (that is, complex distortions at the rater level, applied to many or most ratees), which is sensitive to the constraints of a particular organizational context and appraisal process, generalizes across situations. We do not believe it is reasonable to assume that aside from our sample all other rating situations will be limited to leniency as the only possible intentional rater response. These distortions may be more difficult to observe in more typical industrial appraisal settings. However, if we search for them, it may be possible to capture comparative processes whereby ratings are adjusted to enhance individual outcomes, particularly at critical career junctures.

The big question that remains is whether such adaptations are functional or maladaptive. Should they be tolerated as an integral aspect of the appraisal process in organizations, or should they be controlled and eliminated? Neither the conventional research nor the qualitative research on performance appraisal considered in this chapter can definitively answer this question. *This type of intentional evaluative strategizing, and its effects, represents an entire class of organizational behavior that remains little explored in the performance appraisal literature.*

Impression Management

In addition to the rater's motivation to distort performance ratings, ratees have the potential to exert influence as well. Clearly, the ability of ratees to distort performance appraisals is indirect, as they are rarely in the position of rendering their own ratings. However, there are several ways in which ratees may influence the rater's judgment by selectively behaving so as to enhance their image in the eyes of the rater. The primary means by which ratees engage in these influence attempts is through manipulation of the impressions they convey. Applied impression management theory and research has grown into a substantial field of study (Giacalone & Rosenfeld, 1991).

Theory

Impression management is generally defined as behaviors individuals use to project a certain self-image or to influence others' perceptions (Wayne & Liden, 1995). Tedeschi and Melburg (1984) describe a variety of impression management behaviors intended to achieve short-term (tactical) or long-term (strategic) goals and behaviors that are proactive (assertive) or reactive (defensive) to a given situation. Within the performance appraisal context, tactical-assertive and strategic-assertive impression management techniques are likely to be used by subordinates to create positive impressions of themselves. A common example, ingratiation, can be demonstrated in a variety of ways including the enhancement of the subordinate's own image, enhancing the supervisor's image, conforming to opinions of others, and doing favors for others. An example of impression management is given by a consulting group manager:

> • Phone calls from customers praising a consultant's performance were rarely received except during the month before appraisals. These phone calls were often instigated by the consultants to highlight their importance. *(Consulting Firm)*

Borrowing from social influence theory, Tedeschi, Schlenker, and Bonoma (1973) have proposed that impression management helps shape perceptions of the person. More recently, Wayne and Liden (1995) have proposed that a subordinate's impression management affected the extent to which the supervisor liked the subordinate and perceived similarities with the subordinate. In turn, supervisor liking and perceived similarity directly influenced ratings of that subordinate's performance. Cognitive information processing was used as a theoretical framework to describe how impression management shapes attributions a rater makes about subordinate performance. These attributions help determine what information is recalled for evaluation purposes. Thus impression management was theorized to have indirect effects on performance evaluations.

Research

Much of the early research in impression management has been conducted by social psychologists who examined student ratings of subordinate performance in laboratory experiments. Studies by Kipnis and Vanderveer (1971) and Fodor (1973, 1974) have yielded mixed results on the relationship between subordinate ingratiating behaviors and supervisory performance ratings. These laboratory studies did not have actual subordinates, but programmed written messages from phantom subordinates to research participants playing the role of supervisor.

More recent laboratory studies have involved face-to-face interactions between research participants playing the role of supervisor and confederates playing the role of subordinate. Wayne and Ferris (1990) found impression management that focused on the supervisor was positively related to performance ratings, but this finding was not replicated in the field. In a similar laboratory study, Wayne and Kacmar (1991) found subordinate ingratiating behaviors significantly inflated performance ratings, regardless of the subordinate's objective performance level.

A field study by Wayne and Ferris (1990) surveyed bank employees and their supervisors. Impression management tactics were grouped into three categories: tactics enhancing job performance, tactics praising or doing favors for the supervisor, and tactics presenting the employee as a nice, polite person. The job and supervisor-focused impression management tactics were found to significantly affect the supervisor's liking for the subordinate, which in turn, affected the supervisor's ratings of the subordinate's performance. Thus, impression management's effect on performance ratings was mediated by the supervisor's liking for the subordinate. These results were replicated in a sample of nurses (Ferris, Judge, Rowland, & Fitzgibbons, 1994). More recently, Wayne and Liden (1995), using a sample of nonfaculty university employees, found that supervisor-focused impression management affected supervisor perceptions of similarity to the subordinate, which in turn affected performance ratings. In other words, both studies indicated that impression management affected supervisor performance ratings, although the mediating variables were different.

Additional field studies have examined relationships between specific impression management tactics and supervisory evaluations. Two studies reported by Kipnis and Schmidt (1988) surveyed workers and supervisors and found that the effectiveness of impression management tactics differed for male and female subordinates. More favorable evaluations were given to men who used reasoning tactics to influence their supervisors (for example, writing detailed plans or providing explanations for requests) whereas women were more successful using ingratiation tactics (for example, acting humble or making the supervisor feel important). Regardless of gender, least favorable evaluations were given to subordinates who used assertive tactics, such as setting time deadlines or making demands to influence the supervisor. Thacker and Wayne (1995) surveyed nonfaculty university employees and, contrary to Kipnis and Schmidt (1988), found no relationship between ingratiation and supervisor ratings of a subordinate's promotability. However, consistent with Kipnis and Schmidt, reasoning tactics of impression management were positively related to promotability and assertiveness tactics were negatively related to promotability.

Results from the research on impression management and performance evaluations has shown mixed support for ingratiation effects on performance ratings. Supervisor-focused ingratiation that is viewed as insincere and purely instrumental may backfire and create negative impressions. As one manager described,

> • I have one employee that starts with the impression management several weeks before review time. It begins with a warm cheerful greeting each morning. As review time draws nearer, the morning greeting is expanded to several times throughout the day. This usually increases to include dropping by the office for a social chat or to review the wonderful progress on a particular project. Unfortunately for this individual, this practice has the effect of detracting from rather than enhancing my impression. I find the office chats to be very annoying and wasteful. I often have to get up and excuse myself just to get this person to leave my office. On the other hand I have used this to my advantage. I know that review time is a good opportunity to make requests for special assignments to this person because I know they will get immediate attention and results. After the review is completed, things return to normal. *(Engineering Firm)*

The extent to which certain impression management tactics influence performance evaluations is based on the interpersonal perceptions that result from interactions between the impression management actor and target audience, within a particular situation. What works for one actor may not work for another. Likewise, responses to impression management efforts may vary widely across target audiences. Thus, any effort by individuals to boost their performance evaluations through impression management must take into account a supervisor's interpretations of the impression management behaviors. In addition, there are several actions that organizations can take to minimize the effects of impression management and to control intentional rater distortions in evaluations. However, much more research is needed in this area to determine the effectiveness of these organizational interventions.

Recommendations

Minimizing Appraisal Politics

Most of the literature focuses on the negative consequences of politics and impression management on performance evaluations. The presumption is that failure to accurately report performance appraisals restricts the usefulness of performance information, leading to suboptimal and invalid administrative decisions. Thus many organizations perpetually seek new ways to minimize appraisal politics and impression management.

Several articles and books list prescriptions for organizational action (Bernardin & Beatty, 1984; Longenecker et al., 1987; Longenecker, 1989; Murphy & Cleveland, 1991; Villanova & Bernardin, 1991).These recommendations address the organizational culture and climate for performance evaluation, the nature and administration of the appraisal system, and training for managers on appraisal and impression management consequences. An important organizational climate feature that minimizes the effects of politics and impression management is top management support for the appraisal system. This support includes top management role models for making fair appraisals, discouragement of political game playing, and managerial evaluations of the performance appraisal skills of lower-level managers. An open system that emphasizes employee development and fosters appraisal discussions under a climate of mutual trust and respect minimizes rater motivations to distort evaluations and also minimizes employees' attempts to embellish their performance records. Finally, a climate that encourages organizational members to challenge the appraisal system itself allows review and potential improvement of the system's goals and procedures by raters and ratees.

Characteristics of the performance evaluation system that minimize political and impression management influences tap all phases of evaluation. Villanova and Bernardin (1991) prescribe eight actions: (1) make sure appraisal criteria are relevant to the job, (2) make sure appraisal criteria are clearly defined, (3) train raters on the appraisal process and sensitize them about impression management, (4) conduct appraisals frequently and allow enough time for managers to appraise subordinates thoroughly,

(5) make sure appraisals are appropriate for individual or team goals, (6) avoid overall evaluations, (7) use more than one rater, and (8) make raters accountable for their evaluations.

Although there is little research to indicate that these suggestions improve evaluations, comments from managers support their use:

- The performance results section of the appraisal was made more objective by insisting that the employee's goals, which are established at the end of the year prior to the appraisal year, be both demonstrable and measurable. This minimized the influence of the supervisor's subjective opinion of the employee's performance and gave the employee the opportunity to rely on documented evidence of his accomplishments to justify a given performance rating. In fact, the employee's goals, which include one or two group goals, are derived directly from the supervisor's own goals, thus making it even more likely that the supervisor ends up looking for true results rather than mere image. *(Automobile Manufacturer)*

- To reduce impression management, employees are not evaluated by an individual superior but rather a group of three to five peers selected by the employee and approved by the manager. *(Automobile Manufacturer)*

- All colleagues rated in the top performance category or in the bottom performance category must be reviewed by the next senior level of management. Managers with direct reports of more than one hundred colleagues are required to rank at least 10 percent in the top category and 5 percent in the poor performance category. *(Drug Company)*

Finally, training issues should cover more than how to use a particular appraisal system. Frank discussions on political manipulations of performance evaluations can educate managers on their short- and long-term consequences. Information on how subordinates may use impression management can also help managers make unbiased evaluations. Formal training programs can reinforce organizational support for the appraisal system. Furthermore, informal training or socialization that reinforces good evaluation practices can maintain a positive climate for evaluation. We have synthesized these suggestions into recommendations shown in Exhibit 5.2.

Implementation of these recommendations involves substantial commitments of managers' time and organizational resources. In addition, some of the recommendations diffuse the evaluation

Exhibit 5.2. Recommendations to Manage Politics and Impression Management in Performance Appraisal.

Minimizing Dysfunctional Politics and Impression Management
That Conflict with Organizational Goals

- Make sure appraisal has a single clear purpose—multiple purposes create potential conflicts.
- Make sure the appraisal criteria are well defined, specific, and relevant to the job—generic measures create more opportunities for distortion.
- Train raters on use of appropriate appraisal processes; sensitize raters to impression management and its effects.
- Use developmental appraisals—they are less prone to politics.
- Use more than one rater and make raters accountable to upper-level review.
- Make sure the culture and climate do not promote, support, or tolerate self-serving rating politics.
- Conduct appraisals under a climate of mutual trust and respect.
- Socialize new employees on a fair appraisal process.
- Build top management support for appraisal system integrity.
- Have top management serve as role models and actively discourage political game playing.
- Have raters and ratees periodically review the appraisal system and its organizational context for factors that may promote politics.

Maximizing Adaptive Politics and Impression Management
That Support Organizational Goals

- Clearly communicate the goals of the appraisal process.
- Create consensus on the goals of the appraisal process so as to align political processes with organizational objectives.
- Make sure that appraisal processes are perceived to be uniform across the organization—perceptions that other units are more lenient or less lenient will energize dysfunctional politics.
- Build an organizational culture and climate that promotes integrity and consistency with organizational goals (for example, identify excellent performers, motivate employees) in the application of impression management and politics.
- Foster a climate of openness to encourage employees to be honest about weaknesses so as to promote self-improvement.

Exhibit 5.2. Recommendations to Manage Politics and Impression Management in Performance Appraisal, cont'd.

- Recognize employee accomplishments that are not self-promoted.
- Socialize raters and ratees on the developmental role of the rating process.
- Consider using a separate rating process for appraisals that are linked to important outcomes.
- Make sure external constraints (such as budget) do not drive the process when appraisals are linked to important outcomes—perceived accuracy and fairness are critical to the integrity of the system.
- Give raters some latitude to identify specific performance objectives and criteria for their ratees.
- Allow raters some flexibility to recognize ratees for value-added contributions that are not well-defined performance criteria.

across a number of appraisers, thus relieving some of the responsibility of the ratee's direct superior. Managers who do not want to give up this power may react negatively. One manager noted potential problems with a new 360-degree feedback system:

- The whole process was received favorably by employees. However . . . as the newness of the process wore off, the president was not sure he liked the process. He found that 360-degree feedback removed much of his discretion from the process. The president also began grumbling that the process was too time intensive to administer and was not worth the effort. *(Software Firm)*

The Adaptive Potential of Appraisal Politics

Recommendations to improve the performance appraisal system need to be considered in terms of their own utility, acceptance by managers, and vulnerability to new political games and impression management tactics. For example, at the time our case study was conducted, other military services plagued by similar forms of appraisal politics had embarked on control programs to make raters accountable. Although each program was somewhat different, they all essentially monitored rater behavior using archival data and held raters accountable for distortions. Three years after our study was conducted, a computer-based rater compliance program was instituted in the sample organization. Anecdotal reports suggest that such programs are effective in controlling distortions that are monitored. Of course, the broader implications of such monitoring are unknown. If the political processes are deeply embedded in the culture and widely viewed as adaptive, strong efforts to suppress them are likely to have unanticipated and undesirable consequences. Indeed, if appraisal politics have developed in an effort to accomplish important organizational goals (that is, identify the best performers) in spite of poorly designed, rigid, or ineffective appraisal systems, efforts to control or eliminate appraisal politics may themselves be maladaptive.

Although the prevailing assumption is that intentionally distorted performance evaluations are undesirable for the organization, positive outcomes may be realized. Political strategies that enhance the identification of excellent performers or motivate employees to improve their performance benefit the organization. When performance appraisal politics become deeply ingrained in the culture, are consistent with organizational goals, and contribute to effectiveness, one has to consider them adaptive. In addition, creative, innovative, or iconoclastic employees who do not conform to conventional performance standards may make value-added contributions to the organization that deserve recognition. Appraisal politics may provide a means to accomplish this. Likewise, impression management theory submits that individuals may engage in these behaviors to ensure that accurate images are communicated—not all impression management is deceptive. Thus, not all impression management should be discounted. The big dilemma is identifying when appraisal politics are adaptive and when they are dysfunctional.

We believe that this dilemma is a consequence of the differences between the way organizations use performance appraisal as a control system, and the assumptions human resource (HR) professionals make about the function of appraisal systems. From an HR perspective, appraisal is viewed as a motivational and developmental tool. Individual strengths and weaknesses are identified through appraisal, and development allows the individual to improve. With skill development, superior merit is rewarded with desired outcomes, including pay and promotion. This perspective, however, assumes an open system; one in which a sufficient pool of rewards is always available to reward superior performance.

In reality, the process is typically tightly constrained. Organizations often link performance-based merit awards to their budgeting process. Although this is clearly reasonable from a cost control perspective, it distorts the appraisal process. The pool for merit awards is established in advance of actual appraisals to conform to budget projections. Months later, when managers rate their subordinates, they already have a merit pay target. Should we be surprised that the amount of merit pay, and therefore the performance ratings that justify its award, tend to be right on target? Raters manage the rating process to hit their budgets. Although, in theory, a manager can request an exception to increase the merit pool, in reality the negative impression this may convey for the rater makes this rare. In fact, the way that many appraisal systems operate make them inconsistent with the motivational and developmental assumptions of appraisal. Hence there are appraisal politics ploys that manage ratings to fit the budget and appraisal politics to get around those constraints to reward superior performers and maintain motivation in spite of the appraisal system.

In our view, appraisal politics are likely to be prevalent in all organizations. They comprise the same types of organizational behavior that emerge around all important and salient features. They have the potential to be negative and harmful, but that is probably determined by the organization's climate and culture. If appraisal politics are maladaptive, other dysfunctional behaviors are likely to be present as well. We think that appraisal politics will more often be driven by appraisal system constraints and well-intended efforts to get around those constraints to recognize superior performers and maintain motivation. Hence, in applied contexts, appraisal accuracy in a traditional psychometric sense may have no real meaning. In the case study, it is likely that rating distortions *enhanced* the quality of decision making with respect to the important organizational goal of promoting the best candidates. We offer some recommendations to enhance the effectiveness of appraisal politics in Exhibit 5.2. Of course, this perspective is speculative. There has been very little research on the effects of appraisal politics, and until organizations and HR practitioners focus attention on this phenomenon, we will not be able to generate more definitive answers.

Summary

The potential effects of the appraisal context on intentional rater behavior has been acknowledged for half a century (McGregor, 1957; Sisson, 1948). Rater distortions of employee appraisals and employee attempts to embellish apparent performance are facts of organizational life that can never be completely eliminated. Yet performance appraisal research has generally neglected this important source of variance (Banks & Murphy, 1985). The primary contributions of this chapter are to stretch and empirically ground conceptualizations of the appraisal context and strategic rating behavior, to demonstrate the potential pervasiveness of this activity, and to suggest its potential adaptiveness given the organizational context. We argue for the value of combining the functional perspective of performance appraisal rating process models with expanded conceptualization of the context drawn from organizational theory. Many complex forms of intentional and adaptive rater behavior and ratee impression management have remained little explored because our perspective as a field has been somewhat narrow. Efforts to improve the applied value of appraisals must address this neglected phenomenon.

References
Ashford, S. J., & Northcraft, G. B. (1992). Conveying more (or less) than we realize: The role of impression-management in feedback-seeking. *Organizational Behavior and Human Decision Processes, 53,* 310–334.
Ashforth, B. E., & Lee, R. T. (1990). Defensive behavior in organizations: A preliminary model. *Human Relations, 7,* 621–648.
Banks, C. G., & Murphy, K. R. (1985). Toward narrowing the research-practice gap in performance appraisal. *Personnel Psychology, 38,* 335–345.
Bernardin, H. J., & Beatty, R. W. (1984). *Performance appraisal: Assessing human behavior at work.* Boston: Kent.
Bernardin, H. J., Orban, J. A., & Carlyle, J. J. (1981). Performance ratings as a function of trust in appraisal, purpose for appraisal, and rater individual differences. *Proceedings of the Academy of Management,* pp. 311–315.

Bernardin, H. J., & Villanova, P. J. (1986). Performance appraisal. In E. A. Locke (Ed.), *Generalizing from laboratory to field settings* (pp. 43–62). San Francisco: New Lexington Press.

Bjerke, D. G., Cleveland, J. N., Morrison, R. F., & Wilson, W. C. (1987). *Officer fitness report evaluation study* (NPRDC TR 88–4). San Diego, CA: Navy Personnel Research and Development Center.

Chatman, J. A., Bell, N. E., & Staw, B. M. (1986). The managed thought: The role of self-justification and impression management in organizational settings. In H. P. Sims and D. A. Gioia (Eds.), *The thinking organization: Dynamics of organizational social cognition* (pp. 191–214). San Francisco: Jossey-Bass.

Cleveland, J. N., & Murphy, K. R. (1992). Analyzing performance appraisal as goal-directed behavior. *Research in Personnel and Human Resources Management, 10,* 121–185.

Creswell, M. B. (1963). Effects of confidentiality on performance ratings of professional health care personnel. *Personnel Psychology, 16,* 385–393.

Curran, C. R. (1983). Comments on Vineberg and Joyner. In F. J. Landy, S. Zedeck, & J. N. Cleveland (Eds.), *Performance measurement and theory* (pp. 251–256). Hillsdale, NJ: Erlbaum.

De Cotiis, T., & Petit, A. (1978). The performance appraisal process: A model and some testable propositions. *Academy of Management Review, 3,* 635–646.

Egli, D. S. (1987). I'm counting on you. *Proceedings, 113*(9), 121–123.

Ferris, G. R., Frink, D. D., Bhawuk, D. P. S., Zhou, J., & Gilmore, D. C. (1996). Reactions of diverse groups to politics in the workplace. *Journal of Management, 22*(1), 23–44.

Ferris, G. R., Frink, D. D., Galang, M. C., Zhou, J., Kacmar, K. M., & Howard, J. L. (1996). Perceptions of organizational politics: Prediction, stress-related implications, and outcomes. *Human Relations, 49*(2), 233–265.

Ferris, G. R., Judge, T. A., Rowland, K. M., & Fitzgibbons, D. E. (1994). Subordinate influence and the performance evaluation process: Test of a model. *Organizational Behavior and Human Decision Processes, 58,* 101–135.

Ferris, G. R., & King, T. R. (1991). Politics in human resources decisions: A walk on the dark side. *Organization Dynamics, 20*(2), 59–71.

Fodor, E. M. (1973). Disparagement by a subordinate, ingratiation, and the use of power. *Journal of Psychology, 84,* 181–186.

Fodor, E. M. (1974). Disparagement by a subordinate as an influence on the use of power. *Journal of Applied Psychology, 59,* 652–655.

Giacalone, R. A. (1985). On slipping when you thought you had put your best foot forward: Self-promotion, self-destruction, and entitlements. *Group and Organization Studies, 10*(1), 61–80.

Giacalone, R. A., & Rosenfeld, P. (1991). *Applied impression management.* Thousand Oaks, CA: Sage.

Ginovsky, J. (1988a, July 25). AF takes offensive against rating inflation. *Air Force Times,* pp. 12–13.

Ginovsky, J. (1988b, July 25). Inflation plagues Army and Navy officers, too. *Air Force Times,* p. 13.

Harris, M. M. (1994). Rater motivation in the performance appraisal context: A theoretical framework. *Journal of Management, 20*(4), 737–756.

Hauenstein, N. M. A. (1992). An information processing approach to leniency in performance judgments. *Journal of Applied Psychology, 77,* 485–493.

Heron, A. (1956). The effects of real-life motivation on questionnaire response. *Journal of Applied Psychology, 40,* 65–68.

Highland, R. W., & Berkshire, J. R. (1951). *A methodological study of forced-choice performance rating* (Research Bulletin 51–9). San Antonio, TX: Human Resources Research Center, Lackland Air Force Base.

Holzbach, R. L. (1979). *Surface warfare junior officer retention. Problem diagnosis and a strategy for action* (NPRDC TR 79–29). San Diego, CA: Navy Personnel Research and Development Center.

Ilgen, D. R., Barnes-Farrell, J. L., & McKellin, D. B. (1993). Performance appraisal process research in the 1980s: What has it contributed to appraisals in use? *Organizational Behavior and Human Decision Processes, 54,* 321–368.

Ilgen, D. R., & Feldman, J. M. (1983). Performance appraisal: A process focus. *Research in Organizational Behavior, 5,* 141–197.

Kane, J. S., & Lawler, E. E., III. (1979). Performance appraisal effectiveness: Its assessment and determinants. In B. M. Staw (Ed.), *Research in organizational behavior: Vol. 1* (pp. 425–478). Greenwich, CT: JAI Press.

Kipnis, D., & Schmidt, S. M. (1988). Upward-influence styles: Relationship with performance evaluations, salary, and stress. *Administrative Science Quarterly, 33,* 528–542.

Kipnis, D., & Vanderveer, R. (1971). Ingratiation and the use of power. *Journal of Personality and Social Psychology, 17,* 280–286.

Kozlowski, S. W. J., & Kirsch, M. P. (1987). The Systematic Distortion Hypothesis, halo, and accuracy: An individual-level analysis. *Journal of Applied Psychology, 72,* 252–261.

Kozlowski, S. W. J., Kirsch, M. P., & Chao, G. T. (1986). Job knowledge, ratee familiarity, conceptual similarity, and halo error: An exploration. *Journal of Applied Psychology, 71,* 45–49.

Kozlowski, S. W. J., & Morrison, R. F. (1990, April). Games raters play: Mapping intentional distortions in the rating process. In J. N. Cleveland & B. R. Nathan (Chairs), *The purpose and politics of performance appraisal: Goals of appraisal constituents.* Symposium conducted at the 5th Annual Conference of the Society for Industrial and Organizational Psychology, Miami, FL.

Kozlowski, S. W. J., & Morrison, R. F. (1991). *Officer career development: Mapping rater strategies in officer fitness report ratings* (Report No. TR–91–2). San Diego, CA: Navy Personnel Research and Development Center.

Kumar, P., & Ghadially, R. (1989). Organizational politics and its effects on members of organizations. *Human Relations, 42*(4), 305–314.

Landy, F. J., & Farr, J. L. (1980). Performance rating. *Psychological Bulletin, 87,* 72–107.

Landy, F. J., & Farr, J. L. (1983). *The measurement of work performance: Methods, theory, and applications.* Orlando, FL: Academic Press.

Larson, G. E., & Rimland, B. (1984). *Officer performance evaluation systems: Lessons learned from experience.* San Diego, CA: Navy Personnel Research and Development Center.

Lawler, E. E., III. (1971). *Pay and organizational effectiveness: A psychological view.* New York: McGraw-Hill.

Longenecker, C. O. (1989). Truth or consequences: Politics and performance appraisals. *Business Horizons,* pp. 76–82.

Longenecker, C. O., Sims, H. P., & Gioia, D. A. (1987). Behind the mask: The politics of employee appraisal. *Academy of Management Executive, 1,* 183–193.

McGregor, D. (1957). An uneasy look at performance appraisal. *Harvard Business Review, 35*(3), 89–94.

McIntyre, R. M., Smith, D. E., & Hassett, C. E. (1984). Accuracy of performance ratings as affected by rater training and perceived purpose of rating. *Journal of Applied Psychology, 69,* 147–156.

Meyer, H. H., Kay, E., & French, J. R. P. (1965). Split roles in performance appraisal. *Harvard Business Review, 43,* 123–129.

Mize, D. M. (1987). The answer is at hand. *Proceedings, 113*(11), 127–131.

Mohrman, A. M., Jr., & Lawler, E. E., III. (1983). Motivation and performance appraisal behavior. In F. J. Landy, S. Zedeck, & J. N. Cleveland (Eds.), *Performance measurement and theory* (pp. 173–189). Hillsdale, NJ: Erlbaum.

Morrison, R. F., & Maher, H. (1958). Matching indices for use in forced-choice scale construction. *Journal of Applied Psychology, 42,* 399–403.

Morrison, R. F., Martinez, C., & Townsend, W. F. (1984). *Officer career development: Description of aviation assignment decisions in the antisubmarine warfare patrol community.* San Diego, CA: Navy Personnel Research and Development Center.

Murphy, K. R., Balzer, W. K., Kellam, K., & Armstrong, J. (1984). Effects of purpose of rating on accuracy in observing teacher behavior and evaluating teacher performance. *Journal of Applied Psychology, 76,* 45–54.

Murphy, K. R., & Cleveland, J. N. (1991). *Performance appraisal: An organizational perspective.* Needham Heights, MA: Allyn & Bacon.

NAVMILPERSCOMINST 1611. 1 (1982). *Detailed instructions and guidance for completion and submission of reports on the fitness of officers.* Washington, DC: Department of the Navy.

Pritchard, R. D., Peters, L. H., & Harris, A. (1973). *The effects of confidentiality on the distribution of naval performance appraisals* (Tech. Rep. No. 1). West Lafayette, IN: Department of Psychological Science, Purdue University.

Sharon, A. T. (1970). Eliminating bias from student rating of college instructors. *Journal of Applied Psychology, 54,* 278–281.

Sharon, A. T., & Bartlett, C. J. (1969). Effect of instructional conditions in producing leniency on two types of rating scales. *Personnel Psychology, 22,* 251–263.

Sisson, E. D. (1948). Forced choice: The new Army rating. *Personnel Psychology, 1,* 365–381.

Staff, Personnel Research Section. (1946). The forced-choice technique and rating scales. *American Psychologist, 1,* 267.

Swenson, C. C., Jr. (1987). Where do you really stand? *Proceedings, 113*(8), 112–113.

Taylor, E., & Wherry, R. J., Jr. (1951). A study of leniency of two rating systems. *Personnel Psychology, 4,* 39–47.

Tedeschi, J. T., & Melburg, V. (1984). Impression management and influence in the organization. *Research in the Sociology of Organizations, 3,* 31–58.

Tedeschi, J. T., Schlenker, B. V., & Bonoma, T. V. (1973). *Conflict, power, and games.* Hawthorne, NY: Aldine de Gruyter.

Thacker, R. A., & Wayne, S. J. (1995). An examination of the relationship between upward influence tactics and assessments of promotability. *Journal of Management, 21*(4), 739–756.

Van Maanen, J., & Schein, E. H. (1979). Toward a theory of organizational socialization. *Research in Organizational Behavior, 1,* 209–264.

Villanova, P., & Bernardin, H. J. (1991). Performance appraisal: The means, motive, and opportunity to manage impressions. In R. A. Giacalone & P. Rosenfeld (Eds.), *Applied impression management: How image-making affects managerial decisions* (pp. 81–96). Thousand Oaks, CA: Sage.

Voyer, J. J. (1994). Coercive organizational politics and organizational outcomes: An interpretive study. *Organization Science, 5*(1), 72–85.

Waters, L. K., & Wherry, R. J., Jr. (1962). The effect of intent to bias on forced-choice indices. *Personnel Psychology, 15,* 207–214.

Wayne, S. J. (1995). Coworkers' response to others' ingratiation attempts. *Journal of Managerial Issues, 7*(3), 277–289.

Wayne, S. J., & Ferris, G. R. (1990). Influence tactics, affect, and exchange quality in supervisor-subordinate interactions: A laboratory experiment and field study. *Journal of Applied Psychology, 75,* 487–499.

Wayne, S. J., & Kacmar, K. M. (1991). The effects of impression management on the performance appraisal process. *Organizational Behavior and Human Decision Processes, 48,* 70–88.

Wayne, S. J., & Liden, R. C. (1995). Effects of impression management on performance ratings: A longitudinal study. *Academy of Management Journal, 38,* 232–260.

Wherry, R. J., Jr. (1952). *The control of bias in rating: A theory of rating.* (Personnel Research Board Report 922). Washington, DC: Department of the Army.

Williams, K. J., De Nisi, A. S., Blencoe, A. G., & Cafferty, T. P. (1985). The role of appraisal purpose: Effects of purpose on information acquisition and utilization. *Organizational Behavior and Human Performance, 35,* 314–339.

Zedeck, S., & Cascio, W. F. (1982). Performance appraisal decisions as a function of rater training and purpose of the appraisal. *Journal of Applied Psychology, 7,* 752–758.

PART 2

Methods of Appraising Performance

CHAPTER 6

Creating Performance Management Systems That Promote Perceptions of Fairness

Stephen W. Gilliland
Jay C. Langdon

Jill Carington had been a manager at Suntronics for the past twelve years and was really getting fed up with the management fads that Human Resources kept thrusting upon her. The latest was the most ludicrous yet. Instead of doing its job, HR was "decentralizing" and "empowering" department managers to create their own performance appraisal forms and develop their own performance management process. In the words of HR, "This will allow each department to match its performance management strategy to its strategic business goals." Jill suspected it was simply a way to get everyone else to do HR's job.

HR had suggested that each department form a performance management committee to spearhead the development process. *We already have enough people tied up in management committees,* Jill thought. *If I form yet another committee and assign it the task of developing a new "performance management strategy," who will be left to actually do some work?* Instead of forming a committee, Jill called a friend of hers who worked with the county and asked him to fax her a copy of the performance appraisal form used in his department. She looked it over and was impressed with its simplicity: Job Knowledge, Initiative, Quality, Quantity, and Attendance were the performance dimensions and the entire form was a single page. Jill had her secretary copy the form onto department stationery. *That should keep HR off my back,* thought Jill, as she turned her attention to the real problems that faced her department.

When performance feedback time came at the end of the year, Jill pulled her new performance appraisal form out and began the task of reviewing the twenty-two employees in her department. *Good thing I opted for a single-page form,* she thought as she began the task, *otherwise this would have taken forever.* As she thought about the performance of her employees, however, she realized that she had not worked directly with many of them and really did not know how they were doing. She could go talk with some of the workgroup leaders, but the deadline for getting signed performance appraisal forms to HR was rapidly approaching, so she would simply do the job herself based on what she knew. She had had some trouble with a couple of employees coming in late and missing deadlines, so gave each of them "Unsatisfactory" ratings on the Initiative and Attendance dimensions. She then thought about which employees deserved the biggest annual bonuses and gave each of them "Outstanding" ratings on all dimensions. She rated the rest of the employees of her department "Satisfactory" or "Good," depending on what she remembered about them. *That should do it for another year,* she thought as she finished off the stack of evaluations.

To provide the mandatory annual performance feedback (which she felt was a waste of time since they all knew if they were doing well or poorly), Jill scheduled a fifteen-minute meeting with each employee. In these meetings, she told the employees that they would receive their annual bonus with their next paycheck and then had them sign the performance appraisal form. She told them not to worry about the ratings since the performance appraisals were just a formality that HR required. In the weeks following the feedback sessions, Jill noticed that attitudes among her employees were noticeably worse. The two employees that received "Unsatisfactory" evaluations would barely look at her. A number of those employees that had received "Satisfactory" or even "Good" also seemed to be upset. Two had put in for transfers to other departments. Jill shook her head and wondered how she would solve this latest problem that HR had created.

This opening case demonstrates a performance management system with many problems. Although extreme in its entirety, all aspects of this case were drawn from actual organizational experiences. It exemplifies how a system that is designed to appraise, reward, motivate, and develop can actually have the opposite effect and create frustration and resentment on the part of both the managers that have to use it and the employees that are appraised by it. Evidence of these problems can be seen in the popular press with articles that question whether performance evaluations ever work (for example, Mathews, 1994). In the current chapter we focus on employees' or appraisees' perceptions of the performance management process and generate recommendations on how organizations can develop performance management systems that promote perceptions of fairness.

Perceptions of fairness are central reactions to many organizational decision-making procedures, including staffing, compensation, discipline, and layoffs (Folger & Greenberg, 1985; Cropanzano & Greenberg, 1997). Fairness refers to the extent to which procedures and outcomes are seen as just, consistent, or appropriate. Generally, research indicates that perceptions of fairness arise from evaluations of the outcomes received (outcome fairness), the procedures used to determine those outcomes (procedural fairness), and the way in which the decision-making procedures were implemented and explained (interpersonal fairness). For example, with performance appraisals, fairness perceptions arise from evaluations of the ratings received and rewards tied to those ratings, the appropriateness and consistency of the appraisal process, and the explanations and feedback that accompany the communication of performance ratings.

The importance of considering perceptions of fairness can be demonstrated by examining how fairness perceptions influence important attitudes and behaviors. Research has demonstrated that fair treatment can lead to increased trust in supervisors, commitment to the organization, and job satisfaction (Cropanzano & Greenberg, 1997). Extra-role helping behaviors (such as assisting coworkers) and increased job performance can also result from fair treatment in organizational decisions (Moorman, 1991; Konovsky & Cropanzano, 1991). In addition, fair treatment can decrease the likelihood that employees will file formal grievances or leave the organization (Klaas, 1989; Greenberg, 1990). On the other hand, unfair treatment can lead to adverse behaviors such as sabotage and theft. For example, Greenberg compared two plants that were forced to implement a temporary pay cut and found that shrinkage due to theft was much higher in the plant where workers were given a limited explanation for the pay cut than in the plant where workers were given an elaborate and caring explanation regarding the need for a pay cut. Providing this information with interpersonal sensitivity during the implementation of the pay cut had a significant impact on theft behavior. Similarly, in layoff situations, considerable research has demonstrated that fair treatment leads to more positive attitudes and behaviors among both layoff victims and survivors (Konovsky & Brockner, 1993). Thus the positive impact of fair treatment on a variety of important outcomes has been widely demonstrated.

In the current chapter, we focus our discussion on perceived fairness in performance management systems. We begin our discussion with an examination of reasons for adopting performance management practices that are perceived to be fair. We argue that active consideration of fairness is consistent with a trend toward customer-oriented human resource management. We then address the ways of creating performance management systems that are perceived to be fair. This section begins with definitions of both the performance management process and the determinants of perceived fairness. The main discussion then focuses on recommendations for building perceived fairness into each of the steps in the performance management process. We conclude this chapter with a summary of recommendations and a comparison of our recommendations with those found in the popular literature.

Reasons for Considering Perceived Fairness in Performance Management

It has been argued that for the HR function to be an effective contributor to modern organizations, HR has to adopt a customer service orientation (Bowen & Greiner, 1986; Bowen & Lawler, 1992). The customers of the HR function include line managers and supervisors as well as employees. Customer service means understanding unique customer needs and continually striving to satisfy these needs as they change over time. If the performance appraisal process is perceived by employees as arbitrary and unfair, it is not meeting the needs of the employees as customers. Further, if employees do not agree with and accept the performance appraisal process and outcomes (for example, ratings), then the performance management system is not meeting the needs of the line managers and supervisors because the system will result in conflict, dissatisfaction, and lack of commitment. Recall the problems Jill Carington faced in the opening case from employees that did not accept their ratings. To adopt a customer service perspective, HR must obtain customer input, thereby allowing customers to share in the design of HR procedures and services. The result of this customer-oriented approach to HR is that a large body of the organization supports and recognizes the value of the HR function, and therefore, the perceived value of HR increases. Although research has not directly assessed many of the propositions that underlie the customer-oriented approach to HR, research has demonstrated the impact of perceptions of performance appraisal fairness on a variety of employee attitudes and behaviors. We consider the influence of fair performance management on attitudes and reactions to appraisals, motivation and performance, attitudes toward the organization, and legal challenges. The various outcomes influenced by performance appraisal fairness are also summarized in Exhibit 6.1.

Exhibit 6.1. Consequences of Fair Performance Management Systems.

Improved Employee Attitudes and Reactions to Appraisals
- Acceptance of performance evaluations
- Satisfaction with appraisal process

Improved Employee Motivation and Performance (small effects)
- Motivation to improve performance
- Performance improvements

Improved Employee Organizational Attitudes
- Trust in supervisor
- Organizational commitment
- Intentions to remain with the organization

Improved Company Position in Legal Challenges to Employment Decisions
- Increased legal defensibility
- Decreased likelihood of legal challenges (hypothesized consequence)

Attitudes and Reactions to Appraisals

Most directly related to the performance management process, research clearly indicates that both employee acceptance of the performance evaluation and employee satisfaction with the appraisal process are strongly related to the perceived fairness of that process. Steps taken to improve perceptions of fairness, such as providing due process through adequate notice and allowing employees the chance to offer input into the evaluation process, tend to increase acceptance of evaluations as well as satisfaction with the appraisal process (Taylor, Tracy, Renard, Harrison, & Carroll, 1995). Interestingly, these steps to enhance fairness also appear to enhance supervisors' satisfaction with the appraisal system. From a customer service perspective, it appears that adapting performance management systems to improve perceptions of fairness is an effective means of increasing customer (that is, employee and supervisor) satisfaction. This impact on satisfaction also suggests that supervisors would be more likely to use the appraisal system appropriately and effectively. Indeed, Taylor et al. found that managers reported less tendency to distort or manipulate appraisal ratings after a number of steps had been taken to build fairness into the appraisal process. The impact of perceived fairness on employees' acceptance of ratings and satisfaction with the appraisal suggests that employees will be more motivated to improve their performance when the rating process is perceived as fair.

Motivation and Performance

Several studies have examined the relationship between perceived fairness and motivation to improve, but the results are mixed. In correlational studies, employees' motivation to improve has consistently been related to perceptions of fairness. However, when the performance appraisal process is manipulated to increase perceptions of fairness, the manipulation has not been found to have an impact on motivation to improve (Taylor et al., 1995). Perhaps even more important than motivation to improve is the relationship between perceived fairness and performance improvements. Some research has demonstrated small relationships between perceived fairness or practices that enhance fairness (for example, opportunity to participate in the appraisal process) and changes in performance (Nathan, Mohrman, & Milliman, 1991). Additionally, some laboratory studies have demonstrated an impact of participation in a performance review on performance improvements, but these effects of manipulating fairness and observing performance change have not been found in field settings (Earley & Lind, 1987). Taylor et al. suggest that performance is determined by many factors in addition to motivation (for example, ability and opportunity) and this may be why improving the fairness of the review process has a greater impact on attitudes and commitment than on performance.

Organizational Attitudes

Some attitudes and behaviors that are more directly under motivational control include attitudes toward one's supervisor, commitment toward the organization, and intentions to remain with the organization. A number of studies have demonstrated that perceptions of appraisal fairness are related to trust in supervisor and organizational commitment (for example, Folger & Konovsky, 1989; Korsgaard & Roberson, 1995). Intentions to stay with the organization are related to performance appraisal fairness, particularly among those receiving lower performance evaluations (Magner, Welker, & Johnson, 1996). As with all the research demonstrating the importance of perceptions of performance appraisal fairness, it is important to distinguish research conducted using correlational methods from research using experimental methods. Given that fairness and most attitudes and intentions are assessed perceptually, there are always alternate explanations for correlational results. Additionally, the direction of causality is not known (for example, are committed employees more likely to perceive the performance appraisal as fair, or does fairness lead to more commitment?) and the possibility exists that some third variable accounts for the demonstrated relationship.

Far fewer studies have been conducted in field settings with experimental methods. However, one recent study manipulated fairness through steps to improve due process that included extensive training for employees and managers on all aspects of the appraisal process, as well as meetings to establish realistic expectations and self-appraisals as part of the evaluation process (Taylor et al., 1995). Compared with a control group of employees who continued to use the old system, those evaluated with the new "fair" performance appraisal system indicated that they were more likely to keep working at the agency for at least the next three years. Thus it is clear that perceptions of performance appraisal fairness are important in terms of their impact on employee and manager satisfaction with the appraisal process, as well as employee attitudes toward the organization and intentions to remain with the organization (as shown in Exhibit 6.1).

Resistance to Legal Challenges

A final potential positive effect of attending to perceptions of fairness relates to legal concerns. A number of researchers have suggested that the perceived fairness of the performance appraisal system should be related to decisions about going to court over employment decisions that are based on the appraisal system (see Chapter Two for a more detailed discussion of legal issues in performance appraisal). That is, if individuals feel they have been wronged in some employment decision (for example, promotion or termination) and an unfair appraisal process contributed to this decision, they are more likely to challenge the decision than if they felt they had been fairly appraised and received the same decision. Researchers have not assessed this suggestion, but analyses of legal decisions related to performance appraisals (for example, Barrett & Kernan, 1987; Werner & Bolino, 1997) indicate that features of legal decisions that tend to withstand legal scrutiny are also features that tend to promote perceptions of fairness (for example, providing a formal mechanism for employees to review and appeal appraisal results). Werner and Bolino concluded that issues relevant to fairness and due process were the most salient factors in judicial decisions, whereas more scientific issues of validation and type of rating instrument were virtually ignored.

Creating Fairness in Performance Management Systems

Given the evidence that enhancing the perceived fairness of performance management has positive effects in organizations, the next issue to consider is how to develop performance management systems that are perceived as fair. Specifically, we consider those factors that develop perceived fairness in the performance management process. The basic model that represents the relationships between fair performance appraisal practices, perceptions of fairness, and positive outcome is presented in Figure 6.1. That is, building fairness into the performance management process through practices such as self-appraisals enhances employees' perceptions that the performance appraisal is fair. Perceptions of fairness, in turn, lead to positive outcomes such as increased commitment to the organization.

We begin with a brief overview of the performance management process and identify three related processes that make up performance management. We then identify general determinants of perceived fairness before examining these determinants in each of the three performance management processes. The heart of our discussion is an examination of determinants of fairness as they relate to procedures and features of performance management processes. We use a number of case examples to illustrate these issues and conclude with an examination of the congruence between suggestions based on fairness research and suggestions found in the popular press.

The Performance Management Process

Research on performance management has typically studied the appraisal stage of the process. However, in trying to understand how to create fair performance management systems, it is beneficial to examine the process from beginning to end. In this chapter we examine performance management broadly and suggest that the following three steps are central to the management process: system development, appraisal processes, and feedback processes. The

Figure 6.1. Fairness Impact Model.

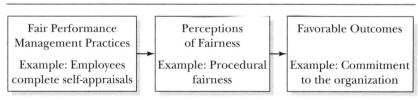

performance management process is summarized in Figure 6.2. Although not a focus of the current chapter, the outermost circle of the figure emphasizes that the three steps in the performance management process are embedded within the organization's culture or environment (for example, values, norms, strategic goals), which can enhance or reduce perceptions of fairness.

• *System development* includes the creation or modification of performance appraisal instruments, the planning of procedures for assessing performance and providing feedback, and the com-

Figure 6.2. Performance Management Process.

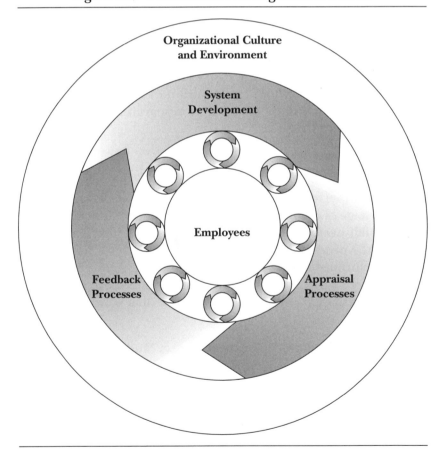

munication of this development to relevant parties. System development also includes communicating business objectives to employees and establishing a process for employee goal setting.

- *Appraisal processes* include observing and collecting information on work-related behavior, evaluating performance, and completing the appraisal form. Decisions regarding rewards and promotions are also part of the appraisal process.
- *Providing performance feedback* is the final step in the performance management process and involves the communication of appraisals and rewards. This feedback process leads into goal setting for the next appraisal period.

As suggested in Figure 6.2, the three performance management processes are not independent, but are in fact cyclically interrelated. After feedback is delivered, the entire performance management process should be reexamined and any necessary improvements should be made through further development. Referring back to the customer service–oriented HR approach suggested earlier, customer (for example, employee and line manager) input should be solicited following feedback delivery and this input used to refine the performance management process. In addition to a customer orientation, this approach to performance management embodies the notion of continuous quality improvement.

By depicting the performance management process as cyclical we are not trying to suggest that each step (for example, providing feedback) should only occur once in a given year. Rather, performance management should be a continuous process. In Figure 6.2, we present an interior ring that contains numerous informal performance management cycles that occur within the context of the larger formal performance management cycle. That is, at many points throughout the formal performance management cycle, employees should be given informal feedback and they should be offering input that can modify their performance goals. This informal feedback and input augment the formal performance management cycle. Nonetheless, the three steps of the performance management cycle do serve as a useful way of organizing our discussion of the performance management processes. In the following sections, we will demonstrate how fairness can be enhanced in each of the steps of the performance management cycle.

Determinants of Perceived Fairness

Considerable research has examined the question, What makes a decision seem fair? It is generally recognized that there are three categories of perceived fairness. These include procedural fairness, interpersonal fairness, and outcome fairness. Table 6.1 provides a summary of these categories of fairness and includes brief definitions and examples.

- *Procedural fairness* refers to the appropriateness of the decision process and is primarily determined by whether or not the recipient has a chance to offer input or a voice in the decision. Additional determinants of procedural fairness include the consistency of treatment and consideration and the relevance and lack of bias in the decision-making procedures.

- *Interpersonal fairness* addresses treatment during the formation and communication of the decision. Whereas procedural fairness addresses the formal decision processes, the primary determinants of interpersonal fairness include honesty, ethicality, feedback, and

Table 6.1. Categories of Perceived Fairness.

Fairness Category	Description	Examples of Determinants
Procedural fairness	Appropriateness of decision process	• Opportunity to participate in process • Consistency of treatment and consideration • Job relevance and lack of bias
Interpersonal fairness	Effectiveness of interpersonal treatment and communication	• Honest and ethical treatment • Timely and thorough communication and feedback
Outcome fairness	Appropriateness of the decision and outcomes associated with the decision	• Outcomes anticipated or consistent with expectations

communication. The feedback and communication dimensions include adequacy or thoroughness as well as timeliness.

- *Outcome fairness* is fairness associated with the outcome of the decision. Outcome fairness is based on a matching of actual outcomes with expected or anticipated outcomes. Further, these expectations are formed through prior experiences and comparisons with relevant others. For example, by communicating with coworkers, employees may form expectations regarding the performance evaluation they will receive and the rewards (for example, bonus or merit increase) that should follow from that evaluation. If the actual evaluation or reward falls short of this expectation, the outcome will be perceived as unfair. Evaluations or rewards that meet or exceed expectations will be perceived as fair.

The three categories of fairness are often interrelated, such that fair procedures and interpersonal treatment tend to be associated with fair outcomes. However, this is not always the case. It is possible to have an unfair decision process or unfair interpersonal treatment, but still receive a fair outcome. For example, you may feel that your supervisor did not know what you were doing in your job and did not seek any input prior to evaluating your performance (thus making the appraisal process unfair), but nevertheless gave you the appraisal and merit increase you feel you deserve (creating outcome fairness).

Research has examined the relationships between process, treatment, and outcomes. One consistent finding to emerge is that fair procedures or interpersonal treatment can make up for negative outcomes (Brockner & Wiesenfeld, 1996). That is, if the decision process is fair, or if decision making is thoroughly and adequately communicated, individuals receiving negative outcomes may actually perceive those outcomes to be fair. Table 6.2 summarizes the effect of procedural and interpersonal fairness on negative outcomes.

Research has demonstrated the power of fair procedures and interpersonal treatment in a variety of contexts with outcomes that range in severity. For example, even layoff decisions (an extremely severe and negative outcome) are perceived to be more fair if the reason for the decision is carefully explained and adequate notice is provided. In the performance management domain, research has demonstrated that providing appraisees the opportunity to

**Table 6.2. The Effect of Fair Procedures
and Interpersonal Treatment on Outcome Fairness.**

	Procedural and Interpersonal Fairness	
	Unfair	Fair
Positive outcome	Fair	Fair
Negative outcome	Unfair	*Fair*

offer input into their evaluation can mitigate negative attitudes that result from an unfavorable performance appraisal (Magner et al., 1996). The implication of this research is that *procedural and interpersonal fairness are particularly important when evaluations and decisions are negative.*

Perceived Fairness and the Performance Management Process

We have broken the performance management process into three stages related to system development, appraisal processes, and feedback processes. We have also broken the fairness notion into three categories of fairness: procedural fairness, interpersonal fairness, and outcome fairness. In this section we examine each type of fairness as it relates to each stage of performance management.

Perceived Fairness of System Development

The development stage of the performance management process is important for fostering initial commitment toward the system. Positive or negative attitudes that form during the development stage are likely to persist once the performance management system is implemented. Procedural and interpersonal fairness perceptions during development are likely to strongly influence these positive or negative attitudes. Although research has not specifically addressed fairness of performance appraisal development, considerable related fairness research provides a number of suggestions for practice.

In this section, we describe four important practices that can enhance perceptions of fairness in the system development process:

- Collect employee input through surveys or interviews.
- Ensure that all employees are treated consistently when seeking input and communicating about the development process.
- Ensure that the information collected from employees is relevant and that the system developed is related to the job.
- Explain why a new performance management system is being developed.

We begin by listing these practices and then discuss them in more detail. We also describe a performance appraisal development effort that exemplifies many of these practices. Our key recommendations for enhancing fairness in system development are summarized in Table 6.3.

- *Collect employee input through surveys or interviews.* Across a variety of decision situations, one of the most consistent factors to influence procedural fairness perceptions is the extent to which the recipient has an opportunity to voice concerns in the decision process (Korsgaard & Roberson, 1995). At the system development stage, this opportunity for voice can be provided by surveying or interviewing employees to determine their primary job performance dimensions. Employees can also be asked to provide input regarding what sort of performance appraisal form should be developed as well as how and from whom appraisal evaluations should be collected. In this way, employees are contributing and having a say in the development of the appraisal system. One long-term employee reacted with dismay and resentment when presented a new "job-related" performance appraisal form without being consulted: "How could they develop a job-related performance appraisal without talking to me? I have been doing this job for eighteen years and that's longer than any of those HR people have been around this company. If anyone knows what's involved in this job, it is me." In addition to this input helping to create a sense of procedural fairness, employees may feel more ownership and commitment to a system that they helped to develop.

- *Ensure that all employees are treated consistently when seeking input and communicating about the development process.* Another

Table 6.3. Fairness in System Development.

Determinant	Description	Recommended Practices
Voice	Collect employee input through surveys or interviews.	• Interview or survey employees to identify primary job dimensions. • Get employee input about appraisal format and rater sources.
Consistency	Ensure that all employees are treated consistently when seeking input and communicating about the development process.	• Seek and use input from everyone in a similar manner. • Keep everyone informed regarding the development process (make sure no one is left out of the loop).
Relevance	Ensure that the information collected from employees is relevant and that the system developed is related to the job.	• Ask job-relevant questions during interviews or surveys. • Ensure the developed appraisal system is related to the job.
Communication	Explain why a new performance management system is being developed.	• Explain the functions of the new performance management system using face-to-face or written communication. • Alleviate concerns about the new system with two-way communication (interviews, conferences, questionnaires).

important procedural fairness dimension is consistency of treatment (Leventhal, 1980). Greenberg (1986a) interviewed managers and found that the consistent application of standards was a common theme to emerge from recollections of fair or unfair performance evaluations. Consistency of treatment in the system development stage can refer to seeking input from everyone in a similar manner and valuing all employee input equally. Consistency can also refer to the communication that is provided regarding the development process and the reasons for the new procedures. Is everyone being kept informed? Is anyone out of the loop? Finding out that everyone else knew about the new performance appraisal process before you can breed instant distrust in the process.

• *Ensure that the information collected from employees is relevant and that the system developed is related to the job.* An additional determinant of procedural fairness in the system development stage is job relevance. The importance of the decision procedure being job related has been discussed in performance appraisal situations (for example, Taylor et al., 1995) as well as a variety of other organizational decision situations (for example, Gilliland, 1993). In the system development stage, job relevance refers to both the relevance of information that is being collected (for example, questions asked during an interview or in a survey appear to be related to the job) and the relevance of the appraisal system that is developed (for example, goals and performance dimensions are related to the job). The closer the connection between the system being developed and the job, the greater the perception of procedural fairness.

• *Explain why a new performance management system is being developed.* One of the strongest determinants of interpersonal fairness is the explanation or communication that is provided regarding the decision and the decision process (Tyler & Bies, 1990). This has been demonstrated to be the case particularly with performance appraisals (Folger & Konovsky, 1989). Explanations are likely to be very important during the development stage. One important explanation to address is why a new performance management system is being developed. Performance appraisals can be used to allocate rewards and make positive decisions (for example, promotion), but in the current era of downsizing, a new performance appraisal process may be interpreted by employees as a tool for conducting layoffs. Explanations can help alleviate these fears. Opening up channels for two-way communication is also likely to be very important in terms of addressing concerns and fears. Again, interviews, questionnaires, memos, and informal conferences can all be used to promote two-way communication.

The discussion so far suggests ways to build procedural and interpersonal fairness into the performance management system development process. Outcome fairness has not been addressed. However, the outcome of the development process is the performance management system. The fairness of this system is most directly evaluated by examining procedural fairness in the appraisal and feedback stages.

Case Example: University of Arizona Intercollegiate Athletics

We can illustrate many of the suggestions we have made regarding procedural and interpersonal fairness in the system development stage by describing our recent experiences developing a new performance management system for the Department of Intercollegiate Athletics (ICA) at the University of Arizona. Although this is a department within a large organization, the University of Arizona's human resources department had recently decentralized and ICA was asked to develop its own performance management system. The ICA department has approximately 150 administrative, coaching, support, and clerical staff members occupying over a hundred different jobs. Even staff with the same job title often have very different duties (for example, the life of an "Assistant Coach, Football" varies greatly depending on whether the job is as an offensive or defensive assistant coach). Therefore, the goals were to develop performance appraisal instruments that tapped the essential duties of each job, but to try to limit the number of different instruments to a manageable total.

Procedural fairness in this development process was managed by allowing all staff the opportunity to offer input during development. Initially, all staff members were interviewed, either individually or in groups. Interview questions addressed job duties and performance standards as well as comments on the existing performance management process. Recommendations and concerns regarding the new system were also collected. Through these steps all staff were able to offer input, and this input was collected consistently across the various levels of the department. Two-way communication was also facilitated with the individual and group interviews.

Interpersonal fairness was largely managed with written and oral communication. All staff members were sent a memo from the director of ICA explaining why a new performance management system was being developed and outlining the steps in the development process. During monthly staff meetings, the staff was informed of the development process by either the director or the administrator who was coordinating the development process. One of the critical issues in this communication was the reasons for the development of a new system. Decisions that would be made with the performance appraisal included merit increases and promotions. Another goal of this new system was to use performance management as a motivation and development tool. Given that performance appraisals had not previously been used consistently for development, and given that merit increases were infrequent, a common fear among staff was that the new system was being developed because of the perception of impending downsizing and layoffs. It is important to note that there were no plans for layoffs, but rather the staff saw the new performance appraisal system as a sign of future layoffs. Communication from the director of ICA and feedback during the interviews from the consultants developing the system helped alleviate these fears. ICA staff on the development team also monitored informal communication networks (for example, an underground newsletter) for concerns regarding use of the new performance management system.

Perhaps as a result of ensuring procedural and interpersonal fairness during the development process, reactions toward the new performance management system were largely positive. Additionally, many of the staff expressed enthusiasm regarding the goal-setting portion of the performance management system, because the goals provide developmental direction and also provide job-related standards by which performance can be evaluated. Although fairness was part of the system development process at this organization, it is important that fairness also be included in the appraisal and feedback processes. If these later stages of the performance management cycle fall short in terms of fairness, the gains realized in the development stage will likely be lost.

Perceived Fairness of Appraisal Processes

After the system is developed, the next stage in performance management is appraisal. Appraisal processes include collecting information on appraisee performance and evaluating performance using some type of evaluation form. Procedural, interpersonal, and outcome fairness are all relevant and important during this stage. In this section, we list and then describe eight important practices that promote perceptions of fairness during the appraisal processes.

- Have employees provide input into the appraisal process.
- Ensure consistent standards when evaluating different employees.
- Minimize supervisor biases during the appraisal process.
- Ensure raters are familiar with the employee's work.
- Ensure appraisal ratings are job related.
- Communicate performance expectations prior to the appraisal process.
- Avoid surprises (for example, unexpected negative evaluations) in appraisal ratings.
- Base administrative decisions on ratings.

These practices are summarized in Table 6.4. We also present a case example of an organization that has included many of these practices in its appraisal process.

- *Have employees provide input into the appraisal process.* As with the system development stage, one of the most important determinants of procedural fairness in appraisal processes is the opportunity for appraisees to have a voice in the evaluation. Korsgaard and Roberson (1995) distinguish between instrumental voice and noninstrumental voice, with the former being the opportunity to influence the appraisal process and the latter being the opportunity to make suggestions but not necessarily influence the process. An example of instrumental voice is when an employee is asked to prepare a self-evaluation and then the supervisor uses this evaluation to develop the final ratings. With noninstrumental voice, self-evaluations allow employees to state their side of the story, but these evaluations may not necessarily influence the supervisor's final ratings. Among a sample of management-level employees, Korsgaard and Roberson found that both forms of voice were equally important in terms of predicting satisfaction with the appraisal review. This demonstrates that having a say in the evaluation process is important above and beyond any influence this say may have in terms of the ultimate evaluation. Therefore, having employees complete a self-evaluation is useful regardless of whether it is simply reviewed by the supervisor or whether it forms the basis for the formal ratings.

In addition to self-appraisals, another mechanism for voice is the opportunity for a formal or informal discussion with the supervisor prior to appraisals being made. When building due process

Table 6.4. Fairness in the Appraisal Process.

Determinant	Description	Recommended Practices
Voice	Have employees provide input into the appraisal process.	• Have employees complete self-appraisals. • Train employees to share information with supervisors. • Train supervisors to solicit information from employees.
Consistency	Ensure consistent standards when evaluating different employees.	• Ensure consistency with respect to advance notice, employee input, and collection of performance information. • Train supervisors to promote consistency. • Standardize and formalize appraisal process and instrument.
Bias	Minimize supervisor biases during the appraisal process.	• Train supervisors and standardize appraisal instrument. • Use multiplier raters and 360-degree feedback. • Increase supervisor accountability by having rating reviewed by supervisor's peers or higher-level management.
Familiarity	Ensure raters are familiar with the employee's work.	• Use supervisor diaries to record employee performance. • Solicit input from coworkers and secondary supervisors.
Relevance	Ensure appraisal ratings are job related.	• Ensure the appraisal system is related to the job.
Communication	Communicate performance expectations prior to the appraisal process.	• Inform employees about performance standards and how they will be evaluated. • Inform employees of any changes during evaluation period.
Feedback	Avoid surprises (unexpected negative evaluations) in appraisal ratings.	• Provide continuous feedback during evaluation period. • Ensure employees have reasonable expectations going into the appraisal process.
Outcomes	Base administrative decisions on ratings.	• Match administrative decisions (such as merit increases, bonuses, promotions) to appraisal ratings. • Communicate structure of incentive system to employees.

into a performance appraisal system, Taylor et al. (1995) provided employees with training on how to conduct a self-appraisal before having them conduct their self-appraisals. They also provided managers with training on how to solicit performance information from employees. All these steps can be seen as encouraging the opportunity for employee voice in the appraisal process.

• *Ensure consistent standards when evaluating different employees.* Consistency is another determinant of procedural fairness that should be part of the appraisal process. It is frustrating to see coworkers in other departments get higher evaluations and merit increases simply because they have a more lenient boss. Supervisors should use consistent standards when evaluating employees in the same department as well as employees in different departments (Greenberg, 1986a). Consistency should also be ensured with respect to the provision of advance notice, the opportunity for employee input, and the collection of performance information from other sources. Perhaps the most direct way to promote this consistency is with training in all aspects of the appraisal process. This training should emphasize the importance of consistency in terms of employees' perceptions of fairness. Standardization and formalization of appraisal instruments can also be used to promote consistency.

• *Minimize supervisor biases during the appraisal process.* Related to consistency is the importance of supervisors' suppressing their personal biases during the appraisal process (Leventhal, 1980). Recall the feeling of injustice of finding out that a low-performing coworker received the same evaluation and bonus as you simply because he or she got along well with the boss. Training and standardization of appraisal instruments can be used to suppress biases, as can the use of multiple raters. Appraisal processes that include 360-degree feedback are likely to be perceived as more procedurally fair because they minimize the chance that any one person's bias will unduly influence an appraisal decision. Training and rating formats can promote consistency and bias suppression; however, they may not be sufficient to motivate accurate ratings. One technique for motivating consistent, unbiased ratings involves increasing supervisory accountability by having ratings reviewed by the supervisors' peers or by higher-level management. For example, at one large communications company supervisors prepare preliminary ratings for managerial and professional employees and then meet to present these ratings to peer supervisors in the department. These peers will often challenge ratings, particularly if they seem excessively lenient, and force supervisors to furnish supporting evidence. After consensus is reached among the peers, ratings are reviewed by higher-level management. Such a system minimizes personal biases and inconsistencies and motivates managers to develop accurate ratings from the onset.

- *Ensure raters are familiar with the employee's work.* Another procedural fairness determinant discussed by Greenberg (1986a) is the evaluator's familiarity with the evaluatee's work. If the supervisor conducting the appraisal is not familiar with the employee's work, his or her evaluations are going to be seen as unfair. Familiarity can be enhanced by the use of supervisor diaries that contain examples of good and poor performance over the course of the appraisal period (Greenberg, 1987). For example, one national food retailer has managers keep daily logs of employees' performance, both positive (for example, making a notable contribution or going above and beyond for a customer) and negative (for example, arriving late to work or treating a customer rudely). Although time-consuming, this system has resulted in substantial improvements in the communication between managers and employees. Solicitation of input from coworkers and secondary supervisors may also increase familiarity. One potential drawback of 360-degree appraisals is that some of the raters may be perceived as lacking adequate familiarity with the target employee being rated. Research has not yet examined this possibility. It would be interesting to see which procedural fairness determinants are perceived as favorable, which are perceived as unfavorable, and how these contribute to form the overall reaction to the 360-degree appraisal.

- *Ensure appraisal ratings are job related.* Another determinant of procedural fairness in performance appraisal processes is the job relevance of the appraisal ratings. This determinant was discussed with regard to system development, and applies similarly in the appraisal stage.

- *Communicate performance expectations prior to the appraisal process.* Appraisal interpersonal fairness is largely influenced by the degree to which performance expectations and standards are communicated ahead of time (Taylor et al., 1995). To some extent, promoting interpersonal fairness through communication in the system development stage should also promote interpersonal fairness in the appraisal stage. Employees want to know how they are going to be evaluated. If the standards or expectations change prior to or during the evaluation period, employees need to be informed of these changes. It is important to note that both communication of standards and adequate notice (that is, timing of this communication) are important to interpersonal fairness.

- *Avoid surprises (for example, unexpected negative evaluations) in appraisal ratings.* In most cases, surprises (unless they are favorable) will lead to perceptions of unfairness. Outcome fairness of the appraisal process arises from both the evaluations that are received and the rewards or punishments that accompany these evaluations (Greenberg, 1986a). If evaluations fall short of expectations based on perceived performance, those evaluations will be perceived to be unfair. To develop realistic expectations, employees should receive continuous feedback throughout the performance evaluation period. Supervisors can also actively manage the expectations of employees before going into the appraisal process. One employee told us that before her first appraisal with her new employer, her manager explained that with her experience level, an average rating would be a remarkable accomplishment. Later, when she received an average rating, instead of being disappointed and discouraged, she was proud of her accomplishments and was determined to gain greater skill and experience to do her job more effectively. In this situation, the rating did not create the outcome fairness, rather the fairness was created by effectively managing expectations through communication.

- *Base administrative decisions on ratings.* The other major determinant of outcome fairness is the relationship between evaluations and administrative decisions (for example, bonuses or promotions). At one restaurant chain, the absence of an observable link between evaluations and bonuses resulted in employees labeling the bonus pay "pennies from heaven." Employees form expectations regarding what decisions should follow a given performance evaluation. Supervisors should make sure employees have realistic beliefs regarding what outcomes they can expect based on their performance. Some organizations have highly structured incentive systems that guarantee a certain bonus or merit increase based on a particular level of performance. If communicated effectively from top management to employees, this structure should help to reduce ambiguity and misperceptions. With less structured systems, increased supervisor accountability through peer or higher-level management review can help ensure that administrative decisions are directly linked to accurate performance evaluations. The organization's past performance with regard to allocating rewards will likely also have a strong impact on the formation of expectations. The more that outcomes have been perceived to be unfair in the past, the less likely employees will be to expect and perceive future actions as fair (Greenberg, 1986b).

Case Example: Promoting Appraisal Process Fairness at FINOVA

One organization that does a good job of promoting fairness in the appraisal process is FINOVA, a provider of corporate financial services. With over two thousand employees around the world, a variety of separate business units, and a centralized performance management system, fairness is somewhat difficult to ensure. A recently developed electronic performance management system has allowed the central human resource department to control the flow of performance-related information to and from employees and managers.

At the beginning of the performance management period, all employees are sent performance objectives forms via the company e-mail system. Across four performance areas, employees are required to set specific, challenging, objectively measurable performance objectives that are related to the company's strategic direction. Employees review these objectives with their supervisors and the completed form is sent back to human resources. Having employees set their own performance objectives builds procedural fairness (through voice and job relevance) and outcome fairness (through the establishment of reasonable expectations). If something in the job or business climate changes, then employees are able to revise these objectives (with the approval of their supervisors). This revisability is also something that has been demonstrated to promote perceptions of fairness (Leventhal, 1980).

At the end of the year, employees and their supervisors are sent the completed objectives form (again electronically) and together they decide the extent to which results met the objectives. Numerical evaluations indicate the extent to which results fell short of, met, or exceeded the stated objectives. Individual evaluations are reviewed by several layers of management and even include discussions between HR representatives and the CEO. This extensive review of individual performance evaluations helps minimize biases that may exist at the supervisory level. The annual incentive plan is tied directly to individual evaluations and is also based on the extent to which the employee's department and the company as a whole meet their respective objectives. These incentives are determined on strictly numeric bases, such that subjective judgments are minimized.

Clearly, the performance management system at FINOVA incorporates many of the recommendations we have suggested to promote procedural, interpersonal, and outcome fairness in the appraisal process. Employees have ample opportunity to offer input. Evaluations are job related and evaluation procedures are consistent across employees. Performance standards are clearly communicated and are in fact set largely by employees. These standards are also modifiable if circumstances change. Outcome expectations are clearly communicated and outcomes are consistently and fairly allocated. Such fairness in the appraisal process sets the foundation for perceived fairness in feedback communication processes.

Perceived Fairness of Feedback Processes

The final stage in the performance management cycle is providing feedback to employees on their performance. As with the appraisal process, all three types of fairness are likely to be important. Additionally, interpersonal fairness is probably the most central and salient fairness perception in the communication stage. In this section we list and then discuss six recommendations for enhancing perceptions of fairness in the feedback processes:

- Ensure that employees are given a voice during the feedback process.
- Allow employees the opportunity to challenge or rebut their evaluation.
- Ensure that feedback is job relevant and does not reflect personal biases.
- Provide timely feedback.
- Provide feedback in an atmosphere of respect and courtesy.
- Avoid surprises during the feedback session.

These recommendations are summarized in Table 6.5. After discussing the recommendations, we present an example of an organization that seems to have included many of these practices in its performance management process.

- *Ensure that employees are given a voice during the feedback process.* We have discussed the importance of both instrumental and noninstrumental voice in the appraisal stage of the performance management cycle. When providing feedback, research has demonstrated

Table 6.5. Fairness in Feedback Delivery.

Determinant	Description	Recommended Practices
Voice	Ensure that employees are given a voice during the feedback process.	• Use two-way communication and a problem-solving approach when providing feedback. • Allow employees opportunity to express their views.
Challenge	Allow employees the opportunity to challenge or rebut their evaluation.	• Have a formal appeals system in place.
Relevance	Ensure that feedback is job relevant and does not reflect personal bias.	• Train managers in effective feedback delivery techniques. • Focus feedback on the behavior, not the person.
Timeliness	Provide timely feedback.	• Use frequent feedback sessions of informal and formal formats. • Provide feedback when the behavior (positive or negative) occurs.
Respect	Provide feedback in an atmosphere of respect and courtesy.	• Train supervisors to use respect and civility regardless of level of performance. • Recognize impact of existing relationship with employees on feedback session.
Surprises	Avoid surprises during the feedback session.	• Provide continuous informal feedback. • Ensure employees have realistic expectations going into the feedback session.

the importance of both types of voice—the ability to influence the appraisal discussion and the opportunity to discuss problems and share ideas (Korsgaard & Roberson, 1995). The notion of voice during feedback also emphasizes the importance of two-way communication. Research on providing performance feedback has demonstrated the effectiveness of adopting a cooperative, problem-solving approach during the feedback session (for example, Wexley, Singh, & Yukl, 1973). Such a problem-solving approach emphasizes employee voice and two-way communication. Research on feedback session satisfaction has demonstrated that employees' participation is the most important predictor of satisfaction in the feedback process (Giles & Mossholder, 1990). Clearly, the more opportunity employees are given to express their views, the more they will perceive the process to be fair and the more satisfied they will be.

• *Allow employees the opportunity to challenge or rebut their evaluation.* Related to the opportunity for voice is providing employees a chance to challenge their evaluation (Greenberg, 1986a). Formalized appeal systems through which employees can challenge and potentially change what they consider to be unfair ratings will improve the perceived fairness of the appraisal and feedback processes. IBM has an extensive program for employees to rebut evaluations. Employees communicate first with their managers, and if disagreements continue to exist, employees can request an "open door" investigation from HR or a panel review from peers and uninvolved managers. These appeal procedures have also been suggested to increase the legal defensibility of the performance management process (Barrett & Kernan, 1987).

• *Ensure that feedback is job relevant and does not reflect personal biases.* In our consideration of the performance appraisal process, we discussed the importance of job relevance and the suppression of personal biases. These suggestions also apply to the feedback process. In fact, steps to ensure accuracy in the evaluation process should promote accuracy and relevance in feedback delivery. Training managers to develop effective feedback delivery techniques can also address both these procedural concerns. Additionally, suggestions in textbooks (for example, Noe, Hollenbeck, Gerhart, & Wright, 1997) and the popular literature (for example, Armentrout, 1993) emphasize the importance of focusing on behavior and results, rather than on the person. Heeding these suggestions should decrease perceptions that the feedback is biased and increase perceptions of job relevance.

- *Provide timely feedback.* Research on feedback delivery has long demonstrated the importance of timely feedback in terms of changing performance (Ilgen, Fisher, & Taylor, 1979), and this recommendation is also valid in terms of promoting interpersonal fairness. Tyler and Bies (1990) review evidence on perceptions of interpersonal fairness and highlight the importance of providing timely feedback. By focusing our discussion thus far on the review session, we may be reinforcing the misconception that feedback delivery is an annual or semiannual event. However, given the importance of timely feedback for fairness perceptions, we are suggesting that feedback (whether formal or informal) should be delivered much more frequently and even on a continual basis. One investment management company conducts formal employee appraisal with feedback sessions on a monthly basis. In this way, the actual performance review session provides a summary of the informal feedback provided throughout the appraisal period.

- *Provide feedback in an atmosphere of respect and courtesy.* Research has shown that an employee's perceptions of trust and the manager's ability to treat employees with courtesy and civility are strong determinants of perceptions of interpersonal fairness (for example, Tyler & Bies, 1990). In the performance feedback session, it is particularly important that this respect and civility is present regardless of the level of performance that is being discussed. While training supervisors to conduct effective feedback sessions helps to promote this interpersonally effective behavior, reactions are also based on the interpersonal relationship that exists between the manager and employee before the review session is conducted. Nathan et al. (1991) demonstrated that the interpersonal relationship before the review strongly predicted employees' perceptions of the quality of the appraisal session and their satisfaction with the appraisal session.

- *Avoid surprises during the feedback session.* As with the appraisal stage, perceived outcome unfairness arises when outcome expectations are not met. When training business students and managers in performance management techniques, we continually remind them that the feedback session should contain no surprises. If supervisors are doing an effective job of providing continual feedback to their employees, the employees will know what to expect when they enter the feedback session. Even if the feedback is negative, it will not be unexpected and therefore will be perceived as more fair. This clearly emphasizes how providing timely feedback can promote outcome fairness, in addition to enhancing interpersonal fairness.

Case Example: Continuous Feedback at Microsoft

A good example of a company building fairness principles into its performance feedback processes is Microsoft Corporation. Formal performance feedback sessions are conducted every six months, but informal feedback is provided continually. Every month, each Microsoft employee participates in a one-on-one feedback session with his or her supervisor. In these sessions, the supervisor informally reviews the previous month's performance and offers advice or developmental counseling as necessary. The manager also allows the employee the opportunity to discuss any concerns.

In the formal performance feedback sessions, performance is assessed in terms of met objectives as well as specific job-related criteria. Given the frequency of informal performance discussions, employees recognize that their supervisors are familiar with their performance and can offer job-related feedback. Employees know that they can challenge their performance evaluation if they disagree with it, but according to one HR representative, this rarely occurs. Employees trust the honesty of their supervisors, and they also know that every appraisal must be approved by a second line manager. All these provisions help enhance employees' perceptions that the appraisal and feedback processes are fair.

Outcome fairness also results from the attention given to procedural and interpersonal fairness. The continuous feedback allows employees to form realistic expectations of their performance. These expectations make it more likely that the outcome or evaluation communicated during formal feedback sessions will be perceived to be fair. Clearly, Microsoft's attention to performance feedback processes results in many positive reactions from employees. One employee enthusiastically stated, "I don't know anyone that does a better job of providing feedback than Microsoft. I always know where I stand and how I'm doing."

Conclusions

In this chapter we have divided the performance management process into three interrelated processes involving system development, appraisal, and feedback delivery. We suggest that within these three processes, organizations should attend to employees' perceptions of fairness along dimensions of procedural fairness, interpersonal fairness, and outcome fairness. Here are the main suggestions regarding procedural fairness:

- Giving employees the opportunity to participate in all performance management processes
- Ensuring consistency in all processes
- Making sure appraisals and feedback are job related and do not reflect supervisor biases
- Providing a formal channel for employees to challenge or rebut their evaluations.

Interpersonal fairness suggestions include

- Keeping employees informed through communicating
- Offering feedback that is both informative and timely
- Ensuring courteous, respectful treatment and trust between employees and managers

Finally, outcome fairness can be conceptualized in terms of

- Providing outcomes (either positive or negative) that are anticipated or expected by the employee
- Maintaining and communicating a formally structured incentive system

Some performance management techniques, such as self-appraisals and supervisor training, can clearly be seen to promote perceptions of fairness. Other techniques, such as 360-degree feedback, would appear to promote fairness in terms of reducing (or diluting) personal biases, but also may be seen as unfair due to rater unfamiliarity with the person and the job being evaluated. Therefore, although there are many obvious advantages of 360-degree feedback, we do not have theoretical or empirical bases for drawing conclusions about its influence on perceptions of fairness. This is definitely an area where future research could make a contribution.

Our discussion also suggested that it is not always sufficient to provide supervisors with the tools and training to complete the performance management process fairly. Steps to build accountability (for example, peer or higher-level management review) into the system may sometimes be required to motivate fair treatment. If we return attention to Figure 6.2 and specifically to the organizational culture and environment in which the performance management system exists, we are suggesting that companies develop a culture that promotes fairness in performance management. The values shared by top management and formal or informal reward systems can develop concerns for fairness. As a senior executive at a large utility company suggested, "The most effective improvement would be a dramatic change in behavior by senior management to endorse, encourage, recognize, and reward effective and fair performance management practices. This should be coupled with an active system of accountability for these practices."

It is interesting to compare the recommendations we have made for development of performance management systems that are perceived to be fair with the recommendations commonly suggested in the popular literature. To a large extent these sets of recommendations are consistent. Specifically, several authors have discussed the importance of soliciting employee input and two-way communication, of focusing on the job and behaviors instead of employee personality, of providing an appeal procedure and opportunity to change ratings, of explaining how performance is evaluated, and of providing feedback on a regular basis (Armentrout, 1993; Fitzgerald, 1995; Miller, 1996). One suggestion from the popular literature that is not consistent with our recommendations is that the formal appraisal system should be abolished entirely and replaced with a dialogue process (McNerney, 1995). Following this suggestion would eliminate consistency and do little to suppress supervisory biases. There are also some suggestions we have made that have not been echoed in the popular literature. Our suggestions for building fairness into the system development stage have not been addressed. Further, the popular literature we reviewed on performance management has not addressed the importance of interpersonal effectiveness—that is, courtesy, respect, and civility regardless of performance. Finally, the popular literature does not capture the importance of supervisor accountability or the impact that an organization's culture can have on promoting fairness.

If we return to the case that opened this chapter, it is easy to see the many ways that Jill Carington failed to consider fairness in her performance management system. Jill did not obtain employee input in the development, appraisal, or feedback stages. She did not attempt to create job-related appraisals or feedback. She did not apply consistent standards when evaluating her employees. Feedback was not timely and two-way communication was minimal. Finally, the ratings she assigned to her staff clearly did not meet the expectations of many of her staff members and therefore lacked outcome fairness. Given the lack of fairness in the performance management process, the employees' morale and commitment were low and their trust in Jill as a supervisor was seriously eroded. In addition to Jill Carington's failings with the performance management system, the HR department could have done more to help Jill and other managers build fairness into their performance management systems. HR could have promoted a culture and environment supportive of fair performance management.

In this chapter we have outlined many suggestions for promoting perceptions of fairness in performance management. With more attention to these fairness issues we hope to see more cases like FINOVA and Microsoft and fewer organizations running into the problems faced by Jill Carington.

References

Armentrout, B. (1993). Eight keys to effective performance appraisals. *HR Focus, 70*(4), 13.

Barrett, G. V., & Kernan, M. C. (1987). Performance appraisal and terminations: A review of court decisions since *Brito* v. *Zia* with implications for personnel practices. *Personnel Psychology, 40,* 489–503.

Bowen, D. E., & Greiner, L. E. (1986). Moving from production to service in human resources management. *Organizational Dynamics, 15*(1), 35–53.

Bowen, D. E., & Lawler, E. E., III. (1992). Total quality-oriented human resources management. *Organizational Dynamics, 20*(4), 29–41.

Brockner, J., & Wiesenfeld, B. M. (1996). An integrative framework for explaining reactions to decisions: Interactive effects of outcomes and procedures. *Psychological Bulletin, 120,* 189–208.

Cropanzano, R., & Greenberg, J. (1997). Progress in organizational justice: Tunneling through the maze. In C. L. Cooper & I. Robertson (Eds.), *International review of industrial and organizational psychology.* New York: Wiley.

Earley, P. C., & Lind, E. A. (1987). Procedural justice and participation in task selection: The role of control in mediating justice judgments. *Journal of Personality and Social Psychology, 52,* 1148–1160.

Fitzgerald, W. (1995). Forget the form in performance appraisals. *HR Magazine, 40,* 136.

Folger, R., & Greenberg, J. (1985). Procedural justice: An interpretive analysis of personnel systems. In K. N. Rowland & G. R. Ferris (Eds.), *Research in personnel and human resources management: Vol. 3* (pp. 141–183). Greenwich, CT: JAI Press.

Folger, R., & Konovsky, M. A. (1989). Effects of procedural and distributive justice on reactions to pay raise decisions. *Academy of Management Journal, 32,* 115–130.

Giles, W. F., & Mossholder, K. W. (1990). Employee reactions to contextual and session components of performance appraisal. *Journal of Applied Psychology, 75,* 371–377.

Gilliland, S. (1993). The perceived fairness of selection systems: An organizational justice perspective. *Academy of Management Review, 18,* 694–734.

Greenberg, J. (1986a). Determinants of perceived fairness of performance evaluations. *Journal of Applied Psychology, 71,* 340–342.

Greenberg, J. (1986b). The distributive justice of organizational performance evaluations. In H. W. Bierhoff, R. L. Cohen, & J. Greenberg (Eds.), *Justice in social relations* (pp. 337–351). New York: Plenum.

Greenberg, J. (1987). Using diaries to promote procedural justice in performance appraisals. *Social Justice Research, 1,* 219–234.

Greenberg, J. (1990). Employee theft as a reaction to underpayment inequity: The hidden cost of pay cuts. *Journal of Applied Psychology, 75,* 561–568.

Ilgen, D. R., Fisher, C. D., & Taylor, M. S. (1979). Feedback on behavior in organizations. *Journal of Applied Psychology, 64,* 349–371.

Klaas, B. S. (1989). Determinants of grievance activity and the grievance system's impact on employee behavior: An integrative perspective. *Academy of Management Review, 14,* 445–458.

Konovsky, M. A., & Brockner, J. (1993). Managing victim and survivor layoff reactions. In R. Cropanzano (Ed.), *Justice in the workplace: Approaching fairness in human resource management* (pp. 171–192). Hillsdale, NJ: Erlbaum.

Konovsky, M. A., & Cropanzano, R. (1991). Perceived fairness of employee drug testing as a predictor of employee attitudes and job performance. *Journal of Applied Psychology, 76,* 698–707.

Korsgaard, M. A., & Roberson, L. (1995). Procedural justice in performance evaluation: The role of instrumental and non-instrumental voice in performance appraisal discussions. *Journal of Management, 21,* 657–669.

Leventhal, G. S. (1980). What should be done with equity theory? New approaches to the study of fairness in social relationship. In K. J. Gergen, M. S. Greenberg, & R. H. Willis (Eds.), *Social exchange: Advances in theory and research* (pp. 27–55). New York: Plenum.

Magner, N., Welker, R. B., & Johnson, G. G. (1996). The interactive effects of participation and outcome favourability on turnover intentions and evaluations of supervisors. *Journal of Occupational and Organizational Psychology, 69,* 135–143.

Mathews, J. (1994, March 20). Do job reviews work? *Washington Post,* pp. H1–H4.

McNerney, D. (1995). Improved performance appraisals: Process of elimination. *HR Focus, 72,* 1–3.

Miller, L. (1996). Do's and don'ts of performance evaluation. *Human Resources Professional, 9*(3), 8–12.

Moorman, R. H. (1991). Relationship between organizational justice and organizational citizenship behaviors: Do fairness perceptions influence employee citizenship? *Journal of Applied Psychology, 76,* 845–855.

Nathan, B. R., Mohrman, A. M., Jr., & Milliman, J. (1991). Interpersonal relations as a context for the effects of appraisal interviews on performance and satisfaction: A longitudinal study. *Academy of Management Journal, 34,* 352–369.

Noe, R. A., Hollenbeck, J. R., Gerhart, B., & Wright, P. M. (1997). *Human resource management: Gaining a competitive advantage* (2nd ed.). Burr Ridge, IL: Irwin.

Taylor, M. S., Tracy, K. B., Renard, M. K., Harrison, J. K., & Carroll, S. J. (1995). Due process in performance appraisal: A quasi-experiment in procedural justice. *Administrative Science Quarterly, 40,* 495–523.

Tyler, T. R., & Bies, R. J. (1990). Beyond formal procedures: The interpersonal context of procedural justice. In J. S. Carroll (Ed.), *Applied social psychology and organizational settings* (pp. 77–98). Hillsdale, NJ: Erlbaum.

Werner, J. M., & Bolino, M. C. (1997). Explaining U.S. courts of appeals decisions involving performance appraisal: Accuracy, fairness, and validation. *Personnel Psychology, 50,* 1–24.

Wexley, K., Singh, V., & Yukl, G. (1973). Subordinate participation in three types of appraisal interviews. *Journal of Applied Psychology, 58,* 54–57.

CHAPTER 7

Performance Appraisal in Team Settings

Richard R. Reilly
Jack McGourty

The movement to team-based work has been one of the most dramatic changes in American business in recent history. Surveys consistently show that organizations ranging in size from the Fortune 500 to small businesses are using teams to accomplish work (Lawler, Mohrman, & Ledford, 1992; Manz & Sims, 1993). Why are organizations embracing the team concept? A cynical response might be that teams are merely one more example of a long line of fads in organizational design and development. Although the wholesale movement to teams by many organizations is often not well thought out, there are some key reasons that team-based approaches are on the increase. First, the pressure on businesses to respond to increased competition has stimulated a search for new ways to work more efficiently and effectively. A foremost consideration in effectiveness is meeting customer needs. Leaders in the Total Quality and Process Reengineering movements such as Juran (1989) and Hammer and Champy (1993) recommend teams as the preferred way to organize and accomplish work. Similarly, concurrent engineering approaches rely on cross-functional teams of researchers, engineers, manufacturers, and marketers to speed the development of new products.

Competitive pressures have also led to wholesale organizational change such as downsizing and flattening of organizations. Because smaller, flatter organizations require employees to be more flexible and to play a greater role in deciding how work gets done, self-directed work teams have become increasingly popular (Lawler et al., 1992). Finally, the increasing complexity of many jobs makes it difficult for one person to perform them, leading to the use of teams as the basic work unit.

A recent survey of companies using teams produced results consistent with these observations. The top three reasons for moving to teams were to improve customer satisfaction, improve products and services, and increase productivity (Gross, 1995).

Although the benefits of team-based structures have only recently become the focus of empirical research (for example, Cohen & Ledford, 1994), it is undeniable that the management of team performance will be a major issue facing organizations for some time.

What Is a Team?

Although teams have been defined somewhat inconsistently in the literature, a broad definition of teams includes the following characteristics: Teams involve two or more people who interact dynamically and interdependently and share a common and valued goal, objective, or mission. Teams also have a limited life-span of membership (Salas, Dickinson, Converse, & Tannenbaum, 1992). Work teams, in particular, are characterized by the following features:

- A dynamic exchange of information and resources among team members
- Coordination of task activities (for example, active communication)
- Constant adjustments to task demands
- Some organizational structuring of members

In historical terms, the movement to team-based structures has occurred rapidly, and our management practices—especially human resource practices—have lagged behind. Some verification of this lag was provided in a 1992 review of research on team performance assessment (O'Neil, Baker, & Kazlauskas, 1992), which found published and unpublished literature on team performance assessment to be almost nonexistent. Traditional HR functions of staffing, performance appraisal, and compensation have been designed for individuals and can frequently create dysfunction when applied to teams. For example, typical appraisal programs assess performance based on individual goal achievement. The emphasis on the individual contributor can inhibit the degree of interaction and collaboration required for a team to function effectively. The development of appropriate and relevant methods for appraising the performance of employees working in teams will be a critical factor in the success of human resource management in the future.

Ultimately, our reasons for establishing appraisal systems are to help achieve strategic organizational goals. We assume that appraisal can serve several purposes, including employee development, employee motivation, and support for rewards and recognition. The development of team appraisal processes requires a set of desired behaviors or performance outcomes that share the following elements:

- Clear definition
- Obvious relevance to team and organizational goals
- Accurate and fair measurement indices
- Effective communication to all team members

What are the desired behaviors in a team-based organization? We identify three classes of behavior: those related to individual competency (that is, knowledge, skills, and abilities relevant to organizationally valued performance), those related to individual team member performance, and those that describe performance at the team level. Appraisal systems should be designed to promote the development of competencies, motivate individuals to contribute to effective team performance, and motivate the team to perform effectively as a unit. Clearly, these behaviors or measures of performance should be relevant to the goals of the organization and the team and should be measured reliably. Finally, behaviors or measures of performance should be clearly communicated to team members and other stakeholders (for example, customers, supervisors) in the organization.

This chapter focuses on ways that organizations can appraise the performance of employees working in teams. Ensuring that the appraisal measures are relevant requires a shift in traditional approaches to validity. With the team as the organizational unit, our common notions of job-relatedness need to be carefully considered, since what is regarded as a job may be a fluid and continually changing construct. The behaviors that we focus on are those related to competency development, those related to individual behavior in a team context, and those related to the performance of the team as a unit.

Strategic and Practical Issues

Before deciding what to measure in each of these areas, several strategic and practical issues should be considered. First, what is the overall organizational strategy and how does the organization of employees into teams align with that strategy? Most organizations move to team-based structures because they believe that work performed in teams can respond to competition better than work performed by individuals. Teams offer several advantages:

- Quick response to rapidly changing environments
- Greater flexibility and versatility than traditional structures
- More effective completion of highly interdependent tasks and objectives
- More openness to continual learning
- More effective integration across organizational units

These features of teams should be aligned with organizational strategy. Groups of individuals working on relatively independent tasks are sometimes designated as teams—but are teams in name only. In such cases, appraisal processes designed to assess team performance may actually be dysfunctional. For example, appraisal processes designed to assess and encourage collaboration among employees performing independent tasks may actually slow productivity. Before considering how to measure and appraise team performance we should be confident that the work group is a true team working interdependently to achieve common goals or tasks.

Case Study 1: A Strategic Approach to Team Appraisal

Allstate Insurance used a strategic approach to the development of teams and the measurement of team performance. As a first step, each work group had to decide if it should be a team by clearly identifying common or shared outputs and customers, work products that could not be produced alone, and results that could not be accomplished alone. Once it was decided that the work group was a team, each team had to develop a team charter that included

- The purpose of the team
- Identification of the team's customers
- The customers' requirements and expectations
- The approach to be used to achieve the necessary results
- The methods and procedures to be used to measure results
- Goals to be set in order to achieve results
- Actions to be taken to achieve goals
- When and how to evaluate results

A second consideration has to do with the characteristics of the teams to be appraised. Teams can vary along a number of different dimensions including the permanence of the team, the extent to which individual member participation varies over time, the degree of task interdependence, the mission or goals of the team, and the extent to which the team is empowered. The design of measurement systems will be dependent upon these characteristics. For example, a team that maintains traditional hierarchical reporting relationships will require different approaches to assessment than a team that is fully empowered to make decisions and self-manage.

Third, what has been current organizational practice in the area of performance assessment? Moving from traditional individual performance appraisals by supervisors to some of the methods suggested here may involve a radical shift in the way the performance of employees is assessed. The transition to these new methods should take current practices into account in deciding how to structure the change process. The more radical the change, the more there is a need for employee participation and careful communication and implementation of the new methods. It is also important to review the intended team appraisal process and its alignment with other key organizational practices as well. Performance management affects and is affected by several key practices including training, career development, and compensation. For example, early in the implementation of one organization's peer assessment program, employees expressed concern over being measured on skills in which there was little or no training offered. In this case, by making team skills and behaviors more salient, the organization highlighted a deficiency elsewhere in the system.

Finally, to what extent are the behaviors and outputs of the team measurable? For some production teams, output may be easily quantifiable. For other teams (for example, management teams) the behaviors and outputs may be less clear and demand more creative and careful specification of team objectives.

Competencies, Individual Performance, and Team Performance

Our model assumes that team performance is a product of the competencies of team members and the effectiveness with which the team members work together. Figure 7.1 illustrates a simple model. These three different aspects of employee behavior—competencies, individual performance, and team performance—should be considered in the definition and measurement of behavior in team-based organizations.

Competencies are defined sets of knowledge, skills, and abilities that allow the employee to perform specific functions related to organizational goals. Although the term *skill* is often used, we prefer the broader term competency. A competency can be defined as a collection of behaviors that contribute to the performance of organizationally valued work. Competencies can be broad or quite

Figure 7.1. A Model of Team Performance.

Team Performance

Competencies, Team Member Behavior,
and Team Performance

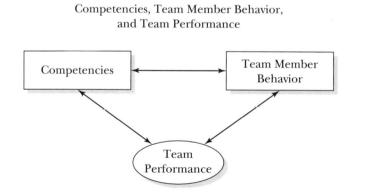

specific. A broad competency such as "team facilitation" will be relevant to the accomplishment of a wide variety of tasks, whereas a more specific competency such as "troubleshooting HVAC systems" will be relevant to a narrow range of tasks. For assessment to occur, competencies must be operationally defined by the organization. Operational definitions can include the demonstration of observable behavior or the demonstration of critical knowledge necessary for the competency.

Individual performance includes behaviors under control of the individual employee. These may include behaviors relevant to the performance of nonintegrated tasks as well as behaviors necessary for the achievement of integrated (team) tasks.

Team performance includes the behavior of the team as an integrated and interdependent unit and focuses on the achievement of measurable team objectives.

Competency Assessment

Surveys conducted in 1987 and 1990 showed that competency-based systems are on the increase. In 1990, 51 percent of the companies surveyed reported use of competency-based pay as compared with 40 percent in 1987 (Lawler, Ledford, & Chang, 1993). Why are organizations focusing on competencies? Downsizing, increased competition, and team-based organizational structures have led many organizations to develop *competency models* that identify and define the competencies employees will need for the future. From an employer's perspective, the competencies are the human software needed to achieve organizational goals. From the employees' perspective, competencies represent personal portfolios of skills, knowledge, and abilities that can establish their value to the organization or to other employers. Team-based organizations can use competency models as a basis for placing value on employee knowledge and skill instead of relying on traditional methods of appraisal. Competency-based pay programs are the most common application, but other applications can include diagnostic feedback, promotion, and requiring employees to demonstrate competency to survive in a job. Competency models can also be a valuable tool for configuring and managing teams. Having the correct mix and level of competencies does not guarantee that desired behaviors will occur or that team performance will be effective, but it does provide the necessary basis for effective performance and can also provide a basis for valuing and rewarding individuals. As noted earlier, the assessment of competencies requires the four elements of definition, relevance, accurate and fair measurement, and effective communication of the desired behaviors.

The definition of competencies begins with the articulation of current and future strategic objectives for the organization. Once the work activities necessary to achieve these strategic objectives are specified, the competencies necessary to effectively perform those activities can be identified. At this stage, the identification of competencies should be done at a general level. These broad categories should encompass all the work activities necessary to achieve the strategic objectives. Sales and customer relations, technical, administrative, and leadership competencies are categories that will apply to a large percentage of the activities in an organization.

Within each of the broad areas, more specific competencies can be identified. There may be many specific technical competencies, for example. Within the marketing division of a telecommunications firm, technical competencies for members of sales teams might include areas such as Telecommunications Knowledge, Sales and Customer Relations Skill, and Marketing Knowledge. Competency definition should be done at the behavioral level and should include criteria for distinguishing between different levels of expertise. Table 7.1 shows how several competencies for a telecommunications marketing organization might be defined. Technical, Sales and Customer Relations, and Marketing Competency are operationally defined in terms of tasks or behaviors that can be observed. Each competency is also divided into three levels depending upon the behavior demonstrated by the employee. Competencies typically represent a collection of tasks or behaviors and are referred to as blocks, or units.

Competency measurement includes the methods and procedures for verifying that the employee has mastered a specific level of a competency. Measurement of competency level is typically accomplished through one of the following types of certification programs: peer assessment, supervisory assessment, accredited external certification, or internal board certification. The methods of measurement can include ratings, structured assessment processes, objective job knowledge tests, and end-of-training testing.

Table 7.1. Competencies for Telecommunications Sales Teams.

Level	Telecommunications Knowledge	Sales and Customer Relations Skill	Marketing Knowledge
Low	• Identify system components • Communicate effectively with customers about their telecommunication needs	• Make effective initial contact with customers • Perform fact finding to identify sales opportunities	• Understand the strategy underlying a marketing plan • Implement most elements of the marketing mix
Intermediate	• Conduct an assessment of a system • Identify problems and how they might be improved	• Build relationships with customers • Develop and present sales proposals effectively	• Contribute to the strategy underlying a marketing plan • Implement all of the elements of the marketing mix
High	• Help customers design and plan their system • Make major improvements to existing system	• Develop a sales plan for a major market • Lead a sales team to develop and present a proposal for a major customer	• Design a strategic marketing plan • Effectively integrate and implement all elements of the marketing mix

Source: Copyright © 1992, Assessment Alternatives, Inc. Used with permission.

Peer assessment programs involve the observation and evaluation of an employee's competence by one or more coworkers. Peer assessment programs are frequently used in mature self-directed teams. For example, Gast Manufacturing designates key nonexempt employees to serve as assessors in determining mastery of certain manufacturing operations. Checklists are used as a guide in observation and evaluation, as described in Case Study 2.

Supervisory assessment is similar to peer assessment and is most useful in newly formed teams, or teams in which the competencies to be certified are not yet possessed by other team members.

External certification relies on an accredited body to certify that the individual possesses a specific competency. External certification is most useful for competencies that can be acquired through well-defined education and training programs. For example, Squibb Manufacturing relies on a local junior college to verify that employees on a maintenance team possess the minimum required competencies in areas such as heating, ventilation, and air conditioning. Another organization with project management teams relies on the Project Management Association to certify the competency of project managers and uses a formal testing program administered by the association.

Internal board certification usually involves assembling groups of recognized experts within the organization who can assess the level of a specific competency or set of competencies. For example, a marketing division of one company has established a board certification process to verify that all market managers are competent in basic marketing skills such as product knowledge, pricing, promotion, and placement.

Development of Certification Programs

The development of certification programs for team members should include the four elements of definition, relevance, accuracy and fairness, and communication.

Competency Definition

As noted earlier, the preparation of competency definitions should begin with consideration of the strategic objectives of the organization and the objectives of the team. Competencies can include not only technical competencies but interpersonal competencies related to effective teamwork (for example, conflict resolution). If possible, team members should be involved in the development of competency definitions to ensure acceptance of the program and commitment to continual learning. It should also be noted that the strategic intent of certification includes the notion of "raising the bar" over time by adding higher levels of competency or adding new competencies as conditions and technology change.

Relevance: Linkage of Competencies to Important Tasks or Behavior

Any program that affects the occupational status of employees should be related to important work performed by those employees. In certification programs, validity studies are done for two reasons: to ensure that the appropriate knowledge, skills, or abilities are being measured, and to comply with legal requirements. The 1964 and 1991 Civil Rights Acts require employers to show that procedures that affect pay, promotion, or other aspects of an employee's status are job-related. Performance appraisal programs have been found to be covered by the Civil Rights Act by the federal courts in *Brito* v. *Zia* (1973). Certification programs can usually be validated by showing that the content of the certification process is related to important work performed by team members. In manufacturing processes, for example, team members can be certified on different phases of the production cycle. Job-relatedness can be established by documenting expert judgments of the relevance of certification content to the work actually performed. An analysis of the tasks involved in production can be directly linked to the knowledge and skill assessed in the certification program.

Measurement of Competency

The choice of certification method will be dependent upon the type of competency to be assessed, the organization's culture, and the objectives of the program. For example, in fully self-directed teams a structured peer review approach may be the best way to manage certification of production competencies. All team members have a common interest in performing effectively, the team is empowered to determine the skill of its members, and some team members should possess the expertise to evaluate the competency of a peer. On the other hand, an organization in which the skills are not routinely possessed by team members, or the teams are not self-directed, should probably rely on another method of certification such as supervisory evaluation or formal internal or external certification processes.

Regardless of the certification method, the criteria applied should be the same. Evaluation procedures should be as reliable and objective as possible and should be fair to the employees. Some steps to ensure fairness include clear communication of the expected behaviors or performance, opportunities for employees to develop the competency, reevaluation provisions for employees who do not pass a certification process, and clear developmental feedback. In addition, an appeals process should be put into place to deal with actual or perceived irregularities in the evaluation process.

For certification processes administered internally, the individuals conducting the certification method should be trained so that all candidates receive a standardized opportunity to demonstrate their knowledge and skill. Training should cover both the administration of the process and the scoring of candidate performance. Regardless of the method of assessment, the administrator should provide standard instructions to all candidates and the conditions of assessment should be the same for all candidates. In the case of processes involving expert judgment a practice session with a mock candidate can help assessors calibrate to a common standard. Behavioral checklists or well-defined rating scales should also be used to help board members accurately and consistently judge performance.

Objective tests are another option. Members of the Merrill Lynch Cash Management Customer Team must demonstrate proficiency in specific areas by answering a series of representative customer questions in a paper-and-pencil test. Depending upon experience, team members are required to demonstrate higher levels of proficiency by passing more difficult and complex tests.

Another option is to build certification into training. Pershing's Customer Service Team members must pass a series of computer-based tests to demonstrate proficiency in each of a series of training modules before certifying into the job. Objective tests offer obvious advantages of standardization and lower administrative costs but also demand the same standards of content relevance required of any job-affecting test.

Certification programs offer several advantages to organizations: they serve as a powerful mechanism for communicating desired competencies and associated behaviors, they provide a common set of standards for defining minimally acceptable competency, and they allow organizations to more effectively manage teams by providing objective information on the competencies possessed by team members. From an employee's perspective, competency programs provide a clear set of goals that are usually realistic and achievable—conditions that are optimal for improvement in employee competence.

Communication in Competency Certification Programs

Before a certification program is implemented, the purpose and nature of the program should be communicated to affected employees. Communication should give employees a clear idea of what is involved in the certification process, how to prepare for certification, when and how the process will be administered, and what the policies are for recertification. Communication should spell out clearly the advantages of certification and the disadvantages and consequences of not certifying. Advantages and disadvantages might be related to pay, bonuses, promotion, or greater internal mobility. In some cases the consequences of not certifying might also include outplacement from the job or the organization. Table 7.2 summarizes recommendation for competency assessment.

Case Study 2: Peer-Based Certification

Gast Manufacturing, a maker of industrial pumps, has instituted a series of competency certification programs for its production teams. Team members are assessed on technical skills related to the manufacturing process and team skills, such as self-management. Certification of technical skills is done by other (certified) peers using a structured observation process. To be certified, team members must demonstrate proficiency on a set of specific production-related skills. Evaluators use a checklist like the one in Exhibit 7.1 to make final evaluations. All evaluators are trained and work with a manual that includes more specific behavioral items and clearly defines acceptable performance on each item.

Table 7.2. Summary of Recommendations for Competency Certification in Team-Based Organizations.

Step	Recommendations
Identification and definition of competency	• Begin with broad, strategic competencies • Define operationally through SMEs and team members if possible
Establishment of relevance	• SMEs link competencies to important tasks performed • Linkages documented
Competency measurement	• Clear communication of desired behaviors • SMEs set standards for certification • Standardized conditions and training of assessors • Reliable measurement • Clear feedback with opportunity to recertify • Peer assessment, supervisor assessment, internal and external certification programs depending upon nature of competency and team
Communication	• Clear description of process and how to prepare • Clear description of policies on readministration • Advantages of certification

Note: SME = subject matter expert.

Source: Copyright © 1992, Assessment Alternatives, Inc. Used with permission.

The assessment of individual performance in a team context would seem to be an oxymoron. Traditionally, individual performance assessment methods have assumed that tasks can be performed independently or that individual contributions to performance can be measured accurately for a given individual. In some so-called teams in which tasks are performed independently or sequentially (Van de Ven, Delbecq, & Koenig, 1976) it might be possible and appropriate to assess and reward individual performance. As task interdependence increases, however, the measurement of individual contributions becomes difficult and individual performance assessment becomes less appropriate. Also, it is recognized that in many organizations individuals function in multiple teams or part-time

Exhibit 7.1. Certification Checklist
for Muffler Housing Technical Skills.

The Team Associate will machine a Quality Product meeting Gast Quality Standards, following ISO procedures and meeting and exceeding all customer requirements in appropriate time frames using the following processes identified below:

	Technical Skill	Satisfactory	Unsatisfactory
1	Read and interpret machine schedule	☐	☐
2	Interpret machine setup sheets and prints	☐	☐
3	Operate fork lift and demonstrate proper handling technique	☐	☐
4	Operate computer terminal	☐	☐
5	Read inspection equipment and perform inspection procedures	☐	☐
6	Interpret CNC program	☐	☐
7	Perform machine procedures	☐	☐
8	Perform machine operations	☐	☐
9	Demonstrate proper use of machine tools	☐	☐
10	Perform certified SPC procedures	☐	☐
11	Identify rough and finished part locations	☐	☐
12	Record machine scrap and identify proper scrap locations and procedures	☐	☐
13	Practice job safety and follow good housekeeping procedures	☐	☐

Evaluator _____

Date _____

Source: Copyright © 1992, Assessment Alternatives, Inc. Used with permission.

teams and that the overall performance of an individual may be a function of performance in several different types of roles (individual as well as team). Our focus here is on those behaviors that contribute to or hamper team performance as opposed to the assessment of overall goal achievement or productivity on independent tasks. Our assumption is that overall team performance involves interdependent activities among the group members and that, ultimately, team performance will be a function of specific behaviors that contribute to effective teamwork as well as task-specific behaviors. Virtually all models of team and work group effectiveness acknowledge that interpersonal processes are a crucial antecedent of team performance (Gladstein, 1984; Hackman, 1983; Nieva, Fleishman, & Reick, 1978; Sundstrom, De Meuse, & Futrell, 1990). This is particularly true in the early stages of team development or for teams that have incorporated new members. Referring again to the model in Figure 7.1, the competencies of team members can only result in effective team performance if the team is able to collaborate, communicate, make decisions, and self-manage as a unit.

Team-based organizations have explicitly or implicitly decided on a strategy for organizing and accomplishing work. Obviously, an important class of behaviors that will contribute to that strategy are those relevant to effective team functioning. Because teams are a relatively new way of working for many employees, the appropriate behaviors needed for effective teamwork are often not clear. Behavioral assessment of team member behavior can be a powerful tool for helping introduce desired behavioral change. Research has shown that behavior can be improved through communicating these behaviors and giving employees periodic feedback (Reilly, Smither, & Vasilopoulos, 1996; Dominick, Reilly, & McGourty, 1997). Repeated exposure to the behaviors as a self-assessor, peer assessor, or recipient of feedback can help team members internalize the behaviors and make them part of the team-based organizational culture.

Identification and Definition of Key Team Member Competencies

Traditional performance appraisal methods focus on the extent to which individuals perform relative to some standard. The standard might be based on key dimensions of performance, a normative comparison to other employees, or specific objectives for an individual employee. It is possible to assess individual behavior within a team, however. As a first step, the key behaviors related to effective team performance must be identified. Behaviors should be described in terms that are understandable and observable by team members and other individuals who might be interfacing with the team.

Although organizations may wish to conduct their own analysis of behaviors needed for effective teamwork, recent research suggests that teamwork is a function of several types of individual competencies grouped into two broad categories (Stevens & Campion, 1994). The first category, *interpersonal,* includes team member competencies related to conflict resolution, collaborative problem solving, and communication. The second category, *self-management,* includes team member competencies related to goal setting and performance management for the team and team planning and co-ordination. One recent model of team behavior (Dominick et al., 1997) incorporates these competencies into a four-dimensional model including self-management, communication, decision making, and collaboration as follows:

Self-management has to do with the facilitation and leadership behaviors displayed by team members during team meetings and other interactions. Individuals can contribute to team self-management by helping lead and facilitate the team; define goals, roles, and responsibilities; and manage the processes involved in team functioning.

Communication includes behaviors related to giving and receiving constructive feedback, listening skills, sharing of information, and articulation of ideas.

Decision making involves helping the team make decisions in a systematic way (for example, polling) or helping ensure that participation in decision making is balanced throughout the team. It also involves avoiding acceptance of the status quo or engaging in groupthink.

Collaboration is the essential ingredient of team performance. Individuals can help or hinder the extent to which their teams function collaboratively. Helping manage or avoid negative conflict, displaying a commitment to the team and its goals, valuing the diversity of background and experience of other team members, and sharing accountability are examples of key collaborative behaviors. It might be noted that many of the behaviors associated with collaboration are related to organizational citizenship. It is likely that highly collaborative teams will be good organizational citizens as a spillover benefit.

Other behaviors can also be added, depending on the team and its goals. Individual behaviors related to specific task performance, customer focus, and quality are examples.

Relevance of Team Behavioral Competencies

An analysis of team processes and the work that the team performs should be the basis for establishing the relevance of the competencies to be assessed. A model of team behavior, such as the one described in this chapter, can serve as a starting point. Team leaders, team members, customers, and other stakeholders can then provide input into determining what will be assessed and who will assess it. In effect, a "team job analysis" can be done by means of approaches such as focus groups and inventory ratings. The same approach can also be used to determine who is in the best position to assess certain behaviors. Lists of specific behaviors can help define the competencies for all raters and ratees and will also allow more precise and comprehensive documentation of relevance. Documentation of the importance of specific behaviors and associated competencies can serve as evidence of relevance to the work that the team performs as a unit. Table 7.3 shows an example of how subject matter experts (SMEs) might rate the relevance of team competencies for specific task areas for a customer service team.

Accuracy and Fairness of Team-Related Behavior Measurement

Methods for assessing team member behavior can include traditional supervisory appraisals, peer assessment, or multisource assessment. For behaviors related to effective team functioning, the ideal rater should be in a position to observe the day-to-day team interaction in functional settings. Team leaders and the team members themselves are usually in the best position to assess relevant behavior. In some cases, customers might be able to provide ratings of specific behaviors. One approach that has been used with

Table 7.3. Ratings of Importance of
Team Member Competencies for Customer Service Tasks.

Team Competency	Planning and Scheduling	Solving Customer Problems	Negotiation	Process Improvement	Order Fulfillment
Communication	4	4	4	3	4
Collaboration	5	4	3	5	4
Decision making	4	3	4	3	2
Self-management	5	3	2	4	3

Rating Scale
5 = Highly Critical for Effective Task Performance
4 = Important for Effective Task Performance
3 = Moderately Important for Effective Task Performance
2 = Minor Important for Effective Task Performance
1 = Not Important for Effective Task Performance

Source: Copyright © 1992, Assessment Alternatives, Inc. Used with permission.

success involves having team members and other raters periodically assess one another using Behavioral Observation Scales (Latham & Wexley, 1977). BOS items describe specific behaviors and ask raters to indicate the extent to which the behavior is demonstrated by the target individual. Simpler methods may also be used. One self-directed work team uses a simple "satisfactory" versus "needs improvement" rating with a third category for "don't know." If this procedure is carried out properly, each team member will be rated on each behavior by all other team members and a team leader. Repeated exposure to the behaviors as an assessor or recipient of feedback can help people internalize the behaviors and make them part of the team-based organizational culture.

Several steps in implementing a multisource assessment program for teams are recommended to ensure that evaluations are as accurate and fair as possible.

As a first step, raters should be instructed to avoid common rater errors. This can be done in group sessions prior to initial ratings or instructions can be embedded in the rating instrument itself. Although paper-and-pencil surveys are commonly used, there are several advantages to using electronic media where possible. One approach (described in Case Study 3) used individualized computer disks that provided instructions on how to make ratings and how to avoid rater errors, and gave sample ratings. The computer program then presented each behavior to be rated separately so that raters were able to consider themselves and their team members on the same behavior. Other electronic media such as Local Area Networks (LANs) can also be used to collect multi-source assessment. Electronic media are especially useful in situations where raters work in different locations. Data collection is accomplished more quickly since printing and mailing are eliminated. All data are also automatically recorded, which can further reduce turnaround time for analysis and reporting.

In most cases, each team member will provide a self-rating and ratings for all other team members (using a form like the one shown in Exhibit 7.2). For example, assessment of a five-person team would involve collecting a total of six ratings from each team member (a self-rating plus five ratings of other team members). It should be made clear that all ratings will be treated confidentially and that only aggregated ratings will be reported.

One of the primary benefits of team member assessment is the feedback that can be provided. Each participant in the process should receive feedback detailing results at the behavioral level. Feedback serves several useful purposes:

- The receipt of feedback can further reinforce the new behaviors necessary for effective teamwork.
- A feedback report can be used as a starting point for a dialogue between team members regarding how they can function more effectively.
- Feedback can help individual team members set goals for themselves.

Typical feedback reports include self-ratings, summary ratings from other sources, and normative ratings. Feedback reports can also identify areas of strength and developmental need and provide guidance on how to use the results developmentally. Research on feedback programs (Atwater, Roush, & Fischthal, 1995; Smither et al., 1995; Reilly et al., 1996; Dominick et al., 1997) shows that feedback can have enhancing effects on performance. Feedback can facilitate performance by allowing participants to compare their own performance to a standard and use the gaps as a starting point in

Exhibit 7.2. Team Peer Assessment Rating Form.

INSTRUCTIONS Think about your experience with your team. You will be rating how frequently you and the other team members engaged in each of the specific behaviors and activities listed. Begin by writing your full name in the column labeled "Self." You will use that column to record your ratings of yourself. Then write in your fellow team members' full names, at the top of each column under the heading "Other Team Members." You will use those columns to record your ratings of them.

Response options are provided to the right of each survey item. For each item, circle only one response per person. Remember:

① This information will remain confidential, so be completely candid.

② Base your responses on actual behavior you observed.

③ Respond to all items.

RATING SCALE:
1=Never 2=Rarely 3=Sometimes 4=Frequently 5=Always N=Does Not Apply

BEHAVIORS		WRITE FULL NAMES AND #'S HERE ⇨	SELF	OTHER TEAM MEMBERS					
Collaboration	1)	Acknowledged conflict and worked to resolve issues	1 2 3 4 5 N	1 2 3 4 5 N	1 2 3 4 5 N	1 2 3 4 5 N	1 2 3 4 5 N	1 2 3 4 5 N	1 2 3 4 5 N
	2)	Helped others by sharing knowledge and information	1 2 3 4 5 N	1 2 3 4 5 N	1 2 3 4 5 N	1 2 3 4 5 N	1 2 3 4 5 N	1 2 3 4 5 N	1 2 3 4 5 N
	3)	Encouraged diverse perspectives and differing points of view	1 2 3 4 5 N	1 2 3 4 5 N	1 2 3 4 5 N	1 2 3 4 5 N	1 2 3 4 5 N	1 2 3 4 5 N	1 2 3 4 5 N
	4)	Promoted balanced participation among team members	1 2 3 4 5 N	1 2 3 4 5 N	1 2 3 4 5 N	1 2 3 4 5 N	1 2 3 4 5 N	1 2 3 4 5 N	1 2 3 4 5 N
	5)	Demonstrated interest and enthusiasm during team activities	1 2 3 4 5 N	1 2 3 4 5 N	1 2 3 4 5 N	1 2 3 4 5 N	1 2 3 4 5 N	1 2 3 4 5 N	1 2 3 4 5 N
	6)	Acknowledged others' contributions and ideas	1 2 3 4 5 N	1 2 3 4 5 N	1 2 3 4 5 N	1 2 3 4 5 N	1 2 3 4 5 N	1 2 3 4 5 N	1 2 3 4 5 N
Communication	7)	Articulated ideas clearly and concisely	1 2 3 4 5 N	1 2 3 4 5 N	1 2 3 4 5 N	1 2 3 4 5 N	1 2 3 4 5 N	1 2 3 4 5 N	1 2 3 4 5 N
	8)	Listened attentively to other team members without interrupting	1 2 3 4 5 N	1 2 3 4 5 N	1 2 3 4 5 N	1 2 3 4 5 N	1 2 3 4 5 N	1 2 3 4 5 N	1 2 3 4 5 N
	9)	Restated what had been said to show understanding	1 2 3 4 5 N	1 2 3 4 5 N	1 2 3 4 5 N	1 2 3 4 5 N	1 2 3 4 5 N	1 2 3 4 5 N	1 2 3 4 5 N
	10)	Demonstrated sensitivity to other team members' feelings and personal interests	1 2 3 4 5 N	1 2 3 4 5 N	1 2 3 4 5 N	1 2 3 4 5 N	1 2 3 4 5 N	1 2 3 4 5 N	1 2 3 4 5 N
	11)	Effectively used facts to get points across to other team members	1 2 3 4 5 N	1 2 3 4 5 N	1 2 3 4 5 N	1 2 3 4 5 N	1 2 3 4 5 N	1 2 3 4 5 N	1 2 3 4 5 N
	12)	Probed for information by encouraging others to elaborate on their ideas and input	1 2 3 4 5 N	1 2 3 4 5 N	1 2 3 4 5 N	1 2 3 4 5 N	1 2 3 4 5 N	1 2 3 4 5 N	1 2 3 4 5 N
Decision Making	13)	Anticipated problems and modified plans accordingly	1 2 3 4 5 N	1 2 3 4 5 N	1 2 3 4 5 N	1 2 3 4 5 N	1 2 3 4 5 N	1 2 3 4 5 N	1 2 3 4 5 N
	14)	Helped the team generate alternative solutions	1 2 3 4 5 N	1 2 3 4 5 N	1 2 3 4 5 N	1 2 3 4 5 N	1 2 3 4 5 N	1 2 3 4 5 N	1 2 3 4 5 N
	15)	Solicited input from other team members	1 2 3 4 5 N	1 2 3 4 5 N	1 2 3 4 5 N	1 2 3 4 5 N	1 2 3 4 5 N	1 2 3 4 5 N	1 2 3 4 5 N
	16)	Analyzed problems from different points of view	1 2 3 4 5 N	1 2 3 4 5 N	1 2 3 4 5 N	1 2 3 4 5 N	1 2 3 4 5 N	1 2 3 4 5 N	1 2 3 4 5 N
	17)	Discouraged team members from rushing to conclusions	1 2 3 4 5 N	1 2 3 4 5 N	1 2 3 4 5 N	1 2 3 4 5 N	1 2 3 4 5 N	1 2 3 4 5 N	1 2 3 4 5 N
	18)	Made decisions based on factual information rather than "gut feel" or intuition	1 2 3 4 5 N	1 2 3 4 5 N	1 2 3 4 5 N	1 2 3 4 5 N	1 2 3 4 5 N	1 2 3 4 5 N	1 2 3 4 5 N
Self-Management	19)	Provided clear direction and defined priorities for the team	1 2 3 4 5 N	1 2 3 4 5 N	1 2 3 4 5 N	1 2 3 4 5 N	1 2 3 4 5 N	1 2 3 4 5 N	1 2 3 4 5 N
	20)	Kept the team focused on its tasks	1 2 3 4 5 N	1 2 3 4 5 N	1 2 3 4 5 N	1 2 3 4 5 N	1 2 3 4 5 N	1 2 3 4 5 N	1 2 3 4 5 N
	21)	Actively monitored progress to ensure completion according to team plan	1 2 3 4 5 N	1 2 3 4 5 N	1 2 3 4 5 N	1 2 3 4 5 N	1 2 3 4 5 N	1 2 3 4 5 N	1 2 3 4 5 N
	22)	Provided nonjudgmental and specific feedback to others	1 2 3 4 5 N	1 2 3 4 5 N	1 2 3 4 5 N	1 2 3 4 5 N	1 2 3 4 5 N	1 2 3 4 5 N	1 2 3 4 5 N
	23)	Helped the team devise procedures for working together	1 2 3 4 5 N	1 2 3 4 5 N	1 2 3 4 5 N	1 2 3 4 5 N	1 2 3 4 5 N	1 2 3 4 5 N	1 2 3 4 5 N
	24)	Acknowledged team accomplishments	1 2 3 4 5 N	1 2 3 4 5 N	1 2 3 4 5 N	1 2 3 4 5 N	1 2 3 4 5 N	1 2 3 4 5 N	1 2 3 4 5 N

Source: Copyright © 1992, Assessment Alternatives, Inc. Used with permission.

goal setting and behavior change. In addition to written feedback reports, workshops that help participants use the results of assessment to structure a personal developmental plan are recommended.

Communications in Team Behavioral Assessment Programs

Although peer or multisource feedback has become more common in recent years (Timmreck, 1995), it still represents a major paradigm shift for most employees and should be introduced and managed carefully. Clearly, other factors can influence team success. Figure 7.2 shows a model of team behavior that incorporates organizational influences external to the team, team member competencies, and team performance. Organizational influences such as organizational culture and structure, reward systems, the resources available to the team, and the nature of the task can influence team effectiveness directly (for example, resources) or indirectly (for example, rewards) by moderating the strength of the relationship between team member behavior and team performance outcomes. Organizational factors should be considered before introducing a team member assessment program. For example, an organization with historically low levels of trust requires a different and more careful approach than one with historically high levels of trust.

The introduction of the assessment program should be accompanied by a statement of the program's purpose and the administrative uses, if any, of the resulting assessments. A strong recommendation is that, at least initially, the data be used primarily for developmental purposes. In addition, the initial communication provides the first opportunity to present the behaviors that reflect the desired model of team behavior. This aspect of communication is extremely important as it represents a way of enhancing a change in the organization's culture. If done properly, the implementation and continued application of the assessment process will reinforce this cultural shift and change the behaviors that are regarded as normative. One other issue that should be addressed in the initial communication has to do with the confidentiality of individual rating data. In most multisource feedback programs, ratings provided by individual raters are aggregated. Typically, average ratings and ranges are provided based on a minimum of three ratings. This helps ensure anonymity of individual

Figure 7.2. Relationships Among Organizational Factors, Team Member Behavior, and Team Performance.

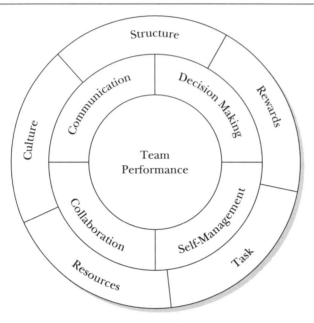

Source: Copyright © 1992, Assessment Alternatives, Inc. Used with permission.

raters and provides a comfort level for raters to be as candid as possible. Table 7.4 summarizes recommendations for appraisal of team member behavior.

Case Study 3: Appraisal and Feedback for Team Member Behavior

Warner-Lambert, a large pharmaceutical firm, established a series of management teams in its financial organization. Each team had a designated team leader and met on a regular basis to plan and make decisions relevant to a specific organizational unit. A peer assessment process was introduced shortly after team formation. The process included a four-dimensional model of team behavior organized around collaboration, communication, self-management, and decision making. All team members evaluated themselves and their teammates using a computerized system that provided rating instructions, sample ratings, and a confidential password that allowed members to rate themselves and their teammates. All employees received detailed feedback reports that showed their self-assessment, their teammates' assessment of them, and normative data for their team and

Table 7.4. Summary of Recommendations for Assessment of Individual Performance in Team-Based Organizations.

Step	Recommendations
Identification and definition of behaviors	• Identify and define key behaviors related to effective team performance • Behaviors related to self-management, communication, decision making, and collaboration are suggested • Behaviors related to specific task performance, customer focus, and quality can be identified and added
Establish relevance	• Team leaders, team members, customers, and other stakeholders can determine relevance of behaviors for effective team performance • Linkages to team performance documented
Measurement of team member competency	• Supervisors, peers, or multisource assessment should be considered • Team leaders and team members can assess behaviors related to effective team functioning • Multisource assessment can be used for appropriate (observable) behaviors • Feedback and developmental planning should be a feature of assessment
Communication	• State program's purpose and administrative purposes • Use of assessment for development only is recommended • Description of desired behaviors should be included in the communication • Confidentiality of raters should be ensured

Source: Copyright © 1992, Assessment Alternatives, Inc. Used with permission.

the entire organization. Feedback reports were used as a discussion point for improvement of team functioning. In addition, postadministration focus groups were conducted to answer questions and discuss concerns about the team assessment process. This was especially important since the overall program strategy was to move team assessment feedback from its initial developmental focus to a full integration with the existing performance management and compensation system within a two-year period. The process was repeated twice over a twelve-month period and results showed significant improvement in average team member ratings.

Assessment of Team Performance

Referring again to our model of team performance (Figure 7.1), we focus on the final aspect of measurement, team performance outcomes. Team-based organizations, whether by design or accident, replace the organizational unit known as the "worker" or "employee" with the team. From an organizational perspective, a customer service team is the key entity to be evaluated in terms of its impact on customers and other organizational units. The members of the team are *fungible*—that is, any member can be exchanged for another employee with similar skills without changing the team. Clearly, a true team-based organization will send the wrong message by continuing to emphasize individual performance exclusively. Waldman (1997) offers evidence that employees working in teams tend to favor team-based systems of appraisal though the preference is not universal. In particular, individuals with high need for achievement still prefer individual appraisal. From a strategic perspective, however, it would seem not only desirable but necessary to appraise performance of the team as a unit if the organization wants to send the message that team performance is the key to organizational success.

Definition and Relevance of Team Performance Measures

For many teams, it is possible to specify objective indices of performance at the team level. If objective indices are used, they should have a clear relevance to the organization's mission and strategy. For example, customer service teams might be measured on the number of calls handled, the number of complaints by customers, or the number of commendations by customers. Sales teams can be measured by dollar volume of sales or by booked revenues for a specified time period. A concurrent engineering team might be measured on product development cycle time or the number of products brought to market. Indices should have a clear relationship to the strategic goals and objectives of the organization. For example, a customer service team might be measured on the number of calls handled—but sheer volume of calls may have little relationship to the strategic goal of service excellence and, in fact, may be negatively correlated with it. On the other hand, indices such as repeat calls, customer complaints, and customer commendations might be more closely aligned with the strategic objective. One important step that should be incorporated if objective measures are to be used is the participation of the team in identifying measures and in setting goals. Team members are good sources of information about what performance outcomes can be achieved, measured, and linked directly to team activities. Line-of-sight issues are an important consideration in team goal setting. The team members must perceive that they can have a legitimate impact or influence on the specified outcomes. If this line of sight is not clear, the team will not focus on the desired outcomes. Team participation will help team members focus on the right measurements and the steps needed to achieve the goals that were set. Other approaches involve multisource assessment and integrated measurement of team objectives. These approaches should also involve the participation of the team members in defining what is to be measured and how it is related to the organization's mission and strategy. As a final step, the relevance of team performance measurements should be documented. This will serve two purposes: as a basis for establishing the job-relatedness of the performance measures, and as a communication device for new team members.

Measurement of Team Performance

What are some of the approaches that can be used to assess the performance of the team as a unit? We offer the following approaches:

- Direct measures of output or quality
- Multisource assessment
- Integrated assessment of objectives

Direct Measures of Quality and Quantity

The use of directly measurable indices can be effective assuming that several characteristics of the measurements hold:

- *Adequate information systems.* For effective use of direct measures of output, the information must be readily available and easily understood by team members. In one organization, a telecommunications sales team was being measured on the dollar volume that customers charged on telephone credit cards sold. Unfortunately, the team had no readily available information on how much a particular customer would actually use the card sold until six months later, making it difficult for team members to modify their behavior to target high-use customers.

- *Reliability.* The measurements should be reliable over time. To put it another way, indices that are highly volatile and unstable will not be perceived as meaningful or fair to employees. Baseline data on measurements should be examined prior to implementation to determine whether sufficient reliability exists for use as a performance indicator. Typically, reliability is assessed by correlating the performance indices over two time periods for a number of times. Although reliability need not be perfect a minimum level is needed to be acceptable. A correlation of .6 is suggested as a minimum reliability.

- *Controllability.* A second desirable feature of directly measurable indices is controllability or independence from context effects. For example, indices of sales performance might be so heavily influenced by territory or shifts in local economic conditions that sales data might be meaningless. Unless the index can be transformed to account for the influence of the contextual factors, such indices should not be used. One customer service team was able to participate in the design of its own measurement systems. Members were able to separate controllable measures such as schedule adherence and the number of mailings sent to customers from the number of calls and letters received and handled in a given day, which were uncontrollable. At ALCOA, teams are measured on controllable indices of quality, costs, and safety rather than the uncontrollable index of profit, which is subject to wide variability due to fluctuations in the price of aluminum.

- *Feedback to teams on performance.* Direct measurements of performance can be used most effectively by the team if feedback can be provided at appropriate intervals. This will allow the team members to adjust their efforts or to adjust the goals when necessary. For example, Lucent Technologies measures the performance of its product development teams by using a number of metrics that can be measured at various stages of the project. Measures such as cycle time between key development checkpoints are collected and fed back to the team to alert it to potential delays to market.

House and Price (1991) described a similar approach for product development teams at Hewlett-Packard.

Case Study 4: Measurement of Performance for a Multifunctional Team

Hewlett-Packard uses a "Return Map." The map tracks time, costs, and return on investment for product development teams. Additional metrics include Break-Even Time, Time-to-Market, Break-Even After Release, and the Return Factor.

Break-Even Time is the time from the start of investigation until product profits equal the investment in development.

Time-to-Market is the total development time from the start of the development phase to manufacturing release.

Break-Even After Sales is the time from manufacturing release until the project investment costs are recovered in profits from the product.

Return Factor is a calculation of profit dollars at a specific point in time after a product has moved into manufacturing and sales.

During the investigation phase the team generates estimates of all four metrics. By focusing on the accuracy of the forecasts, marketing, R&D, and manufacturing are forced to examine problems as a team whose members have equal stakes in the outcome. All four metrics are tracked using graphical output and continually revised. Information from these metrics can be used to monitor progress and set consensual goals for the next phase of a project.

Multisource Assessment

Teams, as organizational units, have internal or external customers and reporting relationships as well as interaction with other teams. Any one or all these sources can provide assessment of the performance of the team. Multisource assessments of teams can be especially useful when the performance is not easily quantified into direct output measures. An interesting example is provided by the legal department of a large financial institution. The legal staff was reorganized into teams, and an instrument designed to assess the quality, timeliness, and effectiveness of legal services was designed and administered to in-house clients, team leaders, and the director of the organization. Each team was thus evaluated by multiple clients and a report was generated for each legal team. This kind of approach can be used with team leaders, supervisors, parallel teams, or external customers providing input. Most of the same issues discussed in using multisource assessment for individual team members apply to multisource assessment for the team as a unit. Feedback reports can be used by the team to identify areas of developmental need or areas where goals might need to be adjusted.

Integrated Assessment of Objectives

For some teams it may be appropriate to combine direct measures of performance and multisource assessment into an integrated program of assessment of objectives. As noted earlier, teams should be involved in objective setting and the objectives should meet all the criteria that have been already specified (that is, adequate information systems, reliability, controllability, and feedback). One advantage of integrating the two approaches is that team members will be able to balance their efforts in a way that better aligns with long-term strategy. As an example, a sales team may have dual objectives related to booked revenue and building long-term relationships with customers. Overemphasis on the former objective could interfere with the attainment of the latter objective. By assessing the team on both objectives through direct measurement of booked revenue and multisource customer feedback, the team can set balanced objectives and better gauge its efforts for the long term.

Case Study 5: Integrated Assessment for a Product Development Team

GTECH, the world leader in the lottery industry, uses an integrated approach to measuring its product development teams. For direct measures of performance, it designed three indices based on product quality, cost, and delivery—called *QCD* indices. Within each of the categories, several specific metrics were defined, with the help of the teams, to measure the effectiveness of the product and its development process. For example, within the delivery category, there were specific measures related to product development cycle time, including how long it would take the team to move the product through each major milestone toward the marketplace. In this case, this performance outcome was a direct reflection on the team's ability to coordinate and manage the development process efficiently. Product development teams also complete a multisource behavioral survey focusing on key behaviors and team skills required throughout the product development process. Team members rate each other on such behaviors as effective cross-functional communication, supporting the product development process, and resolving technical and interpersonal conflicts. Since product development efforts can take between one and two years, the multisource feedback is collected several times throughout the development process.

Communication in Team Performance Assessment Programs

Team performance assessment represents a major change for many employees and therefore should be communicated carefully. The greater the extent to which teams can be involved in the planning of the performance assessment programs, the easier the communication will be. Communication of team appraisal programs should be kept as clear and simple as possible. Also, since team performance is likely to be linked to rewards and recognition, a clear explanation of how performance affects rewards should be included. Table 7.5 summarizes recommendations for assessment of team performance outcomes.

Evaluating Team Appraisal Processes

Once the appraisal process has been implemented, provisions should be made for maintaining the quality of the program by conducting periodic evaluations of program effectiveness. Assessment of team performance has multiple goals. One is to provide a basis for consistent, accurate feedback to the team. A second goal is to provide a fair and equitable basis for determining rewards and recognition. A third goal is to allow a determination to be made of team effectiveness so that organizations can take appropriate actions. In the case of dysfunctional or ineffective teams, the information can be used to take a variety of actions such as additional training, work redesign, or reconfiguration of the team. To achieve these goals, team performance measurement systems should be assessed on four criteria: attainment of objectives, reliability and validity, perceived

Table 7.5. Summary of Recommendations for Assessment of Team Performance in Team-Based Organizations.

Step	Recommendations
Definition and relevance of team performance measures	• Objective indices should have clear relevance to the organization's mission and strategy • Teams participate in identification of measurements and setting of goals • Document relevance of measurements

Measurement	• Direct measures of output or quality—characteristics
	  • Adequate information systems
	  • Reliability
	  • Controllability
	  • Feedback
	
	• Multisource assessment—assessment of team as a unit
	
	• Integrated assessment of objectives

Communication	• Team participation can facilitate communication • Clear explanation of how performance is linked to rewards and recognition

Source: Copyright © 1992, Assessment Alternatives, Inc. Used with permission.

fairness, and legal compliance. In this definition, *reliability* refers to consistency of measurement whether the measures are objective tests, ratings, or objective performance outcomes. For ratings, consistency within a source is more important than consistency between sources (for example, peers versus customers). For objective tests, standard notions of test reliability can be applied (for example, Cronbach's alpha, test-retest) and for objective performance outcomes (for example, number of customer complaints, sales), consistency over time is an appropriate way to assess reliability. *Validity* will typically be measured by content validity standards; that is, expert judgment of the relevance of the measures. It may be possible, in some cases, to conduct follow-up criterion studies showing that short-term measures of team performance tracked by the system correlate with longer-term remote measures of performance; for example, number of customer complaints should be negatively correlated with amount of repeat business.

- *Program objectives.* Program evaluation should first assess whether the program is meeting its objectives. For certification programs, two important measures of program effectiveness are the number of employees undergoing certification and the number of employees successfully certifying. Both these measures are indicators of the extent to which the program is motivating employees to undertake the training necessary to broaden their competencies. For individual and team performance assessment, teams can be surveyed on the usefulness of the program in helping the teams perform effectively.

- *Reliability and validity.* Regardless of the method of appraisal, evaluations should be assessed periodically to ensure that ratings provided by evaluators meet reasonable standards for reliable measurement. Reliability refers to consistency of measurement over time or between raters. For multisource assessment programs, the reliability of ratings within each source should be reviewed. For objective measures, consistency over specified time intervals can be monitored (for example, odd versus even months). Validity should also be reviewed periodically as conditions and work processes change. In many cases, work processes can change rapidly and measures used to assess team performance may become less relevant than they were initially. Periodically obtaining SME judgments on the relevance of measures will allow a current assessment of validity to be made.

- *Employee perceptions.* Employee perceptions of the program should also be monitored to determine whether the program is perceived as fair and accurate, especially when evaluations are used for decisions related to rewards and recognition. Periodic surveys and focus groups can be used to gather the reactions of participants.

- *Legal compliance.* Employee appraisals, like employment tests, are subject to laws protecting employees from discrimination. Title VII of the Civil Rights Act, the Age Discrimination in Employment Act, and the Americans with Disabilities Act are the primary federal statutes, but states also have laws that protect employees. Legal compliance can be achieved to a large extent if the reliability and validity of the measurement system is well established. One additional step that can ensure legal compliance is the careful and thorough documentation of the reliability and validity of the processes as well as the consistent application of the policies established for the process.

References

Atwater, L., Roush, P., & Fischthal, A. (1995). The influence of upward feedback on self and follower ratings of leadership. *Personnel Psychology, 48,* 35–59.

Brito v. *Zia Co.,* 478 F.2d 1200 (10th Cir. 1973).

Cohen, S. G., & Ledford, G. E., Jr. (1994). The effectiveness of self-managing teams: a quasi-experiment. *Human Relations, 47*(1), 13–43.

Dominick, P. G., Reilly, R. R., & McGourty, J. W. (1997). The effects of peer feedback on team member behavior. *Group and Organization Management, 22,* 508–520.

Gladstein, D. (1984). Groups in context: A model of task group effectiveness. *Administrative Science Quarterly, 29,* 499–517.

Gross, S. E. (1995). *Compensation for teams.* New York: AMACOM.

Hackman J. R. (1983). *A normative model of work team effectiveness* (Tech. Rep. No. 2, Research Program on Group Effectiveness). New Haven, CT: Yale School of Organization and Management.

Hammer, M., & Champy, J. (1993). *Reengineering the corporation.* New York: HarperCollins.

House, C. H., & Price, R. L. (1991, January-February). The return map: Tracking product teams. *Harvard Business Review,* pp. 92–100.

Juran, J. M. (1989). *Juran on leadership for quality.* New York: Free Press.

Latham, G. P., & Wexley, K. N. (1977). Behavioral observation scales for performance appraisal. *Personnel Psychology, 30,* 255–268.

Lawler, E. E., III, Ledford, G. E., Jr., & Chang, L. (1993, March-April). Who uses skill-based pay and why? *Compensation and Benefits Review.*

Lawler, E. E., III, Mohrman, S. A., & Ledford, G. E., Jr. (1992). *Employee involvement and total quality management: Practices and results in Fortune 1000 companies.* San Francisco: Jossey-Bass.

Manz, C. C., & Sims, H. P., Jr. (1993). *Business without bosses: How self-managing teams are building high performance companies.* New York: Wiley.

Nieva, V. F., Fleishman, E. A., & Reick, A. (1978). *Team dimensions: Their identity, their measurement and their relationships* (Tech. Rep. No. DAHC19–78–C–0001). Washington, DC: Advanced Research Resources Organizations.

O'Neil, H. F., Baker, E. L., & Kazlauskas, E. J. (1992). Assessment of team performance. In R. W. Swezey & E. Salas (Eds.), *Teams: Their training and performance* (pp. 3–29). Norwood, NJ: Ablex.

Reilly, R. R., Smither, J. W., & Vasilopoulos, N. L. (1996). A longitudinal study of upward feedback. *Personnel Psychology, 49,* 599–612.

Salas, E., Dickinson, T. L., Converse, S. A., & Tannenbaum, S. I. (1992). Toward an understanding of team performance and training. In R. W. Swezey & E. Salas (Eds.), *Teams: Their training and performance* (pp. 3–29). Norwood, NJ: Ablex.

Smither, J. W., London, M., Vasilopoulos, N. L., Reilly, R. R., Millsap, R. E., & Salvemini, N. (1995). An examination of the effects of an upward feedback program over time. *Personnel Psychology, 48,* 1–34.

Stevens, M. J., & Campion, M. A. (1994). The knowledge, skill, and ability requirements for teamwork: Implications for human resource management. *Journal of Management, 20,* 503–530.

Sundstrom, E., De Meuse, K. P., & Futrell, D. (1990). Work teams: Applications and effectiveness. *American Psychologist, 45,* 120–133.

Timmreck, C. W. (1995). *Upward feedback in the trenches: Challenges and realities.* Paper presented at the Annual Meeting of the Society for Industrial and Organizational Psychology, Orlando, FL.

Van de Ven, A. H., Delbecq, A. L., & Koenig, R. (1976). Determinants of coordination modes within organizations. *American Sociological Review, 41,* 322–338.

Waldman, D. A. (1997). Predictors of employee preferences for multirater and group-based performance appraisal. *Group and Organization Management, 22,* 264–287

CHAPTER 8

Using Multisource Feedback for Employee Development and Personnel Decisions

Anthony T. Dalessio

"Seek to know yourself, which is the most difficult knowledge to acquire that can be imagined." This quote from the character Don Quixote is an elegant statement of the importance and difficulty of gaining self-knowledge, which has been extolled as a human virtue throughout philosophy and literature. One important key to self-knowledge is understanding how others perceive our behavior. This knowledge can be used to gain insight into the pattern and texture of competencies we possess, and can be used to help us leverage our strengths as well as identify areas for self-development and self-acceptance. Multisource feedback can be used as one method for obtaining information about how others perceive us and how we perceive ourselves.

Multisource feedback is defined as evaluations gathered about a target participant from two or more rating sources, including self, supervisor, peers, direct reports, internal customers, external customers, and vendors or suppliers. By definition, what has been referred to as 360-degree feedback in the literature falls under the

Note: The author thanks Dick Reilly, Jim Smither, Amy Hirsch, Lisa Kuller, John Mallozzi, and Anna Marie Valerio for their helpful comments.

heading of multisource feedback, and includes an opportunity to receive feedback from individuals in positions above, below, and lateral in the organizational hierarchy, as well as from individuals outside the organization. Feedback processes referred to as upward feedback and team member feedback (or peer feedback) also fall under the rubric of multisource feedback when evaluations are provided by additional sources such as self-ratings.

Brutus, Fleenor, and London (1998) have likened the multisource feedback process to a thermostat-control system that begins with participants' setting performance goals on job-relevant competencies, then gathering feedback on competencies from various sources, effectively processing the feedback, making adjustments by changing behavior based on the feedback, and finally looping back to establish new performance goals. In applications of multisource feedback, evaluations of a participant are typically gathered from the sources through ratings and written verbatim comments on a set of common items assessing job-relevant dimensions or competencies. This information is then compiled into a feedback report for the participant that protects the anonymity of the individual raters. The participant is provided with instruction on how to read and interpret the feedback report, as well as how to use the information to construct developmental plans and follow-up actions.

Based on a recent telephone survey of organizations and consulting firms, London and Smither (1995) concluded that multisource feedback currently is widely used by businesses. For example, seven of the consulting firms contacted in the survey indicated that they each have applied multisource feedback with over a hundred companies. Three of the consulting firms indicated that they have sold their multisource feedback instruments to over a thousand organizations. Companies are also spending large amounts from their training and development budgets on multisource feedback. Romano (1994) noted that Personnel Decisions, Inc., estimated that companies spent $152 million on multisource feedback processes in 1992. London and Smither point out that multisource feedback has also received attention in popular practitioner publications. Another indication of the popularity of multisource feedback is the recent establishment of the Upward Feedback Forum (UFF) by practitioners in organizations with active multisource feedback processes in place. The UFF is an informal consortium of approximately twenty-five major organizations that began meeting semiannually starting in mid-1993 to discuss best practices regarding multisource feedback (Timmreck & Bracken, 1996). Also, multisource feedback has become increasingly popular in industrial and organizational (I/O) psychology. For example, at the 1995 through 1997 Society for Industrial/ Organizational Psychology conferences, a total of fourteen symposia, practitioner forums, or workshops were devoted to the topic.

What has spurred the recent popularity of multisource feedback programs? Reasons include the perennial issue of dissatisfaction with traditional performance appraisal, and an increasing focus by organizations on issues of empowerment, participation, and customer focus (Bracken, 1996). Multisource feedback is one way to open the appraisal and feedback process and include the perspectives of internal and external customers, as well as others in the organization who work with the employee, besides just the supervisor. The process empowers the employee to use the feedback to achieve growth and self-development. The popularity of the technique also stems from its use as a way to communicate critical organizational behaviors and values that need to be practiced to move the organization forward (London & Beatty, 1993). It can be one component of a larger culture change effort to convey the importance of critical organizational competencies and values. Finally, a multisource feedback process may be a more efficient, less time-consuming method for providing participants with developmental feedback than other methods such as traditional assessment, which many organizations no longer have the resources to support.

With the increasing popularity of multisource feedback processes, many practitioners will be faced with a number of important implementation questions. Research and practice relevant to these questions will be examined in this chapter, and recommendations for practice offered. After a discussion of applied measurement issues associated with multisource feedback processes and the practical implications of current research, the following implementation questions will be addressed: What issues need to be considered and resolved when planning a multisource feedback process, including use of the process for development versus for personnel decisions, communications to participants and raters, and working with consultants? How should a multisource feedback questionnaire be constructed, including issues of identifying and developing competencies, item development, response scales, and open-ended questions? What issues need to be resolved regarding administration, such as choosing raters and developing rater training? How should feedback reports be constructed, including data aggregation and presentation? How can an organization facilitate support for developmental activities, including the feedback workshop and follow-up activities? How can it evaluate and revise the process?

Measurement and Validation: The Source of Multisource Feedback

Often practitioners suggest that multisource feedback instruments need not meet strong validation standards, if the instruments are used only for developmental feedback purposes rather than for personnel decisions. Nonetheless, regardless of the purpose, a multisource feedback instrument must still meet the same standards of validity (Bracken, 1996; Dalessio, 1996). Even when the instrument is used purely for the purpose of developmental feedback, the participant will still need to be provided with a valid measure of job-related competencies for constructing a job-relevant developmental plan. And if the results of the instrument are used either intentionally or inadvertently to make a job performance, compensation, promotion, or downsizing decision, it must meet the validation standard for any instrument used for a personnel decision.

Tornow (1993) and Dunnette (1993) provide an interesting dialectic for framing a discussion of measurement issues for multisource feedback instruments. Tornow contrasts a traditional psychometric measurement approach for multisource feedback instruments with a practitioner's approach. On the traditional psychometric end of the continuum, Tornow views the goal of the scientist as "to reduce the error of measurement, and rater variations, in order to enhance the accuracy of measurement" (p. 222). On the other side of the continuum, according to Tornow, "the manager/practitioner values multiple perspectives of different raters because they represent significant and meaningful sources of variation from which much can be learned" (p. 222). Dunnette elaborates on these points by stating that "good measurement—no matter how elegant or wonderful—is sterile unless it is accompanied by meaningful findings. Likewise, provocative interpretations may be rendered illusory if they cannot be firmly supported by solid methodology" (p. 378). For scientist-practitioners, what methodologies constitute evidence for reliability and validity of multisource feedback instruments, yet still allow for provocative interpretations that practitioners can provide to participants to assist in meaningful development and growth?

Reliability

Reliability can be defined "as the extent to which a set of measurements is free from random-error variance" (Guion, 1965, p. 30). Multisource feedback instruments should be able to adequately demonstrate internal consistency reliability for the dimensions assessed with coefficient α reliabilities in the .70 range (Van Velsor & Leslie, 1991a), although lower coefficients may be acceptable, depending on the construct being assessed. Also, reasonably systematic agreement among raters *within* a source (for example, peers) would be expected for multisource feedback. A meta-analysis by Conway and Huffcutt (1996) concluded that raters who are supervisors, peers, and subordinates can provide a reliable *within*-source index, and that within-source reliabilities for peers and subordinates can be increased by including from four to six raters for each of these sources. Conway and Huffcutt report lower within-source agreement for subordinates (.27) than for other sources (supervisors, .51; peers, .39). These results may be partially due to supervisors' behaving differently toward different subordinates, as suggested by the vertical dyad linkage model of leadership (Dansereau, Graen, & Haga, 1975).

Lower agreement *between* rating sources (for example, supervisors and peers, or peers and subordinates) may not necessarily be random error variance, because different rating sources may perceive real behavior differences by the participant (Conway & Huffcutt, 1996; Tornow, 1993). Also low test-retest correlations may not provide evidence for poor reliability, especially when retest intervals are long enough to allow participants to develop and change, which is the major objective of most multisource feedback processes. So reliability for multisource instruments may be best estimated through internal consistency methodology and interrater agreement methodology within sources.

Validity

Validity is traditionally defined as the extent to which an instrument measures what it is purported to measure (Guion, 1980). Although the concept of validity can generally be unified under this theme, evaluative judgments regarding evidence for validity can be drawn from all three conventional aspects of validity—content, criterion-related, and construct (Guion, 1980). What types of evidence would result in judgments regarding evidence for validity of a multisource instrument?

Content Validity

Content validity, or a content-oriented strategy, is an evaluation of the extent to which the items in the multisource feedback instrument represent the defined job performance content domain (American Educational Research Association, American Psychological Association, & National Council on Measurement Education [AERA et al.], 1985; Goldstein, Zedeck, & Schneider, 1993; Guion, 1980; Society for Industrial and Organizational Psychology [SIOP], 1987). Evidence for the content validity of a multisource feedback instrument can be established through a traditional job analysis–content validation process (Goldstein et al., 1993) where subject matter experts (SMEs)—people who know the job—are used to identify important job tasks; define and identify the important knowledge, skills, and abilities required to perform the tasks; and then link multisource feedback items to the critical knowledge, skills, and abilities. The process can be accomplished through facilitated SME meetings and structured questionnaires (Goldstein et al., 1993).

Most applications of a multisource feedback process involve developing a content-valid questionnaire that can be used with managers at many different levels, for example, senior management through first-level management, and with managers in many different functional areas, for example, marketing, sales, production, operations, human resources, finance, and so on. For such applications, a content-validation process would involve using SME meetings and questionnaires to behaviorally define generic management competencies and establish their importance for the successful performance of all the relevant management jobs in the organization. Behavioral items on which employees could initiate change would need to be developed and then linked to the management competencies.

Criterion-Related Validity

Evidence for *criterion-related validity* is based on the extent to which evaluations from various sources are related to outcome criteria (AERA et al., 1985; SIOP, 1987). Two major issues that need to be taken into account when establishing criterion-related validity are first, that the predictor consists of ratings from multiple sources, and second, that the outcome criterion needs to be a measure of effective managerial job performance. For criterion-related validity, each particular source or combination of sources, for example, peers and customers, should be considered separately. It should be kept in mind that ratings from some sources may not necessarily need to demonstrate criterion-related validity to provide valuable information. Ratings from each source represent a legitimate view of job performance, if the source of variation is providing ratings on behaviors linked to important organizational competencies and is used as input to a comprehensive job-related developmental plan.

The other side of the equation is the outcome criterion measure. Choosing an appropriate criterion should be based on clearly defining effective managerial performance (Van Velsor & Leslie, 1991a). Effective managerial performance may be defined as profitability of the unit, high team performance, high job satisfaction for the unit, or low unit turnover. Ratings from particular sources may be more logically related to certain criteria. For example, subordinate ratings may be related to job satisfaction and turnover for the unit, whereas supervisor ratings may be less related to these criteria and more highly related to unit profitability. Also, outcome criteria may not be practically available for some sources, for example, self-ratings. The outcome criterion used to establish criterion-related validity should be under the control of the manager, and will be less appropriate for use in establishing criterion-related validity to the extent that it is influenced by variables other than effective management behaviors (Van Velsor & Leslie, 1991a).

Finally, evidence for criterion-related validity can also be established by demonstrating that the instrument is able to differentiate between groups of managers considered overall to be performing effectively on a relevant criterion variable compared to those considered to be performing ineffectively.

Construct Validity

Evidence for *construct validity* focuses primarily on the extent to which scores on the instrument measure the psychological characteristics of interest (AERA et al., 1985; SIOP, 1987). The process of construct validity involves establishing meaningful, logical patterns of relationships among items, scales, and sources of measurement. The value of multisource feedback is that information about the participant does not come from just one perspective, such as the supervisor, but rather from many different perspectives. The assumption is that each source provides relevant information about a performance dimension, but may evaluate the participant somewhat differently because the participant actually behaves somewhat differently toward each source. Variations also arise because each source does not have the opportunity to view the same behaviors on the dimension, or because the sources differ somewhat in terms of which behaviors they view as most critical for a dimension. This assumption may lower patterns of relationships between certain sources of measurement, for example, subordinates and peers, and subordinates and supervisor, as compared to other sources, such as supervisors and peers (Conway & Huffcutt, 1996). However, these results would not indicate that subordinates' ratings, for example, are useless or not valuable. Subordinates' ratings still provide a legitimate source of feedback to the participant that needs to be considered and used for planning developmental activities.

The constructs measured by the multisource instrument may not be defined by precisely the same behaviors for each source, because the sources differ in their opportunities to view the participant's behavior. Most multisource feedback processes allow raters to endorse an option of "not applicable" if they have not had a chance to view a behavior adequately. The most obvious example involves items that ask about supervisory style or about performance feedback. These items are observed clearly by direct reports but much less clearly by sources such as customers. Factor structures for multisource feedback items may be difficult to establish with data from all sources combined, because a certain percentage of raters from a given source may not be able to evaluate some behavioral items. Within-rating-source data may produce clearer factor structures.

Finally, evidence for construct validity can be established through correlations between ratings made by a particular source and other measures of the same competency, such as assessment center ratings or certification tests.

Aspects of Validation: Summary

Given the nature and objectives of multisource feedback, the key aspect for inferring validity for an instrument is establishing that the items represent the content of the job performance domain, that is, demonstrate genuine content validity. Criterion-related validity for the multisource feedback process can be established when ratings predict appropriate outcome criteria, but not all sources necessarily need to be directly related to outcome criteria to demonstrate value as part of the process. Although ratings among some sources would be hypothesized to show convergence, other sources may not show strong convergence yet still provide meaningful information to participants. Constructs may be defined by somewhat different behavioral items for different sources. Appropriate measures of the same construct should be related to multisource feedback ratings.

Multisource Feedback Research: Implications for Practice

The results of research conducted on multisource feedback processes provide suggestions and guidance that practitioners should consider for implementation purposes. Nearly all multisource feedback research has been completed in the context of a developmental setting rather than a personnel decision setting, so results primarily apply to developmental uses. Research falls into three main categories: implications for administration, implications for feedback of results, and implications for outcomes of the process.

Implications for Multisource Feedback Administration

Should Raters' Evaluations Be Anonymous or Identified?

In an experimental field study of upward feedback, Antonioni (1994) randomly assigned thirty-eight managers and their subordinates from an insurance company to either an anonymity or an accountability condition. In the accountability condition, raters signed their completed upward feedback forms and supervisors received completed individual subordinate questionnaires. In the anonymity condition, by contrast, raters did not sign and supervisors received reports only of summary results. Participants and raters were informed that the process was being used solely for the purposes of developmental feedback, and would not be used for personnel decisions. The results indicated that ratings were less inflated in the anonymous condition, and subordinates were more comfortable providing ratings in this condition. The research suggests that better quality ratings will be provided to participants when raters are anonymous. This conclusion is also consistent with survey data of raters' reactions to an upward feedback process reported by London and Wohlers (1991). When subordinates were asked, "Would you have rated your boss any differently if feedback had not been given to them anonymously," 24 percent indicated that they would have done so (p. 388). Supervisors in the Antonioni study did view the process more favorably when subordinates were identified, which may improve their acceptance of the results, but the results still suggest the best practice is rater anonymity. Future research should investigate the anonymity variable for potentially different effects with other rating sources, including peers, supervisors, and internal and external customers.

Is the Quality of Ratings Affected by Use for Developmental Versus Appraisal Purposes?

Research has indicated that ratings collected for the purposes of personnel decisions are significantly higher than ratings of the same individual collected for development or feedback purposes. For example, Farh, Cannella, and Bedeian (1991) have demonstrated that peer ratings from class project teams of university management students showed greater leniency and halo and were less differentiating when gathered for evaluation purposes than when gathered for developmental purposes. Other studies also "have shown that ratings collected for administrative purposes (for example, salary administration) are significantly higher than ratings of the same individual collected for other purposes, such as feedback or research" (Murphy & Cleveland, 1995, p. 246). Furthermore, London and Wohlers (1991) report that when employees who participated in an upward feedback process were asked whether they would have rated their boss differently if the feedback was used for performance appraisal (rather than development), 34 percent indicated that they would have done so.

The research suggests that when multisource feedback is used for personnel decisions rather than purely developmental purposes, practitioners should be prepared for ratings that are potentially contaminated by rating errors, which may make distinguishing between genuinely good versus mediocre performers difficult and limit the value of such ratings to guide development. Attempts could be made to reduce these errors through more intensive rater training and more extensive employee communications about the importance of providing accurate ratings.

Who Should Choose the Raters?

Research is needed to determine how the quality and acceptance of ratings is affected by participants choosing their raters versus others providing input. No research has been conducted on this question to date.

Do the Rating Sources Included in the Multisource Feedback Process Affect Participants' Attitudes Toward the Process?

Bernardin, Dahmus, and Redmon (1993) examined whether the attitudes of first-line supervisors in a large federal agency differed toward upward appraisal depending on whether they received feedback from both their manager and their subordinates, from their manager only, or from their subordinates only. The results indicated that the most positive attitudes were displayed toward upward feedback when supervisors received feedback from both their manager and their subordinates. Supervisors who received feedback from just their subordinates expressed more cautious attitudes toward upward appraisal, as well as more concern about possible negative implications such as supervisors focusing too much attention on simply pleasing subordinates. Bernardin et al. (1993) suggest that the implication of their results for practice is that, whenever possible, a more comprehensive approach to feedback should be implemented where feedback from all qualified sources is sought. With a more complete multisource feedback process, attitudes toward subordinate feedback as well as feedback from other sources may be more tempered.

Implications for Feedback of Multisource Results

*Should Feedback to Participants Focus on Discrepancies
Between Self-Ratings and Others' Ratings?*

Research that has focused on examining discrepancies between
self- and others' ratings provides insight for interpreting multisource feedback results. The research results suggest implications
for the meaning of particular discrepancies and suggest prescriptive actions that participants should consider as a result of their
feedback.

Meta-analytic work by Harris and Schaubroeck (1988) has concluded that ratings between peers and supervisors agree to a greater
extent than ratings between self and others (that is, self and peers;
self and supervisors). Self-ratings also tend to be higher on average
than ratings provided by others (for example, Bass & Yammarino,
1991; Brutus, Fleenor, & McCauley, 1996; Harris & Schaubroeck,
1988; Smither et al., 1995). Nilsen and Campbell (1993) have shown
that the size of these self-other discrepancies tends to show a high
degree of stability over a period of time using scales from the Campbell Leadership Index. The median correlation reported by these
researchers between self-other discrepancies over a period of one
month for a sample of thirty-one female managers was .71. Although
the time interval was short in this study, it seems appropriate, since
much longer intervals could have resulted in changes due to systematic intervening variables such as experience or training. Nilsen
and Campbell also provided data showing that self-other discrepancies were stable across different types of measures, such as personality and skill measures. Without interventions, participants are likely
to display stability in these discrepancies over a period of time and
across measures.

The size and nature of these discrepancies may be related to
managerial effectiveness. For example, Bass and Yammarino (1991)
conducted a study where 155 Navy officers completed self-ratings
of leadership behavior, and their subordinates also rated the leadership behavior of these officers. Also, Navy records for the 155 officers were obtained to gather performance and promotion data
used as an index of each officer's success. The results of the study
indicated that generally less successful officers showed greater discrepancies between self- and subordinate's ratings of leadership

behavior, whereas more successful officers showed lower discrepancies. In a study addressing a similar question, Van Velsor, Taylor, and Leslie (1993) analyzed data from three samples of managers who completed self-ratings using Benchmarks, which is a multisource feedback instrument developed by the Center for Creative Leadership. The samples consisted of 648 managers randomly selected from the Benchmarks database, 168 upper-level managers from a Fortune 100 organization, and 79 hospital administrators. Subordinates also rated these managers using Benchmarks. The managers were coded into three groups—underraters, agreement, and overraters—based on the discrepancy between average self-ratings and average subordinate ratings across fifteen of the sixteen Benchmark scales. (The self-awareness scale from Benchmarks was not included as part of the coding process.) Overraters in all three samples received the lowest mean overall rating from subordinates across all the Benchmark scales, and had the highest self-ratings. This is consistent with the Bass and Yammarino (1991) results. However, in the Van Velsor et al. (1993) study, the underrater group (rather than the agreement group) received the highest mean overall rating from subordinates, and the lowest self-ratings. Analysis of the self-awareness scale from Benchmarks revealed that subordinates evaluated underraters as highest on self-awareness.

Workshop facilitators should be aware of and use this research to underscore the need for managers to be cognizant of, and consider, others' perceptions of their behavior. This information is especially important if a participant has consistently high self-ratings on the feedback report. The research suggests that these managers may be evaluated as less effective by superiors and direct reports, as well as be perceived as being less self-aware of their behavior. As part of their developmental planning efforts, these managers in particular may need to focus on bringing their self-views more in line with others' views.

Practitioners should also be aware that recent research by Fleenor, McCauley, and Brutus (1996) suggests that level of performance needs to be considered as much as self-other discrepancies in interpreting results and focusing developmental efforts. Facilitators need to focus participants' attention not only on self-other discrepancies but also on behaviors receiving low to average ratings as opportunities for development, and behaviors with high ratings as strengths to be leveraged.

Subordinate-other discrepancies in ratings also received attention in the research literature recently. A meta-analysis by Conway and Huffcutt (1996) confirmed the Harris and Schaubroeck (1988) conclusions and extended this research to show that agreement between peers and supervisors is also higher than agreement between subordinates and peers and subordinates and supervisors. These results suggest that it is important to include subordinates' ratings in multisource feedback, because of their unique perspective relative to peers and supervisors.

Should Participants Be Open to Seeking Negative Feedback?

One approach that could be suggested to participants in multisource feedback workshops is to be open to seeking negative feedback about their behavior from supervisors, subordinates, and peers, as a way to gather information that can be used to narrow the gap between self- and other perceptions, and to improve in developmental need areas. Based on questionnaire data from a sample of 387 mid-level managers in a public service agency, Ashford and Tsui (1991) concluded that the tendency to seek negative feedback was positively associated with self-other agreement for supervisors, subordinates, and peers, as well as with overall effectiveness ratings from all three groups. Their research also suggested that the tendency to seek positive feedback was not a useful strategy for the managers. Results indicted that seeking positive feedback was negatively related to effectiveness ratings from all three sources, and with self-other agreement for subordinates. Positive feedback seeking was not related to self-other agreement for supervisors and peers.

Implications for Outcomes of Multisource Feedback Processes

Does Instituting a Multisource Feedback Process Improve Performance?

This question will eventually be asked by senior management at most organizations. Research on this topic has indicated that performance improvements do result from multisource feedback processes, although improvements appear to be moderate. Practitioners can cite this research as support for instituting or continuing a multisource feedback program within an organization. In a study by Hazucha, Hezlett, and Schneider (1993), forty-eight managers from a large

Midwestern utility company, and their supervisors, peers, and subordinates, completed the Management Skills Profile (MSP) (which assesses nineteen job-related dimensions) at two points in time, two years apart. The results showed that average ratings by others increased from Time 1 to Time 2. Also the correlation between self-other ratings were more similar at Time 2 ($r = .32$) compared to Time 1 ($r = .07$).

Research conducted by Smither et al. (1995) with data from an upward feedback program showed similar results when effects for regression to the mean were controlled. In the Smither et al. study, data were collected from 238 managers and their subordinates in the international operations division of a large organization at two points in time, about six months apart. Ratings were gathered on thirty-three behavioral items. Analyses of subordinates' ratings showed that the managers whose initial level of performance was moderate or low improved over the six-month period. The improvement could not be attributed solely to regression to the mean. Reilly, Smither, and Vasilopoulos (1996) extended the Smither et al. study by following 171 of the original 238 managers for a third administration of the upward feedback questionnaire, and 92 of the managers for a fourth administration two and a half years later. Managers whose initial level of performance was low sustained improvements over the later administrations. Atwater, Roush, and Fischthal (1995) obtained similar results, indicating that leaders' behaviors improved after receiving feedback from followers in a sample of 978 student leaders at the U.S. Naval Academy. A recent study by Walker (1997), examining upward feedback for 252 managers in a financial institution, also showed steady improvements in subordinates' ratings of their supervisor on a composite of leadership behavior items over five yearly administrations. Consistent with previous research, Walker also found improvements primarily for supervisors with initial low and moderate ratings, and these improvements could not be accounted for solely by regression to the mean. An additional important finding from Walker's study was that managers who held feedback sessions with subordinates showed greatest improvements in ratings. So holding feedback meetings may be one potential key to improvement. Walker also showed that subordinates' ratings were correlated with independent annual performance appraisal ratings made by supervisors with stronger correlations in later administrations.

Bernardin, Hagan, Ross, and Kane (1995) examined not only the effects of a multisource feedback process on managerial performance ratings but also outcome variables such as sales volume and turnover with a sample of forty-eight assistant store managers in a retail clothing chain. The managers were divided into two groups, one of which received multisource feedback while the other served as a control group and received only top-down appraisal. Data were collected from each of the groups at two points in time, one year apart. In the multisource feedback group, ratings were gathered on twenty behavioral items from the participant, subordinates, peers, and supervisor at Time 1 and Time 2. Also "professional customer" role-players came into the stores at Time 1 and Time 2 to test system policy as implemented by each manager, and rated the manager using a fifteen-item instrument. In the control group, supervisor and self-ratings were gathered at both times, and customer ratings at Time 2 only. Also, two outcome measures (voluntary termination of employees supervised by the assistant manager, and "sale to target") were collected for both groups at both times. Mean subordinate, peer, and customer ratings increased significantly at Time 2 for the multisource feedback group. Ratings by supervisors and self-appraisals did not improve significantly for either group. The two groups did not show significant differences at Time 1 or Time 2 on either of the outcome measures. The results show moderate support for the effects of multisource feedback on performance variables. Further research on the relationship between multisource feedback and outcome variables is needed, although at least one rating source included in multisource feedback (that is, peer assessments) has shown relationships with outcome variables (for example, see Kane and Lawler, 1978; Mayfield, 1970, 1972).

Do Managers Need to Receive Feedback to Show Improvements in Performance?

Or do managers improve performance as a result of just participating in a multisource feedback process? In the field studies conducted by Smither et al. (1995) and Reilly et al. (1996), managers with initially low or moderate performance improved whether or not they received a written feedback report. Simply participating in the multisource feedback process may have familiarized the managers with the organizational competencies and helped them focus on improvement. These results have also been demonstrated in a more controlled experimental study conducted by Dominick, Reilly, and McGourty (1997). The participants in this study were seventy-five graduate and undergraduate students in an organizational behavior and group dynamics course who participated in the study as part of a class assignment. The participants were randomly assigned to teams of four or five, and then the teams were randomly assigned to one of three conditions: feedback, exposure, or control. In the feedback condition, participants completed ratings on themselves and teammates following completion of a first group task. Before a second group task, they received their written feedback reports and were given time to review the feedback. Participants in the exposure condition also completed ratings on themselves and teammates following the first task, and were told they would receive feedback sometime in the future, but did not actually receive written feedback before the second group task. Participants in the control condition completed a questionnaire on task content, but did not complete self- or team member ratings. Videotapes of each team's second task were made and then evaluated by experienced assessors on the same rating form completed by participants in the feedback and exposure conditions. The results showed that assessor ratings were significantly higher both for the feedback versus control group and for the exposure versus control group, but were not different between the exposure and feedback group. Taken together, these three studies suggest that instituting a multisource feedback process can help communicate and reinforce key organizational competencies and culture change initiatives. Also, managers who do not receive written feedback in upward feedback programs (because less than three subordinates rated them) may still benefit from the process (Smither et al., 1995).

Summary of Research Implications

Based on this research, there are several major implications for practice. First, participants in multisource feedback processes are more likely to receive higher quality ratings if ratings are anonymous and used just for developmental feedback. Including input from all sources is also an important planning consideration. Second, workshop facilitators should emphasize the importance of developmental planning that considers bringing self-other ratings more in line, especially when self-ratings show a tendency to be consistently higher than others' ratings. Facilitators also should encourage participants to consider the level of feedback received on competencies in developmental planning. Also, encouraging participants to seek more negative feedback, if this is not being done, may be helpful for improvement. Finally, participation in multisource feedback processes appears to be related to subsequent improvements in performance. Greater improvements in performance may be associated with holding feedback sessions with subordinates.

Implementation of Multisource Feedback Processes for Best Practice

When practitioners develop and implement a multisource feedback process, there are a number of questions that need to be addressed at each step of the process. Possible options exist for completing each step and resolving the questions. These options will be discussed along with recommendations for best practice based on research and practitioner experience.

Planning the Multisource Feedback Process

How to Link the Multisource Feedback Process to Important Organizational Objectives?

One of the best methods for linking a multisource feedback process to organizational and human resource strategies is to base the process on competencies that have been identified as key to the organization's success now and in the future. The multisource feedback process can be used both as a mechanism for communicating these competencies and as a way to provide feedback and develop these competencies. To the extent that these competencies are the basis of other human resource systems, such as performance appraisal, compensation, or succession planning, the multisource feedback process will also provide relevant feedback and input to these systems.

The multisource feedback process can also be linked to organizational strategies by integrating it with organizational change efforts. For example, if the organization is moving toward a team-based environment, the multisource feedback process can be integrated into this change effort by providing feedback on team skills as part of an organization-wide development program.

How to Gain and Display Senior
Management Support for the Process?

Linking the process to important organizational strategies is the first step to gaining senior management buy-in to the multisource feedback process. Besides these links, senior management will also need to be convinced that the process is resulting in improved performance. This consideration may not be critical at the initiation of the process, but it certainly will be important to sustain the process. Establishing that the process is related to improved performance can be done through citing the previously discussed research that has shown positive improvements. Such research can also be planned as part of the process, although collecting and analyzing the data can become quite complex. (For examples of such research, see Reilly et al., 1996, and Smither et al., 1995.) The value of the process to senior management can also be demonstrated by defining the outcomes in measurable terms, such as having all the participants write a developmental plan and incorporating specific activities from the plan into their performance appraisal objectives. These measures can be monitored and summarized.

Once senior management buy-in is obtained, it is also critical to the success of the process to demonstrate management's support to participants and raters. In large organizations, cascading the implementation of the process from the senior levels down is a way to demonstrate the importance and support for the process. Also, communication and feedback of results by senior managers to their direct reports for the purpose of action planning and follow-up activities can build support and credibility for the process.

Will the Multisource Feedback Be Used
for Development or Personnel Decisions?

This is a major question that needs to be answered as part of the planning process, because it will be the first question that participants ask. Many organizations seem to demonstrate approach-avoidance behavior when deciding whether to use the process for development or for personnel decisions. Dalton (1996) suggests that over the past ten years the use of multisource feedback instruments has evolved from a purely confidential developmental process to include more applications as an appraisal and administrative process. For example, in a survey of twenty-nine multisource feedback processes conduced through the UFF, Timmreck and Bracken (1995) reported that 28 percent used the process as input to appraisal and 45 percent were moving toward using it as part of the performance appraisal process, although most were still used for development and coaching (93 percent). Yet, in follow-up work, Timmreck and Bracken (1996) suggest that about half the companies either using or intending to use multisource feedback for appraisal purposes backed off from this use. Reasons tend to focus on employee reactions and inflated ratings. Timmreck and Bracken (1996) caution, however, that these conclusions are based on small sample sizes.

Results of a carefully developed, well-validated multisource feedback instrument can either be provided confidentially to the participant, purely for development, or shared with the supervisor as input to personnel decisions. Locating the use of the multisource feedback process at either end of this continuum has benefits as well as costs that need to be weighed by practitioners. If the process is used by the supervisor for personnel decisions, these decisions will benefit by drawing on many sources for input resulting in a more complete picture of the participant's job performance (Bracken, 1996; Murphy & Cleveland, 1995). As discussed earlier, the cost is that the quality of the ratings from these additional sources may be poorer when the raters know their evaluations will be used for personnel decisions (for example, Farh et al., 1991; London & Wohlers, 1991; Murphy & Cleveland, 1995).

When multisource feedback processes are located at the other end of the continuum, and are provided confidentially to participants solely for developmental purposes, better-quality ratings with less leniency may result. These ratings will provide better information to the participant for constructing a development plan. However, if the feedback is completely confidential and left entirely up to the participant, accountability for constructing the developmental plan and completing developmental activities becomes questionable. Participants may have very good intentions in group or individual feedback sessions, but not have the motivation to thoroughly review their results and follow through on developmental activities.

Organizations often begin at the developmental end of the continuum, using the multisource process purely to provide feedback, where only the participant receives the results. With subsequent administrations, the organization may require that the feedback move down the continuum and become more available to the supervisor—first requiring the participant to share the developmental plan with the supervisor; then requiring the participant to share the feedback with the supervisor for the purpose of joint developmental planning; and finally requiring the participant to share the results with the supervisor as input to personnel decisions (that is, performance appraisal, compensation, promotion, or downsizing).

For example, one organization introduced a multisource feedback process such that feedback was available to participants at the same time that midyear appraisals were being completed and developmental plans were being designed between supervisors and direct reports. This administration of the process was purely developmental, where only participants received feedback reports. Participants were told that a second administration of the process would be completed six months later to coincide with the year-end appraisal process, at which time supervisors would also be provided with their feedback reports and use the results as input into the performance appraisal process. The process allowed participants to first receive feedback about strengths and developmental needs, and voluntarily share the information with their supervisor at midyear for the purpose of developmental planning if so desired. The process also incorporated later feedback into the appraisal process.

Rather than move completely to the personnel decision end of the continuum, organizations can adopt various middle positions on the continuum to enhance accountability yet still produce high-quality evaluations for participants. One approach may be to provide the actual multisource feedback report just to the participant in a confidential manner such that it would not be shared with the supervisor, then require the participant to use the report to construct a development plan that would be shared with the supervisor. Agreed-upon self-development activities would then become part of the employee's yearly objectives, and completion of the developmental objectives could be evaluated. Although supervisors do not view the participant's feedback report with this process, they do have access to some information from the process. Sharing information at this level with supervisors may not be inordinately difficult for employees in most instances.

Another middle position on the continuum that can enhance accountability was recently put into practice at a large company. With this multisource feedback process, copies of the feedback report go both to the manager being reviewed and to a consultant (either internal or external). The consultant and the manager meet to review the report, for example, clarify, interpret, identify some areas of strength and areas of concern, and discuss some possible developmental plans and actions. The manager sets up a meeting with the team of direct reports where both the manager and the consultant are present. The manager shares some of the feedback results and tells the group some areas where additional input and clarification would be appreciated. The manager then leaves the meeting, and the group and consultant discuss specific reactions and responses to the manager's questions. The manager returns to the meeting and the group (facilitated by the consultant where necessary) provides more detailed feedback and reactions. The manager summarizes the feedback to make sure that it is accurately understood, and commits to some specific areas and steps for improvement. After the meeting, the manager prepares a developmental action plan and shares it with his or her supervisor.

These positions on the continuum require that at least some feedback be shared with the supervisor. Dalton (1996) has suggested, however, that requiring that such information be shared with the supervisor creates a stressful and threatening situation that may lead the participants to use coping strategies that produce movement away from personal development. Dalton has pointed out that counseling principles suggest that feedback will be most readily accepted in a confidential interaction between a qualified feedback giver and the participant, thus locating the process closely to the purely developmental end of the continuum. The feedback giver, for example, could be an outside consultant who works with the participant as a coach in planning and completing developmental activities. Using outside coaches for large-scale multisource feedback applications may be extremely costly. Another less costly option may be to use consultants inside the organization or peers as coaches, although quality and consistency of the coaching as well as confidentiality would need to be addressed.

There is no definitive answer regarding where multisource feedback processes should be located on the developmental–personnel decision continuum. Practitioners and their clients need to weigh the costs and benefits of any approach in light of business needs. As a general recommendation, multisource feedback processes are better used as developmental tools. Under these circumstances, the process is more easily introduced to an organization in a positive light and is better accepted by participants, but it is still necessary to address accountability for development.

What Up-Front Communication Should Be Provided?

Up-front communication is very important to gain buy-in, and to promote understanding about the purpose, benefits, and expected outcomes of the process, as well as to explain to participants and raters what they will be asked to do, and in what time frame. An essential part of the communication is a clear statement regarding whether the results will be provided solely to the participant for developmental purposes, or will be shared with the supervisor for administrative purposes. The reasoning behind this decision also needs to be communicated. Whether or not results are provided to supervisors in any form, raters and participants should be informed that raters' evaluations will remain anonymous by reporting data for a source only if a minimum number of raters (for example, three or more) provide ratings. If an outside consultant is aggregating the ratings and producing the reports, this procedure can also be communicated as an additional way that rater anonymity will be maintained.

Besides these issues, participants and raters should be provided with clear information that reflects sound planning on both scheduling and content issues relevant to questionnaire development, administration, scoring, and feedback; how frequently feedback will be provided; what follow-up support will be in place once feedback is delivered; and how long the process will be in place. Meetings with participants, the project manager, and the upper-level manager responsible for the project can be held to communicate the information. A brochure containing the information and contact persons also can be provided.

How to Work with an Outside Consultant to Develop and Implement Multisource Feedback?

Many organizations planning a multisource feedback process work with a consultant in the development and implementation. Several models exist for contracting with a consultant that range from using the consultant's off-the-shelf questionnaire to customizing this type of questionnaire to contracting only for administrative services. To a large extent, the model that is most appropriate depends on the resources and staff that are available within the organization.

The competencies assessed with off-the-shelf products are applicable for most organizations. However, a content validation process linking the competencies to job activities should be completed to provide evidence for the instrument's job-relatedness. The extent to which these competencies adequately describe specific behaviors that can be influenced and changed should also be evaluated. The psychometric properties and national norm database of these products are potentially strong because of the large amount of available data. Van Velsor and Leslie (1991a, 1991b) present a useful framework for evaluating multisource feedback products in terms of psychometric properties, as well as feedback displays and support materials. Van Velsor and Leslie (1991b) also have reviewed a number of multisource feedback products available from vendors. An additional product developed more recently has been reviewed by Dalessio (1996). Finally, the City of Hampton, Virginia, also has available a brief report completed in 1994 that describes several multisource processes and their costs. These reviews will be useful to organizations considering implementation of multisource feedback.

Customization of at least some items on vendor-developed questionnaires may be necessary for the purposes of focusing the competencies or making the questionnaire more congruent with the organization's culture. A balance needs to be struck when modifying items—useful as it is, this process will undercut the advantages of the national norm and psychometric data because the national data will not be applicable to the modified items.

A useful addition to the multisource feedback questionnaires offered by vendors is a technical manual that includes data on the psychometric properties of the questionnaire items (Dalessio, 1996). This information would be helpful to users with technical backgrounds for choosing items to include in a multisource feedback instrument. Such a manual could provide information on the internal consistency reliability of items composing the dimensions, item-total correlations for items within dimensions, the variability of ratings on each of the items for the sources, and average ratings on the items and the dimensions for the sources.

Consultant services could also be used for purely administrative purposes, including distributing, receiving, entering, processing, and analyzing questionnaires, as well as generating and distributing feedback reports. The content of the questionnaire items, feedback reports, and workshop could be developed within the organization. This approach will result in a questionnaire and process that is very tailored for the organization, but the organization would need to dedicate professional staff time and resources for the development.

Constructing the Multisource Feedback Questionnaire

How to Identify Competencies for a Multisource Feedback Process?

Multisource feedback questionnaire items should measure clearly defined behavioral competencies that are important for successfully performing the manager's job. Exhibit 8.1 provides an example of such competencies that have been used as a basis for a multisource feedback process.

One very good source of competencies is a well-developed, organization-specific managerial competency model that is the result of a sound job analysis and content validation process. This type of model will provide behavioral definitions that can be used as the basis for developing behaviorally based multisource feedback questionnaire items relevant for the current and future direction of the organization. The competency model should contain a core set of general managerial competencies, as well as separate sets of specific competencies for disciplines such as sales, finance, marketing, engineering, and so forth. An advantage of using a competency model is that its purpose is to form the foundation of the organization's HR systems, such as selection, performance management, development, promotion, compensation, and succession planning. As Sparrow and Bognanno (1993) point out, linking the multisource feedback process to it will horizontally integrate this process with other HR systems, creating consistency, coherence, and mutual reinforcement across the organization's HR practices. Sparrow and Bognanno note that linkage to the competency model will also result in vertical integration, tying this HR practice to business strategy by

Exhibit 8.1. Example of Competencies That Have Been Used as a Basis for a Multisource Feedback Process.

Competencies

- *Communication.* Clearly articulating performance expectations to staff, providing them with all relevant information to do their jobs, and creating an environment where candid communication is the norm.

- *Motivation.* Motivating group members by rallying them around a common goal, highlighting episodes of good performance, being considerate of their personal needs, and creating an environment where collaboration is the norm and where each group member feels valued.

- *Participation and Empowerment.* Encouraging and valuing the input and feedback of subordinates, providing the opportunities and resources for them to make decisions and accomplish work on their own, and supporting them in their decisions.

- *Performance Management.* Providing meaningful and timely performance feedback to direct reports, encouraging them to take advantage of personal development opportunities, and utilizing their input when setting each individual's objectives.

- *Planning.* Anticipating the resources needed to meet group or team objectives and ensuring understanding of short-term goals and long-term strategic direction.

- *Problem Solving.* Being accessible and willing to share knowledge and expertise to solve problems and resolve conflicts and disagreements when necessary.

- *Quality.* Stating and demonstrating commitment to quality and customer satisfaction and encouraging others to do so.

- *Valuing Diversity.* Demonstrating the willingness and ability to effectively manage groups consisting of diverse individuals and capitalizing on that diversity to achieve group goals.

Source: Copyright © 1992, Assessment Alternatives, Inc. Adapted from Assessment Alternatives, Inc., *Survey of Leader Behavior;* used with permission.

assessing important competencies required for the success of the business. Besides using organization-specific competency models as a basis for developing multisource feedback items, generic management competencies developed by outside consultants can be used, taking into account the considerations described earlier.

How Should the Multisource Questionnaire Be Constructed?

The multisource feedback items should describe observable behaviors, so that participants can use the resulting feedback from raters to behave more effectively. Yukl and Lepsinger (1995) suggest that the items should describe positive rather than negative behaviors, because feedback on negative behaviors may make managers feel more defensive, and does not tell participants what they should be doing, only what not to do.

The various sources may need to have somewhat different versions of the questionnaire items because they have the opportunity to view different behaviors. This may be especially true for rating sources outside the organization. However, for ease of administration, one version of the questionnaire is typically developed, with a rating option of "does not apply." London and Smither's (1995) survey results are consistent with this conclusion, with only three of the twenty respondents indicating that they sometimes develop customized versions for different sources.

Length of the questionnaire is an important consideration because it can affect response rate, especially if raters are completing questionnaires for more than one participant (Bracken, 1994). Experience suggests that this situation becomes especially important when all the managers in an organization of one hundred or more are participating, and direct report, supervisor, and peer ratings are being collected. For example, some managers may be asked to complete as many as fifteen or more questionnaires in such applications. Under these circumstances, a central coordinator may need to monitor and limit the number of questionnaires sent to any single rater. To facilitate responding, Bracken (1994) suggests that instruments contain forty to sixty items. However, where possible, even shorter questionnaires may be required to facilitate responding.

In the questionnaire instructions, raters should be assured of the confidentiality of their responses by stating the minimum number of respondents needed for data to be reported separately for the source. In their survey, London and Smither (1995) report that the typical number of raters required to present feedback for a source is three to five. Timmreck and Bracken's (1995) data are somewhat more skewed toward a minimum of three raters, with 57 percent of the processes requiring a minimum of three raters, 21 percent a minimum of four raters, and 7 percent a minimum of five raters. If the number of respondents falls below the minimum, then item data for this source are combined with another source that results in meeting the requirements for the minimum number of raters. Supervisors are the only exception. Their data are reported individually (if the participant lists only one supervisor) as would be the case with a performance appraisal.

What Types of Response Scales Should Be Used?

Research cited by Bracken (1996, 1994) recommends the use of "agreement scales" with anchors that range from "strongly agree" to "strongly disagree," or "satisfaction scales" with responses ranging from "very satisfied" to "very dissatisfied." Timmreck and Bracken's (1995) survey data indicated that "extent scales" with anchors ranging from "a great extent" to "a little extent" were most often used followed by the "agreement" and "satisfaction" scales. Research discussed by Bracken (1996, 1994) has also suggested that "frequency scales" with anchors such as "always," "usually," "sometimes," and "never" have some serious deficiencies. Much more systematic research is needed, however, to determine which types of response scales produce the most psychometrically sound multisource feedback data. Based on current research and practice, either agreement scales, satisfaction scales, or extent scales would be reasonable to use.

Some multisource instruments include, or have the option to include, an "expected frequency of performance scale" (anchors range from "never" to "always") and an "importance scale" (anchors range from "not important" to "very important"). Survey data from Timmreck and Bracken (1995) indicate that these scales are not often used. Including such scales is generally not recommended, because the items on the questionnaire should all be relevant for effective job performance, and so should all be rated relatively high on these scales (Dalessio, 1996). However, "importance scales" may be useful for identifying job-relevant items to be included in feedback reports when generic or off-the-shelf questionnaires are being used.

Consideration should also be given to the number of points on the rating scale, so that enough variance is produced to detect meaningful changes in behavior over time (Bracken, 1994), and meaningful differences between rating sources. Timmreck and Bracken (1995) report that rating scales ranging from four to seven points were most often used, and appear to afford reasonable choices.

Should Verbatim Comments Be Gathered?

Verbatim comments (or write-in comments) can provide the participant with very useful additional information that will be helpful with the interpretation of ratings, and are recommended as part of most multisource feedback processes. These comments are often collected as indicated by Timmreck and Bracken's (1995) survey, where 66 percent of the processes included verbatims. Verbatim comments can be collected by asking the rater at the end of the questionnaire to summarize the participant's key strengths and provide comments on how the participant could be more effective. Another approach to verbatim comments is to furnish the rater with the opportunity to write comments on ratings for each item. Although some raters may like this option, others may feel it is too cumbersome, and it could result in the participant receiving very few, or poor quality, verbatim comments (Bracken, 1996, 1994; Dalessio, 1996).

Verbatim comments are typically typed and included as a section in the feedback report, or attached to the report. Usually deleted from the comments are the names of other employees, as well as any expletives that may appear. The confidentiality of raters providing verbatim comments needs to be protected. Confidentiality becomes a real issue when relatively few raters respond to the multisource questionnaire. Under these circumstances, the participant may know (or believe he or she knows) who provided the comments. An approach that can be used in this situation is to content-analyze the comments and produce generic statements to the same effect. The relevant generic comments can then be fed back to the participant.

One potential downside to the use of verbatim comments is that some participants may focus on one or two comments that are not representative of the larger body of quantitative feedback. This misplaced focus can result in dwelling on a negative comment and ignoring the preponderance of positive ratings from raters who did not offer any written comments. This potential problem can be handled in two ways. First, by asking raters to provide comments on strengths as well as developmental needs, and second by having a skilled facilitator discuss this issue as part of the feedback workshop and warn participants not to focus too much on any single verbatim comment, but rather weigh all the information in the feedback report.

Administration of the Multisource Feedback Process

How Should an Organization Choose Raters?

A number of issues must be considered when choosing raters for a multisource feedback process. Research discussed earlier provides several suggestions for current best practice that include maintaining the anonymity of the raters (Antonioni, 1994) and obtaining feedback from as many qualified sources as possible (Bernardin et al., 1993; Conway & Huffcutt, 1996). As discussed earlier, research is not available on how the quality and acceptance of ratings is affected by participants choosing their raters versus others providing input. The suggestion based on current practice is participants should play the major role in selecting raters to promote empowerment and acceptance of the results. Supervisor input or review of the selected raters becomes important if the results are to be shared with the supervisor.

Another relevant issue is the number of raters that participants should be allowed to select. Allowing selection of an unlimited (or very large number) of raters can result in giving questionnaires to raters who have a limited opportunity to view the participant's behavior, and can affect the quality of ratings (Bracken, 1994). Selection of all direct reports typically is important so that the participant receives a complete picture from this source. However, this practice may not be possible in some line organizations where supervisors can have as many as thirty to forty direct reports. In these situations, a smaller number of direct reports (for example, ten to fifteen) may need to be randomly selected for participation. Random selection allows for the opportunity to receive differing views, yet not have others feel undervalued. All direct reports should be informed that random selection has been used in this situation. If the participant has as many as ten to twelve direct reports, all should receive the questionnaire, then the combined number of peers and internal customers sent the questionnaire may need to be limited to a total of approximately six to eight for practical reasons. When there are very few or no direct reports, the combined number of peers and internal customers sent the questionnaire could be increased to approximately ten to fifteen. Numbers at the higher end of these ranges should be selected if lower response rates are expected.

If external customers or vendors are included, similar limits may also need to be required. Including these sources complicates the process, because different questionnaires may need to be structured for them, and motivation to provide high-quality input may not be the same as for employees (Bracken, 1994). The participant and the supervisor should also complete a questionnaire. In their survey, London and Smither (1995) indicated that the typical number of raters from which ratings were obtained ranged from three to nine. Depending on the response rate, the ranges suggested here would probably result in a larger number of respondents.

Yukl and Lepsinger (1995) suggest that raters should be chosen who have interacted with the participant for a year or more on a regular basis. This is good advice, because if raters have not had enough opportunity to observe the participant, more ratings may show central tendency, and more items may not be rated.

What Type of Rater Training Should Be Provided?

Timmreck and Bracken's (1995) survey indicated that 66 percent of the multisource feedback programs included rater training. Bracken (1996, 1994) and Yukl and Lepsinger (1995) have suggested that rater training is a useful component for improving the quality of a multisource feedback process, and should be provided in some form. Such training could include information on the purpose of the process, instrument design, questionnaire administration, as well as training on behavioral observation, rater errors, and the psychometric quality of the ratings. Smith (1986) concluded that rater training processes where raters become more actively involved in the training, for example, participating in group discussions along with practice and feedback exercises, produce the best results with regard to rater errors and psychometric quality. Chapter Eleven in this volume addresses these issues in more depth.

The type of rater training discussed in this section would require bringing raters together for facilitated meetings. The participants, who will also serve as raters for the process, could possibly complete rater training as part of the communication process. However, given that some potential raters may be in different units within the organization—or outside the organization—such as internal customers and external customers, training all raters may not be logistically possible. At a minimum, rater training information could be provided to these raters in the format of a short memo or booklet.

How to Distribute and Return Questionnaires?

Distribution and return of questionnaires is a major administrative task that may positively or negatively affect participants' attitudes toward the multisource feedback process depending on how it is handled. To be effective, raters need to feel that the distribution and return of questionnaires protects the anonymity of their responses, and participants must feel that they are receiving feedback from as many raters as possible in a timely fashion. Outside consultants provide a very useful service in the distribution and return of questionnaires, because they can act as a neutral party and maintain the anonymity of raters during the process.

Three main activities need to be accomplished in this process: participants need to identify their raters for the administration; raters need to receive questionnaires and participants need to receive their self-questionnaire; and raters and participants need to return their questionnaires by the due date for analysis. The main methods for administration and distribution are mailing (either paper-and-pencil questionnaires or questionnaires on 3.5-inch computer disks); electronic mail via local area networks, the company intranet, or the Internet; or an automated telephone system.

When the mail is used, the names and addresses of participants can be given to the vendor by a company administrator. The vendor can then send out a form through the company mail to participants, asking them to list the names, addresses, and phone numbers of their raters. The vendor can then assemble a packet for each selected rater that contains all the multisource questionnaires for the participants that they need to evaluate, along with the self-questionnaire (if appropriate). The packet can then be distributed through the company mail. This is an efficient way to distribute the questionnaires, because all raters and participants receive only one packet. Within the packet is a generic cover letter explaining the process and a postage-paid return envelope addressed to the vendor via U.S. mail. Such a process saves costs by completing the initial distribution through company mail and the more sensitive return through U.S. mail.

Another method that uses the mail for questionnaire distribution involves having the vendor mail each participant a packet that contains a self-questionnaire and a specified maximum number of questionnaires for the participant to distribute. Each questionnaire would need to be enclosed in an envelope that could be sent through company mail to the rater. A generic cover letter explaining the project and a U.S. postage-paid return envelope addressed to the vendor also would need to accompany each questionnaire in the envelope. A problem with this latter method is that raters do not receive a single packet of questionnaires, but rather individual questionnaires from each participant, and no central control can be put into place to limit the questionnaires given to a single rater.

With both mail methods, the vendor would need to know the number of raters selected by the participant from each source so that a tally of the number of responses can be kept. Prior to the return date, each participant should be notified by the vendor or a company administrator of the number of returns for each participant for each source. If less than a minimum number of raters has returned questionnaires for a source, the participant then needs to e-mail or voice mail all participants to ask them to return questionnaires as soon as possible.

A promising alternative to the mail process is distribution and return of questionnaires via e-mail through a local area network, the company intranet, or the Internet. This type of administration has the advantage of speeding the questionnaire distribution and return process, easing the modification of the questionnaire, and facilitating the data coding for analysis. Potential challenges for such a system are securing the transmission of data and maintaining and ensuring the anonymity of the raters. Also, such systems can be expensive to develop.

A final alternative distribution and return system is through use of an automated phone system. With such a system, participants and raters can enter their questionnaire ratings through following a menu activated by a call-in number. Participants can check the tally of the number of respondents and request the generation of a report when they wish. Like an e-mail system, the process can speed data collection, coding, and analysis, but can be expensive to develop.

Constructing Feedback Reports

How Should Data Be Aggregated for Presentation?

Participants in multisource feedback processes receive a feedback report summarizing ratings from the various sources on the items and competency dimensions, as well as verbatim comments. Practitioners will need to make decisions regarding options for aggregating data and for the content of various sections of the feedback report.

Mean ratings are typically calculated for reports. For example, in the Timmreck and Bracken survey (1995), 76 percent of the multisource processes reported presenting means on the feedback report. Average ratings for each source are often calculated on items and dimensions. Overall mean ratings that include data from all sources (except the self-ratings) are also commonly calculated. Practitioners responsible for designing the process will need to decide whether all individual raters should be equally weighted when calculating these averages, or whether the rating sources should be equally weighted. Equally weighting the sources will give more weight to supervisor ratings and sources with fewer raters.

Weighting all raters equally is the preferred method, so that the participant's interpretation of the overall rating is not overly influenced in particular by the supervisor's rating. The supervisor's rating usually is presented as a separate source in the feedback report, so the participant has an opportunity to understand the supervisor's perspective. Furthermore, participants receive input from supervisors at annual performance appraisal reviews. Multisource feedback is an opportunity to emphasize information from other sources.

Olympic scoring—where the highest and lowest ratings are eliminated before calculating means—is another option for consideration. Bracken (1996) has strongly suggested that Olympic scoring is not appropriate because it may eliminate useful data from raters with a large amount of information on the participant. Olympic scoring is inconsistent with the assumption that participants need to consider input from all raters to better understand their behavior.

Including an index of item variance within the source (for example, range or standard deviation) can help participants interpret their evaluations, and may be a better approach than Olympic scoring to addressing variation and degree of agreement in ratings. The extent to which indices of item variance are used on feedback reports is unclear. Only 17 percent of Timmreck and Bracken's (1995) multisource processes indicated that a range was included on the feedback report, while 70 percent of the London and Smither (1995) respondents indicated providing an indicator of within-source agreement. The range is probably the best method for summarizing within-source agreement, because it is easiest to understand in comparison to the standard deviation, for example. Strong consideration should be given to providing an item variance index on the feedback report. However, this consideration needs to be balanced against possibly overwhelming participants with so much information that they are not able to use the report effectively to identify their major strengths and areas for development. If an index of item variance is added to a report, perhaps another aspect of the report should be streamlined.

How Should Feedback Report Sections Be Presented to Facilitate Interpretation?

The purpose of any feedback report section is to assist the participants with interpreting their results and gaining insight into their behavior. The various report sections should provide the participants with views of their behavior from each of the different sources, and with feedback regarding strengths and developmental needs that when considered together will lead to a complete picture and quality conclusions. Most report sections present summaries of numerical ratings, but as discussed earlier a section of verbatim comments is often included.

One typical report section presents overall average ratings (excluding self-ratings) for the competency categories listed from the highest to lowest rated. This section provides a quick summary picture of how others view the participant's strengths and developmental needs on the broad competency categories, and can help identify common themes among competency categories that are viewed as strengths as well as developmental needs. Generally, these overall mean ratings, as well as mean ratings for the individual sources, tend to be skewed in such a way that they are above the scale midpoint for most participants. Participants need to be cautioned that the scale midpoint in most cases should not be used as a benchmark for average performance; a scale value above the midpoint is generally a better benchmark. A consensus of subject matter experts could be used to define the benchmark. Participants need to understand that they should use this information just as a benchmark and consider their overall pattern of results, trying to focus on their relative top strengths and developmental needs in action planning.

Another report section will list from five to ten of the highest and lowest overall average rated items. The competency dimension under which the item is categorized can be listed next to each item. This section can help participants identify more specific behaviors within each of the competency dimensions that are strengths and developmental needs, as well as allow participants to determine whether the highest or lowest rated items are concentrated in one or two dimensions, or are spread across dimensions.

After the report sections focusing on the presentation of overall average ratings (excluding self-ratings), other sections of the report typically compare item and competency dimension information for each of the rating sources. They present information from the self-rating and from supervisor, direct reports, peers, and customers, as well as an overall average. Results of the London and Smither (1995) survey indicated that 80 percent of their respondents contrasted ratings from different sources on the same page and 90 percent explicitly contrasted self- with other ratings. An example of a report section presenting these types of comparisons for self-, supervisor, direct reports, and overall average ratings is shown in Exhibit 8.2.

Graphic displays are usually presented at the competency dimension level and allow for quick visual comparisons of similarity and differences among the various sources. A graphic display may show, for example, key competencies where the sources agree or disagree in their ratings, or may show that the various sources perceive the same pattern of strengths and developmental needs, but

Exhibit 8.2. Example Report Comparing Self-, Supervisor, Direct Report, and Overall Ratings on Items and Dimensions.

Behavioral Statement Ratings by Performance Category

In this section, you can compare your Self-Assessment for each individual statement about leadership behavior that appeared in the survey to the ratings made by your supervisor, your direct reports, and the overall average of ratings.

(1 = Not at all, 3 = To an average extent, 5 = To a very great extent)
Your "Overall" rating is based on 11 people.

	Self	Supervisor	Direct Reports	Overall
Communication	**3.7**	**3.3**	**2.8**	**2.9**
__ Clearly stated expectations regarding team's performance.	3.0	3.0	2.6	2.7
__ Provided direct reports with all relevant information necessary to effectively do their jobs.	4.0	3.0	2.4	2.5
__ Encouraged open and honest communication among team members.	4.0	4.0	3.5	3.7
Motivation	**3.8**	**3.0**	**3.0**	**3.0**
__ Encouraged and facilitated teamwork and collaboration.	3.0	4.0	2.9	3.2
__ Rallied team members around a common goal.	4.0	3.0	2.8	2.8
__ Made all team members feel valued.	4.0	3.0	2.6	2.6
__ Let direct reports know when they did a good job.	4.0	2.0	3.3	3.3
__ Were considerate of the personal needs of direct reports outside the workplace.	4.0	3.0	3.2	3.1
Participation/Empowerment	**3.8**	**3.0**	**3.4**	**3.3**
__ Allowed direct reports to participate in making decisions that affected them.	4.0	3.0	3.0	3.0
__ Empowered direct reports to make decisions on their own.	4.0	4.0	3.4	3.5
__ Assisted direct reports in obtaining the necessary resources to effectively do their jobs.	4.0	3.0	3.9	3.7
__ Supported the commitments direct reports made to their customers.	4.0	2.0	2.9	2.8
__ Requested and acted on feedback from direct reports about ways to improve your effectiveness.	3.0	3.0	3.4	3.3

Performance Management	**3.5**	**2.5**	**2.9**	**2.7**
Provided direct reports with coaching and guidance on ways to improve their effectiveness.	3.0	3.0	3.1	3.0
Provided direct reports with timely, specific feedback on their performance.	3.0	3.0	3.5	3.4
Informed and encouraged my direct reports to take advantage of personal development opportunities.	4.0	2.0	2.6	2.4
Encouraged and utilized each direct report's input when setting his or her objectives.	4.0	2.0	2.5	2.3
Planning	**4.0**	**3.3**	**2.4**	**2.6**
Clearly communicated short-term goals and long-term strategic direction.	4.0	4.0	2.5	2.7
Planned in advance and anticipated resources that would be needed to meet the team's objectives.	4.0	3.0	2.4	2.6
Clearly explained to each direct report how his or her individual function relates to long-term strategic direction.	4.0	3.0	2.4	2.5
Problem Solving	**4.3**	**3.3**	**4.0**	**3.7**
Willingly shared knowledge and expertise with all direct reports.	5.0	3.0	4.5	3.8
Were readily accessible if direct reports needed to discuss a problem or a particular issue.	3.0	3.0	3.8	3.5
Took steps to resolve conflict and disagreement within the team.	5.0	4.0	3.6	3.8
Quality	**4.0**	**4.0**	**4.1**	**4.1**
Regularly challenged direct reports to continuously improve their effectiveness.	4.0	4.0	3.7	3.6
Encouraged direct reports to use creative and innovative ways to satisfy the customer.	4.0	4.0	3.8	4.1
Demonstrated a strong commitment to customer satisfaction with day-to-day actions.	4.0	4.0	4.3	4.1
Regularly stressed the importance of quality and continuous improvement.	4.0	4.0	4.3	4.3
Valuing Diversity	**3.8**	**3.5**	**3.7**	**3.7**
Encouraged and accepted points of view that differed from your own.	4.0	3.0	3.6	3.6
Utilized the expertise of all direct reports when appropriate.	4.0	4.0	3.8	3.9
Valued the contributions of all individuals, regardless of level.	4.0	4.0	3.6	3.7
Utilized the diverse knowledge, skills, and abilities of team members.	3.0	3.0	3.8	3.6

Source: Copyright © 1992, Assessment Alternatives, Inc. Adapted from Assessment Alternatives, Inc., *Survey of Leader Behavior,* used with permission.

at different levels of effectiveness. Numerical displays are used effectively to compare ratings from the various sources at the item level, which allows the participant to see how the sources differ in terms of ratings of specific behaviors.

When ratings from these displays show that all sources are high and agree, this is a strength to be leveraged. When all sources agree, and the rating is low, this is a priority for developmental efforts. When some sources rate high and agree, while other sources agree and rate low, this may be a behavior that is displayed in some situations and not others. The participant may need to consider how to display this behavior more consistently. If all sources agree and rate low, but the self-rating is high, the participant should keep in mind that self-ratings tend to be lenient (for example, Harris & Schaubroeck, 1988) and this may be an area for developmental planning.

Norms should be presented for items and competency dimensions when available. Norms show how the participant compares to other managers, and will further facilitate interpretation (Yukl & Lepsinger, 1995). Norms can be based on national samples, or large samples from the organization. National norms will be available from vendors that administer multisource feedback in a wide variety of organizations. The quality of these norms should be evaluated in terms of sample size, relevance of managerial level, and relevance of industry. Norms from the organization are also useful, but an adequate sample size on which to base these norms may take a long time to gather.

A final report section could provide suggestions for on-the-job developmental activities, readings, and seminars relevant to the key behaviors for each of the lowest-rated competency dimensions. Rather than actually being placed in the report, this information could be consolidated into a separate booklet with all the competency dimensions included. The participant could use this booklet as a reference for obtaining developmental suggestions for any dimension. An example of a page providing on-the-job suggestions for two competency areas is shown in Exhibit 8.3.

How Should the Department (or Group) Feedback Report Be Used?

Often a department-level or group-level feedback report will be produced as part of the multisource feedback process to help identify group strengths and developmental needs for the purpose of

Exhibit 8.3. Developmental Suggestions
for Two Competencies.

Suggestions for Your Development

This section provides several specific recommendations for improving your performance in each performance category that has been listed as a "developmental opportunity." Remember, these are only suggestions to guide your own developmental efforts.

> It is important to keep in mind that an indication of developmental opportunity in a particular category does not imply that you have *no* skill in that area. By the same token, an indication of strength in a performance category does not imply that you should not focus on maintaining or improving your performance in that area. The purpose of this report is to guide your efforts as you continuously monitor and improve your performance in *all* areas.

Performance Management

- Start keeping a performance diary by writing down positive or negative examples of performance by your subordinates. Share the feedback with subordinates in a constructive, nonthreatening way at regular intervals.

  Set a goal to review each subordinate's performance once every two weeks and provide developmental feedback the next day.

- Keep an updated list of developmental opportunities for your subordinates and actively encourage them to take advantage of the activities at regular intervals.

  Encourage subordinates to actively seek feedback from you.

- Develop a plan for assessing employee needs for coaching. Have each employee prepare a list of areas in which he or she feels coaching is needed. Meet individually with each employee and develop an agreement as to what coaching will be provided.

- Plan to meet with each subordinate at regular intervals for the purpose of giving feedback. Make feedback clear and specific and link feedback to objectives.

- When delivering negative feedback to your subordinates, focus on maintaining their self-estcem at all times. Keep the discussion focused on the behavior you have observed rather than your overall impressions.

- Allow employee input in setting objectives. Work toward mutually agreed-upon goals for the employee and review progress at regular intervals.

Exhibit 8.3. Developmental Suggestions
for Two Competencies, cont'd.

Planning

- Solicit employee input on resource problems. Work with employees to develop methods to ensure that resources are not a problem.

- With employees, develop a plan to ensure that any commitments made to customers are realistic and are communicated clearly to all relevant parties. Ensure that the resources necessary to meet those commitments are available.

  Formally communicate short-term goals and long-term strategic direction via written documents or video presentation.

  Check with each subordinate to see that he or she understands short-term goals and long-term strategic direction.

- Take personal interest in developing a career path for each of your subordinates. Regularly monitor progress and provide feedback and suggestions for aligning current responsibilities with long-term goals.

- Explain to each subordinate, informally in conversation and formally in goal-setting, how his or her specific function relates to long-term strategic direction.

Source: Copyright © 1992, Assessment Alternatives, Inc. Adapted from Assessment Alternatives, Inc., *Survey of Leader Behavior;* used with permission.

departmental goal setting. The sections of this report will parallel those of the participant report, but will be based on average ratings for all participants in the group. For example, this type of report could be used to identify whether employees in a group of succession candidates are managing well upward with their supervisors, but less well with peers, customers, and direct reports. If such trends are apparent, then the group head can develop appropriate action plans together with the participants. The group report can be shared with participants during the feedback workshop and used as a stimulus to practice goal setting and action planning. Suggestions resulting from the discussion could be considered for implementation.

Facilitating Support for Developmental Activities

What Should Be Included in a Facilitated Feedback Workshop?

The purpose of the feedback workshop is to provide participants with an opportunity to learn how to interpret their feedback reports, and begin to write follow-up action plans to improve in areas that are opportunities for development and leverage areas that are strengths. Workshop facilitators can be more effective in achieving these purposes if they have completed a multisource feedback process themselves, so that they can speak about the various aspects of the process from direct experience.

The feedback workshop can begin with a discussion of the purpose, objectives, value, and benefits of multisource feedback. Next, background should be provided about how the multisource feedback instrument was developed and the competency model on which it is based. The workshop provides an opportunity to communicate and clarify critical organizational competencies. Then protection of the anonymity of the raters should be discussed, along with the confidentiality of the results. Who does (and does not) have access to the results needs to be clarified, and reasons provided for access.

The information in the various sections of the feedback report should be explained next, so that participants understand their data. Also, various interpretations of discrepancies among the rating sources should be discussed so that participants can use their data effectively for action planning. As discussed earlier, research by Bass and Yammarino (1991) and Van Velsor et al. (1993) suggests that as part of the feedback workshop facilitators should focus the attention of participants on large self-other discrepancies, especially when self-ratings are consistently high. These participants should consider working to bring their self-views more in line with those of others. Research by Fleenor et al. (1996) emphasizes the need for facilitators and participants to consider not only discrepancies but also behaviors receiving low to average ratings as opportunities for development. Yammarino and Atwater (1997) present a model that takes into account both the degree of discrepancy between self-other ratings and the level of the rating. The model presents four different self-other agreement categories, each of which is associated with different possible consequences. The categories are *overestimators* (who tend to rationalize negative feedback and may be headed for career derailment), *in-agreement/good* (who are effective managers and leaders), *in-agreement/poor* (who have accurate self-perceptions, but are poor performers and currently may be taking little action to improve performance), and *underestimators* (who do not appear to recognize their strengths and may not be realizing their full potential). Workshop facilitators can use the model to illustrate why different patterns of results require action to be taken by participants. Facilitators need to emphasize that self-other discrepancies point out behaviors that are salient to others, and need greater awareness and consideration on the part of the participant in developmental planning. Acceptance of such feedback can often be difficult for participants.

The work of Ashford and Tsui (1991) also indicates that facilitators should suggest that participants be more open to seeking negative feedback about their behavior from supervisors, direct reports, and peers as part of the developmental process. Finally, participants should be directed to use the information in the report for identifying strengths as well as developmental needs. Participants more naturally focus on developmental need areas, but they should be reminded to also consider their strengths so that these can be leveraged where possible to further increase effectiveness.

In the workshop, participants should also be provided with guidance on how to develop written action plans that direct their effort toward a specific goal. Facilitators need to discuss topics such as prioritizing strengths and developmental needs, setting specific goals, analyzing and choosing developmental activities, developing an action plan with time frames, taking action, and measuring results. Goals should be set for the highest-priority developmental needs. The goals that are set in these areas should be specific and challenging yet attainable. The goals also should be consistent with the mission of the organization. Time should be set aside during the workshop to actually begin setting goals and writing developmental plans. The participants should be left with a workbook that covers the topics in the workshop for reference purposes (Bracken, 1994).

What Follow-Up Activities Should Be Available?

Once a multisource feedback process is completed, participants need to take the information from the feedback workshop and incorporate it into follow-up developmental activities. Hazucha et al.'s (1993) research indicated that self-ratings and others' ratings of effort to change following the implementation of multisource feedback were related to whether the organization was reported as having a formal and active career development program. Organizations may vary to a large extent in terms of whether multisource feedback processes are linked to career development programs. Results from London and Smither's (1995) survey showed that only 40 percent of their respondents reported that multisource feedback is linked to a specific development program. Linking multisource feedback to these programs may be one key to gaining the greatest benefit from the process.

A process put into place by a company in the financial and insurance industry provides a good example of how multisource feedback can be linked to a development program. In this organization, managers were rated by their direct reports and peers on a few key organizational competencies prior to attending a weeklong development program. On each morning of the program, the participants received the multisource feedback relevant to the competency that would be developed during the remainder of the day. For example, if the day's training focused on conflict management and negotiation skills, then the participants would start the day by receiving feedback about these competencies first thing in the morning. At the end of day, the participants set goals and action plans in these areas.

On a similar issue, Yukl and Lepsinger (1995) suggest that the benefits of multisource feedback are more likely to be achieved if other follow-up activities also support the process. These activities include not only supporting formal training sessions, but also on-the-job learning opportunities for competencies identified as developmental needs. Also, participants should be provided with the opportunity to obtain on-the-job coaching from supervisors or peers on identified strengths and developmental needs. Follow-up administration of the multisource feedback questionnaire can also provide participants with information on what changes in behavior are being perceived. The London and Smither (1995) survey suggested that about 60 percent of their organizations administered the process to participants more than once. Finally, the Walker (1997) study suggests that holding feedback meetings with subordinates may be an important follow-up activity to assist improving performance.

Evaluation and Revision of the Process

Program evaluation should be built into the process to determine whether the multisource feedback is achieving its objectives. For example, the process may include objectives such as: having all employees design a formal written developmental plan, incorporating specific achievable developmental activities from the plan into performance appraisal objectives, or increasing involvement of employees in formal development programs. Data could be collected to evaluate the extent to which these objectives had been achieved.

As part of the evaluation, employee reactions to the process could also be solicited through a questionnaire or focus groups. Information should be sought to improve major aspects of the process, including adequacy of communications, definitions of competencies, questionnaire content, administration process, usefulness of feedback reports, feedback workshops, and adequacy of developmental activities. Finally, longitudinal studies could also be conducted to evaluate the extent to which improvement in performance is affected by the multisource feedback process. As mentioned earlier, these studies are often difficult to conduct because of complex methodological issues. Based on the results of the program evaluation, changes could be made that include administering it more frequently, stopping it, requiring more accountability in writing developmental plans, or providing more support for developmental activities.

Summary and Conclusions

Exhibit 8.4 provides a summary of recommendations for implementing multisource feedback processes based on current research and practice.

Multisource feedback processes are popular means for providing managers with helpful developmental feedback. The extent to which the process is successful in an organization depends to a large extent on how well it fits with the strategy and culture of the organization and is supported by a set of mutually reinforcing HR practices. As discussed previously, one approach to accomplishing

Exhibit 8.4. Summary and Recommendations for Implementing Current Multisource Feedback Practices.

Planning the Multisource Feedback Process

Linking the Process to Organizational Objects

- Base the process on important organizational competencies identified as key to the organization's success.
- Link the process to critical organizational change efforts.

Gaining and Displaying Senior Management Support for the Process

- Plan data collection to demonstrate improvements in performance as a result of the process.
- Define outcomes of the process in measurable terms, and summarize measures.
- Cascade the implementation of the process from the senior level down.
- Have senior managers feedback their results to their direct reports to act as role models and supporters of the process.

Using Multisource Feedback for Development or Personnel Decisions

- Use validated competencies as the basis for a developmental or decision tool.
- Address the issue of holding participants in a purely developmental multisource feedback system accountable for completing development planning and activities.
- Address the issues of quality of ratings and participant reactions in a multisource feedback system used as input to personnel decisions.
- Note that multisource feedback processes are generally suggested for use as developmental tools.

Providing Up-Front Communications

- State clear reasons why the process is being used for development or personnel decisions.
- State how rater anonymity will be maintained.
- Provide information on plans for scheduling, questionnaire content, frequency of feedback, follow-up support, and how long the process will be in place.

Working with Outside Consultants

- Request psychometric data on vendor's items for the purposes of evaluating, selecting, and modifying items.
- Request and evaluate vendor's norms for purposes of feedback.

Exhibit 8.4. Summary and Recommendations for Implementing Current Multisource Feedback Practices, cont'd.

- Use outside consultants to distribute, return, and analyze questionnaire data so that rater anonymity is ensured.

Constructing the Multisource Feedback Questionnaire

Identifying Competencies

- Base the questionnaire on an organization-specific competency model that is linked to other HR systems and organizational strategies.
- Establish job-relatedness through a content validation process for programs that use generic vendor-developed competencies.

Constructing the Questionnaire

- Have each item describe observable behavior linked to job-relevant competencies.
- Limit questionnaire length to forty to sixty items if at all possible.

Choosing a Response Scale

- Use "agreement," "satisfaction," or "extent" scales with four to seven points, bearing in mind that more research on the psychometric soundness of scales is needed.
- Avoid "expected frequency of performance" scales, as they will not provide much information if all questionnaire items are job-relevant.

Verbatim Comments

- Include verbatim comments as a supplement to ratings in most multisource feedback processes.
- Collect verbatim comments by asking raters at the end of the questionnaire to summarize strengths and areas for development.

Administration of the Multisource Feedback Process

Choosing Raters

- Have participants choose raters with whom they have interacted for a year or more on a regular basis.
- Maintain rater anonymity.
- Have participants complete a self-questionnaire.
- Send questionnaires to ten or twelve direct reports. With larger numbers of direct reports, random selection should be used—and communicated.
- Choose ten to fifteen peers or customers when the participant does not have direct reports. When there are direct reports, peers or internal customers may need to be limited to six to eight.

Exhibit 8.4. Summary and Recommendations for Implementing Current Multisource Feedback Practices, cont'd.

Providing Rater Training

- Provide rater training in group settings where possible, or through written materials.

Distributing and Returning Questionnaires

- Accomplish these activities: participants identify raters; raters receive questionnaires; raters return questionnaires for analysis.
- Select one of these methods for distribution: mailing paper-and-pencil questionnaires or questionnaires on 3.5-inch disks; electronic distribution via local area networks, the company intranet, or the Internet; data collection through the automated telephone system.

Feedback Reports

Aggregating Data for Presentation in Report

- Weight all raters equally when calculating overall average ratings that include data from all sources (except self-ratings).
- Avoid use of Olympic scoring.
- Use the range if an index of within-source agreement is included.

Presentation of Feedback Report Sections to Facilitate Interpretation

- Present overall average ratings (excluding self-ratings) for the competency categories listed from highest to lowest.
- Present from five to ten of the highest and lowest overall average rated items.
- Present average item and competency ratings for each source.
- Use graphic display to present visual comparisons among various sources at the competency level.
- Present norms for items and competency dimensions where available.
- Provide suggestions for relevant on-the-job developmental activities, readings, and seminars in the report or as a separate booklet.
- Caution participants not to rely on the midpoint as a benchmark for average performance because ratings are typically skewed, but rather to use a scale value above the midpoint.

Using Department or Group Feedback Reports

- Present the group report in a form parallel to the participant report, but based on average ratings from all participants.

Exhibit 8.4. Summary and Recommendations for Implementing Current Multisource Feedback Practices, cont'd.

- Use the group report as a stimulus during the feedback workshop to practice goal setting and action planning.
- Use the group report to identify and implement developmental activities for the entire department.

Facilitating Support for Developmental Activities

Facilitated Feedback Workshop

- Use workshop facilitators who have completed a multisource feedback process themselves, so that they can speak from direct experience.
- Discuss purpose, objectives, value, and benefits of the feedback process.
- Provide background on competencies and questionnaire development.
- Discuss how rater anonymity will be maintained.
- Explain the sections of the feedback report, and how to interpret potential results.
- Provide participants with guidance on developing action plans and directing efforts to a specific goal.
- Leave participants with a workbook that covers workshop topics.

Follow-Up Activities

- Link multisource feedback to specific developmental programs.
- Support the multisource feedback process with on-the-job learning opportunities and coaching from supervisors or peers on strengths and developmental needs.
- Provide opportunities for follow-up administration of the process.
- Encourage participants to share their feedback results with subordinates in a group meeting.

Evaluating and Revising the Process

- Determine whether the process is achieving specific objectives such as designing a written developmental plan, incorporating identified developmental activities into performance appraisal objectives, or increasing involvement of employees in formal developmental programs.
- Assess employees' reactions and use this information to revise the program.
- Conduct longitudinal studies to evaluate whether the process affects improved performance.

this integration is through linking the multisource feedback process to a competency model that has been strategically designed to build skill sets required to successfully position the organization in new and changing markets, and is the foundation of other HR systems in the organization. Also, the multisource feedback process should be linked to specific company development programs and follow-up activities to facilitate and sustain the development of the participants. The value of the process also needs to be demonstrated by improved performance.

Only time will tell whether this methodology is here to stay, or will metamorphose into an alternative approach to feedback. Continued focus on validation issues, improved design of the multisource feedback programs, and research on the topic will result in a better process to improve self-understanding, human interactions, and effectiveness.

References

American Educational Research Association, American Psychological Association, & National Council on Measurement Education. (1985). *Standards for educational and psychological tests* (3rd ed.). Washington, DC: American Psychological Association.

Antonioni, D. (1994). The effects of feedback accountability on upward appraisal ratings. *Personnel Psychology, 47,* 349–356.

Ashford, S. J., & Tsui, A. S. (1991). Self-regulation for managerial effectiveness: The role of active feedback seeking. *Academy of Management Journal, 34,* 251–280.

Atwater, L., Roush, P., & Fischthal, A. (1995). The influence of upward feedback on self- and follower ratings of leadership. *Personnel Psychology, 48,* 35–59.

Bass, B. M., & Yammarino, F. J. (1991). Congruence of self and others' leadership ratings of naval officers for understanding successful performance. *Applied Psychology, 40,* 437–454.

Bernardin, H. J., Dahmus, S. A., & Redmon, G. (1993). Attitudes of first-line supervisors toward subordinate appraisals. *Human Resource Management, 32,* 315–324.

Bernardin, H. J., Hagan, C., Ross, S., & Kane, J. S. (1995, May). The effects of a 360-degree appraisal system on managerial performance. In W. W. Tornow (Chair), *Upward feedback: The ups and downs of it.* Symposium conducted at the Tenth Annual Conference of the Society for Industrial and Organizational Psychology, Orlando, FL.

Bracken, D. W. (1994). Straight talk about multirater feedback. *Training and Development, 48,* 44–51.

Bracken, D. W. (1996). Multisource (360-degree) feedback: Surveys for individual and organizational development. In A. I. Kraut (Ed.), *Organizational surveys: Tools for assessment and change* (pp. 117–143). San Francisco: Jossey-Bass.

Brutus, S., Fleenor, J. W., & London, M. (1998). Elements of effective 360-degree feedback. In W. W. Tornow & M. London (Eds.), *Maximizing the value of 360-degree feedback: A process for successful individual and organizational development.* San Francisco: Jossey-Bass.

Brutus, S., Fleenor, J. W., & McCauley, C. D. (1996, April). *Self-other rating discrepancy in 360-degree feedback: An investigation of demographic and personality predictors.* Paper presented at the Eleventh Annual Conference of the Society for Industrial and Organizational Psychology, San Diego, CA.

City of Hampton. (1994). *Multi-rater assessments: Study of features and costs.* Hampton, VA: Department of Human Resources.

Conway, J. M., & Huffcutt, A. I. (1996, April). *Testing assumptions of 360-degree feedback: A meta-analysis of supervisor, peer, subordinate, and self-ratings.* Paper presented at the Eleventh Annual Conference of the Society for Industrial and Organizational Psychology, San Diego, CA.

Dalessio, A. T. (1996). Review of *20/20 Insight (Version 2.1 for Windows). Personnel Psychology, 49,* 1050–1056.

Dalton, M. (1996). Multirater feedback and conditions for change. *Consulting Psychology Journal, 48,* 12–16.

Dansereau, F., Jr., Graen, G., & Haga, W. J. (1975). A vertical dyad linkage approach to leadership within formal organizations. *Organizational Behavior and Human Performance, 13,* 46–78.

Dominick, P. G., Reilly, R. R., & McGourty, J. W. (1997). The effects of peer feedback on team member behavior. *Group and Organization Management, 22,* 508–520.

Dunnette, M. D. (1993). My hammer or your hammer? *Human Resource Management, 32,* 373–384.

Farh, J. L., Cannella, A. A., Jr., & Bedeian, A. G. (1991). Peer ratings: The impact of purpose on rating quality and user acceptance. *Group and Organization Studies, 16,* 367–386.

Fleenor, J. W., McCauley, C. D., & Brutus, S. (1996). Self-other rating agreement and leader effectiveness. *Leadership Quarterly, 7,* 487–506.

Goldstein, I. L., Zedeck, S., & Schneider, B. (1993). An exploration of the job analysis–content validity process. In N. Schmitt & W. C. Borman (Eds.), *Personnel selection in organizations* (pp. 3–34). San Francisco: Jossey-Bass.

Guion, R. M. (1965). *Personnel testing.* New York: McGraw-Hill.

Guion, R. M. (1980). On trinitarian doctrines of validity. *Professional Psychology, 11,* 385–398.

Harris, M. M., & Schaubroeck, J. (1988). A meta-analysis of self-supervisor, self-peer, and peer-supervisor ratings. *Personnel Psychology, 41,* 43–62.

Hazucha, J. F., Hezlett, S. A., & Schneider, R. J. (1993). The impact of 360-degree feedback on management skills development. *Human Resource Management, 32,* 325–351.

Kane, J. S., & Lawler, E. E., III. (1978). Methods of peer assessment. *Psychological Bulletin, 85,* 555–586.

London, M., & Beatty, R. W. (1993). 360-degree feedback as a competitive advantage. *Human Resource Management, 32,* 353–372.

London, M., & Smither, J. W. (1995). Can multisource feedback change perceptions of goal accomplishment, self-evaluations, and performance-related outcomes? Theory-based applications and directions for research. *Personnel Psychology, 48,* 803–839.

London, M., & Wohlers, A. J. (1991). Agreement between subordinate and self-ratings in upward feedback. *Personnel Psychology, 44,* 375–390.

Mayfield, E. C. (1970). Management selection: Buddy nominations revisited. *Personnel Psychology, 23,* 377–391.

Mayfield, E. C. (1972). Value of peer nominations in predicting life insurance sales performance. *Journal of Applied Psychology, 56,* 319–323.

Murphy, K. R., & Cleveland, J. N. (1995). *Understanding performance appraisal: Social, organizational, and goal-based perspectives.* Thousand Oaks, CA: Sage.

Nilsen, D., & Campbell, D. P. (1993). Self-observer rating discrepancies: Once an overrater, always an overrater? *Human Resource Management, 32,* 265–281.

Reilly, R. R., Smither, J. W., & Vasilopoulos, N. L. (1996). A longitudinal study of upward feedback. *Personnel Psychology, 49,* 599–612.

Romano, C. (1994). Conquering the fear of feedback. *HR Focus, 71*(3), 9–19.

Smith, D. E. (1986). Training programs for performance appraisal: A review. *Academy of Management Review, 11,* 22–40.

Smither, J. W., London, M., Vasilopoulos, N. L., Reilly, R. R., Millsap, R. E., & Salvemini, N. (1995). An examination of the effects of an upward feedback program over time. *Personnel Psychology, 48,* 1–34.

Sparrow, P. R., & Bognanno, M. (1993). Competency requirement forecasting: Issues for international selection and assessment. *International Journal of Selection and Assessment, 1,* 50–58.

Society for Industrial and Organizational Psychology. (1987). *Principles for the validation and use of personnel selection procedures.* Lake Mill, IA: Graphic.

Timmreck, C. W., & Bracken D. W. (1995, May). Upward feedback in the trenches: Challenges and realities. In W. W. Tornow (Chair), *Upward feedback: The ups and downs of it.* Symposium conducted at the

Tenth Annual Conference of the Society for Industrial and Organizational Psychology, Orlando, FL.

Timmreck, C. W., & Bracken D. W. (1996, April). Multisource assessment: Reinforcing the preferred "means" to the end. In W. W. Tornow (Chair), *360-degree feedback systems: Another look at their uses and impact.* Symposium conducted at the Eleventh Annual Conference of the Society for Industrial and Organizational Psychology, San Diego, CA.

Tornow, W. W. (1993). Perceptions of reality: Is multi-perspective measurement a means or an end? *Human Resource Management, 32,* 221–229.

Van Velsor, E., & Leslie, J. B. (1991a). *Feedback to managers: Vol. 1. A guide to evaluating multi-rater feedback instruments.* Greensboro, NC: Center for Creative Leadership.

Van Velsor, E., & Leslie, J. B. (1991b). *Feedback to managers: Vol. 2. A review and comparison of sixteen multi-rater feedback instruments.* Greensboro, NC: Center for Creative Leadership.

Van Velsor, E., Taylor, S., & Leslie, J. B. (1993). An examination of the relationships among self-perception accuracy, self-awareness, gender, and leader effectiveness. *Human Resource Management, 32,* 249–263.

Walker, A. G. (1997, April). *Upward feedback: Incremental improvement in managers' performance over five years.* Paper presented at the Twelfth Annual Conference of the Society for Industrial and Organizational Psychology, St. Louis, MO.

Yammarino, F. J., & Atwater, L. E. (1997, Spring). Do managers see themselves as others see them? Implications of self-other rating agreement for human resources management. *Organizational Dynamics,* pp. 35–44.

Yukl, G., & Lepsinger, R. (1995). How to get the most out of 360-degree feedback. *Training, 32,* 45–50.

CHAPTER 9

The Advantages and Pitfalls of Self-Assessment in Organizations

Leanne E. Atwater

Self-assessment, the process whereby individuals evaluate their own performance, skills, or attributes, is used for a variety of purposes in organizations. Included among the uses of self-appraisal are input in the performance appraisal process, a means of identifying developmental needs (in some cases by comparing self- and other perceptions for discrepancies), and input in employment selection decisions. This chapter describes the ways self-assessment is used in organizations, discusses factors that can contribute to more and less accurate self-perceptions and self-appraisals, and—most important—provides recommendations for optimally using self-assessments as a tool for self-development and as input for performance appraisal.

Approximately 5 percent of U.S. companies use some type of self-evaluation as part of their performance appraisal process (Ivancevich, 1995). In one application, self-ratings are used as input for the supervisor doing the evaluation as an additional source of information. For example, a number of law enforcement agencies incorporate self-assessment into appraisal on some dimensions because officers typically work alone, without observation by their supervisor (Love & Hughes, 1994). Self-appraisal can

Note: The author thanks Priscilla Cartier for her assistance in preparing this chapter.

331

also be used as an additional data point, added to appraisals by supervisors or others. Some organizations use self-assessment merely for discussion purposes in the appraisal interview. In this case, employees are asked to complete a self-assessment and this information is used by the supervisor as a springboard for discussions about the employee's performance. To date, however, most organizations still rely on supervisor ratings without input from ratees for evaluative or administrative decisions.

Another use of self-ratings in organizations is to help supervisors identify employee developmental needs, or areas where the individual believes he or she needs to improve. Alternatively, self-assessments may identify areas where the supervisor sees a need for development that the employee does not. One way developmental needs are being identified in many organizations today is with the implementation of upward and 360-degree feedback processes.

The 360-degree feedback process includes assessments of performance on various dimensions by a number of evaluator groups (for example, superiors, subordinates, peers, and customers) as well as a self-evaluation. Upward feedback relies on feedback from subordinates to supervisors. An estimated one-quarter of U.S. business organizations now use upward or 360-degree feedback as part of their management development or performance evaluation systems (Antonioni, 1996). In most cases, ratings of the manager on a number of managerial behaviors are made on a numeric scale, and averages (and, in some cases, written comments) from each rater group are fed back to the manager to compare with his or her self-ratings. The comparison of self- and other ratings is expected to promote behavior change in those areas where the manager has been rated lower than he or she expected. In other words, the discrepancies between self- and other ratings will highlight developmental needs or differing perceptions that need to be remedied. In addition, as organizations move to teams, self-management, telecommuting, and less supervisor-subordinate contact, it seems only natural that employees should share some responsibility for evaluating their own performance and identifying their own developmental needs.

A third purpose of self-assessment in organizations is input in the selection process. However, the usefulness of this application has been questioned. George and Smith (1990) found that when self-assessment was used in selection, self-ratings were dramatically skewed to the excellent end of the scale. Clearly, applicants were behaving in their own best interest, though applicants generally do believe the process is fairer if self-assessments are included. Other uses of self-appraisal include promoting team member development and increasing the acceptance of the performance appraisal process. Exhibit 9.1 summarizes the potential uses of self-appraisal.

If the use of self-assessment is going to increase, a number of issues need to be addressed so that practitioners can optimally understand the self-appraisal process and the best ways of implementing it. This chapter will identify the many variables that contribute to self-perception and self-assessment processes, identify factors that contribute to accurate and inaccurate self-appraisals, address the advantages and disadvantages of using self-appraisal for a variety of purposes, and suggest recommendations for optimally using self-assessment in organizations. This chapter will also address the difficulties associated with helping individuals deal with and accept negative feedback.

The Self-Assessment Process

If self-appraisal is to be most useful, it needs to be accurate and reflect reality. This process requires realistic self-perception, as well as self-assessments that reflect that self-perception. London (1995) suggested that self-perception or self-insight requires three primary processes: (1) information reception or perception, that is, receiving and acknowledging information about oneself; (2) remembering and interpreting that information; and (3) recalling and using that information by applying it to behaviors and attitudes. The transition

---

Exhibit 9.1. Potential Uses of Self-Appraisal in Organizations.

- Promote self-awareness.
- Provide data for performance appraisal.
- Foster acceptance of the performance appraisal process.
- Promote team member development.
- Identify training and development needs.
- Contribute to feedback interventions such as 360-degree feedback.

from self-perception to self-assessment involves additional steps, such as weighting various pieces of information, making inferences about the cause or meaning of the information, predicting future behaviors, and interpreting and evaluating consequences. Self-assessment can also be influenced by moods and transient states of mind. Some days we are much more likely to see our strengths; other days our weaknesses seem most obvious (Podsakoff & Organ, 1986). Moreover, even if self-perceptions are accurate, individuals may not rate themselves consistently with their self-insights. For example, there may be ulterior motives to purposely inflate or otherwise distort self-ratings so they do not clearly represent one's self-view.

Atwater and Yammarino (1997) point out a number of factors that influence the self-insight and self-assessment processes in organizations. These factors include biographical characteristics of the self-rater, individual and personality characteristics of the self-rater, cognitive processes, job-relevant experiences, and contextual factors within the organizational setting. It is important to understand the myriad factors that affect self-perception and self-assessment in order to increase their accuracy and to know how and when to optimally use self-assessments.

Biographical Characteristics

A sample of the biographical characteristics that affect self-perception and self-assessments includes gender, age, tenure, and minority status. Some important ways these biographical characteristics affect self-perceptions and self-ratings are highlighted in Exhibit 9.2. Most research on the impact of gender on self-ratings has indicated that males tend to evaluate themselves more positively than females (see Deaux, 1976). One study found over twice as many male as female job applicants overrated their abilities in the areas of sales and marketing (69 percent of males overrated, whereas 33 percent of females overrated) (Lindeman, Sundvik, & Rouhiainen, 1995). More recent work has suggested that this tendency may disappear when males and females rate themselves confidentially, suggesting that females are more sensitive to social pressure to appear modest than males (Daubman, Heatherington, & Ahn, 1992). Additional research has suggested that women may rate themselves less favorably than men because they are more responsive to negative feedback than men. For example, Roberts and Nolen-Hoeksema (1994) found that women perceived others' evaluations of them to be more informational and more accurate portrayals of them than men did. Men were more likely to discount negative feedback than women were. These gender differences have implications for providing feedback to males and females, which will be addressed more thoroughly in a later section.

Age and tenure have been shown to have a somewhat surprising relationship to self-assessment. Generally, older individuals and those with longer tenure in the organization provide higher self-ratings, but these self-assessments are less in agreement with those of others (such as supervisors) than are self-assessments by younger individuals or those with less tenure (Lawler, 1967; Brief, Aldag, & Van Sell, 1977). This relationship seems somewhat counterintuitive. One would expect employees with more experience on the job to be better judges of their own performance or behavior. Again, reactions to feedback may be the culprit. Ashford (1989) found that employees

Exhibit 9.2. Biographical Characteristics and Their Impact on Self-Perception and Self-Assessment.

Gender

- Males are more likely to inflate self-ratings.
- Females are more likely to accept negative feedback as valid.

Age and Tenure

- Older employees and those with more tenure provide higher self-ratings, but their self-ratings show less agreement with others' ratings.
- Older employees and those with more tenure are less likely to seek feedback.

Minority Group Membership

- Ratings of minority group members by members of majority groups are more likely to be affected by stereotyping.
- Good and bad behaviors of minority group members are more likely to be noticed.
- Minority group members' self-perceptions may be affected by biased perceptions of others.

with longer tenure were less likely to seek feedback about their performance than newer employees, perhaps because they feared feedback seeking might be seen by others as a sign of insecurity.

Minority status, or that status given to any member of a group where their age, race, gender, or other characteristic is underrepresented, may influence self-perceptions and self-assessments. Others' ratings of the minority group members may be affected by stereotyping, higher visibility of the minority, and exaggeration of differences between members of minority and majority groups. If the biased others' ratings become incorporated into self-perceptions, minority group members' self-assessments may also change. For example, if others in the group believe the minority group member is less capable, over time the minority group member may start to agree with that assessment.

Individual and Personality Characteristics

Mabe and West (1982), in their review of the literature on self-evaluation, concluded that those with higher intelligence were more likely to provide accurate self-evaluations, probably because they were more capable of processing self-relevant information. Self-esteem and narcissism also have been shown to be related to self-assessment. The impact of these characteristics on self-perception and self-assessment is summarized in Exhibit 9.3.

Exhibit 9.3. Individual and Personality Characteristics and Their Impact on Self-Perception and Self-Assessment.

Intelligence

- More intelligent individuals provide more accurate self-assessments, reflecting better memory and better use of information than those with lower intelligence can bring to bear.

Self-Esteem

- Individuals with high self-esteem rate themselves more positively.
- Individuals with high self-esteem are more likely to question the validity of negative feedback.

Narcissism

- Narcissistic individuals are more likely to inflate self-ratings.

Many studies have found a positive relationship between intelligence and accuracy of self-evaluations of ability. The explanation for this positive relationship is that those with higher intelligence generally have better information-processing capabilities. As London (1995) indicated, one central component in the self-perception process is information gathering and processing. Those individuals with higher intelligence collect, process, and remember more self-relevant information, which results in more accurate self-assessments.

Self-esteem has also been widely studied in relation to the accuracy of self-perception. In general, individuals with high self-esteem rate themselves more highly than those without high self-esteem, even when their performance is the same (Brown, 1986). As an example, when viewing a videotape of their performance, high-self-esteem individuals thought their performance was better than those with low self-esteem did, when it was really comparable (Shrauger & Terbovic, 1976). Additionally, when those with high self-esteem were given negative feedback, they were more likely to question the evaluator's ability to judge than those with lower self-esteem (Shrauger & Lund, 1975). While high self-esteem has been shown to have a number of positive effects, such as higher motivation, better performance, and increased persistence at difficult tasks, it may not be conducive to accurate self-perception. Baird (1977), for example, found that disagreement between self- and supervisor ratings of performance was greatest when the self-rater had high self-esteem and was a poor performer. These individuals tended not to accept negative feedback because it was inconsistent with their self-perceptions. This pattern creates a vicious cycle wherein the high self-esteem perpetuates inaccurate self-perception by causing individuals to deny information that contradicts their high opinions of themselves. The implications of these findings about self-esteem for self-assessment suggest a particular problem if the high self-esteem is unfounded and negative feedback is needed. If the feedback is discounted so as to maintain the positive self-view, it will be difficult to convince these individuals that change is necessary.

Self-efficacy is similar to self-esteem, but with a performance referent. In other words, self-efficacy represents the extent to which an individual believes he or she can carry out the behavior required to do a task. People who believe they can successfully carry out behavior required to do a task are more likely to perform well (Robertson & Sadri, 1990). To the extent that self-rated competencies reflect self-efficacy, we can expect them to have an impact on work performance. This relationship can work in a negative or positive direction. For those who believe they can be successful, performance increases, but for those who believe they cannot be successful, performance decreases. Self-efficacy also is likely to have an impact on task choice (Arnold & Davey, 1992). Individuals will tend to select tasks at which they believe they can be successful and avoid those for which they anticipate failure.

Narcissism (the tendency to exaggerate one's own self-importance) also appears to influence self-perception and contribute to inflated self-ratings. Robins and John (1997) conducted a test where narcissists and non-narcissists rated their performance on a group task following its completion. Narcissists evaluated themselves more positively than non-narcissists even though there were no true performance differences between the groups. Even more interesting was the reaction of narcissists and non-narcissists after viewing their performance on videotape. The narcissists' self-ratings increased after viewing the tape, whereas the non-narcissists' self-ratings decreased to approximately the true score level. Clearly, a narcissistic personality may contribute to the tendency to inflate self-ratings.

How We Process Information

How people gather, process, store, retrieve, and use information from a variety of sources can influence their self-perceptions and self-assessments. For example, some individuals actively seek feedback, whereas others tend to avoid it. Also, some individuals rely more on data in making judgments, whereas others are more intuitive. Most of us have seen presenters come away from a presentation with a very different perception of their success than members of the audience. Differences in attention to, and processing of, the nonverbal and verbal cues of audience members during the presentation generally account for the differences.

Job-Relevant Experiences

Whether individuals have had success or failure experiences in the past or received prior feedback from their jobs can influence the ratings they provide. More feedback should lead to more accurate self-ratings. For example, a stand-up comedian receives more direct feedback about job performance than a librarian. Therefore, the type of job experiences an individual has had can affect the individual's self-perception, and in turn, his or her self-assessment. There are also jobs in which giving feedback is commonplace and those where it rarely occurs. For example, in the military, before a junior officer makes a presentation (or, as they say, "gives a briefing") to a senior officer, the junior officer goes through a number of dry runs (often called "murder boards") in front of others. The job of the audience members is to identify any weaknesses in content or delivery and provide this feedback to the presenter so the briefing can be perfected before being given to the senior officer. In other words, candid feedback in this case is expected. At the other extreme, a bus driver (like many automobile drivers) rarely receives feedback about driving skill levels unless he or she causes an accident.

Context and Situation

Beyond characteristics of the raters, there are job and organizational factors that can influence self-perceptions and self-assessments. Self-assessments can be affected by job pressures, prior rating experience, and the availability and specificity of information pertinent to the self-assessment. For example, students who have taken a number of graded exams or quizzes during the semester will be better able to estimate their course grade near the end of the course than those who have spent the semester working on a class project that will determine the course grade. Research suggests that experience in the rating process is also important and that self-assessments become more accurate as raters gain more experience (Kooker, 1974). Also, if self-assessments are going to be used as part of a formal evaluation on which rewards are based, pressures to inflate assessments will be present.

Self-Other Discrepancies in Perception

Given the large number of factors that can influence self-perceptions and self-assessments, it is no wonder that they are not always accurate or dependable. And, somewhat surprisingly, individuals are not much better at assessing how well they have performed in the past than how well they will do in the future (Ashford, 1989).

Characteristics of Self-Ratings

Self-raters have the most complete information about their behavior, but not necessarily the best information about the results of that behavior nor the clearest idea of how it was received by others. For example, a poet knows how long he or she struggled to compose a poem and all the thought and effort that went into the composition. The poet does not know how good the poem is, nor how it will be received by readers.

Self-raters look at their behavior more in terms of skills and competence rather than of the level of performance it represents. Self-raters also are more likely to compare their performance to that of others rather than to objective standards. A salesperson is more likely to compare monthly sales with those of others on the staff than with sales goals set by the company. For example, if a car dealership had a sales goal of eight cars per month per salesperson, but the person with the highest number of sales only sold four cars, the individual who sold the four cars will likely see his or her performance as quite good compared to others, regardless of the sales goal.

In addition, self-raters base judgments of their own behavior on *intentions* but base judgments of others on observable behavior. If I had every intention of getting to work on time, but the power in my neighborhood went out during the night and my alarm did not go off, I am likely to judge my tardiness to work as acceptable and unavoidable. My peers, who are unaware of my intentions, may judge my tardiness as a sign of laziness.

Self-ratings have been compared to supervisor, peer, and subordinate ratings in a number of studies. The conclusion from these studies (see Mabe & West, 1982; Harris & Schaubroeck, 1988) has been that self-ratings are less related to superior, subordinate, or peer ratings than the superior, subordinate, and peer ratings are to each other. That is, correlations among ratings from supervisors, peers, and subordinates are higher than correlations between self-ratings and ratings of any of the other groups. While much of the empirical research suggests that self-ratings differ from other ratings, others' ratings should not always be used as valid because self-descriptions have some accurate components (Dunnette, 1993). Agreement cannot be considered synonymous with accuracy. Two judges can agree and both be perfectly wrong, or disagree and both be right given their different perspectives. Nevertheless, when compared to objective criterion measures, ratings by supervisors, subordinates, and peers are more likely to be related to those criteria than self-ratings.

There are a number of factors that may contribute to self-other differences in ratings. The differences may be caused by information constraints (that is, different rater groups have different information); different understandings of the job requirements (that is, supervisors may believe different aspects of the individual's job are more important than his or her subordinates do); and biases such as halo or leniency (tendencies to inflate ratings). Supervisor ratings have also been known to involve a wide range of political motives, and thus their primary purpose is not always to accurately reflect behavior but rather to affect outcomes such as rewards and punishments (Longnecker, Sims, & Gioia, 1987). However, when self- and supervisor ratings are compared, most organizations assume supervisor ratings are capturing the true score. In fact, each source may just be capturing different perspectives, or suffering from different biases.

Disagreement between rater groups also goes up when that which is being rated is ambiguous or more difficult to observe (Wohlers & London, 1989). The following section will highlight the ways in which the accuracy and value of self-ratings can be improved.

The Problem of Self-Rating Inflation

One of the most common problems associated with self-appraisal is *leniency bias,* or the tendency for self-appraisals to be inflated. This bias tends to touch individuals at all levels in organizations. Even highly intelligent individuals with many years of experience (for example, top-level executives) seem to suffer from inflated self-ratings. In one study, twenty-four of twenty-seven aspects of behavior rated by top executives about themselves were higher than the ratings given them by their managers. Self-ratings on over half of the behaviors were uncorrelated with supervisor ratings. To make matters worse, those that were more likely to inflate their ratings compared to the ratings given by others were less likely to score high on a promotability index that was decided by a team of managers (Thornton, 1968). Thus, these inflated self-ratings are dysfunctional for the individual and the organization.

When individuals were asked to do self-ratings prior to an appraisal discussion with their supervisor, again, ratings were inflated. The individuals were asked to compare their own performance with those in comparable positions. Over 40 percent of the group put themselves in the top 10 percent, while only 2 percent put themselves below 50 percent (Meyer, 1980). Among high-level professional and managerial employees, over 80 percent placed themselves in the top 10 percent of their job category, yet 85 percent expected to receive lower ratings from their supervisor than they had given themselves. A similar example of inflation was provided by a sample of engineers. When ninety-two engineers were asked to rate their performance relative to others, the average self-rating was at the 78th percentile in a range from 0 to 100. On the average, participants thought they were doing better than three-quarters of their peers. Only two engineers rated themselves below the 50th percentile, and both of these placed themselves at the 45th percentile (Meyer, 1980).

It is possible that narcissism underlies some self-enhancement bias. Individuals with unrealistically exaggerated beliefs about their true abilities and achievements and a grandiose sense of their own self-importance will be less likely to receive positive evaluations from others; yet they are also likely to provide very inflated self-ratings. These individuals also tend to be defensive in response to criticism.

Clearly, few of us see ourselves as below average, and as David Campbell from the Center for Creative Leadership often points out, the vast majority of people consider being "average" an insult. The question becomes, What can be done to help individuals develop more realistic self-perceptions, and get them to provide more realistic, less inflated self-assessments?

Increasing the Accuracy of Self-Ratings

First and foremost, individuals need accurate feedback from others. Clearly, few of us enjoy giving or receiving negative feedback. As a result, much of the feedback we do receive is sugar-coated. In fact, some supervisors simply avoid giving feedback at all if that feedback is negative. They have taken the old adage "if you can't say anything nice, don't say anything at all" to heart. As a consequence, the feedback we do receive is often positively biased, which contributes to an inflated self-perception.

Feedback Seeking

A number of studies have suggested that individuals with self-assessments that are similar to the assessments of relevant others in the workplace are more effective (compare Atwater & Yammarino, 1993). Van Velsor, Taylor, and Leslie (1993) found that those with the most inflated self-ratings were the poorest performers and had the lowest self-awareness as rated by others.

Individual effectiveness may rest on how well employees and managers can use the feedback provided by their constituencies to detect discrepancies between others' assessments and self-assessments and modify their behavior accordingly. In other words, others' perceptions are highly important because it is these perceptions, not some objective reality, that are acted upon. "Organizations are downsizing, restructuring, merging and retooling with striking frequency in response to more turbulent, more competitive and more global marketplaces. One consequence of these trends is an intensifying of the complexity of managerial work. Managers are now held responsible for a wider array of activities than before, including making rapid adjustments to external changes. . . . The processes most needed in the ambiguous and complex situations just described would seem to be those of self-regulation and self-control on the part of managers themselves" (Tsui & Ashford, 1994, p. 93). Self-regulation depends on adequate and accurate feedback.

This feedback can come in a number of forms. Formal performance reviews are one avenue for providing feedback. However, in the majority of organizations these reviews occur once a year and last less than one hour. Obviously, this is insufficient feedback if increased self-awareness is the goal.

Feedback also can occur informally throughout the year if supervisors, subordinates, and peers share evaluative information with one another. Individuals should be encouraged to seek informal feedback by asking others specific, open-ended questions

(questions that cannot be answered simply with yes or no) about their performance. For example, an employee could ask a peer, "What do you think I could have done to have handled that customer's concerns better?" Or a subordinate could ask a supervisor, "Did I make all the relevant points in that presentation I gave?"

Feedback can also be solicited anonymously via survey as is done in 360-degree and upward feedback. Because the rater does not have to worry about being identified, or about a face-to-face interaction, anonymous feedback tends to be more honest.

Giving feedback, however, is only half of the story. The feedback recipient also must be receptive and responsive to the feedback. There are a number of factors that affect the types of feedback individuals receive and the ways in which they are likely to react.

First, social psychological research has demonstrated that evaluative feedback that is perceived as accurate has direct and rapid effects on self-perception (Shrauger & Schoenemann, 1979). Atwater, Roush, and Fischthal (1995) showed that feedback from subordinates can alter leaders' self-ratings of leadership. After receiving feedback, the leaders' self-ratings more closely matched those of their subordinates. Overestimators lowered their self-ratings and underestimators raised their self-ratings. If the feedback comes from multiple sources and it is consistent across sources, the feedback is even more likely to alter self-perceptions than feedback from a single source.

Second, information that is inconsistent with what was expected is likely to be distrusted, discredited, and distorted. Therefore, discrepant information must be based on highly incontrovertible evidence that can not be negated. More sources make the negative feedback more difficult to discount. In addition, information that is behaviorally specific such as "rarely provides positive feedback when followers exceed expectations" will be more difficult to discount than more general information such as "rarely provides feedback."

Third, individuals are more likely to react favorably to positive than to negative feedback (both to the feedback and its source) even if negative feedback is expected. In some cases, if individuals believe they might receive negative feedback, they will avoid the feedback altogether, or seek only those sources or activities that will lead to positive feedback. The feedback problem is also compounded in that few individuals enjoy giving negative feedback and often positively distort the negative feedback they do provide.

The organization's culture also affects the feedback individuals receive in that some organizational cultures sanction and encour age feedback seeking while others do not. For example, Arizona Public Service (a utility company) encourages supervisors to seek feedback from all relevant constituents before completing the performance evaluation. Other organizational cultures treat feedback seeking as a weakness, that is, they assume the supervisor should have all the relevant information and should not need to seek additional perspectives.

The extent to which feedback is provided by the job or is encouraged in the organization is also important. For example, Corning requires frequent performance reviews for all new employees during their first year, so they obtain adequate feedback about their performance early on.

Because negative feedback tends to be avoided by feedback providers and discounted by feedback receivers, special care needs to be taken to help individuals develop more realistic self-views. Recommendations are provided later in the chapter for increasing self-perception accuracy.

360-Degree Feedback

Nilsen and Campbell (1993) demonstrated that in the absence of feedback self-other discrepancies were stable over time and across instruments, suggesting that individual characteristics may underlie these rating tendencies. That is, overraters tended to overrate no matter what was being measured, or when. Similarly, underraters tended to underrate. Given the negative outcomes associated with inaccurate self-ratings and self-perceptions, many companies have adopted formal strategies aimed at increasing feedback to individuals in an attempt to increase their self-awareness of their strengths and weaknesses as perceived by relevant others.

One of these strategies has been the introduction of upward and 360-degree feedback processes. As described earlier, this approach allows individuals to anonymously rate a focal individual on a number of behaviors the organization considers important for the job. The feedback is then aggregated by source and provided to the focal individual to compare with his or her self-rating. The goal is for employees to compare their self-ratings to those from others, identify discrepancies (particularly areas where the focal individual believes he or she is doing better than others believe), reevaluate the self-ratings, and set goals for improvement where necessary. (Chapter Eight in this volume discusses multi-source and 360-degree feedback in more depth.)

However, when individuals receive feedback that is negative, that is, when self-ratings are higher than others' ratings, accepting the feedback and setting goals for improvement is only one of the options available to the individual dealing with the feedback. Other strategies include the following:

- The individual may rationalize the feedback or decide it is invalid.
- The individual may deny that the discrepancy is meaningful.
- The individual may leave the situation, such as change position or organization.
- The individual may decide that change is unrealistic or impossible and abandon it.
- The individual may attempt to change the others' ratings by using threats or intimidation so future discrepancies will not occur.
- The individual may change the self-rating but not really change the underlying self-assessment.

While the goal of upward and 360-degree feedback processes is increased self-awareness and positive behavior change, these may not always be the outcomes. However, as mentioned earlier, if the negative feedback comes from multiple sources (as is the case with 360-degree feedback), it is more difficult to discount, and more likely to have the greatest chance of promoting positive behavior change. Feedback about one's own behavior is important, but information about the behavior or performance of relevant others also helps individuals provide more accurate self-appraisals.

Comparisons Between Self and Others

Social comparison theory suggests that to validate our self-perceptions, we make comparisons between ourselves and others. For example, to assess our ability or competence, we compare our performance with that of others who apply similar skills. Some individuals may choose to compare against a group of poor performers so as to enhance their opinion of themselves or confirm their positive self-views. In other words, "Among those I have selected for comparison, I look good." The fact that the comparison group selected is below average is ignored. Those with low self-esteem may select the most capable individuals for their comparison group, thereby validating their low opinions of themselves. Consequently, individuals need relevant comparison groups and information about the performance of others in order to make more accurate judgments about themselves. For example, the supervisors may want to create teams of individuals where those with the most experience and proven track records are identified as the team leaders. In this way, the team leaders will be implicitly encouraged to select other team leaders as their comparison base.

Information About Others

Normative information (information about the performance of comparable others) improves self-assessment accuracy. Whether information is presented directly in terms of observing others' work or indirectly in terms of being informed about others' work, having information about others increases the accuracy of self-assessments. Normative information is important even if the self-assessments will be used in making administrative decisions such as reward allocations (Dobbins, Farh, & Lehr, 1990; Farh & Dobbins, 1989). Supervisors could be encouraged to share normative information with individuals. For example, rather than merely stating that an individual's sales were at 80 percent of target for the quarter, they could add "and the range among sales personnel in this group was from 50 percent to 120 percent with over half exceeding the 100 percent target." In this way, the individual who is at 80 percent knows he or she is far below the majority.

Providing employees with comparative information as part of their appraisal not only increases agreement between the self-ratings and other's ratings, it reduces defensiveness and conflict and makes it more difficult for the self-rater to question the accuracy of the evaluation. Thus the feedback will more likely be accepted and used as input for needed changes in behavior. Therefore, if the intention is to get an individual to accept feedback in a performance appraisal interview, comparative information is helpful.

While research has demonstrated that providing feedback (for example, upward feedback via surveys) influences future self-assessments (Atwater et al., 1995), we do not know whether these self-assessments truly represent a change in self-perception or a desire to have self-ratings more in line with those of others. For self-perceptions to be enhanced, the individual may need to formulate action plans and see improvements or receive additional, more positive feedback.

Maximizing the Impact of Feedback
What We Do, See, and Remember

Self-enhancement theory suggests that individuals want to see themselves in a favorable light. Consequently, information is selectively perceived or remembered—or perhaps even distorted—to maintain this favorable perception. Individuals may also elect to participate in particular activities or tasks in which they are more likely to succeed and avoid those where failure is expected so as to maintain their positive impression of their competence. For example, individuals with poor interpersonal skills may seek solitary activities where those skills are not needed. Therefore, because they do not receive negative feedback from others about their interpersonal skills, they can maintain a perception of competence. That is, they can tell themselves that they have the necessary interpersonal skills, they just have not needed to use them. As a result, the information recalled as a basis for self-evaluations tends to be positive. Again, the implication is that accurate feedback is essential to counter the effects of selective perception.

Public Announcements

What can be done in addition to providing feedback and social comparison data to individuals to help reduce inflation bias and improve the accuracy of self-assessments? Requiring individuals to publicly announce their ratings tends to reduce inflation. Individuals seem less willing to announce their inflated self-assessments to others than to provide them confidentially or anonymously.

Validation

Beliefs that ratings will be validated or checked also decreases leniency. When self-raters are told that their scores will be validated against a criterion, they are more likely to report accurate rather than inflated scores. For example, subjects who knew a biochemical measure of smoking would be taken were more likely to self-report smoking than those who did not know a measure would be taken (Bauman & Dent, 1982). Faculty members required to provide documentation of student evaluations and publication acceptances are more likely to report accurately. Those who know attendance records are kept are more likely to accurately report absences. Those who know that the number of client calls per day is randomly monitored will be less likely to exaggerate.

Focus on Behaviors

Being asked to rate oneself on ambiguous characteristics may promote inflation in self-ratings. Dunning, Meyerowitz, and Halzberg (1989) asked individuals to compare their abilities to those of their peers. When the characteristic was ambiguous (for example, "congenial"), self-assessments were lenient. When the characteristic was made less ambiguous ("attends social functions"), less inflated evaluations occurred.

Know What Will Be Rated

Providing raters with information about the constructs on which they will be rating themselves before asking them to do the assessment will increase accuracy. Raters are more likely to attend to and remember those things that will be measured. They are also more likely to notice and remember what was not done if they know in advance what will be measured (DeNisi & Summers, 1986).

Scale Manipulations

Given that a very small percentage of individuals rate themselves below average, another way to minimize leniency is to skew the scale. Ratings can be made on an asymmetrical scale (for example,

1 = marginal, 2 = satisfactory, 3 = good, 4 = very good, 5 = outstanding). In this way, above average or good performance is associated with the middle of the scale. When ratings are made on a skewed scale, mean scores can be expected to be less inflated (Dobbins, Farh, & Lin, 1992). However, while the ratings obtained on a skewed scale were less lenient, they were no more highly correlated with other performance measures than the other types of self-ratings. In other words, minimizing leniency errors does not necessarily increase the accuracy of the ratings (Bernardin & Pence, 1980). Future research is needed to determine the value of manipulations for reducing leniency.

A method of self-assessment that has been advocated for assessing change is *retrospective pretest*. This method asks raters to evaluate their performance as it is now and as it was in the past. These retrospective pretests are used instead of actually measuring performance before and after an intervention. There is some research to support the retrospective pretest as a more accurate measure of change than the pre-post method (Howard & Daily, 1979). This improved accuracy is largely because the mind-set of the raters may change between the pretest and the posttest, thereby affecting the standards they use to evaluate themselves. Rating myself as a "4" (above average) on the pretest and a "4" six months later on the posttest does not necessarily mean I have not changed but rather that my interpretation of above average has shifted. There are still cautions concerning the retrospective pretests because of questions concerning the degree to which we can accurately remember our own performance months ago.

Team Self-Assessment

Teams are becoming increasingly popular in organizations as a means to maximize creative input and synergy in problem solving and task accomplishment. Estimates are that over 80 percent of organizations use teams in at least some operations ("How to ensure . . . ," 1994). A variety of instruments are available for teams to assess overall team effectiveness (such as teamwork or conflict resolution skills). In addition, SYMLOG (see "Tools to fine-tune a team," p. 11), and the TEAM-Q (developed by this author and her colleagues), have been developed to give individual team members feedback about their team skills. (Exhibit 9.4 offers samples of items from this survey and feedback report.) As an example, the TEAM-Q asks each team member to rate each other team member on items addressing collaboration skills and contribution to task accomplishment. Then each team member receives individual, aggregated feedback about his or her skills as viewed by the other team members. As in the upward and 360-degree feedback process, the team member also provides a self-assessment, and self-other comparisons can be made.

Anecdotal accounts from individuals who have received this team feedback suggest that the individualized feedback, where team members can compare self- and team member ratings of their skills, is far more helpful than assessing overall team competencies because overall team assessments do not allow individuals to point the finger at others. Instead, individual developmental needs are clearly identified. (Chapter Seven in this book deals with team appraisals in greater depth.)

Self-Assessment in the Performance Appraisal Process

As mentioned earlier, a number of organizations currently use self-assessment as part of the appraisal process, and given the changing nature of work, this practice will probably increase in the next decade. Some of the anticipated advantages of using self-appraisal as part of the performance appraisal process are highlighted in Exhibit 9.5. First, self-assessment enhances the self-rater's dignity and self-respect, in that it signals that the self-rater has valuable input in the assessment process (Meyer, 1991). Another advantage of including self-appraisal in the performance appraisal process is that it generally increases employees' perceptions of the fairness of the appraisal process (Greenberg, 1986). Being asked to provide a self-assessment gives the self-rater a greater sense of control over the performance appraisal process. Ratees do not feel as much at the mercy of the evaluator's opinion. Instead, they feel they have some input into the appraisal and outcomes (such as raises) that may be based on the appraisal. However, if the self-rating is substantially higher than the supervisor's rating, the time, effort, and involvement the self-rater puts into the self-appraisal process may strengthen the ratee's confidence in the accuracy of his or her own rating and decrease acceptance of a

Exhibit 9.4. Team Effectiveness Questionnaire and Report.

In the first section the employee evaluates himself or herself and team members on collaboration and contribution.

	SELF	TEAM MEMBERS 1	2	N
Use this scale for your answers: 1 = not at all or rarely 2 = sometimes 3 = often 4 = always or almost always	*First, Last Name*	*First, Last Name*	*First, Last Name*	*First, Last Name*
1. Can be depended on to do what he or she says......................	1 2 3 4	1 2 3 4	1 2 3 4	1 2 3 4
2. Provides valuable input to decisions......................................	1 2 3 4	1 2 3 4	1 2 3 4	1 2 3 4
3. Acknowledges mistakes without becoming defensive....................	1 2 3 4	1 2 3 4	1 2 3 4	1 2 3 4

Space for written comments about team members follows the first section.

If you have specific comments about any team member, please provide them, along with the team member's name, in the space provided.

The next set of questions addresses organizational issues such as management practices and organizational systems.

22. Team members have an adequate say in selecting team members.........	1 2 3 4
23. Systems are in place to allow the team adequate access to other groups on which it depends..	1 2 3 4
24. The team receives adequate recognition for its accomplishments..........	1 2 3 4

Space for written comments about the organization follows this section as well.

In the space provided, please include additional and more detailed comments about managerial or support systems that affect team performance.

Exhibit 9.4. Team Effectiveness Questionnaire and Report, cont'd.

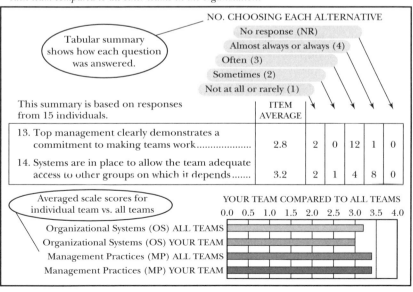

Self-scores can be compared to various aggregated group scores.	AVERAGE RATINGS FOR EACH ITEM				
	FOR RATINGS GIVEN BY				
			YOUR TEAM:		ORG:
	YOUR-SELF	ALL SELF	YOUR RATERS	ALL RATERS	ALL RATERS
CL 1. Can be depended on to do what he or she says..................	3	3.0	3.4	3.0	2.9
CN 2. Provides valuable input to decisions..............................	3	3.0	3.3	2.8	2.4
CL 3. Acknowledges mistakes without becoming defensive ...	2	3.0	3.6	3.3	3.1

2.5 2.6 2.7 2.8 2.9 3.0 3.1 3.2 3.3 3.4

CONTRIBUTION

Average scale scores for various groups appear in graphic form.

COLLABORATION

☐ YOURSELF
■ YOUR TEAM: ALL SELF
☐ YOUR TEAM: YOUR RATERS
■ YOUR TEAM: ALL RATERS
■ ORG: ALL RATERS

This next section addresses ratings of management practices and organizational systems for each team compared to all other teams in the organization.

Tabular summary shows how each question was answered.

NO. CHOOSING EACH ALTERNATIVE

No response (NR)
Almost always or always (4)
Often (3)
Sometimes (2)
Not at all or rarely (1)

This summary is based on responses from 15 individuals.	ITEM AVERAGE					
13. Top management clearly demonstrates a commitment to making teams work.....................	2.8	2	0	12	1	0
14. Systems are in place to allow the team adequate access to other groups on which it depends.......	3.2	2	1	4	8	0

Averaged scale scores for individual team vs. all teams

YOUR TEAM COMPARED TO ALL TEAMS

0.0 0.5 1.0 1.5 2.0 2.5 3.0 3.5 4.0

Organizational Systems (OS) ALL TEAMS
Organizational Systems (OS) YOUR TEAM
Management Practices (MP) ALL TEAMS
Management Practices (MP) YOUR TEAM

supervisor's rating that is substantially lower (Klimoski & Jones, 1989). In this case, the ratee does not perceive the rating process as fair, and tensions between the ratee and the supervisor may increase.

If disagreement between the self-appraisal and other sources is not extreme, overall reliability will be increased. The more people appraising an employee, the more likely it is that the biases of the raters will tend to cancel one another out, and the more their perspectives will combine to give a complete picture of performance (Borman, 1974; Kane & Lawler, 1978).

Allowing the ratee to provide a self-rating increases communication between the supervisor and the ratee. Too often performance reviews end up being a monologue by the supervisor. If the employee has completed a self-appraisal, there is more opportunity for dialogue and input from the evaluatee. When a self-appraisal is included, the supervisor tends to act more as a counselor than a judge (Meyer, 1991).

Since employees probably implicitly make self-ratings even when they are not explicitly asked to make them, formalizing the self-rating process provides a way for discrepancies between self- and

**Exhibit 9.5. Role of Self-Assessment
in the Performance Appraisal Process.**

- Enhances self-raters' sense of dignity and self-respect.
- Increases employees' perceptions of the fairness of the process.
- Reduces the impact of any individual's biases by providing ratings from more sources.
- Provides a tool to increase communication in the appraisal interview.
- Highlights any discrepancies between self- and supervisor perceptions of performance.
- Minimizes halo error; self-raters see more differentiation across rated dimensions than observers.
- Helps clarify differences of opinion regarding performance requirements.
- Increases acceptance of feedback because it promotes self-reflection about performance.
- Increases commitment to development plans and goals formulated.

supervisor ratings to be identified and discussed. The process of discussion wherein expectations and perceptions are clarified on both parts should result in greater acceptance of the appraisal process, more agreement in evaluations, and heightened motivation on the part of subordinates to change in areas that need improvement.

Asking ratees to provide self-assessments may also help clarify differences of opinion regarding performance requirements. It allows the supervisor to recognize areas in which the employee believes he or she is performing well that may be at odds with the supervisor's opinion. Thus, the self-ratings can give the evaluator a heads-up about where opinions differ and can help the supervisor act as coach in these areas. However, when self-ratings are provided to the supervisor they may result in inflation by the supervisor in an effort to avoid conveying information that is neither expected nor desired by the ratee. This is what Klimoski and Inks (1990) found. When the self-rating level was high and the feedback session was face to face, ratings by the supervisor were much higher than when feedback was not shared. For those individuals who rated themselves lower than the supervisor had, there was no inflation or distortion in the supervisor's ultimate ratings.

Self-appraisal can assist individual development by stimulating reflection, promoting problem solving, and increasing receptivity to suggestions. Those who provide self-appraisals also tend to be more committed to any development plans or goals that are formulated. When used as part of the appraisal interview to stimulate communication, self-appraisals can help clarify goals and expectations and force employees to focus more directly on what is expected in the job. Discussions in these interviews should focus more on the future than the past, emphasizing how the employee will perform and what his or her capabilities are, rather than how he or she has performed.

Self-ratings can also be valuable if one wants to minimize halo error. Self-ratings suffer less from halo error than ratings provided by others. Those individuals rating others tend to generalize from one dimension to another, whereas self-raters show greater differentiation across dimensions. Kraiger (1986) for example, found average correlations between dimensions of .41 for self-ratings and .55 for supervisor ratings. In other words, the self-raters are less likely than other raters to generalize high or low ratings from one dimension to another.

Self-appraisals are valuable for assessing individual abilities and intentions (Fox & Dinur, 1988). Self-raters are in the best position to know their inner states and feelings and changes over time. Individuals are more sensitive than observers to external determinants of their own behavior. Observers are more likely to overattribute causes of others' behavior to internal dispositions. This tendency is referred to as the "fundamental attribution error," because it is counterintuitive that observers would know about others' internal states. Self-raters do not share the tendency to overattribute their own behavior to internal dispositions, unless they are attempting to explain their own success or failure. In this case, they may attribute failure to external causes and success to themselves.

Self-Assessment in Employee Selection

Self-assessment has not generally been recommended in the selection process due to its lack of validity. In a study by George and Smith (1990), those individuals who gave themselves the highest self-ratings were more likely to be rated as poor by personnel administrators in terms of suitability for employment than those who did not rate themselves as highly. Also, those with high self-ratings who were selected were more likely to leave before their contract was up than those with lower self-ratings.

In another application of self-assessment to selection among mid-level managers, self-ratings were compared to assessment center ratings done as part of a selection process. Self-ratings were unrelated to assessment center ratings and unrelated to subsequent peer ratings of performance after one year on the job (George & Smith, 1990).

Wicklund and Gollwitzers (1983) discussed anti-validity of self-ratings used in selection. They suggested that poor validity for self-assessment in selection situations is due to applicants with self-perceived weaknesses hiding deficiencies by reporting high and inaccurate ratings. Thus, worse than merely being inaccurate, those with the highest ratings may be covering deficiencies and actually deserve the lowest ratings. Additionally, if taken seriously, those who are being honest and reporting weaknesses may be seen as less suitable than those who purposely distort their ratings.

Self-assessments as estimates of ability have fared equally poorly. DeNisi and Shaw (1977) had subjects rate themselves in ten ability areas. They were then given a battery of tests. The correlations between the self-assessments of ability and the test scores were too low to have any practical significance. Thus the researchers concluded that self-assessments should not be used to measure abilities.

Even in cases where self-assessments have been shown to correlate with performance tests, we have to be skeptical. For example, if the correlation between self-assessment and the test score is .5 and the correlation between the test score and performance is .5, the relationship between self-assessment and performance can range from –.67 to 1.0 (McNemar, 1969). Thus we cannot conclude that because self-assessment can predict test scores, they can be substituted as predictors of performance.

On a more positive note, as with the use of self-appraisals in the evaluation process, job applicants are more likely to consider selection processes fair if self-ratings are used as one piece of evidence in evaluation. However, because most research results suggest that self-ratings in selection are so inflated that they are hardly useful, it may make sense to ask for evidence of self-rated abilities or accomplishments as well as self-ratings. For example, one Native American was asked to rate her negotiation skills as part of a selection battery. As evidence of her high self-rating, she provided copies of the oil leases she had negotiated for her tribe. Accomplishment records, as opposed to ratings of abilities or skills, may be more useful as input into selection decisions.

One tactic that has been used to increase the validity of self-assessments in selection is to use an inflation scale as part of the self-assessment. Asking self-raters to rate themselves on bogus tasks or abilities such as "cleaning chartels" or "monitoring fiscal binaries" and then using self-ratings on these bogus tasks to correct the self-assessment improves the validity of self-assessments (Anderson, Warner, & Spencer, 1984). For example, if an individual gives himself a high rating on a bogus task, corrections for inflation can be made to his other self-assessments. By contrast, if an individual acknowledges that his skill level for a bogus task is zero or that he has no knowledge of such a task, self-assessments may be more trustworthy.

It is also possible that self-appraisals of suitability for a job might increase after individuals have been exposed to the content of the job through realistic job previews. Once they have seen the specific characteristics of the job, individuals may be more accurate in their self-appraisals of their abilities to do the job. For example, I may think I can work as a customer service representative, but once I've actually watched individuals deal with angry customers, I may be more willing to admit that my personality is probably not a good fit with that type of work.

Methods of Self-Assessment in Performance Appraisal

There are a number of methods that can be used to obtain self-ratings for appraisal purposes. Among the most common are both-rate appraisal, joint appraisal, and self-only appraisal.

Supervisor and Subordinate Both Rate

In the both-rate appraisal, both the self-rater and the other appraiser complete the same rating form and compare their ratings. As mentioned earlier, there are hazards with this procedure if the self-rating is substantially higher than the appraiser's rating. Specifically, the self-rater may become defensive and may be less likely to accept input from the appraiser if the ratings were much lower than expected.

Two of the companies that currently use a both-rate system and find it quite satisfactory are Glendale Savings and Loan in Glendale, California, and Lincoln Electric in Cleveland, Ohio. In these organizations, both the supervisor and employee independently complete an evaluation form and then discuss the employee's performance. A higher-level manager then reviews the completed appraisal. At Lincoln Electric, the president of the company personally reviews the performance evaluations of each of the more than two thousand employees in the company (Perry, 1990). Some organizations have used a shortened form for the self-rater. For example, the appraiser completes a thorough evaluation and the self-rater may be asked to complete a subset of questions. Or, rather than a subset of questions, the self-rater may be asked to simply compile a list of accomplishments for the rating period. This can be used by the appraiser as he or she prepares the evaluation.

Supervisor and Subordinate Create a Joint Appraisal

An alternative approach that has been used is for the appraiser and appraisee (self-rater) to create a joint appraisal during the appraisal interview. In other words, the appraiser and appraisee discuss aspects of the appraisee's performance and come to an agreement or understanding about ratings that will be recorded. This approach works best in organizations where supervisors and subordinates have an open, participatory relationship. Supervisors in traditional hierarchical organizations will likely find this method threatening to their positional authority. Joint appraisal also is useful to help supervisors diagnose subordinates' training needs. Areas where subordinates rate themselves low may signal areas where additional training is needed.

Self-Only Appraisal

Another approach that has been used with some success is for the subordinate (self-rater) to prepare the appraisal, and then the supervisor can modify it if he or she thinks it is necessary. This is the approach taken informally by a number of supervisors who ask subordinates to write up their own appraisal, even when it is formally the supervisor's responsibility. When the self-only method was studied in comparison to the supervisor rating method, both managers and subordinates were more satisfied with the process, subordinates were less defensive, and subsequent performance was more likely to be improved. The reasons cited for the success of this method were better upward communication, more serious thought by the employee about his or her own performance, and smoother clarification of differences of opinion about job expectations (Bassett & Meyer, 1968).

GE used self-only appraisals for discussion in performance review. These were only developmental reviews—a chance for supervisors and employees to discuss goals and developmental needs. GE did not recommend the self-only appraisal if evaluative decisions were going to be made; they believed that self-ratings for decision purposes are very likely to be inflated (Farh, Werbel, & Bedeian, 1988).

At the Michigan State Employees' Credit Union, employees complete self-appraisals prior to their performance reviews. During the review, 20 percent of the time is spent reviewing past performance, 20 percent is spent discussing present performance, and 60 percent is spent planning future performance. Each employee writes a performance plan with his or her supervisor (Jooss, 1994).

Cautions in Using Self-Assessment in Performance Appraisal

High-Involvement Organizations Fare Best

There are some caveats in terms of using self-appraisals in the appraisal process. For example, the advantages mentioned earlier are most likely to be realized in organizations that display a high-involvement style of management. In this case, the supervisor is asking the employee to share in the evaluation and to supplement the information he or she already possesses. If self-appraisals are to be introduced into more traditional, hierarchical organizations, managers must first address the belief that self-assessment threatens the traditional hierarchy and management prerogatives. It may be useful to initially adopt a more participatory style for less threatening decisions, such as task accomplishment or scheduling. As participation in decision making becomes more accepted, it will be easier to introduce self-appraisals in the performance appraisal process.

Informal Self-Ratings

Roberson, Torkel, Korsgaard, Klein, and Diddams (1993) found in a field experiment that informal self-ratings (thinking about how I should be rated but not actually doing a rating) were more useful than formal self- and supervisor ratings. In this study, evaluations were used for reward decisions. Those who formally self-appraised (that is, completed a performance appraisal instrument like that completed by their supervisor) felt they had less influence over the appraisal discussion and less agreement with their supervisor's ratings than non-self-appraisers or those who said they had informally engaged in some self-appraisal prior to their review. The researchers point out that past experiments demonstrating positive effects of self-appraisal have been of the self-rate method, rather than the both-rate method.

Self-Assessment and Career Progression

Self-assessment is crucial to optimal human development. According to Ashford (1989), self-assessment or awareness plays a critical role in self-regulation. "When making decisions about how intensely to work and how to allocate their efforts in making major career decisions, self-assessments of strengths, and weaknesses, and the success of previous performances play an important role in individuals' abilities to regulate their behavior successfully" (p. 135).

High self-awareness improves the likelihood that individuals will seek jobs that match their skills and personality (Stumpf & Colarelli, 1980). A case in point, in a study by Heneman (1980), 32 percent of unemployed persons failing to apply for jobs they had heard about cited their self-assessment of their lack of ability as their reason for not applying.

Biased self-estimates of ability, skill, and aptitude also may lead individuals to mistakenly rule out areas of career exploration or to consider inappropriate options. People quit jobs for which they are highly qualified because they have misassessed their value to the organization and believe they are likely to be laid off. At the other extreme, individuals with severely inflated assessments of their capabilities may never find a suitable job because they do not believe potential employers recognize their value.

Inflated self-assessments can also lead to career derailment. McCall and Lombardo (1983) found that those individuals who provided inflated self-evaluations when compared with evaluations provided by others were less likely to advance within the organization. These individuals' careers plateaued at low levels of management. In a similar vein, McCauley and Lombardo (1990) found that managers who provided self-evaluations consistent with those provided by their coworkers and customers were more likely to be promoted. This same pattern has been demonstrated with naval officers; those officers with self-ratings most similar to those provided by their subordinates attained higher ranks and were rated as more promotable (Bass & Yammarino, 1991).

Self-assessment also is used as a tool to guide training and development for employees. In this application, employees are asked to personally identify their training or developmental needs. Motorola asks employees to report to their supervisors on a quarterly basis the extent to which they have the training they need to do their jobs effectively. Employees at all levels then meet with their supervisors quarterly to discuss training needs. Intel has a competency model that guides its training and development for employees who work in semiconductor clean rooms. Employees are asked to assess their own level of competence in several areas. The supervisor does the same. The two then meet to create a developmental plan that is linked to the competency model.

Recommendations for Using Self-Appraisals

The potential uses of self-appraisal in organizations are summarized in Exhibit 9.6. They include increased accuracy, performance appraisal, selection, team member development, training and career development, and feedback interventions.

Summary and Conclusions

This chapter has summarized the current thinking and research in the area of self-assessment as it relates to appraising performance. Self-assessment cannot be discussed apart from self-perception. Numerous factors influence self-perception as well as self-assessment, and these factors must be considered when deciding on the value of self-assessments in different applications. Clearly, self-assessment can provide valuable information in some applications and should not be discarded as unreliable or biased for all purposes. Self-assessment can provide valuable information if the cautions and recommendations cited in this chapter are taken into consideration.

In addition, as organizations continue to adopt upward and 360-degree feedback processes in organizations, the use of self-assessment for self-other comparisons will increase. And as feedback becomes more common and more accurate, the accuracy of self-assessments should also increase. As a result, self-assessments may become a more useful and valid tool for performance appraisal in the next decade.

Exhibit 9.6. Recommendations for Using Self-Appraisal in Organizations.

Increasing Accuracy of Self-Perceptions and Self-Appraisals

- Provide individuals with frequent and accurate feedback about their performance.
- Provide individuals with information about how others in comparable jobs are performing.
- Encourage individuals to seek specific feedback from others.
- Ask individuals to make their self-evaluations public.
- Let individuals know that their self-assessments will be validated whenever possible.
- Caution individuals about typical rating errors, such as leniency and halo.
- Provide self-raters with the criteria that will be evaluated prior to the self-assessment so they can be sensitive to performance relevant to the criteria.
- Specify behaviors to be rated as clearly as possible.
- Consider scale manipulations in order to reduce leniency effects, such as moving "average" to the lower half of the scale rather than the midpoint.

Performance Appraisal

- Self-appraisal is useful as input to performance appraisal, but should not be used as the sole source if evaluative decisions will be made on the basis of appraisal.
- Self- and other raters should rate the same aspects of performance, and should refer to the same time period.
- Dimensions to be assessed should be behaviorally specific rather than general or ambiguous.
- Raters should have training and experience with the rating process.
- New employees should receive supervisor-only appraisals before being asked to begin self-rating.
- Evaluations should be tied to a reference group such as coworkers performing similar jobs.
- Raters should know in advance of the appraisal the criteria on which they will be evaluating themselves.
- Informal self-ratings (such as asking individuals to reflect on their performance) are more useful than formal self-ratings for increasing acceptance of the appraisal.

Exhibit 9.6. Recommendations for Using
Self-Appraisal in Organizations, cont'd.

- If self-assessments in performance appraisal are to be introduced into traditional hierarchical organizations, it is useful to first introduce participation in less evaluative decisions such as task accomplishment practices or scheduling.

Selection

- Self-appraisals used to assess skills and abilities as part of the selection should not be considered valid unless accompanied by objective data.

Team Member Development

- Feedback to individual team members from one another, which they can compare with their self-ratings, is recommended.
- Feedback to individuals about individual performance must be coupled with feedback to team members about team performance.

Training and Career Development

- Self-assessments of training needs are useful as individuals have valuable information about their weak areas.
- Self-perception accuracy is important to successful career progression and can be enhanced with formal feedback interventions such as 360-degree feedback or team feedback that require self-other comparisons.
- Self-assessment as part of an appraisal review can be valuable in attempts to identify developmental needs.

Feedback Interventions

- Feedback will be more genuine and honest if it is provided anonymously.
- Individuals with high self-esteem may need more negative feedback than those without high self-esteem to be convinced of the validity of the feedback.
- Males may be less likely to accept negative feedback as valid than females.
- Those individuals with longer tenure and more experience should be encouraged to seek feedback as they may have a tendency not to seek feedback.
- Organizations should cultivate cultures in which feedback is valuable and feedback seeking is encouraged.

References

Anderson, C., Warner, J., & Spencer, C. (1984). Inflation bias in self-assessment examinations: Implications for valid employee selection. *Journal of Applied Psychology, 69,* 574–580.

Antonioni, D. (1996, April). *Panel discussion: 360-degree feedback gone amok: Where are the data?* Paper presented at the Meeting of the Society for Industrial and Organizational Psychology, San Diego, CA.

Arnold, J., & Davey, K. M. (1992). Self-ratings and supervisor ratings of graduate employees' competencies during early career. *Journal of Occupational and Organizational Psychology, 65,* 235–250.

Ashford, S. J. (1989). Self-assessments in organizations: A literature review and integrative model. *Organizational Behavior, 11,* 133–174.

Atwater, L., Roush, P., & Fischthal, A. (1995). The influence of upward feedback on self and follower ratings of leadership. *Personnel Psychology, 48,* 35–59.

Atwater, L., & Yammarino, F. J. (1993). Personal attributes as predictors of superiors' and subordinates' perceptions of military academy leadership. *Human Relations, 46,* 645–668.

Atwater, L., & Yammarino, F. J. (1997). Self-other rating agreement: A review and model. *Research in Personnel and Human Resource Management, 15,* 121–174.

Baird, L. S. (1977). Self and superior ratings of performance: As related to self-esteem and satisfaction with supervision. *Academy of Management Journal, 20,* 291–300.

Bass, B., & Yammarino, F. J. (1991). Congruence of self and others' leadership ratings of naval officers for understanding successful performance. *Applied Psychology, 40,* 437–454.

Bassett, G. A., & Meyer, H. H. (1968). Performance appraisal based on self-review. *Personnel Psychology, 21,* 421–430.

Bauman, K. E., & Dent, C. W. (1982). Influence of an objective measure on self-reports of behavior. *Journal of Applied Psychology, 67*(5), 623–628.

Bernardin, H. J., & Pence, E. C. (1980). Effects of rater training: Creating new response sets and decreasing accuracy. *Journal of Applied Psychology, 65,* 60–66.

Borman, W. C. (1974). The rating of individuals in organizations: An alternate approach. *Organizational Behavior and Human Performance, 12,* 105–124.

Brief, A. P., Aldag, R. J., & Van Sell, M. V. (1977). Moderators of the relationships between self and superior evaluations of job performance. *Journal of Occupational Psychology, 50,* 129–134.

Brown, J. D. (1986). Evaluations of self and others: Self-enhancement biases in social judgments. *Social Cognition, 4,* 353–376.

Daubman, J., Heatherington, L., & Ahn, A. (1992). Gender and self-presentation of academic achievement. *Sex Roles, 27,* 187–204.

Deaux, K. (1976). Sex: A perspective on the attribution process. In J. Harvey, W. Ickes, & R. Kidd (Eds.), *New directions in attribution research* (pp. 335–352). Hillsdale, NJ: Erlbaum.

DeNisi, A. S., & Shaw, J. B. (1977). Investigation of the uses of self-reports of abilities. *Journal of Applied Psychology, 62,* 641–644.

DeNisi, A. S., & Summers, T. P. (1986, August). *Rating forms and the organization of information: A cognitive role for appraisal instruments.* Paper presented at the 46th Annual Meeting of the Academy of Management, New Orleans, LA.

Dobbins, G. H., Farh, J. L., & Lehr, C. (1990). *Social comparison theory and self-evaluations.* Paper presented at the National Meeting of the Academy of Management, San Francisco.

Dobbins, G. H., Farh, J. L., & Lin, T. R. (1992). *Rating anchors and self-assessments of ability: A field study.* Paper presented at the Annual Meeting of the Society for Industrial and Organizational Psychology, Montreal, Canada.

Dunnette, M. D. (1993). My hammer or your hammer? *Human Resource Management, 32,* 373–384.

Dunning, D., Meyerowitz, J. A., & Halzberg, A. D. (1989). Ambiguity and self-evaluation: The role of idiosyncratic trait definitions in self-serving assessments of ability. *Journal of Personality and Social Psychology, 57,* 1082–1090.

Farh, J. L., & Dobbins, G. H. (1989). Effects of comparative performance information on the accuracy of self-ratings and agreement between self and supervisor ratings. *Journal of Applied Psychology, 74,* 606–610.

Farh, J. L., Werbel, J. D., & Bedeian, A. G. (1988). An empirical investigation of self-appraisal-based performance evaluation. *Personnel Psychology, 41,* 141–156.

Fox, S., & Dinur, Y. (1988). Validity of self-assessment: A field evaluation. *Personnel Psychology, 41,* 581–592.

George, D. I., & Smith, M. C. (1990). An empirical comparison of self-assessment and organizational assessment in personnel selection. *Public Personnel Management, 19,* 175–190.

Greenberg, J. (1986). Determinants of perceived fairness of performance evaluations. *Journal of Applied Psychology, 71,* 340–342.

Harris, M. M., & Schaubroeck, J. (1988). A meta-analysis of self-supervisor, self-peer, and peer-supervisor ratings. *Personnel Psychology, 41,* 43–62.

Heneman, H. G., III. (1980). Self-assessment: A critical analysis. *Personnel Psychology, 33,* 297–300.

How to ensure sourcing team effectiveness. (1994, July 14). *Purchasing,* pp. 32–44.

Howard, G., & Daily, P. (1979). Response shift bias: A source of contamination of self-report measures. *Journal of Applied Psychology, 64,* 144–150.

Ivancevich, J. M. (1995). *Human resource management.* Burr Ridge, IL: Irwin.

Jooss, R. (1994, September). Monitoring performance: Part II. *Credit Union Management, 17,* 40–42.

Kane, J. S., & Lawler, E. E., III. (1978). Methods of peer assessment. *Psychological Bulletin, 85,* 555–586.

Klimoski, R. J., & Inks, L. (1990). Accountability forces in performance appraisal. *Organizational Behavior and Human Decision Processes, 45,* 194–208.

Klimoski, R. J., & Jones, R. G. (1989, August). *Acceptance of feedback as a function of self-appraisal.* Paper presented at the National Academy of Management Convention, Washington, DC.

Kooker, E. W. (1974). Changes in ability of graduate students in education to assess own test performance as related to their Miller Analogies scores. *Psychological Reports, 35,* 97–98.

Kraiger, K. (1986). *Self, peer, and supervisory ratings of performance: So what?* Paper presented at the First Annual Conference of the Society of Industrial and Organizational Psychology, Chicago.

Lawler, E. E., III. (1967). The multitrait-multirater approach to measuring managerial job performance. *Journal of Applied Psychology, 51,* 369–381.

Lindeman, M., Sundvik, L., & Rouhiainen, P. (1995). Under- or overestimation of self? Person variables and self-assessment accuracy in work settings. *Journal of Social Behavior and Personality, 10,* 123–134.

London, M. (1995). *Self and interpersonal insight: How people learn about themselves and others in organizations.* New York: Oxford University Press.

Longnecker, C. O., Sims, H. P., & Gioia, D. A. (1987). Behind the mask: The politics of employee appraisal. *Academy of Management Executive, 1,* 183–193.

Love, K. G., & Hughes, F. V. (1994). Relationship of self-assessment ratings and written test score: Implications for law enforcement promotional systems. *Public Personnel Management, 23,* 19–30.

Mabe, P. A., & West, S. G. (1982). Validity of self-evaluation of ability: A review and meta-analysis. *Journal of Applied Psychology, 67,* 280–296.

McCall, M. W., & Lombardo, M. M. (1983). *Off the track: Why and how successful executives get derailed.* Technical Report No. 21. Greensboro, NC: Center for Creative Leadership.

McCauley, C. D., & Lombardo, M. M. (1990). Benchmarks: An instrument for diagnosing managerial strengths and weaknesses. In K. E. Clark & M. S. Clark (Eds.), *Measures of leadership* (pp. 535–545). West Orange, NJ: Leadership Library of America.

McNemar, Q. (1969). *Psychological statistics* (4th ed.). New York: Wiley.

Meyer, H. H. (1980). Self-appraisal of job performance. *Personnel Psychology, 33,* 291–295.

Meyer, H. H. (1991). A solution to the performance appraisal feedback enigma. *Academy of Management Executive, 5,* 68–76.

Nilsen, D., & Campbell, D. P. (1993). Self-observer rating discrepancies: Once an overrater, always an overrater? *Human Resource Management, 32,* 265–281.

Perry, T. A. (1990). Staying with the basics. *HR Magazine, 35*(11), 73–76.

Podsakoff, P. M., & Organ, D. W. (1986). Self-reports in organizational research: Problems and prospects. *Journal of Management, 12,* 531–544.

Roberson, L., Torkel, S., Korsgaard, A., Klein, D., & Diddams, M. (1993). Self-appraisal and perceptions of the appraisal discussion: A field experiment. *Journal of Organizational Behavior, 14,* 129–142.

Roberts, T., & Nolen-Hoeksema, S. (1994). Gender comparisons in responsiveness to others' evaluations in achievement settings. *Psychology of Women Quarterly, 18,* 221–240.

Robertson, I. T., & Sadri, G. (1990). Self-efficacy and work-related behaviour: A review and meta-analysis. Unpublished manuscript, available from Professor Ivan Robertson, Manchester School of Management, UMIST, PO Box 88, Manchester M60 1QD, UK.

Robins, R., & John, O. (1997). Effects of visual perspective and narcissism on self-perception: Is seeing believing? *Psychological Science, 8,* 37–42.

Shrauger, J. S., & Lund, A. K. (1975). Self-evaluation and reactions to evaluations from others. *Journal of Personality, 43,* 94–108.

Shrauger, J. S., & Schoenemann, J. (1979). Symbolic interactionist view of self-concept: Through the looking glass darkly. *Psychological Bulletin, 86,* 549–573.

Shrauger, J. S., & Terbovic, M. L. (1976). Self-evaluation and assessments of performance by self and others. *Journal of Consulting and Clinical Psychology, 44,* 564–572.

Stumpf, S. A., & Colarelli, S. M. (1980). Career exploration: Development of dimensions and some preliminary findings. *Psychological Reports, 47,* 979–988.

Thornton, G. C. (1968). The relationship between supervisory and self-appraisals of executive performance. *Personnel Psychology, 21,* 441–455.

Tools to fine-tune a team. (1995, April). *Management Today,* pp. 10–11.

Tsui, A. S., & Ashford, S. J. (1994). Adaptive self-regulation: A process view of managerial effectiveness. *Journal of Management, 20,* 93–121.

Van Velsor, E., Taylor, S., & Leslie, J. B. (1993). An examination of the relationships among self-perception accuracy, self-awareness, gender, and leader effectiveness. *Human Resource Management, 32,* 249–263.

Wicklund, R. A., & Gollwitzers, P. M. (1983). A motivational factor in self-report validity. In J. Suis & A. G. Greenwald (Eds.), *Psychological perspectives of the self: Vol. 2* (pp. 67–92). Hillsdale, NJ: Erlbaum.

Wohlers, A. J., & London, M. (1989). Ratings of managerial characteristics: Evaluation difficulty, subordinate agreement, and self-awareness. *Personnel Psychology, 42,* 235–261.

CHAPTER 10

Evaluating Executive Performance

Mirian M. Graddick
Pamela Lane

Corporations today face dramatic and unprecedented change. News headlines are replete with daily stories announcing a new technology, product, or service, a major merger, acquisition, or takeover, a significant downsizing or company restructure, or the ousting of key senior executives and the hiring of new ones. Marketplace demands are changing the roles of executives. Leaders today are under tremendous pressure to produce results and deliver value to their shareholders, customers, and people. Given the complexity and importance of these positions, assessing and evaluating executive performance has become a key question for modern firms.

The process of evaluating executives has always remained somewhat mysterious. While research on the appraisal process abounds, for executives there is very little research, very little documentation, and increased levels of politics as one moves up the organization (Gioia & Longenecker, 1994). It is well known that the performance appraisal process can increase motivation, foster productivity, improve communication, encourage employee growth and development, and help resolve work-related performance problems (Bernardin & Beatty, 1984; Landy & Farr, 1983). The appraisal process can also form the basis for compensation, promotion, transfer, termination, training, and development (Latham & Wexley, 1980). While the work that executives perform is often the most uncertain, unstructured, ill-defined, and arguably the most important, Longenecker and Gioia (1993) have found that performance reviews at senior levels are less frequent, systematic, informative, and useful. Gioia and Longenecker (1988) also suggest that executives may need performance reviews more than any other group in the organization due to factors such as the sophisticated and ambiguous nature of their jobs, the fact that their responsibilities and priorities tend to change often, the serious organizational consequences of ineffective performance at their level, and their typically high need for achievement, recognition, and career progress.

This chapter focuses on some of the unique issues and challenges pertaining to evaluating and managing the performance of executives. Topics will include defining leadership competencies, setting performance goals, linking pay to performance, and managing the appraisal and feedback process including multisource feedback interventions. It will also discuss the role of executive coaching and issues unique to evaluating CEOs. The goal is to review the published literature and highlight examples of practices and trends in industry. It will conclude by highlighting where we have made progress, acknowledge critical gaps, and attempt to stimulate additional research.

To highlight practices and trends in other companies, we developed a short survey and sent it to members of the Council on Executive Compensation (sponsored by the Conference Board). AT&T is a member of this organization. The group meets formally twice a year and routinely collaborates on state-of-the-art policies and practices related to executive compensation and linking pay to performance. The survey covered topics such as leadership competencies, establishing performance goals, financial and non-financial performance measures, use of assessment tools (for example, 360-degree feedback) and executive coaching, formal appraisal processes, and evaluating CEO performance. Of the twenty-seven members, we received data from ten companies and were able to conduct follow-up interviews when necessary to clarify the information. The companies surveyed consisted of Fortune 500 companies in various industries. There was a broad range of approaches used by the various companies to evaluate executives and we will refer to various themes throughout the chapter.

Executives in Today's Dynamic, Competitive Environment

By any objective measure, the amount of significant and often traumatic change in organizations has grown tremendously and will continue to grow over the next several decades (Kotter, 1996). Change can either create terrific opportunities for organizations or, if ignored or unanticipated, be devastating.

The external marketplace trends driving the need for major change in organizations include an increasing rate of technological change; global expansion, which is both opening up new markets and intensifying competition; significant regulatory changes bringing an end to monopolies; and fierce competition, where the quality of a product or service is becoming a point of entry. To anticipate and respond to these marketplace forces, companies have sought ways to reduce costs and locate new opportunities to grow. This has resulted in the launching of initiatives such as:

- Reengineering
- Restructuring
- Mergers, acquisitions, and alliances
- Downsizing
- Quality efforts
- Cultural renewal

There is a wealth of current literature on the "leader of the future" and the critical roles and competencies required for success (Bass, 1997; Farkas & Wetlaufer, 1996; Heifetz & Laurie, 1997; Hout & Carter, 1995; Kotter, 1988, 1996; Locke, 1991).While our intent is not to provide an exhaustive review of the literature, we will briefly highlight some themes related to the critical role executives play as they navigate through a sea of change.

One thing is certain, the traditional "command and control" authoritarian executive will have difficulty leading effectively in today's dynamic, complex environment. It is impossible for a single individual to have all the necessary information and insights to orchestrate major change. Executives now more than ever must rely on the skills and talents of their people throughout the organization. Leaders demonstrating solo acts of heroism are being replaced by executives who are adept at teaming across organizational boundaries and being able to consider the customers' and the company's best interests ahead of those of any specific unit or division. Executives must have the ability to rise above the detail, recognize emerging patterns, make unexpected connections, and identify the points of maximum leverage (Hout & Carter, 1995). They play a key role in ensuring clarity of purpose and direction, creating alignment of systems and processes to support the direction, and building organizational commitment to common goals (Farkas & Wetlaufer, 1996). Another critical role for executives is to foster an environment where people throughout the company confront challenges, take on new roles and form new relationships, change perspectives, and learn new habits (Heifetz & Laurie, 1997). Truly adaptive leaders will develop their skills through lifelong learning and adopting new ways of operating to meet the marketplace challenges (Kotter, 1996).

Most companies we surveyed translated these "ideal leader" characteristics described in the literature into a set of leadership competencies. While there were common themes similar to the ones we just described, each list was somewhat different both in number of competencies and content. Some organizations even combined the values and competencies into a single list. Each company developed the leadership competencies based on what it believed was important for success in their culture. The competencies manifested themselves in describing how work gets done rather than what gets done (results). Brisco (1996) conducted a survey examining how various companies develop and use competencies for selecting and developing executives. Brisco generated four approaches to developing competencies based on a review of company practices and recommends that different approaches are appropriate for different companies. Exhibit 10.1 depicts the four different approaches—Data-Based, Value-Based, Strategy-Based, and Learning-Based—with the advantages and disadvantages of each, and how each approach links to the direction of the business.

In reviewing the empirical literature on leadership competencies, Bass (1997) studied the characteristics of transformational and transactional leaders and whether there are correlations among leadership styles and outcomes in effectiveness, effort, and satisfaction. Bass found a clear link between transformational leadership competencies and firm performance. Key characteristics of

Exhibit 10.1. Competency Foundations.

Foundation	Description	Advantages	Disadvantages	Company Fit
Data-Based	Competencies based in behavioral data compiled from superior performers based on current and past performance. Validated against average and good performers.	Grounded in actual behavior. Scientific basis adds legitimacy. Involves executives heavily via interviews. Facilitates the development of behaviorally anchored competency illustrations useful in development.	Measured behaviors may not in fact reflect emerging and future competency needs. May omit intangible and immeasurable competencies. Requires extensive financial, temporal, and human resources.	Fits best with companies whose executives have proved track records and whose emerging business needs are continuous and predictable.
Value-Based	Competencies based formally or informally on normative or cultural values held by a specific manager or the company.	Values have strong motivating power and sometimes provide strategic direction and continuity across long periods of time.	Poorly selected values may lead to misguided competencies. Can be difficult to define behaviors congruent with values. Development of such competencies can lack rigor.	Most appropriate where values are key to organization's identity or success. May be suitable when future is uncertain.
Strategy-Based	Competencies based on anticipated future and represent proactive or reactive responses to that future in the form of forecasted competency needs.	Competencies are based on future rather than past. This focuses executives on learning new skills. Works well with organizational change efforts.	The anticipated future or the company's response to it may be inaccurate. Forced to speculate about competencies instead of basing them on actual behavior.	Companies with a clear and new strategic direction may benefit, especially when future is uncertain and when values are not strong.
Learning-Based	Competencies emphasizing abilities and skills executives possess related to their abilities to learn new competencies and to adapt to changing roles, circumstances, and environments.	Competencies focus executives on developing ongoing abilities to match quickly changing environment. Engages more basic and enduring dimensions of personal skills.	If used exclusively, may omit other important established competencies. May prove too ambiguous for executives as well as HR staff.	Companies in very rapidly changing environments may benefit when they cannot rely on strategy or even values to endure for predictable lengths of time.

Source: Adapted from Brisco, 1996.

transformational leaders revealed by the Bass research include the following:

- *Charisma*
  Take stands on important issues.
  Present key values.
  Emphasize ethical consequences of decisions.
  Create alignment around shared purpose.
  Generate pride, loyalty, and confidence.
- *Inspirational Motivation*
  Articulate an appealing vision of the future.
  Challenge followers with high standards.
  Talk optimistically and with enthusiasm.
  Provide encouragement and meaning for what needs
    to be done.
- *Intellectual Stimulation*
  Question old assumptions and traditions.
  Stimulate in others new perspectives and new ways
    of doing things.
  Encourage the expression of new ideas.
- *Individualized Consideration*
  Consider individual needs, abilities, and goals.
  Listen attentively.
  Support followers' development.
  Advise, teach, coach.

In subsequent sections of this chapter, you will see how these leadership competencies are incorporated into performance appraisals and multisource feedback processes and, in some cases, linked to pay decisions.

In addition to demonstrating critical leadership competencies, executives must also find creative ways to simultaneously manage the needs and expectations of three major constituencies: customers, shareholders, and employees. This includes being held accountable for the company's financial commitments, meeting the current and emerging needs of customers, and fostering an environment where people can maximize their effectiveness and continuously learn and grow. Many organizations now set goals and objectives related to all three stakeholders—shareholders, customers, and employees. The next section focuses on ways organizations establish performance goals to support the business direction and how they link pay to performance.

Setting Executive Performance Objectives

One of the most consistent findings in social science is that goal setting is a major determinant of subsequent performance (Locke & Latham, 1990). Before defining the performance required of an executive, however, a company must first understand and agree on how to measure the performance of the business itself. Our recognition of the increasingly complex executive role is, in fact, an outgrowth of a more sophisticated understanding of what makes a business successful—both in terms of its current value and its capability to create value in the future.

Over the last five years, work in such areas as Total Quality Management systems, the Malcolm Baldrige Quality Award process, and Kaplan and Norton's development of the balanced scorecard approach has expanded our appreciation for the multiple factors leading to organizational success and has contributed to a growing methodology for assessing business performance and performance drivers.

In response, many companies are developing key measurement or balanced scorecard systems driven by their particular business strategy, then tying executive performance requirements to them. Typically these systems combine short- and long-term measures as well as financial and nonfinancial indicators, and represent both internal and external performance perspectives (Kaplan & Norton, 1996a, 1996b; Conference Board, 1995). By marrying outcome measures to performance drivers, it is argued, key measurement systems can not only capture historical results, but may also provide an indication of future performance.

A 1996 AT&T study of performance measurement approaches in twelve selected companies found that best-practice firms use a combination of value drivers (such as sales productivity or inventory turns), nonfinancial or strategic metrics (such as development of a new technology platform, customer satisfaction, or entry into strategic alliances), and economic and market information (such as Economic Value Added, market share, or product penetration), as well as traditional financial measures in their performance measurement systems. The categorization of a measure may vary among companies, depending on what is strategic to the firm in the relevant time frame. Companies combine these measures into a formal framework to create focus on key outcomes and stakeholders, better predict future outcomes or potential problems, influence behavior toward improving results, and provide balance.

Performance measurement frameworks vary in the number of measurement categories used and the number of metrics tracked within each category. Work on strategic performance measurement by Atkinson, Waterhouse, and Wells (1997) organizes primary and secondary measures by stakeholder group (for example, shareholders, customers, employees, and community), where primary measures relate to the objectives of the firm's owners and secondary measures relate to the processes used to generate results. The Kaplan and Norton balanced scorecard approach (1996a, 1996b) focuses on four perspectives: financial, customer, internal business process, and learning and growth. Examples of the types of measures that can be used in each perspective are provided in Exhibit 10.2.

Increasingly, balanced scorecards or other key measurement systems provide the "what" of executive performance. Our research of company practice reveals broad acceptance of the key measurement approach—all but one of the responding companies report that they now include financial and nonfinancial measures as well as customer and employee perspectives in their evaluation of executive performance. The linkage to individual performance planning, however, is less strong, with only half the companies reporting a formal process for establishing individual performance goals for executives. In part this is due to the infancy of many of the metrics, the difficulty of cascading goals related to nonfinancial objectives, and the dynamic nature of business today.

Eastman Kodak accepted these challenges and implemented its "Management Performance Commitment Process" for roughly nine hundred middle and senior managers in 1995. The program uses three categories: shareholder satisfaction, customer satisfaction, and employee satisfaction and public responsibility to determine executives' performance objectives, base salaries, and annual incentive awards. Currently, the shareholder satisfaction category carries the dominant weight (50 percent), but that could change in the future. As baselines and trends are established for the employee

Exhibit 10.2. Common Performance
Measurement Categories and Measures.

Financial

- EVA (Economic Value Added)
- EPS
- Operating Profit
- Cash flow
- Return on Capital
- Return on Assets
- Return on Equity

Customer

- Customer satisfaction (survey)
- Customer churn or retention
- Market share
- Share of most profitable segments
- Brand image
- Share of wallet
- Segment performance

Internal Process

- Cycle time
- Asset utilization
- Unit cost
- Customer-defined service levels
- Product availability
- Speed to market
- Complaint resolution time

Learning and Growth

- Employee satisfaction (survey)
- Employee turnover or retention by critical skill
- Workforce diversity
- Performance-based compensation
- Skill mix in place versus need
- Percent of sales from new products

and customer satisfaction metrics, their importance in the performance system could increase (*Rochester Business Journal,* 1995).

A second barrier to robust individual performance planning is that the traditional practice of focusing on individual performance in hierarchically boxed jobs no longer fits the reality of today's organization or the role of today's executive. Overcoming the common managerial belief that managing performance is primarily managing individual excellence and the common cultural belief that individual contributions should be recognized and rewarded above all others is a challenge at all levels of the organization (Mohrman & Mohrman, 1995). It is particularly difficult at the executive level, where individual achievement has generally been the path to success.

As Mohrman and Mohrman report, today's organizations are increasingly lateral, with cross-functional teams, task forces, and mini-business units performing in dynamic patterns. This collaborative and fluid mode of work occurs at the executive level as well as on the factory floor. In this environment, many companies are realizing that *how* executives carry out their activities is as important as *what* they accomplish. As a result, behavioral and leadership competency objectives are now common supplements to key measurement systems in establishing executive performance goals. All but one of our responding companies include such objectives in their programs.

How companies weight these behavioral and competency objectives in assessing overall executive performance varies, and in many cases is not precisely defined. Four of the responding companies each place roughly equal weight on the what and the how. For example, executives at American Express receive both goal (G) and leadership (L) ratings based on their performance against objectives set at the beginning of the year. These G and L ratings are equally important in driving all compensation decisions—base pay, annual incentives, and long-term incentives. Other companies in the sample either weight the achievement of financial objectives significantly more heavily or do not specify the relative importance of the different categories.

We also saw variation in whether or not performance against nonfinancial, behavioral, and competency objectives carries through to appraisal and pay decisions at the executive level. While many firms employ some form of multisource feedback to gather information on leadership behaviors and competencies, only four formally link these data to the pay decision (including the American Express example cited earlier). Other firms restrict the use of such data to development purposes, explicitly excluding them from pay decisions. In its 1995 study, the Conference Board also found that few companies had put in place a full-fledged and systematic program to link new performance indicators to compensation (Conference Board, 1995).

Part of the difficulty in establishing a tight pay linkage is the fluid nature of early scorecards (McWilliams, 1996). Most companies go through a learning process in developing a new measurement system. If pay is tied to the system in the early stages, employees will assume the measures are strategically right, reliable, and permanent. Often this is not the case, so moving cautiously with pay can make sense.

The sheer number of objectives that can result from a broader view of performance also creates problems for pay linkage. Some companies cope by developing a weighted average of financial metrics for a portion of the annual bonus, then draw on representative indicators from other sections of their scorecard for the remainder (Kaplan & Norton, 1996a, 1996b). Leadership competencies and behaviors, when included in the pay decision, may also affect a portion of the annual bonus or may be reflected in salary increases or long-term incentive grants. For companies not using such performance to determine pay, competency and behavior outcomes are reflected more often in promotion, succession, and development decisions.

A third complication stems from a reluctance to employ formulaic approaches to the impact of behavioral and competency results on pay. Distrust over the reliability of survey-based measures and disagreement over the relative importance of different skills and behaviors suggest that a more cautious, discretionary approach may be appropriate. Finally, the continuing focus on short-term financial outcomes by shareholders and financial analysts continues to encourage companies to emphasize those results in pay, particularly for the top tier of executives. This is particularly true for proxy officers like the CEO (see section on evaluating the CEO).

Setting performance objectives that can adequately capture the multifaceted role of the modern executive is a challenge facing all the companies we surveyed. The task is complicated by a lack of robust measures covering leadership competencies and behaviors and, often, nonfinancial performance as well. In addition, a continuing focus on short-term financial outcomes by shareholders and investment analysts limits the degree to which nonfinancial and behavioral achievements are reflected in executive pay. This lack of full linkage between the objective-setting process, the executive appraisal, and the company reward system sends mixed messages to executives about what is truly important for personal career success. This problem becomes more clear when we look at the state of executive appraisals in business today.

The Appraisal and Feedback Process

While a plethora of research exists on the appraisal process, there are very few published studies focusing on executive appraisals. Gioia and Longenecker (1988) conducted in-depth interviews with executives to better understand the appraisal process. The sample represented sixty upper-level executives from eleven different functional areas and seven large companies. The executives averaged more than twenty years of work experience and more than thirteen years of managerial experience. Each company had performance appraisal programs (including rater training) and a requirement that annual appraisals be conducted using a structured instrument.

Results revealed that 40 percent of the executives had not had a formal appraisal within the preceding year—even though each organization required formal evaluations. Executives who had received an appraisal reported being frustrated with the quality of the process. Comments from these executives suggested that the evaluations were done infrequently and irregularly, were rushed and informal, and lacked specific details about performance. Amazingly, all the executives had a strong desire to have a performance review. They acknowledged that the review process is an excellent opportunity for them to understand how they are doing, determine ways to improve personal effectiveness, discuss long-term big picture issues that often get lost in day-to-day operations, and calibrate on career development and advancement opportunities.

In 1992, Longenecker and Gioia published another study about the executive appraisal paradox. They concluded that the widespread disappointment about the quality of the executive appraisal process is a result of dysfunctional beliefs or myths that exist about that process. In this study, eighty-four executives from eleven major organizations in manufacturing and service industries were interviewed. Again, all organizations had a formal appraisal process in place. The reported myths that emerged from the study were as follows:

- *Executives neither need nor want structured performance reviews.* Not true according to the executives—in fact, they saw systematic feedback as both crucial and sorely desired.

- *A formal review is beneath the dignity of an executive.* This stems from a belief that once you reach the executive ranks a rite of passage is achieved and you no longer need to conduct or receive formal reviews.
- *Top-level executives are too busy to conduct performance reviews.* This was the rationale provided by many executives for not doing them.
- *Lack of feedback fosters autonomy and creativity.* This was a less prevalent myth, but some executives believe that it "builds character" to force young executives to figure out for themselves the appropriate actions to take.
- *Results are the only basis for assessing executive performance.* Many executives focus only on bottom-line financial results and do not put much emphasis on individual contribution or personal effectiveness.
- *The comprehensive evaluation of executive performance simply can not be captured via formal performance appraisal.* This is a belief that there are many intangibles that are a part of an executive position, such as intuition and gut feelings, that are difficult to capture and measure.

Finally, Gioia and Longenecker conducted another study in 1994, focusing on the politics of the executive appraisal process. Even if appraisals were done more frequently at the executive level, significant factors potentially confound the process. In this study, eighty-two executives were interviewed from eight large manufacturing and service organizations representing twelve functional areas. Results centered on five key themes:

- The higher one rises in the organization, the more political the appraisal process becomes.
- Because of the dynamic, ambiguous nature of executive work, appraisals are susceptible to political manipulation.
- Performance is not necessarily the most important factor that influences ratings at the executive level. Other factors include the boss's agenda, the reputation factor, and the organization's current political climate.
- Senior executives have extraordinary latitude in assessing subordinate performance because they often fail to specify

meaningful performance goals and standards and fail to communicate about the desired style and means of goal accomplishment.

- The appraisal can be used as a political tool to control people and resources.

The authors acknowledge that it is impossible to totally eliminate politics, but offer ways to help minimize its detrimental effect on the individual and the organization. Some of their suggestions include articulating specific goals and standards, linking specific actions and performance results to rewards, conducting structured reviews with specific examples of performance, offering performance feedback on an ongoing basis, leading by example, and providing training on executive appraisal politics. The remainder of this section will look at a few specific examples of practices that exist to address some of the issues raised in the literature.

Unfortunately, many of the issues and concerns raised by Gioia and Longenecker still exist. While all the companies we reviewed had formal performance management systems in place, including requirements for written appraisals and feedback, use of the tools and processes was often optional at the executive level. When asked to describe the major barriers to effectively evaluating executive performance, many companies cited the lack of ongoing, candid feedback (particularly when it comes to delivering news about improving leadership skills). Another important barrier was the difficulty in getting executives to articulate and document individual performance goals and developmental objectives.

We thought it would be useful to provide an example of a company that has implemented a fairly comprehensive executive appraisal process and then summarize by assessing where we have made progress and where gaps still exist.

Several years ago Honeywell modified its executive performance appraisal plan and rolled out a fairly elaborate process. It included the following elements:

- *Rationale.* A rationale for why the process was being introduced—simply put, to better align the actions of executives with the Honeywell vision and values and reinforce the need to "walk the talk" and build a world-class organization.

- *Requirements Versus Variables.* Honeywell provided a description of what was required and where flexibility was permitted.

    All executives had to use the company performance measures (focus is on executive competencies and leadership behaviors and results), but they did not have to use the form that human resources provided. (More than 90 percent of the executives did use the form, but other forms of documentation were permitted.)

    Obtaining multiple sources of feedback was required.

    An individual development plan had to be created and implemented. The specific interventions and job experiences are based on the individual and the situation.

    While a formal appraisal discussion was required at least once a year, the timing of these sessions could vary by unit. It was, however, required that the performance discussion and documentation be completed prior to salary treatment.

- *Performance Measures.* Honeywell developed and articulated a comprehensive list of leadership and behavior competencies required for success (the how) and a focus on results (the what) in three areas, customer delight, people value, and shareholder value.

- *Multisource Feedback Process.* There was a requirement to obtain multisource feedback from a minimum of three sources for the appraisal and feedback process.

- *Formal Documentation.* While the use of a standardized form was optional, executives had to document strengths and areas for improvement related to the leadership competencies; performance goals against results in the areas of customer delight, people value, and shareholder value (and any market conditions or organizational changes that affected goals); and development plans based on the feedback. On the standardized form, there is an opportunity to provide an overall rating of performance based on the leadership competencies and results.

Honeywell also supplied guidelines for providing constructive feedback, and defined roles and responsibilities of the executive, supervisor (coach), and the individuals providing multisource feedback. Finally, they offered external executive coaches as a resource to help with the feedback or to work with an individual on improving performance. Honeywell attributes much of the success of the process to the top-down support and commitment of the CEO.

Table 10.1 summarizes the strengths and gaps of executive appraisal, based on the literature and by examining company practices.

All but two of the companies we surveyed incorporate a list of formal leadership competencies required for success into the appraisal process. As stated earlier, companies are beginning to emphasize how work gets done as an important part of performance. Unfortunately, there remains a lack of rigor in goal setting, provision of open and candid feedback, and formal documentation of performance.

Several other issues could potentially have an impact on the executive appraisal process. First, many companies are increasing the number of outside hires at the executive level. These executives negotiate employment contracts that often commit the company to pay the executive a certain amount over a specified period of time. These commitments may or may not be linked to the individual's performance. Obviously, when negotiating employment contracts, every attempt should be made to link pay commitments to results on the job. It is also important that external hires receive candid and frequent feedback, since they may initially have difficulty interpreting corporate culture and nonverbal cues regarding how well they are doing.

Table 10.1. Executive Appraisal Process and Feedback: Summary of Key Strengths and Gaps.

Strengths	Gaps
• Use of leadership competencies and values to assess how results are achieved	• Lack of open, candid performance feedback from supervisors
• Increased focus on non-financial performance measures (people and customer resources)	• Very limited written documentation
• Feedback is often enhanced by using multisource interventions	• Executives not held accountable for conducting regular performance reviews (no consequences for not doing them)

The Office of Federal Contract Compliance (OFCC) has increasingly targeted companies for glass ceiling audits. Any company that has already been a target of such an audit has become aware of the need to have processes and documentation describing the rationale for how decisions regarding promotions and compensation are made. These audits may encourage companies to have a more formal process for evaluating executives and linking pay to performance.

Methods for Evaluating CEO Performance

Since the early 1990s, a growing furor over executive pay has turned a thousand-watt spotlight on the performance of top executives, particularly the CEO, and the linkage of performance to executive pay. Many of the issues that complicate the definition of performance for other executives—the multifaceted role required of global leaders, the variety of stakeholder interests that must be served, the balancing of short- and long-term imperatives—are intensified at the level of the CEO.

In 1995, the National Association of Corporate Directors (NACD) tackled the topic in its Blue Ribbon Commission Report on *Performance Evaluation of Chief Executive Officers, Boards and Directors.* Stating that evaluation of senior management performance is a fundamental duty of directors, the commission recommended annual objective setting and assessment of CEO performance by the board. The suggested process included development of a job description for the CEO and mutual agreement on performance objectives between the CEO and board in advance of each fiscal year. NACD also suggested the following examples of performance objectives for the CEO:

- Integrity
- Vision
- Leadership
- Ability to meet corporate performance objectives
- Succession planning
- Shareholder relations
- Stakeholder relations (employees, customers, community)
- CEO-board relations

While this model can provide valuable input to the pay decision, the NACD is, perhaps understandably, silent on the methodology for translating the CEO evaluation into compensation treatment. Formulas will not work here. Of the total pay reported in the annual proxy, boards typically have discretion over only the annual bonus to reflect the previous year's performance of the firm and CEO. In most cases, salary treatment and long-term incentive grants have been made twelve months prior. Realized profits from the exercise of options or the removal of restrictions from stock grants, also reported in the proxy, are the result of pay decisions made up to ten years before. Given the trend toward increasing emphasis on long-term incentives and the extended bull market, these amounts can be substantial enough to dwarf the annual bonus. If, in addition, the CEO has met strategic goals not yet reflected in the company's stock performance, the board members may struggle with shareowner perceptions of the value of the CEO's performance for the year versus their own view of the extent to which agreed-upon objectives have been met.

A 1997 report on CEO pay from the American Compensation Association provides some guidance in dealing with the pay decision. Both practitioners and consultants suggest that it is critically important for the board to establish a compensation philosophy and communicate it to investors, to position CEO pay consistent with the strategy, and to externally benchmark both the pay opportunity and the actual compensation paid versus actual company performance relative to peers. Relative financial performance must support the relative pay position (Cook et al., 1997). Where deviations occur, they must be explainable in terms of the strategy and the performance contract established with the CEO.

The process recommended by the NACD also highlights the importance of clear and shared understanding of performance expectations to the success of the subsequent performance evaluation. A review of the list of sample objectives reveals how difficult it may be to reach a precise or quantifiable performance standard in most areas of CEO accountability.

As with other executive positions, it may be easier to define excellent or substandard performance in hindsight than in advance, and financial performance may be at odds with accomplishments, or the lack thereof, in other important areas. In addition, a number of the most important responsibilities of the CEO, such as allocating capital and selecting people for senior management, bear fruit far beyond the annual time horizon reflected in the executive bonus. Here again, the linkage to pay at the end of the process is more likely to be based on informed discretion than on a formulaic approach.

Despite these difficulties, monitoring and assessing performance—at least in terms of its implications for CEO pay—has become not only desirable but necessary. Since 1993, proxy rules have required company Compensation Committees to disclose the performance criteria used to set executive compensation and, in particular, the considerations employed in determining the pay of the chief executive. All the companies we spoke with reported a formal annual review process of the CEO by the board, and validated the heavy use of qualitative objectives in addition to quantitative goals.

For companies wanting to institute a board review of CEO performance, the NACD report provides guidance as to a useful process. While acknowledging that some companies may prefer an informal oral procedure over a formal written process, the NACD recommended the following model:

- Designation of an independent director or directors to serve as leader of the process
- Self-evaluation by the CEO, covering each performance objective and the major duties and responsibilities outlined in the CEO's job description
- Discussion of the CEO's self-assessment by the outside directors
- An independent evaluation by outside directors, which is then consolidated by the lead director
- Review and approval of the consolidated evaluation by the outside directors
- A private meeting between the lead director and the CEO to discuss the consolidated evaluation
- A meeting between the CEO and the outside directors to react to the evaluation and discuss appropriate next steps

In addition to providing guidelines for compensation decisions, a process such as that put forth by the NACD has significant other benefits to the CEO and to the board. It facilitates board-

CEO communication regarding company and CEO performance expectations, helps the CEO identify personal strengths and weaknesses as well as ways to capitalize on or correct them, and provides early warning signals of potential problems to the CEO and the board. It also helps foster a sense of teamwork between the board and the CEO, increases the likelihood that the board will support the CEO in times of crisis, and provides a clear signal to shareholders and regulators that the board is monitoring and evaluating the actions of the CEO and senior management (NACD, 1995).

Diagnostic Interventions

Many companies have struggled with ways to focus simultaneously on the "what" and the "how" of performance. Currently, most companies are using diagnostic interventions to assess and develop leadership behaviors and competencies. As previously discussed, only a few companies incorporate the "how" into pay decisions. In this section, we describe several diagnostic interventions designed to help executives focus on critical leadership behaviors in the context of achieving business results.

Multisource Feedback

One significant trend is the increasing number of companies that are using some type of multisource (360-degree) feedback process for executives. Eight of the companies we surveyed use some form of multisource feedback, although the results are primarily used for ongoing development. Companies reported several benefits from the process. It is an excellent way for executives to receive candid feedback, and an opportunity to obtain perspectives from people at different levels of the organization. The latter helps identify executives who are masters at managing up, but are viewed as "destructive achievers" by others in the organization. It also provides a way to have an open dialogue with supervisors about strengths and areas for improvement. We will first describe a recent approach used by AT&T and then summarize some of the advantages and disadvantages of multisource feedback based on our experiences and those of other companies.

In 1996, AT&T launched a multisource feedback process designed for its senior officers. At an individual level, the intervention was designed to give the officers an opportunity to receive feedback from peers, direct reports, and supervisors and then have an open dialogue with the supervisors about strengths and areas requiring development. At the organizational level, it was an opportunity to profile the collective leadership strengths and gaps to better understand the organization's bench strength and design relevant developmental experiences.

The initial phase of the project was designed to include the officers from the various operating units, as opposed to those officers in common support functions (for example, human resources, public relations, finance, law). The rationale for excluding the common support function officers in the first phase was that they had all recently participated in an assessment and selection process during the AT&T restructuring in 1996.

For each operating unit officer, the process involved collecting the following data:

• *Multisource Feedback.* A survey instrument was developed to assess individuals on AT&T's seven operating behaviors (examples: Communicate Openly, Seize Opportunities) and five company values (examples: Respect for Individuals, Dedication to Helping Customers). Survey instruments were sent to each officer's supervisor, all of his or her direct reports, and five peers. The officers and their supervisors jointly agreed on the selection of the five peers. In addition, each officer completed self-ratings.

• *Business Skills and Knowledge Areas.* A set of critical business skills and knowledge areas were identified for AT&T and each operating unit had the opportunity to add critical skills that were unique to that unit (for example, systems integration). The supervisor rated each individual's proficiency on each skill using a behaviorally anchored scale. This information was gathered for use in individual development planning and to assess skill gaps at an organizational level.

• *Business Performance Results.* Since performance appraisal ratings did not exist for officers in most cases, each officer's supervisor was asked to document the individual's accomplishments for the past two years and rate those accomplishments using a four-point behaviorally anchored rating scale (providing a rating for each year).

A summary of this information was captured on a single form, including some space to include an individual developmental action plan based on a discussion between each officer and his or her supervisor.

An important element of this process was top-down support and commitment among the senior team. The process was championed by the senior team and all the members were responsible for introducing it within their operating units. Although the process was designed at the corporate level, the operating unit human resource leaders were quite instrumental in facilitating the effective execution within the units they supported. They were trained on all aspects of the process so they could help facilitate the initial meeting with the officer team to introduce the process, ensure the data were collected in a timely fashion, and so on. Once the process was introduced to each officer team within a unit, the design included the following sequence of sessions:

- *Multisource Feedback Survey Distribution.* In some cases the officer had a discussion with his or her supervisor to determine the five peers who were to receive feedback instruments. This face-to-face session was not mandatory. In other cases the officer identified the peer group and sent it to the supervisor for approval. This sends mixed signals to the executives and causes a tremendous amount of cynicism among employees who are asked to provide feedback.

- *Partner Discussion.* Once all the surveys were returned and analyzed, a face-to-face meeting occurred between the officer and his or her supervisor to review the feedback in depth and discuss the performance and skill ratings. Based on this discussion, a preliminary development plan was established. External coaches were made available either to help the supervisor interpret the data and prepare for the feedback sessions or as a resource to the officer to help absorb the feedback in a constructive manner and develop an action plan for enhancing performance.

- *Organization Review.* Once all the partnering discussions were completed within a unit, the plan was to have all the operating unit senior officers share a summary of their organizations' performance by reviewing key themes related to leadership strengths and gaps, along with specific action plans for some individuals (such as a planned job change to another unit or a recommended promotion).

- *Partnering Debrief.* Once the organizational review sessions were completed for a unit, the design included an opportunity for each officer to have a follow-up meeting with each individual to discuss any proposed modifications to the original development plan.

Thus far, fifty-five officers (65 percent of the operating unit officers) have participated in the first phase of the intervention (that is, completed the partnering discussions). A few units delayed participation because of timing (for example, critical projects being implemented that required significant focus). While a formal evaluation of the process has not yet been done, anecdotal feedback from the officers thus far has been quite positive, including feedback from those who were initially reluctant to participate.

AT&T's experiences with multisource feedback and those of other companies have yielded the following themes:

- Multisource feedback interventions for executives, like the one implemented by AT&T, can only work if they are driven and supported by the CEO and senior team.
- Multisource feedback can be extremely time-consuming, particularly if multiple peers and direct reports are included. While the data can be quite rich, many supervisors and peers can be inundated with surveys if the entire organization does it simultaneously. On the other hand, while selecting a smaller sample can simplify the process, it could also potentially skew the results.
- Most companies such as AT&T use multisource feedback for development. A few were using the information to influence performance appraisal and pay. Edwards and Ewen (1995) highlight critical pitfalls and legal issues associated with using the data for appraisal and pay decisions.

If multisource feedback interventions are used, it is critical to develop valid, reliable feedback instruments and provide executives with the appropriate training on how to both give and receive feedback. Since many executives rarely get candid feedback from their supervisors, multisource feedback can be very enlightening. Many were surprised by how their actions and behaviors are perceived by others. For example, preliminary data from the fifty-five officers who participated in the AT&T multisource feedback process showed that

41 percent rated themselves more favorably than their supervisors rated them, 56 percent rated themselves more favorably than their direct reports rated them, and 61 percent rated themselves more favorably than their peers rated them.

A critical question is whether these interventions really change behavior. Our observation is that they do not unless the company simultaneously realigns its key HR mechanisms (that is, who is hired, promoted, fired, and rewarded) to reinforce the desired behavior. All too often, companies say they value executives who achieve results and demonstrate leadership competencies, yet they promote destructive achievers—people who get visible results while interfering with the ability of others to act in the organization's interest. This sends mixed signals to the executives and causes a tremendous amount of cynicism among employees who are asked to provide feedback.

The Role of Executive Coaching

Another increasingly popular trend in corporations is the use of external executive coaches. Over half the companies we surveyed provide their executives access to external coaches. We found two major reasons why executive coaches are hired. First, to help talented executives who are in trouble because of behavioral or style deficiencies (Hagberg, 1996), and second, to help executives through critical transitions such as having to lead a major change effort (Harrison & Betof, 1996). Some executives who are very competent and have unique skills still lack the ability to lead effectively and get along with others. While in the past companies did not always take action to help these individuals (except by giving them a pep talk—or in some cases, easing them into retirement), they cannot afford these options today. It is too expensive to keep a nonfunctioning executive on the payroll, and it is both difficult and legally risky to ignore problematic or inappropriate behaviors (Koonce, 1994).

Hagberg (1996) cited several reasons why competent executives get themselves into trouble. Examples include a lack of social and communication skills, difficulty in letting others make decisions, and limited leadership skills.

Lombardo and McCauley (1988) conducted a study designed to better understand the reasons why executives derail. Using items derived from McCall and Lombardo's (1983) ten reasons for derailment, results from a factor analysis revealed six "flaw" scales:

- *Problems with Interpersonal Relationships:* The individual finds it awkward to develop comfortable working relationships with others.
- *Difficulty Molding a Staff:* The individual does not select and build a team smoothly.
- *Difficulty Making Strategic Transitions:* The individual fails to move from the tactical level to the general strategic level as needed.
- *Lack of Follow-Through:* The individual has difficulties in following up on promises, really completing a job, and paying attention to detail.
- *Overdependence:* The individual tends to rely too much on a boss, powerful advocate, or natural talent.
- *Strategic Differences with Management:* The individual disagrees with higher management about business strategy, how the business should be run.

To help executives with these deficiencies, many companies hire an outside consultant (executive coach). The intent is to help executives overcome obstacles that are preventing them from being effective leaders. A key question is what exactly do these coaches do? While executive coaches use different techniques, most interventions include several phases:

- *Precoaching:* This is a meeting with the executive, his or her supervisor, and the coach to discuss specific issues the coaching should address. Often the human resource leader plays a role in these meetings. These meetings are critical to calibrate expectations and set goals.
- *Data gathering:* This phase is designed for the coach to gather as much data and information as possible from the executive as well as others in the organization to diagnose problems and develop action plans. Table 10.2 shows a summary of the strengths and limitations of various assessment techniques (Harrison, 1997).

Table 10.2. Relative Strengths and Limitations of Each Approach to Assessment.

Approach	Strengths	Limitations
Idiographic: Understanding of individual in the context of his or her own uniqueness (history)—a more "clinical" perspective	• Acknowledge uniqueness of the individual • Contributes to understanding of why an individual developed in a certain way • Provides clues for what kinds of developmental activities may work best in the future	• Subjective—open to interpretation and distortion • Makes comparison between individuals or groups difficult
Nomothetic: Understanding of individual through quantifiable data that can be used to reliably predict future behaviors	• Quantitative and objective • Allows for normative comparisons • Changes can be measured and monitored	• May miss important information that is not easily quantified • Indicates what's going on but not why
360-Degree Feedback: Understanding of individual from multiple perspectives (for example colleagues, direct supports)	• Yields important information about the culture of the organization or work group • Provides information about what may be most important development activities	• Instrument may not be psychometrically valid • Inter-rater reliability problems

Source: Reprinted with permission from Raymond P. Harrison, Ph.D., *The Manchester Review,* Spring 1997, Vol. 2, No. 1. "DIAS©: A Three Dimensional Method for Assessment and Development Planning," Figure 2.1 Relative Strengths and Limitations of Each Approach to Assessment, p. 25. Copyright 1997 Manchester Inc., Publishers.

- *Coaching:* This long phase involves the development of a relationship of candor and trust between the executive and coach. The executive and coach meet regularly (often two to four times a month) for several months to review the data, develop a plan of action, and monitor progress. Telephone contact is frequent between meetings. Some coaching relationships last a year or more.

Executive coaches are generally hired as per diem consultants, although some have a retainer contract. The minimum period for working with an executive is three months, but six to twelve months is more common. The expense varies depending on the issues to be addressed and the resources to be employed (for example, the amount of data gathering).

As organizations go through dramatic change, executives are also expected to rapidly transform themselves. As an alternative to the long-term approach, Harrison and Betof (1996) have designed a transformational coaching intervention designed to produce rapid, dramatic new executive behaviors. They work with executives in a very short time frame (less than a week) and focus on identifying dramatic critical events, depicting inappropriate behaviors, and learning more desirable ways to handle situations. They have also tailored other interventions to focus on newly appointed leader coaching and change leader coaching (that is, assisting leaders charged with planning and implementing a major organizational change).

Ironically, the executive coaches are offering executives the most candid, direct feedback many of them have ever had. Many executives find it easier to be vulnerable, hear bad news, and be willing to admit they need help with an external coach. A key question is whether this is a fad of the 1990s. As companies struggle to reduce cost, will this be perceived as a luxury that companies can no longer afford? Does an overreliance on executive coaches exacerbate the problem of allowing supervisors to escape from having to provide meaningful feedback? Much as in a therapeutic relationship, the chemistry between the coach and the executive influences the success of the effort. Another potential issue is the quality of various executive coaches. There is considerable diversity in the backgrounds of executive coaches. Typically, executive coaches have been outside consultants, corporate executives, human resources specialists, outplacement professionals, or psychologists before setting up in the field. Currently, the qualifications of executive coaches vary and there is no certification requirement. Our recommendation is that organizations closely scrutinize the backgrounds of executive coaches, request multiple references, and look for examples of successes and nonsuccesses.

Conclusions

We began the chapter by suggesting that the process of evaluating executive performance has been somewhat mysterious. Our conclusion is that this statement still holds true. Very little published literature exists on the topic. While many companies say that they have methods for evaluating executives, the lack of formality and the inconsistency make it difficult to assess the effectiveness of these processes. It is also quite clear given the critical roles executives play in today's dynamic marketplace that they both want and need clear goals and objectives, ongoing candid feedback, and a system that tightly links pay to performance. Based on a review of current company practices, we suggest several research topics and ways to improve the process of evaluating executive performance.

Companies are expanding their performance measures to include nonfinancial metrics. As they attempt to link these metrics to pay decisions, further research is needed to determine the most robust set of measures and the smallest number of measures that will do the job. As an initial step, companies need to better understand the relationships among their people, their customers, and their financial measures.

Fortunately, what began in some companies as an intuitive belief in a relationship between employee satisfaction, customer satisfaction, and financial outcomes has engendered increasingly sophisticated research into the linkages among stakeholder results. Work on the service-profit chain by members of the Service Management Interest Group at the Harvard Business School has established links between employee outlook (satisfaction, loyalty, and productivity), customer loyalty, and firm profitability (Heskett, Jones, Loveman, Sasser, & Schlesinger, 1994). Data from companies like Southwest Airlines, BancOne, and Taco Bell demonstrate the success that can come from a focus on front-line employees and customers. The authors posit that the initial link in the chain, employee satisfaction, is created through the internal quality of the working environment. Huselid's work on the impact of human resource practices on firm performance supports the importance of a high-quality work environment. High-performance work practices, such as formal appraisal systems, information-sharing programs, performance-based pay and incentives, and performance-based-promotion-from-within policies, are associated with lower employee turnover, greater productivity, and stronger corporate financial performance (Huselid, 1995).

Several companies are already beginning to examine these stakeholder relationships and are using the data, for example, to identify the specific people measures that have the strongest link to delivering value to customers and improving the financial performance of the company. Over time, as baseline and trend data become available, it will also be possible to determine the most effective way to weight the different measures. In addition, as companies become more experienced with using nonfinancial measures, they can more easily examine how these measures fluctuate over time, particularly as actions are taken to improve performance. Executives are always looking for the most effective interventions that will drive improvements in the business.

While numerous "ideal leader" characteristics and leadership competencies exist in companies, very little empirical research is available that links these competencies to business results. Brisco (1996) eloquently describes the various ways competencies have been developed. However, more empirical studies like the Bass (1997) research are needed to demonstrate the relationship between leadership competencies and business outcomes.

It would be interesting to examine the factors that seem to influence the stability of executive appraisals—both process and content. Based on our review, there are several major factors that can stimulate change. First, the number of CEOs and senior executives who are moving from one company to another is increasing. They are often hired to transform the culture of the organization and improve business results. New performance standards and expectations are created, causing executives who were once well thought of to be perceived as ineffective. Many executives transport processes and programs that worked well in their previous environment and attempt to apply them in the new one. For example, some CEOs have strongly supported multisource feedback interventions, even for evaluative purposes. These new perspectives (that is, peers, direct reports, and customers), incorporated into the appraisal process, can drastically change the way someone is perceived. Another important factor influencing change is the dynamic nature of the marketplace. To remain competitive, organizations are having to shift strategies and enter new markets. These important changes alter the criteria for success and render previous skills and accomplishments obsolete. Frequent organizational changes such as restructuring can also contribute to change or even the abandonment of an existing process. All these organizational factors can lead to frequent modifications to the performance management process. This certainly creates challenges in evaluating the effectiveness of the process and people over time.

Another important issue is the rapid movement of executives from one position to another and how that influences the accuracy of evaluations. Sometimes executives move so quickly that it is impossible to assess the impact of decisions they make. For example, an executive can be given an excellent appraisal for the launch of a product that later flops in the marketplace—after its initial champion has moved on to another position. Executives should be left in some assignments long enough to permit accurate assessment of the impact of their decisions on business results and to ensure that they learn from their successes and failures.

A key question is how human resource leaders can sell the value of executive appraisals and other performance management interventions to executives. Many successful executives never conduct or receive formal appraisals and performance reviews and they therefore do not see the value of these processes. Based on the data we gathered from other companies, it is clear that senior leadership buy-in and support has a significant impact on the success of implementing performance management processes for executives. These interventions will fail if they are positioned as HR programs.

In some cases, such as at Honeywell, the CEO strongly believes that managing the performance of executives improves the bottom-line results of the firm. In these circumstances, selling the value of the process is not an issue. More often than not, executives are skeptical.

Some of our key learnings in introducing processes designed to enhance the performance of executives include:

- *Find an executive in one of the business units who is willing to serve as a champion.* Select an individual who is influential and has a good reputation and appreciation for effectively managing the performance of his or her people. These individuals can ultimately sell the success of the process to their peers.
- *Appreciate the fact that executives are extremely busy.* Processes must be simple, user friendly, require minimal paperwork and time, and—most important—be structured in a way that executives can see the link between what they are doing and how it can help them with their business challenges and opportunities.
- *Highlight the costs associated with neglecting effective performance evaluation for executives.* It's obviously easier to make a sale when the business results are suffering or executive turnover is high. One approach might be to demonstrate the costs associated with bringing in new executives or removing a poorly performing executive (that is, severance packages). The impact on customers and employees should also be included in the analysis of such costs.

Table 10.3 is a summary of the key trends, issues, and implications of evaluating executive performance.

Our overall assessment is that there is still important work to be done to strengthen our approaches for evaluating executive performance. Given the cost of hiring and retaining executives as well as the significant impact of their decisions on the business, doing this well can truly become a firm's competitive weapon.

References

Atkinson, A., Waterhouse, J. H., & Wells, R. B. (1997, Spring). A stakeholder approach to strategic performance measurement. *Sloan Management Review*, pp. 25–37.

Bass, B. M. (1997, February). Does the transactional-transformational leadership paradigm transcend organizational and national boundaries? *American Psychologist*, pp. 130–139.

Bernardin, H. J., & Beatty, R. W. (1984). *Performance appraisal: Assessing human behavior at work.* Boston: Kent.

Table 10.3. Summary of Key Themes: Evaluating Executive Performance.

Positive Trends	Continuing Issues	Implications
Expanding definition of performance to include: • Impacts on all stakeholders • Leadership competencies and behaviors	• Lack of robust, time-tested measures to quantify results in nonfinancial and competency performance categories	• Reluctance to link significant pay decisions to nonfinancial and competency outcomes • Inability of executives to identify and leverage performance drivers for success • Tendency to minimize leadership effectiveness by deemphasizing how work gets done
Increasing presence of formal appraisal processes as part of the performance management system	• Lack of specific, documented goals and objectives for individual executives • Discomfort with giving and receiving candid feedback • Persistence of myths that executive appraisals are neither desired nor appropriate	• Reinforcement of belief that executive appraisals are highly politicized • Inability of executives to acknowledge and address performance issues before they develop into career-threatening problems • Tendency to exempt executives from the formal appraisal process
Expanding adoption of multisource feedback as input to the executive evaluation process	• Lack of valid, reliable feedback instruments • Access to training and support on how to give and receive feedback • Alignment of key HR mechanisms (selection, promotion, succession, and reward systems) to reinforce desired outcomes and behaviors	• Executive distrust of the process and resistance to its implementation • Meaningful data never communicated to executive; limited ability to institutionalize and cascade the process • Mixed signals regarding what's really important to success diminish the likelihood of enduring behavior change

Source: Adapted from Harrison, 1997.

Brisco, J. P. (1996, October). *Competency-based approaches to selecting and developing executives: current practices and suggestions for improvement.* Boston: Executive Development Roundtable, Boston University.

Conference Board. (1995). *New corporate performance measures: A research report.* New York: Author.

Cook, S. W., Kay, I. T., Graef, B., Crystal, B. R., Ellig, L. C., & Thurow, P. M. (1997). CEO pay: A comprehensive look. *ACA Journal.*

Edwards, M. R., & Ewen, A. J. (1995, Winter). Moving multi-source assessment beyond development. *ACA Journal,* pp. 82–92.

Farkas, C. M., & Wetlaufer, S. (1996, June). The ways chief executive officers lead. *Harvard Business Review,* pp. 110–122.

Gioia, D. A., & Longenecker, C. O. (1988). Neglected at the top: Executives talk about executive appraisal. *Sloan Management Review,* pp. 41–47.

Gioia, D. A., & Longenecker, C. O. (1994). The politics of the executive appraisal. *Organizational Dynamics,* pp. 47–57.

Hagberg, R. (1996, August). Identify and help executives in trouble. *HR Magazine,* pp. 88–93.

Harrison, R. P. (1997). A three-dimensional method for assessment and development planning. *Manchester Review, 2*(1).

Harrison, R. P., & Betof, E. H. (1996). Transformational coaching: A new paradigm for rapid executive change. *Manchester Review, 1*(2), 17–24.

Heifetz, R. A., & Laurie, D. L. (1997, January-February). The work of leadership. *Harvard Business Review,* pp. 124–134.

Heskett, J. L., Jones, T. O., Loveman, G. W., Sasser, W. E., Jr., & Schlesinger, L. A. (1994, March). Putting the service-profit chain to work. *Harvard Business Review,* pp. 164–174.

Hout, T. A., & Carter, J. C. (1995, November-December). Getting it done: New roles for senior executives. *Harvard Business Review,* pp. 133–145.

Huselid, M. A. (1995). The impact of human resource management practices on turnover, productivity, and corporate financial performance. *Academy of Management Journal, 38,* 635–670.

Kaplan, R. S., & Norton, D. P. (1996a). *The balanced scorecard.* Cambridge, MA: President and Fellows of Harvard College.

Kaplan, R. S., & Norton, D. P. (1996b, January-February). Using the balanced scorecard as a strategic management system. *Harvard Business Review,* pp. 75–85.

Koonce, R. (1994, February). One-on-one training and development. *Training Development,* pp. 34–40.

Kotter, J. P. (1988). *Leadership factor.* New York: Free Press.

Kotter, J. P. (1996). *Leading change.* Boston: Harvard Business School Press.

Landy, F. J., & Farr, J. L. (1983). *The measurement of work performance: Methods, theory, and applications.* Orlando, FL: Academic Press.

Latham, G. P., & Wexley, K. N. (1980). *Increasing productivity through performance appraisal.* Reading, MA: Addison Wesley Longman.

Locke, E. A. (1991). *The nature of leadership in the essence of leadership.* San Francisco: New Lexington Press.

Locke, E. A., & Latham, F. P. (1990). *A theory of goal setting and task performance.* Upper Saddle River, NJ: Prentice Hall.

Lombardo, M. M., & McCauley, C. D. (1988). *Dynamics of management derailment.* Technical Report No. 34. Greensboro, NC: Center for Creative Leadership.

Longenecker, C. O., & Gioia, D. A. (1992). The executive appraisal paradox. *Academy of Management Executive, 6*(2), 18–28.

Longenecker, C. O., & Gioia, D. A. (1993). Executives need appraisals too. *Executive Development, 6*(1), 21–24.

McCall, M. W., & Lombardo, M. M. (1983, February). What makes a top executive? *Psychology Today,* pp. 26–31.

McWilliams, B. (1996, February). The measure of success. *Across the Board,* pp. 16–20.

Mohrman, A. M., Jr., & Mohrman, S. A. (1995, August). Performance management is "running the business." *Performance Management,* pp. 69–75.

National Association of Corporate Directors. (1995). *Performance evaluation of chief executive officers, boards, and directors.* Report of the NACD Blue Ribbon Commission. Washington, DC: Author.

CHAPTER 11

Training Raters to Increase the Accuracy of Appraisals and the Usefulness of Feedback

Neil M. A. Hauenstein

In writing this chapter, I have assumed that in spite of findings of appraisal ineffectiveness (Dorfman, Stephan, & Loveland, 1986; Napier & Latham, 1986), appropriately conducted performance appraisal and employee feedback benefits organizations (see Murphy & Cleveland, 1995, pp. 326–332). However, it would be naive to think of performance appraisal as anything other than a political process (Longenecker, Sims, & Gioia, 1987). Rating accuracy is not always the goal of appraisers (Ilgen, 1993), and there are many situations where providing inaccurate appraisal data is sound management (Murphy & Cleveland, 1995). Nonetheless, rater training programs are based on the notion that accurate ratings and honest feedback are in the best interests of the organization and the overall development of employees. In a sense, rater training is like the pursuit of truth in science, which scientists must attempt even though they know full well that the truth never can be achieved.

Note: Many thanks to Carolyn Facteau, Laura Finfer, Tom Ruddy, and Steven Walker for sharing insights and making materials available. Also, thanks to Jeff Facteau and Jean Anne Schmidt for reading earlier drafts.

Bretz, Milkovich, and Read (1992), summarizing results from three different surveys, reported that most organizations use some form of rater training. There are incentives for organizations to invest in rater training and feedback training. If appraisal data are used in promotion or termination decisions, then rater training is an important protection in the event of a lawsuit (Barrett & Kernan, 1987). On a broader level, given that performance appraisal is a political process, then rater training is a symbol of organizational commitment to a fair process. Unfortunately, the commitment to rater training often goes only as far as what can be trained in one or two hours, most of which is spent explaining how to fill out new forms. As Latham and Wexley (1994) point out, it takes time and resources (two of the rarest commodities in a human resource department) to train raters.

This chapter is organized around two major training issues. First is the traditional issue of training raters to increase the accuracy of their evaluations. Issues covered in this section include how to structure rater training programs, alternative training goals, and the identification of situations most appropriate for each training goal. The second major training issue is training raters to give feedback. The focus of this section is what types of feedback are most effective and maintaining procedural fairness in the process.

Training Raters to Improve Rating Accuracy

The practice of rater training is traditionally associated with training raters to improve the accuracy of the numbers assigned to those being evaluated. In one sense, there is a general consensus about how to structure rater training programs to improve rating accuracy. Effective rater training programs include three elements: explanations of the performance dimensions, opportunities for trainees to make practice ratings, and feedback to the trainees concerning the practice ratings (Smith, 1986). I first address these three structural recommendations and then discuss potential variations of training content.

Performance Dimension Training

The first recommended structural component, performance dimension training (PDT), is fundamental in rater training programs.

PDT focuses on familiarizing raters with the performance dimensions used in the evaluation system. At the simplest level, PDT involves reviewing the definitions associated with each performance dimension. For example, Exhibit 11.1 presents the definitions of two core performance expectations ("leadership" and "coaching and development") used in the 360-degree rater training program at the Tennessee Valley Authority (TVA). Such presentations and discussions are fundamental in assisting trainee understanding of what the appraisal instrument is intended to measure.

However, it is best if this review of the dimensions is supplemented by activities that reinforce understanding of the dimensions. The most common supplemental training activity is to present or generate and discuss examples of performance behaviors associated with each dimension. The TVA rater training program uses a matching game to relate behavioral examples to dimensions. In this matching game, teams are formed at different

---

Exhibit 11.1. Performance Dimension Rating Example.

360-Degree Feedback Performance Expectations and Rating Guidelines

Leadership

Leading Others

- Consistently communicating a clear direction and vision for the work group
- Gaining commitment and participation for the work group's direction
- Recognizing others for their contributions
- Demonstrating behaviors that he/she asks of others
- Acting with urgency when appropriate
- Inspiring me to perform to my full potential

Coaching and Developing

- Providing ongoing feedback
- Providing support and resources for the professional development of employees
- Evaluating performance based on established expectations
- Working with employees to identify and improve development needs

Source: Tennessee Valley Authority University, 1995, p. 33.

tables and each team goes through a stack of cards that give behavioral performance statements. Each team matches each behavior with the most appropriate (or primary) dimension and any other (or secondary) dimensions for which the behavior in question conveys diagnostic information. Here is a sample game statement: "Neal, Cornelia, and Marsha met to discuss the budget proposal. Everyone offered ideas for consideration except Marsha. She remained detached from the group despite the attempts of others to draw her into the discussion." This statement is considered primary for the dimension of "group cooperation" and secondary for the "organizational support" dimension. Each group records its answers and points (two points for primary, one point for secondary) are tallied. As an incentive, prizes are given to the winning group.

It is unlikely that PDT by itself profoundly affects the quality of the evaluations because the dimensions themselves do not convey goals to improve rating accuracy (Smith, 1986; Woehr & Huffcutt, 1994). Nonetheless, PDT is a necessary condition for effective rater training (Stamoulis & Hauenstein, 1993). Understanding of the performance dimensions facilitates the comprehension of any other training content and enhances the benefits of practice ratings and feedback given in relation to the practice ratings.

Practice and Feedback

In contrast to the frequent use of PDT, rater training programs often do not include the recommended practice ratings activity and the provision of feedback on the practice ratings. Instead, PDT is usually supplemented by lectures and discussions of relevant performance appraisal concepts (for example, rating errors), and that is where the training ends. Practice and feedback are important in that they facilitate training effectiveness through active participation and discussion. More specifically, making a series of practice ratings allows the raters to calibrate their individual performance standards to the rating scales. That is, it gives the raters an idea of the scale anchors they personally associate with different levels of competence. Subsequent feedback then allows the raters to check their internal calibration against an external standard. In this manner, each rater can adjust performance standards to more closely model organizational expectations.

Practice Rating Stimuli

Use of a practice rating activity requires examples of performance that trainees can evaluate during training. The initial development issue for a practice rating activity is the content of performance descriptions. This content can be generated by a project team consisting of incumbents, people familiar with the jobs being evaluated, and people familiar with the performance standards the organization is trying to foster. Someone familiar with organizational performance expectations facilitates the group and the goal of this project team is to develop a set of behavioral descriptions that represent a wide range of effectiveness on all the performance dimensions. A critical decision in this process is the comprehensiveness of each performance example. At the simplest level, a performance example can be a single behavior representing performance on one performance dimension. At the most complex level, each performance example can convey multiple performance incidents relevant to all dimensions. A middle ground of conveying performance diagnostic of two or three dimensions in each example is probably best in that it is more realistic than the simplest strategy and less likely to overwhelm trainees than the most complex strategy.

After the development of the content of the performance examples, the next decision is the mode of presentation during training. The obvious dynamic in this decision is the cost-realism trade-off. The lowest-cost–lowest-fidelity option is to use written vignettes to convey the performance examples. Exhibit 11.2 presents an example of a performance vignette used for practice ratings in the TVA rater training program. The vignette gives a series of incidents where Kevin (the fictitious employee to be evaluated) exhibits multiple behaviors relevant to the performance dimensions under the core performance expectations of "teamwork" and "integrity." In this particular practice rating exercise, the trainee assumes the role of Kevin's peer and the incidents reflect various notes to and from Kevin, along with incidents from team meetings and information gleaned from Kevin's own work. As can be seen in Exhibit 11.2, Kevin had several performance lapses. Among other things, he missed two team meetings, he was reminded three times to submit the contract information, and he turned in his contract information two weeks late and incomplete. After examining the incidents, the trainee evaluates Kevin on teamwork and integrity dimensions.

Exhibit 11.2. Example of
Performance Vignette Used for Practice Rating.

360-Degree Feedback Rater Training Module 2:
Rating Behavior in the 360-Degree Feedback Process

Practice Activity 3—Assigning 360-degree feedback ratings

3A) "Teamwork" and "Integrity" Behaviors

Ratee:	Kevin
Position:	Specialist
Rater:	You are Kevin's peer and team member.

Information Source	*Incident*
Note on calendar **1/15/95**	First Team Meeting for Contractor Study. Meeting Notes: Pressing timeline. Crucial to meet deadlines.
Note from Team Leader: **1/20/95**	Agenda for next team meeting on 2/10/95. First team member assignments outlined: All team members to determine the amount spent on contracting with vendors and outside labor sources for the assigned departments.
Planning Notes **2/10/95**	A-1 Priority—Compile all team member information into summary report by next meeting (2/25/95). A-2 Priority—Call Kevin to ask him to fax his vendor contract information to me.
Message from Kevin **2/11/95**	Got your message. Sorry to miss the meeting. Running a little behind schedule. Will get the information to you by next week.
Message to Kevin **2/17/95**	Reminder to send contract information.
Message to Kevin **2/21/95**	Reminder to send contract information.
Work Sample: **Contract Report** **from Kevin** **2/24/95**	Contract report was incomplete.
Work Sample: **Summary Report** **for Team** **2/25/95**	Incomplete. Some of Kevin's information was left out.
Note on To-Do List **2/25/95**	To Do List: Contracting Team Assignment—Benchmarking research by 3/26.

Exhibit 11.2. Example of
Performance Vignette Used for Practice Rating, cont'd.

Information Source	Incident
Message to Kevin 2/27/95	Reminder to send supplemental contract information. Requested to meet with him to clarify how he got some of his information.
Meeting Minutes from 2/25/95 3/2/95	Action item: Kevin to deliver updated contract information.
Message from Kevin 3/6/95	Asked for the names of departments he omitted.
Memo to Kevin 3/6/95	Sent Kevin his list of departments.
Fax from Kevin 3/24/95	Supplemental contract information
Phone call from Kevin 3/24/95	Offered to meet 3/25/95 P.M. —
Meeting Agenda 3/26/95	1: Go over completed summary report of contract information.
Memo from Team Leader 4/1/95	Meeting agenda for 4/12/95 meeting.
Conversation with Kevin 4/14/95	Requested an update on what happened in the 4/12 meeting.
Meeting with Kevin 4/14/95	Reviewed agenda items and action items from 4/12 meeting. Reminded him about final team presentation on 4/25/95.
Meeting Minutes from 4/25/95	Final team report delivered. All team members present.

(Now rate Kevin's behaviors on the next page.)

Source: Tennessee Valley Authority University, 1995, pp. 91, 93.

The most likely choice of an organization seeking greater fidelity is to use videotapes of simulated performances. Lucent Technologies uses such videotapes in their rater training program. After watching a performance episode, trainees fill out a form where, among other things, they describe the central event in the scene, the circumstances of the situation, and the consequences of the incident. At the end of the form, trainees evaluate the effectiveness of the central character in the videotape.

Overall, increases in rating quality as a function of increases in fidelity are difficult to gauge. The use of performance vignettes in performance appraisal research is actively discouraged (Murphy, Herr, Lockhart, & Maguire, 1986). The general opinion is that performance vignettes are not appropriate because "paper people" do not realistically convey performance. However, there should be no hesitation to use paper people in rater training programs if resources are unavailable for more elaborate modes of presentation. It is better to have trainees practice and receive feedback for evaluations of paper people than to have no practice or feedback at all.

Content of Feedback

The final structural issue is the development of the feedback associated with the practice ratings. There are two types of feedback content that I will label as qualitative and quantitative. Exhibit 11.3, taken from the TVA rater training, presents an example of feedback given to trainees after they rate the description of Kevin seen in Exhibit 11.2. The top half of Exhibit 11.3 is the quantitative feedback concerning the numerical evaluations that Kevin should have received. The bottom half of Exhibit 11.3 is the qualitative feedback that provides a review of the evidence that justifies the low ratings received by Kevin.

A similar qualitative feedback strategy appears in the rater training program that Chase Manhattan Bank uses for its 360-degree appraisal instrument called Living the Values. In training, participants are shown a videotape of a manager-subordinate meeting and are asked to evaluate the manager. The trainees' numerical ratings are put on a flip chart and participants discuss the reasons for their different ratings.

Qualitative feedback is not limited to the types of justifications seen in the TVA and Chase Manhattan Bank examples. Rather, qualitative feedback refers to the wide variety of information that can be discussed after the practice ratings are rendered. For example, in the Lucent Technologies rater training program, discussion questions include "What behavior did you see?" "How did you categorize the behavior in terms of dimensions?" and "What would have been more/less effective?"

The issue of accuracy is dealt with in two ways when using qualitative feedback. First, there is an accuracy issue in terms of the recording or memory of performance incidents. If trainees have

Exhibit 11.3. Example of
Qualitative and Quantitative Feedback.

360-Degree Feedback Rater Training Module 2:
Rating Behavior in the 360-Degree Feedback Process

Practice Activity 3—Assigning 360-degree feedback ratings

3A) "Teamwork" and "Integrity" Behaviors (continued)

Teamwork: Group Cooperation

1. Cooperating with others to achieve group goals	1 ② 3 4 5 ?
2. Contributing actively to group projects and meetings	1 ② 3 4 5 ?
3. Developing positive working relationships with other people and team members	1 2 3 4 5 ⑦

Teamwork: Organizational Support

4. Vocally supporting TVA's vision and values	1 2 3 4 5 ⑦
5. Supporting efforts to make TVA a world-class organization	1 ② 3 4 5 ?

Reason for Rating:

Kevin demonstrated less than "effective (3)" performance on three behavioral statements (for example, "Cooperating with others to achieve group goals," "Contributing actively to group projects and meetings," and "Supporting efforts to make TVA a world-class organization") for the following reasons:

• He missed two team meetings (one on 2/10 and one on 4/12).

• Kevin was reminded three times to submit the contract information.

• He turned in his contract information two weeks late and incomplete.

• Kevin had to ask to get the names of the departments he omitted.

• He did not totally complete this assignment until one month after turning in the incomplete report.

• Kevin's lack of speed and inability to do his work correctly the first time run counter to TVA's goal to be "Customer Driven" and its value of flexibility.

Source: Tennessee Valley Authority University, 1995, p. 94.

recorded the observations upon which they base their judgments, then they can be informed how accurately they recorded the behavioral information. If trainees did not write down the behavioral information, this information can be elicited in discussion, and feedback can be provided as to the accuracy of the memories. The second way that accuracy is conveyed through qualitative feedback is to compare practice ratings to an external standard of quality (other than a quantitative estimate of performance).

Raters are often trained to avoid judgment errors. For example, raters are usually trained to avoid being too lenient when rating employees. Thus practice ratings that are distributed over a wide range of scale anchors have ostensibly met the desired quality standard of not being lenient. Feedback can be provided (via the trainers or through group discussion) that addresses the extent to which practice ratings accomplish such training prescriptions.

As seen in the top half of Exhibit 11.3, quantitative feedback provides the trainees with the *target ratings* associated with the performance examples. The target ratings represent the organization's estimate of the effectiveness levels demonstrated in the performance examples. The target ratings used in quantitative feedback must match the anchors used in the practice ratings. Often the anchors are numerical, as seen in the TVA example in Exhibit 11.3. In the Lucent Technologies training program, the quantitative feedback that is given to trainees uses adjective scale anchors. For example, when rating "impact on productivity," the rating scale anchors and quantitative feedback use the terms of "low," "medium," or "high."

When using quantitative feedback, each trainee's ratings are typically displayed along with the target ratings. The trainer then facilitates discussion of rating accuracy by focusing on discrepancies between the target ratings and the practice ratings rendered by trainees. For those trainees whose ratings are discrepant, discussion focuses on whether inaccuracy was due to the trainees' failure to notice or understand critical performance incidents, or due to poor calibration in terms of rating critical incidents too leniently or too severely. Finally, an important issue for the development of quantitative feedback is how to generate the target ratings. A normative process is generally used whereby people familiar with the jobs and familiar with performance expectations estimate the effectiveness of the rating practice stimuli. Final target ratings can be established by averaging the ratings or by raters' coming to consensus agreements about the final target ratings.

Summary of Structural Recommendations

Of the three structural recommendations, PDT is a defining characteristic of rater training. It is difficult to imagine conducting a rater training program without beginning with the explanations of the performance dimensions that raters will use to evaluate employees. In contrast, practice ratings and feedback are used much less frequently. There are a multitude of possible reasons why rater training programs do not include practice and feedback. Perhaps the main reason is that it is just much easier and less time-consuming to put together a lecture than to develop practice stimuli and associated feedback. Whatever the reasons, developers of rater training programs should commit to including practice and feedback as often as possible.

Rater Training Content

Of course, it is best to provide some content in relation to the practice and feedback components of rater training. The content of rater training conveys the goals that the organization, or at least the human resource department, is hoping to achieve in actual evaluations. In terms of increasing the accuracy of ratings, four general goals are currently used or suggested. First, the most traditional goal is to increase rating accuracy by decreasing various judgmental biases in raters (often called rating errors). The second goal used to guide rater training is to train raters to increase the accuracy of evaluations. Third, a goal often included in rater training is to increase behavioral accuracy. That is, to improve trainee observation skills as a strategy for improving the final evaluations. Finally, the fourth rater training goal is to increase employees' confidence in their ability to evaluate.

Decreasing Rater Biases

The first goal of decreasing rater biases is the foundation of what is traditionally called rater error training (RET). RET is predicated on the assumption that raters possess certain biases that decrease rating accuracy. The most frequently discussed rater biases are related to the failure to differentiate among ratees, and fall into three classes commonly known as leniency error, severity error, and central tendency error. Of these three, rater training tends to emphasize *leniency error*—the tendency to give all employees good ratings—because that is generally the major problem with performance evaluations (Hauenstein, 1992). Another commonly discussed source of bias is *halo error,* the failure to discriminate the performance of one individual employee across the different performance dimensions. The most common assumption of the cause of halo error is that raters use their general impression of overall performance to bias their ratings on the individual dimensions. While leniency and halo error are the most frequently discussed, there are several other errors that can be discussed in RET, including first impression errors, contrast errors, and friendship bias.

Focusing on leniency and halo, classic RET content instructs raters to increase variability in observed ratings by not committing rating errors (for an extensive discussion of implementing RET, see Latham & Wexley, 1994, pp. 152–161). In its simplest form, RET includes definitions of the various rating errors and examples of ratings and rating distributions that represent rating errors. The RET program used at the TVA defines the error in question, provides possible causes of the error, and gives suggestions of how to avoid the error. Exhibit 11.4 presents an overhead the TVA uses when covering leniency.

When feedback of practice ratings is included in RET, the feedback is qualitative with a focus on avoiding the error in question. As Latham and Wexley (1994) point out, such feedback allows trainees to observe others making rating errors, to discover the extent to which they were or were not prone to making the rating error, and to practice reducing the errors. Historically, research that measured rating quality as the absence of rating errors generally found that RET was effective in reducing at least one measure of rating error (Bernardin, 1978; Fay & Latham, 1982; Latham, Wexley, & Purcell, 1975). In a review of the rater training research, Woehr and Huffcutt (1994) indicated that RET training was modestly effective in reducing halo and leniency.

Exhibit 11.4. Example of RET for Leniency Error.

**360-Degree Feedback Rater Training Module 2:
Rating Behavior in the 360-Degree Feedback Process**

Understanding How Your Ratings Can Be Influenced or Biased

Leniency Tendency

The rater gives ratings higher than the ratee deserves. That is, the rater gives ratings at the upper end of the scale even though the ratings do not reflect the actual performance observed. The rater could be described as being "too easy" in his or her evaluation.

Possible Reasons:	What to Do:
• Being uncomfortable with giving negative or average feedback	• Remember that accurate feedback is needed for any improvement to occur
• Having unusually low performance standards	• Recognize the need to use published rating guidelines, not personal standards
• Assuming that other raters also inflate their ratings	• Understand that "second-guessing" defeats the rating process
• Fearing retaliation from ratees for giving negative feedback	• Recognize the anonymity safeguards built into the rating process

Source: Tennessee Valley Authority University, 1995, p. 69.

Increasing Accuracy

The design of rater training programs to directly improve rater accuracy is relatively new. Until 1975, there was a general reluctance on the part of appraisal researchers to measure rating accuracy. The main reason for this was the lack of recognized procedures for generating estimates of "true performance" (that is, target ratings) to serve as comparisons to observed ratings. This avoidance of accuracy issues in performance appraisal research led to the general emphasis on rating errors in the practice of rater training. Borman (1975) developed a procedure for estimating target scores and that opened the door to performance appraisal research on rating accuracy. It was not long before rating accuracy became the focus of rater training research, and this naturally led to the proposal of rater training programs designed to improve rating accuracy.

The best-known rater training program with the goal of increasing accuracy is frame-of-reference (FOR) training. FOR training evolved from Bernardin's work (Bernardin & Buckley, 1981; Bernardin & Pence, 1980) on rater training. Bernardin and Pence conducted a RET study that included both rating error and rating accuracy measures. They found that RET reduced leniency and halo, but rating accuracy actually decreased. Bernardin and Pence concluded that raters had replaced an erroneous rating strategy (lenient and haloed ratings) with another erroneous rating strategy (no leniency and no halo).

This led Bernardin and Buckley to propose FOR training as a strategy that focuses specifically on improvements in rating accuracy. The typical steps of FOR training include performance dimension training, presentation and discussion of multiple behavioral incidents representing different effectiveness levels of each performance dimension, and practice rating using vignettes or videotaped performances, followed by both quantitative and qualitative feedback. The inclusion of quantitative feedback allows raters to make direct comparisons of how close they are to the target scores (that is, accuracy feedback). The orientation of this quantitative feedback is to focus on one ratee at a time and to discuss performance discrepancies between practice ratings and target scores on each dimension. In the previous discussion of quantitative feedback, examples were given from rater training programs at the TVA (see Exhibit 11.3) and Lucent Technologies. Both of these examples were taken from FOR training programs designed to improve rating accuracy.

Over the years, research has established that FOR training is the most effective in improving rating accuracy, at least in laboratory settings over fairly short periods of time (Athey & McIntyre, 1987; Hedge & Kavanaugh, 1988; McIntyre, Smith, & Hassett, 1984; Pulakos, 1984, 1986). Woehr and Huffcutt (1994) reported that FOR training was the single most effective training strategy with respect to increasing rating accuracy. Although the effect of FOR training on rating accuracy is well established, the reason why FOR works is not totally understood (see Day & Sulsky, 1995; Stamoulis & Hauenstein,

1993; Sulsky & Day, 1992, 1994; Woehr, 1994). Without detailing the complexities of the debate, it appears that FOR training fosters accurate judgments of ratee performance, but probably decreases the accuracy of memories for the behaviors upon which the judgments are based.

Perhaps the most daunting practical aspect of implementing FOR training is the creation of the performance standards used in training. As previously mentioned, PDT usually includes working with trainees to correctly associate performance examples with the various dimensions used in the evaluation. FOR training extends PDT in that the effectiveness levels also are conveyed. That is, when trainees are exposed to performance examples, they are also given quantitative estimates about how high or low this performance example should be rated.

Techniques for creating performance standards are well established. For example, Hauenstein and Foti (1989) worked with police departments to create a comprehensive frame of reference for the patrol officer job. Using a variation on the process used for creating behaviorally anchored rating scales, they had incumbents generate target effectiveness ratings for a list of over three hundred performance statements. However, a comprehensive process like that used by Hauenstein and Foti is probably not necessary. It may be sufficient if the performance standards are based on some extension of performance dimension training. For example, simply grouping behavioral examples of performance as effective, average, or ineffective within each performance dimension is a viable alternative. It may even be possible to use the trainees to develop the standards during the training. As to the actual target scores, it is important to remember that the target ratings represent truth as defined by the organization (Day & Sulsky, 1995; Hauenstein & Foti, 1989; Stamoulis & Hauenstein, 1993). The goal should be to produce reasonable target scores without being overly concerned that the target scores represent truth in the abstract sense.

A second, more embryonic rater training program that emphasizes increasing rating accuracy is rater variability training (RVT). Stamoulis and Hauenstein (1993) conducted a study in which they compared traditional RET, FOR training, and a third training format that merged RET's emphasis on distinguishing among different ratees with quantitative accuracy feedback from

FOR training. They found that RVT was as good as or superior to other forms of rater training in terms of making accurate distinctions between individuals. This led them to propose RVT training as a viable training alternative. RVT has three steps: train raters to increase the variability in observed ratings to correspond to the variability in actual ratee performance, provide systematic practice at differentiating among ratees, and offer quantitative and qualitative feedback on practice ratings. RVT feedback orients discussion toward relative differences between employees, whereas FOR feedback orients toward differences between the practice ratings and the performance standard.

There is yet to be a systematic evaluation of RVT, but I have used the first RVT learning goal in two organizational settings. In conversations with managers going through this abbreviated RVT, I found that what conveyed the RVT concept best was an analogy. I asked the managers to consider using a sieve to sort a pile of pebbles by size—when the holes in the sieve are so large that all the pebbles pass through. It is abundantly clear to managers that the effort to sort the pebbles is completely wasted, and this realization drives home the point that performance appraisals that fail to make distinctions also represent wasted effort. What is less clear to managers is that the sieve itself is perfectly accurate in its own terms. It makes no mistakes in sorting the pebbles. Discussion turns to tightening standards so that distinctions can be made. In the sieve analogy, conversation focuses on the acquisition of a set of sieves that have progressively smaller holes, so as to make reliable size distinctions. This example is then related to tightening performance standards, and discussions proceed concerning behavioral examples that denote discernible differences between ratee performances.

Increasing Observational Skills

The third goal in rater training is to improve observational skills. The notion underlying this goal is that raters who have accurate information about what employees have done over the evaluation period will provide more accurate ratings. RET, FOR training, and RVT are primarily designed to improve judgment processes. In contrast, behavioral observation training (BOT) is designed to improve the detection, perception, and recall of performance behaviors.

There are two basic strategies in BOT. The first is to focus on increased sampling of employee performances and avoidance of observational errors, so that raters have accurate memories of work behaviors. For example, Thorton and Zorich (1980) used lecture and discussion about observing as much detailed performance as possible and avoiding processing errors. The processing error lectures included loss of detail through simplification, making snap judgments, and forcing observations into categories instead of remembering the differences between people. In the TVA 360-degree rater training program, emphasis is given to distinguishing behaviors from judgments. Trainees are asked to determine if statements describing hypothetical employees represent a behavior or an inference. Examples include "Terry went to the flip chart and drew a model to illustrate his ideas" (a behavior) and "Gene was sensitive to others in the group" (an inference).

The second strategy is to train raters to maintain observational aides such as notes about employees or more sophisticated behavioral diaries. Open-ended notes have been criticized for the potential of sampling bias (Maroney & Buckley, 1992). That is, supervisors will over- and undersample behaviors related to certain performance dimensions, leading to incomplete perceptions of employee performance. A more systematic approach is to organize behavioral diaries by performance dimensions. Although there are different suggested training guidelines for denoting performance incidents, Bernardin and Beatty's (1984) appear to be the best. They suggest that raters record a predesignated number of behaviors on each dimension in an established time period, and that the recorded incidents on each dimension reflect the distribution of performance exhibited by each employee.

Behavioral diaries are clearly useful, especially for providing feedback to employees. The problem with behavioral diaries is the effort involved. Managers have a multitude of tasks and activities and are rarely rewarded for how well they do evaluations, let alone how well they keep notes about employees. When dealing with managers, my preference is to disassociate diary keeping from performance appraisal. Instead, diary keeping is presented as a management development technique that benefits managers, as opposed to a technique that provides better performance evaluations for the organization.

My arguments follow this pattern. Effective leaders have few surprises when talking to employees about performance issues (Latham & Wexley, 1994). Furthermore, effective leaders have a good understanding of what each subordinate has done in terms of results and how each employee accomplished his or her results in terms of work activities (Komaki, 1986). Finally, behavioral diaries allow greater understanding of employee performance, and lead subordinates to ascribe more leadership qualities to managers who maintain diaries. If a personal computer is available, it is easy to create a separate file for each subordinate. I recommend that managers allot thirty minutes a week to recording performance observations of subordinates. Information recorded should include the date of the observation, the observed behavior, outcomes stemming from the behavior, and the manager's impression of performance effectiveness.

As to the effectiveness of BOT, Woehr and Huffcutt (1994) reported improvement in rating accuracy similar to that of FOR training. Measures of rater memories for worker behaviors (that is, observational accuracy) are also common in BOT studies, and Woehr and Huffcutt report a moderate improvement in behavioral accuracy as a function of BOT. Although Woehr and Huffcutt's results are based on only four studies, examination of the broader literature on the relationship between observation and accuracy is typically positive. For example, Heneman and Wexley (1983) found that rating accuracy increased as rater opportunity to observe performance increased.

Increasing Rater Confidence

The final goal suggested for inclusion in rater training is to improve raters' self-confidence in their ability to conduct evaluations. Bernardin and Buckley (1981) are often cited for introducing FOR training concepts, but it typically is ignored that in the same article Bernardin and Buckley also discuss training to improve rater confidence. Neck, Stewart, and Manz (1995) extend this improving-confidence notion and propose Self-Leadership Training (SLT) where raters are trained to use techniques such as positive self-talk, mental imagery, and positive beliefs and thought patterns. The notion is that raters trained in this manner will develop confidence in their ability to conduct performance evaluations, ultimately leading to better evaluations.

Choosing Training Content Goals

In reviewing the four content goals and associated training pro
grams I have avoided the question of whether one goal is superior
to any other goal. Of the four content goals, the goal to decrease
rater biases through RET is the most problematic. As previously
mentioned, early research in performance appraisal did not use
accuracy measures. Instead, researchers used concepts like leniency and halo to describe the quality of ratings. In general, the
use of these concepts was based on the assumption that greater
variability in observed ratings indicates greater rating accuracy. Unfortunately, without some estimate of true performance levels, it is
impossible to know the validity of the assumption that greater variability equals greater rating accuracy. In fact, after performance
appraisal researchers had used both measures of rating errors and
rating accuracy for a few years, Murphy and Balzer (1989) reviewed
the performance appraisal literature and concluded that there is
little or no relationship between measures of rating errors and rating accuracy. That is, higher or lower scores on rating error measures are not associated with improvements or decrements in rating
accuracy.

Findings such as Murphy and Balzer's have led to the general
rejection of rating error concepts in performance appraisal research. This is also true in rater training research. Currently, the
popular research position is that FOR training is superior to RET.
For example, Day and Sulsky (1995) conclude that "FOR training
appears to be the most promising of all rater training programs
presently in use" (p. 166). Yet in practice, decreasing rater biases
through RET remains the most common strategy for rater training. One reason for the continued use of RET is that practitioners
may be unaware of recent developments in performance appraisal
research. A second explanation is that developing an accuracy-
oriented training program requires practice rating exercises and
target scores for the quantitative feedback. As shown earlier, these
issues can be overcome with a modicum of time and resources. As
a result, it is time to recognize that RET is not logically justified
and that the teaching of rating error concepts should stop in rater
training. It is better if the major RET goals of differentiating within
and between employees are achieved through accuracy-oriented
training content.

Obviously, if RET training is not used, then developers of rater training programs need to choose among the other three content goals. Of these content goals, the goal to increase rater confidence should be used in conjunction with either the goal of increasing rating accuracy or the goal of increasing observational skills. Although including a SLT component in a rater training program is reasonable, the most direct way to increase rater confidence is to impart skills relevant to doing evaluations, which is precisely what is being attempted in FOR training, RVT, or BOT.

In summary, five rater training content programs have been reviewed. It is recommended that RET no longer be used, and confidence-building rater training always be paired with another training goal. We now consider in what situations it is appropriate to employ any, or some combination, of the three remaining strategies (FOR training, RVT, and BOT).

Matching Training Goals and Rating Formats

Contingency approaches to rater training are not new (Feldman, 1986; Lee, 1985; Pulakos, 1984; Stamoulis & Hauenstein, 1993). At the simplest level, decisions about rater training should be based on the rating format used and the intended use of the appraisal data. Although there are many rating formats, the judgments called for are either frequency-based or subjective evaluations of performance. These judgments can be relative (ranking of employees) or absolute (judgments against an abstract standard). Given that most appraisals call for absolute judgments, the issue of ranking formats will be ignored.

Frequency-based formats include task checklists, behavioral observation scales, and productivity and quality indices. I also include Management by Objectives (MBO) in this category. Although MBO deals with reaching jointly established performance goals, these goals tend to be quantitative in nature. In that sense, MBO deals with the frequency with which an employee achieves performance goals. In frequency-based formats, the quality of the evaluation depends on accurate memories or records of how often workers emit certain behaviors or accomplish certain outcomes. Subjective evaluations include such formats as graphic rating scales, behaviorally anchored rating scales, and mixed standard scales, where the quality of judgments depends on the accurate comparison of employee performance to abstract performance standards.

The second contingency dimension concerns the intended use of the appraisal data. Although there are potentially many organizational uses of appraisal data (see Murphy & Cleveland, 1995), the administrative-developmental dichotomy is used here. Examples of administrative decisions include pay decisions, promotions, and terminations. If the intended use of the appraisal data is developmental, then the goal of appraisal is to provide employees with useful feedback that will ultimately lead to performance improvements.

If the rating format factor (frequency versus subjective) and the intended use factor (administrative versus developmental) are crossed, then four situations are defined:

- *Frequency-Administrative.* Assuming the appraisal dimensions adequately capture the jobs, the training goal in this situation is to make the rater an accurate recorder of employee performance. Thus raters must understand the critical behaviors and outcomes associated with job performance (it is best if supervisors can do the job that is being evaluated), and must seek to remember or document how frequently employees emit critical behaviors and properly document outcomes. Observational training is the obvious choice. However, BOT contains two strategies, the strategy to monitor performance and to avoid observational errors, and the behavioral diary strategy. Although emphasizing both strategies is best, if there is little need to justify ratings to employees, then there is no great need to document behaviors. If justifications are not needed, the emphasis of BOT for the frequency-administrative situation can be on the first strategy of adequately sampling employee performance, documenting relevant outcomes, and avoiding observational errors.

- *Frequency-Developmental.* If the frequency format is being used for developmental purposes, then BOT remains the choice for training content. However, the emphasis should be on behavioral diary keeping. For example, Xerox recently replaced its subjective format system with an MBO system called Performance Feedback Process. This new system emphasizes coaching and development of employees, although raises are also based on the evaluations. As a result, managers are expected to monitor and record behavioral incidents related to the negotiated objectives. Effective feedback for such jobs will focus either on a more efficient and productive way to produce the desired outcomes or on instilling greater motivation in employees to do the job. Either way, the greater the documentation of the behavioral evidence, the more likely the supervisor will be effective at persuading employees about necessary changes.

• *Subjective-Administrative.* If graphic rating scales or other subjective rating formats are being used to make administrative decisions, then the concern is accurate differentiation among employees. The goal of RVT is most congruent with this situation. Given the lack of research on RVT, practitioners may be reluctant to use RVT, and instead opt for traditional RET. Those who make this choice should be careful not to use Bernardin and Pence's (1980) RET strategy—where "correct" and "incorrect" rating distributions are presented—this strategy tends to decrease rating accuracy. Rather, use Latham et al.'s (1975) RET presentation of rating errors (see Latham & Wexley, 1994, pp. 152–161) because it is more likely to increase rating accuracy.

• *Subjective-Developmental.* Of the four combinations of format and purpose, the subjective-developmental cell is by far the most challenging for rater training because the format and purpose are not well matched. Subjective dimensions tend to summarize performance across tasks. For example, evaluating someone on verbal communication skills or leadership skills reflects performance across the various tasks performed by the employee. The first requirement to use subjective formats effectively for development is that ratings accurately differentiate the strengths and deficiencies of each employee. Differentiation between employees is not important. FOR training is the most appropriate training content for this first requirement.

The problem, however, is that FOR training is unlikely to foster accurate memories of exactly what the employees did to deserve their ratings. Accurate ratings are not enough to foster employee development. That is, informing an employee that he or she has poor leadership skills does little to help the employee improve those leadership skills. The second requirement for using subjective formats effectively for development is accurate behavioral feedback. Behavioral information is needed to aid understanding of performance deficiencies and to facilitate behavioral strategies for changing performance. In this situation, FOR training should be supplemented with BOT (Bernardin & Buckley, 1981; Pulakos, 1986), with emphasis on the behavioral diary component of BOT.

Issues That Complicate Contingency Decisions

Examination of the contingency model presented in the previous section suggests that rater training decisions are rather simple. If the contingencies were that straightforward in organizational settings, then the only issue would be an organization's level of commitment to rater training. Obviously, choices are not usually that simple because the contingencies are not that clear. Organizations often expect appraisal systems to accomplish goals related to both administrative decisions and employee development (Kane & Lawler, 1979; Ostroff, 1993), as is the case with Xerox's Performance Feedback Process. For this situation, within a given format, the recommended contents of training for both administration and development could be combined into one training program.

For example, if a frequency format was used for both administrative decisions and development, then BOT could be used with an equal focus on monitoring employees and diary keeping. If subjective formats are intended for both administrative and developmental purposes, then training is more complex. A hybrid accuracy-training program could be used that incorporates aspects of RVT into FOR training. For example, once the practice ratings are rendered, the quantitative feedback could be given twice. The first time could use FOR feedback, where the focus is on discrepancies between the practice rating and target scores within each ratee. The second review could use RVT feedback, where discrepancies are examined in terms of accurate distinctions among the different ratees on each dimension. This hybrid accuracy training could then be supplemented with BOT. Although such a training program can be developed, perhaps it is asking too much of raters to accomplish all these goals.

Rater training is more manageable if an organization has a single purpose for the use of appraisal data, even if frequency and subjective formats are both used to evaluate a job. The use of mixed formats appears common, given Bretz et al.'s (1992) report that

MBO (a frequency-oriented format) is the most popular format, but that MBO is often supplemented with graphic rating scales (a subjective format). For example, the performance appraisal system at Chase Manhattan Bank is based on MBO, subjective ratings of a general set of competencies (for example, "conceptual skills," "administrative skills," and "communications/interpersonal skills"), and subjective ratings on core organizational values (for example, "teamwork," "quality," and "customer focus"). If the purpose of appraisal is administrative, then BOT and RVT readily can be combined in a training program. Similarly, if the formats are mixed and the purpose of appraisal is developmental, then the combination of BOT and FOR training will work best.

Another complication for decisions about rater training is the extent to which appraisal systems are tailored to particular jobs and job families. Rater training is easiest when the supervisors are all being trained to use the same appraisal system. Complexity increases significantly when managers are expected to evaluate different jobs using different appraisal forms. BOT and RVT, with less emphasis on performance standards, are easier to adapt in this situation than FOR training. Developing comprehensive performance standards, rating practice stimuli, and the target scores needed for FOR training would be a daunting task if many different forms existed for many different jobs. Furthermore, if administrative decisions are to be made from the appraisal data generated from different rating forms, then the conversion of appraisal data to a common measurement scale that allows direct comparisons among employees is a problem. Rater training will have to address this unless the human resource department does this activity.

In closing, the choice of training content is simple if there is only one appraisal purpose and one universal format. In general, rater training is easier and less costly when using frequency-based scales or when ratings are used for administrative decisions. As multiple formats or multiple purposes are introduced, then effective rater training requires greater resources. The most challenging training situation is when subjective ratings are used, where dimensions vary by job, and ratings are used for both administration and development.

Other Rater Training Issues

To this point, several relevant issues have been avoided because there is a lack of research and understanding necessary to make strong recommendations, or these issues represent a "wish list" of points to consider in the future. Space limitations prevent an elaborate discussion of these issues. Nonetheless, they will be mentioned for completeness.

Motivation to Rate Accurately

Except for the self-leadership approach to rater training, none of the training programs mentioned above make assumptions about rater motivation (Banks & Murphy, 1985), friendship bias (Kingstrom & Mainstone, 1985), or resisting upward influence attempts (Wayne & Ferris, 1990). Longenecker et al. (1987) described performance evaluation as a political process, and gave insights into how managers inflate or deflate ratings in order to justify merit raises or to facilitate the social environment. (See Chapter Five in this volume for more extensive discussion.) This is not surprising given that managers view fairness, not accuracy, as the most important appraisal issue (Bretz et al., 1992).

The political nature of performance appraisal is irrefutable, as is the fact that raters vary in their motivation to conduct evaluations. The relevant issue here is what can be done in rater training to counteract the politicization or facilitate rater motivation. Training modules addressing these issues can readily be integrated in rater training programs. For example, the TVA 360-degree rater training program treats friendship bias as a type of rating error in the RET component of training.

Dealing with this problem through rater training is not as effective as holding raters accountable. For example, at AT&T, supervisors evaluating managers and professional employees meet with other peer supervisors to review initial evaluations. The role of the peer supervisors is to challenge other supervisors to provide evidence that justifies the evaluation. Higher-level managers also review the evaluations. The AT&T process of holding raters accountable is likely to do far more to limit politicization and facilitate rater motivation than any rater training program. If raters are held accountable for how well they conduct performance evaluations, the quality of the rating data improves (Mero & Motowidlo, 1995; Salvemini, Reilly, & Smither, 1993). Yet Bretz et al. (1992) reported that only one-quarter of organizations make any attempt to hold raters accountable, and such attempts are usually minimal.

Rating Ability

Raters differ in their ability to rate accurately. Rater intelligence (Borman, 1979), beliefs about human nature (Wexley and Youtz, 1985), beliefs in how performance behaviors go together (Hauenstein & Alexander, 1991), and experience (Zalesny & Highhouse, 1992) have all been shown to relate to rating accuracy. Individual differences have two implications for rating and rater training. First there is the issue of identifying raters most likely to be in need of training. For example, Bernardin and Buckley (1981) proposed that FOR training should be targeted toward raters with idiosyncratic standards, but this suggestion is virtually ignored (Hauenstein & Foti, 1989; Stamoulis & Hauenstein, 1993).

Perhaps more interesting is the issue of retraining and coaching managers. Managers typically receive rater training only when a new evaluation system is implemented (Bretz et al., 1992). Given that raters are likely to vary in their ability to rate employees, organizations may benefit from a more focused training and coaching intervention for those managers who are assessed as not doing well at evaluating employees. This issue again strikes at holding raters accountable. If part of the supervisory evaluation process deals with how well the supervisor does at evaluating employees, then poorly performing supervisors can be identified and improving these skills can become part of the development goals for these supervisors.

Training Subordinates

Bretz et al. (1992) reported that ratees receive virtually no training about the appraisal process. Hauenstein and Foti (1989) demonstrated that supervisors and subordinates differ in terms of performance standards, especially in terms of what constitutes poor performance. They argued that rater training should be extended to include training ratees in the performance appraisal process. The emphasis of such training would be to ensure that employees understand the performance standards used in training supervisors.

The growing exception to the lack of ratee training is in the multirater feedback rating systems. However, training for multirater systems tends to focus on preparing ratees to receive feedback as opposed to conveying performance standards.

Summary of Training Raters to Make Accurate Evaluations

Table 11.1 summarizes the five training content programs presented here. Examining Table 11.1 allows comparisons of the different learning goals, nature of the feedback given for practice rating exercises, and situations where each program is recommended. The two aspects of Table 11.1 that I would emphasize are the recommendation that BOT be used any time evaluations are done for the purpose of development and that content programs can be merged based on the situation. In closing this section, it is important to remember that rater training is limited in terms of solving problems associated with performance appraisal systems. If an organization does not invest in the development of a fair system, does not send unambiguous messages about the benefits of fair and accurate ratings, and does not hold raters accountable for the appraisal process, then what realistic benefits can be expected of a rater training program? Finally, although determining content of the rater training program is important, the structure of rater training may well be more critical. Whatever content is used, designers of rater training programs should strive to include practice rating activities and provide feedback on practice ratings.

Training to Give Feedback

In this age of empowerment of workers (Cascio, 1995), there appears to be a growing consensus that feedback to employees has a high probability of ultimately improving performance. Examples of research that facilitate this belief include the virtually universal finding that goal setting works (Locke & Latham, 1990), the notion that employees are active seekers of feedback (Ashford, 1989; Ashford & Cummings, 1983), and early successes with 360-degree feedback (Smither et al., 1995). The reality is that the likelihood of a feedback intervention working in an organization is far less

Table 11.1. Summary of Rater Training Content Programs.

Program	Training Program Goal	Nature of Feedback	Recommended Uses
RET	Improve rating accuracy by training raters to avoid rating errors.	Qualitative feedback that indicates the extent to which practice ratings are free from rating errors.	Not recommended because rating errors may say little about rating accuracy.
FOR	Provide accurate ratings of each employee on each performance dimension.	Quantitative feedback that allows for assessing accuracy of practice ratings. Qualitative feedback that justifies practice ratings in relation to performance standard.	When using subjective scales for developmental purposes.
RVT	Provide accurate distinctions among employees.	Quantitative feedback that allows assessment of accuracy of practice ratings. Qualitative feedback that compares performance across employees.	When using subjective scales for administrative purposes.
BOT	Improve rating accuracy by improving observational skills.	Qualitative feedback that focuses on the accuracy of memories or recording of performance incidents.	When using frequency-based scales or when ratings are used for developmental purposes.
SLT	Increase rater confidence in ability to evaluate employees.	Not applicable.	Use in conjunction with other rater training programs.

Note: RET = Rater Error Training, FOR = Frame-of-Reference Training, RVT = Rater Variability Training, BOT = Behavioral Observation Training, SLT = Self-Leadership Training than certain. Dorfman et al. (1986) found that appraisal feedback had no effect on performance evaluations one year later. On a broader scale, a comprehensive review of feedback intervention research by Kluger and DeNisi (1996) reported performance decrements in approximately one-third of the studies.

In contrast to the rater training literature, there is no systematic body of evaluation research on training raters to give feedback. The literature abounds with practical recommendations based on collections of empirical findings from feedback-related literature and insights of practitioners published in books and trade journals. For example, the *Successful Manager's Handbook* (Davis, Skube, Hellervik, Gebelein, & Sheard, 1996) recommends that the person providing the feedback explain the purpose of the feedback, establish trust, work to *really* understand the employee, invite the employee to shape the feedback process, be genuine, and treat feedback as information, not a value judgment. Specific organizational examples include Xerox's focus on active listening, problem resolution, and promoting ownership. The Lucent Technologies training program emphasizes employee participation, constructive attitude, mutual goal setting, problem solving, minimization of negative feedback, and allowing employees to have a voice in the process.

Feedback Intervention Theory

Although these recommendations are reasonable, there is no comparative research that indicates one learning goal or one strategy is more or less effective than the others. The major problem with the feedback literature has been the lack of a comprehensive theory to guide research. Most empirical feedback studies are based on Ilgen, Fisher, and Taylor's (1979) communication model of feedback. This model emphasizes characteristics of the person giving feedback (Fedor, Eder, & Buckley, 1989), message content (Ilgen & Moore, 1987) and characteristics of the people receiving feedback (Korsgaard, 1996). Unfortunately, Ilgen et al.'s communication model does not handle the dynamic nature of the feedback process well. The lack of critical variables in the model, such as employees' self-perceptions of how well they do the job (Albright & Levy, 1995), raises questions about the practical utility of this research.

At the same time, theoretical progress is being made in feedback research. London and Smither (1995) postulated a control theory model concerning reactions to self-other discrepancies in 360-degree feedback systems. On a more general level, Kluger and DeNisi (1996) proposed a general feedback intervention theory (FIT) that deals specifically with the explanation of why feedback interventions succeed or fail. Simplifying FIT and phrasing it in work-related terms, discrepancies between feedback and employees' perceptions of how well they perform the job are fundamental. Similar to goal setting, FIT is predicated on the notion that workers will strive to reduce differences between others' perceptions of how well they do the job and their own perceptions of job performance. What is different about FIT is the notion that employees can interpret feedback at three different levels—task, motivation, and self.

Task-level feedback focuses on learning how to perform the job better. For example, if an employee has problems making presentations, then task-level feedback might include suggestions to develop an introduction that grabs the audience's attention, formulate key statements that convey the main points, and provide a conclusion that gives the audience a sense of closure. *Motivational feedback* focuses on exertion and direction of effort to perform the job. An example of motivational feedback is telling an employee to set work deadlines and to reward himself or herself for meeting these deadlines, or telling an employee to set aside time each day for planning activities. *Self-level* feedback deals with abstract, general statements regarding personal characteristics and tendencies as related to work. For example, telling an employee that he or she is not a team player or that he or she needs greater interpersonal impact in team situations.

FIT postulates that task-level and motivational feedback are more likely to succeed, whereas self-level feedback is more likely to fail or lead to performance decrements. Task and motivational feedback provide specific strategies for improving performance. Self-level feedback by itself is not as helpful in that it does not provide strategies for improvement. To improve performance based on self-level feedback, an employee must develop task and motivational strategies on his or her own. Kluger and DeNisi argue that this is unlikely. At the self level, negative feedback is likely to threaten self-esteem and generate feelings of incompetence. In the face of such negative feelings, an employee is more likely to discount the feedback, avoid the task, or lower performance expectations.

FIT is a powerful framework from which to examine recommendations for rater feedback training in that most are consistent with FIT. There are many recommendations that guard against the use of self-level feedback, including prescriptions to avoid personality issues, to be supportive, to be nonevaluative, to have more concern about the recipient than yourself, to focus on the changeable, to avoid attempts to change too much too quickly, and to maintain a pleasant atmosphere (Burke, Weitzel, & Weir, 1978; Blanchard, 1996; Dorfman et al., 1986; Fowler, 1996). All these recommendations are intended to prevent the recipient from processing feedback in relation to his or her self-image as a success or a failure.

Many other recommendations foster the use of task and motivational feedback. Examples of such recommendations include the use of specific and difficult goals, discussion and resolution of barriers to job performance, discussion of ways to improve job performance, focus on changeable behaviors, and taking a problem-solving approach to effective coaching (Burke et al., 1978; Dorfman et al., 1986; Latham & Wexley, 1994). The use of these recommendations will facilitate strategies for improving job performance.

Procedural Fairness

Although FIT potentially explains the effectiveness of recommendations for providing feedback, there is one category of prescriptions that resides outside the explanatory power of FIT. Most lists of feedback recommendations make reference to providing a clear reason for conducting the interview, encouraging ratee participation in the discussions, and giving employees a voice in the process (Burke et al., 1978; Dorfman et al., 1986; Latham & Wexley, 1994). These recommendations foster perceptions of procedural fairness in ratees. (See Chapter Six in this volume for more extensive discussion.) Performance appraisal is a popular topic in the procedural justice literature. One of the strongest and most consistent findings is that participation, that is, having a voice in the feedback process, is related to both perceptions of fairness (Greenberg, 1986; Landy, Barnes, & Murphy, 1978) and satisfaction (Dipboye & de Pontbriand, 1981). Voice reflects trust in the opinions and abilities of employees, and enhances ratees' opportunities to influence decisions (Folger & Greenberg, 1985).

Rater Training in Multirater Feedback Systems

Multirater systems are the exception to the previously mentioned point that ratees are not trained. However, most multirater systems typically do little training to increase the accuracy of ratings, regardless of the source. Instead, training in 360-degree feedback systems emphasizes preparing the ratees to receive their feedback. Practical concerns often dictate that ratees are simply given workbooks that provide formats and suggestions for feedback meetings, and listings of internal and external resources tied to the targeted skill areas (Bracken, 1994). In contrast, internal and external facilitators often are used to prepare ratees for feedback, even to the point of having an external consultant present when individuals receive peer feedback.

Beyond dealing with the nuts and bolts of the feedback forms, the intention of this training is to break down resistance to accepting feedback. For example, in Chase Manhattan Bank's feedback workshop there is a facilitated discussion of the utility of feedback information. After employees receive their feedback booklets, facilitators are given discretion to pair employees to discuss reactions to their feedback reports, or even to discuss reactions to feedback using the Kübler-Ross model of the grief process (shock followed by anger, followed by rejection, followed by acceptance). Finally, there is discussion about seeking clarification and more feedback. Guidelines are given for this feedback-seeking activity (for example, solicit feedback on other's turf, use open-ended questions, and carefully monitor your nonverbal behaviors).

Multirater systems clearly form an area where practice is moving much faster than research (London & Smither, 1995). However, drawing on FIT, multirater training is consistent with the goals of avoiding threats to self-esteem and facilitating feedback processing at the motivational or task level.

Recommendations for Feedback Training

In conclusion, there is no evaluative research in feedback training upon which to base recommendations about specific interventions. However, with the introduction of FIT, it is likely that better

436 PERFORMANCE APPRAISAL

understanding will soon follow concerning factors that affect feed-back intervention effectiveness. Although specific content recom-mendations cannot be made, it is clear that three general principles should guide the development of rater training to provide feed-back. First, training activities should discourage the use of self-level feedback. If self-level statements are made, they should be accom-panied immediately by motivational or task-level feedback. Second, training activities should teach employees how to develop and de-liver motivational and task-level feedback. Third, training activities should emphasize fairness in the process and allowing employees to have a voice. These three principles should be used whether training managers to give feedback in a traditional rating system or a 360-degree feedback system.

In terms of designing training activities to reinforce these prin-ciples, a behavioral modeling program is well suited to the matter at hand. The previously mentioned Living the Values exercise from the Chase Manhattan Bank training program is a simple example of behavioral modeling. The manager-subordinate interaction that trainees evaluate is that of a feedback meeting. Through discus-sion of the video, trainees gain understanding of effective tech-niques to model and ineffective behaviors to avoid when giving feedback. From a design perspective, it would be a straightforward project to develop a series of modeling videotapes (along with as-sociated learning points) and trainee role-plays that could be done during training.

Final Thoughts

The view of performance appraisal is changing rapidly in organiza-tional settings because the performance management movement is redefining the performance evaluation process. Organizations are less likely to view performance appraisal as a yearly activity for which raters have little incentive. Instead, the performance management perspective is that performance appraisal is a formal supervisor ac-tivity embedded in the larger context of coaching performance from day to day (see Davis et al., 1996; Day, 1989; Schneier, 1989). From this viewpoint, rater training, especially for providing feedback, be-comes less of a performance appraisal issue and more of a manage-ment development issue.

Latham and Wexley (1994) use the example of an athletic coach to drive home this idea. Any coach who waited to give feedback until after the season would probably be fired in short order. Coaching is an ongoing activity that requires informal evaluation and feedback within fairly short performance cycles. If managers openly discuss daily performance issues, then the yearly evaluation is little more than a formality. Although training employees in terms of performance management is a broader issue, formal rater training is consistent with the performance management perspective in that it reinforces the day-to-day nature of monitoring performance and providing feedback.

In closing, here is a summary of the many recommendations that have been given throughout this chapter. In terms of training for rating accuracy, the more important prescriptions include the need to structure training programs to include performance dimension training, practice ratings, and feedback on practice ratings, and the point that traditional rater error training is not theoretically justified and its usage should therefore stop. In addition, it is desirable to promote greater utilization of rater accuracy training and behavioral observation programs, and to make sure that rater training programs are consistent with the rating format and purpose of the appraisal.

For feedback rater training, recommendations were less specific given the paucity of evaluative research. Feedback intervention theory (Kluger & DeNisi, 1996) was used as a theoretical model from which to organize the feedback literature. It was concluded that feedback training should always orient ratees toward task-level and motivational solutions to performance problems and attempt to minimize ratee interpretation of feedback in terms of self-images of success and failure. Furthermore, raters should be trained to encourage participation from ratees to facilitate perceptions of procedural justice. These recommendations for feedback training apply equally to traditional rater training systems and 360-degree feedback systems.

References

Albright, M. D., & Levy, P. E. (1995). The effects of source credibility and performance rating discrepancy on reactions to multiple raters. *Journal of Applied Social Psychology, 25,* 577–600.

Ashford, S. J. (1989). Self-assessments in organizations: A literature review and integrative model. In L. L. Cummings & B. M. Staw (Eds.), *Research in organizational behavior: Vol. 11* (pp. 133–174). Greenwich, CT: JAI Press.

Ashford, S. J., & Cummings, L. L. (1983). Feedback as an individual resource: Personal strategies of creating information. *Organizational Behavior and Human Performance, 32,* 370–398.

Athey, T. R., & McIntyre, R. M. (1987). Effect of rater training on rater accuracy: Levels of processing theory and social facilitation theory perspectives. *Journal of Applied Psychology, 72,* 567–572.

Banks, C. G., & Murphy, K. R. (1985). Toward narrowing the research-practice gap in performance appraisal. *Personnel Psychology, 38,* 335–345.

Barrett, G. V., & Kernan, M. C. (1987). Performance appraisal and terminations: A review of court decisions since *Brito* v. *Zia* with implications for personnel practices. *Personnel Psychology, 40,* 489–503.

Bernardin, H. J. (1978). Effects of rater training on leniency and halo errors in student ratings of instructors. *Journal of Applied Psychology, 63,* 301–308.

Bernardin, H. J., & Beatty, R. W. (1984). *Performance appraisal: Assessing human behavior at work.* Boston: Kent.

Bernardin, H. J., & Buckley, M. R. (1981). Strategies in rater training. *Academy of Management Review, 6,* 205–212.

Bernardin, H. J., & Pence, E. C. (1980). Effects of rater training: Creating new response sets and decreasing accuracy. *Journal of Applied Psychology, 65,* 60–66.

Blanchard, K. (1996). Giving and receiving feedback. *Manage, 48,* 31–32.

Borman, W. C. (1975). Effects of instructions to avoid halo error on reliability and validity of performance evaluation ratings. *Journal of Applied Psychology, 60,* 556–560.

Borman, W. C. (1979). Format and training effects on rating accuracy and rater errors. *Journal of Applied Psychology, 64,* 410–421.

Bracken, D. W. (1994). Straight talk about multirater feedback. *Training and Development, 48,* 44–51.

Bretz, R. D., Jr., Milkovich, G. T., & Read, W. (1992). The current state of performance appraisal research and practice: Concerns, directions, and implications. *Journal of Management, 18,* 321–352.

Burke, R. J., Weitzel, W., & Weir, T. (1978). Characteristics of effective employee performance review and development interviews: Replication and extension. *Personnel Psychology, 31,* 903–919.

Cascio, W. F. (1995). Whither industrial and organizational psychology in a changing world of work? *American Psychologist, 50,* 928–939.

Davis, B. L., Skube, C. J., Hellervik, L. W., Gebelein, S. H., & Sheard, J. L. (1996). *Successful manager's handbook: Development suggestions for today's mangers*. Minneapolis, MN: Personnel Decisions Inc.

Day, D. (1989, August). Performance management year-round. *Personnel,* pp. 43–45.

Day, D. V., & Sulsky, L. M. (1995). Effects of frame-of-reference training and information configuration on memory organization and rating accuracy. *Journal of Applied Psychology, 80,* 158–167.

Dipboye, R. L., & de Pontbriand, R. (1981). Correlates of employee reactions to performance appraisals and appraisal systems. *Journal of Applied Psychology, 66,* 248–251.

Dorfman, P. W., Stephan, W. G., & Loveland, J. (1986). Performance appraisal behaviors: Supervisor perceptions and subordinate reactions. *Personnel Psychology, 39,* 579–597.

Fay, C. H., & Latham, G. P. (1982). Effects of training and rater scale on rating errors. *Personnel Psychology, 35,* 105–116.

Fedor, D. B., Eder, R. W., & Buckley, M. R. (1989). The contributory effects of supervisor intentions on subordinate feedback responses. *Organizational Behavior and Human Decision Processes, 44,* 396–414.

Feldman, J. M. (1986). Instrumentation and training for performance appraisal: A perceptual-cognitive viewpoint. In K. N. Rowland & G. R. Ferris (Eds.), *Research in personnel and human resources management: Vol. 4* (pp. 45–99). Greenwich, CT: JAI Press.

Folger, R., & Greenberg, J. (1985). Procedural justice: An interpretive analysis of personnel systems. In K. N. Rowland & G. R. Ferris (Eds.), *Research in personnel and human resources management: Vol. 3* (pp. 141–183). Greenwich, CT: JAI Press.

Fowler, A. (1996). How to: Provide effective feedback. *People Management, 2,* 44–45.

Greenberg, J. (1986). Determinants of perceived fairness of performance evaluations. *Journal of Applied Psychology, 71,* 340–342.

Hauenstein, N. M. A. (1992). An information processing approach to leniency in performance judgments. *Journal of Applied Psychology, 77,* 485–493.

Hauenstein, N. M. A., & Alexander, R. A. (1991). Rating ability in performance judgments: The joint influence of implicit theories and intelligence. *Organizational Behavior and Human Decision Processes, 50,* 300–323.

Hauenstein, N. M. A., & Foti, R. J. (1989). From laboratory to practice: Neglected issues in implementing frame-of-reference rater training. *Personnel Psychology, 42,* 359–378.

Hedge, J. W., & Kavanaugh, M. J. (1988). Improving the accuracy of performance evaluations: Comparison of three methods of performance appraiser training. *Journal of Applied Psychology, 73,* 68–73.

Heneman, R. L., & Wexley, K. N. (1983). The effects of delay in rating and amount of information observed on performance rating accuracy. *Academy of Management Journal, 26,* 677–686.

Ilgen, D. R. (1993). Performance appraisal accuracy: An elusive and sometimes misguided goal. In H. Schuler, J. L. Farr, & M. Smith (Eds.), *Personnel selection and assessment: Individual and organizational perspectives* (pp. 235–252). Hillsdale, NJ: Erlbaum.

Ilgen, D. R., Fisher, C. D., & Taylor, S. M. (1979). Consequences of individual feedback on behavior in organization. *Journal of Applied Psychology, 64,* 347–371.

Ilgen, D. R., & Moore, C. F. (1987). Types and choices of performance feedback. *Journal of Applied Psychology, 72,* 401–406.

Kane, J. S., & Lawler, E. E., III. (1979). Performance appraisal effectiveness: Its assessment and determinants. In B. Staw (Ed.), *Research in organizational behavior: Vol. 1* (pp. 425–478). Greenwich, CT: JAI Press.

Kingstrom, P. O., & Mainstone, L. E. (1985). An investigation of rater-ratee acquaintance and rater bias. *Academy of Management, 28,* 641–653.

Kluger, A. N., & DeNisi, A. S. (1996). Effects of feedback intervention on performance: A historical review, a meta-analysis, and a preliminary feedback intervention theory. *Psychological Bulletin, 119,* 254–284.

Komaki, J. L. (1986). Toward effective supervision. *Journal of Applied Psychology, 71,* 270–279.

Korsgaard, M. A. (1996). The impact of self-appraisals on reactions to feedback from others: The role of self-enhancement and self-consistency concerns. *Journal of Organizational Behavior, 17,* 301–311.

Landy, F. J., Barnes, J., & Murphy, K. (1978). Correlates of perceived fairness and accuracy of performance appraisals. *Journal of Applied Psychology, 63,* 751–754.

Latham, G. P., & Wexley, K. N. (1994). *Increasing productivity through performance appraisal* (2nd ed.). Reading MA: Addison Wesley Longman.

Latham, G. P., Wexley, K. N., & Purcell, E. D. (1975). Training managers to minimize rating errors in the observation of behavior. *Journal of Applied Psychology, 60,* 550–555.

Lee, C. (1985). Increasing performance appraisal effectiveness: Matching task types, appraisal process, and rater training. *Academy of Management Review, 10,* 322–331.

Locke, E., & Latham, G. (1990). *A theory of goal setting and task feedback.* Upper Saddle River, NJ: Prentice Hall.

London, M., & Smither, J. W. (1995). Can multisource feedback change perceptions of goal accomplishment, self-evaluations, and performance-related outcomes? Theory-based applications and directions for research. *Personnel Psychology, 48,* 803–839.

Longenecker, C. O., Sims, H. P., & Gioia, D. A. (1987). Behind the mask: The politics of employee appraisal. *Academy of Management Executive, 1,* 183–193.

Maroney, P. M., & Buckley, M. R. (1992). Does research in performance appraisal influence the practice of performance appraisal? Regretfully not! *Public Personnel Management, 21,* 185–196.

McIntyre, R. M., Smith, D. E., & Hassett, C. E. (1984). Accuracy of performance ratings as affected by rater training and perceived purpose of rating. *Journal of Applied Psychology, 69,* 147–156.

Mero, N. P., & Motowidlo, S. J. (1995). Effects of rater accountability on the accuracy and favorability of performance ratings. *Journal of Applied Psychology, 80,* 517–524.

Murphy, K. R., & Balzer, W. K. (1989). Rating errors and rating accuracy. *Journal of Applied Psychology, 74,* 619–624.

Murphy, K. R., & Cleveland, J. N. (1995). *Understanding performance appraisal: Social, organizational, and goal-based perspectives.* Thousand Oaks, CA: Sage.

Murphy, K. R., Herr, B. M., Lockhart, M. C., & Maguire, E. (1986). Evaluating the performance of paper people. *Journal of Applied Psychology, 71,* 654–661.

Napier, N. K., & Latham, G. P. (1986). Outcome expectancies of people who conduct performance appraisals. *Personnel Psychology, 39,* 827–837.

Neck, C. P., Stewart, G. L., & Manz, C. C. (1995). Thought self-leadership as a framework for enhancing the performance of performance appraisers. *Journal of Applied Behavioral Science, 331,* 278–302.

Ostroff, C. (1993). Rater perceptions, satisfaction, and performance ratings. *Journal of Occupational and Organizational Psychology, 66,* 345–356.

Pulakos, E. D. (1984). A comparison of rater training programs: Error training and accuracy training. *Journal of Applied Psychology, 69,* 581–588.

Pulakos, E. D. (1986). The development of training programs to increase accuracy. *Organizational Behavior and Human Decision Processes, 38,* 76–91.

Salvemini, N. T., Reilly, R. R., & Smither, J. W. (1993). The influence of rater motivations on assimilation effects and accuracy of performance ratings. *Organizational Behavior and Human Decision Processes, 55,* 41–60.

Schneier, C. E. (1989). Capitalizing on performance management, recognition, and reward systems. *Compensation and Benefits Review, 21,* 20–30.

Smith, D. E. (1986). Training programs for performance appraisal: A review. *Academy of Management Review, 11,* 22–40.

Smither, J. W., London, M., Vasilopoulos, N. L., Reilly, R. R., Millsap, R. E., & Salvemini, N. T. (1995). An examination of the effects of an upward feedback program over time. *Personnel Psychology, 48,* 1–34.

Stamoulis, D. T., & Hauenstein, N. M. A. (1993). Rater training and rating accuracy: Training for dimensional accuracy versus training for ratee differentiation. *Journal of Applied Psychology, 78,* 994–1003.

Sulsky, L. M., & Day, D. V. (1992). Frame-of-reference training and cognitive categorization: An empirical investigation of rater memory issues. *Journal of Applied Psychology, 77,* 501–510.

Sulsky, L. M., & Day, D. V. (1994). Effects of frame-of-reference training on rater accuracy under alternative time delays. *Journal of Applied Psychology, 79,* 535–543.

Tennessee Valley Authority University. (1995). *360-degree feedback rater training.* Knoxville, TN: Author.

Thorton, G. C., III, and Zorich, S. (1980). Training to improve observer accuracy. *Journal of Applied Psychology, 65,* 351–354.

Wayne, S. J., & Ferris, G. R. (1990). Influence tactics, affect, and exchange quality in supervisor-subordinate interactions: A laboratory experiment and field study. *Journal of Applied Psychology, 75,* 487–499.

Wexley, K. N., & Youtz, M. A. (1985). Rater beliefs about others: Their effects on rating errors and rater accuracy. *Journal of Occupational Psychology, 58,* 265–275.

Woehr, D. J. (1994). Understanding frame-of-reference training: The impact of training on the recall of performance information. *Journal of Applied Psychology, 77,* 525–534.

Woehr, D. J., & Huffcutt, A. I. (1994). Rater training for performance appraisal: A quantitative review. *Journal of Occupational and Organizational Psychology, 67,* 189–205.

Zalesny, M. D., & Highhouse, S. (1992). Accuracy in performance evaluations. *Organizational Behavior and Human Decision Processes, 51,* 22–50.

PART 3

Linking Appraisal to the Larger Human Performance System

CHAPTER 12

Linking Appraisals to Individual Development and Training

Paul Squires
Seymour Adler

With the rapid diffusion of technological innovations and the move toward a service economy, it is the quality of the people in the organization that gives companies the edge in a competitive marketplace. The development and retention of talent has become, for many companies, the key to survival. This will be particularly true in the difficult recruiting climate of the next decade, with a smaller labor pool of qualified employees in the prime age group, thirty to forty-five years old.

In light of continuous, rapid change, organizations are attempting to anticipate the skill requirements for future work and prepare their workforces. Effective performance in last year's environment may not be strongly predictive of next year's performance if the environment changes significantly. But it is often possible to evaluate, based on performance exhibited over the past year, the extent to which an employee already has the skills that will be required next year and to take action to ameliorate deficiencies before they affect future performance.

There is a growing appreciation for the "dual nature" of the performance appraisal process first identified by Meyer, Kay, and French (1965) so long ago. Not only must an effective appraisal accurately evaluate past performance as an equitable basis for rewards, it should also guide future development, leverage existing strengths, and address skill deficiencies. This second function of the appraisal process is going to be more critical than ever in tomorrow's workplace.

Yet against this increasing need to link appraisal and employee development processes stands an imposing set of practical and theoretical challenges. The practical challenges include:

- *Time.* Development is an ongoing process, not a once-a-year event—and today's managers are already stretched.
- *Organizational support.* Managers operate in a business environment that emphasizes short-term performance. The payoff from development is not likely to have an impact on next-quarter profits.
- *Expertise.* Fairly sophisticated diagnostic and people-management skills are needed to provide constructive coaching—and these skills are not consistently considered in selecting managers.
- *Diagnostic tools.* Developmental planning requires appraisal processes that not only have sufficient construct validity but also have high levels of both inter- and intra-individual discriminability.
- *Developmental resources.* Training must be customized to address specific developmental needs in a cost-effective way.
- *HR planning.* Individual development must be linked to business strategy so that employees are prepared to meet tomorrow's challenges.

Along with these practical challenges and directly influencing practice there is a set of theoretical challenges that must be successfully addressed. Important theoretical challenges include:

- Better understanding of skill dimensions so as to define the constructs we seek to appraise and develop more vigorously. Are we measuring knowledge, skill, the aptitude to perform effectively in the future, expressive style, or personality traits? Are these attributes different from the term *competency*? Do constructs have to be defined differently for appraisal and development purposes?
- Better understanding of processes for skill development so as to determine the employee's stage of development for a particular skill. On what dimensions do novices and experts differ in

the way they perform a task? Which skills are malleable and which are fairly resistant to change in adult populations?

- Developing an adequate prescription based upon a diagnosis so as to identify cost-effective strategies for addressing developmental weaknesses.

- Applying a theory of instruction and effective instructional methodology for the prescription specified so as to deliver the right training at the right time to achieve maximum impact.

To what extent have human resource practitioners and industrial-organizational psychology researchers and theoreticians met these challenges and established an effective linkage between performance appraisal on one hand and employee development on the other? A review of the current state of appraisal practice and research leads us to a number of initial observations:

- Nearly all performance appraisals include professional and personal development sections but experience indicates that these items are rarely carefully tracked and followed to ensure implementation.

- There is a gap between research and practice. Within the field of industrial-organizational psychology, the focus has been almost exclusively on the validity or accuracy of appraisal ratings, and more recently on appraisal feedback. The most current textbook on performance appraisal (Cardy & Dobbins, 1994) thoroughly reviews the literature relevant to appraisal but includes nothing about how appraisal can be used to enhance employee skill. This is just as true of the practitioner literature. Typical of this phenomenon is a recent how-to article on performance management appearing in *HR Magazine* (Campbell & Garfinkel, 1996), which provides sound advice on measurement and feedback but makes no mention of subsequent development activity.

- We believe there have been significant advances in a number of areas of psychological research and theory that can help guide practice in leveraging appraisal as a tool to develop employees in the workplace. Some of these advances have occurred within the field of industrial and organizational psychology. Others have occurred in the study of personality and social psychology. In our view, the advances with the most far-reaching implications for appraisal and development have occurred in research conducted by experimental psychologists working in such areas as cognition, skill acquisition, and motivation and emotion.

From our perspective, the process of linking performance appraisal to employee development can be conceptualized as a special case of the broader psychology of diagnosis, intervention, and change. In this case, change at the level of the individual employee consists of learning. This view places the issue of linking appraisals and development within a well-established theoretical and empirical literature on the mental process models that mediate human learning (Newell, 1990).

In this chapter, we will first describe several attempts in world-class organizations to use appraisal for development. We will then introduce a concept from experimental and instructional psychology, the mental process model, and discuss how this model can help us think more systematically about the link between appraisal and employee development. We will selectively review psychological research and theory relevant to the mental process model that can guide future appraisal research and practice. We will describe steps for the creation of a mental model–based developmental appraisal. We will provide samples of mental model–based competency models that can be used to develop performance appraisals that provide diagnostic information and guide curriculum decisions. Finally, we will evaluate recent trends in human resource practice in the area of developmental appraisal in light of the model and associated research findings.

The State of Practice

As we noted earlier, most organizations—certainly the larger and more HR-sophisticated organizations—have long (that is, since the early 1970s) had sections for diagnosing developmental needs and creating developmental plans in their regular performance appraisal forms. In a few of these organizations, those plans are reviewed the following year, and the extent to which developmental plans have been implemented actually affects the next year's appraisal.

More recently, many of these larger organizations have embraced the strategy known as "competency modeling." In some of these firms, an entire Competency Modeling Unit has been created whose sole function is to define the dimensions required for effective performance in specific jobs or job families. Human resource magazines are filled with ads from vendors offering software that can help organizations identify relevant competencies from defined lists. Biannual conferences on competency modeling draw a thousand HR professionals or more. Using the term *competency* instead of *KSAOs* (knowledge, skills, abilities, and other characteristics) and the title *competency modeler* instead of *job analyst* has certainly enhanced the appeal—if not the substance—of this activity! A laudable outgrowth of this trend is that companies are applying a consistent set of competencies to select, appraise, and train.

Today, large organizations are increasingly conducting developmentally oriented appraisals outside the context of the regular supervisor appraisal process. What follows are a few current examples from world-class organizations:

• One electronics manufacturer recently installed a new developmental appraisal process as part of a reengineering initiative. An analysis of this organization's product cycle time process indicated that there were thirty-nine steps and approval points in the process and ten different job functions involved. This process was adhered to by some five hundred professional engineers. Process reengineering resulted in fewer steps and approval points. Changes were made to the content of jobs, that is, their duties and component tasks. Following the redesign, different combinations of skills were required for the remaining and revised job functions. The organization developed a paper-and-pencil, developmentally focused performance appraisal process that obtained ratings on skill dimensions to arrive at a skill gap analysis to aid in placing people in the newly redesigned jobs and determining the training needs of the engineers.

• A technology sales organization needed to prepare its sales force for a more competitive marketplace. The organization developed and implemented a developmentally oriented diagnostic appraisal aimed at measuring the competency model defined for the targeted sales jobs. The appraisal was developed and delivered as a two-hour structured interview and administered over the telephone to each salesperson by a two-person team comprising the interviewee's manager and an outside assessor (a doctoral or master's-level psychologist). The results were used by the manager and salesperson to create and implement an individual development plan that addressed the competency gaps identified by the appraisal. The final report contained courses and instructional suggestions for each of the areas of developmental need. Nearly two thousand salespeople participated in the diagnostic appraisal in a six-week period.

• A large computer company is preparing senior managers to champion organizational change into the next century. To appraise change leadership skill, the organization developed a four-hour simulation of a "year in the life" of a senior executive, with waves of restructuring and downsizing, emerging marketplace opportunities, and key staff additions and departures. In the course of the simulation, the executive's change leadership skill is appraised by a team of external assessors. The diagnosis is far more detailed than the typical skill appraisal and includes an analysis of competency strength and weakness for each type of change situation encountered. Following a feedback session discussing the results of the leadership appraisal, the manager works closely with an outside coach, implementing a six-month skill development plan. Developmental activities include formal training, standard resources (books, tapes, videos), and on-the-job action learning (experimentation and reflection).

These examples illustrate that major organizations are recognizing the value of systematic appraisal as a tool in the more effective deployment and development of staff. These organizations are creating detailed, behaviorally based appraisal tools, using different methods (such as paper and pencil, interview, and role-play), to focus specifically on gathering information for use in development. It is significant, though, that many of these organizations have created new processes for developmental appraisal outside the structure of the existing traditional, supervisor-driven performance appraisal system. This strategy may reflect an explicit or implicit recognition of the serious challenges in implementing an effective developmentally oriented appraisal process. In addition, even the best of these new processes make little use of emerging mental process models to guide the appraisal of factors underlying performance.

Diagnosis, Development, and the Mental Process Model

In linking appraisal and developmental planning, the appraisal is the diagnostic measurement event that must provide information to guide decisions about an individualized, prescriptive development plan. This is a fundamentally different application of appraisal than is usual in organizations. Diagnostic assessments are more commonly used in an educational setting such as an elementary or secondary school to make curricular decisions. The typical evaluation used in organizations focuses on a dichotomous decision: hire–no hire, promote–don't promote, train–don't train. Diagnostic assessment is more complex and extensive and must provide information that can be used to design an individualized development plan. Therefore these assessments are much more difficult to develop and validate and are critically dependent on the development and construct validity of a mental process model. Effective diagnostic assessment measures each of the components of the mental process model. However, appraisals used as a basis for employee development in organizations today are not based upon a well-articulated, validated mental process model.

A *mental process model* is a complete description of the psychological components of performance. A fully developed model specifies all the critical cognitive and social-emotional processes, and the interactions among these processes, that when functioning properly result in skilled performance. Most appraisals measure traitlike skill dimensions. For example, a typical appraisal contains rating scales for skill dimensions such as planning and organizing, coaching, decision making, and problem solving. But ratings on these competencies provide no information about *why* the ratee performed well or poorly—and these appraisals therefore have little diagnostic value. The assessment must answer the "why" question to be instructionally valuable.

For example, two employees with exactly the same poor rating for the problem-solving dimension may have very different developmental needs. One person may lack knowledge of problem-solving strategies and the other may lack self-confidence in problem-solving situations. On the positive side, the overall rating for the employees will indicate that neither can be depended upon to perform well on problem-solving tasks at this time. In a selection situation, this alone is important and sufficient information. But for the purposes of creating a development plan, more is needed than an overall skill dimension rating. For development, the two employees' assessments must diagnose different cognitive and emotional explanations for the overall performance to create developmental plans that reflect the true training and development needs. An appraisal designed on the basis of a properly specified mental process model will provide the necessary diagnostic information to create a development plan.

The notion of the mental process model has its origins in the work of Newell and Simon (1972), who laid out the framework for much of the research in cognitive psychology and information processing conducted during the following two decades. The "new look" stimulated by their work represented a shift from a trait- or abilities-based approach to human cognition to a process approach. This was a critical shift for those interested in diagnostic assessments and training. This shift, first apparent in research on human memory, yielded new information about mental process models and the components required for successful performance in different skill and knowledge domains.

Two important components of the mental process model are *knowledge structures* and *executive control processes.* Knowledge structures are the compiled facts, if-then relationships, taxonomies, rules, heuristics, techniques, and procedures that are learned through extensive direct experience and purposeful learning in a specific domain. Constructs similar or identical to the notion of knowledge structures include procedural knowledge, schema, scaffolding, scripts, tacit knowledge (Wagner & Sternberg, 1985), productions (Anderson, 1982), and thinking frames (Perkins, 1990). With learning, knowledge structures become larger, richer, and more interconnected. When addressing a problem, an experienced manager will analyze the situation more quickly, organize information into more sophisticated taxonomies, and solve the problem rapidly, often automatically, with little need for attentional resources. Understanding the knowledge structures underlying effective managerial problem-solving performance helps the appraiser more precisely identify existing weaknesses and suitable developmental strategies.

Executive control processes, by contrast, direct mental activity—the stream of consciousness. The functions of these processes include prioritization of mental tasks, searches of long-term memory for appropriate knowledge structures, selection of problem-solving strategies, allocation of attentional resources, goal setting, monitoring of progress toward goals, and start-task and stop-task decisions.

Researchers in recent years have learned much about the components of mental process models beyond knowledge structures and executive control processes (Brown, 1989; Newell, 1990). Constructs such as schema, heuristics, metacognitive strategies, attributional style, learning orientation, goal setting, and feedback, as well as of the impact of anxiety, worry, and stress on learning and performance, have been explored and their roles in theories of performance and instruction have been investigated. This literature provides useful direction for the development of appraisals and the practical design of training and development programs that are linked to appraisal.

Development plans must be based on the results of a valid diagnostic assessment. If the diagnostic assessment is based on an incorrectly specified mental process model, then the resulting development plan will be misguided. Figure 12.1 depicts the dependence of diagnostic assessment and of development planning on a mental process model. It illustrates that while the diagnostic assessment drives the creation of the development plan, they are both built on a valid mental process model.

Thus a fully specified mental process model is a complete description of the constructs or skill dimensions that are the targets of diagnostic assessment and the training. It contains a description of the cognitive and social-emotional components and constructs that make up the skill dimension as well as of the way they interact. A diagnostic assessment based upon a fully specified mental process model provides the information needed to create an individualized development plan. Such a diagnostic assessment can identify that (to return to the earlier example) the first employee's poor problem-solving performance was due to an incorrect knowledge structure and misdirected executive control processes, whereas the second performed poorly because problem-solving tasks created anxiety, which led to task-irrelevant mental ruminations that interfered with performance. Such an appraisal has actionable diagnostic value.

Figure 12.1. Importance of a Comprehensive, Valid Mental Process Model.

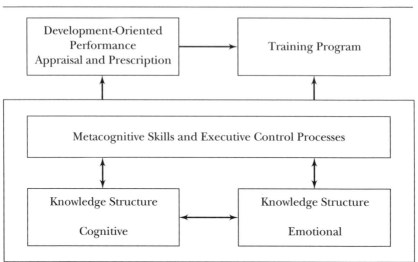

The Appraiser as Diagnostician

What are the responsibilities of the individual assigned to complete an appraisal if the goal of an appraisal is employee development? The requirements would include, of course, the valid differentiation among the employee's levels of skill across a number of critical competencies. However, as we have been arguing, this degree of differentiation would not be sufficient to provide a valid diagnostic assessment. Like a physician reviewing a patient's symptoms, the rater needs to identify the reasons underlying the employee's current level of skill on each critical dimension. This requires the rater to rely on relevant information to triangulate on potential underlying cognitive, emotional, and physical causes in order to arrive at a reasonable diagnosis. Moreover, diagnostic appraisal further requires an indication of the developmental strategies to which the employee is most likely to respond, or whether the skill deficiency is treatable at all.

Indeed, there is evidence that less diagnostically detailed appraisals are actually more susceptible to rater bias. For example, a recent field study by Varma, DeNisi, and Peters (1996) revisited the old question of whether performance appraisals are biased by the degree to which the appraiser likes the employee. They found that liking does in fact influence performance appraisals and that this influence is significantly stronger on ratings of traits than on ratings of specific task behaviors. Thus designing more discriminating appraisal forms may help appraisers generate more objective appraisals. But what are the appraiser skills that are needed for effective diagnosis?

The existing literature on rater training provides very limited guidance to organizations seeking to define and develop the rater skills required for diagnostic appraisals. Judging by the published literature (see Woehr & Huffcutt, 1994, for a review), most rater training consists of instruction on the evils of rating errors (halo, leniency, central tendency). This may reduce the errors that are the target of training at the expense of errors that are not stressed. Some training also focuses on providing raters with a mental model of the dimensions on which subordinate performance should be appraised and the evaluation standards (frames of reference) to be applied in providing an overall assessment of these dimensions. This enhances interrater consistency, though not intra- and interratee discriminability. Very rarely, again judging by the number of published studies, does training also seek to enhance observational skills. Yet sophisticated observational and diagnostic skills are needed to generate appraisals that are truly useful in development. What is needed here is a more detailed job analysis of the KSAOs required for diagnostic assessment as a guide to appraiser training practice and research.

Considering the Employee's Proficiency Level

There is an additional consideration when developing a diagnostic assessment. Diagnostic appraisals need to consider the proficiency level of the employee. Proficiency has been conceptualized as stages of learning (Anderson, 1982) and as the novice-master continuum.

Anderson (1982) described three stages of learning—declarative, procedural, and automaticity. According to Anderson's ACT model, skill acquisition begins with the learning of simple facts that must be rehearsed in working memory to be learned. This first stage of learning is called the *declarative* stage. During this stage, skill and knowledge are inert and not well integrated into existing knowledge structures. Performance using these skills and knowledge makes a large demand on attentional and general intellectual resources (Kanfer & Ackerman, 1988). Next, these facts are operated on by procedures; with sufficient repetition, the knowledge becomes proceduralized. This transition from the declarative knowledge stage is called knowledge compilation and it moves the learner to the *procedural* stage of learning. During the procedural stage, the learner performs more skillfully. Separate pieces of knowledge and procedures now operate as one and the new skills are integrated into existing knowledge structures. The skill is now more context sensitive and operates more quickly. Finally, when the skill is well practiced, it reaches the stage of *automaticity*—that is, it occurs automatically and in the appropriate context, with little need for attentional resources.

Differences in the mental process models of expert and nonexpert performers correspond to different stages of proficiency development. When employees learn a new skill domain, they act and think like novices. They possess novice mental process models. As their proficiency increases, they begin to act and think like experts as they develop expert mental process models.

Expert-novice comparisons entail careful analyses of the strategies, techniques, and thought processes used by experts and novices as they perform tasks. For example, researchers (Chi, Feltovich, & Glaser, 1981; Baker, 1989) have investigated differences between expert chess players and novices, novice and expert physics students, and superior and less skilled readers. Results indicate that experts think in terms of *sets* of actions or ideas; their ability to remember and reconstruct the information is aided by a more complex and deeper approach used for input processing. They are able to move from big picture thinking to detail thinking and back continually during task performance.

Wagner and Sternberg (1985) examined a different class of knowledge structures and executive control processes across proficiency levels. They studied the "tacit knowledge" that distinguished successful managers and faculty members from less successful managers and faculty members. While they did not explicitly describe successful managers as experts and less successful managers as novices, the approach they used was very similar to that used in expert-novice research. They found that expert managers and faculty members were better than novice managers at managing themselves, managing their careers, and managing others. Sternberg and Wagner provide a list of behaviors and rules of thumb that characterize a manager with tacit knowledge (see Exhibit 12.1).

These studies and others identify specific knowledge structures, executive control processes, and techniques stored in long-term memory, which experts use when learning or solving problems. To learn successfully and achieve higher levels of performance, novices must learn to behave cognitively like experts. Incorporating these proficiency concepts within a diagnostic appraisal requires the appraiser to specify for each employee the stage of learning (declarative, procedural, or automaticity) for a given level of competence (novice-master) for a given skill dimension. Equipped with this diagnosis, a

**Exhibit 12.1. Rules of Thumb
for Managerial Tacit Knowledge.**

I. Componential
   A. Metacomponents
      1. Recognizing the existence of a problem
         a. Find ways to recognize problems as they arise before they become serious.
      2. Defining a problem
         a. Know what the problem is before you tackle it.
         b. Find out whether others in authority agree with the way you have defined the problem.
         c. Make sure the level at which you define the problem can lead to a solution.
         d. If the problem seems insoluble, try reformulating it.
      3. Selecting a strategy for problem solution
         a. Formulate strategies with built-in flexibility.
         b. Get approval of the strategy from those who matter so they don't try to sabotage it later.
         c. Make sure the people who should know, do know.
      4. Allocating resources
         a. Make sure the time you put in is commensurate with the importance of the problem.
         b. Make sure the company resources you put in are commensurate with the importance of the problem.

Exhibit 12.1. Rules of Thumb
for Managerial Tacit Knowledge, cont'd.

5. Solution monitoring
   a. Step back on occasion to take stock of the situation.
   b. Seek hard, concrete data regarding how the solution is going.
   c. Set up multiple independent tests to see how the solution is going.
   d. Monitor results frequently enough to redirect if you need to.
6. Solution evaluating
   a. Have a built-in evaluation procedure for the strategy.
   b. Make sure others will accept the tests as valid.
7. Using feedback
   a. Seek out feedback on your performance from those who matter.
   b. Evaluate the utility of the feedback you receive.
   c. Selectively use the feedback you receive.
B. Performance Components
   1. Balance short-term losses or inefficiencies against long-term gains, and vice versa.
   2. Make sure you hear what someone is saying.
   3. Take a second look at first impressions.
   4. Consider doing the opposite.
   5. Seek to understand things from other points of view
   6. Follow through on your commitments.
   7. Know when to let people off the hook.
   8. Learn from your mistakes and those of others.
   9. Use humor to defuse difficult situations.
   10. Know when to admit your mistakes.
   11. Know the capabilities, interests, and values of those with whom you are working.
   12. Figure out ways to turn crises into opportunities.
   13. Know when to wait and when not to wait.
   14. Accept criticism nondefensively.
   15. Admit when you don't know something.
   16. Know when to seek help.
   17. Know whom you can and whom you cannot trust.
   18. Know when and how to criticize.
   19. Know what people expect of you.
   20. Know when to give up and when not to give up.

Exhibit 12.1. Rules of Thumb
for Managerial Tacit Knowledge, cont'd.

21. Know the weaknesses as well as the strengths of your positions.
22. Find ways of getting around your weaknesses, such as delegating.
23. Know what you need to know and what you don't need to know.
24. Let others save face.
25. Treat others the way you would like to be treated.

  C. Knowledge-Acquisition Components
    1. Selective encoding
      a. When barraged with information, ask yourself what the important parts are.
    2. Selective combination
      a. Put together disparate sources of information.
    3. Selective comparison
      a. Draw upon past experience, but recognize its limitations as well as its domains of generalization.

II. Experiential Subtheory
  A. Coping with novelty
    1. Ask yourself whether there are better ways of doing things that are now done in ways you take for granted.
  B. Automatization
    1. Devise effective standard operating procedures for handling routine activities.

III. Contextual Subtheory
  A. Adaptation
    1. Know your managerial strengths and make the most of them.
    2. Know your managerial weaknesses and find ways to compensate for them.
  B. Selection
    1. Try to place yourself in an environment that matches your interests, abilities, and values.
  C. Shaping
    1. Determine the extent to which the environment can be shaped into what you want it to be.

meaningful development plan can be created that takes employees from their current level of proficiency to the level of an expert.

This conceptualization is actually an oversimplification. There are more stages between declarative knowledge and procedural knowledge and more levels of competence. In fact, there is a continuum between these two points and not discrete stages. One may reasonably assume that the characteristics and interrelationships of knowledge structures and executive control processes change as the learner moves from the declarative stage of a novice to the automaticity stage of a master performer. A complete diagnostic appraisal should be based on a competency model that includes information about the ratee's status on these levels of proficiency and content similar to that contained in Exhibit 12.1.

Developing Diagnostic Performance Appraisal

The steps involved in the development of a performance appraisal are well known and practiced by industrial psychologists. The development of a diagnostic performance appraisal based on a mental process model follows similar steps with some modifications. Table 12.1 contains a list of those steps. The outcome from following these steps is two competency models—one for experts and one for novices. The competency models contain the critical knowledge, skills, heuristics, metacognitive skills, and other characteristics that describe and distinguish expert and novice performers.

There are several unique features to this approach compared to the usual job analysis. First, novices as well as expert job performers are included as subject matter experts. Novices serve as subject matter experts about how novices perform work. They are needed to present their view of KSAO requirements, even if this view is incorrect in many respects. Second, the job analyst's goal is not only to identify critical job requirements but also to characterize the mental process models used by experts and novices. This is a different focus from that of researchers in the usual job analysis work. Third, the content captured by the job analyst is different. In the traditional job analysis, the job analyst captures knowledge, skills, abilities, and other characteristics. In a job analysis whose goal is to develop competency models based on mental process models, the job analyst peels back the onion on the skills and knowledge dimensions and captures other characteristics including metacognitive skills, heuristics, knowledge structures, thinking frames, strategies, and executive control processes used by experts and novices. Special emphasis is given to identifying those characteristics that distinguish experts and novices. And finally, a job analysis for the development of competency models based upon mental process models includes the social-emotional characteristics that characterize experts and novices. These characteristics are often overlooked in traditional job analysis, but recent research has demonstrated their importance in learning, problem solving, and job performance.

When the job analyst completes Step 6 from Table 12.1, the job analysis work is completed and the development of the performance appraisal tool can begin. The work from this stage forward proceeds much like the work entailed in the development of any measurement tool. The method must be selected (for example, interview, paper-and-pencil test, rating scales, and so on). Instructions must be developed and the content must be selected and formatted. There are two important differences, one of which involves the selection of content. The content must be selected in a way that enables the appraiser to identify where on the expert-novice, declarative-automaticity scale the appraisee falls. The other important difference is that the diagnostic assessment will be longer than a traditional appraisal. The job analyst cannot use a "domain sampling" approach, but must provide accurate measurement for all components of the mental models to diagnose the appraisee's deficiencies and provide a training prescription.

The expert and novice competency models based on mental process models serve an additional purpose. The models form the basis for the design of developmental curricula. The KSAOs become the content of training. The goal of the curriculum designer is to create training programs that move the trainee from whatever point on the novice-expert scale he or she currently is toward the expert-automaticity point on the scale. It is the curriculum designer's challenge to select the training content and design instructional methods, experiences, and exercises to achieve that goal.

Samples of expert and novice competency models for a research analyst are provided in Exhibits 12.2 and 12.3, while Table 12.2 presents examples of methods for the development of a performance appraisal based upon a mental process model. There are several

Table 12.1. Steps in the Development of a Mental Process Model.

Step	Action	Comments
1	Identify novice and expert "subject matter experts" who can provide input about critical job requirements, learning, and problem solving for the target job.	
2	Specify the organization's learning objectives for the training and then identify the critical job components for the learning objectives of the target job.	The critical job components are associated with learning objectives. The learning objectives are based on the goals the organization has established for the training.
3	Based upon the critical job requirements, develop a hierarchical knowledge taxonomy of job knowledge components by interviewing subject matter experts and reviewing job information such as training material, job aids, and technical documentation.	This work involves specifying a knowledge domain much like the work done when creating a job knowledge test but reflects how experts organize their knowledge.
4	Interview novices and develop a hierarchical knowledge taxonomy that reflects a novice's view of the knowledge domain.	This work involves specifying a knowledge domain much like the work done when creating a job knowledge test, but reflects how novices organize their knowledge—including mistaken and inaccurate constructions.

5	Identify expert and novice metacognitive skills and executive control processes by reviewing the relevant research literature and interviewing experts and novices about strategies, heuristics, techniques, rules of thumb, and schema they use when applying their knowledge to learn and solve problems.	Note in particular skills and processes that differentiate experts and novices.
6	Identify expert and novice social-cognitive and emotional processes by reviewing the relevant research literature and interviewing experts and novices about strategies, heuritics, techniques, rules of thumb, and schema they use when setting goals, motivating themselves, dealing with frustration, and so on when learning and solving problems.	Note in particular skills and processes that differentiate experts and novices.
7	Summarize the results of Steps 4, 5, and 6 into two mental process models, one for novices and one for experts.	
8	Use the competency models to create the performance appraisal tool. Select content from the expert and novice models to develop a tool. Choose appropriate methods to measure the content.	Blending the content from the two competency models will provide an appraisal tool that scales the appraisee from novice at the declarative knowledge stage to expert at the automaticity stage.

points to note when examining these models. First, the expert list is considerably longer than the novice list. This is to be expected because an expert knows more than a novice and this difference is reflected in the models. Second, the structure for expert statistics knowledge is more sophisticated and has more levels than the statistics knowledge structure for novices. This is reflective of a common characteristic that distinguishes experts and novices. Experts organize their knowledge differently such that it enables them to process information more quickly, more deeply, and more complexly. Third, the novice model includes errors of omission and commission. Compared to the expert model, many items are not included in the novice model—errors of omission. Also, several items in the novice model are known to be associated with poorer performers—errors of commission. For example, under goal setting, the novice performer sets "do best and general goals." The research (Latham & Locke, 1990) is clear that this leads to performance that is less than optimal. Fourth, novices are not without skills. The novice competency model does not consist only of incorrect knowledge and errors of commission. Novices are not completely incompetent. In fact, depending upon the target population chosen for the job analysis, the researcher might find that the novices are moderately competent. This should not present a problem. As in any effort to develop a measurement tool, the developer must ensure that the tool adequately measures the range of ability for which the tool will be applied. Fifth, note that much of the content of the competency models comes from the research literature. The job analyst developing competency models based on mental process models will find the research literature a valuable source of content for competency models. For example, findings regarding mastery goals, attributional style, and checking and organizing written material are well supported by the research literature and readily adaptable to a competency model. Finally, the job analyst should be sure to include a knowledge structure for the job knowledge information that reflects how experts process and organize their knowledge domain. The research literature is very clear that this is an important feature of experts and distinguishes them from nonexperts. The job analyst should be sure to interview experts and novices and identify the knowledge structures that they use. This distinction has much diagnostic and instructional significance.

Exhibit 12.2. MPM-Based Performance Appraisal Research Analyst—Expert Model.

I. Hierarchical Taxonomy of the Knowledge Domain
  A. Knowledge Domain for Critical Incidents: Statistical Methods
    1. Nonparametric Methods
      a. One-Sample Data
        • Binomial Test
        • Kolmolgorov-Smirnov
        • Chi-Square
      b. Two-Category Data
        • Fischer Exact Test
        • Kolmolgorov-Smirnov
        • Mann-Whitney U Test
        • Sign Test
        • Chi-Square
      c. Multiple-Category Data
        • Chi-Square
        • Kruskal-Wallis
        • Friedman two-way analysis of variance
        • Odds ratios
        • Loglinear methods
      d. Correlational Methods
        • Contingency Coefficient
        • Spearman rank correlation
        • Kendall coefficient of concordance
    2. Parametric Methods
      a. Descriptive
        • Measures of Central Tendency
        • Measures of Dispersion
      b. Inferential
        • One-sample means test
        • Two-sample means test
          Independent samples
          Related samples
        • General Linear Model
          Multiple regression
          ANOVA
          ANCOVA
        • Multivariate
          MANOVA
          Canonical correlation
          Discriminant analysis

Exhibit 12.2. MPM-Based Performance Appraisal Research Analyst—Expert Model, cont'd.

- Data reduction techniques
  - Factor analysis
  - Cluster analysis
  - Multidimensional scaling
  c. Correlational techniques
    - Pearson correlation
    - Partial correlation
    - Part correlation
  d. Bayesian methods
B. Knowledge Domain for Critical Incidents: Research Design
  1. Proof, and the logic of the scientific method
  2. Validity
    a. Internal validity
      - Threats to internal validity
    b. External validity
      - Threats to external validity
  3. Quasi-experimental design
    a. One-Group Posttest only
    b. One-Group Pre- and Posttest
    c. Control Group Pre- and Posttest
    d. Repeated measure designs
  4. True experimental design
    a. Randomized control group designs
    b. Randomized block designs
    c. Factorial designs
    d. Fractional factorial designs
  5. Time-series designs
    a. Simple time series
    b. Interrupted time series
    c. ARIMA models
C. Knowledge Domain for Critical Incidents: Software
  1. Windows operating system
  2. Basic file manager functions including copying, saving, deleting, moving
  3. Basic knowledge of a spreadsheet including formatting, sorting data, and simple statistical calculations
  4. Basic knowledge of database software including creating fields, changing formats of fields, editing fields, adding fields and records, and producing reports

Exhibit 12.2. MPM-Based Performance Appraisal Research Analyst—Expert Model, cont'd.

5. Basic knowledge of database design including creation of flat files and relational databases

II. Processes

  A. Metacognitive and executive control processes

    1. Clearly defines the hypotheses being tested.

    2. Clearly defines the independent and dependent variables.

    3. Evaluates the psychometric quality of the metrics used.

    4. Assesses whether or not the measurements and research approach answer the questions posed.

    5. Considers threats to the internal and external validity of the study design.

    6. Considers previous research findings and what results should be expected.

    7. Considers the type of measurement used and suitable statistical methods.

    8. Considers the practical field limitations of the study and recommends appropriate research methods.

    9. Considers previous research findings for similar studies and recommends appropriate research methods.

    10. Distinguishes between parametric and nonparametric methods.

    11. Distinguishes among types of statistical methods such as descriptive, inferential, univariate, bivariate, and multivariate.

    12. Organizes and cleans data to ensure that calculations are based on correct data.

    13. Applies correct statistical methods to the problem.

    14. Applies statistical methods whose assumptions are satisfied by the data.

    15. Correctly interprets the results.

    16. Recognizes incorrect results and improbable findings.

    17. Follows a systematic approach to analyzing and reporting data.

    18. Recognizes the weaknesses in the analysis and recommends actions to overcome them.

    19. Analyzes the data using more than one method to ensure results are not dependent upon the method.

  B. Social-cognitive and emotional processes

    1. Interpersonal skills

      a. Expresses understanding of others' concerns.

      b. Listens carefully to speaker without interrupting.

Exhibit 12.2. MPM-Based Performance Appraisal Research Analyst—Expert Model, cont'd.

    c. Demonstrates empathy and concern.
    d. Modifies communication approach according the listener.
    e. Is sensitive to the moods and feelings of others.
    f. Understands the strengths and weaknesses of others.

2. Communication skills
    a. Oral communication
- Considers the listener when deciding what to say.
- Considers what the listener needs to know.
- Speaks in clear, well-paced complete sentences.
- Considers how much information should be provided.
- Considers the current level of knowledge of the listener.
- Considers the ability of the listener to grasp the concepts and information to be presented.
- Asks the listener to repeat what was said to confirm understanding.
- Summarizes what has been said by the speaker to confirm understanding.
- Considers whether what was said makes sense.
- Remembers what was said.

    b. Written communication
- There are no grammar, spelling, and punctuation errors.
- Vocabulary is appropriate for the context and correctly used.
- The information is factually correct.
- There is no illogical or contradictory information in the text.
- The information presented is well organized.
- Checks to ensure there is no missing information.
- Writes in a way that is sensitive to the audience in tone and complexity.

3. Problem Solving
    a. Defines the problem.
- Defines terms.
- Organizes thoughts and articulates them concisely and coherently.
- Can identify the essential and irrelevant information surrounding the problem.

Exhibit 12.2. MPM-Based Performance Appraisal Research Analyst—Expert Model, cont'd.

- Can structure informally represented problems in such a way that formal techniques (such as mathematics) can be used to solve them.
  b. Obtains facts.
    - Uses evidence skillfully and impartially.
    - Knows how to seek information.
  c. Analyzes the facts and information.
    - Attempts to anticipate the probable consequences of alternative actions before choosing among them.
    - Uses mental models, heuristics, thinking frames, and so on.
    - Sees similarities and analogies that are not superficially apparent.
    - Can represent differing viewpoints without distortion, exaggeration, or caricaturization.
  d. Plans how to solve the problem.
    - Looks for similarities with familiar problems.
    - Makes drawings to represent the problem.
    - Looks for unusual approaches to complex problems.
    - Makes and considers several hypotheses for solving the problem.
  e. Attempts to solve the problem.
    - Suspends judgment in the absence of sufficient evidence to support a decision.
    - Avoids logical fallacies.
  f. Evaluates progress.
    - Distinguishes between logically valid and invalid inferences.
    - Understands the difference between reasoning and rationalizing.
    - Recognizes that there is usually more than one correct answer to a problem.
4. Goal-Setting
  a. Sets specific goals.
  b. Sets challenging goals that are attainable.
  c. Seeks positive and negative feedback.
  d. Uses feedback to determine the need to increase effort or change strategy.
  e. Sets mastery goals.

Exhibit 12.2. MPM-Based Performance Appraisal Research Analyst—Expert Model, cont'd.

---

    f. Compares progress against own previous performance, not against others.

    g. Demonstrates positive affectivity.

5. Attributional Style

    a. Focuses on improvement.

    b. Recognizes and focuses own improvement.

    c. Objectively analyzes the cause for failure.

    d. Blames failure on approach and effort.

    e. Attributes failure to external events and success to own skills.

    f. Uses failure as a signal to increase effort.

    g. Recognizes setbacks are temporary.

    h. Believes that failure represents an opportunity for learning and improvement.

    i. Believes that skills are trainable.

6. Persistence

    a. Works hard.

    b. Reacts to failure by spending additional hours solving the problem.

    c. Recognizes that errors are a part of learning and problem solving.

    d. Continues to work in the face of failure.

    e. Tries different approaches.

    f. Experiments with several different approaches before selecting one.

7. Self-Efficacy

    a. Believes in own ability to learn and perform successfully.

    b. Makes positive self-statements while learning and problem solving.

    c. Believes in own ability to control events.

    d. Accentuates the positive aspects of own performance.

Exhibit 12.3. MPM-Based Performance Appraisal Research Analyst—Novice Model.

I. Hierarchical Taxonomy of the Knowledge Domain
   A. Knowledge Domain for Critical Incidents: Statistical Methods
      1. Descriptive and Inferential Methods
         a. Binomial Test
            • *t*-test
            • ANOVA
            • Multiple regression
            • Chi-Square
         b. Correlational Methods
            • Contingency Coefficient
            • Pearson Correlation
            • Spearman's rho
   B. Knowledge Domain for Critical Incidents: Research Design
      1. Validity
         a. Internal validity
            • Threats to internal validity
         b. External validity
            • Threats to external validity
      2. Experimental design
         a. One-Group Posttest only
         b. One-Group Pre- and Posttest
         c. Control Group Pre- and Posttest
         d. Repeated measure designs
         e. Randomized Control Group designs
         f. Factorial designs
   C. Knowledge Domain for Critical Incidents: Software
      1. Windows operating system
      2. Basic file manager functions including copying, saving, deleting, moving
      3. Basic knowledge of a spreadsheet including formatting and sorting data
      4. Basic knowledge of database software including creating fields, changing formats of fields, editing fields, adding fields and records, and producing reports
II. Processes
   A. Metacognitive and Executive Control Processes
      1. Clearly defines the hypotheses being tested.
      2. Clearly defines the independent and dependent variables.
      3. Considers previous research findings and what results should be expected.

Exhibit 12.3. MPM-Based Performance Appraisal
Research Analyst—Novice Model, cont'd

4. Considers the type of measurement used and suitable statistical methods.
5. Distinguishes among types of statistical methods such as descriptive, inferential, univariate, bivariate, and multivariate.
6. Organizes and cleans data to ensure calculations are based on correct data.
7. Applies correct statistical methods to the problem.
8. Correctly interprets the results.
9. Follows a systematic approach to analyzing and reporting data.
10. Recognizes the weaknesses in the analysis and recommends actions to overcome them.

B. Social-Cognitive and Emotional Processes
  1. Interpersonal skills
    a. Expresses understanding of others' concerns.
    b. Is sensitive to the moods and feelings of others.
    c. Does not readily share information.
    d. Views relationships as "friends versus others."
    e. Understands the strengths and weaknesses of others.
  2. Communication skills
    a. Oral communication
      • Considers the listener when deciding what to say.
      • Considers what the listener needs to know.
      • Considers the current level of knowledge of the listener.
      • Considers the ability of the listener to grasp the concepts and information to be presented.
      • Speaks too quickly and does not enunciate.
      • Considers whether what was said makes sense.
      • Remembers what was said.
    b. Written communication
      • There are no grammar, spelling, and punctuation errors.
      • Vocabulary is appropriate for the context and correctly used.
      • The information is factually correct.
      • There is illogical or contradictory information in the text.
      • Checks to ensure there is no missing information.

Exhibit 12.3. MPM-Based Performance Appraisal Research Analyst—Novice Model, cont'd.

3. Problem Solving
   a. Obtains facts.
      - Uses evidence skillfully and impartially.
      - Knows how to seek information.
   b. Analyzes the facts and information.
      - Attempts to anticipate the probable consequences of alternative actions before choosing among them.
      - Sees similarities and analogies that are not superficially apparent.
   c. Attempts to solve the problem.
      - Suspends judgment in the absence of sufficient evidence to support a decision.
      - Avoids logical fallacies.
   d. Evaluates progress.
      - Distinguishes between logically valid and invalid inferences.
      - Understands the difference between reasoning and rationalizing.
4. Goal-Setting
   a. Sets "do best" goals.
   b. Goals are general.
   c. Seeks positive feedback
   d. Uses feedback to determine the need to increase effort or change strategy.
   e. Compares own progress against the progress of others.
   f. Demonstrates positive affectivity.
5. Attributional Style
   a. Focuses on improvement.
   b. Recognizes and focuses own improvement.
   c. Objectively analyzes the cause for failure.
   d. Blames failure on own level of ability.
   e. Attributes failure to self and success to luck.
   f. Is discouraged by failure.
   g. Believes that skills are based on ability and not amenable to training.
6. Persistence
   a. Work effort is inconsistent.
   b. Reacts to failure by spending fewer hours solving the problem.

Exhibit 12.3. MPM-Based Performance Appraisal Research Analyst—Novice Model, cont'd.

    c. Sticks with one approach.

    d. Selects the approach that is used habitually without considering uniqueness of the situation.

  7. Self-Efficacy

    a. Makes negative self-statements while learning and problem solving.

    b. Feels powerless to control certain events critical to success.

    c. Ruminates about occurrences of failure.

Cognitive and Emotional Components of the Mental Process Model

Until the 1980s, research on mental process models had an almost exclusively cognitive flavor (Newell, 1990). The learner's emotional reactions were not considered in the models that cognitive researchers developed; emotional reactions were studied by a separate group of psychologists. Research on the role of emotions and cognition in anxiety, depression, learning orientation, attributional style, motivation, and self-efficacy—and their joint effects on performance—has expanded greatly in recent years. These findings have contributed to the development of a more complete mental process model of performance, one that includes emotional reactions, self-esteem, motivation, and anxiety. This fuller model offers the possibility of developing a more valid assessment and more effective training and development programs.

As an example, let us briefly review some valuable work that identified the causes and effects of cognitive interference on learning. Researchers (for example, Sarason, Pierce, & Sarason, 1996) estimate that the average person experiences about four thousand thoughts per day. This represents the stream of consciousness that includes purposeful, on-task thinking. Effective task performance requires the control of this stream of thoughts. This control is exercised by the executive control processes. Studies of state and trait anxiety demonstrate the extent to which executive control processes are interrupted by anxiety. There are two aspects to the interfering

Table 12.2. Examples of
Developmental Performance Appraisal Methods.

There are different approaches to the creation of a developmentally oriented performance appraisal based upon a mental process model. One approach is to present the rater with the target knowledge, skill, or ability, or other characteristic and the rater then rates the appraisal items on a scale that represents the novice-declarative–expert-automaticity continuum. This approach is created by using the following rating scale and, in this example, selecting non-parametric statistics knowledge content from the expert mental model.

Use a rating of	If the statement describes the appraisee
1	Possesses little or no knowledge of basic concepts and knowledge for this domain. Cannot perform effectively in this domain.
2	Possesses knowledge of basic concepts and knowledge for this domain, but has not integrated the concepts and knowledge. Performs and solves problems as a novice.
3	Has demonstrated understanding of the relationships among the different concepts and knowledge. Can perform and solve problems somewhat effectively in this domain with moderate amounts of help from experts.
4	Has demonstrated a nearly thorough understanding of the relationships among the different concepts and knowledge. Can perform and solve problems effectively in this domain with little help from experts.
5	Has demonstrated a thorough understanding of the relationships among the different concepts and knowledge. Can perform and solve problems in this domain as an expert.

Table 12.2. Examples of
Developmental Performance Appraisal Methods, cont'd.

Nonparametric Methods

	1	2	3	4	5
One-Sample Data					
Binomial Test					
Kolmolgorov-Smirnov					
Chi-Square					
Two-Category Data					
Fischer Exact Test					
Kolmolgorov-Smirnov					
Mann-Whitney U Test					
Sign Test					
Chi-Square					
Multiple-Category Data					
Chi-Square					
Kruskal-Wallis					
Friedman two-way analysis of variance					
Odds ratios					
Loglinear methods					
Correlational Methods					
Contingency Coefficient					
Spearman rank correlation					
Kendall coefficient of concordance					

Another approach is to obtain statements that are characteristic of novices and experts and the rater rates the statements with respect to the extent that they characterize the appraisee. An example rating scale and appraisal form are provided. The content of the appraisal was obtained from the novice and expert mental models.

Use a rating of	If the statement describes the appraisee
1	Not characteristic.
2	Characteristic to some extent.
3	Moderately characteristic.
4	Characteristic to a large extent.
5	Extremely characteristic.

**Table 12.2. Examples of
Developmental Performance Appraisal Methods, cont'd.**

Appraisee Characteristic	1	2	3	4	5
Clearly defines the hypothesis being tested.					
Clearly defines the independent and dependent variables.					
Evaluates the psychometric quality of the metrics used.					
Fails to assess whether or not the measurements and research approach answers the questions posed.					
Considers threats to the internal and external validity of the study design.					
Does not consider previous research findings and what results should be expected.					
Considers the type of measurement used and suitable statistical methods.					
Does not consider the practical field limitations of the study and recommends inappropriate research methods.					
Considers previous research findings for similar studies and recommends appropriate research methods.					
Does not distinguish between parametric and non-parametric methods.					
Organizes and cleans data to ensure calculations are based upon correct data.					
Inconsistently applies correct statistical methods to the problem.					
Applies statistical methods whose assumptions are satisfied by the data.					
Correctly interprets the results.					
Fails to recognize the weaknesses in the analysis.					
Analyzes the data using more than one method to ensure results are not dependent upon the method.					

anxiety. One is the occurrence of non-task-related cognitions and the other is physiological arousal. When a learner feels unduly anxious, attentional resources are drawn to non-task-related stimuli associated with the anxiety. The source of the stimuli many be external or internal.

The nature of the cognitive interference can be explained, in part, by worry and rumination. People who are depressed report a larger portion of their stream of consciousness is spent thinking depressive thoughts compared to nondepressed subjects, and anxious subjects report that they have less control over the content of their stream of consciousness (Kroll-Mensing, 1992). Worry and rumination are not easily controlled. Evidence suggests that negative thoughts gain attention even at an unconscious level.

This line of research shows that emotion-related constructs can have significant effects on executive control processes and ultimately on task performance. In addition, these constructs are significantly influenced by cognitions that define and maintain anxiety, depression, worry, and stress. At best, current appraisals may attempt to evaluate the extent to which the employee concentrates on task performance during the work day. Equipped with appraisal content about the part emotions play in mental process models, future appraisals can focus on both the emotional and cognitive factors that underlie the employee's attention and performance. Such an appraisal can be the basis of developmental strategies specifically directed at, for example, learning to avoid external cues that trigger worrisome thoughts.

Other lines of research that have yielded useful content for appraisals based on mental process models include work done by Dweck on mastery orientation and work by Bandura on self-efficacy. Dweck's studies (1986) of school-age children identified two work orientations that affect academic performance. For those with a mastery orientation, the learner's attentional focus is on developing competence. Failure represents a skill deficit needing improvement, and feedback about skill deficiencies is viewed as an opportunity for improvement. In contrast, those with a performance orientation constantly compare their performance to that of others, see failure as reflective of a lack of ability, and consequently view performance feedback as threatening. The negative effects of having a performance orientation are greater for those with low self-efficacy than for those with high self-efficacy.

Self-efficacy has been found to have a strong impact on goal setting, motivation, attributions of success and failure, perseverance, anxiety, and the risk of depression (for example, see Bandura, 1991). Low self-efficacy results in more negative thoughts and negative affect while working on a task, which in turn interferes with executive control processes and reduces attention to task-relevant feedback (Sarason et al., 1996). Self-efficacy also influences the goals and personal standards one sets for oneself prior to task performance. Persons with higher self-efficacy set more challenging goals to begin with and then persevere longer in the face of failure (Latham & Locke, 1990). In addition, self-efficacy influences affective reactions to failure through its impact on attributions. People lower in self-efficacy are more likely to attribute failure to their own lack of ability and those higher in self-efficacy tend to attribute it to a lack of effort. Failure, then, has a more emotionally crippling effect on those low in self-efficacy. In learning situations that routinely involve failure, the role of self-efficacy becomes particularly important.

We have seen, then, that mastery versus performance orientation, arousal, expectations, self-appraisals, and self-efficacy, among other factors, affect how people learn and perform. Further, as we have argued, development naturally involves failure and frustration as the employee progresses from incompetence to competence. The research we have reviewed here sensitizes us to two important processes that influence learning and performance. First, in the face of failure, some individuals experience significant cognitive interference, with less efficient strategic plans, fewer self-provided instructions, and more time on off-task thoughts. Second, orientation toward performance can significantly facilitate or inhibit learning. A more complete appreciation of both the cognitive and the emotional factors can help us design and implement more effective developmental programs.

The literature reviewed provides some intriguing examples of how research findings can be used by a job analyst to develop a competency model based on a mental process model. Referring back to Exhibits 12.2 and 12.3, note how these research findings were translated into content for the competency model. For example, in Exhibit 12.3, under the category of self-efficacy, the literature identified that poor performers make negative self-statements and this finding is used as an item in the competency model and can be rated with respect to how well it characterizes the appraisee.

Cognitive Components of Mental Process Models and Employee Development

Thus far we have discussed how research findings and a mental process model approach to competency models and performance appraisals provide a new approach to the appraisal-development challenge. Next we will focus on the development part of the challenge. We have defined development as a process of learning. Research on the mental process model has contributed to the development of a theory of instruction that can guide employee development. This research answers the question, What should be taught? Putting the answer succinctly, development must be designed to teach novices the executive control processes and knowledge structures used by experts. The following describes the use of research findings on mental process models to design training curricula.

According to Glaser and Bassock (1989), effective curricula provide instruction in three areas: functional, proceduralized skill and knowledge (progressing from declarative to procedural knowledge); self-regulatory skills (or executive control processes); and knowledge structures and the organization of knowledge for problem solving. Glaser and Bassock argue that every developmental plan should be evaluated with respect to the extent that it addresses all three components.

A few researchers have used the influence of these three components on the effectiveness of training design. In one line of research, Nisbett (1993) looked at a number of studies in which abstract, general knowledge structures were used to teach students to apply the "law of large numbers" in statistical problem solving. The law of large numbers states that for a given attribute, a larger sample is required to obtain an accurate estimate of the overall average when the attribute is variable than when the attribute has little variability. Nisbett found that when abstract rules were made more concrete by casting them in pragmatic terms involving familiar concepts, instruction was more effective. For example, permissions and obligations are abstract logical rules that can be taught by using concrete, familiar concepts. The rules are similar and related. Permission enables action only when it has been obtained, and obligation requires action when a specific situation (such as permission) occurs. Nisbett reported an obligation study in which subjects were asked to check for certain words on the reverse side of a form if it contained the word *entering* on the front side. Many subjects were unable to perform this task successfully. But subjects were much more successful when given a concrete context and rationale: they were airline passengers deplaning in a new country. If they had the "entering" form, they were required to indicate whether they had been exposed to any of the diseases listed on the reverse side. In Nisbett's view, making the abstract obligation more concrete and familiar by providing context and rationale prompted the subjects to draw on their existing knowledge structure of obligations, and these knowledge structures then facilitated their ability to comprehend and perform the task.

Brown (1989) investigated methods to teach reading comprehension, and developed a method—*reciprocal teaching*—based on studies of the differences between expert readers and those less expert. Reciprocal teaching develops executive control processes and knowledge structures for reading comprehension. Sternberg and Davidson (1989) developed a similar instructional approach to teach thinking skills. The approach comprises four stages: familiarization, group analysis of problem-solving procedures, labeling of mental processes and strategies, and application of labeled processes to initial problems.

A final example of the use of the components of a mental process model to guide instructional design comes from the field of artificial intelligence. Various forms of expert systems have been developed that are built on what we have been calling knowledge structures and executive control processes. Knowledge engineering is an approach that expert-systems researchers use to define the knowledge structures and executive control processes that experts used to solve problems, based on an analysis of expert-novice differences. An example of this approach is an intelligent tutoring system developed by Anderson (1993). He defines intelligent tutoring as computer-based systems for instruction using artificial intelligence, applying an approach he calls "model-tracing." This involves developing a cognitive model (that is, a mental process model) of the target skill from a set of rules or strategies that can solve the problems. The system is built on the assumption that learning and problem solving require the acquisition of knowledge structures and rules guided by executive control process.

Common to the approaches used in this research is the explicit use of mental process models as a basis of the design and the content of instruction. This work demonstrates that the value of mental process models is not limited to better diagnosis. Effective instruction starts with the learner's current knowledge structures and executive control processes and facilitates the learner's development toward expert performance by providing instruction in the mental process models used by experts.

Emotional Components of Mental Process Models and Employee Development

Findings concerning the emotional components of mental process models can also help guide instructional design. Similar to the research on cognitive components discussed earlier, this research provides answers to the question, What should be taught? Traditionally, it is within the domain of psychotherapy to teach someone to overcome emotions and cognitions that interfere with the performance of basic tasks of day-to-day life. An otherwise well-adjusted employee whose cognitions and emotions inhibit development is not necessarily mentally ill, but he or she does require remediation for these problems in order to become more effective at work.

While numerous studies indicate that people who worry excessively perform poorly in terms of learning and performance, little research exists regarding the direct impact of interventions aimed at "emotional remediation." The evidence that does exist, however, provides some guidance for the design of interventions aimed at remediating the emotional components of the mental process model.

In one study, Wege and Moller (1995) examined the effectiveness of training to improve the social problem-solving skills of students. Poor social problem solvers were characterized by low self-efficacy for this skill, poor executive control processes in the form of inattention to task-related cues and a focus on interfering emotional responses, and an orientation to believe that failure was due to a lack of innate ability. The remedial program, eight weekly fifty-minute training sessions directly aimed at the emotional components, proved successful. The gains attained by the students were sustained in follow-up measures collected one week and two months after training.

Fiedler (1995) found that, under stressful conditions, the leadership performance of highly intelligent but inexperienced leaders deteriorated more than the performance of those with more experience but lower intelligence. Both groups of leaders received three two-hour sessions consisting of muscle relaxation training, practice with breathing exercises to reduce stress, and cognitive restructuring. This intervention improved the leadership performance of both groups, as measured with an in-basket exercise. Leaders with high intelligence performed more poorly than those with low intelligence before and during training, but performed better on a posttest three months later.

In an entirely different performance domain, Smith examined a variety of interventions designed to enhance athletic performance. Successful interventions included increases in social support from coaches and teammates in order to reduce distracting self-devaluative cognitions and negative emotions (Smith, Smoll, & Barnett, 1995); teaching a refocusing technique called "centering" as a means to regain attentional control and reduce physiological arousal (Nideffer, 1993); mental rehearsal with imagery to gain attentional control, increase attention to task-relevant cues, and avoid negative cognitions; and a "soft focus–hard focus" technique that enables the athlete to focus or "zoom in" on a critical stimulus such as a tennis serve at precisely the right moment. Several stress management interventions have proven to be effective, including self-regulation to control task-irrelevant responses (Smith, 1980); relaxation training to reduce physiological arousal (Smith & Ascough, 1985); cognitive restructuring to counter self-defeating ruminations; and self-instructional training to refocus attention to task-relevant stimuli. These latter techniques were found to have the additional benefit of increasing self-efficacy and reducing anxiety-induced arousal (Smith & Nye, 1989).

These various lines of research suggest two conclusions. Emotional components are important constructs in a mental process model and have direct effects on the learning process, and successful interventions that make explicit use of mental process model constructs can be designed. As in the case of the cognitive components, a well-articulated understanding of the emotional components of mental process models can guide instructional design and development.

Emotional Components and Feedback

In our discussion, we have seen how cognitive and emotional components mediate the linkage between diagnosis and development. Consider the typical supervisory feedback session. Explanatory style and locus of control may affect an employee's self-diagnosis, which in turn influences the way the employee reacts to the diagnosis presented by a supervisor or an assessor and the approach the employee takes to implementing a developmental plan. Similarly, these reactions may be influenced on the emotional side by trait anxiety or positive affectivity.

Given the critical role played by self-efficacy in learning, we would expect that self-esteem would mediate the appraisal-development linkage. Those high in self-esteem should invest more effort in development, given their stronger expectation for the development to result in enhanced proficiency. Renn and Prien (1995) recently varied the frequency with which experimental subjects received feedback on task performance. They found that subjects high in self-esteem reacted more positively to frequent feedback than subjects low in self-esteem did. Notwithstanding these preferences, Brockner's (1988) programmatic research on behavioral plasticity has demonstrated that feedback is more likely to affect the subsequent behavior of those low in self-esteem. Those low in self-esteem are more likely to be socially insecure and as a consequence more sensitive to cues relevant to social approval. Thus they are more likely to attend to performance information provided by supervisors and use that information to guide future behavior to avoid the risk of future disapproval. In contrast, those high in self-esteem would be less likely to respond to supervisor feedback information. Moreover, Korman (1976) has demonstrated that those low in self-esteem are more likely to expect negative feedback and consequently more likely to attribute the causes of performance problems to their own lack of skill relative to those high in self-esteem. We would expect, then, that attributing poor performance to lack of skill is more likely to stimulate efforts at skill improvement than attributing poor performance externally—to bad luck, for instance.

We need to be aware, however, that potentially offsetting the receptivity of those low in self-esteem to negative feedback is a lower sense of self-efficacy concerning the extent to which acting on the developmental feedback will actually result in successful learning.

As in other applications of theories of cognitive-emotional components to complex, real-world work settings, the linkages between key components and the criteria we expect those constructs to influence need to be carefully thought out (Adler, 1996). As in the case of self-esteem, these relationships tend to be complex and mediated by a number of important factors, and as a consequence the role of personality variables may be obscured without consideration of the underlying mental process model.

Appraisal and Development

Before leaving this topic, it might be worth flipping around the essential thrust of this chapter: Does the conduct of performance appraisal make subsequent development more effective? Interestingly, this question has not been much addressed. There is a recent Australian study (Tharenou, 1995) that sheds some light on this issue. Tharenou performed a field experiment in an Australian federal agency that was introducing a formal performance appraisal process. She was able to collect both attitudinal and performance data from employees who were subjected to the new appraisal process and from a parallel group of employees not yet part of the appraisal process. Her results indicated that the presence of an appraisal process, while enhancing employee satisfaction, did little to enhance the perceived effectiveness of employee training. Of course, this might be the result of the lack of resources assembled to support postappraisal development in that particular organization. Nonetheless, these results should serve as a caution to any expectation that training programs are somehow automatically enhanced if they are positioned as a follow-up to appraisal.

Kluger and DeNisi (1996) recently conducted an exhaustive meta-analysis of the effects of performance feedback on subsequent job performance. The review analyzed 607 effect sizes and a pooled sample of over 23,000 subjects. Scholars in our field have generally assumed that the effects of feedback are uniformly positive. Indeed, the provision of feedback—compared to a no-feedback control—generally does enhance later performance (the average effect size was 1.41). However, in a third of the studies, the provision of feedback actually had a negative impact on subsequent performance. Control theory would predict, for example, that someone who has invested very little effort but is told his customer service skills are adequate, if not exceptional, might in fact decrease the effort invested in serving customers. In addition, Kluger and DeNisi (1996) suggest that feedback may focus attention on the self, rather than on the task, inducing a performance rather than a mastery orientation—which in turn leads to performance decrements.

More germane to our interest, feedback may indicate the need to improve performance but not provide a sufficiently clear and detailed path to improvement. If reviewers fail to specify in detail particular developmental needs and action to be taken in pursuit of them, employees may be left more frustrated and confused than they were prior to feedback.

Evaluating Emerging Practice

As we noted at the outset, there is a growing appreciation of the value of appraisal as a basis for developmental planning. This appreciation is manifest in several areas of the appraisal process.

• *Timing.* Driven in part by the increasingly dynamic workplace, annual reviews are being complemented by more frequent appraisals. Quarterly and even monthly performance reviews, long common in sales positions, are now true of other functions. Increasingly these reviews also examine developmental needs. More frequent appraisal allows for supervisors and subordinates alike to track learning, changed behavior, and development. It also allows for "small wins" to help sustain behavior change.

For example, one major credit card company uses an external group of professional assessors to remotely and unobtrusively monitor a random sample of calls and evaluate the customer service skills of their telephone representatives. Supervisors are provided with behaviorally detailed reports on a monthly basis, identifying each representative's relative strengths and weaknesses. These reports are initially used as the basis for developmental planning and coaching. Over the course of time, these monthly evaluations, generated by a remote staff of objective assessors who are blind to the interventions taking place at the workplace, are used to track improvements in customer service skills.

- *Source.* Supervisors remain the most common source of appraisals. Nonetheless, the use of multisource appraisals has grown dramatically over the past decade (London & Smither, 1995). This trend, too, may signal at least an implicit recognition of the developmental value of appraisals. Judgment about the economic value of an employee's outputs to the business objectives of his or her unit may indeed best be placed in the hands of the manager responsible for that employee. However, an accurate description of the *activities* of the appraisee and the skills brought to bear on the conduct of those activities requires multiple perspectives. This is especially true in today's downsized organizations, where managers may have insufficient opportunity to observe each employee enough to accurately diagnose specific developmental needs. Moreover, while self-appraisals may have relatively little value in the context of outcome evaluation for the purposes of, say, reward allocation, there is real value in soliciting self-appraisal to identify areas for development. Employees are more likely to act on feedback that is consistent with their own self-appraisals (Korsgaard, 1996).

- *Value of Third-Party Assessment and Observation.* In line with the increased use of multisource feedback, including in some cases customer input, there appears to be an increasing use of external third-party assessors to provide developmental appraisal. We have already described the use by a major credit card company of third-party assessors to monitor and assess the customer contact skills of telephone service representatives. Other firms are using third-party monitoring for stock brokers, software help lines, travel agents, and telecommunications company service representatives. This trend may also be reflected in the advent of "executive coaches" who shadow managers through their day and provide objective feedback and personal training on an ongoing basis.

What we may be seeing here is an implicit (and occasionally explicit) recognition that the task of providing effective diagnosis and remediation may be too complex and burdensome for most managers and is best given over to "performance enhancement professionals."

- *Content.* Appraisals are making increasing use of competencies. The focus of appraisal has been pushed back from outputs to the activities that produce those outputs to the competencies that drive those activities. The titles of the target competencies used in a particular organization have become artifacts of that organization's culture; the organization's particular competency model helps structure how people in that organization see themselves and others.

We are suggesting that the focus of appraisal be pushed back yet another step to the roots of an individual's current skill level in a given competency. The research and theory around the notion of the mental process model indicates strongly that to diagnose and develop a person more effectively, it is insufficient merely to ascertain, say, that interpersonal skills are weak and need improvement, even if this appraisal is absolutely accurate. A finer level of analysis is required.

There are many skills that are contained in appraisals. For example, cognitive ability, problem solving, decision making, planning and organizing, reasoning, teamwork, strategic thinking, written and oral communication, and interpersonal skills are on almost every organization's list of required manager skills. These skills are usually defined by listing behavioral statements that exemplify the skill. While these behavioral descriptions are helpful, they must be understood within the rubric of a valid mental process model that identifies the components of performance and the interactions of these components. The mental process model, then, becomes the definition of the skill.

Once the skills are defined as processes, it becomes possible to design diagnostic appraisals that provide information about all the elements of the mental process model required to create individualized, prescriptive development plans. A diagnostic appraisal provides a comprehensive picture of the learner's needs, including information about the correctness of the learner's knowledge structures compared to the knowledge structures of an expert. The appraisal identifies where the learner's skills are on the novice-expert continuum. It identifies whether the learner is at the declarative knowledge or knowledge compilation stage for the skill. The appraisal also provides similar information regarding the executive control processes. Finally, the appraisal assesses the learner's self-efficacy for the skill domain and other social-emotional reactions and responses that might facilitate or inhibit learning.

As is the case with the appraisal, more finely defined skills enable the design of training programs that address all elements of the mental process model. Armed with a valid model, the course developer has a psychologically sound basis on which to build instruction. The instruction must address all elements of the model because, for each learner, the diagnostic assessment will identify the unique set of elements that require remediation and the instruction must be able to address each unique set of remedial needs.

Additional Consideration for the Appraisal-Development Process

There are other changes that will influence the future of performance appraisal and development programs. These trends include the following:

Manager and Employee

Coaching skills are now a basic element of virtually every management training program we have encountered. Entry-level management development programs commonly have participants take on mentoring roles prior to assuming formal management responsibility in order to develop both a sensitivity to, and skill at, employee development. Effectiveness as a coach-mentor is an element in many managerial competency models. Not surprisingly, management selection has, in the past decade, increasingly attempted to evaluate candidates on coaching-mentoring skill. Coaches are well positioned to provide developmental appraisals, but few are well equipped to do so.

As so many have noted (for example, Hall, 1996), we live in the era of the protean worker. Employees need to take personal responsibility for their own career development. It is for this reason that some of the individual difference variables (self-efficacy, self-esteem, explanatory style, and so on) we discussed earlier will be such critical moderators of the linkage between appraisal feedback and actual learning.

Interventions

Individual Development Plan

In line with the notion of career self-management, organizations are encouraging the creation of individual development plans (IDPs), at least for professional, managerial, and higher-level sales positions. Sometimes the plan is part of a succession planning program. The IDP document typically lists:

- Competencies that are targeted for development
- Developmental action steps (both formal and on the job) to be undertaken
- Milestones and (more rarely) metrics to assess progress

Organizations vary considerably in what is done with these documents. In most cases, IDPs are developed and reviewed with the individual's direct supervisor. In other cases, a mentor or field development coordinator out of the training department is responsible for reviewing, approving, facilitating, and tracking the plan. Unfortunately, too often there is little or no personal accountability for achieving or failing to achieve developmental milestones. And, as we have been arguing, even the best IDPs lack the specificity of a well-articulated mental model that would tightly define the targets, methods, outcomes, and mediators for successful learning.

Compensation and Certification

There is much talk of "pay for skills" instead of pay for performance. Some major organizations have selectively established certification programs that reward employees for skill development. One major telecommunications firm, for instance, designed a systematic technical knowledge and skill assessment process for Major Account Representatives, a unionized position. The certification process defined four competency levels from novice to expert. Incumbents went through assessment and received very specific written feedback against the standards for the next competency level. The feedback identified, for example, the particular product or procedure in which competency was at less than that required for a Level 1 Representative to be certified at Level 2. Incumbents were entitled to retest for certification at the next competency level every six months. Employees received compensation adjustments as they certified at higher and higher levels.

Global Needs Identification

Using available information technology, training departments are aggregating data from multisource surveys and assessments to identify needs common across employees in order to focus broader interventions. Rarely, though, are similar data aggregated from the developmental sections of the regular performance appraisal form or from IDPs.

Resources

Organizations run a risk in providing developmental feedback without also providing appropriate developmental resources. In one field study, Maurer and Tarulli (1996) found that the degree to which employees felt that such resources were available to them directly affected employee beliefs in their own capacity to improve. In turn, this "developmental self-efficacy" influenced the attitudes of employees toward the entire appraisal process.

Organizations are beginning to understand the linkage between appraisal and development. A number of guides to training tools are now organized around competency models. One example is the *Successful Manager's Handbook* (Davis, Skube, Hellervik, Gebelein, & Sheard, 1995), which provides specific resources (books, tapes, courses, and on-the-job experiences) that are assumed to address weaknesses in a specific competency. Several vendors now produce software in which the user chooses the particular competency weakness and the system provides developmental suggestions. The problem with these resources is that a critical mass of systematic evaluation research has not yet been built to impart confidence that the developmental suggestions will indeed address particular deficiencies in the specific target competency.

Conclusion

In 1978, Glaser stated, "Progress is now being made toward the integration required for building a psychology of instruction based on research and theory in learning and cognition. Some of the particular areas that show this interaction include: psychological task analysis of the subject matter of instruction [and] the interpretation of intelligence and aptitude in terms of cognitive processes." Twenty years have passed and there are very few appraisal and development programs that fulfill the prediction made by Glaser. But there is reason for optimism. Industrial psychologists are in a unique position to advance the development of a psychology of instruction and vastly improve the quality and effectiveness of training and development programs. Organizations spend over $50 billion on training each year and virtually none of the training is designed on the basis of research and theory in learning and cognition. There are a number of steps that industrial psychologists can take to advance the theory and practice of instruction:

- Based upon mental process models and cognitive theory, develop new skill definitions for the skills most frequently used to create selection, appraisal, and training programs.
- Design appraisal and training programs on the basis of mental process models and cognitive theory.
- Develop an instructional research foundation and perform meta-analyses and utility studies that demonstrate training's value.

Although a complete mental process model is essential for the design and development of appraisal and training programs, it does not ensure that the resulting remedial program will be successful. The practitioner interested in creating a development plan that will improve performance is faced with one more challenge—the selection of an instructional method. For example, how does one correct an improper knowledge structure? Or how does one correct a propensity to engage in task-irrelevant mental ruminations?

Glaser (1976) proposed three criteria for a theory of instruction: a description of competent performances (knowledge structures and executive control processes), analysis of the initial state of the learner's knowledge (diagnostic assessment), and explication of the process of learning—the transition from initial state to desired state (changes in knowledge structures and executive control processes). Teachers and clinical psychologists have struggled with the challenges of applying these guidelines for a very long time. Successful techniques and methods exist. But there is, currently, only the beginning of a theory of instruction based on mental process models. Such a theory is developing along with advances in specifying mental process models.

Organizations will not benefit from advances in learning and cognitive theory unless they create development programs that thoughtfully incorporate the findings of theory-guided research. An applied research base must be developed to establish empirically sound methods of diagnostic appraisal linked to development.

References

Adler, S. (1996). Personality and work behavior: Exploring the linkages. *Applied Psychology, 45,* 207–224.

Anderson, J. R. (1982). Acquisition of cognitive skill. *Psychological Review, 89,* 369–406.

Anderson, J. R. (1993). Problem solving and learning. *American Psychologist, 48,* 35–44.

Baker, L. (1989). Metacognition, comprehension monitoring, and the adult reader. *Educational Psychology Review, 1,* 3–80.

Bandura, A. (1991). Social cognitive theory of self-regulation. *Organization Behavior and Human Decision Processes, 50,* 248–287.

Brockner, J. (1988). *Self-esteem at work.* San Francisco: New Lexington Press.

Brown, A. (1989). Knowing when, where, and how to remember: A problem of metacognition. In R. Glaser (Ed.), *Advances in instructional psychology: Vol. 1* (pp. 77–165). Hillsdale, NJ: Erlbaum.

Campbell, R. B., & Garfinkel, L. M. (1996). Strategies for success in measuring performance. *HR Magazine,* pp. 98–104.

Cardy, R. L., & Dobbins, G. H. (1994). *Performance appraisal: Alternative perspectives.* Cincinnati, OH: South-Western.

Chi, M. T. H., Feltovich, P. J., & Glaser, R. (1981). Representation of physics knowledge by experts and novices. *Cognitive Science, 5,* 121–152.

Davis, B. L., Skube, C. J., Hellervik, L. W., Gebelein, S. H., & Sheard, J. L. (1996). *Successful manager's handbook.* Minneapolis, MN: Personnel Decisions International.

Dweck, C. (1986). Motivational processes affecting learning. *American Psychologist, 41,* 1040–1048.

Fiedler, F. E. (1995). Cognitive resources and leadership performance. *Applied Psychology, 44,* 5–28.

Glaser, R. (1976). Components of a psychology of instruction: Toward a science of design. *Review of Educational Research, 46,* 1–24.

Glaser, R. (1978). Introduction: Toward a psychology of instruction. In R. Glaser (Ed.), *Advances in instructional psychology: Vol. 1* (pp. 1–12). Hillsdale, NJ: Erlbaum.

Glaser, R., & Bassock, M. (1989). Learning theory and the study of instruction. *Annual Review of Psychology, 40,* 631–666.

Hall, D. J. (1996). Protean concerns of the 21st century. *Academy of Management Review, 10,* 8–16.

Kanfer, R., & Ackerman, P. L. (1989). Motivation and cognitive abilities: An integrative/aptitude treatment interaction approach to skill acquisition. *Journal of Applied Psychology, 74,* 657–690.

Kluger, A. N., & DeNisi, A. S. (1996). Effects of feedback intervention on performance: A historical review, a meta-analysis, and a preliminary feedback intervention theory. *Psychological Bulletin, 119,* 254–284.

Korman, A. K. (1976). Hypothesis of work behavior revisited and an extension. *Academy of Management Review, 1,* 50–63.

Korsgaard, M. A. (1996). The impact of self-appraisals in reactions to feedback from others: The role of self-enhancement and self-consistency concerns. *Journal of Organizational Behavior, 17,* 301–311.

Kroll-Mensing, D. (1992). *Differentiating anxiety and depression: An experience sampling analysis.* Unpublished doctoral dissertation, University of Minnesota, Minneapolis.

Latham, G. P., & Locke, E. A. (1990). *A theory of goal setting and task performance.* Upper Saddle River, NJ: Prentice Hall

London, M., & Smither, J. W. (1995). Can multisource feedback change perceptions of goal accomplishment, self-evaluations, and performance-related outcomes? Theory-based applications and directions for research. *Personnel Psychology, 48,* 803–839.

Maurer, T. J., & Tarulli, B. A. (1996). Acceptance of peer/upward performance appraisal systems: Role of work context factors and beliefs about managers' development capability. *Human Resource Management, 35,* 217–241.

Meyer, H. H., Kay, E., & French, J. R. P. (1965). Split roles in performance appraisal. *Harvard Business Review, 43,* 123–129.

Newell, A. (1990). *A unified theory of cognition.* Cambridge, MA: Harvard University Press.

Newell, A., & Simon, H. A. (1972). *Human problem solving.* Hillsdale, NJ: Erlbaum.

Nideffer, R. M. (1993). Concentration and attention control training. In J. M. Williams (Ed.), *Applied sport psychology: Personal growth to peak performance* (2nd ed., pp. 243–261). Palo Alto, CA: Mayfield Press.

Nisbett, R. E. (1993). *Rules for reasoning.* Hillsdale, NJ: Erlbaum.

Perkins, D. (1995). *Outsmarting IQ: The emerging science of learnable intelligence.* New York: Free Press.

Renn, R. W., & Prien, K. O. (1995). Employee responses to performance feedback from the task. *Group and Organization Management, 20,* 337–354.

Sarason, I. G., Pierce, G. R., & Sarason, B. R. (1996). *Cognitive interference: Theories, methods, and findings.* Hillsdale, NJ: Erlbaum.

Smith, R. E. (1980). A cognitive-affective approach to stress management training for athletes. In C. H. Nadeau, W. Halliwell, K. M. Newell, & G. C. Roberts (Eds.), *Psychology of motor behavior and sport, 1979* (pp. 54–72). Champaign, IL: Human Kinetics.

Smith, R. E., & Ascough, J. C. (1985). Induced affect in stress management training. In S. R. Burchfield (Ed.), *Stress: Psychological and physiological interactions* (pp. 359–378). New York: Hemisphere.

Smith, R. E., & Nye, S. L. (1989). Comparison of induced affect and covert rehearsal in the acquisition of stress management coping skills. *Journal of Counseling Psychology, 36,* 17–23.

Smith, R. E., Smoll F. L., & Barnett, N. (1995). Reduction of children's sport performance anxiety through social support and stress-reduction training for coaches. *Journal of Applied Developmental Psychology, 16,* 125–142.

Sternberg, R. L., & Davidson, J. (1989). A four-prong model for intellectual development. *Journal of Research and Development in Education, 22,* 22–28.

Tharenou, P. (1995). The impact of a developmental performance appraisal program on employee perceptions in an Australian federal agency. *Group and Organizational Management, 20,* 245–271.

Varma, A., DeNisi, A. S., & Peters, L. H. (1996). Interpersonal affect and performance: A field study. *Personnel Psychology, 49,* 341–360.

Wagner, R. K., & Sternberg, R. J. (1985). Practical intelligence in real-world pursuits: The role of tacit knowledge. *Journal of Personality and Social Psychology, 49,* 436–458.

Wege, J. W., & Moller, A. T. (1995). Effectiveness of a problem solving training program. *Psychological Reports, 76,* 507–514.

Woehr, D. J., & Huffcutt, A. I. (1994). Rater training for performance appraisal: A quantitative review. *Journal of Occupational and Organizational Psychology, 67,* 189–205.

CHAPTER 13

Performance-Based Pay Plans

Robert L. Heneman
Maria T. Gresham

A revolution is taking place in compensation and incentive systems. Many organizations today are reengineering their compensation and incentive systems to link pay to achieving organizational strategies. New pay-for-performance plans are used to compensate employee performance at all levels in the organization. These new reward systems are now referred to as *alternative rewards* (McAdams & Hawk, 1995), the *new pay* (Schuster & Zingheim, 1992), and *strategic pay* (Lawler, 1990). In this chapter they will collectively be referred to as *performance-based pay plans*.

The purpose of this chapter is to show how organizations can most effectively make the link between performance appraisal and compensation and incentive systems. This requires an understanding of the need for performance-based pay, the compensation context, types of reward systems, design issues, and implementation issues. Each of these topics will be addressed in turn.

The Need for Performance-Based Pay

Although there has been explosive growth in performance-based pay plans (Lawler, Mohrman, & Ledford, 1995), not all employees

Note: The authors would like to thank Jim Smither and Sara Rynes for their helpful comments on an earlier version of this chapter.

prefer pay increases based on performance. For example, research has shown that exempt employees tend to be more in favor of performance-based pay plans than nonexempt employees. Nonexempt employees tend to favor pay based on seniority and cost of living (Heneman, 1992). As a result, a critical starting point for the linking of pay to performance is to assess whether this concept is a viable method of pay for organizations.

The thesis of this chapter is that pay-for-performance plans are not only desirable but are a necessity in most organizations. Traditional pay plans, which reward people for the value of their job and time in the job, are a huge expenditure for organizations, but have not been a source of above-average returns. Traditional pay plans simply reward employees for the status quo as depicted in job descriptions that are often static and fail to capture behaviors outside the boundaries of the job that are critical to organizational effectiveness (Ilgen & Hollenbeck, 1991). Incentives have traditionally been provided only to a small and elite portion of the labor force, usually executives and sales representatives. As competition in product and service markets intensifies in domestic and international markets, bureaucratic organizations that perpetuate the status quo are finding it very difficult to compete (Lawler, 1990). For a company to gain a competitive advantage, employees must be empowered to be more flexible in their jobs. The accomplishment of results must be emphasized over mere participation in activities, and there must be continual upgrading of employee knowledge, skills, abilities, and competencies. It is our contention that these objectives are more likely to be met with performance-based pay plans than with traditional pay plans.

It should be noted that the use of performance-based pay plans often requires some fundamental changes in the way organizations are managed. Operational and financial information previously reviewed only by management may need to be shared with employees. Along with open information, management may need to empower employees to make decisions previously made by management such as deciding which performance standards are to be used to assess performance. Management may also need to provide much more support to employees in the form of training and development opportunities for employees to be successful in a performance-based environment.

Opponents of pay-based reward systems point to many flaws with performance-based pay plans, suggesting that they may actually detract from organizational effectiveness. While these flaws are very interesting and certainly do arise upon occasion, empirical research usually shows little support for these positions. Criticisms of performance-based pay plans and rebuttals to these claims are shown in Table 13.1.

In conclusion, the preponderance of current research suggests that the concept of pay-for-performance has an important role to play in the operation of organizations. Later in this chapter, this conclusion will be further bolstered by reviewing the research literature on the effectiveness of various plans. While we support the

Table 13.1. Criticisms of Performance-Based Pay.

Criticism	Empirical Rebuttal
• Performance-based pay doesn't work in other cultures.	• Performance-based pay has been used for years in Russia (Gaga & Kaz, 1996) and is now being tried in Japan (Pollack, 1993).
• Performance-based pay doesn't work with unionized employees.	• About 25 percent of union contracts have performance-based pay clauses (Heneman, von Hippel, Eskew, & Greenberger, 1996).
• Performance-based pay leads to decreased intrinsic motivation (Deci, 1972; Kohn, 1993).	• Performance-based pay does not decrease intrinsic motivation (Scott, Farh, & Podsakoff, 1988; Montemayer, 1995; Podolske, 1996; Eisenberger & Cameron, 1996).
• Individual performance-based pay is inconsistent with total quality management (Deming, 1986).	• TQM organizations see greater rather than less importance for individual performance-based pay (Risher, 1992; Knouse, 1995).

concept of pay-for-performance, we are very aware that the implementation of this concept is very difficult. Our hope is that we can show the important steps needed to use these plans successfully. There have been highly publicized cases where pay-for-performance plans have had devastating consequences when not properly designed and implemented (Wright, 1994). Notable examples here include Sears and Salomon Brothers. At Sears, quotas with incentives were set for mechanics to complete a certain number of jobs in a day. It appears that mechanics cut corners to save time, resulting in poor quality repairs (Lorant, 1992). At Salomon Brothers, a performance-based pay system with limitless bonuses pitted executives against each other and may have promoted unethical behavior (Norris, 1991). Although horror stories like these do occur, the preponderance of the empirical evidence points to success with performance-based pay plans.

Pay Context

The fundamental building block in traditional pay systems is the *job* (Ash, Levine, & Sistrunk, 1983). The process of job analysis is used to define the job and the job is summarized in a job description that lists the duties and responsibilities of the job and a job specification that lists the knowledge, skills, abilities, and other factors required to perform the job. Wages and salaries are determined on the basis of the value of the job. In turn, the magnitude of the wage or salary determines the size of the benefits and incentives received. Value is established by assessing the internal value of the job through a process known as job evaluation and by assessing the external value of the job through market surveys (Milkovich & Newman, 1996). Hence, under a traditional plan, the job directly determines direct pay and indirectly determines benefits and incentives received.

Another fundamental building block in a traditional pay system is a *pay range* that spells out the minimum, midpoint, and maximum pay rates for each collection of jobs with similar value to the organization known as a pay grade. The minimum value is the lowest wage or salary that the organization will pay to people holding a particular job. The range is designed such that the legally required minimum wage is paid, but also so that the job holder is being equitably paid relative to others in different pay grades. The midpoint is usually set at or around the market average to make the jobs in the pay grade competitive with the external market. The maximum of the pay range is the maximum level that the organization is willing to pay for the contribution of this job to the organization. Even if a person has above-average credentials, the maximum he or she can earn is at this level because the duties performed only add so much value regardless of the job holder, and the organization must keep control of labor costs to be competitive.

In traditional organizations, movement within a pay grade is based on seniority. Each year on the job, a permanent pay increase is granted based upon position in range. Employees near the bottom of the pay range receive a larger pay adjustment than employees at the top of the pay range. Employees at the bottom of the range receive more so that they move up to the market average quickly and do not leave the organization for a job at another organization paying at the market average. Employees at the top of the pay range receive smaller increases so that they do not exceed the maximum of the pay grade.

In terms of individual pay increases, performance assessment can be used in addition to, or in replacement of, seniority as the basis to determine movement in the pay range. The better the performance of the individual, the better the pay increase or bonus. As with seniority, however, for purposes of retention and cost minimization, good performers lower in the pay grade may receive larger increases than good performers higher in the pay grade.

Performance-based pay systems provide an additional fundamental building block to the pay system. The building block is an *assessment of performance* that in turn can influence the size of the pay budget and the method used to determine pay increases. In terms of the budget, performance of the organization can increase the size of the budget available for pay increases in a given year. In effect, this budget may increase the levels of the minimum, midpoint, and maximum wages of the pay range. In turn, employees are eligible for larger raises. If the organization does not want to incur any additional fixed costs in the budget, then good performance by the organization can be passed along in the form of a one-time bonus to employees that does not become a permanent addition to their wage or salary.

Performance-based pay systems also challenge the building blocks of traditional pay systems in several ways. First, pay may be increased on the basis of accomplishments not spelled out in the traditional job description. For example, someone may receive an increase or a bonus on the basis of being a member of a cross-functional task force. Second, pay may be increased on the basis of the mastery of new skills or competencies not spelled out in the traditional job description. Third, pay may be allocated on the basis of team accomplishments rather than individual accomplishments. Fourth, pay may be allocated on the basis of the results that are produced rather than the activities undertaken. Fifth, pay may be allocated on the basis of cost savings or organizational improvements. Finally, pay increases may be in the form of bonuses, benefits, or nonmonetary rewards rather than wage or salary adjustments. Moreover, these payouts may be more substantial in size than usual because they are not part of the base wage or salary and do not therefore push the base pay near or above the maximum pay level for the pay range.

In short, performance-based pay plans force organizations to clearly define effective performance and to determine what factors are likely to lead to effective performance (Campbell, 1990). Rewards are then provided for the accomplishment of those outcomes that constitute effective performance and the successful development of those factors that are likely to lead to the accomplishment of these outcomes. As will be seen in the next section, organizational results that are rewarded include so-called hard measures of performance such as costs, revenues, and profits. Factors that lead to these results and may also be rewarded include critical behaviors such as customer service, teamwork, and attention to quality, as well as underlying capabilities such as skills and knowledge. These criteria are very different from the traditional criteria of job duties and seniority. They serve as additions to duties and seniority in order to motivate improved performance. They do not always replace duties and seniority because duties and seniority may be needed to build equity, commitment, and retention in the organization.

Types of Pay and Performance Plans

A multitude of different pay and performance plans exist. As shown in Table 13.2, they vary along two dimensions: performance measure and measurement level. *Performance measure* refers to the type of measurement that is used by the organization to assess the contribution of the employee to the organization. *Measurement level* refers to the level at which employee performance is measured. At the individual level, the performance directly attributed to the employee is measured. At the team or group level, performance attributable to the entire work group is measured. At the organizational level, performance attributed to the entire organization is assessed. Parenthetically it should be noted that pay is given to the individual even if performance is measured at the group and organization level.

Plan types corresponding to the level of each dimension are entered into the cells in Table 13.2. These are pure types of each plan that are helpful for illustrative purposes. In reality, many of these pure plan types are being blended together, as will be discussed in a later section.

A brief description and analysis of each plan will be presented based in part on materials from the American Compensation Association (1996a). The operational details of the various plans are spelled out in the body of literature listed in Table 13.3.

Merit Pay

Merit pay has been referred to as the "grandfather" of all pay-for-performance plans (Milkovich & Newman, 1996). Over 80 percent of organizations use some form of merit pay (Peck, 1984.) Merit pay provides a pay increase to employees for their individual behavioral contributions to the organization. Performance is usually assessed on an annual basis using a multidimensional graphic rating scale. Occasionally, more advanced measures of employee behaviors such as Behavioral Observation Scales (BOS) or Management by Objectives (MBO) are used. Once merit pay ratings have been generated and an overall score for each employee determined, the rater then uses a merit pay matrix to make a pay increase decision for each employee. A merit pay matrix shows the

Table 13.2. Performance-Based Pay Plan Typology.

Performance Measure	Measurement Level		
	Individual	Group	Organization
Behaviors	• Merit pay	• Team-based merit pay	
Knowledge and Skills	• Skill-based pay • Competency-based pay		
Output	• Piece-rate pay	• Group incentives	
Time Savings	• Standard hour plan	• Standard hour plan	• Gainsharing: Improshare
Cost Reduction and Revenue Enhancement	• Employee suggestion systems	• Team recognition	• Gainsharing: Scanlor Plan • Gainsharing: Ruckers Plan • Gainsharing: Goalsharing
Sales	• Commissions	• Sales teams	
Profit			• Profit sharing • Stock ownership • Executive pay

Table 13.3. Sources of Detailed Descriptions of Pay Plan Types.

Author (Date)	Book Title
Belcher (1991)	*Gain Sharing*
Graham-Moore & Ross (1990)	*Gainsharing*
Gross (1995)	*Compensation for Teams*
Heneman (1992)	*Merit Pay: Linking Pay Increases to Performance Ratings*
McAdams (1996)	*The Reward Plan Advantage*
Milkovich & Newman (1996)	*Compensation*
Nelson (1994)	*1001 Ways to Reward Employees*
Schuster & Zingheim (1992)	*The New Pay*
Wilson (1995)	*Innovative Reward Systems for the Changing Workplace*

range of pay increase percentages that can be granted for each level of performance and each position in the pay range. The pay increase is granted as a percentage of base pay. The increase can be granted as a permanent base pay increase or as a lump-sum bonus not built into base pay. Average merit pay increases are usually set at the level of the cost of living or the level of the average pay increase for unionized employees. In the 1990s, average merit increases have been about 3 percent to 4 percent.

Merit pay works well when behaviors that contribute to the effective functioning of the firm are rewarded. Behaviors critical to organizational effectiveness include innovation, empowerment, and customer service. Behaviors rather than results are especially important to measure when the results are outside of the control of employees. Employees would be unfairly penalized, for example, in a retail establishment when sales declined as a function of a decline in the economy rather than poor sales behaviors.

Merit pay plans have been criticized because they may promote an entitlement culture and because they fail to differentiate between high and low performers. The perception of merit pay systems is multidimensional, consisting of performance assessments and merit pay allocation. Fairness in performance assessments and the distribution of merit pay is important if merit pay systems are to work effectively (Montemayer, 1994). To prevent problems, organizations must be willing to grant no increase to employees who are not performing up to standard. By doing so, a pay increase is not automatic and additional money can be allocated to high performers to distinguish their contributions.

Team-Based Merit Pay

Another criticism of merit pay is that it leads to competition rather than cooperation. Employees are pitted against one another to compete for a limited fund. Paying for individual performance strikes some companies as too difficult. In response, team-based merit pay has supplemented traditional merit pay plans by making teamwork a performance standard that is now evaluated by team members and the supervisor. By including the teamwork criterion in individual performance appraisals, individuals cannot reach for their own goals at the expense of others. Dimensions of teamwork that have been identified by a review of the psychological literature (Stevens & Campion, 1994) and case studies in industry (Katzenbach & Smith, 1993) include dedication to a common purpose, sense of mutual accountability, mutual respect and support, technical and functional expertise, collaborative problem-solving skills, interpersonal skills, cooperation, trust-based relationships, conflict resolution, communications, goal setting and performance management, and planning and task coordination (Heneman & von Hippel, 1995). Team-based merit pay is combined with individual merit pay by adding criteria such as these to the evaluation form to supplement individual criteria such as output quality and quantity. An example of this approach is Johnsonville Foods, where the coach (supervisor) and job incumbent evaluate the job incumbent's contribution to groups, communication, willingness to work together, and attendance and timeliness at group meetings (Stayer, 1990). Other organizations such as AT&T, Xerox, and Motorola use a 360-degree review process to assess the evaluations of the individual to the team. That is, peers are used along with the job incumbent and supervisor to assess team contributions.

Skill-Based Pay

The focus of skill-based pay is on the underlying ability, skill, and knowledge possessed by employees rather than their manifest behavior. Pay increases are based upon skill mastery. Administering such a program requires the organization to define the skill sets required of employees in certain positions. Skill sets are described with great precision rather than relying upon general skill designations such as education levels or experience levels. Skill sets are also very job specific. Peers and supervisors are usually used to certify that the employee has mastered the required skills. Skill certification should include not only the mastery of knowledge but the successful demonstration of that knowledge back on the job. Once the skill has been certified, a pay increase is granted.

Skill-based pay is used by organizations to enhance organizational learning and to promote flexibility. Employees learn new and better methods of conducting their work and become cross-trained so that they can pitch in and do whatever work is required even if it is outside their traditional job descriptions.

A major problem with skill-based pay is the substantial expense associated with this plan in the form of direct costs (increased pay) and indirect costs (training). The skill-based pay system may enhance flexibility in the workforce. However, higher labor costs may ensue if most or all employees are certified to receive top pay. Employers can avoid this possibility by controlling the rate at which employees can be certified, requiring that new skills must be used on the current job, or hiring fewer people. Skill-based pay only makes financial sense when the efficiencies of flexibility outweigh the increased costs.

Early examples of skill-based pay plans can be found at General Mills, Northern Telecom, and Honeywell (Ledford, 1991). General Mills put its plan in at a new manufacturing facility with continuous process technology and a high level of employee involvement. Skill blocks were formed based on steps in the production process. Ratings of skill mastery were obtained by peers. Northern Telecom used skill-based pay for service technicians. Skill blocks were developed for specific job families. Skill block mastery was certified by supervisors, a management review committee, and human resources. Honeywell used skill-based pay in a new assembly plant with high-involvement work practices. Generic skill sets were developed across different work areas. Skill mastery was assessed by supervisors with input from team leaders, engineers, and peers. The wide range of skill-based pay practices can be seen from these examples.

Competency-Based Pay

Skill-based pay has been extended to competency-based pay. In addition to rewarding the acquisition of knowledge, skills, and abilities as with skill-based pay, competency-based pay also rewards other underlying attributes of performance including motivation and personality traits. Caution must be exercised with this approach due to the difficulty of measuring motivation (Lawler, 1996) and the legal problems associated with the measurement of employee traits for purposes of performance appraisal (Nathan & Cascio, 1986). It is, however, an important advancement in performance-based rewards because performance is actually modeled in terms of its determinants (Campbell, 1990). That is, job performance is broken down into its basic components rather than simply being viewed as an end result. Components of job performance include declarative knowledge (facts, principles, goals, self-knowledge), procedural knowledge and skills (cognitive, psychomotor, self-management, interpersonal), and motivation (choice to perform, level of effort, persistence of effort) (Campbell, 1990). Many performance-based reward systems simply measure end results and hope that employees know how to get there. Competency pay directs employees how to achieve results rather than assuming that the paths to success are readily apparent. As a starting point, firms are developing competency dictionaries to guide organizations on the development of competencies associated with organizational effectiveness. However, Zingheim, Ledford, and Schuster (1996) and Lawler (1996) suggest that while dictionaries are helpful, it is the definitions of those competencies that are specific to the business strategy of the organization that help a firm achieve a competitive advantage. Highly successful companies develop their own competency sets consistent with their strategic plans. For example, the Limited is a $10 billion retailer of specialty items. One of the competencies assessed at the Limited is "fashion sense." This competency is defined in very specific behavioral terms appropriate to the culture and history of the organization. This type of approach helps organizations derive sustained competitive advantage because the competencies are not easily imitated by other companies (Barney, 1991).

Piece-Rate Pay

Under this plan, pay is provided for individual output above a predefined standard. Pay increases are in the form of a pay bonus rather than a permanent adjustment to base pay. Output is usually determined on the basis of individual productivity where productivity is defined by output divided by input. In manufacturing, productivity may be measured, for example, as parts produced divided by number of hours for each employee. In the service sector, a bank, for example, productivity may be assessed as number of checks processed divided by number of hours for each employee. If productivity enhancement is the organizational goal, piece-rate systems align as an appropriate reward system assuming that individual productivity can be assessed and that employee effort, more than technology, influences productivity. Problems do exist with piece-rate plans. They may discourage quality because the amount of output rather than the quality of output is counted. Teamwork may also be jeopardized because employees compete against one another to receive the largest reward. Time spent on assisting others in being productive detracts from one's own productivity, and as a result piece-rate pay plans can have a dampening effect on teamwork.

Standard Hour Plan

This approach sets pay standards based on the time per unit of output. Standard hour plans place the incentive rate based on the completion of a task in some expected time period (Wagner & Hollenbeck, 1992). If tasks can be completed in less than the designated time, then employees will receive a higher hourly wage than those employees who do not complete the tasks in less than the designated time. Task completion can be measured at the individual or group level. Standard hour plans are more suitable for complex, nonrepetitive tasks that require numerous skills for completion (Milkovich & Newman, 1996).

Group Incentives

When work is designed such that the group produces an identifiable output and where it is difficult to assess the contribution of individual team members, then group incentives can be offered for output. As with piece-rate pay, incentives are paid out for production above a certain standard. The incentive is usually divided up equally among group members. This approach works well if it can be assumed that all members of the team contributed equally to the final point of service.

Suggestion Systems

Under this approach rewards are offered to individual employees for individual suggestions that produce actual cost savings. Rewards are also sometimes provided for new products or services that enhance revenues, but these rewards are built into suggestion systems far less frequently than are rewards for cost-reduction suggestions. Rewards are usually a fixed amount per successfully implemented suggestion or a percentage of the labor cost savings. Suggestions are usually reviewed by top management or an appointed committee. These plans would seem to motivate individuals to carefully guard their ideas rather than share them with others and this may be a problem in team-based environments. Criteria for selecting winning suggestions must be clearly stated so that employees understand, for example, why a money-saving idea that conflicts with the mission statement may win nothing.

Team Recognition Plans

Suggestion systems can be elevated to the team level, where teams of employees compete against one another for rewards. In some organizations with team recognition plans a monetary prize is offered; in most, a nonmonetary recognition award is offered. Rewards are usually granted on the basis of the team that comes up with a more efficient way to produce their product or service. Unlike employee suggestion systems, the team is given the reward rather than the individual. Both individual suggestion systems and team recognition plans motivate employees to think outside the confines of the job description.

Gainsharing

An organizational-level pay intervention that takes many forms is known as *gainsharing*. There have been several generations of these plans, with each generation emphasizing different performance measures (Wallace, 1990). The first generation consisted of Scanlon and Ruckers plans, both of which provided rewards for cost savings. Second-generation plans—known as Improshare—emphasized time savings. Third-generation plans, sometimes called goalsharing, performance sharing, and win sharing, emphasized revenue enhancement along with cost or time savings. Cost savings were also expanded to include costs other than labor (for example, materials). Revenue enhancement measures include customer service and quality. As can be seen by the measures used, earlier plans emphasized the reduction of inputs to increase productivity (the ratio of outputs to inputs). Later plans emphasized the reduction of inputs *and* the increase of outputs in the form of revenues. One of the desirable features of these plans is that they can pay for themselves. Bonuses are not allocated unless productivity increases.

Productivity is enhanced under these plans by joint committees of employees (labor union representatives in unionized organizations) and managers. These committees solicit suggestions from employees on ways to decrease costs (and increase revenues, in plans that deal with both sides of the ratio), screen the suggestions for the best ones, help implement the suggestions, and administer the pay system. Hence there is a heavy component of employee empowerment in these reward plans. Payouts under these plans are set such that both employees and management gain. Cost savings and increased revenues are split between the parties so that employees' efforts are rewarded and management can reinvest money in the organization for further improvements.

Equal percentage payouts are usually granted to employees regardless of individual contributions in terms of suggestions or committee participation. This approach is intended to foster a spirit of teamwork and camaraderie among employees. It may also, however, foster feelings of resentment and inequity on the part of those employees whose individual contributions are the greatest.

Corning Technologies presents an excellent example of a third-generation gainsharing plan (Altmansberger & Wallace,

1995). Labeled *goalsharing,* it was implemented in partnership with the American Flint Glass Workers Union (AFGWU), AFL-CIO, and other unions. The plan was first instituted in 1988 to improve quality, and it now covers fifteen thousand manufacturing and non-manufacturing employees. It consists of sixty different goalsharing plans. Plans vary by performance measure. For example, the first plan initiated bases payouts on cost per unit, process loss, quality, and customer service. Both attitudinal and financial data gathered by Corning Technologies suggest that the plan has had a positive impact.

Sales Commissions and Team Sales Plans

Traditional sales plans are very similar to piece-rate pay plans. Sales outputs are rewarded with a commission. Sales outputs include new accounts, revenues, and profits. There are two problems with traditional sales commissions. First, making the sale becomes more important than customer service if sales quantity is rewarded rather than sales quality. In response to this situation, an educational distribution company established sales teams consisting of salespeople, support staff, and customers. The teams design—with management input—measures of both sales quantity and quality to be rewarded. By using this approach, a premium is placed on customer service. In the absence of an emphasis on customer service, long-term customer retention is a problem.

A second problem with traditional sales commissions is that sales output measures tend to be contaminated. For example, some products sell better than others and some sales territories have better customers than others. As a result, care must be taken to adjust the sales output standards for sales representatives to reflect the demand for their products or services and to reflect the territory they serve relative to other sales representatives.

Profit Sharing and Stock Sharing

The profit sharing approach is a group incentive pay plan that uses profitability as the standard for organizational-level incentives. There are three primary types of profit sharing plan. First, full payment plans allocate rewards to employees soon after profits have been determined. Second, deferred payment plans credit an employee's account, paying cash at the time of retirement. Finally, some plans involve a combination of the immediate and deferred methods. Employee stock ownership plans are not considered performance-based pay plans because they reward membership in the organization rather than performance.

Stock-sharing is another approach to group incentive-based pay created through employee stock ownership plans. Providing employees with the ability to buy company stock at a reduced rate per share is one method of stock sharing.

Under profit sharing and stock sharing, rewards are distributed to employees on the basis of the financial performance of the entire organization. Financial measures of performance of the firm include returns on assets, economic value-added formulas, and earnings per share. With profit sharing, cash rewards are distributed on an annual basis. With stock sharing, stock is distributed as a reward.

A goal of both approaches is to foster employee identification with the goals of the organization at large. Profit sharing fosters identification with short-term organizational goals, while stock sharing fosters identification with long-term interests of the organization. A downside to both of these plans is that the "line of sight," especially for lower-level employees, is unclear between individual employee behavior and organizational performance. Consequently, the motivational value of these reward programs may be diminished.

To improve the line of sight at 3M, profit sharing for managers is a tiered system where profit is measured not only at the organizational level but at the division and group levels as well (Milkovich & Newman, 1996). Other methods to shorten the line of sight include providing employees with financial data, the training needed to interpret financial data, and the authority to act on financial data. In the absence of these important steps, employees may become very frustrated with profit sharing because it asks them to risk their bonus on factors outside their control.

Executive Pay

Profit sharing and stock sharing for the top level of the organization form what is known as executive pay. While cash bonuses are issued for successful organizational performance under this plan, most of the reward is issued in the form of company stock in order to ensure that executives' activities are consistent with the shareholders' interest, and to encourage executives to tend to the long-term performance of the organization. The line-of-sight problem previously described is less of an issue with executives as they make strategic decisions, which indeed influence organization performance and shareholder value. It should be noted, however, that the line-of-sight problem does not disappear with executive pay. Many factors, such as the state of the economy, still lie outside the control of executives. As a result, boards of directors might consider evaluating executive performance on the basis of individual behavior (much like merit pay plans), as well as organizational results. Behaviors evaluated might include development and execution of strategic and operational plans. Interestingly, a recent development is the use of stock options for members of the board of directors. Traditionally, cash bonuses have been provided, but increasingly stock is being issued to ensure that the long-term interests of the company are represented by the board.

Pay and Performance Plan Effectiveness

Many empirical studies and literature reviews have been conducted on the effectiveness of pay and performance plan effectiveness. This literature is summarized in Table 13.4. Several important general themes emerge from this literature. Unlike other areas of human resource research, a large number of studies have been amassed on the impact of performance-based plans on actual productivity. In general, the results are very impressive for the magnitude of the impact of performance-based pay relative to other human resource interventions such as employee empowerment (Locke, Feren, McCaleb, Shaw, & Denny, 1980).

Actual productivity gains associated with each type of plan seem to vary by the purpose of the pay plan type. Productivity gains are substantial (averaging around 20 percent) for plans such as piece-rate that emphasize specific short-term results. Plans that are designed to foster identification with the organization, such as profit sharing, have smaller productivity gains (averaging around 5 percent). Plans such as gainsharing that have specific goals at the business unit level (and thus attempt to motivate individual performance

Table 13.4. Evaluation of Various Performance-Based Pay Plans.

Plan	Frequency of Use	Average Productivity Increase	Attitudinal Reactions	Benchmark Companies
Merit pay	Large and declining	Too few studies to tell	Positive pay satisfaction and job satisfaction	Hewlett-Packard, Motorola
Piece-rate and sales	Moderate and steady	Large	Few studies, mainly case studies; dated	Lincoln Electric
Gainsharing	Small and rapidly increasing	Moderate	Positive job satisfaction	Herman Miller, General Electric
Profit sharing and Stock ownership	Small and moderately increasing	Small	Too few studies to tell	3M, PepsiCo
Skill-based pay and Competency-based pay	Small and moderately increasing	Too few studies to tell	Positive employer reactions; employee reactions unknown	Procter & Gamble

Sources: Kruse (1993); Blinder (1990); McAdams and Hawk (1995); Heneman (1992); Lawler, Mohrman, and Ledford (1995); Welbourne and Gomez-Mejia (1995); Blasi, Conte, and Kruse (1996); Gerhart and Milkovich (1992); Lawler and Jenkins (1992); Jenkins, Ledford, Gupta, and Doty (1992); Schuster (1989); Peck (1989, 1991); O'Dell (1987).

through the group) have moderate productivity gains (averaging about 10 percent). Unfortunately, the most frequently used performance-based pay plan, merit pay, has undergone too few studies to allow us to reach any meaningful conclusions regarding productivity. A similar problem exists with the most recent innovations in performance-based pay, skill-based and competency pay.

With the exception of merit pay and to a lesser extent gainsharing, there is very little data available on employee reactions to performance-based pay. Merit pay has repeatedly been shown to be related in a positive manner to both job and pay satisfaction. Gainsharing has been repeatedly shown to be positively related to job satisfaction, but for the most part is missing data on the relationship with pay satisfaction. Very few studies have looked at employee reactions to piece-rate pay, profit sharing, and stock sharing. Only employer perceptions, which are favorable, have been reported for skill-based and competency-based pay. This summary of attitudinal data points to the crying need for additional research. Perhaps employers could band together in a consortium to further explore reactions to performance-based pay plans. An excellent model to follow here is the Mayflower group, a consortium of employers that has built a large descriptive database on employee attitudes across organizations (Johnson, 1996). Development of a database such as this for attitudinal reactions to pay would provide organizations with norms to compare themselves against. Such an effort is important as employee reactions toward pay have been shown to be related to absenteeism, turnover, and union vote (Heneman, 1985).

In terms of frequency of use, many employers appear to have become disillusioned with merit pay. Factors that may contribute to this disillusionment include small merit budgets (3 percent to 4 percent) in recent years, the use of poorly developed rating instruments, and the treatment of pay increases under traditional merit plans as a fixed rather than variable cost. On the other hand, gainsharing has taken off in popularity. The increased popularity of these plans may be due to the increased use of teams in organizations and to the emphasis in many of these plans on cost reductions.

Overall, it is difficult to say whether performance-based pay plans affect attitudes, productivity, or both attitudes and productivity. Unfortunately, within any of the pay plan types, researchers have focused on either attitudes or productivity. Future researchers and organizations evaluating the effectiveness of their performance-based pay plans need to gather both sets of evidence. We hope that this can become the norm as newly created performance-based pay plans are more frequently used and evaluated.

Design Issues

Integration with Business Strategy and Organizational Culture

When designing a reward plan, careful consideration must be given to matching the reward plan with the objectives of the business and the culture of the organization. As can be seen in Figure 13.1, business strategy and organizational culture affect the selection of performance criteria. These criteria reflect the goals that the organization strives toward, and the culture needed to meet these organizational goals.

The reward plan must also be consistent with these factors. Plans that match with various business objectives are shown in Table 13.5. Plans consistent with different cultures are shown in Table 13.6. *Culture* refers to the shared set of beliefs and values held by members of the organization (Ott, 1989). Traditional cultures emphasize top-down decision making, vertical communications, and clearly defined jobs while involvement cultures emphasize shared decision making, lateral communications, and loosely defined roles (Lawler, 1990).

Figure 13.1. Reward Plan Design Model.

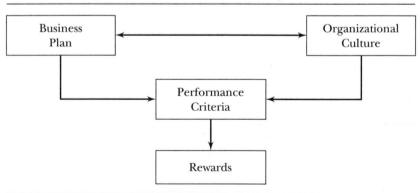

Table 13.5. Matching Reward Plans with Business Objectives.

Business Objective	Reward Plan
Employee development	Competency-based pay Skill-based pay
Customer service	Merit pay Competency-based pay Gainsharing
Productivity: Individual	Piece-rate Sales Standard hour
Productivity: Group	Gainsharing Standard hour Group incentives
Teamwork	Team recognition Team sales Team-based merit pay Gainsharing
Quality	Merit pay Gainsharing Competency-based pay
Profit	Executive pay Profit or stock sharing
Cost reduction and Revenue enhancement	Gainsharing Employee suggestion systems

Ameritech offers an excellent example of linking performance criteria to the business plan (Heneman & von Hippel, 1996). Core competencies of the business, spelled out in the business plan, are taken directly from the business plan and then used to establish performance criteria for evaluating employees on each competency. For example, customer service is a core business competency. In turn, it is used to establish dimensions of customer service performance such as "Personalizes Customer Contacts." Ultimately, behavioral indicators of each performance dimension serve as performance criteria for customer service representatives. For example, behavioral indicators of personalized customer contact include "Treats each customer as an individual with individual needs,"

Table 13.6. Matching Reward Plans with Organizational Culture.

Plans for Traditional Cultures	
• Merit pay	• Sales commissions
• Piece-rate pay	• Employee suggestion systems
• Standard hour plans	• Executive pay

Plans for Involvement Cultures	
• Team-based merit pay	• Stock sharing
• Team recognition plans	• Skill-based pay
• Gainsharing	• Competency-based pay
• Profit sharing	• Team sales and recognition
• Executive pay	• Group incentives

"Incorporates customer information in conversations," and "Recognizes different personality types and responds appropriately."

Several organizations are known for having appraisal and reward systems tied to the culture of the organization (Heneman, Waldeck, & Cushnie, 1996). Performance standards at US West and Levi Strauss, for example, are based on diversity criteria and in turn these criteria are related to the respective business plans (Mitchell & O'Neal, 1994). At Hoechst Celanese, performance relative to diversity criteria is also used to determine pay increases (Rice, 1994).

The absence of a match between the reward system, culture, and business objectives can create problems (Lawler & Jenkins, 1992). For example, organizations with a traditional culture that want to improve productivity through team-based pay may be in for a shock. Productivity gains hoped for with teams may not be instantaneous because an involvement culture is needed for teams to work. While team-based pay can be used to change the culture, it will take time. An example of an organization with a critical alignment of the business plan, culture, and reward system is Time Warner Cable in Columbus, Ohio. The senior author of this chapter was brought in at a transitional time in the company, when it was shifting from a traditional culture to an involvement culture to be more responsive to customer and employee needs. A new mission statement was developed that stated: "We are committed to becoming the premier multimedia company through our collective talents, quality service, innovation, and technology." To emphasize employee talents, a skill-based pay plan was put in place. To deliver quality service, innovation, and technology, team-based pay was used. To ease the transition from a traditional to employee involvement culture, the merit pay system was retained. As a result of these innovations and others, Warner Cable is one of the most profitable groups in the Time Warner cable system network.

This example from Time Warner also shows the reward system being used as a *lag* system (Lawler, 1981). That is, the reward system was used to reinforce the shift from a traditional to involvement culture. In other organizations, according to Lawler, the reward system is used as a *lead* system to move the culture from traditional to innovative. That is, the reward system is developed to bring about a change in the culture. In essence, pay as a lead system provides shock therapy to the organization to free it from the traditional culture. An example of a lead system is the educational system in Kentucky, which shifted from a time-in-grade pay system to a gain-sharing plan where pay increases are based on improvements in student achievement scores at the school level. This approach was mandated by Kentucky state law (Odden & Kelley, 1997).

Performance-based pay plans should only be used for organizational change under limited circumstances. There should be a perceived need for change in the existing reward system and there must be the resources needed to bring about a change (Lawler, 1991). For example, in 1984 Baker Supermarket was rapidly losing market share to other grocery chains entering the Omaha market. As a result, management met with its seventeen hundred employees to communicate the urgency of the situation. Employees concerned about the situation (and the security of their jobs) asked how they could increase their productivity. Management and employees held a series of meetings to identify areas of operations in which sales might be increased. Once these ideas were communicated, employees had a better understanding of how to improve their performance, and profitability improved. ("Case History . . . ," 1986).

A final strategic consideration is the need for performance criteria to guide the selection of reward systems rather than using reward systems as a guide to the selection of performance criteria. Performance-based reward plans are popular these days and receive considerable publicity. As a result, a senior executive may say, "We should consider using a profit sharing plan like I read about in our trade association magazine." The human resource manager is likely to receive this suggestion as a command and look for profit measures (such as return on assets or economic value added) to guide pay decisions. A better approach would be for the human resource manager to say to the executive, "Do you realize that profit sharing conflicts with our corporate goal of increasing market share? What we really need to focus on is customer service to improve market share. Perhaps we should consider using competency-based pay to be consistent with our performance measure (customer service) and our corporate goal (market share)?"

The point being made in the previous example is that the performance measurement system needs to be developed prior to the pay mechanism. One only need look to the federal government for a case study on the problems that can arise when the pay mechanism is developed prior to the performance measurement system. The Civil Service Reform Act of 1978 shifted the basis of pay in the federal government from seniority to merit. This change was done with little consideration given to performance measurement and the plan led to very unfavorable reactions by all those employees affected, as documented in many studies (Perry, 1988).

Unfavorable reactions under this type of system change are very predictable from a fairness perspective (Greenberg, 1987). Performance standards should always be spelled out in advance of rewards so that employees know what is expected of them. In the case of the federal government, performance standards were never made clear due to the absence of a well-developed appraisal system. As a result, employees were not clear about what was expected of them and in turn, were unsure how to influence their pay.

Motivational Considerations

Rewards will have more motivational influence when the employee recognizes a direct relationship between activities, performance results achieved, and rewards gained. A primary concern in the design of reward systems is how well the plan will work in motivating employees. The theory base behind this design consideration is *ex-*

pectancy theory (Heneman, 1992). According to this theory, a reward plan needs to have the following motivational properties: expectancy, instrumentality, and valence. *Expectancy* means that employees must see a link between their efforts and performance. *Instrumentality* means that performance must be seen as being linked to outcomes or consequences. *Valence* means that the outcomes or consequences must be attractive to employees. There are many outcomes other than cash that may have as much positive valence as cash, or more. Time off, for example, is often critical to employees and may be viewed as being more attractive than cash.

An important strategic decision that organizations must make in designing reward systems is how to best influence these motivational properties of expectancy, instrumentality, and valence. There are currently four major motivational philosophies to guide these decisions, as shown in Table 13.7.

Table 13.7. Matching Reward Plans with Motivational Philosophies.

Motivational Philosophy	Reward Plan
Pure pay	Piece-rate Sales commissions Standard hour plan Executive pay Group incentives
Employee development	Skill-based pay Competency-based pay Merit pay
Participation	Profit sharing Stock sharing Gainsharing Employee suggestion plans Merit pay
Teamwork	Team-based merit pay Gainsharing Team-based sales Team recognition Group incentives

The pure pay perspective is based on reinforcement theory and suggests that pay should be made contingent on specific and observable measures of performance (Heneman, 1992). Under this approach, performance must be very clearly defined for employees and a direct link made to their pay. If performance is not clearly defined, then undesirable consequences may occur. For example, if performance is solely defined as output, then quality may suffer. A pure pay perspective lends itself to the use of performance-based reward plans with countable indicators of performance as in a piece-rate pay plan. It should be noted that a pay plan of this type may need to be supplemented with a merit pay plan to compensate for the undesirable consequences of measuring countable indicators only. For example, at Lincoln Electric, merit pay is used along with piece-rate pay to reinforce both quantity and quality.

The employee development perspective is based on human capital theory (Becker, 1996). It suggests that rather than specifying outcomes for employees to pursue, inputs or human capital should be emphasized. Human capital consists of knowledge, skills, and abilities. From this perspective, pay should be provided for capabilities rather than results to serve as a motivational factor. The employee development perspective is used when the organization wishes to emphasize flexibility in its workforce. That is, it wants employees who are qualified to perform whatever work is needed at a particular time. A company with this perspective sees no need to shut down an assembly line when a stoppage occurs, for example, or to call in a specialist to fix it. Instead, employees on the line should have the competencies needed to immediately repair the line and keep the product moving. Thus, although it may seem unusual to pay for capability rather than actual results, it can be seen from this example how capabilities can be directly related to business results. Moreover, to make the link between capabilities and results even more clear, some organizations like Westinghouse define competencies in terms of observable behaviors and results.

The participation perspective suggests that employees should become active participants in decisions that affect the business and have traditionally been decided by managers (Lawler, 1995). Some pay plans like gainsharing make employee participation a cornerstone of the pay plan. Other reward plans like piece-rate pay rely on subject matter experts, involving industrial engineers and executives to make decisions. The motivational value from plans with participation is believed to come from the process of participation as well as the amount of pay received. Participation is motivational to employees because it gives them a sense of ownership to the work process as they have input into how it is to be best accomplished. That is, they can see a relationship between their efforts and company performance. Participation also helps the employees feel that the pay system is a fair one. Research has shown that in terms of pay fairness, not only is the amount of pay that people receive important, but so too is the manner in which the amount of pay was determined (Folger & Konovsky, 1989). Pay decisions are more likely to be viewed as fair when employees have input into the process used to determine pay increases than when pay decisions are unilaterally decided by management. Input might include, for example, employees and managers jointly setting performance standards.

A teamwork perspective suggests that employees are energized by their work with others (Gross, 1995). Team members work with one another to advance their collective aims and issue sanctions to group members who fail to comply. Under this approach the social aspects of work are believed to be motivating to people. To emphasize the importance of social interactions, rewards are offered. This approach differs from the participation philosophy in that participation can be used regardless of whether work is designed for individuals or collections of individuals to perform.

As shown in Table 13.7, reward plans lend themselves to different motivational philosophies. Design teams need to fully consider these perspectives and their implications when designing the reward plan. Also, they need to consider these perspectives regarding their own functioning. Research has shown that a participatory approach to pay plan design seems to work best (McAdams & Hawk, 1995). A design team needs to have representation from all business units and levels of the organization for the results of its work to be acceptable to all those affected. Special expertise is also needed, including help from finance, operations, and human resources.

Performance Measurement Levels

Many performance constructs, productivity as an example, can be measured and rewarded at the level of the individual, group, or organization. The levels selected are of primary concern in the design of performance-based pay plans because there are distinct virtues and problems with measures at each level.

Measurement at the individual level has the distinct advantage of usually being under the control of the individual. As a result, it strengthens by expectancy and instrumentality links. The downside, however, is that employees may become so engrossed in their individual accomplishments that they ignore the larger goals of their team and organization.

Group- or team-level performance measures have the advantage of putting the goal of the team before that of the individual. This approach is often advocated in team environments. Unfortunately, some employees may take advantage of this system by "social loafing" or "free riding" (Heneman & von Hippel, 1995). That is, some employees may not put forth their best efforts because others in the group will carry the slackers to group goal accomplishment through their own extra-hard efforts.

When performance is measured at the organizational level, an important advantage is that the measures of performance are very closely related to the goals of the organization. Hence, they fulfill the goal of many reward plans to bring employee goals in alignment with organizational goals. Unfortunately, however, in many circumstances these organizational-level measures of performance are outside the control of individual employees, which may weaken expectancy perceptions needed for employee performance.

Given the strengths and weaknesses of performance measures at each level and the fact that many organizations have business goals at each level, an argument can be made that there should be multiple performance-based pay plans. In this fashion, the weaknesses of one plan may be offset somewhat by the strengths of another plan and multiple business goals may be accomplished. A combined reward strategy of this nature is used by Lincoln Electric, where financial rewards are provided for individual, group, and organizational performance measures (Perry, 1990). This plan has been successfully used at Lincoln Electric for over eighty years.

Rigorous empirical assessment of the combined reward strategy has produced mixed results. On one hand, Wageman (1995) found that with intact work teams at Xerox, combining individual and group pay led to deleterious effects on group performance. The groups performed better as a group when the pay plan was based on group or individual performance rewards rather than a combination of group and individual rewards. On the other hand, Crown and Rosse (1995) found in a study of sports teams that a combination of group and individual performance goals resulted in better group performance than did individual performance goals alone, but that the combined group and individual goals resulted in less effective group performance than did group goals alone. Unfortunately, neither study measured the impact of these approaches on individual performance.

The results of these two studies and the Lincoln Electric case suggest that it is possible to successfully use a combined reward strategy, but that to do so may require considerable time and that the attempt may not be appropriate in all situations. Considerable time may be required because in many organizations, employees have grown accustomed to pay increases based on individual or group performance rather than individual and group performance combined. Not all situations lend themselves to a combined plan (Lawler, 1990). Some do, of course. For example, baseball teams have both group and individual business objectives—that is, winning games and maintaining the players' own batting averages and other statistics. A combined plan may make sense for organizations that have both group and individual goals. Other settings, such as process manufacturing, may only have group output goals. In this environment, combined group and individual rewards may not make sense.

Organizations might also consider integrated individual and group reward plans instead of combined individual and group reward plans. Under this approach, often called team-based merit pay, a group-level outcome such as teamwork is measured at the individual level in terms of critical incidents that reflect desired behavior on the part of the individual (Heneman & von Hippel, 1995). In the case of teamwork, individual behaviors that are consistent with being a good team player are measured. Organizations using this approach include Motorola, Hewlett-Packard, and Levi Strauss (Shaw & Schneier, 1995). This approach led to higher group performance than did a combined plan in the Crown and Rosse (1995) study. Team-based merit pay plans keep more of the focus on the individual than do combined plans. As a result, they might be used to help individual-based reward organizations make the transition toward becoming more group focused.

Implementation Issues

The Achilles heel of many pay-for-performance plans is the implementation stage. Issues of implementation that must be considered prior to the pay plan intervention include measurement, fairness, and communications. Each of these issues will be addressed in turn.

Measurement

Pay-for-performance plans are highly dependent upon the measures of performance that are used. If the measures used are not reliable and valid, then the organization may incur large costs as a result of rewarding employees for factors not related to the effectiveness of the organization. In addition, employees are unlikely to be motivated because reliable and valid measures are needed for employees to perceive the expectancy and instrumentality links necessary for employee motivation.

It is sometimes mistakenly assumed that valid measures refer to those indexes that the organization currently measures. While these measures may be convenient, they are not necessarily valid because they may have no relationship to the business plan. Instead, for example, they may be collected as part of an off-the-shelf applications package. The data collected by this package may have been put together without regard to the specific goals of any one particular organization.

It is also sometimes mistakenly assumed that countable indicators of performance are more objective and hence more valid. Absenteeism, for example, can be a count of employees who are not at work. There are two potential problems with this count. First, the count may not be consistently made. Recorders may apply different standards (for example, excused versus unexcused) in counting absences. Second, concentrating on countable, objective indicators may lead an organization to overlook less countable but equally important indicators of performance, such as customer service.

For performance measures to be valid, they must be consistent with the business plan of the organization and be measured in a consistent and reliable manner. Methods to improve the reliability and validity of performance measures include the use of a mission statement and job analysis to develop performance measures, participation by employees in scale development, rater training, and the use of multiple raters (Heneman, 1992).

Fairness

More reliable and valid measures of performance are likely to lead to greater perceptions of fairness by employees. In turn, perceptions of fairness are likely to lead to employee acceptance of the new pay plan and a greater willingness to act in accordance with the plan. A survey of Fortune 100 firms by Bretz, Milkovich, and Read (1992) indicated that the most crucial issue organizations faced in terms of their performance appraisal systems was the fairness in how the system was used.

Fairness has two components: distributive justice and procedural justice (Greenberg, 1987). *Distributive justice* refers to the fairness of the outcome associated with the performance-based pay plan (for example, size of bonus), while *procedural justice* refers to the fairness of the procedures used to determine the outcomes (for example, performance ratings). As noted earlier, research has shown that it is not only the amount of money that is important in determining pay satisfaction, it is also the procedures used to establish pay (Folger & Konovsky, 1989). To increase the perceived procedural justice of a performance-based pay plan, the following steps can be taken (Heneman, 1992):

- Have employees participate in pay plan design.
- Create an appeals system.
- Use reliable and valid performance measures.
- Train raters to eliminate rating errors.
- Follow laws and regulations.
- Use a written policy and procedure for pay decisions.
- Send out a periodic newsletter.

For a more detailed review of issues and recommendations concerning fairness and appraisal, please see Chapter Six in this book.

Communications

An excellent example of a newsletter comes from McDonnell Aircraft Company (Handshear, 1988, supplemented by personal communication from N. A. Handshear, 1989). Known originally as *Merit Review News*, it was issued to all employees on a periodic basis to update them on the merit pay program at McDonnell Aircraft. Topics included discussion of the size of the merit budget, rate range movement, and performance review guidelines. Surveys of employees' reactions at McDonnell and those of compensation professionals outside McDonnell were very positive. As a result, the newsletter was expanded to include more detail on the merit pay guidelines and to include other compensation topics like the bonus plan. A more formal survey of this plan several years later indicated that employees who were familiar with the newsletter saw their pay as being more fair, were more committed to the organization, and were less likely to leave their jobs than those employees that were not familiar with the newsletter (McCarty-Kilian, 1992).

Pay Secrecy

One issue regarding the communication of performance-based pay plans is how much information should be revealed to employees about their performance and pay and the performance and pay of other employees. Plans can range from being very closed (employees are only told their performance ratings and pay raises) to very open (employees are told everyone's performance ratings and pay raises).

The research on which approach is best is mixed (Heneman, 1992). On one hand, secrecy may result in supervisors doing a better job at differentiating among employee performance levels. On the other hand, employees are less likely to be satisfied with secrecy because they have a tendency to overestimate the rewards of others. Confronted with this mixed evidence, most organizations take a middle ground and let employees know the average ratings and raises, as well as the range of ratings and raises around that average, rather than letting employees know the specific figures for each employee.

Split Reviews

General Electric pioneered a concept in the 1960s known as *split reviews* (Meyer, Kay, & French, 1965). Under a split review, the performance review for purposes of development is separated from the performance review for purposes of pay raises. In essence, two reviews are conducted: one for pay and one for development. This split is done so that the supervisor is not required to be a coach and judge in the same session. This practice was carried out at General Electric for many years and many other organizations adopted this model.

Interestingly, Lawler, Mohrman, and Resnick (1984) returned to General Electric many years later and found that employees were not supportive of split reviews. Employees wanted pay discussed in their reviews and felt that it was not being done enough. Although it is difficult to be a coach and evaluator, it appears that supervisors should play both roles in appraisals. Employees are more likely to be satisfied (Giles & Mossholder, 1990; Prince & Lawler, 1986; Dorfman, Stephan, & Loveland, 1986) and may also be more motivated because it is easier for the employee to establish instrumentality perceptions when both topics are discussed at the same time.

In those organizations using 360-degree review systems, caution needs to be exercised in combining developmental and evaluative reviews. Recent research by the American Compensation Association (1996b) suggests that most organizations with competency models are using them for the purposes of selection and development rather than for purposes of selection, development, and compensation combined. A story from a compensation director of a large manufacturing firm illustrates why it may be advisable to couple pay with performance in a 360-degree review environment only after employee reactions to the 360-degree review process are favorable. The story goes that for a research and development facility with scientists, a 360-degree feedback process was hastily implemented for pay decisions. It immediately failed because the appraisal system was brand new and not well thought out. The scientists worked in teams. Each team got together at a remote site and set up a circle of chairs in a room. The person being evaluated sat in the middle and was grilled by the other team members.

Needless to say, this procedure did not conform to the principles of a sound performance appraisal system. Coupling pay increases to this poorly developed performance appraisal system further sensitized employees to problems with the appraisal system.

Summary and Conclusion

Performance appraisal is only one component of the performance management process. Another important component of the performance management process is the linkage between performance judgments and rewards. Prior to the publication of this book, previous books on performance appraisal have devoted very little attention to the reward system. As demonstrated in this chapter, rewards can and should be viewed as an integral part of the performance management process. Reward systems have been shown to be related to individual and organizational effectiveness. A detailed summary of the conclusions reached for practice in this chapter is shown in Exhibit 13.1. They are grouped by general principles, which list practices having wide scale applicability, and by contingency considerations, which list practices that need to be adapted to local circumstances.

References

Altmansberger, H. N., & Wallace, M. J., Jr. (1995, Winter). Strategic use of goalsharing at Corning. *ACA Journal,* pp. 64–73.

American Compensation Association. (1996a). *Certification course 12: Alternative reward systems: Improving productivity and competitiveness.* Scottsdale, AZ: Author.

American Compensation Association. (1996b). *Raising the bar: Using competencies to enhance employee performance.* Scottsdale, AZ: Author.

Ash, R. A., Levine, E. L., & Sistrunk, F. (1983). The role of jobs and job-based methods in personnel and human resources management. *Research in Personnel and Human Resources Management, 1,* 45–84.

Barney, J. B. (1991). Firm resources and sustained competitive advantage. *Journal of Management, 17,* 99–120.

Becker, G. S. (1996, March 11). Human capital: One investment where America is ahead. *Business Week,* p. 18.

Belcher, J. G., Jr. (1991). *Gainsharing.* Houston: Gulf.

Exhibit 13.1. Summary of Recommended Reward Practices.

General Principles

- Performance-based pay plans have been shown to be effective in many different organizational settings.

- There has been a rapid increase in the use of performance-based pay plans by organizations.

- Performance-based pay plans are more likely to be motivational when they help employees clearly see links between their effort and performance and between their performance and rewards.

- Performance-based pay plans are more likely to be effective the more reliable and valid their measures of performance.

- Performance-based pay plans are more likely to be effective the more that employees consider the outcomes of the reward process and the procedures used to determine the outcomes to be fair.

- Pay increase parameters (minimum, average, maximum) and not individual pay increases should be communicated to employees.

- Employees are more likely to be satisfied with performance reviews when a discussion of their performance and pay is conducted in the same session than when their performance and pay are discussed in two separate sessions.

Contingencies to Consider

- Exempt employees are more likely than nonexempt employees to prefer performance-based pay plans.

- The attractiveness of different forms of rewards for employees (for example, bonus pay versus time off) varies by individual.

- The selection of the most appropriate performance-based reward plans depends upon the business objectives, culture, and motivational philosophy of the organization.

- The type of pay plan used is determined by the types of performance measures used and the level of performance measurement.

- The strengths and weaknesses of performance-based pay plans depend on the type of pay plan used.

Blasi, J., Conte, M., & Kruse, D. (1996). Employee stock ownership and corporate performance among public companies. *Industrial and Labor Relations Review, 50,* 60–79.

Blinder, A. S. (Ed.). (1990). *Paying for productivity: A look at the evidence.* Washington, DC: Brookings Institution.

Bretz, R. D., Jr., Milkovich, G. T., & Read, W. (1992). The current state of performance appraisal research and practice: Concerns, directions, and implications. *Journal of Management, 18,* 321–352.

Campbell, J. P. (1990). Modeling the performance prediction problem in industrial and organizational psychology. In M. D. Dunnette & L. M. Hough (Eds.), *Handbook of industrial and organizational psychology: Vol. 1* (2nd ed., pp. 687–732). Palo Alto, CA: Consulting Psychologists Press.

Case history: Employee feedback helps bottom line. (1986). *Small Business Report, 11,* 98.

Crown, D. F., & Rosse, J. G. (1995). Yours, mine, and ours: Facilitating group productivity through the integration of individual and group goals. *Organizational Behavior and Human Decision Processes, 64*(2), 138–150.

Deci, R. L. (1972). The effects of contingent and noncontingent rewards and controls on intrinsic motivation. *Organizational Behavior and Human Performance, 8,* 15–31.

Deming, W. E. (1986). *Out of the crisis.* Cambridge, MA: MIT Center for Advanced Engineering Study.

Dorfman, P. W., Stephan, W. G., & Loveland, J. (1986). Performance appraisal behaviors: Supervisor perceptions and subordinate reactions. *Personnel Psychology, 39,* 579–597.

Eisenberger, R., & Cameron, J. (1996). Detrimental effects of reward: Reality or myth? *American Psychologist, 51,* 1153–1166.

Folger, R., & Konovsky, M. A. (1989). Effects of procedural and distributive justice on reactions to pay raise decisions. *Academy of Management Journal, 32,* 115–130.

Gaga, V. A., & Kaz, M. S. (1996, November-December). The post-privatization period: A look at personal motivation systems for Russian enterprises. *American Compensation Association News,* pp. 8–11.

Gerhart, B., & Milkovich, G. T. (1992). Employee compensation: Research and practice. In M. D. Dunnette & L. M. Hough (Eds.), *Handbook of industrial and organizational psychology: Vol. 3* (2nd ed., pp. 1009–1055). Palo Alto, CA: Consulting Psychologists Press.

Giles, W. F., & Mossholder, K. W. (1990). Employee reactions to contextual and session components of performance appraisal. *Journal of Applied Psychology, 75,* 371–377.

Graham-Moore, B., & Ross, T. L. (1990). *Gainsharing*. Washington, DC: Bureau of National Affairs.

Greenberg, J. (1987). A taxonomy of organizational justice theories. *Academy of Management Review, 12*, 9–22.

Gross, S. E. (1995). *Compensation for teams*. New York: AMACOM.

Handshear, N. A. (1988, May). News preferred over mystery—members favor *Merit Review News*. *American Compensation Association News*, p. 10.

Heneman, H. G., III. (1985). Pay satisfaction. In K. N. Rowland & G. R. Ferris (Eds.), *Research in personnel and human resource management: Vol. 3* (pp. 115–139). Greenwich, CT: JAI Press.

Heneman, R. L. (1992). *Merit pay: Linking pay increases to performance ratings*. Reading, MA: Addison Wesley Longman.

Heneman, R. L., & von Hippel, C. (1995). Balancing group and individual rewards: Rewarding individual contributions to the team. *Compensation and Benefits Review, 27*(4), 63–68.

Heneman, R. L., & von Hippel, C. (1996). The assessment of job performance: Focusing attention on context, process and group issues. In D. Lewin, D. J. B. Mitchell, & M. A. Zaidi (Eds.), *Handbook of human resource management* (pp. 587–617). Greenwich, CT: JAI Press.

Heneman, R. L., von Hippel, C., Eskew, D. E., & Greenberger, D. B. (1996). Strategic rewards in unionized environments. *ACA Journal*.

Heneman, R. L., Waldeck, N., & Cushnie, M. (1996). Diversity considerations in staffing decision making. In E. E. Kossek & S. Lobel (Eds.), *Managing diversity: Human resource strategies for transforming the workplace* (pp. 74–101). Cambridge, MA: Blackwell.

Ilgen, D. R., & Hollenbeck, J. R. (1991). The structure of work: Design and roles. In M. D. Dunnette & L. M. Hough (Eds.), *Handbook of industrial and organizational psychology: Vol. 2* (2nd ed., pp. 165–208). Palo Alto, CA: Consulting Psychologists Press.

Jenkins, G. D., Ledford, J., Jr., Gupta, N., & Doty, D. (1992). *Skill-based pay: Practices, payoffs, pitfalls, and prescriptions*. Scottsdale, AZ: American Compensation Association.

Johnson, R. H. (1996). Life in the consortium: The Mayflower Group. In A. I. Kraut (Ed.), *Organizational surveys: Tools for assessment and change* (pp. 285–309). San Francisco: Jossey-Bass.

Katzenbach, J. R., & Smith, D. K. (1993). *The wisdom of teams*. New York: HarperCollins.

Knouse, S. B. (1995). *The reward and recognition process in total quality management*. Milwaukee: ASQC Quality Press.

Kohn, A. (1993). *Punished by rewards*. Boston: Houghton-Mifflin.

Kruse, D. L. (1993). *Profit sharing: Does it make a difference?* Kalamazoo, MI: Upjohn Institute.

Lawler, E. E., III. (1981). *Pay and organizational development*. Reading, MA: Addison Wesley Longman.

Lawler, E. E., III. (1990). *Strategic pay*. San Francisco: Jossey-Bass.

Lawler, E. E., III. (1995). The new pay: A strategic approach. *Compensation and Benefits Review, 27,* 14–22.

Lawler, E. E., III. (1996). Competencies: A poor foundation for the new pay. *Compensation and Benefits Review, 28*(6), 20–26.

Lawler, E. E., III, & Jenkins, G. D., Jr. (1992). Strategic reward systems. In M. D. Dunnette & L. M. Hough (Eds.), *Handbook of industrial and organizational psychology: Vol. 3* (2nd ed., pp. 1009–1055). Palo Alto, CA: Consulting Psychologists Press.

Lawler, E. E., III, Mohrman, S. A., & Ledford, G. E., Jr. (1995). *Creating high performance organizations: Practices and results of employee involvement and TQM in Fortune 1000 companies*. San Francisco: Jossey-Bass.

Lawler, E. E., III, Mohrman, A. M., Jr., & Resnick, R. M. (1984). Performance appraisal revisited. *Organizational Dynamics, 12,* 20–35.

Ledford, G. E., Jr. (1991). Three case studies on skill-based pay: An overview. *Compensation and Benefits Review, 23*(2), 11–23.

Locke, E. A., Feren, D. B, McCaleb, V. M., Shaw, K. N., & Denny, A. J. (1980). The relative effectiveness of motivating employee performance. In K. D. Duncan, M. M. Gruneberg, & D. Wallis (Eds.), *Changes in working life* (pp. 363–388). New York: Wiley.

Lorant, R. (1992, June 27). Mechanic sues Sears for firing. *Wisconsin State Journal,* p. A1.

McAdams, J. L. (1996). *The reward plan advantage: A manager's guide to improving business through people*. San Francisco: Jossey-Bass.

McAdams, J. L., & Hawk, E. J. (1995). *Organizational performance and rewards*. Scottsdale, AZ: American Compensation Association.

McCarty-Kilian, C. (1992). *Using a corporate newsletter to communicate pay information: A study of pay fairness*. Unpublished doctoral dissertation, Ohio State University, Columbus.

Meyer, H. H., Kay, E., & French, J. R. P. (1965). Split roles in performance appraisal. *Harvard Business Review, 43,* 123–129.

Milkovich, G. T., & Newman, J. M. (1996). *Compensation*. Burr Ridge, IL: Irwin.

Mitchell, R., & O'Neal, M. (1994, August 1). Managing by values. *Business Week,* pp. 46–52.

Montemayer, E. F. (1994, Winter). Aligning pay systems with market strategies. *ACA Journal,* pp. 44–53.

Montemayer, E. F. (1995). Book review of A. Kohn, *Punished by rewards. Personnel Psychology, 4,* 941–948.

Nathan, B. R., & Cascio, W. F. (1986). Technical and legal standards. In R. A. Berk (Ed.), *Performance assessment: Methods and applications* (pp. 1–50). Baltimore: Johns Hopkins University Press.

Nelson, B. (1994). *1001 ways to reward employees.* New York: Workman.

Norris, F. (1991). Look out for number one. *New York Times,* pp. A1, C5.

Odden, A., & Kelley, C. (1997). *Paying teachers for what they know and do.* Thousand Oaks, CA: Corwin Press.

O'Dell, C. O. (1987). *Major findings from people, performance, and pay.* Scottsdale, AZ: American Compensation Association.

Ott, J. S. (1989). *The organizational cultural perspective.* Florence, KY: Dorsey Press.

Peck, C. (1984). *Pay and performance: The interaction of compensation and performance appraisal.* Research Bulletin No. 155. New York: Conference Board.

Peck, C. (1989). *Variable pay: New performance rewards.* Research Bulletin No. 246. New York: Conference Board.

Peck, C. (1991). *Gainsharing for productivity.* Report No. 967. New York: Conference Board.

Perry, J. L. (1988). Making policy by trial and error: Merit pay in the federal service. *Policy Studies Journal, 17*(2), 389–405.

Perry, T. A. (1990). Staying with the basics. *HR Magazine, 35*(11), 73–76.

Podolske, A. (1996). Tools for defending pay-for-performance against the skeptics. In *Pay-for-performance report* (pp. 1, 12–14). New York: Institute for Management and Administration.

Pollack, A. (1993, October 2). Japanese starting to link pay to performance. *New York Times,* p. A1.

Prince, J. B., & Lawler, E. E., III. (1986). Does salary discussion hurt the developmental performance appraisal? *Organizational Behavior and Human Decision Processes, 37,* 357–375.

Rice, F. (1994, August 8). How to make diversity pay. *Fortune,* pp. 79–86.

Risher, H. (1992). Paying employees for quality. In *Perspectives in total compensation.* Scottsdale, AZ: American Compensation Association.

Schuster, J. R. (1989). Improving productivity through gainsharing: Can the means be justified in the end? *Compensation and Benefits Management, 5,* 207–210.

Schuster, J. R., & Zingheim, P. K. (1992). *The new pay.* San Francisco: New Lexington Press.

Scott, W. E., Jr., Farh, J. L., & Podsakoff, P. M. (1988). The effects of "intrinsic" and "extrinsic" reinforcement contingencies on task behavior. *Organizational Behavior and Human Decision Processes, 41,* 405–425.

Shaw, D. G., & Schneier, C. E. (1995). Team measurement and rewards: How some companies are getting it right. *Human Resource Planning, 18,* 34–49.

Stayer, R. (1990). How I learned to let my workers lead. *Harvard Business Review, 68*(6), 65–72.

Stevens, M. J., & Campion, M. A. (1994). The knowledge, skill, and ability requirements for teamwork: Implications for human resource management. *Journal of Management, 20,* 503–530.

Wageman, R. (1995). Interdependence and group effectiveness. *Administrative Science Quarterly, 40,* 145–180.

Wagner, J. A., III, & Hollenbeck, J. R. (1992). *Management of organizational behavior.* Upper Saddle River, NJ: Prentice Hall.

Wallace, M. J. (1990). *Reward and renewal: America's search for competitive advantage through alternative pay strategies.* Scottsdale, AZ: American Compensation Association.

Welbourne, T., & Gomez-Mejia, L. R. (1995). Gainsharing: A critical review and a future research agenda. *Journal of Management, 21,* 559–609.

Wilson, T. B. (1995). *Innovative reward systems for the changing workplace.* New York: McGraw-Hill.

Wright, P. M. (1994). Goal-setting and monetary incentives: Motivational tools that can work too well. *Compensation and Benefits Review, 26*(3), 41–49.

Zingheim, P. K., Ledford, G. E., Jr., & Schuster, J. R. (1996, Spring). Competencies and competency models: Does one size fit all? *ACA Journal,* pp. 56–65.

CHAPTER 14

Lessons Learned
Research Implications for Performance Appraisal and Management Practice
James W. Smither

True or false: Performance appraisal *research* is not relevant to the *practice* of performance appraisal.

As John Bernardin and his colleagues say at the beginning of this volume, "The appraisal of performance appraisal is not good." Nowhere in industrial-organizational psychology has there been a bigger gap between the interests of scientists and practitioners. For a long time, researchers were asking themselves, "How do people attend to, encode, and recall behavior? How do they translate the behavior they recall into ratings of someone's performance?" They talked a lot about halo errors and the cognitive processes that might cause such errors.

In the meantime, practitioners were asking, "Why do supervisors and employees complain so much about performance appraisals? Why do people say appraisals are unfair or political? Is it possible to design a performance appraisal process that actually motivates (rather than demotivates) employees to behave in ways that benefit the organization? How can appraisals work in team-based or quality-oriented work cultures? How should appraisals be

---

Note: Manuel London served as editor for this chapter.

connected to training investments and compensation decisions?" It's pretty clear that the questions asked by researchers appear very different from the questions asked by practitioners. Thus, when asked the question posed at the beginning of this chapter, I would expect most practitioners to answer, "True."

But things are changing. I think it is premature to conclude that research has nothing to offer the practice of performance appraisal. In fact, I would argue that research has a lot to tell us about the practice of performance appraisal. Each author in this volume tackles an issue that is important to practitioners. The authors show how research can help guide many of the key decisions practitioners make about performance appraisal. They deal with questions about what should be measured, fairness (from the perspective of the law and the employees being appraised), politics, multisource (or what many call 360-degree) feedback, rater training, and appraising executives and CEOs. They consider how to make appraisals work in team, quality, and international contexts. And they show how appraisals can be linked to training and compensation decisions.

In many of the organizations I have observed (through my own work experience or consulting), appraisal is a top-down annual event. Performance dimensions and standards are set unilaterally (usually by a staff member or committee from human resources). The performance appraisal meeting lasts about fifteen minutes (thirty if you're lucky), and there is little or no feedback about performance during the year. Appraisals focus on individuals (even in team environments). Poor performance is generally ignored, unless it is truly abysmal. The process is very political, and there is virtually no accountability to ensure that raters are fair. Appraisals are completely unrelated to training decisions. Everyone receives the same across-the-board salary increase, regardless of performance. (Does this sound like any place you know?)

What would the ideal performance appraisal system look like? I agree with Cardy that there is no easy recipe for the perfect appraisal system. As Bernardin and his colleagues say, no performance appraisal and management system is ideal for all jobs, for all purposes, in all organizations. The authors of this volume cite seven hundred articles and spend hundreds of pages grappling with this issue. Still, the collective insights of these authors (and the voluminous research studies they review) suggest that many of the recommendations summarized in the paragraphs that follow are likely to be useful.

The Context of Appraisals

Appraisal should not be seen as an end in itself but rather as one vital element in a broader set of human resource and management practices that link business objectives, day-to-day performance, development, and compensation. This emphasis on *performance management* includes gathering performance information linked to customer expectations and corporate strategy, providing feedback to individuals and groups, and using the information to improve organizational effectiveness.

The Content of Appraisals

The expectations of key external and internal customers must play a critical role in determining the dimensions and standards of performance that are appraised, thereby eliminating the chance that workers will be rewarded for performance that is valued by their functional area (or supervisors) but is irrelevant to the customers of the product or service. (See Chapter One for examples.)

Appraisals and feedback should focus on performance (not merely on underlying traits). Performance dimensions and standards should be specific and communicate to employees what is expected of them. Raters are not asked to provide a single rating in a broad area like "planning." Instead, there should be separate ratings concerning several aspects of planning, such as quality, quantity, timeliness, cost-effectiveness, interpersonal impact, or need for supervision. The expectations of external or internal customers should help determine what is considered timely, cost effective, high quality, and so on. (Chapter One also provides more information on this point.)

Where feasible, assessments of performance should be combined with customer data (for example, external or internal customer satisfaction or professional mystery shoppers) and so-called objective or countable results, but these countable results must be interpreted in context (for example, sales revenue is interpreted by considering and perhaps adjusting for factors that may facilitate or constrain sales, such as the behavior of competitors in the region). (Chapter One also provides more information on this point.)

Contextual performance (contributions beyond formal or technical role expectations such as helping others, spontaneously offering suggestions for improving work processes, maintaining good relationships with coworkers, staying late to complete a task) should be explicitly assessed. Contextual performance may be evaluated by peers or direct reports (as well as by supervisors) and is rewarded because it contributes to group and organizational performance. (Chapter One also provides more information on this point.)

An explicit assessment of situational constraints (or system factors) helps illuminate areas of difficulty in the work situation and facilitates agreement between workers and supervisors about the causes of performance and appropriate remedies (including changes in the situation). (For examples, see Chapter Four and also Chapter One.)

Ideally, an organization-specific competency model is developed from a job analysis and content validation process that considers the firm's strategic goals. Competencies are defined at the level of observable behaviors and include criteria for distinguishing between different levels of expertise. That is, these competencies do not look merely like a list of traits ("adaptability," "self-confidence," "integrity," "personal maturity," and so on). The model must guide numerous human resource initiatives, including appraisal, selection, development, promotion, and compensation, thereby creating consistency and mutual reinforcement across the organization's human resource practices. (See discussions in Chapters Seven, Eight, and Twelve.)

The Sources of Appraisals

Appraisals ideally combine feedback from multiple sources, including peers, direct reports, (internal or external) customers, and supervisors. Self-appraisals should also play an important role. The reliability (internal consistency, interrater agreement) of ratings is examined. Validity is established via content evidence (importance ratings from subject matter experts), criterion-related evidence (relationship with outcome measures such as satisfaction, turnover, or group or unit performance), or construct evidence (for example, factor structure). Rated behaviors are observable and can be improved with effort or training. Repeated exposure to desired behaviors (for example, as a self-assessor, peer assessor, and recipient of feedback) helps employees internalize the behaviors and make them part of the organization's culture (that is, the measured behaviors become normative). These appraisals also explicitly consider situational constraints or system factors that may inhibit or facilitate performance. The sources selected to provide ratings are the people who are most knowledgeable about the factors that influence the employee's performance. For example, employees in customer contact roles are appraised by customers. At least initially, multisource feedback is used for developmental rather than administrative (pay) purposes. Ongoing (not merely annual) feedback from these sources helps identify gaps between the way employees see themselves and the way they are seen by others. This helps them better regulate and modify their behavior (for example, via goal setting and links to training programs), thereby increasing performance (and the accuracy of self-evaluations) over time. There are tools (workshops, facilitators, coaches) that help employees use feedback to structure personal development plans and create accountability for change. Data from multisource surveys are aggregated across employees to focus organization-wide interventions. (For examples and more information, see Chapters Eight and Nine.)

Raters need training, but traditional rater error training is to be avoided. Instead, rater training should be matched to the purpose and format of the appraisal and includes frame-of-reference training (to increase rating accuracy, especially with respect to each ratee's relative strengths and limitations), rater variability training (to enhance accurate differentiation among ratees), and behavioral observation training (to improve the observation and recall of relevant behavior). During training, raters are given clear explanations of performance dimensions along with the opportunity to make practice ratings and receive feedback about those ratings. Raters learn to provide task-level feedback and avoid feedback that focuses on the employee's self-image. (See Chapter Eleven for examples and a discussion.)

Certification programs help communicate desired competencies and provide common standards. Certification of competencies is accomplished via structured peer or supervisory assessment, accredited external certification, or internal board certification. There are opportunities for employees to develop each competency, reevaluation for those who do not pass a certification process, clear developmental feedback, and an appeal process to deal with any perceived irregularities in the certification process. Certification may be linked to pay, bonuses, promotion, or other career opportunities. (For examples, see Chapter Seven.)

Special Issues in Appraisal

When organizations recognize that team performance is key to organizational success (or when individual performance is highly dependent on the work of others), they should appraise the performance of the team as a unit. Appraisals in team settings should measure the competencies of individuals (for example, knowledge and skills related to organizationally valued performance), each individual's contribution to the team's performance (via communication, collaboration, and supporting the team's goal setting and decision making), and performance at the team level. A team job analysis is used to identify competencies required of team members and indices of team performance that are clearly related to the strategic goals of the organization. Measures used to assess team-level outcomes (for example, booked revenue, customer satisfaction, cycle time) should not be volatile or unstable and should be controllable (that is, the team can influence the outcomes) and supported by adequate information systems that allow the team to monitor its performance. Team-level performance can also be assessed by internal or external customers (especially when team output is not easily quantifiable). (For examples and a discussion, see Chapter Seven.)

Executive goal setting, appraisal, and compensation should be tightly linked. Executive appraisals should reflect *how* work gets done as well as *what* gets done. Executive goals should reflect the interests of shareholders, customers, and employees and include short-term and long-term, financial and nonfinancial, primary (objectives of the firm's owners) and secondary (processes used to generate results), and internal and external perspectives. These may include value drivers such as sales productivity or inventory turns, strategic metrics such as the development of a new technology platform or entry into strategic alliances, economic or market indicators such as economic value added or market share, and traditional financial measures. Executive performance measures such as those described here should drive all compensation decisions including base pay, annual incentives, and long-term incentives. Any market conditions or organizational changes that affect performance and goal attainment must be given explicit consideration. Employment contracts negotiated for outside hires at the executive level should also link pay commitments to results on the job. Executives need to remain in assignments long enough to accurately assess the impact of their decisions (for example, the celebrated launch of a new product that subsequently fails in the marketplace) and ensure that they learn from their successes and failures. Because organizations are becoming less hierarchical and more lateral, fluid, and collaborative, measures of how work gets done (competency and behavioral measures) should be reflected in promotion, succession, and development decisions. The assessment of executive competencies (how the work gets done) is enhanced by multisource feedback (to make sure that executives who are masters at "managing up" are not rated highly while being perceived as destructive by others in the organization) and executive coaches who help otherwise talented executives who are in trouble because of behavioral deficiencies or assist executives through critical transitions (such as a major change initiative). Such interventions must be aligned with other decisions (who is hired, promoted, rewarded, or fired) to ensure that a consistent message is sent. (See Chapter Ten for more information.)

Evaluation of the CEO's performance should include the breadth of factors listed for executives, annual objective setting with the CEO and the board, and annual assessment of CEO performance by outside directors of the board. Informed discretion (rather than a rigid formula) should create a situation where the firm's relative financial performance is consistent with the CEO's relative pay. (See Chapter Ten for a discussion.)

The firm's international human resource strategy (for example, exportive, adaptive, or integrative) should enable it to execute its business strategy in a way that strikes a balance between the need to adapt to local conditions and the need to maintain control throughout the firm's scattered locations. Performance appraisal practices (including criteria, choice of raters, and the way feedback is provided) should be shaped by a careful analysis of social conditions and cultural values in each nation where the firm operates, and local managers must be involved in the development of appraisal practices to ensure a fit with social conditions and cultural values. For example, in cultures where power distance is high (for example, Latin America), autocratic decision making may be viewed as appropriate and managers may resist receiving performance feedback from people lower in status, whereas in cultures where power distance is low (for example, Sweden), autocratic decision making may be viewed as inappropriate. Depending on the international human resource strategy, performance criteria may be exported from the parent country or developed by the local unit (or both). It should be recognized that unit-level financial performance measures (sometimes used to assess the performance of managers who occupy key positions in a foreign unit) may reflect factors beyond the control of the manager to the extent that accounting and financial practices are used to minimize foreign taxes or losses due to changes in foreign exchange rates. Assessment of contextual performance should include cross-cultural adjustment (for example, immersing oneself into the local culture rather than remaining aloof or marginal) and cross-cultural skills (for example, knowledge of host country language and culture, sensitivity to cross-cultural differences in expression and self-presentation). The cross-cultural adjustment of family members can also be a concern, although it is likely to be monitored informally. The difficulty of adjusting to a particular culture (for example, Western managers tend to have difficulty adapting to cultures such as those of India, Pakistan, East and Southeast Asia, the Middle East, and much of Africa) must also be reflected in performance expectations and evaluations. Compensation and reward practices should be adapted to fit local conditions (for example, in cultures with collectivist values, there may be more emphasis on group-based rewards). In some cultures, there may need to be a gradual transition from reward allocation based on seniority, equality, or need to a performance-based pay plan. (See Chapter Three for an extended discussion.)

Using Appraisal Results: Links to Feedback, Training, and Compensation

Formal annual reviews should be complemented by more frequent, timely, developmental feedback that allows employees to track their learning and for "small wins" to sustain behavior change. Feedback sessions must be conducted in a climate of civility and courtesy and be characterized by a cooperative, problem-solving approach that focuses on behavior and results, not the person. Coaching skills (essential for effective feedback) are an element in competency models that guide selection and management development.

Appraisals play a critical role in diagnosing development needs and training interventions. Such appraisals are ideally based on a mental process model developed from novice-expert comparisons, and they identify where the employee's skills are on the novice-expert continuum. The appraisals should consider the employee's knowledge (and structure of knowledge), executive control (or metacognitive) processes, and self-efficacy and other social-emotional reactions that influence performance. Increasingly, external, third-party assessors are being asked to provide developmental appraisals. (See Chapter Twelve for examples and a discussion.)

A performance-based pay plan, linked to individual, group, or organizational performance, is essential. The pay plan should be matched to the organization's business objectives (customer service, quality, productivity, cost reduction, profit, employee development) and culture (traditional or involvement). For example, as task interdependence increases, measuring individual contributions becomes more difficult, individual appraisal becomes less appropriate, and pay plans increasingly need to be linked to team or organizational performance with team-based merit pay, group incentives, team recognition, or gainsharing. (See Chapter Thirteen for examples.)

Fairness and Appraisals

The ideal appraisal system is especially sensitive to fairness. One aspect of this preoccupation focuses on the variety of legal issues that can create unwelcome entanglements for the organization. In addition to discrimination based on gender, race, national origin, age, disability, or other factors, there is widespread awareness and concern with issues such as negligence, defamation, misrepresentation, just cause, and progressive discipline. (See Chapter Two for a detailed summary and case illustrations.)

The preoccupation with fairness extends to a concern with employees' perceptions of fairness. Fairness perceptions are enhanced during system development because employees are given an opportunity to voice their concerns, and there is clear communication about the intended use (for example, to guide development, allocate rewards, select people for layoffs) of appraisal results. Employees help set (and, when circumstances dictate, modify) their performance objectives, are given the opportunity to provide input about their performance (via self-evaluation or discussion with the supervisor) before appraisals are completed, and may challenge or rebut their appraisals (for example, via a panel review by uninvolved managers). To minimize personal bias, performance information is collected from multiple sources and appraisals are reviewed by others (for example, the rater's peers or higher-level management). Employees are convinced that supervisors are familiar with their work because supervisors maintain diaries with examples of effective and ineffective performance. Because feedback is provided frequently, there are no surprises (unexpected negative ratings) in formal appraisals. As found in research, fair treatment often results in even negative decisions being perceived as fair. Input from line managers and employees is used to refine the performance management process. (See Chapter Six for more information and examples.)

People must recognize that some amount of politics is common in appraisal processes. Still, an attempt must be made to minimize the dysfunctional aspects of appraisal politics (for example, via rater accountability) while recognizing that, at least in some instances, appraisal politics can play an adaptive role and may serve legitimate organizational interests. (See Chapter Five for an interesting case study.)

Conclusion

The ideas presented here summarize what the authors in this volume prescribe for practitioners. I would be surprised (perhaps *stunned* is a better word) to find any organization that has been able to consistently implement all of these ideas. Indeed, some of these ideas may not be appropriate for every organization or setting.

Still, the authors' prescriptions can serve as a road map and as a challenge to practitioners. To me, they convincingly demonstrate that the practice of appraisal can be well served by paying attention to the results of research. This, for many of us, is part of what we mean when we talk about being "scientist-practitioners."

Finally, many of the authors in this volume argue persuasively that the practice of appraisal can be advanced only with additional research. For example, Davis notes that we know too little about how culture shapes the behaviors that raters observe, remember, and record during the appraisal process. Graddick and Lane describe how advances in executive appraisals will require companies to determine the relationships among their people, customer, and financial measures and to better understand the links between "ideal leader" competencies and business results. Squires and Adler point to the need for research that examines the value of mental models (for example, based on expert-novice differences) to guide diagnostic appraisals and subsequent training. In all these areas (and many others), progress will be made only when practitioners and researchers develop partnerships to study appraisal practices in real-world settings. When practitioners close their doors to researchers, they have no one but themselves to blame when research appears irrelevant to their day-to-day problems. In the end, being a scientist-practitioner involves using the results of research to shape practice, and conducting or sponsoring research about our day-to-day human resource practices. The authors in this volume convincingly demonstrate the value of the former and the need for the latter.

Name Index

Subject Index

A

Abbott Laboratories, R.G.H. v., 72, 88

ABI/Inform, 108

Accuracy: increasing, 416–419; for self-assessment, 342–348, 363; training to improve, 405–430

Adaptive strategy, in international management, 99–100

Administration: of multisource feedback, 286–288, 307–311, 324–325; in training formats, 424–425

AFL-CIO, 511

Africa, and international management, 116, 117

Age: in discrimination cases, 66–68; and self-assessments, 335–336

Age Discrimination in Employment Act (ADEA): and legal issues, 50, 51, 53, 57, 58, 66–68, 82; and team appraisals, 275

Alabama Department of Economic and Community Affairs, Robertson v., 53

Albemarle Paper Co. v. Moody: and appraisals as tests, 77; and disparate impact, 60

ALCOA, team measures at, 270

Alignment, in international management, 122

Allstate Insurance, team appraisal at, 247–248

Alltel Information Services, Patterson v., 55

Aloha Airlines, Mathewson v., 51, 53, 74, 84, 87

Alternative rewards. *See* Performance-based pay

American Airlines, Kerr-Selgas v., 65

American Compensation Association, 387, 502, 529, 530

American Educational Research Association (AERA), 283, 284, 285, 327

American Express, executive appraisals at, 379

American Flint Glass Workers Union, 511

American Management Association, 8

American Psychological Association, 283, 327

Americans with Disabilities Act (ADA): and legal issues, 50, 57, 59, 68–74, 84, 91; and team appraisals, 275

Ameritech, pay plan at, 517–518

Amirmokri v. Baltimore Gas & Electric Co.: and discrimination, 64–65; and flexible job designs, 90; and subjective criteria, 81

Andersen Consulting, and customer satisfaction, 26

Anthropological Index Online, 108

Appraisal politics: adaptive nature of, 176, 197–200; aspects of, 163–205; background on, 163–166; broader view of, 170–172; case study of, 172–190; defined, 171; and executives, 382–383; facilitating conditions for, 178–182; implications of, 187–190; and impression management, 190–193;